NEW VENTURE CREATION

NEW VENTURE CREATION

SIXTH EDITION

Kathleen R. Allen
University of Southern California

SOUTH-WESTERN
CENGAGE Learning™

Australia • Brazil • Japan • Korea • Mexico • Singapore • Spain • United Kingdom • United States

SOUTH-WESTERN
CENGAGE Learning™

New Venture Creation, Sixth Edition,
Kathleen R. Allen

Vice President of Editorial, Business:
Jack W. Calhoun

Editor-in-Chief: Melissa Acuña

Senior Acquisitions Editor: Michele Rhoades

Developmental Editor: Sarah Blasco

Senior Editorial Assistant: Ruth Belanger

Marketing Manager: Jon Monahan

Senior Marketing Communications Manager:
Jim Overly

Marketing Coordinator: Julia Tucker

Production Manager: Jennifer Ziegler

Media Editor: Danny Bolan

Manufacturing Buyer: Ron Montgomery

Senior Art Director: Tippy McIntosh

Permissions Acquisitions Manager: John Hill

Content Project Management:
PreMediaGlobal

Production House/Compositor:
PreMediaGlobal

Internal Designer: PreMediaGlobal

Cover Designer: Patti Hudepohl

Cover Photo Credits:
  B/W Image: iStockphoto
  Color Image: Shutterstock Images/
  silver-john

Library of Congress Control Number: 2011921726

International Edition:

ISBN-13: 978-0-538-48197-7

ISBN-10: 0-538-48197-8

Cengage Learning International Offices

Asia
www.cengageasia.com
tel: (65) 6410 1200

Australia/New Zealand
www.cengage.com.au
tel: (61) 3 9685 4111

Brazil
www.cengage.com.br
tel: (55) 11 3665 9900

India
www.cengage.co.in
tel: (91) 11 4364 1111

Latin America
www.cengage.com.mx
tel: (52) 55 1500 6000

UK/Europe/Middle East/Africa
www.cengage.co.uk
tel: (44) 0 1264 332 424

Represented in Canada by
Nelson Education, Ltd.
tel: (416) 752 9100 / (800) 668 0671
www.nelson.com

Cengage Learning is a leading provider of customized learning solutions with office locations around the globe, including Singapore, the United Kingdom, Australia, Mexico, Brazil, and Japan. Locate your local office at: **www.cengage.com/global**

For product information: **www.cengage.com/international**
Visit your local office: **www.cengage.com/global**
Visit our corporate website: **www.cengage.com**

Printed in China
2 3 4 5 6 7 15 14 13 12

BRIEF CONTENTS

CONTENTS

All chapters include Chapter Objectives, a New Venture Action Plan, Questions on Key Issues, Experiencing Entrepreneurship, and Relevant Case Studies.

Chapter 3 CREATIVITY AND OPPORTUNITY   44

Chapter 4 TESTING BUSINESS CONCEPTS AND MODELS   64

Part Two Analyzing Feasibility   107

Chapter 8 UNDERSTANDING THE NUMBERS 189

Part Three Organizing the Venture 231

Chapter 9 CREATING THE BUSINESS PLAN 232

Part Four Evolving the Business   409

Appendix 523

PREFACE

Since the fifth edition of this book came out, the world has changed, and it is doubtful that anyone would argue that the impact on entrepreneurs and on the field of entrepreneurship has been enormous. The global economy has experienced a downturn the likes of which has not been seen for decades. The developing world has grabbed the mantle of entrepreneurship out of necessity to grow and create jobs even as the developed world becomes more risk averse, often looking to government to solve problems. This is a very different world than the one that existed when I wrote the first edition of *New Venture Creation* in 1995. Nevertheless, I would argue that the future of the U.S. and certainly the world lies with entrepreneurs who start the innovative businesses that create jobs and produce products and services to fuel the economy. For the foreseeable future, we live in a world characterized by uncertainty rather than risk. Risk is something entrepreneurs are comfortable with because they can calculate probabilities and outcomes for the risks they face. Uncertainty, on the other hand, has no probabilities associated with it; it can't be calculated or predicted. To survive in a world of uncertainty, entrepreneurs must develop businesses that are fast, lean, adaptable, and flexible. Whether a new venture operates in the Internet world, the life sciences, manufacturing, or services, entrepreneurs need to compress the product development timeline, get to an early prototype quickly and cheaply with the minimum number of features needed to meet the customer's requirements, continually refine the business model, and find ways to get traction as fast as possible. An uncertain business environment means more than ever that the winners will be those who launch businesses as entrepreneurs in the true Schumpeterian sense of the word: disrupting what has gone before, looking for the unexpected, and creating new value.

In attempting to mainstream the field of entrepreneurship, entrepreneurship educators and researchers have often forfeited much of what makes entrepreneurship as a discipline unique. One of the earliest leaders in the field, Dale Meyer, wrote about this problem in an article for the *Journal of Small Business Management* called "The Reinvention of Academic Entrepreneurship." He lamented the lack of rigorous metrics for measuring the impact of entrepreneurship education on students and society, the heavy reliance on neoclassical economic paradigms, and the blurring of the boundaries between entrepreneurship and small business management. He called for more emphasis on creative, self-organizing processes that entrepreneurs employ to craft complex, adaptive business systems. I agree with Meyer's assessment. Today, the term *entrepreneurship* has been diluted by overuse in contexts that have nothing to do with new venture development. *Entrepreneur* is being co-opted by everyone, including the media, to describe what is more traditionally referred to as a small business owner, a successful musician, or an effective product manager. The rationale for this dilution is that if you think like an entrepreneur, you're an entrepreneur. I believe that this rationale confuses entrepreneurship with creativity and innovation. In all the editions of *New Venture Creation,* I have attempted to remain true to the Schumpeterian view of the entrepreneurial process as "creative destruction." Now, more than ever before, the world needs entrepreneurs, in the strictest sense of the word—those who challenge the way we think about business, who create innovative business models that solve new problems, and who excel at sense-and-respond processes in the face of great uncertainty.

With all the knowledge we now have about how to operate effectively in a global market, how to build successful companies with extraordinary valuations, and how to innovate, we still have so much more to learn. And that is perhaps why so many of us enjoy the field of entrepreneurship, because it is messy, chaotic, and in a constant state of change. We are continually challenged to revise our ideas—what we knew to be true—in the face of almost daily changes in the countless variables that affect the complex launch and growth of a new business.

New Venture Creation, Sixth Edition, represents the most current thought, ideas, and practices in the field of entrepreneurship. In fact, ever since its first edition, *New Venture Creation* has endeavored to extend the boundaries of what we know about entrepreneurship and to celebrate the uniqueness and creativity of entrepreneurs.

CONTENT, ORGANIZATION, AND UNIQUE COVERAGE

New Venture Creation, is organized around the process of creating a startup, from the recognition of an opportunity to the launch of the business. It is designed to help the reader organize and plan for venture creation by mentally (and sometimes physically) engaging in the various activities that entrepreneurs typically undertake. This book has never sought to be all things to all people. It has a very specific focus on pre-launch activities—those things that entrepreneurs do to prepare to start a business and secure the first customer. Because the book focuses on the pre-launch phase of venture creation, it explores activities, such as opportunity creation and feasibility analysis, in more depth than the average book on entrepreneurship. The book also takes a distinctly entrepreneurial view of new businesses as opposed to a small business perspective. In a complex, global world, any new business owner, whether that owner's business might be the next Google or simply a small restaurant, needs to think like an entrepreneur. He or she needs to be opportunity-focused, innovative, growth-oriented, and constantly looking for new ways to create and capture value for customers. Today the entrepreneurial mindset is essential for survival and growth.

Part One introduces the foundations of entrepreneurship and entrepreneurial opportunity, which are important to understanding the decisions that entrepreneurs make, the environment in which they make those decisions, and the tasks they must undertake before starting a new company. In Chapter 1, readers will learn the nature of entrepreneurial ventures and how they are distinct from other types of businesses as well as the role of entrepreneurship in the economy. Chapter 2 dispels many myths about entrepreneurs and helps readers understand the characteristics and behaviors that work for and against entrepreneurs. Readers also learn about the entrepreneurial mindset, which is so critical for a successful startup. Chapter 3 introduces the subject of opportunity and how entrepreneurs recognize, create, and shape opportunities for themselves. Part One closes with Chapter 4, "Testing Business Concepts and Models," where readers will learn how to define and develop a business model, position it in the value chain, and validate it with customers through the investigative process of feasibility analysis.

Part Two addresses the heart of entrepreneurial activity, the testing of a business model through feasibility analysis. Chapter 5 presents how to analyze an industry, which is the environment in which the new business will operate, and follows that with a discussion of how to effectively conduct market research to understand customer needs and level of demand. Chapter 6 explores the way entrepreneurs develop products and services; it considers product development, prototyping, and intellectual property. Chapter 7 looks at how to build an effective founding team and also discusses how to determine what gaps in experience and expertise may exist in the management team and how to compensate for them with such solutions as strategic alliances and independent contractors. Part Two closes with Chapter 8, which discusses the startup resources entrepreneurs must gather and how to calculate the required capital and other resources to launch the venture and operate it until it achieves a positive cash flow from the revenues it generates.

Part Three focuses on the design of the business, which is the business plan or execution part of the entrepreneurial process. It begins with Chapter 9, which describes how to move from a feasibility analysis to proof of concept and a business plan. Chapter 10 looks at the legal form of the business and discusses the advantages and disadvantages of sole proprietorships, partnerships, and corporate forms. Chapter 11 explores the increasingly important topics of vision, ethics, and social responsibility. The value system of a new business shapes the culture of the business and the image it will have to live up to as it builds its reputation. Readers will be challenged to define a vision for a new venture based on the values they believe to be important. They will also gain a greater understanding of the need for ethics and social responsibility in any business. Chapter 12 is a design chapter that considers how entrepreneurial businesses are organized, how entrepreneurs determine the best business location, and how they develop their initial human resource capability. Chapter 13 focuses on how products and services are produced and addresses issues related to planning the startup operations of a new business, such as production, quality control, customer service, outsourcing, and managing the supply chain. Chapter 14 deals with the role and implementation of the startup marketing plan and how to promote new products and services effectively with limited resources. It pays particular attention to the role of new media, including social media and search engine marketing. The chapter also addresses personal selling and customer relationship management. Chapter 15 addresses the entrepreneur's resource strategy, how to construct a resource plan, and how to finance a start-up venture with equity and debt.

Part Four looks at planning for growth and change in the new organization. It begins with Chapter 16, which explores how to fund a rapidly growing venture, including the cost and process of raising capital, venture capital, and the IPO market. Chapter 17 deals with growth strategies for entrepreneurial ventures, such as strategic innovation, and intensive, integrative, and diversification growth strategies. It also pays particular attention to growing by going global. Chapter 18, the final chapter, discusses how to plan for change and for a successful exit or harvest.

SPECIAL FEATURES IN THE SIXTH EDITION

The sixth edition contains a variety of features of value to instructors and readers.

1. *Chapter Objectives* highlight the key topics for each of the chapters.

2. Entrepreneur *Profiles* that begin each chapter provide real-life examples to illustrate the application of chapter concepts and to inspire readers. Smaller-scale examples are also scattered throughout the chapters to maintain the real-life tone of the book.

3. *"Global Insights"* and *"Social Entrepreneurship: Making Meaning" boxed inserts* highlight additional examples, companies, and organizations that have taken a global or a socially responsible approach to entrepreneurship.

4. The *New Venture Action Plan* serves as a reminder of the tasks that need to be completed at particular stages of the entrepreneurial process.

5. *Questions on Key Issues* at the end of each chapter provoke interesting discussions.

6. *Experiencing Entrepreneurship* is a series of activities at the end of each chapter that give readers a chance to learn about entrepreneurship by getting involved in entrepreneurial activities and interacting with entrepreneurs and others in an industry of special interest to the reader.

7. Six new *Case Studies* have been added to the sixth edition to reflect a wider variety of businesses and types of entrepreneurs. The cases are followed by discussion questions.

NEW TO THIS EDITION

The following are the major changes to the sixth edition.

Overall Changes

- Chapters 4 and 5 from the fifth edition have been merged to provide a tighter focus on business model development and the overview of feasibility analysis; the sixth edition now has 18 chapters.

- The sixth edition has nine cases, six of which are new to this edition and reflect companies started and built since 2000. Command Audio, MySpace, and Crowne Inn were retained from the previous edition.

- More international and environmental/sustainability examples have been included.

- End of chapter material now includes an Action Plan section that prompts the reader with action items that need to be accomplished relative to the topics discussed in the chapter.

- Examples and data have been updated; many of the beginning Profiles, as well as a number of the boxed inserts, are new or have been revised to reflect current company data,

Chapter by Chapter Changes

- Chapter 1: All statistics have been updated, as well as the inclusion of the most recent trends: global economic turmoil, green power, the women's market, the Internet, social media, and mass mingling. The opening Profile on Amoeba Music and the Social Entrepreneurship box on Salesforce.com were updated to reflect the most recent status.

- Chapter 2: New Global Insights box features ecologically friendly Method Home, and new introductory Profile is the story of a student company that is focused on global poverty.

- Chapter 3: Profile 3.1 about inventor Yoshiro Nakamatsu has been updated. New chapter title, "Creativity and Opportunity," underlines the reorganization and rewriting of the chapter to move more effectively from understanding creativity to developing skills, to then applying those skills to problem solving and innovation. New research on creativity has been added, including the new Social Entrepreneurship box featuring the most recent work of Norman Seeff, who identified seven stages that move through the beginnings of an idea to fulfillment or final outcome. The problem-solving section has been expanded to include a process for thinking about and generating problems and refining problem definitions.

- Chapter 4: Rewritten, reorganized, and merged with Chapter 5 from the fifth edition to present a more coherent picture of the development and testing of a business model through a step by step process. This combined chapter now contains the section on "Analyzing the Feasibility of a Business Model," which covers the analytical tools for feasibility analysis, as well as a section on quick screen for multiple business options. New opening Profile is about two U.S. entrepreneurs starting a business in China.

- Chapter 5: A new opening Profile showcases Gemvara, a jewelry industry business. Anthropological techniques for customer observation have been added to the market research section.

- Chapter 6: Renamed "Understanding Product Development" to reflect an emphasis on product design issues. Intellectual property data have been brought current. New box features include Profile 6.1 about a small product company, and a Global Insights box, "Think Less to Tap Emerging Markets."

- Chapter 7: Reorganized for better flow. Profile 7.1 about an Internet company is new, as is the Social Entrepreneurship box on Live Aid. A founding team quiz has been added.

- Chapter 8: New financial examples have been added. The introduction has been expanded to explain the rationale behind not creating a full set of pro forma financial statements at the feasibility stage. Diagrams and tables have been changed significantly. A new section on startup financial metrics has been added to complement the development and validation of the business model. These metrics uniquely describe key elements on the financial health of a new business, such as customer acquisition costs and revenues per salesperson. A special section on metrics for Web 2.0 businesses is included. A new Global Insights topic on informal investment has been added, as well as an updated Profile 8.1 on Crushpad.

- Chapter 9: Now titled "Creating the Business Plan," it has been completely reorganized. A new section, "The Micro Strategy Approach to Proof of Concept," has been added to address how readers can create execution plans for new businesses around a series of proof-of-concept experiments in the market. This approach addresses the failure of most business plans to reflect the reality of the marketplace and to get traction beyond the written document. Profile 9.1 on Future Beef has been updated.

- Chapter 10: All laws and regulations have been updated. The Global Insights box on the Chinese economy has been updated and new Profile 10.1 is on a family business with partnership problems.

- Chapter 11: Profile 11.1 on women entrepreneurs in Bangladesh, and the Social Entrepreneurship box on nonprofit Room to Read have been updated. Table 11.1 is a new table introducing the Character Counts Inventory. New examples throughout, and the Paul Adler framework on awareness has been added.

- Chapter 12: Opening Profile 12.1 on an entrepreneur in the pizza business is new, as is the Social Entrepreneurship box on sustainability. In general, this chapter has been refreshed.

- Chapter 13: Profile 13.1 about a new medical machine was updated and a new Global Insights box on emerging players in outsourcing has been added. The chapter was reorganized and refreshed for better flow.

- Chapter 14: Profile 14.1 is new with Ty's Toy Box and a new Social Entrepreneurship box on entrepreneur Fabio Rosa bringing energy to rural Brazil has been added. The "Internet Marketing and New Media" section has been expanded to recognize its increasing importance to marketers and entrepreneurs.

- Chapter 15: Profile 15.1 on bootstrapping has been updated as has the story of AirTies in Istanbul in the Global Insights box. Overall, it has been refreshed and updated.

- Chapter 16: Opening Profile is new about a company that manufactures in China and the Social Entrepreneurship box on Ocean Power Technologies has been updated. New sections were added, including "Getting to a Term Sheet" and "Super Angels" which reflects a shifting of the venture capital community in response to the economic environment.

- Chapter 17: New Profile focuses on a business in Israel. Reorganized, new sections on "Profit Drivers" and "Strategic Innovation" have been added. New are Global Insights box focused on Africa and a table on the "Friendliest Countries for Startups."

- Chapter 18: New Profile 18.1 deals with a social entrepreneurship business. The section on risk management has been expanded and a new section on leadership succession was added.

SUPPLEMENTAL MATERIALS

Key instructor ancillaries (Instructor's Manual, Test Bank, ExamView, and PowerPoint slides) are available on the companion website, www.cengage.com/international, giving instructors the ultimate tool for customizing lectures and presentations.

The Instructor's Manual is a comprehensive and valuable teaching aid, featuring chapter summaries and author notes, chapter objectives, brief chapter outlines, answers to end-of-chapter questions, suggestions to end-of-chapter activities, supplementary lecture materials, and Case Study teaching notes.

The Test Bank, revised and updated, includes a variety of true/false, multiple choice, and short answer questions in varying levels of difficulty, which emphasize the important concepts presented in each chapter. ExamView™ Testing Software is an easy-to-use test creation software compatible with Microsoft Windows. Instructors can add or edit questions, instructions, and answers, and they can select questions by previewing them onscreen, selecting them randomly, or selecting them by number.

The PowerPoint® Presentation provides instructors with comprehensive visual aids for each chapter in the book. These slides include outlines of each chapter, highlighting important figures, concepts, and discussion points.

Visit the text Web site at www.cengage.com/international to find instructor's support materials and study resources to help students practice and apply the concepts they learned in class. The password-protected site contains resources for both students and instructors. For students it provides online interactive quizzes and flashcards. For instructors it includes downloadable

Instructor's Manual and Test Bank files available in Microsoft Word and Adobe Acrobat format, as well as downloadable PowerPoint® Presentations.

A video package corresponds with the key concepts taught in the text and will be offered on the companion website (www.cengage.com/international) to supplement in-class discussions.

ACKNOWLEDGMENTS

Many people helped make this sixth edition of *New Venture Creation* happen—entrepreneurs, university students, professors, and, of course, the publishing staff at Cengage. In particular, I would like to thank development editor Sarah Blasco, who kept me on track through a very fast production schedule. In addition, I want to express my appreciation to Michele Rhoades, Acquisitions Editor, and our Senior Project Manager at PMG, Karunakaran Gunasekaran.

I want to thank the instructors who used the fifth edition and provided feedback, as well as my students at the Lloyd Greif Center for Entrepreneurial Studies at the University of Southern California, who willingly share their ideas and comments with me. I also want to thank those instructors who provided formal manuscript reviews at various stages of the revision process for this and previous editions:

Donna Albano
Atlantic Cape Community College

Joseph S. Anderson
Northern Arizona University

Rachel Bates
Wichita Area Technical College

Richard Benedetto
Merrimack College

Edward Bewayo
Montclair State University

Bruce Dickinson
Southeast Technical Institute

Janice Feldbauer
Austin Community College

Todd Finkle
University of Akron

Susan Fox-Wolfgramm
San Francisco State University

Frederick D. Greene

Manhattan College

Jeffry Haber
Iona College

Jo Hamilton
Franklin University

Steven C. Harper
University of North Carolina at Wilmington

Timothy Hill
Central Oregon Community College

Sandra Honig-Haftel

Lilly Lancaster
University of South Carolina–Spartanburg

Victor L. Lipe
Trident Technical College

Tom Lumpkin
University of Illinois at Chicago

Clare Lyons

Hagerstown Community College

Steven Maranville

University of Houston–Downtown

Ivan J. Miestchovich, Jr.

University of New Orleans

Stephen Mueller

Texas Christian University

Eugene Muscat

University of San Francisco

Terry Noel

Wichita State University

Robert Novota

Lincoln University

Fred B. Pugh

Kirksville College of Osteopathic Medicine

Juan A. Seda

Florida Metropolitan University

Michael Sperling

Stanly Community College

Randy Swangard

University of Oregon

Charles N. Toftoy

The George Washington University

Lynn Trzynka

Western Washington University

Barry L. Van Hook

Arizona State University

John Volker

Austin Peay State University

Mark Weaver

University of Alabama

David Wilemon

Syracuse University

Dennis Williams

Pennsylvania College of Technology

Gene Yelle

SUNY Institute of Technology

And finally, I would like to thank my husband, John; and our children, Rob, Jaime (a writer herself), Betty, and Greg for their love and support.

K.R.A.

ABOUT THE AUTHOR

Dr. Kathleen Allen is the author of more than 15 books in the field of entrepreneurship and technology commercialization. As a professor of entrepreneurship and the Director of the Marshall Center for Technology Commercialization at the University of Southern California, which she co-founded, Allen works with scientists and engineers to help them identify markets and applications for their technologies and to prepare them to seek funding. Her personal entrepreneurial endeavors include two successful companies in commercial real estate brokerage, development and investment, and two technology-based businesses. She is also director of a NYSE company. As co-founder and CEO of N2TEC Institute, a nonprofit organization, she is advising universities and state government entities in the northern plains states on the commercialization of energy technologies and medical devices, and assisting them in the development of commercialization teams to drive the launch of new technology ventures. Allen also serves as entrepreneur-in-residence at a major aerospace company working to develop commercial applications for space technology. Allen holds a Ph.D. with a focus in entrepreneurship, an MBA, and an MA in Romance languages; as well as a degree in music.

THE OPPORTUNITY

INTRODUCTION TO ENTREPRENEURSHIP

"My son is now an 'entrepreneur'. That's what you're called when you don't have a job."

—TED TURNER,
broadcasting entrepreneur

CHAPTER OBJECTIVES

- Define entrepreneurship.

- Explain the role of entrepreneurship in economic growth.

- Distinguish entrepreneurial ventures from small businesses in terms of their purpose and goals.

- Describe the evolution of entrepreneurship as a field of study since the 1960s.

- Identify today's broad trends in the field of entrepreneurship.

AMOEBA MUSIC: DAVID CAN STILL BEAT GOLIATH

How do you succeed in a tumultuous industry that can't seem to do anything right and regularly sues its customers? Meet Mike Boyder and Marc Weinstein, co-founders of Amoeba Music, a three-store California retailer that is the self-proclaimed "largest independent record store on the planet." They have succeeded where industry giants Tower Records (no longer in business), Sam Goody (closed hundreds of stores), and even Target are struggling. They have succeeded despite a recording industry dominated by major labels that no longer produces huge wins.

In 1990, Boyder and Weinstein opened their first store, a tiny outlet in Berkeley, California, that was jammed to the ceilings with more than 11,000 new and used CDs, from the Top 40 to the best in underground rock and hip-hop, soul, jazz, world, and experimental music. In entrepreneurship, timing is critical, but these two couldn't have picked a worse time to launch their business. In the early 1990s, the major record labels were turning out megahits in record numbers while national retail chains were quickly acquiring the independents and positioning themselves as giants to take advantage of consumers' love of popular music.

Boyder and Weinstein knew that they had to come up with a very clever strategy to have a chance of surviving in that kind of market. They recognized that independents don't have to be small, so one of the first goals was to outgrow their startup location. In 1997, Amoeba moved into its 25,000-square-foot location in San Francisco that housed at that time 100,000 CDs, vinyl records, and audio cassettes, new and used. By comparison, Wal-Mart carried on average 350 titles and Tower Records in its heyday carried 60,000 titles, mostly current hits that the big music companies wanted the public to buy. Diversity and superior merchandising were also important to differentiate Amoeba from the superstores. Amoeba carried an enormously diverse collection of music genres and subgenres and

used every square foot of space for selling merchandise, rather than promoting merchandise as the competitors do.

The second part of Amoeba's strategy involved how customers would view the store not as a music store, but rather as a music exchange where they could buy and sell used CDs. This trading concept proved to be a significant component of their business model and afforded Amoeba margins as high as 70 percent on used CDs (margins are typically 20 percent on new CDs). Whereas the major labels and retailers saw music as a consumable, Amoeba saw it as a commodity for trade with long-term value.

The third component of Amoeba's strategy was to put people first, to make shopping for music a social experience. To make that happen, Amoeba hired salespeople with music and communication skills, people who were obsessed with music. Boyder and Weinstein described them as a "community of independent artists and listeners" looking for something more. Avoiding corporate advertisement and promotion, they created an environment exploding with art, live music, and people—and then stood back to watch the show.

The success of a business model is measured in many ways, but certainly by the more traditional metrics of revenue and growth. Amoeba has added huge stores in Berkeley and Hollywood (a 35,000-square-foot warehouse with more than a million LPs, CDs, and DVDs) and incorporated live shows. In 2005, Amoeba's three-store revenues exceeded $60 million while industry sales fell 7.2 percent. Although they have a successful concept now, Boyder and Weinstein understand that it must continue to evolve as their customers' needs change. They don't want to make the same mistake that their superstore competitors did. One way they stay in touch with their customers is by supporting local bands and artists through their Home Grown program. The Amoeba staff nominates local artists who meet their criteria and they are given opportunities for promotion in the stores and on the website.

Amoeba now has its own record label—Amoeba Records—and a digital store where customers can purchase select music and Amoeba gear. They still see a strong market for "hard copies" of music by fans and their biggest challenge now is how to create the Amoeba experience online.

Sources: R.C. Hart, "Marc Weinstein of Amoeba Music," *American Songwriter* (February 17, 2010), www .americansongwriter.com; S. Perman, "Make Your Own Kind of Music," *Business Week Online* (January 30, 2006), www .businessweek.com; B. Breen, "What's Selling in America," *Fast Company* (January 2003), p. 86; S. Kang, "CDs a Tough Sell? Music Stores Try Toys," *The Wall Street Journal* (June 20, 2003), p. B.1; and N. Wingfield and A.W. Mathews, "Behind the Missing Music: Huge Gaps in Offerings Plague Online Song Sites," *The Wall Street Journal* (July 2, 2003), p. D1.

Entrepreneurship is a phenomenon that continues to excite the imagination of students interested in enjoying the sense of independence that comes with owning a business, inventors looking for ways to commercialize their discoveries, CEOs of large firms seeking to remain competitive in a global marketplace, and even government leaders undertaking economic development initiatives in their communities. Since the early 1980s, when entrepreneurship was identified as a driver of economic growth, both the term and the field of study have rapidly evolved. From the legendary solo entrepreneur of the 1970s and 1980s, to the high-tech entrepreneurial teams and corporate venturers of the 1990s, and the Internet entrepreneurs of 2000 and beyond, entrepreneurs and their unique view of the world have come to be recognized as an essential element to the sustainability of any innovation-driven economy.

What is entrepreneurship? Today the term seems to be applied to all types of businesses, from the one-person, home-based business to the Fortune 500 company. Because the term *entrepreneur* carries with it a positive connotation, there is a tendency to attach it to any activity that involves starting or innovating. Frequently, people say, "I'm being entrepreneurial," when what they mean to say is that they're being creative. From one of the earliest definitions of entrepreneurship, proposed by Austrian economist Joseph Schumpeter, we learn that entrepreneurship is a form of "creative destruction." Breaking down old ways of doing things to create new value.[1] In the early years of the field of entrepreneurship as a discipline, the focus was on the startup of new ventures[2] and the associated activities that defined those ventures. Some research tackled the psychological and sociological traits of the entrepreneur in an attempt to define *who* the entrepreneur is while other research asserted that what the entrepreneur *does* is more important.[3] Many of the more contemporary definitions of entrepreneurship focus on the pursuit of opportunity and its exploitation.[4] One definition that seems to embody the essence of entrepreneurship is Stevenson's:

> The process by which individuals—either on their own or inside organizations—pursue opportunities without regard to the resources they currently control.[5]

This definition suggests that entrepreneurship goes well beyond simply starting a business to encompass a mindset or way of thinking and a set of behaviors. The entrepreneurial mindset tends to be opportunity-focused, risk taking, innovative, and growth-oriented. Although entrepreneurship is still most commonly thought of in the context of starting a business, the entrepreneurial mindset can be found within large corporations, in socially responsible nonprofit organizations, and anywhere that individuals and teams desire to differentiate themselves and apply their passion and drive to executing a business opportunity. The behaviors that entrepreneurs undertake include recognizing opportunity, gathering the resources required to act on the opportunity, and driving the opportunity to completion. At its core, entrepreneurship is about a novel entry into new or established markets, and about exploiting new or existing products and services.[6]

Entrepreneurship is not unique to any country, gender, race, age, or socio-economic sector. Entrepreneurs can be found in some form in every country, in every age group, and (increasingly) in women as often as in men. The entrepreneurial fever does not distinguish between the rich and the poor; in fact, it touches anyone who has the passion to be self-employed or anyone who is determined to be independent and to take charge of his or her life. The mindset of the entrepreneur can be understood and practiced, and the skills and behaviors of the entrepreneur can be learned and applied. The only characteristic of entrepreneurs that is arguably intrinsic is passion, the drive to achieve something. Passion cannot be taught or practiced; it simply exists when the right elements come together—for example, when an entrepreneur recognizes a business opportunity and devotes his or her full attention and resources to bringing it to life. Passion is found in successful people in all disciplines—great musicians, artists, writers, scientists, and teachers. It is what drives a person to go beyond expectations and to be the best that person can be.

This chapter explores entrepreneurship as a phenomenon and lays the groundwork for the skills and behaviors that are the foundation of the remainder of the text.

THE ROLE OF ENTREPRENEURSHIP

To understand the role that entrepreneurship plays in the economy, it is important to describe the process that entrepreneurs undertake as they create and exploit opportunity. There is no agreement on the components and order of the entrepreneurial process, but, in general, three schools of thought dominate this issue: (1) an integrated input/output model proposed by Morris, Lewis, and Sexton that looks at which variables are put into the process in order to achieve a certain level of entrepreneurship;[7] (2) Ronstadt's career assessment approach, which proposes that entrepreneurs make judgments about themselves, the new venture, and the environment based on where they are in their career;[8] and (3) Gartner's conceptual framework for the new venture creation process, which most closely reflects the approach taken in this text. Gartner proposes that the entrepreneurial process is affected by three major categories of variables: the individual entrepreneur and what he or she brings to the process; the environment, which consists of all of the external variables that affect the process such as industry, suppliers, and markets; and the organization, which is all the strategic aspects of the new venture such as focus, resources, and strategic part-nerships.[9] Figure 1.1 depicts a view of this entrepreneurial process. Despite the organized depiction of all the variables the entrepreneur must deal with, the process in reality is not linear, but rather consists of a fluid group of variables that interact at different times with the entrepreneur and his or her team. The suc-cessful execution of the process results in a new venture; however, that venture continues to conduct its business in a dynamic environment that includes all the variables external to the business that have an important impact on the business's

FIGURE 1.1   The New Venture Creation Process

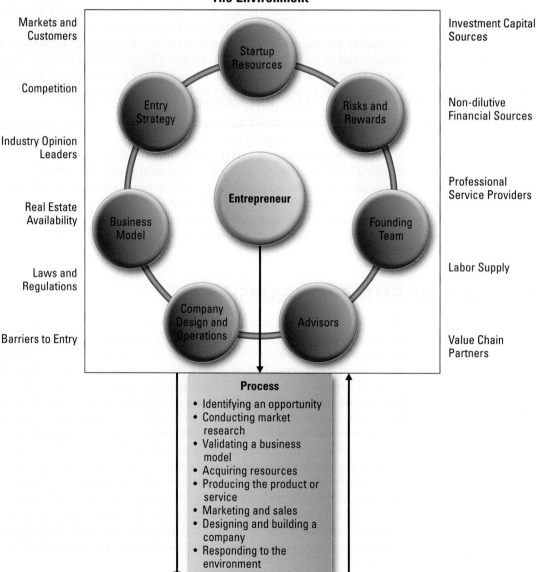

The Environment

Markets and Customers

Competition

Industry Opinion Leaders

Real Estate Availability

Laws and Regulations

Barriers to Entry

Startup Resources

Entry Strategy

Risks and Rewards

Entrepreneur

Business Model

Founding Team

Company Design and Operations

Advisors

Investment Capital Sources

Non-dilutive Financial Sources

Professional Service Providers

Labor Supply

Value Chain Partners

Process
- Identifying an opportunity
- Conducting market research
- Validating a business model
- Acquiring resources
- Producing the product or service
- Marketing and sales
- Designing and building a company
- Responding to the environment

strategy for growth. As the leader, an entrepreneur essentially plays two roles—that of the catalyst, initiating and driving the process, and that of a ringmaster in a three-ring (or more) circus, managing the process through all its changes.

The entrepreneurial process provides many benefits to society. Chief among these benefits are economic growth, new industry formation, and job creation. The following sections offer some insight into these contributions.

Economic Growth

Early economists recognized that technology is the primary force behind rising standards of living[10] and that technological innovation would determine the success of nations in the future. For many years, economic growth was explained solely in terms of inputs of labor and capital. However, in the 1980s—referred to by many as the Decade of Entrepreneurship—the work of Paul Romer and others identified technological change as a critical element of a growth model that responds to market incentives.[11] Romer asserted that technological change happens when an entrepreneur identifies new customer segments that appear to be emerging, new customer needs, existing customer needs that have not been satisfied, or new ways of manufacturing and distributing products and services. Often the resulting game-changing technologies are commercialized in partnership with the inventor. The entrepreneur brings the business experience and acumen to the team.[12] (See Figure 1.2.)

Innovation and invention have also played important roles in entrepreneurship. From inventors like Ben Franklin (bifocal lens), Thomas Edison (light bulb), and Mary Anderson (windshield wipers) to innovators such as Craig Ventner (Celera Genomics) and Larry Page and Sergey Brin (Google), inventing

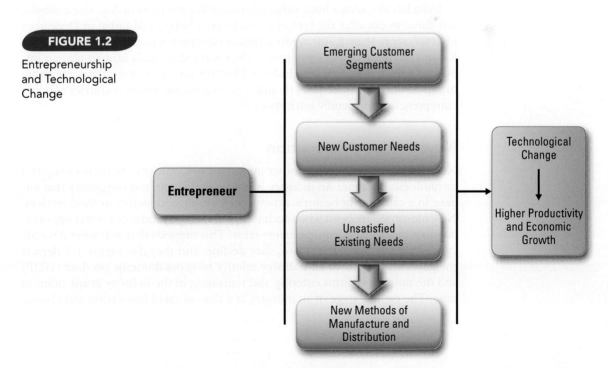

FIGURE 1.2

Entrepreneurship
and Technological
Change

new technologies and innovating or improving on existing technologies have been key drivers of entrepreneurial opportunity. Platform technologies such as the laser, discovered by Gordon Gould in 1957, or the miniautonomous robots created at Sandia National Laboratories serve as fertile ground for startup ventures that license their technologies to other companies to develop and apply them in a number of different ways. Countless examples throughout history illustrate how economic prosperity can result from invention and innovation, even as industries decline.

Technological change has also facilitated globalization and a new form of creative destruction by moving lower-skilled jobs out of the United States to countries where labor costs are substantially less. Although globalization has produced huge economic benefits, it has also resulted in lower costs of information and transportation, allowing for a broader range of goods and services to be traded over greater distances. Today very few markets enjoy freedom from competition in the global arena. For example, where local markets in Florida and California once dominated the market for fresh fruits, today consumers are frequently unaware that much of their fresh produce comes from Chile, New Zealand, and other parts of the world. Even service companies cannot escape the impact of the global economy. India and Pakistan, for example, have become dominant players in the software programming industry by transmitting their services electronically and economically to anywhere in the world.

Today, after reopening its economy, China is growing faster than any modern economy. In 2009, the Chinese economy grew 11.90 percent over the previous year, and is on track to overtake the U.S. economy due to its significant investment in entrepreneurial businesses that produce goods and create value for customers.[13]

India has also seen a huge surge in interest in entrepreneurship. For example, just three weeks after the terrorist attacks on a hotel in Mumbai in December of 2008, more than 1,700 aspiring Indian entrepreneurs gathered in Bangalore for an entrepreneurship conference. They wanted to learn how to play an important role in forging a new India.[14] The bottom line is that entrepreneurship brings about economic growth and wealth creation where countries support entrepreneurship-friendly institutions.[15]

New Industry Formation

New industry formation is another important outcome of entrepreneurship and technological change. An industry is simply the people and companies that engage in a category of business activity such as semiconductors or food services. New industries are born when technological change produces a novel opportunity that enterprising entrepreneurs seize. This suggests that industries have life cycles—they're born, they grow, they decline, and they die. Figure 1.3 depicts the generic life cycle of an industry relative to gross domestic product (GDP) and the number of firms entering and remaining in the industry at any point in time. The earliest stage of an industry is a time of rapid innovation and change

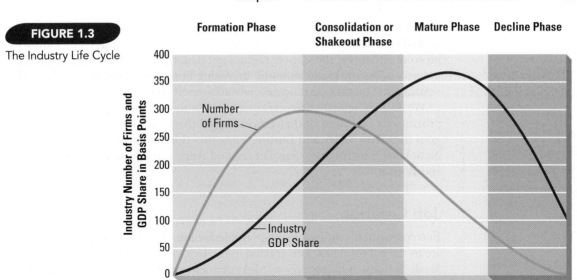

FIGURE 1.3

The Industry Life Cycle

Source: Adapted from M.R. Darby and L.G. Zucker, "Growing by Leaps and Inches: Creative Destruction, Real Cost Reduction, and Inching Up," *Economic Inquiry* (January 2003), pp. 1–19.

as young firms struggle to become the industry standard bearers with their technology. As these entrepreneurial firms achieve noticeable levels of success, more and more firms desiring to capitalize on the potential for success enter the industry. As the industry grows, it generally becomes more fragmented as a result of so many firms competing for position. At some point consolidation begins to occur as the stronger firms begin to acquire the smaller firms. Eventually, the number of firms in the industry stabilizes, and if innovation ceases to occur, the industry output may actually begin to decline.

Nevertheless, as the gross domestic product (GDP) curve in Figure 1.3 depicts, the industry as a whole does not decline when the number of firms declines. In fact, the remaining successful companies have usually achieved economies of scale that make them more productive and efficient, so the industry continues to grow for some time.

Why are so many more firms created than an industry can support? The answer lies in not knowing which new firms will be successful in securing adoption of their game-changing technologies, products, or services. In the case of incremental innovations, or improvements on existing products, research has shown that incumbent firms are generally more successful than new firms; but, with paradigm-shifting technologies, it is anyone's guess who the survivors will be.[16] Take, for example, the recent rivalry between Toshiba's HD DVD and Sony's Blu-ray technology; both are new formats for the distribution of movies. For two years the companies battled for market share with the coveted goal of becoming the industry standard. Finally, in 2008, after Sony had garnered the support of powerhouses Netflix, Wal-Mart, and Best Buy, Toshiba raised the white flag and bowed out, leaving Blu-ray the winner. Now an entire industry is growing up around the Blu-ray technology. This type of shakeout occurs in every industry as it grows; and although the losing firms leave the industry, those that remain grow quickly, creating new jobs to support that growth.

We also know that entrepreneurship tends to happen in clusters because approximately one third of the venture capital that funds high-growth companies goes to Silicon Valley and Boston. Fully two-thirds of ventures capital flows to New York, Los Angeles, San Diego, and Austin in addition to Silicon Valley and Boston.[17]

Job Creation

Entrepreneurial ventures are responsible for job creation that is disproportionate to the net total new jobs created in the U.S. over the past 25 years. The U.S. Small Business Administration (SBA) defines a small business as one with fewer than 500 employees, which by many standards is not very small and includes both high-growth technology ventures and small "mom and pops"—quite a range indeed. The European Union uses a lower cut-off point of 250 people. Nonetheless, businesses classified as small by the U.S. SBA definition represent 99.7 percent of all employers and pay more than 45 percent of the total U.S. private payroll. They have generated 65 percent of net new jobs over the past 15 years.[18] It is important to note, however, that the vast majority of net new jobs created by the small business sector are created by a few rapidly growing firms called "gazelles." Research points to 5 percent of small firms accounting for three of four new jobs.[19] A recent study by the Kauffman Foundation found that in the period between 1977 and 2005, existing firms had a net job loss of about one million jobs a year, while startups added an average of three million jobs per year.[20]

The most recent actual (not estimated) data from 2007 indicate that there were 6,031,344 small businesses (under 500 employees) and 18,311 large firms in existence. In 2007, nonemployers (by definition small businesses) accounted for 21,708,021 of the total number of U.S. firms, which in 2008 was 29.6 million businesses.[21]

On a global level, the *Global Entrepreneurship Monitor* found that only about 14 percent of all attempted startups expected to create 20 or more jobs.[22] In their 2009 report, they discussed the link between economic growth and entrepreneurship and how economic development evolves based on where the country stands in terms of growth. They identified three categories of countries:[23]

- **Factor-driven economies** that rely on unskilled labor and the extraction of natural resources. Here businesses are created out of necessity. Examples are Uganda, Guatemala, and Algeria.
- **Efficiency-driven economies** that are growing and in need of improving their production processes and quality of goods produced. Examples are Argentina, Russia, and South Africa.

- **Innovation-driven economies**, which are the most advanced, are where businesses compete based on innovation and entrepreneurship. Examples are Denmark, Israel, United Arab Emirates, and the United States.

Entrepreneurship occurs in all three categories, but it is clearly driven by different factors in each, and those factors determine the types and size of businesses found in those countries.

THE NATURE OF ENTREPRENEURIAL STARTUPS

Entrepreneurial ventures and small businesses are related, but they are not the same in most respects. Both are important economically but each provides different benefits and outcomes. Schumpeter described entrepreneurs as equilibrium disrupters who introduce new products and processes that change the way we do things, while small-business owners typically operate a business to make a living.[24] Examples of small businesses are small shops, restaurants, and professional service businesses. They form what has been called the "economic core."[25] They tend to be slow growing and often replicate similar businesses already in the market. It should not be forgotten, however, that even entrepreneurial ventures start small. The difference is that the entrepreneur's goal is not small.

In general, entrepreneurial ventures have three primary characteristics. They are

- Innovative
- Value-creating
- Growth-oriented

An entrepreneurial venture brings something new to the marketplace, whether it be a new product or service (Moshi, an alarm clock incorporating artificial intelligence, or Amazon.com, disrupting traditional brick-and-mortar retail), a new marketing strategy (Twitter), or a new way to deliver products and services to consumers (*The Wall Street Journal Interactive Edition*). An entrepreneurial venture creates new value in a number of important ways. Entrepreneurs create new jobs that don't merely draw from existing businesses; and by finding niches in the market, entrepreneurs serve customer needs that are currently unserved. Moreover, entrepreneurs typically have a vision of where they want their businesses to go, and generally that vision is regional, national, or (more often) global.

The Kauffman Foundation distinguishes innovative entrepreneurship from replicative entrepreneurship, which is characteristic of small lifestyle businesses. Lifestyle businesses are usually started to generate an income and a lifestyle for the owner and his or her family. Often referred to as mom-and-pop businesses, they tend to remain relatively small and geographically bound, most often because of a conscious decision on the part of the founder to keep the firm a small, lifestyle business.

Choosing what kind of business to start is very important, because that choice influences all subsequent decisions and determines what kinds of goals the entrepreneur is able to achieve. For example, if the intent is to grow a business to a national level, entrepreneurs will make different decisions along the way than if the intent is to own and operate a thriving restaurant that competes only in the local community. Generally, running a small business requires good management skills on the part of the owner, who must perform all tasks associated with the business as it grows. By contrast, entrepreneurs often do not have the skills to handle the management aspects of the business and prefer to hire experts to carry out that function, leaving the entrepreneur and the founding team free to innovate, raise capital, and promote the business. Chapter 2 will address the behavioral characteristics of entrepreneurs.

New Business Formation

Entrepreneurs engage in a number of activities in the process of creating a new venture. Although there is no universal agreement on where the process starts and where it ends, one view is that the process starts when one or more people decide to participate in the formation of a new business and devote their time and resources to founding it.[26] Empirical research has found that the process of launching a new business is iterative, nonlinear, and nonsystematic.[27] And although entrepreneurs may go in many directions during the creation process, they typically use identifiable milestones to measure their progress.[28] These milestones include deciding to start a business, researching the concept, preparing for launch, securing the first customer, obtaining the business license, and many other activities that signal that the business is in operation.[29]

The process of new venture formation is depicted in Figure 1.4 and is characterized by four stages and three transitions or decision points. The first transition point occurs when an individual, acting independently or as an employee of a firm, decides to start a business. A nascent entrepreneur is an individual who intends to start an independent business; a nascent corporate venturer (or nascent intrapreneur) is someone who intends to start entrepreneurial ventures inside a large corporation. The second transition point comes about during the gestation of a new venture and includes all the startup processes that lead to the birth of a firm and to the resulting infant firm. These startup processes include feasibility analysis, business planning, and resource gathering, among other activities. Once the new venture survives startup, it typically does one of three things: (1) It may grow at a rate higher than normal, (2) it may persist or survive to move into the adolescent (fourth) stage, or (3) it may be abandoned by its founders. Figure 1.4 also depicts three question marks that represent aspects of the entrepreneurial process about which very little is known. The label "?a" stands for the number of nascents that actually complete the process and launch; label "?b" stands for the number that never complete the process; and label "?c" stands for the tasks and times to completion.

Borrowing a term from product development, we can call the period of time prior to firm birth the *fuzzy front end*, which simply means that the activities

FIGURE 1.4

Social, Political, and
Economic Context of
the Entrepreneurial
Process

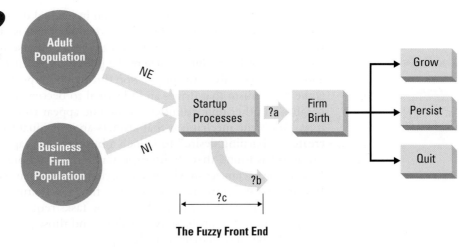

The Fuzzy Front End

NE — Nascent entrepreneur
NI — Nascent intrapreneur
?a — How many entrepreneurs in the nascent stage actually complete the process
and launch an infant firm?
?b — How many startups never complete the process?
?c — What are the tasks and timeline involved in actually completing the startup
process and giving birth to a new firm?

Source: From Paul D. Reynolds, "National Panel of U.S. Business Start-ups: Background and
Methodology," in *Databases for the Study of Entrepreneurship*, edited by J.A. Katz, pp. 153–227.
Copyright © 2000, with permission from Elsevier. Modified by *Launching New Ventures* author to
reflect the concept of the fuzzy front end and its associated probabilities.

undertaken at this point are often unclear and subject to change as more information is obtained. The fuzzy front end has been modeled in economic terms. Simply put, the amount of investment an individual is willing to make in a new product—or, in this case, in a new venture—is a function of the probability of its success, the value of that success, and the cost of failure [Inv = f(PS + VS + CF)]. A change in any one of these values will alter the economics of the bet.[30] In terms of the model in Figure 1.4, the nascent entrepreneur uses the time spent in the fuzzy front end to calculate the probability of success as an entrepreneur, what that success will mean in terms of return on his or her investment of time, money, and effort, and what the risk or cost of failure might be. Those probability estimates are highly subjective; however, if the nascent entrepreneur uses the time in the fuzzy front end to gather information about the industry and market, test the business concept through feasibility analysis, and determine the conditions under which he or she is willing to move forward and start the business, much of the subjectivity will be eliminated. Moreover, the risk of startup will be reduced, and the probability associated with the three outcomes will be more accurate.

It is not entirely clear what actually prompts an individual to become a nascent entrepreneur. Even with the risk assessment and risk mitigation that are part of preparing to launch a new venture, there appears to be no uniform mechanism that consistently results in an individual deciding to put forth the effort to launch a business. One individual may choose to enter the nascent stage despite a high level of risk. Another may choose to reject the nascent phase even under conditions where the perceived risk involved is low. Nascents appear to emerge from the population through both push and pull factors. *Push* is the mechanism that drives an individual to become a nascent entrepreneur because all other opportunities for income appear to be absent or unsatisfactory. *Pull* is the mechanism that attracts an individual to an opportunity and creates a "burning desire" to launch a business and capture a market. Recent research has found that ability expectancies play a more significant role than outcome expectancies in whether a nascent entrepreneur launches a business.[31] In other words, entrepreneurs come to the new venture process with perceptions about their ability to undertake the tasks required to start the business independent of the probability of failure, and those perceptions drive whether or not the business actually launches.

Business Failure

The intent to start a business is not enough to make it happen. Due to the challenging nature of the endeavor, many potential entrepreneurs drop out of the process as they move from intention to preparation and then to execution. In addition, a high number of entrepreneurs give up before the new business makes the transition to an established firm.[32]

The Small Business Administration Office of Advocacy reports that seven out of ten new employer businesses survive at least two years. The survival rate at five years is 51 percent, and these numbers are similar across industries. Survival has been attributed to sufficient capital, having employees, and the entrepreneur's intention in starting the business.[33] (See Table 1.1.) Many factors contribute to new venture failure: lack of legitimacy, lack of resources, an ineffective management team, and a challenging business environment.

One body of research views failure as a liability of newness; that is, the firms that are most likely to survive over the long term are those that display superior levels of reliability and accountability in performance, processes, and structure. Because these factors tend to increase with age, failure rates tend to decline with age.[34] Young firms have a higher chance of failure because they have to divert their scarce resources away from the critical operations of the company in

TABLE 1.1	Category	2004	2005	2006	2007	2008
Starts and Closures of Employer Firms, 2004–2008	Births	628,917	644,122	670,058	633,100[e]	627,200[e]
	Closures	541,047	565,745	599,333	571,300[e]	595,600[e]
	Bankruptcies	34,317	39,201	19,695	28,322	43,546

[e]Estimate using percentage changes in similar data provided by the U.S. Department of Labor, Employment and Training Administration.

Sources: U.S. Bureau of the Census; Administrative Office of the U.S. Courts; and U.S. Department of Labor, Employment and Training Administration.

SOCIAL ENTREPRENEURSHIP: MAKING MEANING

Salesforce.com's Culture Is About Philanthropy

It is easy for a big company to write a check, even a very large one, and feel that it has done its corporate duty with respect to social responsibility. But Mark Benioff, founder/CEO of phenomenally successful Salesforce.com, believes that's not enough. Soon after founding what is now the industry leader in on-demand customer relationship management, Benioff formed the Salesforce Foundation, funding it with 1 percent of the company's stock, and then committing to donate 1 percent of profits to the community through product donations and an additional 1 percent of employee working hours to community service. Called the 1-1-1 integrated model, today more than 85 percent of the company's employees are involved in philanthropy. "We've seen how our 1-1-1 integrated corporate philanthropy model has influenced many companies, including Google, to build philanthropy into their day-to-day operations."

Recently, Benioff and his wife Lynne have decided to focus their personal philanthropic efforts for the next decade on helping to fund the construction of a new UCSF Children's Hospital with a $100 million donation as a way to give back to the San Francisco community, where their company is based.

Sources: Benioff, M. "Benioff's Philanthropic Shift, In His own Words," *The Wall Street Journal*, (June 17, 2010); M. Benioff, "Force for Change," *Inc. Magazine* (November 2006), p. 83; Marc Benioff, CrunchBase, www.crunchbase.com/person/marc-benioff, accessed September 26, 2010; and Barret, V. (July 23, 2010). "Billionaire Marc Benioff: I'm Sold," Forbes.com. www.forbes.com/2010/07/22/salesforcecom-philanthropy-billionaires-intelligent-technology-marc-benioff.html.

order to train employees, develop systems and controls, and establish strategic partnerships. Another body of research sees failure as a liability of adolescence, claiming that startups survive in the early years by relying on their original resources, but that as those resources are depleted and the need to find new and different resources increases the company's chances of failing also increase.

The vital issue for entrepreneurs is not avoiding failure but minimizing the cost of a possible failure and recovering quickly. That comes from starting with a robust business model and testing it in the marketplace prior to starting the business.

A BRIEF HISTORY OF THE ENTREPRENEURIAL REVOLUTION

The United States was founded on the principle of free enterprise, which encouraged entrepreneurs to assume the risk of developing businesses that would make the economy strong. However, it was not until the 1980s that the word *entrepreneur* came into popular use in the United States, and an almost folkloric aura began to grow around men and women who started rapidly growing businesses. These formerly quiet, low-profile people suddenly became legends in their own time, with the appeal and publicity typically associated with movie stars or rock musicians.

Today's entrepreneurs are no different. Elon Musk has changed the game for the space industry by creating a lower-cost solution for sending cargo and satellites into space. Under the leadership of Jeff Bezos, Amazon.com completely

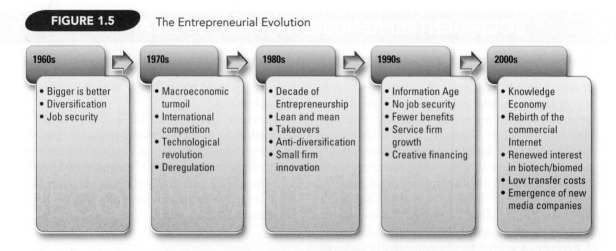

FIGURE 1.5   The Entrepreneurial Evolution

1960s	1970s	1980s	1990s	2000s
• Bigger is better • Diversification • Job security	• Macroeconomic turmoil • International competition • Technological revolution • Deregulation	• Decade of Entrepreneurship • Lean and mean • Takeovers • Anti-diversification • Small firm innovation	• Information Age • No job security • Fewer benefits • Service firm growth • Creative financing	• Knowledge Economy • Rebirth of the commercial Internet • Renewed interest in biotech/biomed • Low transfer costs • Emergence of new media companies

disrupted the brick-and-mortar retail industry. Entrepreneurs such as these shake up the economy and change the game for everyone. They look for unsatisfied needs and satisfy them. Figure 1.5 summarizes the entrepreneurial evolution that has taken place since the 1960s, paving the way for the innovation economy that has been the envy of the world.

The Decades of Entrepreneurship

In the *mid-1960s*, gigantic companies were the norm. General Motors in the 1960s was so large that it earned as much as the ten biggest companies in Great Britain, France, and West Germany combined.[35] The reason why U.S. companies enjoyed such unrestricted growth at that time was that they lacked competition from Europe and Japan. Therefore, job security for employees was high, and companies tended to diversify and grow by acquiring other businesses.

The *1970s* saw the beginning of three significant trends that would forever change the face of business: macroeconomic turmoil, international competition, and the technological revolution. A volatile economic climate the likes of which had not been seen since World War II dominated the 1970s. The Vietnam War economy brought inflation, the dollar was devalued, food prices skyrocketed as a consequence of several agricultural disasters, and the formation of OPEC sent gas prices up 50 percent. Furthermore, by the late 1970s the Federal Reserve had let interest rates rise to a prime of 20 percent with the result that there was no borrowing, no spending, and a recession that spilled into the 1980s, bringing with it an unemployment rate of 10 percent.[36] To compound the effects of the economy on business, by 1980 one-fifth of all U.S. companies faced foreign competitors that had far more favorable cost structures with much lower labor costs. Imports, particularly in the automobile and machine tools industries, were suddenly taking a significant share of the market from U.S. businesses.

The third event affecting business at that time was the technological revolution brought about by the introduction in 1971 of the Intel microprocessor, the Mits Altair personal computer in 1975, and the Apple II computer in

1977. Microprocessors succeeded in rendering whole categories of products obsolete—such things as mechanical cash registers and adding machines, for example—and effectively antiquated the skills of the people who made them.

Increasing the pressure on business, the government ushered in a new era of business regulation with the Environmental Protection Agency, the Occupational Safety and Health Agency, and the Consumer Product Safety Commission, all of which increased costs to businesses. On the opposite front, deregulation forced planes, trucks, and railroads to compete, and in general big companies no longer had control of the marketplace.

By the *early 1980s*, business was in terrible shape. The Fortune 500 saw a record 27 percent drop in profits.[37] Large mills and factories were shutting down; manufacturing employment was declining; and yet, ironically, productivity remained the same or actually increased. New, smaller manufacturers were still generating jobs—and not only manufacturing jobs, but service jobs as well. How was this possible?

To become competitive, the smaller, more flexible, entrepreneurial manufacturers had hired subcontractors who could perform tasks such as bookkeeping and payroll more efficiently. These service firms developed to support the needs of the product sector, but they also inspired the creation of other service firms: people who work often need day-care or maid services, so even more jobs were being created.

With the creation of all these jobs, it is no wonder that the 1980s was called the true Decade of Entrepreneurship by many, including the dean of management science, Peter Drucker, who was not alone in asserting that the United States was rapidly and by necessity becoming an entrepreneurial economy.[38] On the heels of the emergence of Silicon Valley and its legendary entrepreneurs, the mainstream press began to focus on business activities, creating many popular magazines such as *Inc.* and *Entrepreneur.*

Responding to this entrepreneurial drive, big business in the 1980s found it necessary to downsize and reverse the trend of diversification it had promulgated for so long. If big companies were going to compete with the dynamic, innovative smaller firms and fend off the takeover bids so prevalent in the 1980s, they would have to restructure and reorganize for a new way of doing business. This restructuring and reorganizing actually resulted in improved performance, increased profits, and higher stock prices. It also meant, however, that many jobs would no longer exist, employees would receive fewer benefits, and the only "secure" jobs left would be found in civil service.

Toward the end of the 1980s, researchers observed that young entrepreneurial ventures were internationalizing much earlier than expected and at a much smaller size.[39] A significant number of these ventures were in high-tech industries.[40] Large-sample empirical work revealed that directors and managers with significant international experience played a strong role in the internationalization of entrepreneurial ventures at startup.[41] All these events moved this country toward a period in the 1990s that required the vision, the resources, and the motivation of the entrepreneur to seek new opportunities and create new jobs in a vastly different global environment electronically linked via the Internet.

More than perhaps anything else, the *1990s* were characterized as the Information Age. The commercial Internet emerged midway through the decade, and suddenly global competition and resources were more readily available than ever before. The Internet made entrepreneurship and the ability to compete alongside large established companies in the same markets a reality. Furthermore, with more and more jobs being shipped overseas, employees learned that job security was no longer a fact of life. U.S. companies quickly discovered that their competitiveness lay in the control of information and new ideas, and clearly the Internet was to play an important role in this new view of the world. The late 1990s brought the "dot com" bubble and the rush of the venture capital community to position itself for what appeared to be a new way of doing business. At the same time, the interest in non-Internet-related technology was waning as investors saw a much quicker return on their investment in the world of e-commerce.

The *new millennium* ushered in what many refer to as the *knowledge economy*, brought about by increased globalization and the competitive shift to more "knowledge-based economic activity."[42] In the new economy, the primary resource is knowledge rather than raw materials and physical labor.[43] Today, differences in economic performance in regions of the world can largely be explained by the presence or absence of entrepreneurship capital, which is essential to the development of new business models that monetize knowledge. Entrepreneurship capital is characterized by social networks that link entrepreneurs to educational institutions, industries, network brokers, and to resources.[44] California's Silicon Valley and the North Carolina Research Triangle are two examples of environments that have long prospered from knowledge-based economic activity and a high level of entrepreneurial enterprise.

The knowledge economy of the 2000s is also described by low-cost competition from Asia and Central and Eastern Europe that came about when transfer costs were driven down in the telecommunications and computer sectors, making it easier and less expensive to move capital and information.[45] Consequently, most routine tasks in production and manufacturing are now more efficiently accomplished in low-cost locations.

Without a doubt, the 2000s are also influenced by the commercial Internet. In 1998, the media declared that dot com was the business of the future—that it would change the way business is conducted forever. By the spring of 2000, the dot com bubble had burst and funding for dot com ventures virtually disappeared overnight. However, what remained was a distribution channel that had huge potential and merely required good business models to sustain it. Chapter 4 looks at some of these Internet business models. The Internet has also influenced the evolution of the media and entertainment industries with new media companies such as Demand Media pioneering innovative ways to generate revenues from advertising and from providing real-time user-generated content to the Internet.

Renewed interest in non-Internet-related technologies was one of the results of the dot com crash of 2000 as investors turned to solid technologies that could be protected through patents and developed a growing interest in green tech, biotech, and biomedical devices.

ENTREPRENEURIAL TRENDS

Throughout entrepreneurial history, various trends and patterns of change can be observed. For example, in the 1980s, the solo entrepreneur was prevalent; in the 1990s, team-based entrepreneurship became the norm. In the previous edition of this book (copyright 2009), the leading trends at that time were women-and-minority-owned businesses, social responsibility, the Internet and new media, and globalization. Those trends are certainly ongoing, but today four major trends have emerged as significant and will affect entrepreneurs' thinking for the foreseeable future: global economic turmoil, green power, the women's market, and the Gen Y consumer movement called *mass mingling*.

Global Economic Turmoil

Economic cycles are a normal phenomenon, and wise business owners take them into account when they plan their strategies; so normally a book such as this will not talk about the economy from the perspective of the circumstances at the time the book was written. However, the economic turmoil that began in 2008 (the recession officially started in the fourth quarter of that year) and that has continued unabated is predicted by many to be the state of the business environment for many years to come. This is principally because today the economies of individual countries are interlinked in such a way that what happens in one country (for example, the problems in Greece in 2010) has ramifications at some level for every other country around the globe. Economic uncertainty and volatility in the gross domestic product (GDP) of a country produces a sense of caution on the part of consumers and businesses; they delay spending and investment.[46] For entrepreneurs and business owners in general, this means that sustainability in every sense of the word will be critical, whether that is building a company that is transparent and honest in its dealings, interacting more with customers, or taking a bit more risk. Some examples of successful entrepreneurial companies that are already doing this are Zappos, Google, Amazon.com, and Virgin Airlines.

Economic turmoil has a plus side because it produces opportunities for entrepreneurs who are comfortable with instability and environmental factors not in their control. The Kauffman Foundation Index of Entrepreneurial Activity found that in 2009, 558,000 new businesses were started per month by new and repeat entrepreneurs. This was the highest level of startup generation on record.[47]

Green Power

Regardless of where entrepreneurs stand on the climate change and hydrocarbons debate, the fact is that money is flowing toward green solutions for all manner of problems that challenge the goal of a sustainable society. While the biggest problems—water, hunger, large-scale energy projects—will require a consortia of corporations, government, and nonprofits to solve, there remain a multitude of ways that entrepreneurs can participate in the opportunities spawned by the growing interest in everything green. For example, entrepreneurs can take advantage of several subtrends within the green power sector. Consumers generally want to save on the costs of energy consumption and consume less of everything. They're willing to buy green if they don't have to pay a premium for it, and some consumers will pay for brands that give them status as eco consumers. For instance, eco-iconic marketing is about developing a product and brand that makes it possible for consumers who buy it to be instantly recognized as having eco status. Usually these products also incorporate a story that creates meaning and draws the consumer to the product. For example, Crop to Cup is a coffee brand that buys its coffee directly from farmers, but it goes beyond that: the company lets customers trace their actual cup of coffee back to the particular farmer who produced it and start a dialogue. Another example is e-concierges, companies that help consumers go green in every aspect of their life like New York-based Green Irene that offers a green home makeover.

The Women's Market

Women now comprise one-third of all entrepreneurial activity globally. In middle-income countries like Venezuela and Thailand, where necessity is a dominant motivator of entrepreneurship, women exhibit the highest levels of entrepreneurial activity at the early stages; in the high-income countries like Japan and the Netherlands, women exhibit the lowest levels of activity.[48] The National Women's Business Council, compiling estimates from the U.S. Bureau of the Census, estimates that, as of 2006, majority female-owned firms (where 51 percent of the company is owned by a woman) number 8 million (28.2 percent of all U.S. businesses), generating an economic impact of $3 trillion annually and about 23 million jobs.[49] This is the state of entrepreneurship for women, but the big trend goes far beyond the starting of businesses. These facts tell the story.

■ The growing market of women 50–70 today are the healthiest, wealthiest, most educated, and most active generation in history. Their workforce numbers have grown by 52 percent since 2000.

■ Women make 80 percent of the buying decisions for households that control 50 percent of discretionary spending in the U.S.

■ Women control 77 percent of financial assets.[50]

Entrepreneurs dealing in financial services, health care, travel/hospitality, real estate, and automotive sectors particularly will be affected by this important and growing market.

The Internet, Social Media, and Mass Mingling

The Internet will certainly be the foundation for many entrepreneurial trends for some time to come. In the current decade, the Internet has succeeded in disintermediating aspects of the value chain and in lowering the barriers to entry in some industries. Internet businesses now provide tremendous access to information and personalization as well as an easy way for entrepreneurs to sell goods without the need for a physical location. It has also become the vehicle for next-generation media companies like Demand Media, Facebook, and YouTube that create new and interesting ways to attract advertising dollars and major advertisers, who want to do a more effective job of targeting their customers and look to communities of interest to find them. Furthermore, these same activities are now moving to Smartphones because good marketers understand that one-to-one contact with a customer on the phone is more likely to result in a sale than an Internet ad that requires a potential customer to click on it.

The Internet and social media are not new trends but they are producing new trends, particularly in the consumer markets. One new trend is called *mass mingling* and it has been adopted enthusiastically by the Gen Y or New Millennial Generation, those born after 1982. This generation spends a large portion of their day online and connecting with others through Facebook, Twitter, and the current crop of services that help them find, track, connect to, and ultimately meet other people—Google Latitude, Loopt, and FireEagle. Mass mingling is about making it easy for a lot of people to meet up for a common purpose. Twitter has been the leader in facilitating mass mingling. For example, in Los Angeles the traveling Kogi truck is a landmark. It's essentially a mobile restaurant offering "Korean-Mexican tacos" day and night. Its founders, Mark Manguera, Caroline Shin-Manguera, and Chef Roy Choi, use Twitter to communicate the location of their four trucks to their devoted fans who line up for their inexpensive but delicious food.

LOOKING AHEAD: THE ORGANIZATION OF THE BOOK

Starting a new venture is a process that begins long before the business ever opens its doors. That process is rarely linear but rather a more iterative—even chaotic—process; however, the entrepreneurial process does have direction and goals. This book is divided into four sections that reflect the entrepreneurial process. Part One focuses on opportunity and the entrepreneur. Chapter 1 serves as an introduction to the field of entrepreneurship and the environment in which entrepreneurs start new ventures today from a macro perspective. Chapter 2, another foundational chapter, explores the entrepreneurial journey from the entrepreneur's perspective and helps the reader prepare for this journey. At Chapter 3, the process of entrepreneurship begins with the recognition of an opportunity through the development of creativity and problem-solving skills. Chapter 4 covers the development of a business concept and business model for the new venture.

Part Two (Chapters 5 through 8) explores the feasibility analysis of a new venture in detail by examining the various tests that entrepreneurs use to determine the conditions under which they are willing to move forward with a new business concept, and ways to achieve proof of concept.

Once there is a feasible concept, the business plan is the document that explains the execution strategy for the concept. Part Three focuses on the execution strategy for the feasible venture. The business plan documents the creation of a new company including the operations and funding strategy. Chapters 9 through 15 deal with how to move from proof of concept to the execution strategy.

Any business undergoes growth and change, so Part Four focuses on these related issues. Chapters 16 through 18 consider how to fund and grow the business, plan for unexpected changes, and architect a harvest strategy for the entrepreneur and investors.

Entrepreneur skills are key not only to economic independence and success but to business survival. The marketplace puts a premium on creativity, initiative, independence, and flexibility. Entrepreneurs who develop those behaviors and display those characteristics will be more likely to succeed.

New Venture Action Plan

- Read broadly about entrepreneurs and new ventures.

- Interview an entrepreneur.

- Become more aware of new trends, particularly in an industry in which you're interested.

Questions on Key Issues

1. Define the term entrepreneurship.
2. As the mayor of your community, what incentives would you put into place to encourage entrepreneurship?
3. Describe the current environment for entrepreneurship. How does it differ from the environment pre-2000?
4. Which of the entrepreneurial trends discussed in the chapter will have the biggest impact and why?
5. How do entrepreneurial ventures differ from small businesses?

Experiencing Entrepreneurship

1. Interview an entrepreneur in an industry or business that interests you. Focus on how and why this entrepreneur started his or her business. Be sure to include the following:

   a. Contact information

   b. The entrepreneur's name, address, title, company name, and phone number

   c. Background

   d. How did you find this person and why did you choose her or him?

   e. Why is this person an entrepreneur?

   f. What influenced the entrepreneur to identify and pursue this opportunity?

   g. How did the entrepreneur's background (family history, prior education, and work experience) affect the opportunity discovered?

   h. Describe the opportunity that the entrepreneur decided to pursue and the process the entrepreneur used to evaluate the opportunity.

   i. How did the entrepreneur evaluate the opportunity?

j. What criteria did the entrepreneur use to decide whether to pursue the opportunity?

k. What were the perceived risks of this opportunity and how did the entrepreneur expect to manage them?

l. What did the entrepreneur do to turn the opportunity into a business?

m. Identify specific activities the entrepreneur undertook to develop the opportunity into a business.

n. Identify when the entrepreneur did these activities (provide dates: month and year).

o. Identify important contacts and individuals who were helpful during the startup process.

p. What major problems did the entrepreneur encounter along the way?

q. How were these problems solved?

r. What advice would the entrepreneur give to someone thinking about pursuing an opportunity?

s. Why was this entrepreneur successful?

2. Analyze how the factors in question 1 affect the entrepreneur's success.

3. Visit your local Chamber of Commerce and use an Internet search engine to discover how many of the major entrepreneurial trends discussed in the chapter are reflected in businesses in your community. In a two-page report, discuss your findings.

Relevant Case Studies

Case 3 HomeRun.com

Case 7 1-800-Autopsy

CHAPTER 2

BECOMING AN ENTREPRENEUR

"Success isn't permanent, and failure isn't fatal."

—MIKE DITKA,
professional football coach

CHAPTER OBJECTIVES

- Dispel myths about entrepreneurs.
- Understand the many pathways to entrepreneurship.
- Prepare to become an entrepreneur.

Sometimes you start out wanting to launch a simple business and end up creating an entire industry. At least that's what happened to lifelong friends Adam Lowry and Eric Ryan who combined contemporary design and eco-friendly ingredients to produce a line of liquid soaps and cleaners called Method Home that is now worth over $100 million. Lowry is a chemical engineer with a focus on the environment while Ryan is a marketing guru with experience at Gap and Saturn, among other companies.

It was the late 1990s in San Francisco when the two Michigan born and bred friends began brainstorming potential products to reinvent. They used a technique that entrepreneurs often use when they want to see something from a different point of view: they took the most mundane household cleaners and said "what if we. . ." That process led to the idea that, unlike the dominant products from Procter & Gamble and Clorox that contained harsh, toxic chemicals, their cleaners would be eco-friendly and have beautiful, contemporary designs—in other words, both style and substance. In Lowry and Ryan's view, going green did not mean that the consumer had to suffer. Green could be stylish and practical.

Their first product came out in the midst of the recession of 2001, funded with seed capital of $90,000 that they had raised from friends and family. In true entrepreneurial fashion, they had mixed the products up in a bathtub and delivered them in an old pickup truck. However, in the process, they had used up all their capital. They

even remember a dinner with their first investors where they couldn't find a credit card that wasn't maxed out—they had to use their persuasive skills to convince the restaurant owner that they were good for it.

Within a year, they had battled their way into distribution in 800 stores with products that used natural ingredients—palm oil, coconut oil, and corn—bottled in attractive, recyclable containers. Lowry and Ryan knew that their core strategy had to be around brand building and that they were going head-to-head with the dominant players in the market. To succeed, they needed to attract one of their favorite designers, Karim Rashid, who turned out to be intrigued by their bold mission and agreed to come on board as the chief creative officer.

Design was one component of their brand-building strategy; speed and innovation were the other critical elements. To achieve that, they developed a system of 50 subcontractors so they could introduce new products quickly and pull failed products off the shelves just as quickly. Today, they sell 130 products in more than 8,000 stores.

Sources: "How Two Friends Built a $100 Million Company: The Rise of Method Home," Inc.com, June 29, 2010, www2.inc.com/ss/how-two-friends-built-100-million-company; Heffernan, M. "Messy Guys Make Millions Selling Green Cleaning Products," *Reader's Digest*, www.rd.com /money/messy-guys-make-millions-selling-green-cleaning-products; and; Van Schagen, S. "An Interview with the Founders of Method Green Home-care Products," March 13, 2008, www .grist.org/article/fighting-dirty/PALL/print.

E ntrepreneurship is a personal journey that begins in the mind of the nascent entrepreneur. It is a personal journey because business is fundamentally about people—how they interact, make decisions, plan for the future, deal with conflict, and so on. In fact, all of entrepreneurship can be reduced to people. From the entrepreneur's motivation to start a business to the decisions made about growth, customers, facilities, employees, and the exit from the business, everything comes down to people and the needs and motivations of those people. These needs and motivations must be satisfied through the startup of a new venture, or entrepreneurs will not have the motivation to persist in their efforts. The new venture must also satisfy the needs of customers or they won't be motivated to buy. Kim Camarella understood this. Through the eyes of her plus-sized best friend, she learned about the difficulty that larger young women have finding fashionable apparel. This motivated her to solve the problem through the launch of Kiyonna Klothing, now a successful line of plus-sized apparel that is satisfying a real need in the market (www .kiyonna.com).

Finding a market need or "pain" is a vital first step. Another essential step in the entrepreneurial journey is assembling the right team, which can, more frequently than not, make the difference between success and failure. It is very difficult today to start a new company as a solo entrepreneur, mostly because any single person rarely has all the knowledge and skills required to move quickly and make the decisions that will lead to success, so assembling a great team is more critical than many entrepreneurs believe. As part of an enormously successful team, Eric Schmidt stays in the background when it comes to the press about the company he co-founded with his much younger partners Sergey Brin and Larry Page—Google. Brin and Page brought the youthful exuberance and new ideas while Schmidt brought business experience and capital. This is a team that believes in creating a family in their workplace environment—"it's easier to get a family united behind a cause than a bunch of employees," says Schmidt.[1] In the fast-moving Internet marketplace, having a team with compatible values and a laser focus on the company vision is a sure route to success.

How large to grow the business is very much a personal decision. Entrepreneurs who want to balance work with a personal life may choose to start a business that generates significant revenues but does not require a great deal of people and physical assets to manage. That was the position that Neil Johnston took. After several unsuccessful partnerships that had him doing most of the work, in 2001 he merged his label business with one of his customers' businesses, a solo entrepreneur company that sold bar code labels to libraries. Total investment by the parties to this venture was $383,000, but it added substantially to the company's ability to grow. By 2002, ID Label had made the Inc. 500 list of fastest-growing private companies in the United States, with revenues at about $2.2 million. Johnston was able to reduce his workload and finally live the kind of life he wanted. Johnston is a prime example of an entrepreneur who does not want the type of business that employs many people. He realized early on that in his case more employees would not necessarily equal more profits. Furthermore, the challenges of managing all those employees would involve more stress than he wanted to take on. Instead, he kept the business at a manageable size and secured the balanced life he had always wanted.[2]

The decision about when and how to exit the business is also a very personal one because it is based on the entrepreneur's goals and values. Some entrepreneurs start many ventures in their lives, so they experience the exit multiple times. Others, like Bill Gates of Microsoft (co-founder/CEO from 1976–2000) or Michael Dell of Dell Computers, (founder/CEO from 1984–2004 and again from 2007 to the present), stay with their businesses and choose not to exit. And still other entrepreneurs see their exit strategy change in response to unforeseen circumstances. John Lusk co-founded Platinum Concepts Inc. in July 1999 with some of his classmates from the Wharton School of Business at the University of Pennsylvania. Their core product was the MouseDriver, a computer mouse shaped like a golf-club head. Lusk's goal was to build the company up as fast as he could in two years and then sell it to another business. His plan forecasted the company's revenues skyrocketing to $10 million in 6 months. Unfortunately, this did not happen within his predetermined time-frame. It took approximately 18 months to build any sales for the MouseDriver. As a result, Lusk altered his exit strategy, deciding not to sell the company but instead to spend more time diversifying the product line and getting his products into the mass market. Ultimately, Lusk sold the company in 2003 to a large east-coast gift distributor.[3]

As discussed in Chapter 1, entrepreneurship is a very complex process inspired by and driven by the entrepreneur and his or her co-founders. With the entrepreneur playing such an important role, one would think that there would be a definable profile of a successful entrepreneur. But research has failed to find that stereotypical entrepreneur. There are, in fact, no psychological or sociological characteristics that can predict with any certainty who will become an entrepreneur or who will succeed as an entrepreneur.[4] This chapter explores the personal journey to entrepreneurship, what it takes to become a successful entrepreneur, and the many ways to approach entrepreneurship throughout a career.

SAYING GOODBYE TO STEREOTYPES

Given the frequency with which entrepreneurs are discussed in the media, it is not surprising that stereotypes have developed around them. Not all of these stereotypes are flattering and most are simply false. This section attempts to dispel some of the myths surrounding entrepreneurs so that the entrepreneurial journey can begin on a solid, factual foundation.

Myth 1: Entrepreneurs Start Businesses Solely to Make Money

Entrepreneurs start businesses for many reasons, but the number-one reason appears to be their need for independence and to create something new. They don't want to work for someone else; they want to create something they can call their own. Early studies found, and later research confirmed, that entrepreneurs are motivated intrinsically by such things as the desire for independence, the need to be in control of one's destiny, and the satisfaction of being ultimately responsible for the success or failure of the venture.[5] This does not suggest that entrepreneurs don't want to make money; they do. However, the same research found that entrepreneurs are secondarily motivated by extrinsic rewards such as the financial performance of the venture.

Myth 2: It Takes a Lot of Money to Start a Business

Another false assumption about entrepreneurship is that it takes a lot of money to start a business. Nothing could be further from the truth. Every year *Inc. Magazine* profiles entrepreneurs who started their businesses on $1,000 or less. For example, Lori Bonn Gallagher parlayed her love of travel and finding unique jewelry into a $2.8-million business. Starting with $1,000 worth of samples of handblown glass jewelry that she discovered in France and a successful selling strategy, Gallagher secured a deal with Nordstrom to begin selling her imported jewelry in the United States. Today her jewelry is designed at her headquarters in Oakland, California, manufactured in Bali, and sold in retail outlets such as Nordstrom, Discovery Store, and Boston's Museum of Fine Arts museum shop (www.loribonn.com). When it comes to the Inc. 500 Fastest Growing Private Companies, the amount of startup capital is not a predictor of ultimate success.[6] Other factors such as the management team and the market being addressed are far more important. In fact, some research has determined that it is not specifically the amount of capital the entrepreneur possesses at startup that is important but rather how many resources (founding team, network of contacts, connections in the value chain, and so forth) the entrepreneur can access and/or control.[7]

Myth 3: It Takes a Great Idea

Jim Collins's research, which was documented in the bestseller *Built to Last,* dispelled the myth that it takes a great idea to start a business. In fact, most of the great businesses that have been successful for at least 50 years—companies such as Walt Disney, Sony, and Merck—didn't start with a great idea. They started with a great team who simply wanted to create an enduring company. In general, venture capitalists say that they will take a great team and a large market opportunity in a fast-growing area over a great idea any day, because it takes a superior team to execute a successful business concept and it takes customers in a fast-growing market to create the return to the investors.[8] Often it's not the idea, but the execution plan that makes the business a success. Mark Benioff did not invent software as service, but his company Salesforce.com found the pain in hosted solutions and removed it. Instead of having to buy applications to handle each function in the business, companies can access hosted services that can be customized to meet their specific needs. Benioff's success was not a great idea, but rather great execution.

Myth 4: The Bigger the Risk, the Bigger the Reward

Students of entrepreneurship often hear that risk is correlated with reward—the greater the risk taken, the greater the reward expected. Certainly, it appears that investors hold that point of view. But *risk* is a relative term, and the goal of most entrepreneurs and investors alike is to reduce the level of risk in any venture. In fact, investors *expect* entrepreneurs to do what it takes to reduce the risk for them, such as testing the market, acquiring the first customer, and investing some of their own capital in the business, and no one expects the business to be worth less because risk was reduced. It is actually to entrepreneurs' advantage to reduce risk for investors so that entrepreneurs can retain more of the equity when it comes time to negotiate for an infusion of capital.

Myth 5: A Business Plan Is Required for Success

There is no question that lenders, investors, and others want to know that an entrepreneur has done his or her homework before they're willing to risk their capital. But many entrepreneurs have started highly successful businesses without having a formal business plan in place—including recognizable companies such as Pizza Hut and Crate and Barrel that have survived for decades. Others have launched websites and been "in business" within a day, making money within a couple of weeks. The prevalence of business plan competitions and courses requiring a formal plan obscures a potentially troubling fact: researchers do not agree on the relationship between a completed business plan and new venture success. Some believe that a plan takes time away from more valuable activities. Others argue that a plan helps facilitate resource acquisition and management, making goals more achievable. Ultimately, it appears that given the determination that the concept is feasible, time may be better spent in a series of small experiments to prove the concept. The issues of the business plan will be presented in more depth in Chapter 10.

Myth 6: Entrepreneurship Is for the Young and Reckless

Many people believe that if they haven't started their first business by the time they are 30, it is too late. They think that the energy, drive, resources, and risk involved are suitable only for the young. But many great businesses have been started by older entrepreneurs who had the passion to do something original. Ray Kroc started McDonald's at age 52, and Gary Burrell was 52 when he left Allied Signal to start Garmin, now a GPS leader. In fact, the Kauffman Foundation studied 652 American-born heads of technology companies launched between 1995 and 2005 and discovered that the average age of the founder was 39 at startup.[9] Research supports the conclusion that being older can be an asset when starting a business. The 2008 *Global Entrepreneurship Monitor Report* found that men and women in the 45–98 age bracket are responsible for 36 percent of all the entrepreneurial activity in the United States and for 22 percent of the activity globally. In the U.S. this represents an increase of about 9 percent over the previous year, while entrepreneurial activity in the 18–44 age category shrank by an equivalent amount.[10] Entrepreneurship is for anyone, regardless of age, who wants to experience the thrill of building something from scratch and making it a success.

Myth 7: Entrepreneurship Cannot Be Taught

This myth is a corollary to "Entrepreneurs are born, not made." Both are wrong. There is a lot about entrepreneurship that can be taught, including specific skills and behaviors. People who don't naturally have the skills of a successful entrepreneur can certainly learn and apply them. Management guru Peter Drucker asserted, "The entrepreneurial mystique, it's not magic, it's not mysterious, and it has nothing to do with the genes. It is a discipline. And, like any discipline, it can be learned."[11] Scholarly research over a number of years has supported that claim.[12] In fact, a recent twin study by Nicolaou and Shane using 870 pairs of identical twins and 857 pairs of same-sex fraternal twins to study entrepreneurial activity, found that entrepreneurs are about 40 percent born and 60 percent made.[13] The born part was not deterministic but rather explanatory; that is, their results pointed to the strong evidence for the effect of environmental factors, including genetics, on entrepreneurial propensity. Practically speaking, the born part is what cannot be taught, the passion to persist and achieve as well as the willingness to take risk. Some have called it the "fire in the belly." And indeed, what motivates someone to leave Harvard University to start a business (like Bill Gates of Microsoft) or to start by driving a garbage truck (like Wayne Huizenga, who founded Waste Management) cannot be learned. It is simply part of a person's makeup as it is in any successful person in any field of endeavor.

PATHS TO ENTREPRENEURSHIP

Entrepreneurs are as varied as the kinds of businesses they start and the precipitating events that led them to become entrepreneurs. In general, people start businesses out of necessity or driven by opportunity. In the United States, opportunity-driven entrepreneurship is far more prevalent than in efficiency-driven or factor-driven economies such as Brazil and Uganda where entrepreneurship frequently happens out of necessity.[14] Moreover, when capital markets make it difficult to find funding, entrepreneurs are less likely to start new ventures from scratch. They are more likely to start new ventures on their own when the incentives inside large organizations are weak or nonexistent, when the opportunity requires significant individual effort as in the invention of a new technology, and when normal scale advantages and learning curves do not provide advantages to the large organization.[15] Entrepreneurs also choose the startup process when industry entry barriers are low, when the environment is uncertain, and when the opportunity they seek to exploit involves a breakthrough or disruptive technology that will make previous technology obsolete.

There are many paths to entrepreneurship, and in the following section we briefly look at four broad categories apart from the traditional path: the home-based entrepreneur, the serial entrepreneur, the nonprofit entrepreneur, and the corporate entrepreneur.

The Home-Based Entrepreneur

Home-based businesses comprise over two-thirds of all sole proprietorships, partnerships, and S-corporations in the United States. Between 1999 and 2005 (the latest available data from the census) the total population of people working from home increased from 9.48 million to 11.33 million.[16] They represent

52 percent of all small businesses.[17] Many of these are hobby businesses, consulting, and freelance-type businesses; but many others are entrepreneurial ventures that compete in the same arena as brand name businesses with large facilities. Technology has made it possible to do business from virtually anywhere, so entrepreneurs don't have to work in traditional office spaces to start or run businesses. Moreover, home-based business owners can tap into more resources than ever before from their desktops or mobile devices to locate help for any problem they may be facing, from finding business forms to seeking legal advice to learning how to start and run a business. In addition, U.S. tax laws have become friendlier to home-based business owners, who can take a deduction for their home office space and appropriate business expenses.

Many entrepreneurs with aspirations to grow their businesses start from home to save on overhead and reduce the risk of startup. Once the concept has proved itself, they often move out to acquire facilities and other resources that will support the growth of the company and the addition of employees. Some entrepreneurs choose never to have office space but rather to enjoy the ability to move around and do business from their home, boat, car, or vacation home. With Fortune 500 technologies now available to small businesses at affordable prices, business really can be conducted from anywhere.

The Serial or Portfolio Entrepreneur

Many entrepreneurs enjoy the pre-launch and startup phases so much that when those activities are over and running the business takes center stage, they become impatient to move on to the next startup. The thrill of starting a business keeps them going; they prefer to leave the management issues to someone else. An entrepreneur who starts one business and then moves on to start another is called a *serial entrepreneur*. Often these entrepreneurs start another business that builds on the experience from the first venture or a specific expertise that the entrepreneur possesses or has acquired through a previous venture. An entrepreneur who owns a minority or majority stake in several ventures is called a *portfolio entrepreneur*.[18] Portfolio entrepreneurs tend to create a lot of churn in their portfolios as they seek out new business opportunities that link to their existing businesses. They tend to be constantly on the hunt for new opportunities.[19]

Consummate entrepreneur Wayne Huizenga is a classic serial entrepreneur. He started with a single garbage truck and grew his company truck by truck to become Waste Management Inc., the largest garbage hauler and waste management service in the world. Huizenga then went on to tackle the video rental business with Blockbuster Entertainment and the used-car industry with Auto Nation. However, Huizenga could also be considered a portfolio entrepreneur because he typically owns multiple businesses simultaneously. In addition to the businesses cited, he has also owned numerous professional sports teams. Niva Shima, a California entrepreneur and investor, found an effective way to manage his multiple biotech startups. He created an incubator, a program, and a facility to accelerate the development of biotech companies, so he could more easily move among the various startups and they could benefit from their association with each other.

The Nonprofit Entrepreneur

Today many enterprising people are turning to nonprofit types of ventures to realize their entrepreneurial dreams. Nonprofit, socially responsible businesses typically focus on educational, religious, or charitable goals. They generally seek tax-exempt status so that they can attract donations from companies and individuals who believe in their mission. Contrary to popular belief, nonprofit businesses can make a profit, but that profit must stay within the company rather than be distributed to the owners.

Robert Chambers used the nonprofit organizational structure as a vehicle to help low-income people make better purchasing decisions when it comes to cars. Chambers, a retired engineer in Lebanon, New Hampshire, with five years of auto sales experience, was frustrated by how much low-income people were spending because they didn't understand how car dealerships worked. To solve the problem, he launched Bonnie CLAC (car loans and counseling), which not only guarantees car loans for these people at reasonable rates, but also provides them with training in how to manage their finances.[20] Chapter 11 explores nonprofit ventures in more depth from a legal perspective.

The Corporate Entrepreneur

Entrepreneurship is no longer viewed solely as the startup of a new, independent firm; it can also occur inside an existing organization. Known as corporate

GLOBAL INSIGHTS

Nourish International: Students Eradicating Global Poverty

Sustainable development has captured the attention of entrepreneurs around the world. Ryan Allis is one of those entrepreneurs. Founder and CEO of e-mail marketing firm iContact in Durham, NC, Allis didn't want to wait until he achieved huge success before giving back to the world. Nourish International, a nonprofit dedicated to helping eliminate global poverty, was the inspiration for Allis to focus his plans to give back. Founded by Sindhura Cetineni in 2003 as a University of North Carolina at Chapel Hill student group and incorporated as a 501(c)(3) nonprofit in 2006, Nourish International works with undergraduate students during the school year raising money through small businesses they call "ventures." With the money earned, they identify a sustainable development project to fund. During the summer, they travel to the community they are supporting and work alongside community members to complete the project. For example, in 2008, they worked in a squatter settlement in Ciudad de Dios, Peru building a clean water system that would serve 5,000 people. After completion of a project, Nourish stays in touch to ensure that the project continues.

Today Ryan Allis serves on the board of directors for Nourish. "It's a unique and effective model that Nourish is perfecting and then scaling to have a global impact... They have chapters at 23 college campuses now—and it all started right here in Chapel Hill!"

Sources: Nourish International, http://nourishinternational .org; and "Nourishing Socially Responsible Entrepreneurship is Appetizing Goal for iContact CEO," *Local Techwire*, http://localtechwire.com/business/local_tech_wire /venture/story/4271547, January 12, 2009.

entrepreneurship, corporate venturing, or intrapreneurship, this phenomenon is now regularly studied by the research community.[21] Increasingly, large organizations are finding it necessary to provide for entrepreneurial activity to remain competitive. Corporate ventures, those entrepreneurial-like ventures inside large companies, are distinct from other types of projects that these firms take on. For one thing, they involve activities that are typically new to the company so the risk of failure is high. There is also a high degree of uncertainty around such projects, so they are often managed separately from the core business activities. Recognizing that it is nearly impossible to re-engineer and redesign an entire organization, many companies have chosen from several options to simulate the entrepreneurial environment required for innovation to occur: the skunk works, intrapreneurship, and acquisition.

The "skunk works®" route (named for Lockheed's unit that developed the Stealth fighter jet) refers to an autonomous group that is given the mandate to find and develop new products for the company that may even be external to the company's core competencies. They typically operate outside the traditional lines of authority in the organization, which makes for a more flexible, fast, and creative work environment.[22] In 2000, for example, IBM made a bold move and tasked one of its best executives, Rod Adkins, with starting a new business that would help IBM apply wireless technology to extend computing beyond the home and office. Within three years, his new venture was generating annual sales of $2.4 billion. To counteract the natural tendency of the corporate entrepreneurs to want to staff up like a big company, IBM makes them work alone or perhaps with a colleague. They work on a small budget, but they can tap IBM's wealth of expertise.[23]

Other companies try to encourage corporate venturing or entrepreneurship inside the structures of their existing organizations. This approach has been difficult, at best, to achieve because the bureaucratic structures of most large organizations—deep organizational charts, their inherent avoidance of risk, and strict budgets—all challenge even the most enthusiastic corporate entrepreneur.

For an entrepreneurial mindset to succeed inside a large corporation, the following are required:

- *Senior management commitment.* Without the support of senior management, it will be difficult to move any entrepreneurial project forward fast enough and far enough to be successful.
- *A champion or several champions.* At various points in the development of the corporate venture, the corporate entrepreneur needs a champion at the highest levels who can open doors and make valuable contacts and who will lend credibility to the enterprise.
- *Corporate interoperability.* The environment must encourage collaboration and give the entrepreneur access to the knowledge and resources of all the company's functional areas, while at the same time allowing the entrepreneur a high degree of autonomy.
- *Clearly defined stages and metrics.* Entrepreneurial ventures inside large organizations need a timeline with stages at which decisions can be made about whether to proceed and whether additional or different resources are

required. They also need a way to measure progress and success that is not based on the corporation's benchmarks but rather on benchmarks appropriate to startup ventures with limited resources.

■ *A superior team.* Only the best people should be put in corporate entrepreneurship situations, because by definition these ventures are riskier than projects based on the company's core skills and products. The new venture team also requires a champion among the top management who will secure help for the team when the project reaches the inevitable roadblock.

■ *Spirit of entrepreneurship.* Entrepreneurship is about opportunity— recognizing it, seizing it, shaping it, and exploiting it—but it's also about failing sometimes. A company that encourages corporate entrepreneurship must not penalize its entrepreneurs for failure but must support them as they take what they have learned to a new project.

Still other companies prefer to acquire emerging companies who have discovered and developed new technologies but don't have the resources to commercialize them.

This book is not intended to address the specific needs of corporate entrepreneurs, but recognizing opportunities, conducting feasibility analyses, and developing execution plans are as relevant in the corporate environment as they are in a startup.

ENTREPRENEURSHIP AS A WAY OF LIFE: CHALLENGES AND OPPORTUNITIES

Jeff Hawkins, the co-founder of Palm Computing and later Handspring, both successful PDA companies, would argue that entrepreneurship is not a career because "if you're successful at it, you quickly become a business person."[24] In other words, the only people who make a career of entrepreneurship are those who haven't been successful. In some respects, Hawkins is being facetious because he has in fact started more than one business, and Palm, his first, was certainly a successful company. The point is, however, that entrepreneurship is, for the most part, about startup, about identifying an opportunity and gathering the resources to turn that opportunity into a successful enterprise. Entrepreneurship is not for everyone, no more than any other endeavor is. Table 2.1 presents an overview of the challenges and opportunities that come with choosing entrepreneurship as a career path. When reading the table, it is important to ask if the reader would be able to deal with such a challenge and also if the opportunities of entrepreneurship are meaningful to the reader and compatible with his or her life goals.

Readers may come up with even more challenges and opportunities than are presented in the table, but these are the most common. The last challenge listed is "dealing with a sense of isolation and disillusionment." When Susan LaPlante-Dube left her corporate job to start Precision Marketing Group out of her home in Massachusetts, she learned how lonely that could be. "I was used to walking down the hall to bounce ideas off someone...." Now, she had to plan her time to include opportunities to meet with people and to network.

TABLE 2.1	Challenges	Opportunities
Challenges and Opportunities with the Entrepreneur Career Path	Finding the right business opportunity	Becoming independent—taking charge of a career
	Needing to work, often without pay, for long hours	Creating wealth
	Facing uncertainty and high risk	Doing well while doing good—the potential for social entrepreneurship
	Needing to make major decisions, often that affect other people's lives	Working in a business environment that the entrepreneur creates
	Relying on other people for expertise and resources	Doing something the entrepreneur is passionate about
	Having no previous experience on which to rely	Making a difference
	Facing failure at some point	Creating new jobs
	Finding the right people to help grow the business	Supporting the community
	Raising capital and other resources	
	Dealing with a sense of isolation and disillusionment	

The lead-up to the launch of the business is a very exciting time. Everyone wants to see the entrepreneur succeed, so encouragement and support are never lacking. But many entrepreneurs are surprised at what running a business is really like. They have no comprehension of how difficult it is, and so often there is a feeling of being overwhelmed. This is one reason starting a business with a team makes sense; the difficulties and the work can be shared.

To succeed at anything requires a higher-than-average amount of self-discipline and perseverance. Entrepreneurs don't give up easily, and they tend to stick doggedly to a concept until something or someone convinces them that it's time to move on to something else. For example, Todd Stennett spoke with more than 450 people before he found the right person to guide him to the perfect model for his now successful laser mapping business, Airborne 1. If entrepreneurs didn't have this kind of tenacity, there would be no great products and no great businesses, because every entrepreneur faces doubters and naysayers when a business concept is in its earliest stages. The ability to stick to the task and persevere against all odds is what wins the day for an entrepreneur.

One of the biggest problems that scientists and engineers face when they decide to consider entrepreneurship is the expectation that there are formulas for success and right and wrong answers to guide them. In short, they expect linear processes and predictability. People who wish there were no surprises in life and who want an environment that is predictable and stable will find it very difficult to survive in the world of the entrepreneur. One reason why entrepreneurship is such an interesting and exciting field is that it is constantly changing. It is well-known that the greatest, most innovative ideas occur at the edge of chaos when things that aren't normally associated with each other are brought together in new ways. Opportunity is rarely found in stable, predictable settings, so potential entrepreneurs must learn to embrace change.

PREPARING TO BECOME AN ENTREPRENEUR

Starting any business, large or small, requires a tremendous amount of time, effort, and resources. Therefore, it usually makes sense to start a business that has the potential to grow large and provide a good return on that investment, rather than spend the same amount of effort on a very small business that yields only a single job. In fact, research supports that notion.[25] The probability of survival and success tends to go up with businesses that have more potential. Unfortunately, the vast majority of people who start businesses do not think like entrepreneurs. They think like small-business owners, wanting to keep everything under control, to grow slowly, and simply provide a job for the owner. Although there is nothing inherently wrong with looking at business from this perspective, it does, regrettably, expose the entrepreneur to significantly more risk. Because these small businesses do not create new value, innovate, or have a plan for growth, they tend to be undercapitalized, poorly managed, and unable to differentiate themselves from competitors. In a word, they are vulnerable.

How, then, does an entrepreneur increase the chances for success? Through preparation. There are a number of important steps that an individual can take to increase his or her chances of success in entrepreneurship. Figure 2.1 displays these steps, and we discuss them here.

FIGURE 2.1

Preparing for
Entrepreneurship

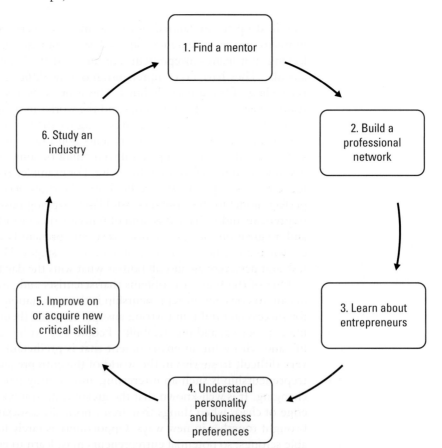

Find a Mentor

One very specific task that an aspiring entrepreneur can undertake to prepare for success is to find a mentor—that is, someone who is leading the type of life that the entrepreneur envisions for his or her own future and who can be the entrepreneur's guide and sounding board as well as champion and gateway to contacts the entrepreneur would otherwise not have been able to meet. Vivek, an Indian entrepreneur, discovered that he had become so passionate about the product side of his computer hardware business that he had stopped listening to the good advice he was being given about the need to diversify his product line. It was not until his business was facing failure, something that is viewed very negatively in India, that he sought the guidance and wisdom of a *guruji* or mentor. The mentor helped Vivek understand that it was his own ego that was standing in the way of his success in finding the right path for his business.[26]

Build a Professional Network

Networking is the exchange of information and resources among individuals, groups, or organizations whose common goals are to mutually benefit and create value for the members. Research in the field of entrepreneurship has revealed much about the positive effects of networking. For instance, entrepreneurship has been found to be a relational process. Entrepreneurs do not act autonomously but, rather, are "embedded in a social context, channeled and facilitated or constrained and inhibited by people's positions in social networks."[27] These social networks consist of strong and weak ties. *Strong ties* are the entrepreneur's close friends and family members whom he or she knows well, whereas *weak ties* are the entrepreneur's acquaintances and business contacts. In general, acquaintances are not socially involved; that is, entrepreneurs do not generally spend their nonbusiness hours with acquaintances.[28] Nevertheless, these weak ties play an important role in the entrepreneurial process because entrepreneurs typically move forward faster with the help and support of weak ties who are not biased by a prior history with the entrepreneur. Entrepreneurs rely on their weak ties for objective advice. Family and close friends, on the other hand, tend to restrict the entrepreneur's potential because they tend to look at the impact on them of the entrepreneur's business activities.

Building a large network with credible partners and maintaining the connections in that network will be important to an entrepreneur's success. However, how does one achieve a large, but meaningful network? Entrepreneurs accomplish this by connecting with network brokers who serve as gateways to other networks. These brokers, or opinion leaders, exert influence between groups or networks rather than within groups.[29] Figure 2.2 depicts such brokering. The entrepreneur in this example initially has a network of family and friends as well as a network of professional engineers. Outside of these networks, the entrepreneur knows only two people: an angel investor and a production person. However, these two people are well connected into communities with which the entrepreneur has no experience. In effect, they are opinion leaders who serve as the gateways to those new communities and can make the

FIGURE 2.2   Brokering Across Networks

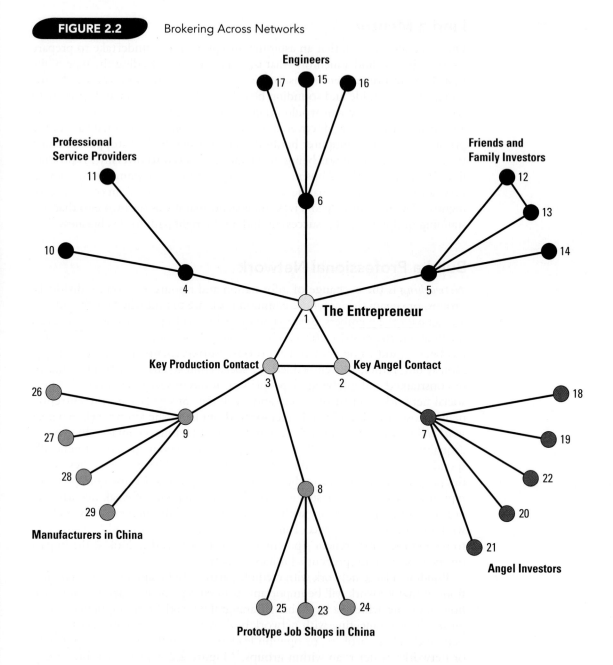

appropriate introductions to provide the entrepreneur with instant credibility. Now it's easy to see why the adage "it's who you know" makes sense. Rather than spending an extraordinary amount of time trying to find all the required contacts, it would be more efficient and prudent for entrepreneurs to figure out who is the gateway to the community and endeavor to meet and cultivate that relationship.

TABLE 2.2	Name	Weak Tie	Strong Tie	Broker	Source of Help
Social Network Participants	Tim Burns	X			Business attorney
	Caroline McCallum			X	Gateway to energy community

Entrepreneurs who successfully use their networks to build their businesses generally are committed to the success of the people in their network, are active listeners, and approach every contact with an open mind.[30] In that way, they derive the maximum value from their network ties. Table 2.2 provides a way for readers to analyze their networks. The first two rows have been filled in to illustrate how to complete the matrix. Networking is discussed in the context of building a startup team in Chapter 7.

Learn About Entrepreneurs

One of the best ways to prepare for entrepreneurship is to learn as much about it as possible by reading magazine articles, books, and newspapers, and—most importantly—by talking to entrepreneurs. Some examples of magazines that focus on entrepreneurs are *Fortune Small Business, Inc. Magazine*, and *Entrepreneur*. University entrepreneur programs, local Chambers of Commerce, Small Business Development Corporations, and industry events are also great sources for meeting entrepreneurs.

Understand Personality and Business Preferences

Although we have dispelled many of the myths surrounding entrepreneurship in this chapter, it is a fact that there are barriers to becoming an entrepreneur that should not be ignored, and many of these barriers relate to the entrepreneur's personality and preferences. Recent research has uncovered six factors that serve as barriers to people becoming self-employed: (1) lack of confidence, (2) financial needs, (3) startup logistics, (4) personal or family issues, (5) time constraints, and (6) lack of skills.[31] The questions in Table 2.3 reflect these factors and others that should be considered as well. The table presents a series of questions that will help entrepreneurs understand more about what they like and dislike about business. The questions are posed as a definitive yes/no choice to force readers to think about these questions independent of any particular opportunity being considered.

Launching a new business requires tremendous amounts of time and energy, as well as a great deal of support from family and friends. During the early stages of a new venture, resources are limited and entrepreneurs must wear many hats. This can be immensely stressful, so it is important that entrepreneurs be in good health and optimal physical and emotional condition. It is often said that entrepreneurs start businesses to be in charge of their lives. The reality is that after they start their own business, they might find themselves working more than they ever did for someone else. The major difference is that

TABLE 2.3	Entrepreneur Personality and Preferences Questionnaire		
		Yes	**No**
1. Are you a self-starter?			
2. Are you able to work for up to a year with no income from the new business?			
3. Do you stick with a project until it's finished?			
4. Do you frequently abandon a project when you grow tired of it?			
5. Do you enjoy working with other people on a regular basis?			
6. Do you enjoy traveling for business purposes?			
7. Are you comfortable with pressure (i.e., deadlines, fast-paced work environment)?			
8. Do you enjoy working with people from other countries?			
9. Are you comfortable hiring people you believe are smarter or more experienced than you are?			
10. Do you enjoy being in an office at your desk for most of the day?			
11. Are you comfortable in selling situations?			
12. Are you comfortable asking for money or other resources?			
13. Are you comfortable with debt?			
14. Is security important to you?			
15. Do you have time to devote to this new business?			
16. Are you comfortable with unions?			
17. Are you willing to work in a government-regulated environment?			
18. Do you have the support of your family to start a business?			

because they are building something they own, it doesn't feel like the work they are accustomed to; instead, they are bringing to life a new business that reflects *their* goals and values.

It is equally important for potential entrepreneurs to think about the kind of lifestyle they are striving to achieve. Not all businesses support the kind of lifestyle that some entrepreneurs want to lead. Is travel important? Is having a large home and all the things that go with it a requirement? Is achieving a balanced life with plenty of time for family and friends important? If so, starting a business that requires a lot of travel or puts the entrepreneur at the mercy of demanding clients probably won't provide that balanced lifestyle.

Most people spend the majority of the day at their work; therefore, the work environment should be an enjoyable place to be. Entrepreneurs who love the outdoors should probably not start businesses that require them to sit at a desk all day. Entrepreneurs who don't enjoy working with people should probably not start businesses that are labor-intensive or involve numerous daily interactions with the public. It is a good idea for future entrepreneurs to take a step back and contemplate their ideal work environment. What does this environment look like or "feel" like? What would spending a day in this environment entail?

Improve or Acquire Critical Skills

Because entrepreneurs operate in a world of uncertainty, the ability to analyze a situation, extract the important and ignore the superfluous, compare potential outcomes, and extrapolate from other experiences to the current one is vital. Entrepreneurs also regularly have to weigh options in complex situations. Critical thinking skills can be improved through practice and by observing how others with well-developed skills work through a problem-solving situation. Many colleges and universities offer courses in critical thinking and there are a number of excellent books on the subject.

People who have a difficult time making decisions or who regularly find that they make poor decisions will probably not be successful as entrepreneurs. Making effective decisions is a critical part of the everyday life of an entrepreneur and is a skill that must be developed and exercised carefully. Poor decisions about hiring, business location, investors, and strategic partners can cost a company a great deal of money and prevent it from achieving its goals. Wise decisions, even in times of crisis, can provide an opportunity for growth.

The saying "the devil is in the details" could not be more true in business. Entrepreneurs who proudly claim that they leave the details to others while they focus on the vision are telling the world that they don't participate in the inner workings of their business. Details matter, and although entrepreneurs should not be micromanagers as the business grows, they should be well aware of the status of critical numbers in their business, and they should make their presence known among employees on a regular basis. It is vitally important to the success of the business that an entrepreneur be detail-oriented. Table 2.4 lists some of the skills that entrepreneurs need to hone to be effective at starting and growing their businesses.

Note in Table 2.4 that storytelling is listed as a critical skill. Research tells us that entrepreneurial stories are a way to facilitate a new venture's identity and legitimacy as well as create a competitive advantage that is difficult to replicate.[32] A compelling story about the founding of the business, how the need was identified, and why customers will choose to buy from the entrepreneur's company over others will help an entrepreneur raise capital, find strategic partners, and build a board of directors. Entrepreneurs, therefore, must become skilled storytellers, crafting tales about who they are and how their new venture and its resources will benefit customers, investors, and society.

Entrepreneurial leaders have a distinct advantage over charismatic or heroic leaders. Being a hero is lonely; there are no peers to confide in or teammates with whom to share the load. Today, more than ever before, entrepreneurs see

TABLE 2.4	Analysis and critical thinking	Persuasion and negotiation
Critical Entrepreneurial Skills	Opportunity recognition	Written and oral communication
	Resource gathering	Leadership and people management
	Organizational and time management	Decision making
	Calculated risk taking	Storytelling

themselves as part of a team, from the founding of the venture throughout all the various stages in the life of that venture. The days of the gunslinging solo entrepreneur are gone. Today it takes a team to succeed and a leader who can inspire others to motivate and lead as well. Entrepreneurial leadership, like any effective leadership, is a balance of passion and pragmatism. It is the entrepreneur's passion that launches the business and keeps it going through the early days when survival is often in doubt. But a different kind of leadership is often required once the business has survived and has entered growth mode. A more pragmatic style of leadership that can deliver the right systems and controls to keep the venture on course is not often found in the same person who founded the venture. Unfortunately, in private companies it is often the entrepreneur/founder who is left to decide when it's time for him or her to hand the reins to a different type of leader, and only the rare entrepreneur recognizes when that moment is at hand. Sometimes, however, the entrepreneur remains as the visionary leader of the company but brings on a CEO with professional management skills. This topic is explored in more depth in Chapter 18.

Study an Industry

One of the best ways to discover an opportunity is to study an industry in depth, perhaps even work in the industry for a time. An industry is a group of companies that are engaged in a similar or related activity; for example, the computer industry consists of all the businesses that provide parts, assembly, manufacturing, and distribution for computers—essentially all of the businesses involved in the value chain for computers. The value chain is all the businesses involved in the production of a product or service from raw materials through delivery to the final customer and is discussed in more depth in Chapter 5. The best opportunities come from entrepreneurs' experience and knowledge of an industry, a market, or a type of business. Since opportunities are not limited to products and services, studying an industry offers the prospect of identifying opportunity anywhere in the value chain of that industry. A method for analyzing an industry is presented in Chapter 5.

When all is said and done, business is about relationships—with partners, with customers, and with suppliers. Successfully building relationships requires honesty and integrity. It requires giving value and delivering on promises. An entrepreneur's core values are the foundation for the business and are always reflected in the business and in the way customers are treated. Their integrity is something that entrepreneurs guard more carefully than anything else because they cannot afford to taint or lose it. The next chapter explores how entrepreneurs cultivate ideas into business opportunities.

New Venture Action Plan

- Complete the personality and preferences questionnaire.

- Find a mentor and begin building a network.

- Pick an industry and begin studying it.

Questions on Key Issues

1. Why do myths emerge around phenomena such as entrepreneurship?
2. How do corporate entrepreneurs differ from other types of entrepreneurs?
3. What are the steps you should take to prepare yourself for entrepreneurship?
4. What might explain the rise in interest in social or nonprofit entrepreneurship?
5. Why are more ventures started by teams than by solo entrepreneurs?

Experiencing Entrepreneurship

1. Identify an entrepreneur who is leading the kind of personal and business life that you aspire to lead. Interview that person to find out more about how she or he achieved that lifestyle. During the interview, and only if the two of you have developed a rapport, approach the entrepreneur about the possibility of becoming your mentor.

2. Entrepreneurship is a journey, and many people contribute to that journey. Begin a contact portfolio that will contain the names of all the people you meet as you network. Record their contact information, how you met them, and what they contributed to your journey. Strive to meet three to five new contacts a week.

Relevant Case Studies

Case 2 MySpace
Case 7 1-800-Autopsy

CHAPTER 3

CREATIVITY AND OPPORTUNITY

"The greater danger for most of us lies not in setting our aim too high and falling short; but in setting our aim too low, and achieving our mark."

—MICHELANGELO

CHAPTER OBJECTIVES

- Understand the nature of entrepreneurial opportunity through discovery and creation.

- Discuss creativity, its challenges, and how to develop creative skills.

- Explain problem solving as it relates to creativity and entrepreneurship.

- Understand types of innovation and the innovation process.

Dr. Yoshiro Nakamatsu, also known as Dr. NakaMats, is truly the essence of a creative, innovative person. An 81-year old genius, he holds the world record for inventions, more than 3,218 inventions and patents, twice as many as the great American inventor Thomas Edison. And with that he claims to be only halfway to his goal of 6,000 inventions in his lifetime. For example, Nakamatsu is responsible for the floppy disk, which he licensed to IBM (and he does get a royalty on the millions of disks sold every year), the compact disk and disk player, the digital watch, and the water-powered engine. So prolific is he that his offices in Tokyo are located just a short walk from the patent office.

At the tender age of 5, he invented an automatic gravity controller for a model plane that he claims made autopilot possible. The patent on that invention has long since expired, and he earns no royalties from autopilot systems. At the age of 14, he invented a plastic kerosene pump on which he still holds the patent. That device can now be found in any hardware store.

Nakamatsu credits his genius to his parents' constant encouragement to be creative and not focus solely on learning. This is contrary to the traditional Japanese upbringing, where children are typically made to memorize great quantities of information and are not allowed to free associate in their thinking until their twenties. These factors, along with his discipline and belief that trying too hard stifles creativity, led to Nakamatsu's stellar career as an inventor.

Nakamatsu believes that successful innovation comes from "freedom of intelligence." By that he means that you have to work with no strings attached. Consequently, Nakamatsu has never sought funding from anyone and uses his own resources to develop and invent. The only licensing of his technologies that he has ever done was to IBM in the 1970s for computer-related patents.

He prefers to hold on to his intellectual property and to make his unique products himself.

Nakamatsu has a very idiosyncratic way of generating ideas. He starts the creative process by sitting calmly in a room in his home that he calls the "static room" because it has only natural things in it, much like the meditation gardens in Kyoto, Japan. Here he opens his mind to the creative flow of new ideas—he free-associates, letting his mind go wherever it wants to. He then moves to the "dynamic room," a dark room with the latest audio/video equipment. Here he listens to jazz, easy-listening music, and Beethoven's Fifth Symphony—one of his favorites. In this room, new ideas begin to form. Following a period of time in the dynamic room, he heads for the swimming pool, where he swims underwater for extraordinarily long periods of time. It is underwater that he finishes the process of "soft thinking," or playing with the idea, and becomes ready to move on to the more practical phase of considering how to implement the idea. He even records his ideas under water on a special Plexiglas writing pad.

Nakamatsu, by the way, also swears by the brain food he eats, which he dubbed "Yummy Nutri Brain Food": dried shrimp, seaweed, cheese, yogurt, eel, eggs, beef, and chicken livers! He has consumed only his own food for the past 30 years and lives on 4 hours of sleep a night. He now has 29 guesthouses on his property where "geniuses" of all types spend time. "There is a waiting list of about 100 people who simply want to live here to get inspired by me and my inventions," asserts Nakamatsu. When faced with a choice between the easiest path and the most difficult path, he always chooses the most difficult because there he can find what no one else has found.

Sources: "Dr. NakaMats: Patently Strange: The World's Most Prolific Inventor," *Motherboard*, March 3, 2010, www.motherboard.tv/2010/3/3/dr-nakamats-patently-strange-the-world-s-most-prolific-inventor; "Twilight

Zone: Dr. NakaMats' Inventions," *Pingmag* (October 20, 2006), http://pingmag.jp/2006/10/20/ twilight-zone-dr-nakamats-inventions; T. Hornyak, "Dr. Naka-Mats: Japan's Self-Proclaimed Savior," *Japan Inc.* (January 2002); L. Betti, "Yoshiro Nakamatsu: Inventing Genius," *Evolution* (September 15, 2002), http://evolution.skf .com/zino.aspx?articleID=425 and Linda Naiman and Chic Thompson, "Dr. Yoshiro Nakamatsu," www.creativityatwork .com/articlesContent/Nakamats1.html.

Ideas are a commodity; everyone has them, dozens of them every day. Entrepreneurs are no different in that regard, but what distinguishes entrepreneurs from others who have ideas is that entrepreneurs know how to extract value from those ideas and turn them into opportunities that have commercial potential. Fundamentally, that is the difference between an idea and an opportunity, and it's an important distinction because when we talk about creativity and problem solving, we typically talk about them in the context of ideas; but the reality is that creativity and problem-solving skills are critical to entrepreneurs' ability to shape an opportunity in such a way that more value is extracted from it.

Research on entrepreneurial opportunity has identified two fundamental theories to explain how opportunities happen: discovery theory and creation theory. Discovery theory sees opportunity arising from shifts in external factors in the market or industry, such as regulation, technological changes, and changes in customer preferences.[1] These opportunities are out there waiting for entrepreneurs to discover them, so they require a more systematic approach to scanning the environment. If opportunities are out there for anyone to find, what explains why entrepreneurs tend to be better at discovering or recognizing opportunity when they see it? Research has learned that what distinguishes entrepreneurs from others is alertness or awareness. Alertness is a combination of a number of attributes such as risk preference, cognitive differences, and information asymmetries—what the entrepreneur knows that others do not.[2] Entrepreneurs often find themselves making decisions about opportunities without having all the required information needed to judge the risks and benefits associated with them. Therefore, a discovery type of opportunity requires decision making under high levels of risk.[3]

The second major theory of opportunity is creation theory. Unlike discovery theory, there is no single coherent theory, but rather a number of assumptions about contexts and behaviors that don't fall within the realm of discovery theory. In creation theory, entrepreneurs are the actors; that is, entrepreneurs create opportunities via their actions, reactions, and experiments around new products, services, and business models.[4] This means that opportunities do not necessarily emerge out of existing industries or markets; therefore, search is not associated with creation theory. Entrepreneurs act and then monitor how customers respond to those actions. Creation theory allows for the fact that there are no "seeds" for opportunities in the industry/market environment.[5] If there are seeds, they lie within the entrepreneur, so these types of opportunities do not exist outside the mind of the entrepreneur. Consequently, a creation opportunity can emerge without any planning or foresight; the entrepreneur acts and then in a sense-and-respond fashion continues to move forward in a direction dictated by the responses he or she receives from the environment and the new information acquired from the experience. In practice this means that creation entrepreneurs, by their very nature, are willing to generalize from small samples, take more risk with less information, and rely on their own abilities to develop the opportunity.

Whether entrepreneurs recognize opportunity in external shocks in the industry or market or they create opportunity by their actions and reactions, entrepreneurs employ their creativity and problem-solving skills. This chapter focuses on the link between creativity and problem solving and how entrepreneurs use these skills to shape the opportunities they exploit.

CREATIVITY: WHAT IT MEANS

What does creativity have to do with entrepreneurship? Everything! Creativity enables entrepreneurs to differentiate their businesses from competitors so that customers will notice them. Creativity is the basis for invention, which is discovering something that did not exist previously, and innovation, which is finding a new way to do something or improving on an existing product or service. Creativity is also fundamental to problem solving. Today, entrepreneurs face a rapidly changing environment brought about in large part by the speed of technological change. The combination of rapid change and the resulting uncertainty about what the future holds presents a fertile ground for new opportunities. Creativity is a critical skill for recognizing or creating opportunity in a dynamic environment and for problem solving, which is necessary to satisfy customer needs.

What exactly is creativity? Many people have attempted to define creativity. Gryskiewicz defined creativity as useful, novel associations.[6] Noller developed a formula that suggests that creativity is a function of three dynamics: knowledge, imagination, and evaluation.[7] Isaksen and others, recognizing the diversity of definitions and not wanting to subscribe to one single version, have adopted four general themes as depicted in the diagram in Figure 3.1: characteristics of

FIGURE 3.1

Creativity Themes

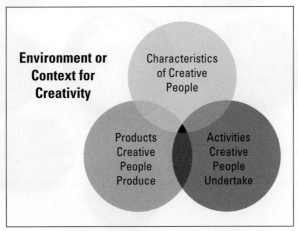

Source: Adapted from Isaksen, S.G., Stein, M.I., Hills, D.A. & Grayskiewicz, S.S. (1984). "A Proposed Model for the Formulation of Creativity Research," *Journal of Creative Behavior,* 18: 67–75.

creative people, processes creative people perform, products produced, and the climate, culture, or context in which creativity occurs.[8]

The earliest research on creativity focused on the individual, in much the same way that early research on entrepreneurship focused on the entrepreneur. Researchers looked at personality factors and cognitive skills such as language, thinking processes, and intelligence to attempt to determine the profile of a creative person.[9] Then they examined the context in which people are creative and found that a number of environmental settings are conducive to creativity, among them the absence of constraints or freedom to do as one pleases, the presence of rewards or incentives to encourage creativity, and team effectiveness or the ability of people to collaborate and support each other's efforts.[10]

The creative process is difficult to study because it generally deals with a person's internal thought processes, which are often not apparent even to the person being studied. One of the earliest descriptions of the creative process came from Wallas who had studied famous artists and scientists and from that identified four stages in the creative process: (1) preparation, or looking at a problem from a variety of perspectives; (2) incubation, or letting the problem lie in the subconscious for a time; (3) illumination, or the discovery of a solution; and (4) verification, or bringing the idea to an outcome.[11]

A more recent view of the creative process comes from photographer and documentary film producer Norman Seeff, who identified seven stages that an individual or a team goes through as they move from the beginnings of an idea to the fulfillment or final outcome (see Figure 3.2).[12] In stage one, the

FIGURE 3.2

The Seven Stage Dynamic of the Creative Process

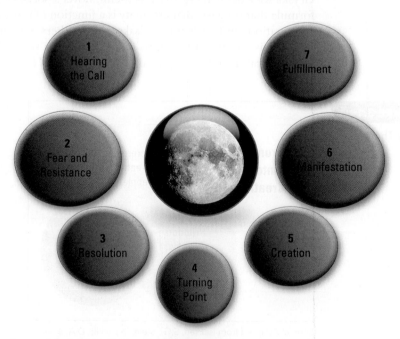

Source: Adapted from Norman Seeff Productions.

honeymoon phase, the new idea is born and it brings with it all the possibilities for what it can become. However, that possibility stage is quickly followed by fear and resistance, typically precipitated by previous experience with failure that causes the individual to consider what might go wrong this time. Stage three is reached when the individual has reconciled the major fears associated with the idea and has answered enough of unknowns to feel comfortable moving forward. Stage four, the turning point, is when the individual either makes the commitment to move forward despite not having all the answers, or he or she gives up on the dream. Stage five represents the implementation of the action plan to turn the idea into reality, while stage six is the outcome of the effort in the form of a new product, a new business, or whatever outcome has been defined. Seeff's process has a stage seven, which represents the emotional fulfillment of the original dream. If Seeff's process is overlaid on the entrepreneurial process, which is typically a team effort, it is clear that stage seven represents the full emotional commitment of the team to each other as individuals and to the new venture as a whole. Seeff believes that this emotional commitment is essential to the successful completion of a creative endeavor and this belief was born out in his experience with the JPL team and the Mars Rover project (see the Social Entrepreneurship box).

SOCIAL ENTREPRENEURSHIP: MAKING MEANING

Tapping into Emotions to Understand the Act of Creation

Breakthroughs in understanding the creative process often come from people who are involved in an active way on a daily basis. Norman Seeff, a South African medical doctor turned photographer, has spent his life exploring the creative process, and through his work has managed to put a very human face on a highly technical project. Seeff is probably best known for his innovative and interactive photo sessions with actors, musicians, and artists that give a unique insight into the act of creation. It was this work that led him to be invited to work with NASA scientists at the Jet Propulsion Laboratory (JPL) in Pasadena, CA, and to produce a documentary film about the Mars Exploration mission of 2004 called *Triumph of the Dream*.

In working with the JPL team, it would have been easy for Seeff to simply recount the events that led up to the successful mission, but Seeff knew that if he could tap into the team's emotions, he might figure out why this mission succeeded while the previous Mars Polar Lander mission had failed. As it turned out, the technical achievements of the mission served merely as the context or backdrop for the very real inner journey the team members experienced as they struggled to overcome the inertia of the previous failures. What Seeff discovered during this journey was that the imagination and emotional commitment the team had to each other and to the dream of successfully landing two Rovers on Mars made all the difference in their success. For the duration of the project, the team essentially became a family who believed in each other as much as they believed they could achieve the mission. And achieve the mission they did in just three and a half years from the date the idea was born. This experience cemented Seeff's belief that to achieve game-changing creativity, a team has to be emotionally connected with a vested interest in succeeding as individuals and as a team for the good of the whole.

Challenges to Creativity

Creativity tends to occur naturally if one lets it, but entrepreneurs often unintentionally erect roadblocks that prevent them from following the creative path. These roadblocks are generally of three types: personal, problem solving, and environmental.

No Time for Creativity

Entrepreneurs are often so busy that there is no time to think and contemplate, and this can keep them from exercising their creative skills. Today we are all bombarded by mobile devices that deliver a constant stream of information. Recent research has found that most U.S. workers complain that they are under a great deal of pressure in their jobs to get things done quickly. They report difficulty concentrating on a single task, so workers never feel that they have accomplished anything.[13] When the same study was conducted in 1994, researchers found that 82 percent of respondents claimed to accomplish at least half their planned work for the day, but in the current study that percentage dropped to 50 percent. One of the biggest contributors to lowered productivity is multitasking. A recent study published in the *Proceedings of the National Academy of Sciences* surveyed 262 students about their media consumption habits. They then took the 19 students who multitasked the most and the 22 who multitasked the least and conducted additional tests. The findings were telling. In every test, those who spent the least amount of time simultaneously e-mailing, texting, talking on the phone, and surfing the Internet performed substantially better than those who spent the most time doing such activities.[14]

The subconscious is the part of the brain responsible for discovery. If the thinking parts of the brain (left and right hemispheres) are constantly active, the subconscious is unable to supply the creative power it was designed for. Entrepreneurs need to set aside some time each day to let their brains free-associate or perhaps to do something creative that is unrelated to work. The simple act of turning off the e-mail notification button or turning off the phone can cut down on distractions and open the door to new ideas.

No Confidence

"Confidence is the expectation of success."[15] Those who expect to be successful generally are willing to exert the effort, spend the time, and expend the money to achieve it. Rosabeth Moss Kanter believes that confidence is comprised of three elements: accountability, collaboration, and initiative.[16] Accountability is personal responsibility for actions taken and is a component of a person's integrity. Collaboration means working with others and being able to count on each other. Initiative is believing that the actions taken will make a difference. Taking the familiar, easiest, or shortest path usually happens when entrepreneurs lack confidence; they act out of fear of being criticized, and that often keeps them from fully realizing their potential. The need for their ideas to be acceptable or seem rational to others is a significant roadblock for some entrepreneurs; however, rationality is not a prerequisite either for innovative ways to seize opportunities or for receiving a patent on an invention! The inventor of patent number 2,608,083 probably thought he was being rational when he invented the Travel Washing Machine, a portable, mobile appliance that is mounted on the wheel of a vehicle and washes the driver's clothes as he or she motors down the road. Unfortunately, the motorist has to jack up the car first to install the device and, for optimum results, cannot travel faster than 25 miles an hour. Ridiculously irrational inventions notwithstanding, many of the products in use every day—the fax machine and the personal computer, to name two—would not have come about if the people who invented them hadn't had the courage to go against the general thinking of the time.

Setting manageable goals that create small wins when they're achieved can help entrepreneurs who lack confidence develop this important attribute. Conducting a feasibility analysis of a new business idea is an excellent way to reduce some of the risk of entrepreneurship and build confidence.

For all the positives associated with creativity, it should not go unmentioned that creativity can also be an obstacle to achieving a goal. Creatives who don't know when to stop improving on an idea or planning their business and start moving into an action orientation face an uphill battle attempting to reach the outcome they seek. This topic will be discussed in more depth in Chapter 9.

DEVELOPING CREATIVE SKILLS

All of the aforementioned roadblocks can stifle creativity, but individuals who believe they are not creative are doing themselves the greatest disservice. They are dismissing ideas before even trying them out and, at the very least, setting themselves up for failure. There are a number of things that can be done immediately to remove the roadblocks along the path to more creative thinking. The process starts with preparing an environment that makes it easier to think imaginatively and then moves to some techniques for enhancing creative skills.

Design an Environment to Stimulate Creativity

Great inventors such as Yoshiro Nakamatsu and highly creative companies like Google owe their success to having provided an environment that simulated high levels of innovation. Thomas Edison's greatest invention was arguably not the light bulb but rather the concept of a research and development laboratory that served as an incubator for radical innovation. Likewise, Disneyland was not the greatest invention of the Walt Disney Company. Disney Imagineering, its Edison-like laboratory, is the source of most of its celebrated ideas.

The environment in which a person works can either stimulate or discourage creativity. No matter what the daily activities an entrepreneur is responsible for, there are ways to make the setting more conducive to creativity and innovation. Entrepreneurs should do the following:

Minimize distractions. Close the door, shut off the phone, and turn off e-mail to prepare to do some creative thinking.

Devote some time each day to quiet contemplation. Maintaining quiet time on a regular basis trains the mind to shift quickly into the creative mode. It also helps make creative thinking a habit.

Pay attention to the places that inspire the most creative thinking and spend more time there. Individuals who find that they think best outside should arrange their day to spend some time outdoors.

Spend more time with people in different fields of interest and move out of the comfort zone. Spending time in new endeavors with people who are very different from the entrepreneur will bring a new perspective to the issues the entrepreneur faces. Neville Hockley found that he had to get away from his traditional New York design firm to do his most creative work. So he and his wife took their 41-foot sloop on a trip around the world. Using satellite communications, he was able to do everything he typically does in the office without the distractions of the day-to-day running of the business. This change of environment freed him up to focus on new ideas.

Log Ideas

The creative journey begins with maintaining a journal of one's thoughts and ideas. Many entrepreneurs keep this type of journal with them at all times, even at their bedside at night, to record whatever pops into their heads. They may not be

MAKE A CONNECTION

Try this exercise with a group of friends. It is sure to get everyone thinking outside the box. Give each person in the group a piece of paper. Then have each person write a noun on his or her paper—any noun. When all of the members have written a noun, everyone then passes his or her paper to the person on the right. Each person will now write an adjective on the paper—any adjective; do not consider the noun when writing it. Then the papers should be passed again to the right. Each person will then write a verb on the paper and pass it to the right. For the final round, each person will write an adverb on the paper. In each case, the word that is written does not have to relate to the previous words on the page.

Then the group should move into the next phase: connecting the words in a relationship so that a potential business opportunity appears. The group should decide on one page only and discard the others. Using the words provided, the group will come up with a business concept that includes product/service, customer, benefit, and distribution.

This exercise is based on the premise that many opportunities are created by going through a process that involves:

- Connecting dissimilar concepts
- Experimentation
- Inventing something new based on connections and experimentation
- Finding applications for the invention/opportunity created

ready to work on a particular idea at that very moment, but they still jot it down so that they can return to it in the future. IDEO, with locations around the world including North America, the United Kingdom, Germany, and Asia, is one of the most successful new product idea companies in the world. One of the reasons for their success is that they stockpile ideas, even those on which they didn't follow through, because these ideas, which can range from glow-in-the-dark fabric to holographic candy, become useful for brainstorming sessions. When they are shared across several IDEO offices through the company's virtual Tech Box, every item, no matter how unusual, has the potential to be the inspiration for the next blockbuster product. The act of putting ideas down on paper reinforces that ideas have value and should be saved. It also serves as motivation for the entrepreneur, who will no doubt see an increase in the number of ideas generated over time.

Put the Familiar into a New Context

It is a myth that entrepreneurs only build businesses based on concepts that never existed before. Most business concepts derive from existing ideas on which the entrepreneur makes improvements. And most business ideas stem from a problem or opportunity that an entrepreneur sees in his or her immediate environment. The local neighborhood or community is a rich source of opportunity, and finding opportunity in things with which an entrepreneur has experience is the most common and effective way to achieve early entrepreneurial success. Playing with a piece of wire while thinking about a debt he had to repay resulted in Walter Hunt's development of the safety pin, and no one could have predicted that such a simple device would have such a long product life.

Great ideas often spring from imagining the opposite of what is normal. For example, think about what can be done with a telephone. A number of years ago, when AT&T was brainstorming some new marketing tactics, the marketing people asked themselves what a telephone is *not*. It's not something that can be eaten, so they came up with a way to eat telephones—chocolate telephones, to be exact, which they sent to their best customers.

Another example can be found in the paradox of recessions. Most people regard recessions, or economic downturns, as negative events, but looking for what is good about a recession is a useful creative exercise. A recession brings about many more needs and problems in which to find opportunity. For example, during a recession, many people lose their jobs and go back to school to retrain themselves for new careers. Educational entrepreneurs know this, so they start private schools offering courses and workshops to people who want to take a new direction in their careers or need retraining after losing a job. Publishers know this as well, so they develop books geared toward retraining and refocusing careers.

Take Advantage of a Personal Network

The second most commonly cited source of new venture ideas is business associates. A personal network—a circle of friends, associates, and acquaintances—is not only a rich source of innovative ideas but it also opens the mind to new ways of thinking and new possibilities. Contacts within a personal network can help an individual connect ideas that might not have been considered because the individual was relying solely on her or his personal experiences. Contacts can help refine ideas and can direct an individual to resources to assist in testing the business concept. Personal networks come about not by accident but from the concerted effort of entrepreneurs to go out and meet new people on a daily basis.

Return to Childhood

Many creativity and innovation gurus use toys to get their clients to respond more creatively. Legos and K'NEX are great for stimulating creativity because they start with a simple brick or connector piece, and from there the sky's the limit. Take that one step further and play with children to see unfettered imagination in action. Suspending the adult intellect for awhile and thinking like a child can stimulate the natural creativity in everyone. Creativity guru Doug Hall, whose famed Eureka! Ranch in Cincinnati, Ohio, has been the birthplace of thousands of new product ideas, uses games and toys to make people more comfortable doing things they've never done before and to come up with ideas that previously they would have dismissed as strange or unworthy. Jose Muñiz was thinking in a childlike fashion when he took a bet from a friend that he could not make a living selling butterflies. He found that releasing scores of butterflies at weddings or other special events was something people were willing to pay for. In 2006, the revenues of his company, Amazing Butterflies, had reached $1 million.[17]

CREATIVITY AND PROBLEM SOLVING

One of the most effective ways entrepreneurs have of finding opportunity is to identify a problem and seek a solution. Most people do this out of habit every day; they just don't realize it. They can't find a particular tool they need (say, a hammer), so they substitute something else (the handle of a screwdriver). That's using creative thinking to solve a problem.

How are creativity and problem solving related? Early research has come up with some answers. For example, it has been suggested that creative thinking

CREATIVITY ACTION PLAN

- Work on your idea individually before you collaborate with the team.
- Capture your creativity in an action plan.
- Divide your action steps into urgent, important, and long term.
- Focus each day on something that implements your idea.
- Decorate your walls with the things you've completed to remind everyone what has been accomplished.

results in new or novel outcomes while problem solving produces original responses and effects in new circumstances.[18] It seems that problem solving often involves creativity, but creativity does not always involve problem solving. "Creative activity appears...simply to be a special class of problem-solving activity characterized by novelty, unconventionality, persistence, and difficulty in problem formulation."[19] In essence then, creative problem solving is about linking imagination and intelligence, emotion, and logic to arrive at the optimal opportunity.

Those who research and consult to large organizations on creative problem solving have developed complex processes by which teams can understand the problem or challenge, generate effective ideas, design a process, and prepare for action.[20] However, entrepreneurs need quick and flexible ways to creatively solve problems. Here we will introduce some techniques that may help entrepreneurs generate ideas and then focus on the best solution.

Define the Problem

In attempting to solve a problem, many entrepreneurs make a number of common mistakes that prevent them from defining the problem correctly and then analyzing potential solutions.[21] They often define the problem incorrectly by asking, for example, "how can I fix this problem?" when the better question is "what is the source of the problem?" Answering the latter question opens the door to many more alternatives than are available with the first question. When we disregard the actual source of the problem, we may take mental shortcuts such as letting our personal biases interfere with the process, or relying simply on our intuition. Unfortunately, many of these mental shortcuts are subconscious; that is, we're not aware of them. For example, entrepreneurs frequently rely on patterns derived from previous experience, so when they face a new problem, they tend to consolidate all their previous biases based on experience and apply them to the new problem, which could be a huge mistake. Moreover, entrepreneurs sometimes draw conclusions before beginning their analysis or identify a solution before adequately defining the problem and analyzing it. Improperly or inadequately defining a problem means that the chances of ending up with the wrong solution increase substantially.

There are a number of effective ways to overcome these challenges. A few of the more popular strategies include:

- Restating the problem so as to uncover the real problem. For example, a problem stated as we need to increase our revenues appears to be an issue of how to generate more sales, but further investigation might conclude that the real problem is how to better serve the needs of the customer. If the value proposition for the customer has not been defined correctly, there is no realistic way to increase revenues and solve the actual problem.

- Identifying the pros and cons for potential solutions. There may be more than one way to solve a problem. In this case, it may be helpful to examine the positives and negatives associated with each solution and determine whether there is any way to convert the negatives to positives. The solutions with negatives that can't be fixed should be eliminated.

■ Develop a decision tree (like the one shown in Figure 3.3) that reflects all
the possible choices to solve the problem and its related outcomes. This
very simple tree depicts the choices available for an entrepreneur who had
developed a simple videoconferencing system to connect the elderly with
their distant family members. Notice that the tree branches are mutually exclusive, meaning that only one choice can be made. The branches are also

FIGURE 3.3   Decision Tree for Simple Videoconferencing System for the Elderly

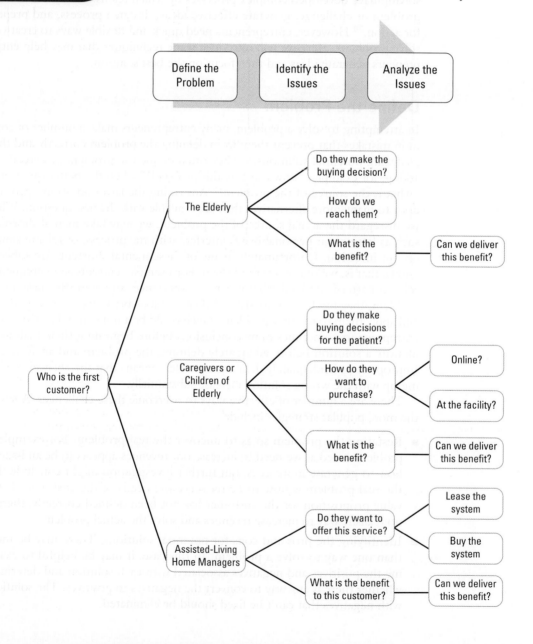

collectively exhaustive; that is, they include all the possible choices (note that due to space limitations, this example does not contain the entire universe of choices and potential outcomes). The decision to sell to assisted-living managers would generate two additional choices that would require additional analysis.

Generate Ideas for Sources of the Problem and Potential Solutions

Idea generation, whether it be to figure out the most likely source for the problem being considered or to generate solutions to a problem that has been defined, is an activity that benefits from few restrictions and no evaluation or criticism. The reason is that either praising or criticizing an idea at this point might shut off the flow of additional ideas or confine the direction of thought too early in the process. Instead, three rules of thumb apply:

- Go for quantity over quality of ideas initially.
- Capture every idea no matter how outlandish it may seem on the surface.
- Piggyback on ideas and create new combinations and modifications, but do this only after first generating ideas at the individual level.

Recent research conducted as a laboratory experiment has determined that where teams generate ideas first as individuals before coming together as a group to brainstorm (a hybrid approach), the number and quality of ideas improve, and the team is better able to discern which ideas are the best.[22] In fact, it appears that the best idea generated by the hybrid process is usually better than the best idea generated by the group approach. Why is this true? Group brainstorming often leads to situations where someone is unable to articulate an idea because others are speaking, an individual self-censors his or her idea before offering it based on evaluating other ideas already presented, or free riding takes place where some members contribute little or nothing because other members participate more actively.[23] The hybrid process, by contrast, produces about three times as many ideas per unit of time and these ideas are generally of much higher quality.[24] The bottom line is collaborative or team processes at the idea generation stage tend to lead to consensus and convergence, neither of which is useful to entrepreneurs looking for ideas that are innovative or game changing. A hybrid approach that involves working individually first to generate a set of ideas, then coming together as a group produces better results.

Other techniques for generating ideas include brainwriting, connecting unrelated things, identifying attributes, and restating the problem. These are now discussed.

Brainwriting

This approach is often used to make sure that everyone on the team feels comfortable offering up ideas. There are a number of ways the exercise can be accomplished, but essentially it's about getting ideas down on paper and then organizing the ideas and creating themes. Each person is given a stack of Post-It® notes. Each individual writes three ideas, one on each of three Post-Its. As everyone finishes, they place their Post-Its in the center of the table. Then each one takes three Post-Its they didn't create, looks at the ideas and once again writes three new ideas on each of three new Post-Its. This continues for three to four rounds. Then all the Post-Its are placed on a white board or flip chart and the process of finding common themes and combining ideas begins.

Connecting Unrelated Concepts

One of the common sources of new inventions is the ability to connect things that don't normally go together. Leonardo Da Vinci saw a connection between the branches of trees and the potential for a canal system in the city of Florence, Italy. He verbalized this connection as a metaphor: *canals are tree branches.* Nature has often served as the metaphor for an invention, including Velcro®, which was inspired by the sticky burr, and the entire field of nanotechnology. Review the "Make a Connection" box for an exercise in connecting things that are not normally associated.

Attribute Identification

This simple technique has the entrepreneur breaking down a problem into its various elements and then generating new approaches or modifications for each of the elements. For example, suppose the problem being worked on is how to differentiate an apparel company from every other apparel company? The attributes of this problem might include, among other things, the actual clothing line, the type of retail outlet, in-store service techniques, and customer acquisition strategies. Each of these attributes will have numerous possibilities for how they might be configured to create a unique product/service differentiation for the entrepreneur.

Restating the Problem

Two simple words, "how" and "why," can often break the logjam created by a problem statement that may be too narrow or too broad, giving the entrepreneur nothing meaningful to use. Look at Table 3.1 to see an example of how a problem statement can be reworked to get at the root problem that was not apparent from the original problem statement. In this case, it appears on the surface that the problem is not enough manufacturing space. One way to explore the source of the problem is to consider the opposite of the original statement or put the statement into a broader or narrower context; for instance, if we had more manufacturing space, what could we do with it? The approach that gets at the root of the problem in this case is asking "why" and then restating the problem until the real cause of the problem emerges.

Focus on the Problem Definition

Once a bunch of ideas are generated, there is a natural tendency to want to kill the "crazy" ideas quickly and rush to judgment on the best ideas. Both of these actions will ensure that the right problem definition gets lost in the scramble.

TABLE 3.1	Restating the Problem
Original problem statement	We don't have enough manufacturing space
The opposite of the original statement	We have too much manufacturing space.
Broaden or narrow the focus. Put the statement into a larger or narrower context	What would we do with more manufacturing space?
Ask "why" to get to the root of the problem	**Original Statement:** We need more manufacturing space.
	Why? Because we don't have room for all our workers.
	Problem Restatement: How can we accommodate all the workers we need?
	Why? Because we have had to hire more workers to complete our contract on time.
	Problem Restatement: How can we get more workers without having to provide manufacturing space?
	Why? Because we don't have the funding to add more manufacturing space right now.
	Problem Restatement: How can we outsource some of the work to another manufacturer?
	Why? Because we need to finish the project on time or we'll lose our major customer.
	Problem Restatement: In what ways can we finish the project on time?
	(We have generated the root of the problem, which is time and an impending deadline.)

To avoid this, Isaksen et al. suggests using the principle of Affirmative Judgment, which is simply looking for the strengths or positive aspects of a problem definition first.[25] In other words, keep the criticism at bay until all the positives are articulated. When offering up criticisms, they should be done in a positive manner by focusing on how the problem might be restated or refocused. Questions should engage the group in developing the definition further rather than simply dismissing it. This same principle will come in handy when it comes time to choose among solutions.

Using a set of predefined criteria is also helpful to establish some standards for the selection of the best problem definition. Alternatively, an evaluation matrix, often used to select product concepts for product development, can be used to select among several options against some critical benchmarks such as identifiable customer or inexpensive to prototype.

The goal of this stage in the problem-solving process is to arrive at a well-conceived problem statement. Going back to the example in Table 3.1, it is easy to see that the final problem statement arrived at by using the "ask why" process is clear and compelling and will make it easier to identify a good solution. An effective problem statement has four components: (1) a "how" question, (2) an answer to who is responsible for dealing with the problem, (3) an action verb, which represents the positive course of action anticipated, and (4) the target or desired outcome. Notice that in Table 3.1, the final problem statement contains all these elements: *In what ways can we finish the project on time?*

Developing Solutions

Identifying the right problem is the most challenging aspect of the problem-solving process because it's important to get it right so that time and money won't be wasted on the wrong solution. Engineers know that design represents about 8 percent of the new product budget but it accounts for about 80 percent of the final cost. For example, every time an engineer has to go back and redesign a solution because the problem was not correctly identified, it adds to the cost and time lost getting to market. Once the problem statement is completed, it's time to turn that statement into action.

The same techniques used to generate and focus ideas related to the problem can now be employed to generate and focus potential solutions. Criteria often play a more critical role in the identification of solutions because there are costs, skills, and timeframes associated with solutions that must be taken into consideration. Criteria can be explicit, which are more formal such as time limits, budget constraints, and the like. They can also be implicit: criteria that may not have been specifically identified, but that are known to be part of what must be considered in any decision about a solution—such things as intuition, team culture, preferences, prejudices, and perspectives often based on previous experience.

For entrepreneurs, the closer the solution relates to the actual problem the customer is experiencing, the more likely that there will be immediate sales upon completion of product development. The issue of customers as problem identifiers and how to find out about customer needs is the subject of Chapter 5.

INNOVATION

Creativity and problem solving are important skills for entrepreneurs to acquire, but they don't in and of themselves solve the entrepreneur's dilemma of how to extract value from an idea, value that someone will pay for. Innovation has been defined in a number of ways, but the following definition reflects the concept that innovation is not simply about products and services but about other aspects of the entrepreneurial process as well.

> Innovation is concerned with the process of commercializing or extracting value from ideas: this is in contrast with "invention," which need not be directly associated with commercialization. Rogers, 1998.[26]

In the 1930s, economist Joseph Schumpeter identified five categories of innovation: (1) a new product or substantial change in an existing product, (2) a new process, (3) a new market, (4) new sources of supply, and (5) changes in industrial organization.[27] Strictly speaking, Schumpeter did not see incremental improvements as innovation even if they generated economic growth. Moreover, an innovation did not become an innovation until it was commercialized, that is, until it realized economic value. So, when we talk about innovation, we're really talking about the process that takes a novel idea and transforms it into a product or service that customers will pay for. *Commercialization* is the process that moves an innovation from the laboratory to the market and develops the business strategy. Figure 3.4 depicts the innovation

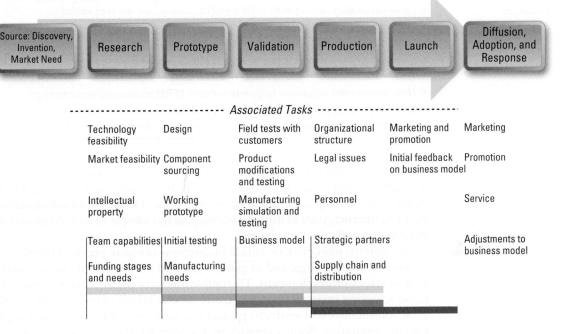

FIGURE 3.4   The Innovation and Commercialization Process

and commercialization process, the associated tasks, and the relationship of the various components. Note that the tasks listed are meant to provide a sense of the kinds of activities associated with a particular stage in the process and do not reflect all of the actual tasks that might need to be undertaken. Moreover, in the case of highly regulated ventures such as biotech and medical devices, the whole area of FDA requirements would need to be included.

How is innovation related to creativity and problem solving? Recall that creativity produces outcomes or results; sometimes those outcomes take the form of an innovation. The solutions that come out of successfully identifying a problem often require the development of something new, and that something new is called an innovation.

Innovation is increasingly a team sport. In 2006, the percentage of successful products developed in collaboration with others was nearly 79 percent, and the return to shareholders in those companies was 1.6 times the return for solo inventors.[28] These statistics are not surprising when one considers that the vast majority of all patents issued by the U.S. Patent and Trademark Office are never commercialized. Two prominent reasons for this are that the inventor did not have the skills to create a business opportunity from his or her invention, or that there was no market for the invention, meaning the invention did not solve a real problem that potential customers experienced.

Innovations can be grouped into two broad groups—incremental and disruptive (or radical)—and each has ramifications for entrepreneurial strategy. The vast majority of innovations today are incremental, that is, they are built on existing technology. For example, the Apple iPad was a huge improvement

TABLE 3.2 Some Sources of Innovation	• Customers (e.g., needs and suggestions for improvements or new products/services) • Newspapers and magazines (source of potential needs in the market) • Observation (e.g., sitting in a hospital and observing how the staff works) • Demographic shifts (e.g., the increase in the Latino population in the United States) • Small businesses (e.g., need for logistics support) • Unexpected news events (e.g., increased security needs resulting from the 9/11 attacks) • Trends and patterns of change (e.g., need for privacy protections on the Internet) • New government regulation (e.g., International (IFRS) accounting requirements) • Emerging industries (e.g., private space enterprise) • Business operations (e.g., new processes that reduce the costs of manufacturing)

over previous tablets but was actually an extension of the very popular iPhone. A number of important technologies had to be invented and available before Apple could develop either the iPad or the iPhone. Delivering an offline service over the Internet, such as distance learning, is an example of an incremental innovation on a distribution channel.

By contrast, disruptive or radical innovations obsolete previous technology or ways of doing things, and in general can find no identifiable market in the earliest stages of development. Disruptive innovations are often patented because achieving mass adoption is a costly process taking many years to accomplish and the inventor wants to protect the time and effort he or she has put into the innovation. Some examples are the Internet, the birth control pill, and the transistor. We will take up the strategic issues that are related to incremental and disruptive innovation in the chapters on marketing and growth. In the meantime, Table 3.2 provides some sources for innovation.

Opportunity is everywhere, and much of it goes unnoticed. Entrepreneurs who make the effort to become more creative and opportunistic will have an unending supply of new ideas available to play with.

New Venture Action Plan

■ Do the exercises under "Developing Creative Skills."

■ Complete the Creativity Action Plan.

■ Practice generating ideas and problems using the techniques provided in the chapter.

Questions on Key Issues

1. Give an example to demonstrate the difference between an idea and an opportunity.
2. Identify the challenges you face in becoming more creative. What three things will you do to address those challenges?
3. Pick a business in the community, and find a creative way to change either the product/ service or the way it is delivered to customers. How does your innovation add value to the business, and how can that value be captured?
4. How is invention different from innovation? Which is more common today, and why?

Experiencing Entrepreneurship

1. Spend an afternoon walking around your community or your university or college campus. Don't look for anything in particular. Observe the things that you don't normally pay attention to when you're in a hurry. Watch people—what they do and don't do. At the end of the afternoon, write down all the thoughts that come to you on the basis of your afternoon of observation. Which of these ideas could possibly become a business opportunity and why?

2. Pick one of the sources of new product/service ideas discussed in the section of this chapter that starts on page 57. Using that source, come up with an opportunity that has business potential. Then, using the Internet or talking to people in that industry (always the best approach), develop a brief report that supports the viability of this opportunity.

Relevant Case Studies

Case 5 B2P
Case 8 Demand Media

TESTING BUSINESS CONCEPTS AND MODELS

"Good design can't fix broken business models."

—JEFFREY VEEN,
Designing the Friendly Skies, 06-21-06

CHAPTER OBJECTIVES

- Explain what a business model is and what it accomplishes.
- Discuss the process for developing a business model.
- Explore the testing of a business model through feasibility analysis.

You would think that even today it is easy to stand out from the crowd in China if you're two U.S. entrepreneurs in the apparel industry. But you would be wrong. Visit any major shopping mall in Beijing or Shanghai and you will see Western brand names everywhere—Quicksilver, Levi's, French Connection, Gap. So when Tor Petersen and Renee Hartmann, U.S. expats, decided to try their hand at a lifestyle fashion brand targeting 18–24-year-old Chinese consumers, they knew they had to get the business model right.

The two were no strangers to China. Petersen joined Nike in China in 1990 and Hartmann was an investor relations consultant working with companies that were going public in the U.S. and Hong Kong. They met in 2005 while Peterson was working at a sports marketing firm that he co-founded. They initially conceived their fledgling company as a sportswear brand, but quickly discovered that the sportswear sector was already saturated with American and Chinese brands. Undaunted, they kept looking and discovered that the street wear sector was just emerging and offered an opportunity if they moved quickly. With a $5 million investment from a Shanghai venture capital firm, they went after the "low hanging fruit"—T-shirts—and then moved on from there to other types of apparel. They trademarked the name Eno (which is one spelled backward) to reflect the fact that Chinese youth love individualism but they need their group, no doubt in part because of China's one child law. Chinese youth have access through the Internet (in 2009, 330 million Chinese were online, up from fewer than 1.2 million in 1998) to people and ideas from all over the world, so they want their clothing to reflect who they are. Understanding this about their customers was important to Hartmann's and Petersen's ability to figure out that the critical success factor in their business model was design. They could do everything else right but if they didn't get the designs right, they would lose customers. Design was the critical success factor. In the beginning, Petersen directed the design staff and had them develop ideas off themes he gave them. That didn't work well because the designers weren't allowed to use their creative talent to its fullest. Learning from his mistake, he then gave the designers, who live in the same culture as Eno's target customers, responsibility for coming up with design concepts. They also used a crowdsourcing approach, getting design submissions from all over the world.

Hartmann and Petersen quickly learned that they really didn't know Chinese preferences as well as they thought they did. For example, Hartmann thought that Chinese youth didn't like having Chinese characters on their t-shirts. But then they had a hit with an environmentally themed shirt with the character for "tree" written three times on the front of the shirt. According to Hartmann, ". . . that T-shirt sold like crazy no matter what color we put it in. We didn't expect that." With the changes in their design process, Eno can now move a T-shirt design from concept to the selling floor in three weeks, and they're working on a supply chain that will enable them to get small batches of new designs out even more quickly.

Another critical success factor that quickly became apparent was the need to get close to the customer in order to quickly respond to their ever-changing needs. Their Shanghai store is a converted karaoke bar where they not only sell their apparel, but provide free monthly music events that have become very popular with their customers. Eno is in an increasingly competitive market and their biggest concern is the rise of other local brands. Current plans have Hartmann and Petersen staying ahead of the competition by constantly innovating and franchising for rapid growth.

Sources: Zouhali-Worrall, M. (October 29, 2009). "China's Street Fashion," www.cnnmoney.com; and "Interviewed: Tor Petersen, Eno CEO and Founder," *Enovate*, http://enovatechina.com, accessed July 5, 2010.

n today's vibrant, fast-paced business environment, it's easy to get the impression that business concepts are developed on a napkin during dinner and that the business is funded and operating within a few days. But even for Internet businesses, that exciting scenario is a stretch. Just because an entrepreneur builds a business does not mean that customers will come. In reality, a substantial amount of thought must take place and a great deal of effort must be put forth before a company's products or services ever successfully reach the market. That thought process includes developing a business concept that meets a real market need and a business model or way to capture value.

Peter Drucker, often referred to as the greatest management thinker of the last century, understood as far back as the 1950s that there is no business without a customer. He regularly challenged entrepreneurs and corporate CEOs alike to answer five important questions about their business model:

- What is our mission?
- Who is our customer?
- What does our customer value?
- What are our results?
- What is our plan?[1]

In the field of entrepreneurship, no matter how many fancy names are given to what entrepreneurs do, no matter how many elaborate frameworks researchers use to explain who entrepreneurs are and why they succeed, it all comes down to these fundamental questions. If the entrepreneur doesn't have a firm grip on the answers to these questions, all the rest is a waste of time.

Drucker's five questions are the basis for the development of the business model. The mission is why we're in business—the big goal that the company is trying to achieve. The customer is the one who pays for the value being delivered, and that customer may be an individual or a business. What the customer values is the most difficult question to answer unless the entrepreneur has spent time in the market trying to understand the problems customers face. Solving those problems is the value or benefit customers are seeking. The results tell us if we're on the right path, but entrepreneurs also need to know what results they're working toward. Entrepreneurs don't predict the future—they create it and then find the means to achieve it. The plan is not the traditional business plan, a huge document that tends to cement ideas in place while the reality around those ideas keeps changing. For entrepreneurs, the plan is an action plan, a series of small experiments to provide feedback and help them test and rework the original ideas until they best meet the needs of the customer.

This chapter explains how to turn an idea into an effective concept for a new business, position that business in a value chain, and develop a business model that creates and captures value for the customer and insures that the business is sustainable.

THE BUSINESS MODEL

The term *business model* has become quite popular in discussions about new businesses, but there appears to be significant confusion about what a business model actually is and how entrepreneurs use them.[2]

A recent study of the current definitions of *business model* has concluded that all these definitions have at their foundation two fundamental activities: the creation and capture of value. These two activities represent the core logic for how the company creates value for the customers and what the organization must do to become or remain viable. First, a successful venture creates value by differentiating itself from competitors and/or by meeting an unserved need in the market. Second, it captures value by monetizing (to use another popular term) its offering; in other words, entrepreneurs find ways to make money from what the businesses do. Both of these activities take place within what has been termed a *value network*, which is the community of partners, suppliers, and other members of the value chain with which the venture does business.[3]

Effective business models address all the aspects of the model, which are depicted in Table 4.1: pricing, revenue, value proposition, process, and Internet commerce. A winning business model is difficult to copy because it builds barriers to entry for competitors. It is also "grounded in reality...based on accurate assumptions about customer behavior."[4] Building an efficient business model

TABLE 4.1 The Business Model Components		
Pricing Model	• Market based • Cost plus • CPM (cost per thousand clicks) • Premium	
Revenue Model	• Transaction fee • Subscription or membership • License or syndication • Advertising • Volume or unit based	
Value Proposition	• Significantly greater value, higher cost, premium pricing • More value at same cost, same price • Less value at lower cost, lower price	
Business Process	• Direct to customer • Through intermediaries: distributors, retailers • Bricks-and-mortar location • Fully Internet based • Combination	
Internet Commerce	• Aggregator • Market maker • Value network • Integrator • Virtual supply alliance	

addresses all these issues and creates a competitive advantage for the company. One difficulty with business models is that they tend to change over time as customer needs change, so the challenge is to find a way to sustain the efficacy of the model over time. It must also be protected from imitation, which could turn the company's products and services into commodities and force the entrepreneur to compete on price.[5]

One of the few really successful business models from the dot com era, eBay, is thriving because its model cannot be replicated in the offline world and because the user/customer controls the buying and selling, which is the value they're seeking. Moreover, over time the eBay brand has engendered trust. Trust is also part of Union Supply Company's highly successful business model. It sells specialty items to correctional facilities that don't have time to search out the kinds of products they're allowed to have in their commissaries. For example, Union Supply offers tennis shoes with wooden shanks, which are safer, rather than the typical metal shanks. Demand is high, government buyers pay up front before receiving the product, and the company has no receivables and no physical inventory to deal with. There aren't too many business models more attractive than that.

Why Business Models Fail

Research has determined that there appear to be four major problems associated with business models that may explain why many fail: (1) flawed logic, (2) limited strategic choices, (3) imperfect value creation and capture assumptions, and (4) incorrect assumptions about the value chain.[6] Here we will consider examples of each.

Flawed Logic

Business models are doomed to failure when the underlying logic about the future is incorrect. When entrepreneurs assume situations and conditions that do not currently exist, they face huge challenges in their ability to execute the model. Napster, the file-sharing music site that pioneered music downloads from the Internet, began with the flawed assumption that it was not going to be held accountable for copyright violations on the MP3 files that its users swapped and downloaded. Because the recording industry was slow to recognize the threat of the digitization of music, Napster presumed that it had a clear path to success, but its model was shut down by court order in 2001. If the story doesn't make sense, the business model will fail.

Limited Strategic Choices

The strategic choices that a business model addresses should reflect both the value creation and the value capture processes. Satisfying only one of these will often lead to problems. During the dot com era, many misguided entrepreneurs thought that the Internet *was* the business model, so they developed businesses that had no compelling reason to exist beyond the fact that they were on the Internet. As a result, they couldn't get customers to patronize their sites.

Pets.com, for example, was built on the notion that customers would find it easier to buy dog food online. What they didn't realize was that most customers purchase dog food when they purchase their own food in a grocery store, so making online purchases was actually an inconvenience for them because it required them to make an additional stop on their computer and pay shipping charges. Funerals.com experienced a similar fate during the run-up to the dot com crash. The founder did not understand that in times of emotional grief, people do not want to turn to their computers for help; they prefer to deal with someone face-to-face.

In the offline world, problems with strategic choices also exist. Entrepreneurs are continually faced with the challenge of maintaining the value of their products and services so that they don't become commodities competing only on price. Avoiding commoditization means following a strategy of continual innovation and searching persistently for new ways to satisfy the changing needs of the customer. This certainly is the challenge that every technology entrepreneur faces.

Imperfect Value Creation and Capture Assumptions

One of the biggest challenges for business models is finding a way to make money from the value that has been created. A poor assumption about the value created by a new venture will mean that there are no customers to pay for that value. Similarly, even if there is a reasonable assumption of value created, it may not be the beneficiary of that value who has to pay for it. This is one of the biggest problems for entrepreneurs in the health care industry. An entrepreneur with a new medical device that can save patients' lives is not collecting revenue from the patient who sees the value but rather from the health care provider or worse yet an insurance company, whose mission is to contain costs, a completely different value proposition. When the numbers don't add up, the business model fails.

Incorrect Assumptions About the Value Chain

Entrepreneurs often assume that the value chain for their product or service is static, that is, that it will continue with the current players and with the current processes and information flow well into the future. This is a faulty assumption. Core competencies enable firms to move into new industries and new value chains unrelated to their current products and services. UPS did this when it examined Toshiba's lengthy and inefficient process for repairing laptops that involved shipping to UPS's hub, then to Japan, then back to UPS, then to the customer. UPS cut out all the excess shipping for Toshiba and now repairs their laptops in UPS's facility.[7] UPS's core competency is designing effective and efficient systems, and it took that competency from the package delivery industry to the computer industry, serving new markets.

DEVELOPING A CONCEPT FOR A NEW BUSINESS

A business concept is a concise description of an opportunity that contains four essential elements: the customer definition; the value proposition (or benefit to the customer); the product/service being offered; and the distribution channel or means of delivering the benefit to the customer. It is useful to think of the business concept as a quick elevator pitch. *Elevator pitch* is a term that has been applied to the idea that entrepreneurs have only a few seconds—the time it takes to ride an elevator up to the twelfth floor of a building—to get an investor (or other third party) interested in the entrepreneur's business concept. But the elevator pitch serves another valuable purpose: it gives focus to the development of the business. It's likely that the first concept conceived will go through many iterations before the business is launched, but coming back to the four critical elements each time will ensure that the fundamentals of the business are intact.

The Value Proposition

The value proposition is the benefit that the customer derives from the product or service the entrepreneur is offering; in other words, the reason the customer will buy—the value for the customer. To understand what the customer values, entrepreneurs need to identify a need or "pain" that customers are experiencing. When entrepreneurs first conceive of the concept for their business, they typically start with the value they believe customers will recognize and pay for. However, it is not until they do some actual market research and learn what customers value from their own words, that they can be confident that there will be someone to buy what they're selling. We talk about effective ways to understand customer needs in Chapter 5.

Entrepreneurs often confuse features with benefits as they design their products and services. In general, benefits are intangibles such as better health, saving time and money, or reliability, while features reflect attributes of the product such as design and characteristics. Table 4.2 offers an example of the distinction between features and benefits for a business where the product is premium hay for thoroughbred racehorses. Note that the benefits for the customer—the retailer—and for the end-user or beneficiary—the horse owner—are different.

TABLE 4.2 Features Versus Benefits for Premium Horse Feed for Thoroughbred Racehorses*

Features	Benefit to Retailer	Benefit to End-User (horse owner)
2-foot length of hay	Revenue potential—this feature makes the product more attractive to end-users, leading to higher potential sales and customer loyalty	Save money because less of it is wasted than is wasted with regular hay
Packaged in plastic bags	Cost savings, because it leads to less waste in inventory	Save money because there is less waste in storage
Flash-baked for greater nutrition and to reduce dust and mold spores	Revenue potential, because of cost savings from longer shelf life	Can prevent common ailments that impede racing performance, so also save money
Made with molasses, giving it a good taste for the horse	More reliable revenue potential—this feature leads to more consistent use among horse owners because horses typically do not switch after trying it	Make more money—its good taste leads horses to eat this high-nutrition feed, which can improve racing performance

*Prepared by Sheryl Sacchitelli, Daniel Wang, and Jason White, MBA class of 2003, University of Southern California.

The Customer Definition

Who is the customer? This vital question is deceptively simple. Many entrepreneurs cannot answer it accurately, because they simply assume that their customer is the user of a product or service they are offering. Although it is more common today than ever before for that to be the case, in many industries it is not. When Jordan NeuroScience first considered who the customer was for its ER-EEG technology designed to remotely monitor the brainwaves of trauma patients in emergency rooms, the founder immediately thought of the patients, the beneficiaries of the technology whose lives would be saved. But when faced with figuring out how to make money, the entrepreneur realized that the patients were not the customers, even the doctors were not the customers. Rather, the hospital administrators who made the purchasing decisions were the customers. This revelation changed everything about the business model. Jordan NeuroScience had to decide what benefit its product was providing to the hospital administrators, which was quite different from the benefit to the patients and doctors. Although hospital administrators are interested in obtaining technologies to improve patients' quality of life, they are primarily focused on increasing revenues and reducing costs. In short, the customer is always the one who pays for the solution.

Defining the customer is a critical part of the business concept, because the customer determines all the other components—what the entrepreneur will offer, what the value proposition is, and how the benefit will be delivered to the customer. A clear and precise customer definition increases the chances that the business concept will meet the customers' needs.

The Solution Being Offered

The product or service the entrepreneur offers at startup is really a solution to a problem the customer is facing, and that is how it should be positioned. Today, most businesses produce both products and services, even if one category dominates. Doing so provides multiple revenue streams, which gives the company a distinct competitive advantage. At startup, it's normal to focus on the lead product or service, but even at launch, entrepreneurs need to show that the company has potential for growth. Growth comes from a plan to add new products and services and enter new markets.

The Distribution Channel

The distribution channel answers the question "How do you deliver the benefit to the customer?" Many options exist, but in general, the best option is the one that fulfills the customer's expectations about where and how the product or service should be sold. Most services are delivered direct to customers, but products often go through channel intermediaries such as distributors and retailers. The distribution channel is addressed in Chapter 5 and again in Chapter 14, which deals with the new venture's marketing strategy.

Creating a clear and concise concept statement or elevator pitch from the four elements is not difficult, but it does require an ability to parse words, something many entrepreneurs have difficulty with. For example, consider the creation of artificial nerves called BIONS, under development at the University of Southern California. BIONS re-animate paralyzed muscles through electrical stimulation. In this case the proposed company, we'll call it BIONNIX, is studying the treatment of pressure ulcers in patients who are bedridden or in a coma. The company plans to sell to hospitals and nursing homes. To attract attention for the business, the entrepreneur needs to convey the magnitude of the pain.

> Every year there are 3.5 to 5 million people in the United States suffering from pressure ulcers, and an estimated 60,000 persons die annually from ulcer-related complications. Pressure ulcers represent a common but preventable medical problem encountered by primary-care practitioners providing care to older patients, particularly in hospital and nursing home settings.

This is the problem that must be solved in order to offer value to the customer. It must be stated in a way that captures attention quickly. If the problem requires detailed explanation, then the real pain has probably not been identified. In other words, the problem statement should be simple and clearly understood.

Adding the four-element concept statement or solution to a condensed problem statement produces the following:

> An estimated 60,000 persons die annually from pressure ulcer-related complications that could have been prevented with muscle stimulation. BIONNIX will provide a proprietary solution to hospitals and nursing homes that seek to reduce the costs and nursing hours associated with preventing and treating pressure ulcers in their immobile patients. BIONNIX will manufacture, sell, and support the implantable BION, which provides patients with an effective, easy, and painless solution to pressure ulcers.

We see here that the primary customer is hospitals and nursing homes that are looking to save money (labor costs) on treating patients with pressure ulcers. The end beneficiary is the patient, who avoids pressure ulcers. The concept statement is not designed to answer all the questions about the solution or how it will be implemented; instead, its goal is to focus the feasibility analysis and generate interest and further discussion.

Note that in the development of the concept statement, money was not mentioned. Money is assumed by inexperienced entrepreneurs to be the most necessary component of a successful venture. But although money is important, it is only an enabler; its presence does not confirm that the business concept is feasible, nor does it ensure success. In fact, the dot com bust of spring 2000 proved that a large investment in a business idea will not make it feasible if customer demand and an effective business model are not also present. Until customers express interest in what is offered and will pay for it, all the money in the world will not make the venture feasible.

The Entrepreneur's Story

Entrepreneurs have rarely understood the value of creating a great story around their ventures. Frequently, investors note that one reason they chose not to fund a particular venture was they couldn't find a compelling story, a reason to invest. Most of the work in the field of entrepreneurship has centered on how entrepreneurs recognize opportunity and mobilize resources to exploit that opportunity.[8] But entrepreneurship is largely a social process and to the extent that entrepreneurs can make sense of their own behaviors as they move through the process of conceiving, designing, and bringing to life a new business, they can use their story to create legitimacy and attract resources for the emerging business. The new venture's story will convey its specific assets and capabilities, particularly those that are rare and inimitable and make the venture more comprehensible to people who might be interested.

Every compelling story has a beginning, middle, and end. For entrepreneurs this translates to how they identified or created the opportunity, the challenges they overcame, and where they are now (prototype, seed round of funding, first customer). The story is designed to appeal to whatever audience the entrepreneur is trying to persuade whether that be customers, investors, potential partners, and anyone else the business might need to be successful. The story must balance the need to demonstrate the company's uniqueness with the need to conform to stakeholder expectations.[9] A well-told story will establish the company's identity and inspire confidence; as a result, it will be repeated and become part of the venture's legend over time.

The business concept is only a small part of the story—it establishes the facts—but the narrative that surrounds the concept adds color and texture and gives meaning to the venture that can't be replicated. For example, craigslist .com made waves in the Internet world not because it was exciting new technology or an unheard of new concept but because of the story behind the company and the legions of fans that story inspired. The founder, Craig Newmark, was the classic nerd who would have fit perfectly in the 1980s Generation X movie *Revenge of the Nerds*, which is about a group of super bright, but socially inept, young college students who succeed despite being constantly ridiculed by the stereotypical popular set—the football players and cheerleaders. Starting with his personal email list of people he regularly advised about art and technology parties at the local art house in San Francisco, Newmark began adding tips about art and culture. His fan base grew, and it was those very fans who got him to launch the website and name it as "Craig's List." As Newmark built the company, he retained his nerd values, which were shared by the growing list of people who frequented the site. The story of craigslist has been told again and again, and it has served Newmark and his business well.

BUILDING A BUSINESS MODEL FROM A CONCEPT

Identifying an opportunity is only part of the equation for new venture success. There also has to be a way to make money with this venture. How do entrepreneurs create value for customers and capture that value so that their business makes a profit? A number of important business decisions associated with the development of a business model can be summarized in a series of questions that should be answered before proceeding further with the model.[10]

1. What are the size and importance of the revenue streams that the business model can generate?

2. What costs most affect the model, and what are their size and importance to the model? In other words, what are the significant cost drivers for the business?

3. How much capital is required to execute the business model and what is the timing of the cash needs?

4. What are the critical success factors to achieving the goals of the business model?

Using eBay as an example, the highly successful company had a very simple business model at launch. Its infrastructure enabled users to communicate with each other for a reasonable fee. eBay "has no responsibility for goods offered at auction, for collecting buyer's payments, or for shipping."[11] It was merely responsible for making sure these transactions occurred. Its revenues came from seller fees; its cost structure included the online infrastructure, marketing, product development, and general and administrative expenses. More importantly, it took only a few salaried employees and partners to implement the startup model.

It is a fact of business life that business models evolve and sometimes radically change over time due to circumstances often beyond the control of the entrepreneur. Change can occur in a number of ways.[12]

1. *Incrementally expand* the existing model geographically, enter new markets, modify pricing, or change product/service lines. An example would be Kiyonna, an apparel manufacturer that moved from boutiques to an online site that better served their young, plus-sized customers. (www .kiyonna.com)

2. *Revitalize an established model* to give it new life and stave off competition. This can be accomplished by introducing new products or services to existing customers as Starbucks did when it began selling CDs of the music it played in its stores.

3. *Take an existing model into new areas.* For example, Amazon.com, known as a highly effective Internet bookseller, began using its successful fulfillment process to market and sell everything from clothing to household goods.

4. *Add new models via acquisition.* For example, a restaurant company might acquire a catering service.

5. *Use existing core competencies to build new business models.* Canadian manufacturer Bombardier originally focused on snowmobiles. Because it sold its products through credit, it developed an expertise in financial services, which enabled the company to move into capital leasing. Its manufacturing

FIGURE 4.1

Building a Business
Model

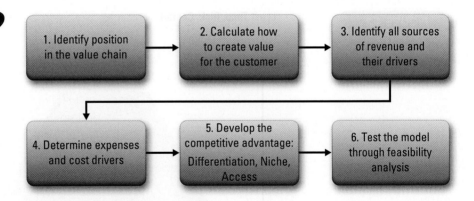

expertise was leveraged into large-scale manufacturing for the aircraft
industry.

6. *Reinvent the business model.* As a company's products become commodities,
it may take an enormous shift in operations, culture, and business model to
add new value to the company's offerings. Apple reinvented itself with the
introduction of the iPod and then again with the iPhone. The case study on
Command Audio in the back of the book is an example of a company that
had to reinvent itself and its business model three times before finding one
that was sustainable.

When building a business model, it's useful to do it in stages, as depicted in
Figure 4.1 and discussed in the following sections.

Stage 1: Identify the New Venture's Position in the Value Chain

The first step in developing a business model is to identify the new venture's
place in the value chain. The value chain consists of all of the companies that
contribute to the development and distribution of a good. If, for example,
the entrepreneur's company is a supplier or producer of raw materials, it will
generally be at the top of the value chain and upstream from manufacturers.
Intermediaries, such as distributors and retailers, will be downstream from
manufacturers and assemblers. Where a company is located in the value chain
normally reflects the entrepreneur's capabilities and risk-taking propensity.
Consider Figure 4.2, which depicts a commitment pyramid. In very simple
terms, the graph portrays the relationship between the location of a business
in the value chain and the time commitment, level of risk, and financial capital
required. Selling a business concept takes the least amount of investment and
requires the least time commitment from the entrepreneur; therefore, it is the
least risky and provides the lowest return. Conversely, starting a retail business
requires a huge time commitment, demands substantial capital, and generally
carries with it a higher level of risk and reward.

The Commitment
Pyramid

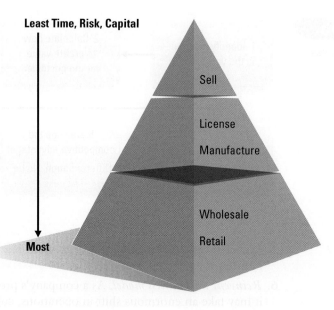

Least Time, Risk, Capital

Sell

License

Manufacture

Wholesale

Retail

Most

Once the business is located on the value chain, it is easier to recognize who pays whom and to determine costs and pricing. Figure 4.3 adds this information to a generic example of a complex indirect channel of distribution. The raw materials producer charges the manufacturer $4 per unit; the manufacturer turns the raw material into product and sells it to the distributor for $6. Alternatively, the manufacturer can use an independent sales representative (sales rep), who will find outlets and receive a commission on sales made. Note that the retailer, who buys from the distributor or sales rep, typically at least doubles its cost in setting the price to the consumer. This is known as keystoning. Also note that as a rule, markups increase as one moves down the channel. This occurs because the cost of doing business increases, as does the risk.

The Value Chain with
Markups

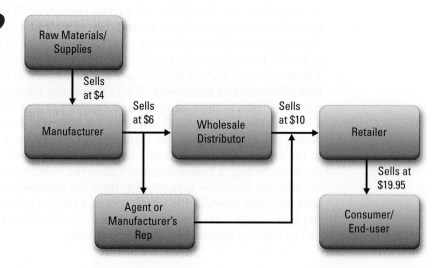

Raw Materials/
Supplies

Sells
at $4

Manufacturer

Sells
at $6

Wholesale
Distributor

Sells
at $10

Retailer

Sells at
$19.95

Agent or
Manufacturer's
Rep

Consumer/
End-user

The value chain now illustrates the various markups, which is helpful in determining the lowest price possible for the product. The highest price possible is determined through market research with potential customers. The markups on the original cost reflect profit and overhead for the channel intermediary and are determined by what is typical in the industry. Every product or service has more than one channel option, so it's a good idea to depict distribution options graphically to compare their effectiveness. Graphing the value chain makes it possible to do the following:

- Measure the time from manufacturing to customer on the basis of the lead time needed by each channel member.
- Determine the ultimate retail price on the basis of the markups required by the intermediaries.
- Figure the total costs of marketing the product. For example, manufacturers have to market to distributors, but to support their distributors, they may also market to retailers and even end-users or consumers.

At this stage, entrepreneurs should decide their business process model, whether they will serve the customer by means of a brick-and-mortar location, via the Internet, or some combination of the two. The business process, which includes the various Internet-based process types, is discussed in Chapter 8 as part of the building of the financial forecasts for the business.

Stage 2: Calculate How to Create Value for the Customer

Market research with customers should give the entrepreneur confidence that the solution being provided is recognized as valuable by customers. It is also important to determine whether the proposed business model will force customers to change the way they use or find a particular product or service. Will that change provide value for customers in a way that they can readily see? In other words, the basic functionality has not changed substantially, but the cost to the customer in terms of time and money is too high to warrant switching. Many products have learning curves associated with them, so it's essential to determine whether the learning curve for the customer will be steep. If customers see that learning to use the new product or service will take some time and require them to change old habits, they will think twice before purchasing.

Stage 3: Identify Revenue Sources

One of the most important components of the business model is identifying the revenue streams that will flow from the products and services being offered. A healthy business model always supports revenue streams from multiple types of customers and multiple products and services. Relying on one revenue stream from one type of customer is dangerous. What happens when the market shifts and that customer goes away? At launch it's not uncommon for new ventures to rely on one source of revenue from their primary product or service, but very quickly they need to move to multiple products and services and multiple markets to diversify their revenue streams and secure their sustainability.

The revenue model describes the various ways that entrepreneurs plan to make money. In general, the following categories of revenue models comprise the most common ways to monetize a product or service.

- **Subscription or membership.** Customers pay a fixed amount to belong or subscribe, generally monthly or annually.
- **Volume or unit-based.** Customers pay a fixed amount per unit and often receive a discount for volume purchases.
- **Licensing and syndication.** Customers pay to use or resell, typically a product, technology, or brand.
- **Transaction fee.** Customers pay for services, generally hourly or on a project basis.
- **Advertising.** In this model, the customer is the advertiser, not the end user of the product or service. Many Internet businesses have advertising as one of their revenue models.

In the mid-1990s, Edmunds Inc., the 32-year-old publisher of automotive information, saw the Internet as just another marketing vehicle. Today, the Internet *is* the business. Edmunds's website provides independent ratings, reviews, and pricing data for every make and model of car, in addition to a variety of other interactive features. Edmunds.com's basic business model is to make its money through ads placed by manufacturers, parts dealers, and others in the automobile industry. Books now account for less than 1 percent of its revenues. Changing its business model with the changing times, Edmunds.com now has revenue streams from books, from advertising, and from selling and licensing information to other companies.[13]

The pricing model (see Table 4.1) works in tandem with the revenue model. Both require significant market research and will be discussed in Chapter 8.

Stage 4: Determine Expenses and Cost Drivers

Equally important are the expenses and cost drivers of the business. The business that can keep its costs low enjoys a significant advantage and will bring more dollars to the bottom line. Every business has costs that produce the biggest impact on the cost structure; they are known as key cost drivers because they impact total costs.[14] These costs can be fixed (rent), variable (manufacturing), or nonrecurring, such as a one-time expense. In some businesses, there will also be semivariable expenses, which are simply a combination of fixed and variable costs. For example, many retail outlets employ a base number of sales people as a fixed cost. During the holiday season, they may supplement with additional sales people to handle the increased volume, so the cost to the business goes up for that time but not proportionate to the volume as in a true variable cost.

Depending on the type of business, the cost structure may be one of the following:

- **Marketing or advertising cost structure.** The primary costs of the business come from customer acquisition.
- **Inventory cost structure.** Here the biggest costs come with the maintenance of inventory, either goods for sale or raw materials.
- **Office or retail space cost structure.** In this type of business the primary cost driver is the cost per square foot of the space required to conduct business.
- **Support centered cost structure.** Here the business has high fixed costs in personnel required to support the activities of the business.
- **Direct cost structure.** These businesses' costs are driven by the direct costs of producing the product or service.

Stage 5: Develop the Competitive Strategy

A business model describes a system and how the various components of that system come together to create a competitive advantage in the marketplace.[15] Strategy is very different from a business model because it considers more than the customer and how the new venture will create and capture value; it considers the competition. An effective competitive strategy either differentiates the new venture from existing ventures, creates a niche in the market that other companies are not serving, or has access to resources that others in the industry do not. In short, it describes how the new business will be superior to existing businesses. Individuals contemplating the launch of a new business will frequently resort to copying what has succeeded in the past. Hundreds of would-be entrepreneurs attempt every day to emulate successful Internet companies like Facebook and Groupon or successful food services companies like Starbucks and The Cheesecake Factory in the offline world without considering why customers would buy from them. A competitive strategy speaks to how a business model is different or unique from the business models of competitors. Competitive strategy is discussed in more detail in Chapter 5.

Stage 6: Test the Model through Feasibility Analysis

Having taken all of these considerations into account, and armed with a clear and compelling concept and business model, entrepreneurs are ready to test the business model through a process called *feasibility analysis*. In this chapter, we provide an overview of feasibility analysis; the individual areas of analysis are then discussed in more detail in subsequent chapters.

GLOBAL INSIGHTS

Business Models for the Developing World

It may surprise many to learn that the "world's 4 billion poor people [are] the largest untapped consumer market on Earth."[16] As a group, they have more buying power than any other, with a total annual income of $1.7 trillion. Fortunately, today many organizations are beginning to address the needs of consumers in the developing world through products and services that meet their very unique requirements. Those organizations that have been successful have been able to transition from a nonprofit business model to a commercial business model.

KickStart (www.kickstart.org) is an East African nonprofit organization that worked with world-famous design company IDEO to develop a water pump that was suited to the needs, budget, and environmental conditions of Kenya. It was designed to employ manufacturing capabilities already available in Kenya; it cost less than $150, could survive the harsh Kenyan environment, and was easy to maintain. More than 24,000 pumps were sold in Tanzania and Kenya. Approximately 70 percent

of those sales were to female entrepreneurs who used the pumps to produce $30 million per year in profits and wages. As of April 30, 2010, 95,500 new businesses generating over $96.5 million in new profits were formed due to a compelling value proposition and a way for everyone involved to make money, an important incentive. KickStart employs a local supply chain from raw materials to manufacturing and distribution. Its execution plan involves five elements: (1) researching the market for small-business opportunities based on local resources; (2) designing new products and technologies as well as business models; (3) training local manufacturers in the production of the new technologies; (4) promoting the technologies to local entrepreneurs; and (5) monitoring the impact of the program to develop best practices.

Sources: www.kickstart.org/about-us, accessed July 5, 2010; and H. Chesbrough, S. Ahern, M. Finn, and S. Guerraz, (2006). "Business Models for Technology in the Developing World: The Role of Non-Governmental Organizations," *California Management Review*, 48(3): 54.

ANALYZING THE FEASIBILITY OF A BUSINESS MODEL

Feasibility analysis is unquestionably one of the most important skills individuals can acquire if they want to become entrepreneurs or use their entrepreneurial mindset inside a large corporation. The reason is simple: feasibility analysis is a tool that is used to assess and reduce risk at startup. All opportunities that entrepreneurs identify or create involve uncertainty—the unknown—and uncertainty is characterized by varying degrees of risk.[17] Risk serves as an incentive for entrepreneurs to achieve success, because with risk come rewards and, in general, the amount of reward the entrepreneur earns is proportionate to the risk taken. At the same time, there are levels of risk that entrepreneurs need to reduce (and investors expect them to reduce) so that the probability of a successful venture increases. Those risks are typically associated with the customer, the size of the market, the technical feasibility of the product, and the ability of the founding team to successfully execute the venture. Feasibility analysis is a way of dealing with the idiosyncratic risk of a new venture. The important thing to remember about risk is that most business risks can be identified and dealt with; the same is not true of uncertainty.[18]

Uncertainty is also a natural part of the launch of any business. Uncertainty means that the outcomes are not known so probabilities cannot be attached to them. For example, with startups, understanding the differences between the market conditions at the development of the original business model and the realities of the market at the time of launch becomes critical.[19] Many new businesses launch under assumptions about the market that were developed a year previously and are no longer valid. This is what happened to Command Audio after it had licensed its broadcast on-demand media software to industry leaders. Development delays on the part of the licensees caused them to postpone deploying Command Audio's technology for three years. This certainly was not part of the entrepreneur's original plan and it caused Command Audio to rethink its business model.

So, how do entrepreneurs deal with uncertainty? Given that in uncertain situations there are choices that have to be made, entrepreneurs apply subjective probabilities (educated guesses) to the choices. Typically, someone who is naïve about starting a business will be more positive about the potential outcome of an effort, while someone who is experienced in startups will be more skeptical about potential success. But it's possible for quite the opposite to occur. In fact, research has found that entrepreneurs introducing pioneering products for which there was no precedent in the market tended to be overconfident about their ability to achieve success.[20] Whether that overconfidence came from underestimating the actual risk is not known, but it suggests that entrepreneurs introducing pioneering products need to be particularly mindful of correctly assessing the risks they face.

To more accurately assess the future for an opportunity, entrepreneurs must understand their capabilities, the capabilities and intentions of their competition, the needs and desires of customers, and the bargaining power that the entrepreneur has in the value chain.[21] The bottom line is that the more information an entrepreneur acquires during the process of feasibility analysis, the higher the chance that his or her predictions will be close to the mark, risk will be reduced and uncertainty managed.

Feasibility and the Business Plan

If feasibility analysis is about conceiving, building, and testing a business model for a new venture, the business plan should be about executing an action plan for a feasible new business. Unfortunately, there is no agreement in the field of entrepreneurship on the value of the business plan. Those that argue for it believe that planning facilitates goal attainment and helps the entrepreneur make quicker decisions. It also reduces the chance that the team will abandon the new venture.[22] Those that argue against business plans assert that it takes time away from more valuable activities[23] and that since there is only a relatively small downside risk from mistakes in the earliest stages of a new venture,[24] the founders are more able to rely on intuition than on planning.[25] Furthermore, in very dynamic industries, the value of planning is lost in the speed required to get to market.[26]

Wherever the reader stands on the issue, it is clear today that investors are moving away from the written business plans of the past in favor of a brief, well-constructed executive summary or better yet, an effective pitch. That doesn't mean that the entrepreneur doesn't have to do all the research and work behind planning for a new venture; it just means that the formal document is no longer as important as it once was. What appears to be more important today is the entrepreneur's ability to demonstrate that they have proved their concept. This text will take up the business plan as an execution plan in Chapter 9.

The Outcomes of Feasibility Analysis

The primary outcome of feasibility analysis is the determination of whether the business model appears feasible, that is, it would work given the conditions defined. Feasibility analysis can be a simple or a very complex process depending on the requirements of the business under consideration and the nature of the environment (industry) in which the business will operate. In industries where the environment is highly dynamic, such as the mobile devices industry, feasibility analysis will require the ability to understand and predict the natural changes that will occur between the time the business is conceived and the time at which it is launched. This is no easy task because it demands that the entrepreneur in such an industry have complete knowledge of all the variables in the equation that might change and what impact those changes might have on the new venture. Industry and market fluctuations affect demand, cash flows, valuation, and even the window of opportunity, and they are very difficult to predict. By contrast, entrepreneurs with concepts that will launch in more stable industries, like the baked products industry, have an easier time planning for an environment that will likely be the same by the time the business launches.

Figure 4.4 depicts the feasibility analysis process and its relationship to the business model it is testing. Throughout the process, the entrepreneur

FIGURE 4.4

Feasibility Analysis: Testing the Business Model

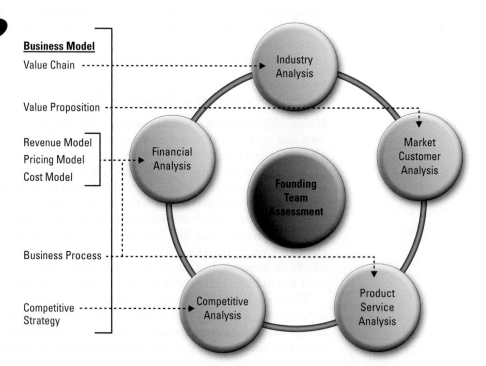

determines the range of outcomes for various aspects of the business model that are being tested—a type of sensitivity analysis—and then assigns subjective probabilities to those outcomes. In simple terms, this means looking at the forecasted outcomes in four ways: (1) what is the probability a change in the forecast will occur, (2) what is the magnitude of the change if it occurs, (3) what is the impact of the change on the business, and (4) what can be done to mitigate the change or reduce the impact substantially. For example, suppose an entrepreneur determines that there is a high probability that the estimates for customer demand might be overstated (a very common problem). The probability of this occurring might be 70 percent (based on the entrepreneur's understanding of the market and how he or she conducted research). The magnitude of the impact of this occurring might be to reduce revenues by 40 percent, which could delay profitability for one year. To mitigate the impact, the entrepreneur might need to plan for additional working capital in the startup funding requirements to carry the business until demand increases. In markets where a lot of information is available to an entrepreneur, it will be easier to assert a high degree of confidence in the robustness of the probabilities assigned to various outcomes, less so where information is not readily available. Recall that with pioneering products, markets are not clear, so the probabilities assigned will be purely arbitrary.

To make these types of risk assessments, feasibility analysis forces the entrepreneur to conduct serious research, to think critically about the business model, to answer fundamental questions, and to achieve a high level of confidence about the willingness to move forward with the business or project. Of course, no amount of feasibility analysis can reduce risk to zero.

Many businesses have launched on the strength of a feasibility analysis alone to get traction and feedback from the market. This is particularly true of Internet-related businesses, where it is relatively easy to create a presence in the market and get quick feedback from customers and end users.

Preparing for Feasibility Analysis

In addition to testing the business model components, feasibility analysis also addresses three critical success factors for any business.

1. *Is there a customer and market of sufficient size to make the concept viable and able to grow?* No business exists without customers, and even if an entrepreneur can determine that there are customers for a new venture, it will be important to calculate whether there are sufficient customers to make the effort worthwhile. Some market niches are not large enough for entrepreneurs to make a suitable profit once competitors enter the market. Knowing in advance that the market is too small permits entrepreneurs to make adjustments in their business models to broaden the market niche or decide not to go forward with the business before time and money have been wasted.

2. *Do the capital requirements to start and operate to a positive cash flow make sense?* Can this business be started with an amount of capital that the entrepreneur has or will be able to raise? Are there ways to reduce startup costs

through outsourcing or strategic partnering with another company? Too many entrepreneurs underestimate the time it will take to establish a presence in the market, acquire customers, and gain acceptance for what they're offering.

3. *Can an appropriate startup or founding team be assembled to effectively execute the concept?* Recall that in today's complex, global environment, most successful startups involve teams rather than solo entrepreneurs. A team consists of the founders, advisory board, and any required strategic partners, which can be people or other businesses with capabilities that the business needs. The team is more important, in most cases, than the idea, so assessing why the founding team is *the* team to execute this business is vital.

Upon completion of feasibility analysis, entrepreneurs should be able to determine whether the conditions are right to go forward with the business concept. If conditions are not favorable, the areas tested, such as industry, market, product, pricing, and so forth, will need to be reviewed to discover whether another approach might make the business viable. For example, suppose an entrepreneur has a concept for a new type of wheelchair that is better suited to disabled people with active lives, for example, those who drive cars or participate in sports. Through the entrepreneur's analysis, she may have determined that the cost to execute the concept (set up a factory, purchase equipment, and so on) is well beyond her means. All it may take to make the concept feasible, however, is to consider outsourcing the expensive aspects (such as product development and manufacturing) to an existing company. Immediately, the direct costs are reduced, and the entrepreneur doesn't have to invest in expensive equipment and a manufacturing facility.

The point is that many concepts can achieve feasibility if the right conditions are in place. The real question is whether the entrepreneur is convinced of the concept's feasibility and is confident enough to put the time, money, and effort into its execution. Has the analysis provided the entrepreneur with enough supporting evidence that he or she is willing to take a calculated risk and begin to plan the launch?

The Feasibility Tests

Table 4.3 provides an overview of the feasibility tests, the questions addressed by each test, and the chapter in this book that discusses in detail that particular aspect of the feasibility analysis and how to accomplish it. Feasibility analysis is not a linear process, but it does help to do an extensive study of the industry first because the industry is the environment or context in which the new venture will operate and it sets the stage for all the decisions related to the business model. Table 4.3 assumes that the business concept and business model have been developed and now need to be tested to achieve some degree of proof of concept. Think of feasibility analysis as field work because it cannot be done simply sitting at a computer and searching the Internet; entrepreneurs must get out into the industry and market to develop the ability to sense and respond to what is happening.

TABLE 4.3 Feasibility Analysis	**Areas to Be Analyzed and Some Questions to Ask** *Industry and Market/Customer (Chapter 5)* 1. What are the demographics, trends, patterns of change, and life-cycle stage of the industry? 2. What are the barriers to entry and are there any barriers you can set up? 3. What is the status of technology and R&D expenditures, and what is the level of innovation? 4. What are typical profit margins in the industry? 5. Who are the opinion leaders in the industry and how do they affect the industry? 6. What are distributors, competitors, retailers, and others saying about the industry? 7. What are the demographics of the target market? 8. What is the profile of the first customer? Are there other potential customers? 9. How have you approached customers to learn about their needs? 10. Who are your competitors, and how are you differentiated from them? *Product/Service (Chapter 6)* 11. What are the features and benefits of the product or service? 12. What product development tasks must be undertaken to achieve a marketable product, and what is the timeline for completion and the associated costs? 13. What is the window of opportunity for this product? 14. Is there potential for intellectual property rights? 15. How is the product or service differentiated from others in the market? *Founding Team (Chapter 7)* 16. What experience and expertise does the team have? 17. What are the gaps and how will you fill them? *Financial Needs Assessment (Chapters 8)* 18. What are your startup capital requirements? 19. What are your working capital requirements? 20. What are your fixed cost requirements? 21. How long will it take to achieve a positive cash flow from the revenues generated? 22. What is the break-even point for the business? 23. What are your funding requirements? Timeline and milestones?

Drawing Conclusions from Feasibility Analysis

Rejecting new ideas is an age-old practice. In the 1940s, von Neumann talked about self-replicating programmable manufacturing architectures, and in the 1960s Feynman revealed that atoms could be arranged in new ways, further supporting the notion that what we know today as nanotechnology was a feasible concept. But most products in common use today—airplanes, automobiles, telephones—were originally thought to be infeasible.[27] Furthermore, even business concepts like eBay and Starbucks were initially considered to be infeasible. So how does an entrepreneur determine whether a new business concept is feasible once all the research is accomplished and the various aspects of the concept tested?

Recall that the process of feasibility analysis is designed to convert an uncertain opportunity to one that has a specific level of risk associated with it.

Uncertainty is reduced by acquiring more information and answering the questions that contributed to that uncertainty. At each point in the feasibility process, entrepreneurs are able to make a judgment about whether to proceed with the analysis. For example, if, during the industry analysis, it was discovered that Congress was planning to pass legislation that would render it difficult for the entrepreneur to do business, he or she might consider designing another business opportunity in that industry that would not be affected.

Each step in the analysis provides information about the conditions that are necessary to make the business feasible. The sum total of these conditions should give an entrepreneur a level of confidence about the risk associated with the concept and his or her ability to execute the concept given that risk. But there is another important decision that must be made, perhaps as important as whether or not the business is feasible. And that is whether this business, given the necessary conditions for success, satisfies the personal needs and goals of the entrepreneur. The feasibility analysis should provide an entrepreneur with significantly more information about how this business would work than was available when the concept was conceived. Sometimes, in learning more about the industry and how businesses operate in that industry, an entrepreneur may discover that he or she is not suited to this type of business. Perhaps the initial excitement over the business has waned and in its place is a reality that is no longer attractive to the entrepreneur. Maybe launching this business will be too difficult a task, more difficult than the entrepreneur first thought it would be.

Alternatively, the process of feasibility analysis might make an entrepreneur even more enthusiastic about the business and its potential, enough so that it compensates for any identified risk associated with it. What is generally certain in all of this is that the process of feasibility analysis will definitely help an entrepreneur draw an appropriate conclusion about the business, and therein lies its real value.

QUICK SCREEN FOR MULTIPLE OPTIONS

Sometimes entrepreneurs are faced with several business concepts that, on the surface, appear to be equally viable. Before undertaking the research associated with a thorough feasibility study on any one of the concepts, it makes sense to do a quick screen of the ideas based on what the entrepreneur already knows about the business and industry and after talking with a few trusted business people. A quick screen starts with a concept statement, as was discussed earlier in the chapter, specifying the pain or need in the market, the potential first customer, the value proposition for that customer, and how the value proposition will be delivered to the customer. Here is an example of such a concept statement.

> Aegis will manufacture integrated snowsports apparel that combines fashion, function, and protection to the risk-conscious snowsports participants, enabling feelings of security, freedom, and peace of mind. Targeted direct customers for the line include specialty snowsports apparel retailers and the end-users will be Generation X and Y, intermediate to advanced snowsports enthusiasts. Products will be shipped directly to retailers who will enjoy high margins and quick product turnover.[28]

Then the industry in which this business will operate should be examined. The industry is the aggregation of all the companies in a value chain that support a common area of business. A quick look on the Internet or through the electronic resources of a library will reveal the trends in this industry, the opinion leaders, and what impact they have on the industry. Is there room in the industry to enter and grow? Here is a brief industry summary for the concept previously presented.

> The snowsports apparel industry is a $1.2 billion industry that is in the midst of significant growth. Given the increased acceptance of the freestyle snowriding popularized by mainstream media in the form of the X Games on ABC/ESPN and the Gravity Games on NBC, the number of snowriders participating in the sport has never been higher. It is a highly fragmented industry and seasonal. Only a few companies have been able to acquire sizable market share. The opinion leaders are companies like Sport Obermeyer and The North Face.

The market is comprised of the customers described in the concept and the competitors for those customers. Knowing who the first customer is and the size of the niche can help to determine if the business can survive and grow to add additional customer niches. At this point, identifying all the possible customers will at least provide a level of confidence that there is potential for growth beyond the original customers.

> The primary target market is specialty retail stores catering to Generation X and Y skiers and snowboarders. The market size is about $650 million with over 8,500 retailers in the United States alone. Additional targets include chain retailers that appeal to multiple sports and carry lower-end products.

With the industry context defined and the market identified, the product or service can be described in a way that provides a benefit to the customer. Without being able to solve a problem customers have, it is unlikely that a new product or service will be successful, so the features that describe the product or service should be associated with an intangible benefit to the customer, such as saving money. It is also important to consider any intellectual-property protections that might afford a competitive advantage, such as patents, trademarks, copyrights, and trade secrets. These are discussed in Chapter 6. In the case of a product, the status of development and time to completion are critical factors in predicting when the business concept can become feasible. Of course, at this point, these estimates will be very broad and based on assumptions that may prove incorrect once the entrepreneur does some market research, but the entrepreneur can certainly determine if the product development will be exceedingly long and costly, for example, due to regulatory issues. Here again is an example from the Aegis feasibility study.

> Initially, the primary focus will be on jackets and pants that offer a proprietary removable, fitted, protective padding layer incorporated into a fashionable shell, as well as integrated knee braces. The focus of protective features will include support and protection for areas of the body identified as being at high risk of injury during participation in snowsports.

The founding or management team is the catalyst that will give the business traction. Examining the capabilities and experience of the team will reveal any gaps that will need to be filled by hiring personnel or outsourcing to an independent contractor or company. Here is the statement about the founding team for Aegis.

> The founding team has experience in the fashion industry and retailing as well as biomedical engineering, with a specialty in tendon and ligament tissue engineering. One of the founders also has experience as an entrepreneur, having founded two web-based companies.

The quick screen does not deal with financial projections, because the purpose of this exercise is to weed out concepts that don't meet the market test. Nevertheless, during the quick screen, it makes sense to list all the resources that might be needed by a business of this type. Such a list might reveal whether this will be a labor-intensive business, require outsourcing of certain capabilities, or need to be located in a specific geographic region.

> Aegis plans to outsource most of the workflow to third parties and use a trading company to oversee the manufacturing of the product line and shipping to the United States. After the initial roll-out of the product line, a sales team and back office support, including customer service, order fulfillment, and office management, will be required. Aegis will need leased office space for a headquarters. Materials will be sourced through fabric sourcing companies. Design work will be done in-house.

The quick screen is an effective way to choose among several business ideas or even make a rapid decision about a single venture. Rather than spending the time undertaking in-depth feasibility analyses on each of the ideas, a quick screen may make it possible to eliminate one or more of the ideas early in the process. It's actually a great way to examine any opportunity an entrepreneur is considering to determine if there is anything that could make the business impossible to achieve.

New Venture Action Plan

- Create a concept statement for a new venture.
- Develop a business model for the venture.
- Craft a story that explains the business and is compelling to others.
- Prepare to conduct a feasibility analysis on the business model.

Questions on Key Issues

1. What is the role of the compelling story in defining the value proposition of the business?
2. What is the relevance of identifying where on the value chain the new venture lies?
3. What is the purpose of the business model, and why do business models typically fail?
4. What are the characteristics of an effective business model?
5. What is the purpose of feasibility analysis?

Experiencing Entrepreneurship

1. Define a concept for a new venture using the four components discussed in the chapter: product/service, customer, benefit, and distribution. Conduct a quick test on some potential customers through a focus group or interviews. Did you secure enough information to make a decision to move forward to conduct a feasibility study? Why or why not?

2. Suppose you intend to start a theme restaurant that can be replicated and franchised. Based on an analysis of some existing theme restaurants, what types of revenue streams could this business generate?

Relevant Case Studies

Case 1 Command Audio

Case 8 Demand Media

COMMAND AUDIO: THREE STARTUPS FOR THE PRICE OF ONE

Introduction

As Don Bogue, CEO of Command Audio, stood before the imposing assemblage of intellectual-property attorneys at the Marcus Evans November 2006 Conference in Washington, DC, he knew he was about to bring them a perspective of their field that only he, as an entrepreneur whose company developed and now licenses patents, could bring. He had facetiously titled his speech "Do Not Try This at Home: A Scarred Entrepreneur's View of Patent Licensing, Litigation, and Law." It was to be his version of how his company successfully developed a sustainable business model based on its intellectual-property assets.

> I am an entrepreneur, not a lawyer. Consequently, I see the world of patent law and litigation through a soda straw. My view of what is important out of the vast body of patent law is very narrowly focused: One company (mine), one technology, one portfolio of patents, and, at any given time, one lawsuit, one opponent, one set of facts, legal maneuvers, relevant law, prior art, etc., etc. While I may say things with which you disagree, just understand that they come from this tightly bounded perspective.

The attorneys listening to Bogue were about to hear an interesting and very unique case study of Bogue's company, Command Audio, which had been granted more than 60 U.S. and foreign patents and which had succeeded in leveraging its patent portfolio in each of the three principal ways that such a portfolio can be monetized: (1) attracting investment capital and protecting the technology position, (2) acquiring customers and strategic partners, and (3) licensing patent rights.

> We are unique (or nearly so) not only because we have had these three very intense, very high-risk business experiences, but also because we have lived to tell the story.

The Founding of a Company

Don Bogue grew up in a middle-class family with a father who worked in law enforcement; as a consequence, the family moved a lot. Nevertheless, Bogue, who was his high school's student body president, followed a reasonably straight path that took him to Harvard University, where he graduated *magna cum laude* with a bachelor's degree in economics. He then spent a decade at Ampex Corp, where he held a number of senior management positions.

In the early 1980s, while Bogue was at Ampex running its audio–video systems business, he met John Ryan, who was chief engineer for the camera group. John, it seems, was about to leave the company to start his own company, called Macrovision, which invented and patented anti-copying technology for VHS tapes, the popular mode of video storage at the time. While at Ampex, Ryan had learned the value of patents; so after filing his initial applications, he proceeded to file for patent protection on all the various ways that someone could defeat his original invention. Meanwhile, Bogue had moved on to join a small publicly held microwave test instrument company, Gigatronics, as CEO. One day in June 1995, Ryan called Bogue to tell him about a new technology he had developed that didn't fit with the Macrovision portfolio. Bogue liked the technology and thought that he might have a good business model for commercializing it. The thought of leaving the relative security of a job in corporate America was a risk, but Bogue believed that as a founder and CEO of a start-up company, "If you're not scared, you're not paying attention. It's thrilling, which is the state between exciting and terrifying." Bogue had no personal start-up experience to follow—he had to learn it as he moved forward. "If you have any self-awareness at all, you realize you have been given a gift: great accountability, but you're in charge of building the entire company from the ground up. It's even more fun than just being CEO." Together Don and John decided in late 1995 to launch Command Audio.

> John Ryan invented the basic functionality of what has come to be known as the personal video recorder, or PVR; you may be more familiar with its best known branded version—TiVo. John's inventions—expressed in a series of patent applications he began filing in early 1993—cover the audio elements of devices that receive broadcast multimedia content, then store it as a database in some sort of random access memory for later replay at the convenience of the user. What you want, when you want it. (Don Bogue)

The technology that Ryan had invented would receive a broadcast signal and store all of it or only those parts that were of interest to the particular user. In other words, Command Audio would broadcast a variety of audio programming and the users could choose what they wanted to store and listen to. The receiver provided the users with an electronic program guide that let them select from the broadcast stream what they wanted to hear. A small hand-held device that was always on automatically captured the latest editions of the users' preferred programs for instantaneous access every time they got into their cars.

> I, for instance, had my receiver set up to give me, whenever I got in my car, instantaneously at a single press of a single button, the latest traffic report for my commute route, NPR's most recent top-of-the-hour newscast, a roundup of NFL action, today's "What's News Business and Finance Column" from *The Wall Street Journal* (in audio, of course), last night's Jay Leno monologue, and *News Hour with Jim Lehrer*. In short, with an RCA Audio-on-Demand receiver and a subscription to the Command Audio service, car commuters could listen to what they wanted whenever and wherever they were. (Don Bogue, Marcus Evans Conference, November 2006)

The receiver's interface was designed for "someone who is essentially blind and paralyzed, which, when you think about it, is a good analog for a person whose primary activity is driving a car at speed and only secondarily wants to access and listen to entertaining content: eyes on the road, not on a complex LCD display; hands on the wheel, not engaged in locating and pushing a dozen or more buttons." CA's research with consumers using driving simulators found, for example, that when people attempted to access content by navigating a three-level information hierarchy they invariably crashed. Two-level hierarchies in conjunction with distinctively shaped, tactile buttons and audio feedback were simple to use, at least as easy while driving as a conventional car radio. Who was the customer CA was trying to reach with its initial product and service? It wasn't the music listener, but rather car commuters who were looking for news and information in choices and amounts that fit their unique listening preferences during their morning and afternoon commute times. They already satisfied their on-demand music needs through conventional methods like tapes and CDs. The CA system would essentially do the same for non-music categories, and the content would be both local and national, although traffic, sports, and weather would have more detailed reports at a local level. The service would carry advertising, but the user would be able to opt out of listening to it. Bogue's market research determined that users actually wanted advertising if it was relevant to their interests and occurred at convenient times. CA placed advertising links at the end of program segments where they might logically occur according to the content presented. Users could also access advertising through a separate product information content menu. To provide such a service, CA had to acquire the content from broadcasters, acquire the rights to broadcast, and actually broadcast an interactive version. CA would receive an automated feed of broadcast material—for example, an NPR show. Then a technician would go through the broadcast and provide segment markers so the listener could choose the parts they wanted to listen to. This could actually be accomplished in a matter of seconds. CA broadcast 80 hours of content every day and, to this day, it believes it is the only company to which NPR has licensed broadcast rights to its "crown jewel" programs: *Morning Edition, Talk of the Nation,* and *All Things Considered.*

Audio content was ubiquitous, inexpensive, and provided by many companies. Moreover, in popular content areas like traffic, weather, news, sports, and business, users were indifferent to brand name, which further contributed to the low cost of the service. The CA system was most threatening to the AM band, which was the primary carrier of news, sports, and talk shows. And, to broadcast the signal, CA could use small pieces of idle spectrum in the FM band. In 1996, there were more than 7,000 licensed FM transmitters.[1] About 16 percent of those were in the top 100 metro areas that CA was targeting. Bogue figured that leasing the idle spectrum would provide the stations with incremental income at no cost. The amount of money involved might not be significant to leading stations, but to stations in smaller markets and to public radio, it would be enormously attractive.

The Command Audio system consisted of three main components:[2]

- A database of news and non-music entertainment material in audio form, which was then compressed, encrypted, and broadcast to hand-held receivers
- Receivers that sifted the incoming material and stored in memory those portions that were of interest to the user
- Specific items that, at the user's convenience, he or she could recall from memory for listening

Implementing the system required a program center where content was gathered, edited, formatted, and distributed by satellite link to local markets for transmission. CA then leased idle frequency spectrum from a network of local FM radio stations and pushed it to users' receivers.

The Industry

Just 30 years ago, most of what we rely on today for entertainment, networking, collaboration, and communication did not exist. With the advent of digital technology in the mid-1990s, the surge in new consumer electronics has been unprecedented. Digital TV (DTV) products emerged in 1998 after being adopted as the industry standard in 1996. As of 1998, one in four U.S. households had the basic equipment to put together a home theater system; VCRs were a commodity item, as were personal computers.[3] In 1996, digital cellular communications became available in the United States, and in June 1998, the first Internet-enabled phones appeared.

The consumer electronics industry actually began with radio, which was commercialized by Radio Corporation of America (RCA), a joint venture of General Electric, Westinghouse, and

[1] "By the Numbers." *Broadcasting & Cable* (March 4, 1996), p. 76.

[2] Command Audio Business Plan, 1996.

[3] J. Anderson. "Industry Focus: Consumer Electronics." *Raytheon* (1998), www.graduatingengineer.com/industryfocus/consumer.html.

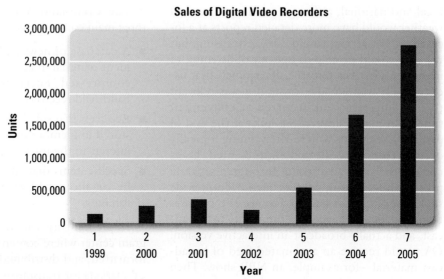

FIGURE 1

Sales of Digital Video Recorders

Source: Media Trends Track, Television Bureau of Advertising, Inc., www.tvb.org.

AT&T; and Telefunken, a joint venture of European companies Siemens and AEG.[4] RCA later led the commercialization of television worldwide, but failed in the 1970s from an ineffective effort to become a conglomerate. Meanwhile, by the late 1980s, Japanese companies Sony and Matsushita became the most important commercializers of electronics, in particular, the Walkman, Triton Color TV, the VCR, the CD, and the DVD, and succeeded in driving American companies out of their own domestic markets.

The personal video recorder industry grew rapidly when in 2001 the satellite and cable television companies began integrating the PVR function into their marketing packages in competition with existing PVR companies. In 1999, TiVo Inc. and ReplayTV Network Inc. were the industry leaders and the first to mass-market to consumers. Their technologies enabled consumers to pause and record live TV as well as enjoy instant replay. Because TiVo developed many strategic alliances with huge consumer product companies like Sony, Toshiba, GE, DirecTV, and Philips, it gained market share

over ReplayTV, which struggled after being acquired by SONICblue. Unit sales of digital video recorders are depicted in Figure 1.

The Market and the Competition

In 1996, Bogue determined that approximately 120 million people in the United States commuted to work each day by car, and of those, 18 million spent 60 minutes or more commuting in their cars. His market research also indicated that more than 90 percent of those commuters were interested in CA's on-demand service. Bogue knew that a new consumer product might take years to be adopted by the mass market. Figure 2 depicts the comparative projected U.S. household penetration of radio-on-demand (ROD) against VCR and CD adoption patterns.

The "early adopters" of CA's service were defined as people who

- Resided in the 100 largest metropolitan areas[5]
- Spoke English as their primary language

---

[4]A. D. Chandler. "Gaps in the Historical Record: Development of the Electronics Industry." *Working Knowledge* (October 20, 2003), http://hbswk.hbs.edu/item/3738.html.

[5]Top 100 Metropolitan Areas per "Metro Market Ranks." *Radio Advertising Source* (December 1995).

FIGURE 2

Overall Interest in Command Audio Concept

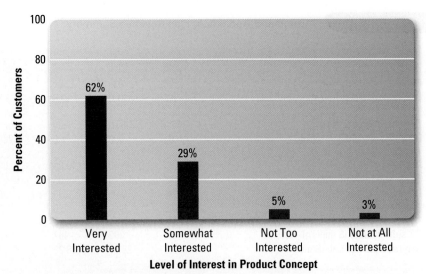

Source: Command Audio Business Plan, 2005, p. 33.

FIGURE 3

Comparative Projected U.S. Household Penetration of Radio-on-Demand (ROD)

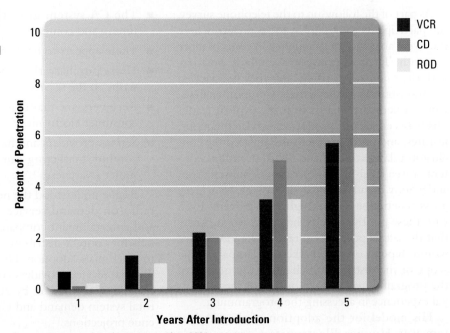

Source: Command Audio Business Plan, 1996.

- Commuted to work by car
- Spent an aggregate of 60 minutes per day commuting

Bogue believed that this target group represented the best chance for entering the market, and it consisted of 18 million people. Customers were disproportionately male, more inclined to purchase electronic devices, and had higher incomes. To validate his estimates and gauge demand, Bogue commissioned an independent market study. In a test in the San Francisco Bay area of 625 residents, respondents were favorably accepting of the concept. Figure 3 depicts the response pattern for this group.

FIGURE 4   Command Audio (CA) Plan Revenue Summary

	1998	1999	2000	2001	2002
Radio-on-demand subs, avg (000)	98	596	1,501	2,778	4,589
U.S. household penetration, end (%)	0.2	1.0	2.0	3.5	5.5
CA market share (%)	100.0	90.0	88.0	70.0	60.0
CA subs, avg (000)	98	556	1,320	2,264	3,428
Activation fee ($)	10.00	10.00	10.00	10.00	10.00
Basic sub fee ($/month)	19.95	19.95	19.95	19.95	19.95
Premium sub fee ($/month)	9.95	9.95	9.95	9.95	9.95
Premium buy rate (%)	80.0	80.0	80.0	80.0	80.0
CA sub revenue ($ million)	38	209	487	835	1,265
Avg revenue per sub ($/mo)	29.28	28.71	28.28	28.17	28.12

As part of the follow-up to the telephone survey, the participants took part in focus groups where they were able to understand the CA concept more in-depth. Their response was similarly positive, with their evaluation rising after they had viewed a demonstration of the system. Conjoint analysis, which asked participants to make explicit trade-offs between various product or service functions, features, and prices, further substantiated the conclusion relative to demand. With premium content, a free receiver, $30 per month subscription, and a Sony brand, the analysis was able to achieve gross penetration rates as high as 75 percent. Even with these positive results, however, Bogue knew that the actual penetration rate of the CA service would depend on the marketing campaign, the scope of the distribution channel, the quality of the programming, and the quality of the individual experience in accessing the programming.

His model for the adoption of the CA system was Hughes Electronics Corporation's DIRECTV®, which has been called the most successful product launch in the history of consumer electronics. The similarities include the following:[6]

- CA is an advanced version of a universally accepted consumer service that does not require the mastery of a complex new technology.
- There appears to be a need in the market.

[6]Command Audio Business Plan, 1996, p. 38.

- The CA system gives the user control over timing and content.
- There appears to be demand for the system.
- Users purchase the receivers and then subscribe to the service.
- Receivers are manufactured by well-known consumer electronics firms.
- Service providers and hardware manufacturers conduct marketing campaigns to build consumer awareness.

Bogue understood the need to license to other radio-on-demand service providers and media and entertainment companies seeking new channels for content distribution if he was ever going to reach mass adoption. He figured that these additional service providers could capture about 40 percent of the market by 2002. Figure 4 displays total system demand and Command Audio's revenue projections.

The Competition

Bogue saw his primary competition as conventional radio, which was free to users because of its advertising business model and because it no longer had a learning curve. Nevertheless, he believed that users wanted more control over what they listened to and they wanted to avoid a clutter of advertising that was not relevant to their interests. For a low price and through a simple method, users could gain that control. Because CA's system could determine audience demographics, it would be easier for CA to convince prospective advertisers to use its medium over conventional radio in order to closely target ads to the interests of specific demographic groups.

One competitor was RBDS (Radio Broadcast Data System), a low data rate data broadcasting service that, in 1996, was being adopted by some FM stations. The service enabled "listeners with specially equipped car radios to receive supplementary program data and text messages that [could] be displayed on the receiver to show station call letters, programming format . . . title and artist of a current piece as well as playlists of the next several selections. In addition the radios could receive and display pager messages and low data rate information such as sports scores."[7] In 1995, approximately 5 percent of licensed stations were broadcasting some RBDS data, and fewer than 800,000 car radios were RBDS compatible.

In 1996, when Bogue wrote the Command Audio business plan, a few companies had announced intentions to bring satellite broadcast radio to market through point-to-multipoint systems that would transmit music and non-music programming to cars equipped with special receivers. These services promised better quality sound, the ability to select a station by format, a broader range of programming, and freedom from terrestrial-induced signal interference. However, satellite radio would not give the user control of what they listen to, how much, and when.

In 1996, wireless communication (cellular or PCS) was facing the same barriers to adoption, and their high cost to install or expand made them an unlikely delivery mechanism for on-demand radio because they could not match CA's pricing. Moreover, wireless did not have the bandwidth to deliver a program at a sufficient level of quality. The other potential competitor was Internet search engines and browsers, but they were not yet capable of providing simple and safe access to program material while driving. With this approach, users could not gain immediate access to current information and breaking events, and downloading would necessarily occur at a particular time when the user was connected to the Internet. So users would have to carry their receivers from the car to their computers and back. In addition, users would have to pay based on how much content they downloaded or they would be required to listen to advertisements. The biggest threat might come with the convergence of the Internet and wireless capability, which in 1996 was still several years away.

A significant advantage that Bogue saw for CA was its low infrastructure costs, which reduced its capital requirements significantly when compared to other information and entertainment service providers. "For example, in 1996 major direct-to-home satellite TV programmers spent between $0.5 billion and $1.5 billion each to purchase transmission licenses and launch satellites. Command Audio, by comparison, [spent] in total just $10 million on facilities and equipment in order to commence service . . . and only $23 million annually to lease the necessary FM subcarriers."[8]

Business Model #1: Raising Investment Capital and Protecting the Technology Position

In December 1999, just before CA launched its service, Audio on Demand, it raised $56 million in venture capital. Although this was a time of intense investment by the venture capital community, CA's funding was successful by any measure. It was designed to provide launch financing into four lead markets and to begin the exploration of another six markets.

The service was officially launched in January 2000, running 24 hours a day, 7 days a week. In March, CA began its media campaign to a lukewarm response; the customer acquisition rate was not nearly as fast as projected. To make matters worse, the service suffered a 25 percent churn

---

[7]Command Audio Business Plan, 1995, p. 48.

[8]Command Audio Business Plan, 1996, p.14.

because of the battery, which was too large and didn't have a long enough life span. Initially, CA charged $200 for the receiver and $9.99 per month for the service, but within three weeks they were forced to lower the price of the receiver to $99 and make adjustments to the service pricing and programming.

As the company also optimistically prepared for a potential initial public offering (IPO) of $150 million to roll out to the top 50 markets, April 2000 brought the crash of the public equity markets, especially for pre-profitability technology companies, and the investment banks CA had chosen to lead the IPO advised the company that the window of opportunity for companies like CA had closed but would likely open again in spring 2001. Although that was only a year away, if their predictions were correct, Bogue couldn't figure out how things would change fast enough to keep the company alive. They would be out of money by September 2000.

> Our senior management team realized very quickly that a seismic and very negative shift in our prospects had occurred. Though crushingly disappointed, we decided almost immediately to shut down our service and downsize the company to conserve capital for a strategic redirection towards software development and licensing. In this new model, we generalized the tools and technologies we already had developed and licensed them to others who wanted to offer similar on-demand media services.

Business Model #2: Licensing Their Tools and Technologies

With a portfolio of valuable technologies and a determination not to give up, Bogue repositioned the company as a software development and licensing company that would license the systems and tools it had developed to companies that wanted to offer on-demand media services. Initial success with digital radio pioneers XM Satellite Radio and iBiquity encouraged Bogue that he had made the right decision. CA's growing patent portfolio was demonstrating to licensees, strategic

investors, and partners that CA was the technology leader in broadcast on-demand media.

However, as optimistic as Bogue was, he soon discovered that his software licensees' plans had also been rather optimistic. Development delays resulted in these industry leaders deciding not to deploy CA's technology for three more years, which meant that CA would not be receiving any royalties for three years. Once again the company was faced with the possibility of a cash shortfall and once again Bogue downsized the company with a plan to reorganize yet again. In August 2002, Bogue sold CA's software development business to iBiquity Digital and licensed to that company all of CA's patents and software. iBiquity had the right to sublicense CA's patents in the terrestrial digital radio field, but CA retained the exclusive rights to license its intellectual property in every other field of use.

Business Model #3: Enforcing Existing Patents and Licensing Agreements

Still searching for a strategy that would enable CA to return its shareholders' capital, Bogue was about to undertake the most unconventional and risky business model of all: licensing and, where necessary, enforcing CA's patents. With digital and satellite radio already under license, Bogue turned his attention to personal video recorders, the sort of device pioneered by TiVo and ReplayTV. This market was potentially very large, but it would prove extremely difficult to penetrate. For the next 15 months, Bogue and his team, now a very small company, worked hard to conserve CA's remaining cash and began to approach the major consumer electronics companies as well as manufacturers of cable and satellite television set-top boxes. Although these companies had an interest in personal video recorders and saw them as the next big thing, they were reluctant to accept the fundamental nature of CA's intellectual property and the need to acquire a license to use it. They figured that if they ignored CA, the company would eventually disappear.

Bogue had not gone into this effort without preparation. The response of the big consumer electronics companies was expected, and it was time to draw a line in the sand. It was clear that TiVo and Replay were using the audio time-shifting functionality embodied in John Ryan's inventions, even though they were focused on television. Their use of the technology could well have been inadvertent; they may simply have been unaware at the time they began developing their products that the same idea had occurred to Ryan a few years earlier. TiVo's founders came out of Silicon graphics and apparently, in their own way, had reached the same solution as John Ryan had. Bogue also foresaw that, down the road when video was delivered to cell phones, it would be delivered through broadcast rather than point-to-point technology and would be cached on the handset by users. That, too, would require manufacturers and service providers to obtain licenses to CA's patents. So now he had two choices: He could either shut down the company or he could fight the big boys. He chose the latter.

Bogue quickly realized that the key to his company's success was in having the money to go after the companies that were infringing his patents, and he had to have enough funding to outlast them. His current investors, as committed as they were, would not be supplying any more capital for this latest business model; in any case, the amount that Bogue needed was significantly higher than they might provide. An exhaustive search produced the answer: an insurance policy that covered the cost of offensive patent litigation and provided several million dollars of financing at a price the company could afford. CA would pay an up-front premium and, upon settlement of the lawsuit, would repay what had been put out plus a premium. This policy was the turning point because the company was now competing on a level playing field with the major electronics manufacturers.

With financing in place, Bogue began to study companies coming into the PVR market and selected a target to focus on for litigation: Sony Corporation. Bogue figured that if he could win this suit, the other companies infringing his patents would be more likely to fall in line and pay royalties

rather than risk infringement litigation. On February 1, 2002, CA filed a patent infringement action against Sony Corporation. The litigation took four years, during which CA prevailed in multiple Markman rulings, summary judgment motions, and a bench trial on inequitable conduct. After the two companies had spent over $15 million, Sony decided to settle the lawsuit. It paid an up-front financial settlement and signed a royalty-bearing license for the use of CA's patents around the world.

This was a monumental win for Command Audio. The personal video recorder market, which consists of cable and satellite TV set-top boxes, DVD recorders, game consoles, and PCs, is perhaps twenty times as large as the digital and satellite radio market. And right behind that is television delivery to cell phones that incorporate broadcast tuners and PVR functionality, which is an order of magnitude larger than personal video recorders. Analysts estimate that in 2006 alone, more than 25 million PVRs were sold, and that number would grow by 30 percent in 2007.[9] In April 2007, CA signed a license agreement with Scientific Atlanta, a leader in cable television set-top boxes and a Cisco company. They intend to use CA's technology in all of their PVR set-top box products. Bogue knows that even with this pivotal win, the game is not over. Although he has aligned his patent and business strategies and prepared his company's financing, will every company infringing his patents agree to pay royalties? Is this a sustainable strategy?

Discussion Questions

1. What was the source of the opportunity for Command Audio?
2. What were the problems with the first business model: building and selling the CA box and service to consumers?
3. Why did the second business model fail? Could that failure have been avoided?
4. Was it necessary for the company to go through three business models before it found the right one to build a sustainable company?

[9]"Scientific Atlanta Purchases License to Use Command Audio's PVR Technology." Press release (April 24, 2007).

MYSPACE: THE ROCKY EVOLUTION OF A SOCIAL MEDIA COMPANY

In the fall of 2006, Chris DeWolfe found himself stepping back in time as he stood before a crowd of alums and current students from the Lloyd Greif Center for Entrepreneurial Studies at the University of Southern California. He was there to receive an award as the Alumni Entrepreneur of the Year for co-founding MySpace, the social networking phenomenon. But more than that, he was there to remember his roots and to tell an eager audience of entrepreneur hopefuls what to watch out for. "Technology does not drive demand," he cautioned the students. "MySpace has always taken a sociological viewpoint—How do people do things? What do they like to do? Then the MySpace team figures out how they can enable their users to do what they want." Asked what he would have done differently, DeWolfe doesn't miss a beat—"I would have started it sooner." He would have expanded aggressively and hired more developers in the early days, because "speed to market is important."

DeWolfe was looking back at the launch of the company he co-founded with Tom Anderson from a new position in that fall of 2006. MySpace had recently been acquired by Rupert Murdoch's News Corporation (News Corp) as part of a $580 million package deal for Intermix Media, MySpace's parent company. With the enormous resources of News Corp behind it, MySpace was taking on an astounding number of new projects: a new Google agreement for text ads, a MySpace

records label, a VoIP feature so their users could call one another, international sites, and another 20 products in various stages of development in the pipeline. How did MySpace go from launch in late 2003 to online media giant by 2007 and back to the drawing boards by 2010?

In the Beginning

Chris DeWolfe hails from Portland, Oregon; both parents were teachers. So it was a bit of a break from tradition when he decided to major in business at the University of Washington. Upon graduation he took a job, but two years into it, he began to have some doubts.

> I looked to my left and looked to my right and saw that my colleagues were twenty years older than me, and it was almost like looking into the future. And I was scared because that wasn't something that I wanted to do. I wanted to create my own business; I wanted to do my own thing; I wanted to innovate.

Frustrated, he decided to further his education by getting an MBA. His friends told him that he had to have a plan to get into a good business school. He had to know whether he wanted to be a consultant, an investment banker, or a marketing manager. Again, DeWolfe sidestepped the traditional route—"My plan is, I'm going to figure out a plan when I get there." He was accepted into the Marshall School of Business at the University of Southern California (USC), and for the first year he immersed himself in the Internet, which in 1995 was just beginning to gain some ground as a commercial channel. Netscape and Yahoo! had gone public and things were getting interesting. In the second year of his MBA, he took a class in the Lloyd Greif Center for Entrepreneurial Studies and was hooked. He knew what he wanted to be—an Internet entrepreneur—that was his passion.

After graduation, DeWolfe and three of his USC Marshall friends took jobs at an Internet data-storage company, Xdrive; DeWolfe became the company's head of sales and marketing. It was in that capacity that he met one of his future partners, Tom Anderson, in 2000. Anderson, a frustrated English major at UC Berkeley and then film school major, responded to an ad to earn $20 for testing an Xdrive product. Although Anderson disliked the product immensely, DeWolfe liked him so much that he offered him a full-time job. Xdrive was not a success, however. It was the typical dot com company of the day, raising $120 million and spending it foolishly on parties, excess advertising, and hiring people it didn't need. That experience told DeWolfe that it was time to start his own company, so he and Anderson left the firm (in bankruptcy) in 2001 and launched an Internet direct-marketing firm called Response Base. They sold that business for several million dollars in late 2002 to eUniverse, a holder of multiple Internet assets. Both joined the company, but just six months later, DeWolfe and Anderson were asking themselves, "What's next?"

A Brief History of the Internet

Although the Internet didn't become the focus of consumer attention until about 1995, its history actually dates back to August 1962, when MIT's J.C.R. Licklider began discussing what he called the "galactic network," a "globally interconnected set of computers," which would enable anyone in the network to access data and programs from any site. While serving as the first head of the computer research program at DARPA, he convinced his colleagues of the significance of his concept. By late 1966, MIT researcher Lawrence Roberts had created a plan to build the ARPANET and by 1969, the first node was installed at UCLA. Within a month, two additional nodes were added at UC Santa Barbara and the University of Utah, and by the end of 1969, there were four host computers connected on ARPANET. Nevertheless, it took until October 1972 to demonstrate ARPANET's capability to the public at an international conference and to introduce its newest application, electronic mail.

ARPANET was the first of what would become many networks linked by an open architecture networking called the Internet. In open architecture, each network could have its own design and user interface, yet they would all be connected seamlessly to the Internet. The 1980s saw the rapid development of LANs (local area networks), PCs, and workstations, which contributed to the swift expansion of the Internet that was now serving a broad base of researchers and developers.

In 1991, the first user-friendly interface was developed at the University of Minnesota. *Gopher*, as it was named after the university's mascot, quickly expanded to over 10,000 systems around the world while other universities developed enhancements to it, such as a searchable index of gopher menus and a spider that crawled gopher menus to collect links and place them in the index. But it was the development in 1993 of Mosaic, a graphical user interface, by Marc Andreessen and his team at the National Center for Supercomputing Applications that became the catalyst for the commercial Internet as we know it today. With the launch of Delphi, the first national commercial online service that offered Internet access to subscribers in 1992, the commercial Internet could not be stopped. In 1995, the National Science Foundation halted funding of the Internet backbone, and commercial networks like AOL and CompuServe were born.

Until 1998, when Microsoft released Windows 98 with a full-scale browser incorporated, Netscape's browser, which was free, was the most popular browser on the market. At this point, there was no stopping the proliferation of Internet sites as more and more companies tried to find business models that would enable them to make money through this exciting new channel. The highly speculative period between 1995 and 2001 has been called the "dot com bubble," because stock markets saw their value explode to unprecedented levels from the growth in Internet companies and related sectors only to crash in the spring of 2000 because these same companies couldn't deliver business models that made sense or contributed to realistic valuations. The dot com bubble was not a unique event. History has witnessed other booms and busts: radio in the 1920s, transistor electronics in the 1950s, and home computers in the early 1980s. Some of the more notable dot com failures were Webvan, the online grocer; Pets.com; and eToys.com.

By 2005, many pundits questioned whether we were heading into another dot com bubble—the sequel—with the acquisitions of MySpace and YouTube at extremely high valuations. These social networking sites depended a good deal on content that their users created and on their users' ability to build large networks among their friends and associates. There were no fees charged to the users, so the sites relied on advertising revenue and sponsorships and often had no proprietary technology. However, if MySpace was the model for the Internet venture at that time, then it predicted more acquisitions by large corporations instead of IPOs by unprofitable Internet companies.

The Birth of MySpace

Ready to start another business, DeWolfe and Anderson surveyed the Internet landscape and recognized a "perfect storm" of activities that seemed to suggest a space to do something that wasn't being done. In late 2002, the term *social networking* was getting some play due to the emergence of Friendster (a dating site), Tribe (a classifieds and local information guide), and Facebook (social networking for college students). DeWolfe and Anderson, then employees at eUniverse, noticed that they were receiving a constant stream of requests through their email to join these networks, so they began to do some research and quickly determined that these were niche players without a lot of potential to become huge. The two had bigger plans in mind, specifically a portal that would bring all of the niche functions together and let users do whatever they do offline in a more productive way: express themselves, send out invitations, blog, discover music, share photos, and play games. DeWolfe's mantra was always "once you've done the research, stop strategizing and jump off the cliff." So he and Anderson pitched the idea to Brad Greenspan, then CEO of eUniverse, who agreed to fund the new project for 66 percent of the equity, and MySpace was born. The duo purchased the myspace.com domain name from a data-storage company, YourZ.com, no longer in existence, and they were off and running.

It took three months to build the site, and they launched at the end of 2003. However, the day after launch the site blew up—in other words, it stopped working. DeWolfe quickly consulted with his developer and learned that the system they had built couldn't survive an assault by more than 200 people at the same time. Realizing the mistake that had been made, DeWolfe instructed the developer to build the site to hold millions of people at the same time. Shortly thereafter they were back in business. Growth did not come quickly for this social networking portal; in fact, the company didn't start to see success for at least six to nine months. At first they attracted their users by inviting bands and club owners in Los Angeles to create pages and then invite others to "become their friends." Because the bands and clubs could use MySpace as their promotional platform, they very willingly invited others onto the site. And everyone came, because MySpace allowed them to do and post what they wanted, whereas rival Friendster made sure that its site did not contain anything that didn't fit its core proposition, which at the time was essentially

Internet dating. MySpace also succeeded in correcting many of the problems that users had with Friendster, such as speed of access to the site. Giving bands an outlet to let users sample and share songs as well as communicate with the bands was the secret sauce that catalyzed MySpace's growth. By 2004, more than 350,000 bands and solo artists, both unknown and famous, had set up pages on the site and invited their friends to join, creating a viral effect. In September 2004, R.E.M. became the first band from a major record label to stream its latest album on MySpace before its release.

The New York Times wrote of MySpace:

> Even with many users in their 20s MySpace has the personality of an online version of a teenager's bedroom, a place where the walls are papered with posters and photographs, the music is loud, and grownups are an alien species.

And that's just what DeWolfe and Anderson intended. Users were able to customize the look of their pages, add personal photographs, and create a network of friends who had to receive permission before being added to someone's site. The biggest celebrity on MySpace was cofounder Tom Anderson because it was his face that popped up when a new member registered, so his list of friends was running over 46 million as of 2006. Of the two, Anderson, who came out of music and film, was the most gregarious and creative while the quieter DeWolfe managed MySpace's finances and kept a lower profile. In fact, it was DeWolfe who shielded Anderson from much of the turmoil surrounding the later acquisition of MySpace.

By 2003, eUniverse was in serious trouble. The company had gone through an SEC investigation, had its stock halted from trading for nearly four months, had to restate the first three quarters of fiscal year 2003, had been delisted from NASDAQ, and was being sued by its shareholders in various class-action and derivative lawsuits. In July 2004, the board of directors voted to change eUniverse's name to Intermix Media (IMIX) and brought on a new CEO, Richard Rosenblatt, a successful serial Internet pioneer who in 1999

had sold his company iMall for $565 million. His challenge was to turn around the struggling company. All of the problems had cost the company a lot of money, so it was soon clear that Intermix needed more funding to support its rapid growth and that of its fastest growing asset, MySpace. This meant talking to venture capitalists, most of whom didn't understand the MySpace concept, didn't know the management team, and thought they were trying to do too much. But Redpoint Ventures, a Silicon Valley firm, did understand the technology–entertainment mix. In December 2004, they agreed to invest $4 million in Intermix Media, Inc., for one million shares of its common stock and a five-year warrant to purchase 150,000 shares of common stock at $4/share. With the ink on that deal still drying, in February 2005, Redpoint Ventures again invested, this time a total of $11.5 million for a minority stake of 25 percent in the newly formed independent subsidiary, MySpace, Inc. Intermix held a 53 percent equity interest in MySpace, Inc. and DeWolfe served as chief executive officer for a three-year term that ended in October 2007.

The Acquisition of Intermix and MySpace

In 2005, a number of large media companies began approaching Rosenblatt, CEO of Intermix and chairman of MySpace, about acquiring Intermix and its three main assets: MySpace, Alena (marketing analytics and e-commerce), and its media network, which consisted of about 30 different websites. At the time, MySpace was supporting approximately 18 million unique visitors and was the fastest growing part of Intermix. DeWolfe was very nervous when News Corp's Rupert Murdoch, the media icon, approached them about an acquisition, because he did not want to risk losing the no-rules culture they were known for and become buried in a huge conservative conglomerate; however, they needed the money to support their blistering growth, and the Intermix board approved the sale. In approximately 18 months from the time he had become CEO of Intermix, Rosenblatt had turned the company around and sold it and its highly successful subsidiary MySpace for a premium, $580 million in cash, to News Corp to become part of its Fox Interactive Media, Inc. Rosenblatt remained a consultant to News Corp to help grow the Intermix properties until he launched Demand Media in 2006, raised $220 million in investment capital, and bought back the non-MySpace assets of Intermix Network LLC from News Corp. DeWolf and the MySpace team were able to purchase equity stakes in MySpace before the sale.

Prior to the acquisition, Murdoch had assured DeWolfe and Anderson that he would not interfere with the running of MySpace; however, shortly after the acquisition of Intermix in July 2005, News Corp decided to move MySpace from its laid-back office a block from the beach in Santa Monica to Beverly Hills, where all of News Corp's Internet companies were housed. It was at that point that DeWolfe and Anderson first realized that they didn't really own MySpace. They soon found that other things had changed as well. Decisions took a lot longer now with all the big corporate processes and the culture was not as casual. The upside, though, was that MySpace had significantly more resources at its disposal to launch multiple projects and products simultaneously.

DeWolfe believed in 2005 that MySpace was at the nascent stage of where it could potentially go. As the number two Internet site in terms of page views, the team needed to make sure that they continued to listen to the market, not the experts, and not "follow the pack." DeWolfe attributed the success of MySpace to several factors: (1) an experienced management team that had worked together for 8 years; (2) great timing on the launch of the site, with social networking taking off and advertising revenues returning to Internet companies; (3) features on the site that were compelling to their users—they provided a solution that made sense and that users couldn't find on other sites; and (4) the use of influencers from entertainment to drive interest in the site. As long as DeWolfe and Anderson remained with the company, the intent was to make sure

that users controlled the site and users dictated the features that MySpace offered. In December 2006, with the resources of News Corp at its disposal, MySpace went mobile on a grand scale with a service that enabled Cingular Wireless subscribers to use many of the social networking features of MySpace on their cell phones for a $2.99 per month premium. This was a way to diversify its business model and again meet one of the requested needs of its users. By late 2007, MySpace was considered the leading social networking site, but its successful run was about to end.

It Matters Who's Leading the Company

For several years, the user base that MySpace had grabbed from Friendster was moving on to Facebook, which was quickly becoming the social network of choice. The biggest problem for MySpace was that it had become simply a place to hear bands and comment rather than a place to build relationships. The company had not changed its business model in years, and it seemed to be stuck in the inertia of its early success. It had not evolved with its user base. Facebook CEO Mark Zuckerburg located his company in tech-centric Silicon Valley where change is a way of life. News Corp moved MySpace to Beverly Hills, not known for change and speed. MySpace had also gone through multiple CEOs, most of which left out of frustration with the slow pace of a giant media company. In 2010, MySpace decided to refocus on the 13–35 age bracket and no longer compete with Facebook. It was satisfied being a niche player in social entertainment. Whether or not MySpace succeeds over the long term is anyone's guess. But research firm eMarketer estimated in 2008 that ad spending on MySpace would decline from $470 million in 2009 to about $297 million in 2011 while Facebook's revenue was expected to reach $1.7 billion in the same period.

Meanwhile, back in Santa Monica, Richard Rosenblatt, CEO and co-founder of Demand

Media, was preparing to form an IPO. (See Case Study 8, Demand Media: Creating a Transformative Business.)

Sources

Helft, M. (October 27, 2010). "For Myspace, a Redesign to Entice Generation Y." *The New York Times*; Van Buskirk, E. (February 11, 2010). "Flailing MySpace Loses CEO, Death Spiral Continues." *Epicenter*, www.wired.com/epicenter/2010/02/flailing-myspace-loses-ceo; "A Brief History of the Internet." *Internet Society*, www.isoc.org, accessed May 29, 2007; Interview with Chris DeWolfe, Alumni Entrepreneur of the Year Event, November 2006, University of Southern California; "Dot-Com Bubble, Part II? Why It's So Hard to Value Social Networking Sites." *Knowledge@wharton*, http://knowledge.wharton.upenn.edu, accessed October 4, 2006; Sellers, P. (2006). "MySpace Cowboys." *Fortune* (September 4): 67; "Interview with Richard Rosenblatt, Intermix and MySpace." *Socal Tech* (January 30, 2006), www.socaltech.com; Williams, A. (August 28, 2005). "Do You MySpace?" *The New York Times*, www.nytimes.com; Weintraub, J. (July 25, 2005). "A, B, C, D, eUniverse." *DM Confidential*, www.adastro.com; "Entry Material Agreement, Other Events, Financial Statements and Exhibits." Form 8-K for Intermix Media, Inc., published February 17, 2005; and Exhibit 99.1, eUniverse Issues Open Letter to eUniverse Stockholders, January 7, 2004, www.edgar-online.com.

Discussion Questions

1. How did DeWolfe and Anderson recognize the opportunity for MySpace?
2. What mistakes were made with Xdrive that ultimately made MySpace go more smoothly?
3. How did MySpace differentiate itself from the competition?
4. Should DeWolfe and Anderson have given up so much equity (66 percent) in the beginning to eUniverse? Was there an alternative strategy available?
5. Evaluate the acquisition of MySpace as part of the Intermix package. Would you have made that decision? Why or why not?

ANALYZING FEASIBILITY

UNDERSTANDING THE MARKET

"A moment's insight is sometimes worth a life's experience."

—OLIVER WENDELL HOLMES (1809–1894)

CHAPTER OBJECTIVES

- Explain the difference between an industry and a market.
- Discover effective ways to research and analyze an industry.
- Determine first customer and the characteristics of the market.
- Understand anthropological techniques for understanding customers.
- Gather competitive intelligence.

The jewelry industry is centuries old, so finding a new business model that stands out from the crowd is not an easy task. In 2006, Matt Lauzon and Jason Reuben were seniors at Babson College in Wellesley, MA, and very much involved in the world of startups, fully intending to start a business before they graduated. Jason's family had been in the diamond business for about 30 years, and the duo believed they could leverage that industry knowledge to find a novel way to enter the industry. In addition, the family's connections in the industry with suppliers would be invaluable. Their plan was to help the old-school jewelry businesses connect with consumers online through their company, Paragon Lake. The opportunity they saw was to take advantage of a trend at the time in mass customization with the creation of a network structure where an intermediary—Paragon Lake—brokered transactions among diverse jewelry retailers and manufacturers. The problem they were solving was to help smaller mom-and-pop jewelers boost sales through the Internet. Others seemed to like the concept as well because they went on to win Babson's annual Business Plan Competition and were featured in *Business Week* on a list of "America's Best Young Entrepreneurs."

Just before the two graduated, they received a call from Bob Davis, a general partner at Highland Capital Partners, a venture capital firm, who offered them a place in the firm's Summer@Highland accelerator program for startups. They were given $7,500, office space, and the ability to get mentoring from Highland as they worked on their business. Lauzon and Reuben set up shop in Highland's Lexington MA office and began the development of a product they called "virtual display case," essentially an online service for jewelry stores who let their customers customize their jewelry and see a 3D model of their design in advance.

To accelerate the startup process, Lauzon tried to raise a first round of funding but with no success. Davis, their venture capital mentor, thought they weren't ready. "The team wasn't well-rounded, and it wasn't totally clear who the customer was, how the market was segmented."[1] Eventually in December of 2007, the team signed a term sheet with Highland for $500,000 in seed capital and continued to work on the website and sign up jewelers. Before too long, Lauzon again believed they were ready for a much larger tranche of investment capital. This time his attempt was successful and in July 2008, the company was able to raise $5.8 million in funding.

Unfortunately, Paragon Lake did not find the demand they had predicted from their target market of jewelry retailers, so it was time to change the business model. By February, 2010, Reuben was no longer with the company and Lauzon had changed the company's name to Gemvara to reflect a new business model that involved selling directly to consumers over the Internet. The site, which is targeting women aged 35 to 45, enables consumers to choose custom jewelry from the comfort of their home. Customers get previews of custom jewelry and an engine that calculates pricing for various combinations of designs, metals, and jewels. Time will tell if this model is a winner in a very tough industry, but so far it shows promise.

Sources: Moore, G. (February 12, 2010). "Paragon Lake Now Named Gemvara, Targets Consumers," *MHT: The Journal of New England Technology,* www.masshightech.com/stories/2010/02/08/daily51-Paragon-Lake-now-named-Gemvara-targets-consumers.html; "Paragon Lake will Let You Customize Jewelry Online," *VentureBeat,* www.venturebeat.com, November 13, 2009; and Kirsner, S. (Jul7 6, 2008). "Incubator Polishes Gem of an Idea," Boston.com. www.boston.com/business/articles/2008/07/06/incubator_polishes_gem_of_an_idea.

Unquestionably, the analysis of the industry in which the business will operate is critical to determining whether a new venture will be feasible. From the broadest perspective, the industry is a grouping of businesses that interact in a common environment as part of a value chain or distribution channel. There is enormous value in knowing an industry well. Ideas for new ventures frequently come from understanding and having experience with an industry. In addition, comprehending how an industry works can help entrepreneurs find strategic partners, customers, venture capital, and strategies for success and also learn where the pitfalls and roadblocks might be. A strategic position in a growing, dynamic, healthy industry can go a long way toward ensuring a successful venture. For example, a young, growing industry with many new entrants, like the new media industry spawned by the Internet and user-generated content technology such as blogs and video, offers an opportunity to position a business to become a major player in the industry. By contrast, occupying a weak position in a mature industry, such as the PC industry, may sound a death knell for the business before it ever opens its doors. Understanding how an industry operates is fundamental to shaping effective entry and growth strategies and to determining the potential for profitability.

A market, by contrast, is a grouping of customers that an entrepreneur targets. Identification of the primary market and the first customer is one of the most important tasks that needs to be undertaken during feasibility analysis. What is meant by "first customer"? The customer is an individual or organization who pays for a product or service, so the first customer for the entrepreneur generally represents that segment of the marketplace that needs the product or service most—in other words, the customer in the most pain. The reason is that entrepreneurs have limited resources so they want to assure that their first sales come quickly, which will happen if they've targeted customers with real problems.

Entrepreneurs identify their primary customers by recognizing a need, or pain, in the market. Gus Conrades and his partner Bryan Murphy saw a need for a central online place where people and businesses could purchase auto parts and car-care products. In the highly fragmented auto products market, customers had a difficult time finding what they needed. Conrades and Murphy launched Wrenchead.com to remedy that situation, and they now sell millions of auto parts and brand name accessories around the world to people who love cars, and at the same time, they provide online business solutions and supply chain management to dealers.

Identifying a pain or need in the market is only the first step. Unfortunately, many entrepreneurs don't place enough emphasis on in-depth market analysis to support the need they have recognized. As a result, they tend to overestimate their market forecasts for demand by as much as 60 percent. And that kind of error can be devastating to a startup venture. This chapter helps the reader do efficient and effective industry and market research within the constraints of the limited resources available to entrepreneurs so that their new venture increases its chances for success.

AN OVERVIEW OF INDUSTRY ANALYSIS

There are two important reasons to study the industry in which a new venture will operate. First, it represents the business's external environment, and no business operates independent of its external environment. Second, entrepreneurs need to understand whether they can make a profit in the industry and if that profit will be significant enough to make the effort to start the business worthwhile. Return on investment (ROI) is a critical factor in any entrepreneur's planning. Two forces influence ROI in an industry: (1) forces that tend not to change such as brand equity and intellectual property and forces that are dynamic, such as the number of potential buyers or changing demographics; and (2) the aggregate strength of the market forces. For example, the airlines and publishing industries have intense forces acting on them, so returns typically are not attractive. Return on invested capital for the airlines industry from 1992 through 2006 averaged 5.9 percent; publishing was 13.4 percent as compared to industries with weak forces acting on them. Software garnered an average of 37.6 percent and pharmaceuticals 31.7 percent in the same period.[2]

Exploring an industry will involve gathering and synthesizing an enormous amount of information as well as talking to people who spend their days working in that industry. Starting with a clear understanding of what information needs to be gathered will increase the chances that the assessment is as accurate as possible.

The data collected should answer the following key questions:

■ *What does the industry look like?* Every industry possesses a particular character that may be described as hostile, collaborative, highly competitive, friendly, and so forth. It is also characterized by its demographics, such as size, number of active companies, revenues, and age.

■ *Is the industry growing?* Growth is measured by sales volume, number of employees, units produced, number of new companies entering the industry, and so forth. A growing industry means more opportunities for new ventures to enter and survive. The appropriate growth measure is determined by the type of industry. For example, the food services industry is typically labor intensive, so looking at growth in the number of employees makes sense. On the other hand, the import/export industry is not necessarily labor intensive so growth in the number of employees is not a good measure of overall industry growth.

■ *Where are the opportunities?* Does the industry provide opportunities for new businesses with strategies involving new products and/or processes, novel business models, innovative distribution strategies, or new marketing approaches? Are there clear examples of new ventures that have succeeded in this industry?

■ *What is the status of any new technology?* How quickly does the industry adopt new technology, and does technology play a significant role in the competitive strategy of firms in the industry?

- *How much do industry companies spend on research and development?* Expenditures on R&D indicate how important technology is, how rapid the product development cycle is, and whether technology is critical to industry success.

- *Who are the opinion leaders in the industry?* Which firms dominate the industry and what impact do they have? How do they influence new firm strategy? Opinion leaders may or may not be a new firm's competitors in its markets depending on how the entrepreneur has defined his or her customers. Nevertheless, opinion leaders will affect the new venture's ability to access the supply chain and distribution channels.

- *Are there young, successful firms in the industry?* This information will provide an indicator of how formidable the entry barriers are and whether the industry is growing rapidly.

- *What does the future look like?* What appears likely to happen over the next five years? What are the trends and patterns of change? Entrepreneurs need to prepare their new ventures for success beyond the date of launch; they need to prepare for sustainability.

- *Are there any threats to the industry?* Is there any chance that new technology will render obsolete either the industry or that segment of the industry in which the entrepreneur is doing business?

- *What are the typical margins in the industry?* Looking at average gross margins in the industry provides an indication of how much room there is to make mistakes. A gross margin is derived by dividing gross profit by sales. It indicates how much money is left to pay overhead and make a profit. If the industry typically has 2 percent margins or less, as the grocery industry does, making a profit will require selling in large volumes and keeping overhead costs to a minimum. Price, therefore, will be a driver of customer purchasing decisions. Where margins run at 70 percent or higher, there is a lot more room to play, but generally these industries (such as the software industry) have relatively short product life cycles, so R&D costs are high. Here customers are more interested in getting a solution to their problem and are willing to pay a premium to get that solution.

For all businesses, there are global trends that offer rich opportunities to innovate.[3]

- For the first time in 200 years, emerging-market countries will generate more growth than developing countries, which will provide a new market of middle class consumers.

- These developing economies need to become productive quickly so there are opportunities to offer innovations that increase productivity.

- Global interconnectedness in economies, markets, and social groups means more volatility and an acceleration of the rate of innovation.

Going into the analysis with a firm grip on which questions need to be answered is the first step. Figuring out where to find this information is the next step.

Gathering Secondary Sources of Industry Information

It's generally wise to begin any research by looking at secondary sources of information to gather background data. Today, Google search engine (or Yahoo!, MSN, and others) and Wikipedia.com are great places to get an introduction to an industry and pick up on some trends by noting what is being talked about. Journals, trade magazines, industry analysts, government publications, and annual reports of public corporations—normally available in a university or community library and on the Internet—are also excellent starting points; they provide more targeted information and generally from experts. For example, a number of industry analysts offer excellent overviews of most of the major industries. Table 5.1 presents a listing of a few of these analytical resources. Trade magazines provide a good sense of key firms and the direction the industry may be taking. LexisNexis and STAT-USA are also fine sources of industry statistics. The important thing to remember is to use multiple sources to draw conclusions because no one source is complete and it's important to get a variety of perspectives to look for patterns.

The North American Industry Classification System (NAICS), the classification system that the United States, Canada, and Mexico developed to identify industries and allow for common standards and statistics across North America, is replacing the traditional U.S. Standard Industrial Classification system (SIC). NAICS covers 350 new industries that have never been coded before. Some of these industries reflect high-tech developments such as fiber optic cable

TABLE 5.1   Resources for Industry Analysis (Available online or at most university libraries)

Alacra Industry Spotlight	Web-based content sources: www.alacrawiki.com
Bureau of Labor Statistics Occupational Outlook Handbook	Describes industry working conditions including employment, occupations, and lists of other organizations with information
Datamonitor Industry Market Research	A collection of industry studies
Encyclopedia of American Industries	Short essays on a number of industries covering trends and forecasts
Encyclopedia of Associations	Contains descriptions of about 120,000 international and U.S. membership organizations
Encyclopedia of Emerging Industries	Inception, emergence, and current status of about 120 U.S. industries and segments
Encyclopedia of Global Industries	Overview of industries worldwide including trends and forecasts
Forrester	Focuses on IT and telecommunications market research
Gartner	Industry insights
Google Business Associations by Industry	http://directory.google.com/Top/Business/Associations
OneSource	Diverse industry coverage
Standard & Poor's NetAdvantage	Detailed overview of 50 industries; updated every six months. Also find "Industry References" for a list of professional and trade associations for a specific industry
Valuation Resources Industry Information Resources	A free guide to industry information, research and analysis for more than 400 industries: http://valuationresources.com/industryreport.htm

manufacturing, satellite communications, and the reproduction of computer software. However, far more of these new categories are not technology-based: bed and breakfast inns, environmental consulting, warehouse clubs, pet supply stores, credit card issuing, diet and weight reduction centers, to name only a few. These codes can be found at www.census.gov/epcd/www/naics.html.

NAICS industries are identified by a six-digit code instead of the four-digit SIC code. The longer code accommodates a larger number of sectors and enables more flexibility in designating subsectors. NAICS is organized in a hierarchical structure much like the SIC. The first two digits designate a major economic sector (formerly division), such as agriculture or manufacturing. The third digit designates an economic subsector (formerly major group), such as crop production or apparel manufacturing. The fourth digit designates an industry group, such as grain and oil seed farming or fiber, yarn, and thread mills. The fifth digit designates the NAICS industry, such as wheat farming or broadwoven fabric mills. The international NAICS agreement fixes only the first five digits of the code. The sixth digit is used for industrial classifications in other countries where necessary. With the NAICS code, one can find statistics about size of the industry, sales, number of employees, and so forth.

It is easy to research common broad industries like consumer goods and technology because they are frequently covered by the government, news sources, brokerage firms, and the financial press. More difficult are small industries, whose data may end up aggregated within a larger industry; new or emerging industries, which are not yet represented in the government classification system; business-to-business industries where information is kept proprietary; and those industries that are not yet perceived to be legitimate industries. However, there are some indirect ways to extrapolate valuable information to guide the feasibility process.

1. *Check the business press.* Often popular business publications and newspapers will write about an industry before it hits the radar of the more established sources.

2. *Talk to trade associations.* Since these organizations are comprised of industry companies, they tend to collect data that describes that industry. The *Encyclopedia of Associations* is a good way to find such a trade organization. Also consider searching online using the ".org" domain, which is typical of nonprofit organizations such as trade associations.

3. *Consult trade association journals.* These journals are often found online or through services like LexisNexis or Factiva.

4. *Check organizations that list government and agency resources.* For example, FedStats lists U.S. government sites that contain statistical information, and it can be searched by topic or agency.

5. *Look at blogs, wikis, websites, and social networking sites.* Find patterns of thought and support or disconfirming evidence for your conclusions.

The Internet is an exciting source of a vast amount of information, most of it for free. When using free sources such as wikis, websites, blogs, etc. it is important to remember that these are, for the most part, sources of opinion that may not have any evidence to support them. Entrepreneurs should ask serious questions about who authored the information, what that person's credentials are, and what their motivation was for writing it. In addition, consider whether the author included citations to original sources and determine the currency of the information. Many significant events have occurred in the business environment since 2000 that will impact business strategy. Relying on outdated information could send the new venture in the wrong direction.

The Importance of Primary Industry Data

Secondary research paints a broad picture of the industry, but given the lead time from data gathering to print, it rarely yields the most current information available. Therefore, to access the timeliest information, it is extremely important to gather primary field data on the industry. Put more simply, entrepreneurs need to talk with people in the industry to validate what they have gathered with their secondary research. Some sources to tap are:

- *Industry observers,* who study particular industries and regularly report on them in newspapers or newsletters or through the media.
- *Suppliers and distributors,* who are in an excellent position to comment on the health of the industry in terms of demand for products and services, as well as on the financial strength and market practices of major firms in the industry.
- *Customers,* who can be a clue to satisfaction with the industry and the products or services supplied by firms in the industry.
- *Employees of key firms in the industry,* who are a good source of information about opinion leaders and competitors.
- *Professionals from service organizations,* such as lawyers and accountants, who regularly work with a particular industry.
- *Trade shows,* which give a good indication of who the opinion leaders are and who has the strongest market strategy.

Understanding Industry Life Cycles

Industries do not remain static or stable over time; in fact, they are constantly evolving. Like people, industries and their products move through a life cycle that includes birth, growth, maturity, and ultimately decline. Today, many industry life cycles are accelerating with a corresponding speeding up of their product cycles; consequently, many companies have been caught in the inertia of believing that their products would live forever. Like companies, industries decline when the story is no longer compelling. When companies in that industry stick to the old strategies while customers move on, the life cycle slows and eventually dies. Currently, the newspaper industry is suffering from disruptive change brought about by the Internet and the new consumer-generated media—blogs, Google, online newsletters, eBay, and Monster.com. Despite this powerful competition, the industry is still focusing most of its resources on print media even after making the shift to the Web.[4]

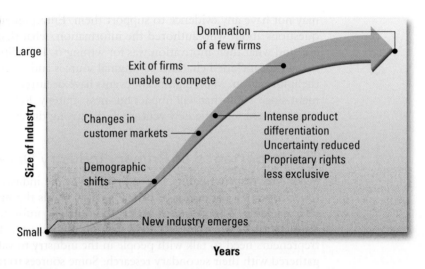

FIGURE 5.1

Industry Life Cycle

The stages of the industry life cycle are identified by the different kinds of activities occurring at each stage. Figure 5.1 displays this life cycle, and we describe the stages and their strategic implications here.

Birth

A new industry emerges, often with the introduction of a disruptive technology, such as the Internet, that displaces previous technology and creates opportunities that didn't exist before. One might argue that the new media sector, discussed previously, is an example of an emerging industry that came about as the result of affordable and accessible production technology via the Internet. Successful examples of early companies in this space are YouTube, Facebook, Twitter, and Wikipedia, and these companies have inspired thousands of service companies designed to help individuals and businesses take advantage of these platforms to better connect with their customers. For entrepreneurs contemplating an industry entry at the earliest stage, it truly is the Wild West, with no rules and plenty of opportunities to try anything and everything. With sufficient resources, an entrepreneurial firm can position its technology to potentially become the industry standard; without them, the new venture's strategy will be influenced by the standards set by more dominant players.

Growth and Adaptation

Following birth, a new industry typically goes through a volatile and rapid stage of growth as companies and their respective technologies jockey for position and the right to determine industry standards. This is an expensive period for most companies because they need to use extensive resources and develop critical partnerships to establish their position in the industry.

Differentiation and Competition

As more firms enter the industry, intense product differentiation occurs, because the industry's established standards and proprietary rights no longer provide the exclusivity they once did. Entrepreneurial ventures that enter the industry at this point must either identify niches that have not been served or differentiate themselves sufficiently in order to attract enough customers to be successful. One of the biggest threats at this stage is commoditization. It is commonly believed that all products eventually become commodities; however, recent research has revealed that this is not always the case. Take, for example, the humble toaster, which has gone through multiple iterations in its product life cycle and is still a prominent fixture in the home appliance industry. Today, the global marketplace in countertop toasting technology is demonstrably driven by differentiation, segmentation, and ongoing technical innovation.[5] When price becomes the most important differentiator, however, it signals to entrepreneurs that the time for innovation has already arrived and that new value must be created quickly.

Shakeout

When competition is the most intense, those companies that are unable to compete leave. The remaining firms then grow more rapidly as they pick up the slack. In fact, it is a curious truism that as the industry goes through its shakeout, the GDP (gross domestic product) actually increases, meaning that firms in the industry become more productive. Nevertheless, although shakeouts may lead to temporary efficiency gains, they also eliminate the possibility of competition and therefore contribute to a social loss from decreased market competition.[6] Entrepreneurial firms will not enter such an industry if they cannot survive the predatory tactics of the dominant players in the industry. The shakeout period moves the industry from many companies and high product costs, to a more stable and mature industry with only a few efficient firms. This is the period in the industry life cycle when the opinion leaders establish themselves.

Maturity and Decline

In this stage, the industry reaches a mature state in which several major players dominate. If new research and development in the industry do not produce a resurgence of growth, the industry could face impending decline as earnings and sales growth slow and prospects deteriorate. Typically, mature industries are described by high-dividend yields and low price-to-earnings ratios, and CEOs of companies in mature industries tend to focus on cost containment. In general, it takes the introduction of disruptive technology to turn a declining industry around. Broad industries like mining, manufacturing, and agriculture are all in decline, although some sectors within those industries have found new life. For example, in Iowa, soy farmers have developed a new soy flour that can substitute for eggs in baked goods with no cholesterol. And miners of mica in South Dakota are finding new applications for their minerals as a result of new technology that can reduce the size of mica granules to the nano level or less than 12 microns in size. Mica, traditionally used as an insulating material in electronics, is now used to dampen sound in automobiles and add shine to cosmetics.

For every industry, these life-cycle stages occur at different times and vary in their duration. The video rental industry presents a classic example of an industry in transition. In the early stages it was made up of small independent (mom-and-pop) owners. Wayne Huizenga sought to consolidate the industry by developing Blockbuster Video, a video megastore. In just a few years, independents were disappearing in favor of large-volume chain outlets. Then the megastores gave way to video on demand, available over cable television and even the Internet. And then Netflix made DVDs easily available through the mail at an even lower cost and more convenience and more recently streams its movies to the user's television or other playback device.

Recent research has identified four major industry trajectories that signal how fast change occurs in a particular industry.[7] Figure 5.2 depicts these trajectories from the most prevalent, progressive and intermediating through radical and creative change. Progressive change takes place as companies in the industry grow geographically and increase profits through innovations in operations, processes, distribution, and technology. Examples are discount retailers like Wal-Mart and airlines like Jet Blue. Intermediating change, by contrast, is industry change that comes about when there are major shifts in the value chain in the form of forward and backward integration, strategic partnerships, and new ways to transact business with customers. A good example is the automobile industry, where dealers have moved onto the Internet in an effort to reach more customers and bring down costs.[8]

Radical change occurs in industries when an innovation results in the obsolescence of previous technology and drives old-line companies out of business. The Internet produced such a change for the automobile industry, and the PC drove typewriter manufacturers out of business. Radical change is transformative, but the transformation typically happens over decades. Finally, creative change is found in industries where resources turn over frequently and must continually be replaced. Companies in industries like the film production industry tend to undertake multiyear projects to develop new assets for customers (the moviegoers) who constantly seek new forms of entertainment.

It is important to identify which stage of the life cycle an industry is in. Reading the analyses of industry watchers in trade magazines and talking with people who regularly work in that industry are good ways to learn where an industry is in the life cycle. Using a framework such as Porter's Five Forces, discussed in the next section, will assist entrepreneurs in determining the competitive characteristics of an industry or market as well as the industry's trajectory.

FIGURE 5.2   Industry Trajectories

Progressive Change	Intermediating Change	Radical Change	Creative Change
• Neither core assets nor activities threatened	• Core activities threatened	• Core assets and activities threatened	• Core assets threatened

ANALYZING AN INDUSTRY

It is often helpful to attach a framework to the concept of an industry to organize all the data collected and to be able to effectively evaluate the industry. Many frameworks have been proposed, and several have been adopted successfully by entrepreneurs. Perhaps the most commonly used competitive framework is Porter's Five Forces. Porter's work has been challenged on several levels, most notably, that a "sixth force," the government or public, should be included and that the attractiveness of an industry cannot be evaluated independent of the resources the company brings to the industry. Keeping these criticisms in mind, Porter's framework still provides an excellent exercise for entrepreneurs as they seek to characterize the industry and markets they will enter.

Porter's Five Forces

For years, the work of Michael Porter has provided a way of effectively looking at the structure of an industry and a company's competitive strength and positioning relative to that industry and to the markets it serves. Porter's basic premise is that sustaining high performance levels requires a well-thought-out strategy and implementation plan based on knowledge of the way the industry works and the attractiveness of markets. Porter asserts that there are five forces in any industry that affect the ultimate profit potential of a venture in terms of long-run return on investment.[9] By contrast, such things as economic forces, changes in demand, material shortages, and technology shifts affect short-run profitability. Figure 5.3 depicts the Five Forces framework, which is discussed in more detail in the following sections.

Barriers to Entry

An entrepreneurial venture's success in a given industry or market is affected by the ability of new firms to enter the entrepreneur's market. If the costs are low and few economies of scale exist, then competitors can easily enter and disrupt the entrepreneur's competitive strategy. In some industries and markets, however, barriers to entry are high and will discourage competitors from entering. Note that these factors may also present a challenge for the entrepreneur entering new markets or a new industry. These barriers may include the following:

Economies of Scale: Many industries have achieved economies of scale in marketing, production, and distribution. This means that their costs to produce have declined relative to the price of their goods and services. Typically, economies of scale are found in more mature industries. A new venture cannot easily achieve these same economies, so it is forced into a "Catch-22" situation. If it enters the industry on a large scale, it risks retaliation from those established firms in the industry. If it enters on a small scale, which is the more common strategy, it may not be able to compete because its costs are high relative to everyone else's. Another version of this dilemma occurs in an industry in which the major players are vertically integrated; that is, they own their suppliers

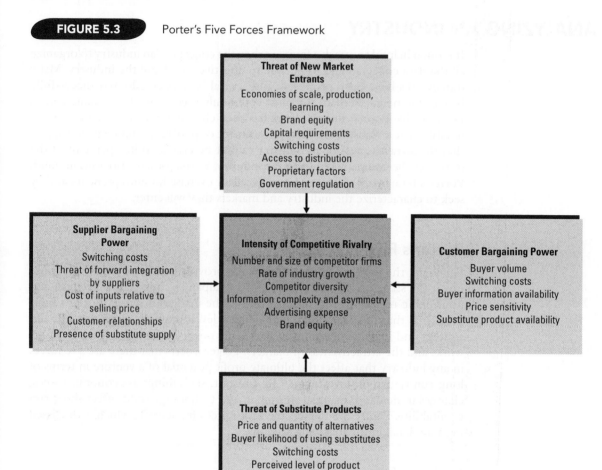

FIGURE 5.3   Porter's Five Forces Framework

Threat of New Market Entrants

Economies of scale, production, learning
Brand equity
Capital requirements
Switching costs
Access to distribution
Proprietary factors
Government regulation

Supplier Bargaining Power

Switching costs
Threat of forward integration by suppliers
Cost of inputs relative to selling price
Customer relationships
Presence of substitute supply

Intensity of Competitive Rivalry

Number and size of competitor firms
Rate of industry growth
Competitor diversity
Information complexity and asymmetry
Advertising expense
Brand equity

Customer Bargaining Power

Buyer volume
Switching costs
Buyer information availability
Price sensitivity
Substitute product availability

Threat of Substitute Products

Price and quantity of alternatives
Buyer likelihood of using substitutes
Switching costs
Perceived level of product differentiation

and/or distribution channels, which effectively locks out the new venture. What most new ventures do when they must compete with companies that have achieved economies of scale is attempt to form alliances with other small firms to share resources and thus compete on a more level playing field. This type of collaboration is occurring more and more often as businesses realize that the industry is too complex for any one company to have all the resources and intellectual property required to control a portion of it. An example of this strategy is the grocery industry, where independent grocers have joined forces in consortia to achieve more buying power in their industry.

Brand Loyalty: New entrants to an industry face existing products and services with loyal customers who are not likely to switch easily to something new. A new firm will need to undertake an extensive marketing campaign focused on making the customer aware of the benefits of the new venture's products. The cost of undertaking this strategy can be a significant barrier to entry unless customers are dissatisfied with the competing brands. On the Internet, it has become clear that when incumbents like Gap and Barnes & Noble set up shop online, they retain the brand presence they have already established in their bricks-and-mortar stores—consequently, they can be profitable immediately. By contrast, it takes a company like Amazon.com (with the strongest online brand recognition), which had no bricks-and-mortar presence, years to become profitable. In Amazon's case, another factor in its slow pace to profit was that it was trying to grow the business into multiple areas—books, DVDs, music, and so forth—simultaneously and that kind of growth is very costly in terms of marketing and inventory.

Capital Requirements: The cost of entering many industries is prohibitive for a new venture. These costs may include up-front advertising, research and development (R&D), and expenditures for plant and equipment. Entrepreneurs often overcome this barrier by outsourcing to or partnering with established companies to leverage their resources and industry intelligence.

Switching Costs for the Buyer: Buyers in most industries don't readily switch from one supplier to another unless there is a compelling reason to do so. Switching costs the buyer money and time. For example, a manufacturing business that has spent a lot of time and money finding the best supplier for the raw materials it needs to produce its product will not easily change suppliers, because that would mean going through the whole process again.

Access to Distribution Channels: The new venture must persuade established distribution channel members to accept its new product or service and must prove that it will be beneficial to distributors to do so. This persuasion process, like any sale, can be costly for a new venture in terms of time, personnel, and travel. One solution for some types of businesses is distributing via the Internet, which is a direct method of reaching the customer.

Proprietary Factors: Barriers to entry also include proprietary technology, products, and processes. Where established firms hold patents on products and processes that the new venture requires, they have the ability either to keep the new venture out of the industry or to make it very expensive to enter. Most favorable location is another form of proprietary barrier. Often entrepreneurs will discover that existing firms in the industry own the most advantageous business sites, forcing the new venture to locate elsewhere, perhaps in a less desirable location. The Internet diminishes such location advantages somewhat, but the ability of customers to find a Web address quickly through the major search engines also becomes a location advantage. Making sure the website is optimized so that the business name comes up near the top of the search list is important. Other proprietary factors include trade secret supplier and customer lists.

Government Regulations: The government can limit entry to an industry or market through strict regulation, licensing requirements and by limiting access to raw materials via laws or high taxes and to certain locations by means of zoning restrictions. Food products and biochemicals must obtain FDA approval, which is a significant barrier to entry.

Threat from Substitutes

A new venture must compete not only with products and services in its own industry but also with logical substitutes that other industries bring to the market. Generally, these substitute products and services accomplish the same basic function in a different way or at a different price. For example, movie theaters regularly compete with other forms of entertainment for the consumer's disposable dollars. The threat from substitute products is more likely to occur where firms in other industries are earning high profits at better prices than can be achieved in the new venture's industry. It is also likely to happen where an incumbent firm has deep resources and technical talent so that it can move quickly into new markets.

Threat from Buyers' Bargaining Power

In industries where buyers (customers) have bargaining power, it is more difficult for a new entrant to gain a foothold and grow. Examples of buyers that have this type of bargaining power include Price/Costco, Barnes & Noble, and Wal-Mart. Buyers like these can force down prices in the industry through volume purchases. This is particularly true where industry products constitute a significant portion of the buyers' requirements—books for Barnes & Noble, toys for Wal-Mart. Under this scenario, the buyer is more likely to be able to achieve the lowest possible price, a price that entrepreneurs will find difficult to compete with. Buyers also gain bargaining power where they face few switching costs; where the industry's products are standardized or undifferentiated, so there are plenty of substitutes; or where the industry's products don't affect the buyer in a significant way. The largest buyers also pose a threat of backward integration; that is, they may actually purchase their suppliers, thus better controlling costs and affecting price throughout the industry.

Threat from Suppliers' Bargaining Power

In some industries, suppliers exert enormous power through the threat of raising prices, limiting the quality or quantity of goods they supply, or changing the quality of the products that they supply to manufacturers and distributors. If the number of these suppliers is few relative to the size of the industry, or the industry is not the primary customer of the suppliers, that power is magnified. A further threat from suppliers is that they will integrate forward—that is, they will purchase the outlets for their goods and services, thus controlling the prices at which their output is ultimately sold. And entrepreneurs must remember that where switching costs are high, it's difficult for firms to make the needed changes to increase their profitability.

Competitive Rivalry Among Existing Firms

The four factors just discussed all work together to create competitive rivalry. In general, a highly competitive industry serving highly competitive markets will drive down profits and ultimately the rate of return on investment. To position themselves in a competitive market, firms often resort to price wars and advertising skirmishes. Once one firm decides to make such a strategic move in the market, others will usually follow. The clearest example is the airline industry; when one airline discounts its prices significantly, most of the others immediately follow. The problem with this tactic is that it ultimately hurts everyone in the industry and may even force out some smaller firms because competitive prices drop below costs. Most new ventures can't compete on price and can't afford costly advertising battles to build an image. To compete in a market that is highly competitive, they must instead identify a niche that serves an unmet need for customers and that will enable them to enter quietly and gain a foothold. Southwest Airlines did that effectively by understanding an unmet need for customers to more directly fly to regional airports and pay less per ticket in exchange for giving up some non-essential services. Many entrepreneurs seeking entry into industries such as software, biomedical, biotech, and telecommunications deliberately position themselves to be acquired eventually by the larger rivals rather than try to compete against them.

In general, competitive rivalry in an industry will be the most intense where there are numerous competitors of generally similar size and power, where growth is stagnant and exit barriers are high, and where the competitive strategies among the rivals are very diverse.

Using the Framework to Draw Conclusions

Entrepreneurs can quickly become overwhelmed by the amount of information and the inconsistencies they confront when they begin their search process. That is why it's important to understand how the author defined the industry they're talking about, and be careful of sources that define the industry in such a way as to make it appear larger than it actually is. The demographics in the industry are also difficult to get a handle on because if the industry is comprised of a lot of private firms (and most are), then government data broken down into SIC or NAICS codes is valuable because it includes private and public companies. The extent of supplier power can be gauged by looking at a representative public company's income statements to determine what percentage of its direct costs were spent on suppliers. Economies of scale are a barrier to entry for entrepreneurs, so it's critical to examine government data from the census to calculate the percentage output of an average firm in the industry relative to the total output of the industry. If the firm's output is large relative to total output, it suggests that economies of scale are in play, so the entrepreneur's entry strategy must involve rapid scale up to survive.[10] When it comes to the issue of customer power, the general rule is that where the industry supplies many downstream markets, customers have little power. That means that if the entrepreneur has only one or two customers, those customers have significant power to affect the entrepreneur's strategy.

Some additional things to watch out for include the following:

- A fast-growth industry may not be attractive because suppliers typically gain power and charge higher prices. Moreover, products reach commodity status much faster, which means that profit margins decline.

- A "sexy" industry that everyone is writing about will tend to attract more competition and will often have price-insensitive buyers, high switching costs, and high barriers to entry.

- The need for industry complements to enable a new venture to grow must be considered. For example, electric cars have been slow to take hold for a number of reasons, but the lack of an infrastructure (recharging stations) is a significant roadblock.

Using the Porter framework to characterize an entrepreneur's industry and target market is just the first step. To be able to use this information to refine a business model and entry strategy requires drawing some conclusions based on the information gathered. One way to do this is to start by determining the impact of the variables that describe each of the five forces. The following scale will help to differentiate the direction and strength of the impact.

Threat of new entry or substitution is extremely high and impact will be very negative = ↓ ↓

Threat of new entry or substitution is high or strong = ↓

Threat of new entry or substitution is moderate = +

No threat = 0

Supplier/buyer power is extremely high and impact will be very negative = ↓ ↓

Supplier/buyer power is high or strong = ↓

Supplier/buyer power is moderate = +

Supplier/buyer power is not a threat = 0

Once the strength and direction of impact of the various variables is defined, it is important to analyze how this knowledge will affect business strategy. For example, suppose the entrepreneur finds that in the particular industry being considered, competitive rivalry is extremely high and there are few barriers to entry (market entry is not a threat). Suppose also that buyer power is strong, signaling that buyers could exert downward pressure on prices, forcing a commodity pricing situation, and that there appear to be viable substitutes for what the entrepreneur is offering. This scenario is certainly not a very positive one for the entrepreneur who must either figure out a way to change the conditions by perhaps modifying the business model or ultimately deciding that the business is not feasible under these circumstances.

When making decisions based on the Five Forces, it is important to consider the core competencies and resources that the new venture brings to the equation. For entrepreneurial ventures, an industry has to enable the venture to access the supply chain and distribution channels; however, it does not mean that existing markets must be favorable. Entrepreneurs typically enter with a niche strategy serving an unmet need in the market, so by definition, there will be no competitive rivalry for a time. In the end, the Five Forces Model should be used as one of several tools to aid in the decision making that entrepreneurs must do when judging the feasibility of their new business concepts.

PEST Analysis

In addition to viewing the industry and market through the lens of the Five Forces Model, it may be helpful for an entrepreneur to also conduct a PEST (or STEP) analysis to examine the environment in which the new venture will operate and to ensure that the entrepreneur's strategies are aligned with the trajectory of the industry and the markets in which the new business will compete. PEST analysis (Figure 5.4) examines specific aspects of the macro-environment: its social, technological, economic, and political facets. Social factors consist of demographic and cultural aspects of the environment, such as age distribution and health consciousness or attitudes toward the environment. Technological factors include such things as R&D activity and rate of technological change. Economic factors deal with the firm's cost of capital and customers' purchasing power as well as inflation, employment rate, and economic prospects over time. Political factors involve government regulation and the various legal issues that affect the business's operations in addition to the stability of the government and trade agreements. Depending on the needs of the entrepreneurs, the PEST analysis can be extended to include environmental, legal, and ethical factors (STEEPLE).

A PEST analysis should begin with the identification of the macro-environmental factors that apply to the new business and then an examination of the potential impact these factors might have on the business. For example, factors that make it more difficult to do business—high taxes, real estate costs, and labor costs—may cause an entrepreneur to consider a different location for doing business where these items are more favorable. However, these negatives are often found in high-economic-growth regions like major metropolitan areas, so the trade-off is that going to a more favorable location from an economic perspective may not provide the type of skilled labor required for the business operations. The bottom line is that for any new business, a thorough understanding of the context in which the business will operate is essential to success and long-term survivability.

CHARACTERIZING THE TARGET MARKET

Starting a new business might be as relatively simple as launching a website, but securing enough customers to survive is another matter entirely. Savvy entrepreneurs rely heavily on their market research to substantiate their intuitive

FIGURE 5.4

PEST Analysis

Political Government, Regulatory, and Legal	Sociocultural Demographics and cultural
Economic Cost of capital, Inflation, Customer purchasing power, Employment rate	Technological R&D, Rate of change

SOCIAL ENTREPRENEURSHIP: MAKING MEANING

Having It All

Imagine an entrepreneurial venture competing against the likes of AT&T and Verizon. Sound impossible? Not at all. Working Assets is a long-distance, wireless, credit card, and broadcasting company that was started in 1985 to "build a better world." It donates 1 percent of its revenues to nonprofits nominated by its customers. Customers can also round up their bills to the next dollar amount, and the difference is contributed to charity. Working Assets has funded nonprofits such as Doctors Without Borders, Planned Parenthood, the National Center for Science and Education, and the Children's Defense Fund. It works with socially responsible companies such as Ben & Jerry's Ice Cream to create joint promotions and is internally consistent in its environmental message.

It uses recycled paper for billing and recycled plastic for its calling card. And in an industry that is not known for customer loyalty, Working Assets has a loyal customer base. The company also enhances its customers' ability to speak out on important issues by allowing them to place free calls to decision makers on critical issues of the month. Since its inception, the company has raised $65 million by helping its customers make a difference in the world through philanthropy and political activism, while still succeeding as an entrepreneurial venture.

Sources: www.workingassets.com (July, 2010); and J.G. Dees, J. Emerson, and P. Economy, *Enterprising Nonprofits* (New York: Wiley, 2001), p. 224.

belief that they have a winner, but the market research that entrepreneurs undertake doesn't resemble in any great degree the research conducted by large, established companies. In the first place, entrepreneurs are limited by a lack of sufficient resources, time, and high levels of uncertainty, so the data they collect is far from perfect and just enough to give confidence that the entrepreneur should go forward with the new business.

The previous discussion of frameworks for analysis of the industry and market also provides an effective way to describe the characteristics of the potential market the entrepreneur wishes to serve. However, it is not until an entrepreneur gets into the field and actually talks to potential customers and those who deal with potential customers that a clearer understanding of various customer segments and the first or entry customer is revealed. Ashbury Images, a San Francisco-based nonprofit screen printer that serves as a source of transition jobs for the homeless, had always viewed its primary customers as small nonprofits. The problem was that these businesses were not profitable customers for Ashbury. As the company began to analyze its customers in depth, it discovered that its best customers, the ones whose needs were actually being served, were larger corporate clients. These clients understood Ashbury's value proposition: a high-quality product and a social mission. Ashbury has now refocused its efforts to put more emphasis on its best customers.[11]

In the beginning stages of market analysis, the customer definition will be fairly loose and may even change substantially as field research is conducted.

It is easy to become overwhelmed by the amount of information available about the target market, so it's important to keep in mind the key questions that should be answered:

- What are the potential markets for the product or service? How big is each market? How dynamic is the market? Is it growing?
- Of these potential markets, which customers are most likely to purchase the product or service at market introduction? In other words, who is in the most pain?
- How much do these customers typically buy, how do they buy, and how do they hear about the product or service?
- How often do they buy? What is their buying pattern?
- How can the new venture meet these customers' needs?

It is important to remember that for a new company, the goals of market research are to (1) identify and profile the first customer; (2) estimate potential demand from that customer; and (3) identify subsequent customer segments and needs to grow the company. Markets that are growing generally experience two types of turbulence: market turbulence, which is the rate at which customer tastes and preferences change; and competitive turbulence, which is the rate at which competitors in the market change their strategies, such as introducing technological innovations.[12]

Targeting the First Customer

Target market research provides some of the most important data that one needs to decide who the first customer is. Recall that the first customer is the one who has a problem the entrepreneur can solve. Therefore, the first customer may not be the biggest market, but rather be an unserved niche that enables the entrepreneur to enter the market with no direct competition for a time. To narrow the focus of market research and to save time and money, entrepreneurs should consider identifying two to three prototypes of a business that seem to be the most feasible. For any product, for example, the entrepreneur could be a manufacturer, distributor, or a retailer. If the product has patents associated with it, licensing the technology to another company is yet another business opportunity. By narrowing the focus, market research can be more targeted, take less time, and generally be more productive.

The market data the entrepreneur collects is only as good as the research methods used to collect them. To ensure that useful and correct conclusions can be drawn from the data collected, sound research methods must be employed. Table 5.2 depicts a four-step process for ensuring that the right information is gathered and that it is used correctly.

As was true with the industry analysis, the Internet is a good starting point for gathering secondary data. Many of the traditional resources found in libraries are now available in online versions; for example, U.S. census data can be found at www.census.gov. Using census data, entrepreneurs can determine whether the geographic area they have defined for the business is growing or declining,

TABLE 5.2	A Four-Step Market Research Process
Assess your information needs.	• How will the data be used?
	• What data need to be collected?
	• What methods of analysis will be used?
	• What are the potential business designs under consideration?
Research secondary sources first.	• What are the demographics of the target market?
	• What are the psychographics of the customer (i.e., buying habits)?
	• How large is the market?
	• Is the market growing?
	• Is the market affected by geography?
	• How can you reach your market?
	• How do competitors reach the market?
	• What market strategies have been successful with these customers?
Measure the target market with primary research.	• What are the demographics of the first customer?
	• Would they purchase your product or service? Why?
	• How much would they purchase?
	• When would they purchase?
	• How would they like to find the product or service?
	• What do they like about your competitors' products and services?
Forecast demand for the product or service.	• What do substitute products/services tell you about demand for your product/service?
	• What do customers, end-users, and intermediaries predict the demand will be?
	• Can you do a limited production or test market for your product or service?

whether its population is aging or getting younger, or whether the available work force is mostly skilled or unskilled, along with many other trends.

Some demographic data (data on age, income, race, occupation, and education) help identify the likelihood that a person will choose to buy a product. Demographic data also make it possible to segment the target market into subgroups that are different from one another. For example, if the target market is retired people over age 65, their buying habits (such as product requirements and quantity or frequency of purchase) may vary by geographic region or by income level.

Finally, census data can be used to arrive at an estimate of how many target customers live within the geographic boundaries of the target market. Then, within any geographic area, those who meet the particular demographic requirements of the product or service can be segmented out.

It is not only consumer markets that are described by demographic data. Business markets can also be described in terms of their size, revenue levels, number of employees, and so forth. Online sources are not the only sources of secondary market data. Most communities have economic development departments or Chambers of Commerce that keep statistics on local population trends and other economic issues. Some communities have Small Business Development Centers (SBDCs), branches of the Small Business Administration that offer a wealth of useful information, as well as services, for small and growing businesses. Table 5.3 provides some secondary sources available at most university libraries or online. Some of the resources listed in Table 5.1 will also help to study the market.

Exploring the Market with Primary Data

The most important data that entrepreneurs can collect on potential customers are primary data, in particular, data collected through observation or customer interviews. The general process involves collecting data based on the questions from Table 5.2, forming some hypotheses or educated guesses about the potential first customer, and then testing the hypotheses by conducting additional research with the customer.

There are many ways to collect primary data on the target market, some more effective than others. We'll talk about them generally in the order of importance to the entrepreneur: observation using anthropological techniques, interviews, informal focus groups, online or in-person surveys, and phone surveys. Notice we did not include mail surveys because entrepreneurs neither have the time nor the money to invest in this type of market research, particularly since it achieves a very low response rate and requires multiple reminders.

Anthropological Techniques for Customer Observation

The problem with most market research is that entrepreneurs don't get at the heart of the customer's problem and, to make matters worse, they often lead the customer to a solution, which just happens to be theirs! Approaching the

TABLE 5.3	Market Research Resources
Frost & Sullivan	Available at many university libraries
Global Market Information Database	Available at many university libraries
MarketResearch.com	A free, searchable index to market research reports. Not all reports are free
Market Share Reporter	Contains market share information on products aggregated from articles and market research reports. Available at many university libraries
FedStats	Statistics and information from more than 70 agencies of the U.S. government: www.fedstats.gov
IES (International Economic Statistics) Database	Links to site of various countries and NGOs: http://liber8.stlouisfed.org/iesd
EIU Country Data	Economic indicators, forecasts, and trends in foreign trade. Available at many university libraries
ISI Emerging Markets	Country and company information from more than 500 sources on Asia, Latin America, Eastern Europe, the Middle East, and North Africa
Portals to the World	Links to statistical sources for most countries: www.loc.gov/rr
Social Technographics®	A free site that lets the user look at the social technographics profile of a customer base: www.forrester.com/empowered/tool_consumer.html
PRIZM Segmentation System from Nielsen Claritas	Free look at the psychographics of a neighborhood by zip code: www.claritas.com/MyBestSegments/Default.jsp

customer as an anthropologist would approach a family of gorillas being studied is actually a very effective approach. It consists of five steps, with step one arguably being the most important.

Step One: Induction. Inductive reasoning is learning from observation. It has the goal of understanding the nature of the customer and the customer's needs in a way that does not intrude on customers in their natural habit. In terms of what the entrepreneur is trying to accomplish, this step involves observing customers in action, where this makes sense, or engaging customers in conversation with the goal of getting the customer to reveal problems they face. An example of pure observation is what Hewlett-Packard's medical division does when it wants to consider the development of new products. They embed their people in a hospital to observe how hospital personnel go about their day. Are there points where they may not have a tool or solution for something they need to do so they create a work-around? What do they struggle with most? Their goal is to identify problems.

Where pure observation would not give the results needed, engaging customers in conversation is effective. For example, suppose an entrepreneur wanted to improve on the standard alarm clock but wasn't sure customers had any pain associated with alarm clocks. She might engage some random consumers in conversation about how they make sure they wake up in time to meet their obligations. She will hear everything from *I set an alarm clock*, or *I set my alarm clock and the clock on my cell phone* to *My husband wakes me up*. That's the easy part of the conversation. What the entrepreneur really wants to know is how customers would like to be awakened. Why? Because alarm clocks are essentially a commodity and the entrepreneur wants to change the game. To develop a game-changing product, the customer can't be tethered to something they already know. They have to be free to think beyond what they know and focus on their problem. So the answer to the question *how would you like to be awakened* might be *I want to hear music and then say 'OK, I'm up' and that would turn off the alarm*. The problem the customer has revealed is that they don't want to have to touch the alarm clock—they want a kinder, gentler way of waking up. The customer doesn't know how to solve this problem, but that's not the customer's job; it's the entrepreneur's job. And one entrepreneur, Jonathan Nostrandt, actually solved this very problem using artificial intelligence and creating an alarm clock the user can talk to—Moshi.

Step 2: Abduction. Abduction is a method of reasoning logically. What this means is that the entrepreneur takes what has been observed or gained from talking with customers and tries to explain it in some logical fashion. In the case of the alarm example, the explanation would be that the customer is looking for a kinder, gentler way of waking up. Essentially, the entrepreneur attempts to explain what he or she has observed.

Step 3: Deduction. In this step the entrepreneur deduces or draws a hypothesis or theory from the explanations or premises generated in step 2. The entrepreneur's theory might be that the customer might want to talk to their alarm clock.

Step 4: The Test. Armed with a hypothesis about the customer, the entrepreneur goes back into the field to test it with customers. *If we could provide an alarm clock that you could talk to, would that solve your problem?* Because this type of solution involves developing a prototype, it's important that the entrepreneur be confident that if the alarm clock were created and worked, there would be customers ready to buy before making the investment of time and money. That confidence comes from testing the solution of the customer.

Step 5: Conclusions. The final step involves drawing conclusions from the responses of customers. It is particularly important here not to bias the conclusions but to make them based on the preponderance of evidence provided by the customer, whether positive or negative.

This observation technique takes time, but it's time well spent because the results will better ensure that the solution the entrepreneur develops is the right solution for the right customers.

Structured Interviews

Although personal interviews are more costly and time-consuming than surveys, they have many advantages:

- They provide more opportunity for clarification and discussion.
- The interviewer has an opportunity to observe nonverbal communication and hence assess the veracity of what the interviewee is saying.
- The response rate is high.
- Interviews permit open-ended questions that can lead to more in-depth information.
- They provide an opportunity for the entrepreneur to network and develop valuable contacts in the industry.

Where time and money permit, structured interviews are an excellent source of valuable information from customers, suppliers, distributors, and anyone else who can help the entrepreneur determine who the first customer is. If the entrepreneur is interviewing a number of people, it would be important to have questions in common so that there is a basis for response comparison and useful patterns can be identified. It is critical to prepare for interviews by developing questions that focus on the information required to answer the market research questions, and by conducting some background research on the person being interviewed and the company. That way, more insightful questions can be asked rather than wasting the interviewee's time with questions that can be easily answered from material on the company website.

Informal Focus Groups—The Group Interview

One efficient way to gain valuable information and feedback from customers and others is to conduct an informal focus group, in which a representative sample of potential customers is brought together for a presentation and discussion session. It is often used to elicit feedback on customer needs relative to a potential product or service or to compare products. It is essential to ensure that the person leading the focus group have some knowledge of group dynamics and be able to keep the group on track. Often these focus group sessions are videotaped so that the entrepreneur can spend more time later analyzing the nuances of what occurred. It is important to get the written permission of attendees before videotaping.

Survey Techniques

Survey techniques, whether online, in-person, or by phone require drawing a representative sample from the population of customers in which the entrepreneur is interested. The sample must be selected with great care, for it will determine the validity of the results. In general, to avoid bias, a sample should be random—that is, one in which the entrepreneur has as little control over the selection of respondents as possible. Most entrepreneurs, because of limitations of cost and time, use what is called a convenience sample. This means that not everyone in the defined target market has a chance of being chosen to participate. Instead, the entrepreneur may, for example, choose to select the sample from people who happen to be at the airport on a particular day. Clearly, this method will not reach all possible customers at the airport, but if the target customer is typically found at airports, there's a good chance of obtaining at least a representative sample from which results can be derived fairly confidently. Even if a convenience sample is used, there are ways to ensure the randomness of selection of the participants. Using the airport example, an entrepreneur can decide in advance to survey every fifth person who walks by. Thus the respondents are not chosen on the basis of attractiveness or lack of it—or for any other reason, for that matter. Whatever system is employed, the key point is to make an effort not to bias the selection so that the outcomes are more meaningful.

Conducting a survey, whether in person or online, entails designing a survey instrument, usually a questionnaire that, once filled out by the respondent, provides the desired information. Questionnaire design is not a simple matter of putting some questions on a piece of paper. There are, in fact, proven methods of questionnaire construction to help ensure unbiased responses. It is not within the scope of this text to present all the techniques for questionnaire construction; however, a few key points should be remembered:

- Keep the questionnaire short, with lots of white space, so that the respondent is not intimidated by the task.
- Be careful not to ask leading or biased questions.
- Ask easy, simple questions first, progressing gradually to the more complex ones.
- Ask demographic questions (questions about age, sex, income, and the like) last, when the respondent's attention may have waned. These questions can be answered very quickly.

The Internet has made it easy for small businesses to collect valuable data without having to enlist the help of costly market research firms.[13] Internet surveys such as SurveyMonkey and ZapSurvey are less expensive than traditional surveys, the response time is greatly reduced, and it's easier to include global respondents seamlessly. Posting surveys on the Internet is a convenient way to conduct research if the primary customer is an Internet user. The survey can be posted in user groups, social networks, sent via email to target customers, or placed on a website (as long as the people who need to respond to the survey have a way of knowing that it's there). More information about this topic, including examples of question types, can be found at "Online Survey Design Guide," which is a project of the University of Maryland (http://lap .umd.edu/survey_design/index.html).

Some entrepreneurs prefer to conduct their surveys in person at a location where their target customer can be found, for example, a shopping mall if the respondent is a consumer. Alternatively, a trade show is another popular source for these types of surveys. The advantage of this approach is an immediate and more targeted response as well as the opportunity to perhaps delve deeper into a particular response, not to mention the ability to observe nonverbal communication.

Each of the techniques discussed has advantages and disadvantages associated with it. In general, surveys have a response rate of only about 2 percent, and several follow-ups are usually required to get a sufficient sample. Phone surveys are typically ineffective because in the past few years, people have been bombarded by telemarketers and now resist responding to a telephone survey. Whatever method is chosen, nothing beats feedback from the customer, whether it be at the design stage or as part of an effort to profile the customer and calculate demand.

Segmenting the Market with a Customer Matrix

One useful way to look at various customer segments to determine which should be the primary or first customer is to construct a customer matrix that lays out the benefits, distribution channel, product/service, and potential competition for each of the identified customer segments. The matrix in Table 5.4 represents an initial hypothesis about three potential customers for a proprietary hand-held ultrasound device. This is an example where the primary customer (the one who pays) is not the primary beneficiary or end user. To give some context to the matrix, millions of ultrasound-guided catheter insertion procedures are performed annually, and a significant percentage of them fail because the doctor is forced to look away to view the images. This requires reinsertion, which is uncomfortable for the patient and wastes time. The product being introduced solves that problem because the probe and image display are integrated in a single miniaturized device.

Notice in the matrix how the benefit to the customer changes to meet the customer's specific pain. Once the customer segments are identified, the entrepreneur has to make a choice. Which of these three customers should the entrepreneur go after first? The decision about where to enter the market first is affected by size of the market, customer demand, and resources, but the most important consideration is which customer is most likely to buy. Market

TABLE 5.4   Initial Customer Matrix for a Portable Ultrasound Device*

Customers	Pain	Benefit	Distribution	Competition
Hospital Administration - customer who pays	Need to increase productivity and reduce risk in patient procedures	Save money and decrease potential for litigation	Medical equipment distributor	Siemens (Acuson), General Electric, SonoSite, Zonare, Pocketsonics, Signostics - Australia
End User Catheter Specialists	Guidance is difficult and causes patient discomfort; time consuming; reinsertion rate high	Guidance is easier, increased patient throughput so save time	Medical equipment distributor selling to hospital	Siemens (Acuson), General Electric, SonoSite, Zonare, Pocketsonics, Signostics - Australia
Rural practitioners in underdeveloped regions of various countries	Scarce imaging capability, travel for diagnosis is risky, e.g. in rural India about 317 image centers service 742M people	Provide imaging capability at village level for basic diagnosis so potential to save lives	Government agency, or charitable relief agencies	International - Brazil, Russian, India, and China (BRIC) medical device manufacturers/ suppliers likely have home-field advantage

*Example adapted from feasibility study conducted by Clifford Cousins, Masaru Nakagawa, and Ali Ziaee, University of Southern California, 2009.

research with customers may suggest, for instance, that the quickest early sales will come from rural practitioners because the entrepreneur is not dealing with the bureaucracy of a hospital. Note also that, in this example, the different benefits and distribution strategies for each of the three customers actually produce two distinct types of businesses: a manufacturer that sells to distributors and a company that manufactures, markets, and distributes to organizations in developing countries. The type of business the entrepreneur wants to own then also influences the decision on first customer.

The Customer Profile

Out of the primary research will come a complete profile of the customer in great detail, that is, a description of the primary customer, be it a consumer or a business. The profile is critically important to the eventual marketing strategy, because it provides information vital to everything from product/service design to distribution channels and the marketing plan to attract the customer. Here is a list of some of the information that goes into the customer profile, whether that customer be a consumer or a business:

- Age
- Income level
- Education

- Buying habits—when, where, how much
- Where these customers typically find these types of products and services
- How they would like to purchase these products and services

If the customer is a business, it can be described in essentially the same way—for example, the first customer is a small to midsized construction company with annual revenues of $5 million that makes purchases quarterly, buys primarily over the Internet, and pays within sixty days. The customer profile will also play an important role in the development of the marketing plan, as we will see in Chapter 14.

Gathering Demand Data

It is no easy task to figure out what the demand for a new product or service might be. Even large, experienced companies have failed at it. (Remember the Apple Newton, the first PDA? Its handwriting recognition capability was poor; customers became frustrated, and demand went to zero.)

If entrepreneurs are attempting to give customers what they need, something they will demand, the first thing they must understand is that customers can describe their problems and they can describe what they need to be able to do—their outcomes, but they are typically not effective at describing solutions to their problems.[14] For example, if entrepreneurs ask customers to identify what they like and don't like about the entrepreneur's product or the competitor's product, customers will typically respond in the context of something they know. "I wish this smart phone had a scroll wheel on the right side." Customers are merely providing a missing feature that perhaps a competitor offers. By contrast, if the entrepreneur asks a question that seeks an outcome—"how do you want to use a communication device?" (or better yet, "how do you want to communicate?")—he or she has put no boundaries on the customer. Customers are free to think about how they want to communicate in various scenarios without describing features. With these outcomes understood, the entrepreneur can better design a solution to the customer's problem. More importantly, with this knowledge in hand, the entrepreneur is better prepared to gather demand data.

The question that entrepreneurs do not want to ask is "Would you buy this product?" The simple reason is that in many cases, the respondent will be reluctant to offend the entrepreneur and so will say "yes," knowing full well that they won't be asked to purchase it that day so there is no commitment on their part. A better approach is to identify a problem, confirm that the respondent is experiencing that problem, and then ask if the entrepreneur's solution would interest them. This approach makes it easier for the customer to respond sincerely.

Talking to customers to gauge demand is only the first step. It is also important to discuss demand with industry people such as suppliers and retailers. Getting estimates from at least three different sources enables the entrepreneur to derive a range of values and then triangulate to a best estimate. More detail about this process is found in Chapter 8.

Drawing Conclusions from Market Research

Entrepreneurial decision making is more art than science, so the data gathered during the market research process must be analyzed, synthesized, and result in some conclusions about market feasibility. One of the first steps in working toward a conclusion is to organize the data into meaningful categories—customer profile, market demographics, demand indicators, and so forth. This organization makes it possible to more easily analyze the data and seek patterns or trends that might provide vital information. A thorough review of all the data collected may also enable the entrepreneur to develop some sense of whether there are more positive aspects to the market than there are negative aspects. Furthermore, from the review, threats and challenges to the business goals can be identified and opportunities or courses of action that can include potential business models, customers, distribution channels, and business strategies can be taken. It is the entrepreneur's job to interpret all the raw data and turn it into business intelligence. With a complete picture of the market in hand, an entrepreneur will be in an excellent position to draw a conclusion regarding the market feasibility of the new venture.

GATHERING COMPETITIVE INTELLIGENCE

One of the weakest portions of any feasibility analysis or business plan is the competitive analysis. Why do entrepreneurs frequently underestimate the competition? For one thing, their information is incomplete because competitors don't reveal their most proprietary strategies and tactics. Entrepreneurs also tend to underestimate what it takes in the way of resources and skills to establish a presence in a market and they don't identify all the roadblocks along the way. That talent comes from experience. Furthermore, it is difficult for entrepreneurs to know what they don't know! The competition generally possesses market share, brand recognition, management experience, customer knowledge, value chain relationships, industry knowledge, and resources. That is a formidable package of competitive strength. By contrast, many entrepreneurs take the naïve view that their concept is so new that they have no competition. Sadly, that is rarely the case. Even a niche strategy, probably the most effective strategy for a startup, will only leave an entrepreneur competitor-free for a very short time. Add to that the very real fact that entrepreneurial startups are short on resources and long on commitment and it is easy to see why it would be difficult for a small startup to respond effectively to a competitor attack.

In assessing the competition, the idea is not to benchmark the new venture against a competitor but rather to find ways to create new value that customers will pay for. To undertake effective competitor research, one has to first determine the target market that the entrepreneur's venture is serving (which was discussed in the previous section), because entrepreneurs compete in markets.

Identifying the Competition

There are generally three types of competitors for a product or service: (1) direct, (2) indirect or substitute, and (3) emerging or potential. Identifying exactly who these companies are, including their strengths, weaknesses, and market strategies, will put the new venture in a better position to be a contender in the market.

The noteworthy research of M.I. Chen[15] on competitor analysis suggested that to correctly assess the competitive market, one must view it from two sides: the supply side, which includes resource capabilities such as R&D and production, and the demand side, which is represented by the customer and the customer's needs. Figure 5.5 depicts this framework and enables a clearer understanding of competitor types based on resources and customers addressed. Direct competitors, as the figure shows, are those businesses that serve the same customer needs with the same types of resources, while indirect competitors serve the same customer needs but with different resources as in substitute products or services. Potential competitors are those that are not currently serving the same customer needs but have the resources to quickly move into that space and compete.[16] Therefore, it is important to look outside the immediate industry and market for alternatives. An entrepreneur also needs to look beyond existing competition to emerging competitors. In many industries today, technology and information are changing at such a rapid pace that the window of opportunity for successfully starting a new venture closes early and fast. Consequently, entrepreneurs must be vigilant in observing new trends and new technology that might portend new competitors.

Sometimes the most threatening aspect of a competitor is not readily visible in the typical facts that are reported, and frequently competitors come from outside the entrepreneur's industry and market. For example, understanding

FIGURE 5.5

Competitive Framework

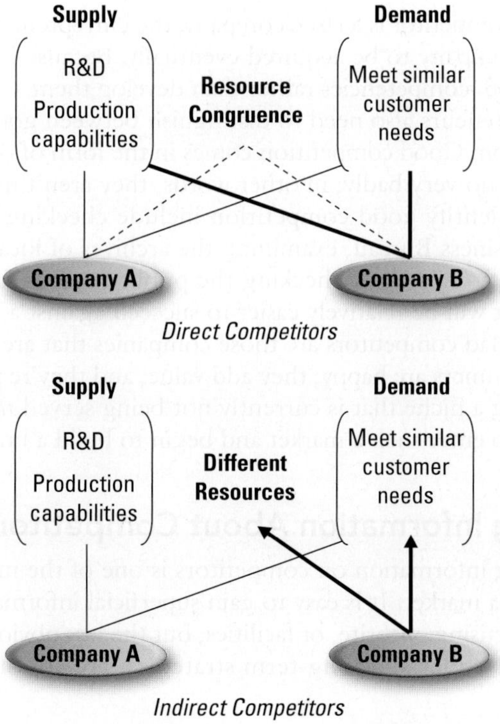

a competitor's core competency helps to determine whether that competency can ever be shifted to the entrepreneur's niche market. Suppose the entrepreneur's business is to train unskilled workers for well-paying jobs in industry. The entrepreneur looks at all the competitors in the training industry and decides that he can compete because he has created a unique niche in the market. What the entrepreneur has failed to do is look outside his industry to companies that might have the same core competency and might have the deep resources required to shift to his niche very rapidly. Those companies are not always obvious. For example, one of Marriott's core competencies is training unskilled workers in the language and work skills they need to perform the various jobs in Marriott's hotel chain. It certainly has the resources to take this competency into any niche it desires. Another example is substitutes and new entrants to the market in the form of disruptive innovation coming from outside the market.[17] These game-changing innovations can destroy the profitability of existing firms. That is why so many companies are continually innovating their products and processes, because of the strong competitive advantage it gives them. Therefore, to make certain that a potential threat like this one is not missed, entrepreneurs should:

- Determine what the competitor has to do to be successful in its own core business. Are there any core competencies that it must acquire?
- Determine whether the competitor has a competency in the same area as the entrepreneur.
- Determine which of the competitor's core competencies are transferable to the entrepreneur's business.

If the competitor is a large company, the entrepreneur may strategically position his company to be acquired eventually, because large companies typically acquire core competencies rather than develop them.

Entrepreneurs also need to distinguish between good competition and bad competition. Good competition comes in the form of companies that are doing what they do very badly; in other words, they aren't making customers happy. Ways to identify good competition include checking complaint levels at the Better Business Bureau, examining the archives of local newspapers for stories about the company, or checking the public records for financial or legal difficulties. It will be relatively easier to succeed against a good competitor than a bad one. Bad competitors are those companies that are doing everything right. Their customers are happy; they add value; and they're prosperous. In this case, identifying a niche that is currently not being served might be the most effective way to enter such a market and begin to build a brand.

Finding Information About Competitors

Collecting information on competitors is one of the most difficult parts of researching a market. It is easy to gain superficial information from the competitor's advertising, website, or facilities; but the less obvious types of information, such as revenues and long-term strategies, are another matter. Information on publicly held competitors can be found in annual reports and other filings required by the Securities and Exchange Commission (SEC). Unfortunately, however, most startup companies are competing against other private companies that will not be willing to divulge these sensitive data. Data that are important to gather include current market strategies, management style and culture, pricing strategy, customer mix, and promotional mix.

The following are some suggestions on where to look for this information.

- Visit competitors' websites or the outlets where their products are sold. Evaluate appearance, number of customers coming and going, what they buy, how much, and how often. Talk to customers and employees.
- Buy competitors' products to understand the differences in features and benefits and to learn about how they treat their customers.
- Use Internet search engines such as Google.com to read what customers are saying about the company.
- Find information on public companies to serve as benchmarks for the industry. Public companies can be investigated through Hoover's Online (www .hoovers.com), the U.S. Securities and Exchange Commission (www.sec.gov), and OneSource (www.onesource.com), to name a few.

Dealing with Competition

Undoubtedly the best way for entrepreneurs to stave off competition is to provide meaningful differentiation in their solutions to customer needs. In a complex world that strategy needs to be bolstered by additional strategies that recognize the new venture's market position. One way to provide meaningful differentiation is to identify new market space—a niche that is not currently being served. That strategy gives entrepreneurs a temporary monopoly in which to establish themselves before having to face competition.

Entrepreneurs should also have a plan in place to maintain a market focus after launch. Market research does not end with the launch of the business. It's an ongoing process over the life of the business. The venture must constantly scan the environment for new competitors, trends, disruptions, and new opportunities. Entrepreneurs should plan for a continual stream of disciplined experiments, always looking for ways to attract noncustomers and venture into new markets.

Finally, entrepreneurs need to quickly focus on developing relationships with key people in the supply chain as well as key customers. It creates a significant competitive advantage because business relationships take time to develop and once that trust is in place, it's difficult for a competitor to overcome it.

Studying the industry and market the new venture will serve is a difficult and time-consuming task, but it is perhaps the most important information an entrepreneur can collect because it helps the entrepreneur understand the business context or environment, and the entrepreneur will learn whether the business will have customers. This is the heart of feasibility analysis and the foundation for launching the business.

New Venture Action Plan

- Identify the NAICS codes for the industry in which the new venture will operate.

- Collect secondary data on the industry.

- Conduct field research by interviewing suppliers, distributors, customers, and others.

- Develop an industry profile that will indicate whether the industry is growing, who the major competitors are, and what the profit potential is.

- Define the target market and first customer for the product or service.

- Gather primary data on the target market to generate a customer profile and evidence of demand.

- Gather competitive intelligence and determine the impact on the new venture launch strategy.

Questions on Key Issues

1. Which primary and secondary information will tell you whether the industry is growing and favorable to new entrants?
2. What kinds of information can suppliers and distributors provide?
3. How should a market entry strategy be determined? What factors should be considered?
4. What is the value of defining a market niche?

5. Suppose you are introducing a new type of exercise equipment to the fitness industry. What would your strategy for research with the customer look like?
6. Given the definitions of direct and indirect competitors, provide an example of each for a product of your choosing.

Experiencing Entrepreneurship

1. Choose an industry that interests you. Create a status report using the Internet, LexisNexis, or other industry source, current periodicals, and interviews with people in the industry. In your estimation, does this industry have potential for new business opportunities? If so, where do those opportunities lie? Write your analysis in a two-page report, indicating sources.

2. Pick a product or service, and formulate a plan for researching the customer. Identify what information needs to be collected (secondary and primary) and how to collect it. Justify the plan in a two-page report.

Relevant Case Studies

Case 3 HomeRun.com
Case 5 B2P

UNDERSTANDING PRODUCT DEVELOPMENT

> *"When each thing is unique in itself, there can be no comparison made."*
>
> —D.H. LAWRENCE,
> British author

CHAPTER OBJECTIVES

- Discuss the current trends in product/process design and development.

- Describe the product development cycle.

- Compare the advantages and disadvantages of outsourcing product development.

- Explain the process of intellectual-property development for patents, trademarks, copyrights, and trade secrets.

Anyone who enjoys scuba diving knows that the walk from the parking lot to the dive boat can easily exceed 200 yards over uneven, slippery terrain. The problem is not the walk itself (it's exercise after all); it's that divers have to lug 25 to 50 pound scuba tanks on their shoulders or attached to their hands, which can make the trek dangerous, harmful to the diver's lower back, and very exhausting.

Kimberly Isaac's favorite pastime is scuba diving and every time she had to lug her tanks she thought about how she might solve the problem. Because she was working full-time, Isaac hadn't gone further than thinking about a solution. However, when she got laid off from her accounting job, she decided it was time to see if she could turn her solution into a business. She managed to recruit fellow diver Thomas Spiegle to join her as her business partner and they began playing with ideas for a compact scuba-tank dolly—like the roller bags that so many business people use to carry their laptops and books.

Isaac and Speigle are not engineers by any means, but they didn't let that stop them from putting together a primitive prototype out of spare metal and foam and gluing it together with a glue gun, which gave them the ability to show manufacturers how they wanted the product to look and function. It wasn't a simple matter of creating a dolly. It had to be designed to safely transport compressed gas cylinders without putting the diver at risk or losing the equipment.

Product development for entrepreneurs is a process of trial and error. What Isaac and Spiegle did right was to transform their product idea into a physical state as quickly as possible so that potential customers could actually see the benefit. As of July 2010, Isaac and Spiegle had sold thirty units and had thirty more in production.

Sources: Shark Bite Scuba, www.sharkbitescuba.com, accessed July 18, 2010; and Needleman, S.E. (July 4, 2010). "A Sample Can be Simple and Cheap," *The Wall Street Journal Online*.

E very business—large or small, product or service—is involved in product/ service design and development at every stage of its life cycle. Each time a new product or service or an improvement on an existing product or service is introduced, it will have gone through a complex design and development process. The goal of the product development process is to bring new products to market at the right time and for the right cost so that customers will pay a price that reflects value to them. However, accomplishing this is no simple task because most organizations are limited by budgets, people, and time.[1] Moreover, in the midst of design and development, entrepreneurs also have to think about how to protect their new products. The importance of intellectual property protections cannot be overstated.

On a sleepless night in 1957, Gordon Gould conceived the idea for the laser. He wrote down all his thoughts, sketched the design and its components, and forecasted future uses. He had a notary witness, sign, and date his notebook in anticipation of applying for intellectual-property protection in the form of a patent. But then he made a critical mistake. Thinking that he had to build a working model of the laser before filing for a patent, he went to work for

Technical Research Group Inc. (TRG) to begin the development of laser applications. In the meantime, a pair of scientists, Charles Townes and Arthur Schawlow, filed for a patent on the optical maser (it used microwave energy instead of light, as Gould's did), and it would come to be considered the true laser patent for many years. Gould spent the next 30 years of his life battling the U.S. Patent and Trademark Office (USPTO) before he could finally lay claim to one of the most important inventions of all time. His laser applications are used in 80 percent of the industrial, commercial, and medical applications of lasers. Had Gordon Gould understood the patent process, and secured an intellectual property attorney early on, he might have saved himself years of struggle.

Product development and intellectual-property development are closely intertwined. This chapter describes the product development process from an entrepreneur's perspective and discusses how to protect the various assets created from that process: patents, copyrights, trademarks, and trade secrets.

ENTREPRENEURS AND NEW PRODUCT DESIGN

Since the 1980s, there has been an enormous increase in the number of companies competing in the global marketplace. Coupled with the fact that most new products are derivatives of something that already exists, this means that an intensely competitive arena for product development has emerged. U.S. companies find they are no longer competing only with U.S. firms; now, they must also compete with companies from diverse regions of the world who put their own stamp on processes and products. This volatile environment actually is good news for entrepreneurs who realize that the most innovative new products emerge when uncertainty, risk, and ambiguity are present. In this type of environment, small companies often shine because of their high degree of flexibility and ability to respond quickly.

Today's customers can differentiate products on a very subtle level; therefore, they demand products that reflect their individual lifestyles and value systems. As a result, product designers must create offerings that distinguish themselves on many levels in the marketplace. Whereas product performance and price were the main competitive measures in the past, today these two factors are givens. A company must offer superior performance and value-based pricing to even begin to be competitive and then it must offer products and services that address niche markets. This means that a manufacturing company can never stop improving its design and manufacturing processes, and a service company must continually find ways to improve its delivery methods and customer service.

Product design can be defined as the activity that transforms a set of requirements into a format that brings all the elements into an integrated whole or system.[2] This system consists of form, texture, color, fit, user interfaces, production and assembly processes to manufacture the parts, and the methods for joining all the parts together. The design of a product is critical because it determines the features and performance, reliability, price, and appeal to the customer. More importantly, perhaps, design determines cost, in fact, as much as 80 percent of the final cost.[3]

Design is also affected by the fact that technology has shortened product life cycles. A product life cycle is analogous to an industry life cycle with periods of product development, market introduction, growth, maturity, and decline. A complete product life cycle can be as short as 90 days for fads or as long as 100 years as in the case of automobiles. Whereas 50 years ago a new tool product had a life cycle of 18 years and a new game or toy a life cycle of 16 years, today those life cycles have shrunk to 5 years or fewer. Consequently, companies must always be researching and developing new products and improving existing ones to stay ahead of the competition.

The same can be said of service companies. New products often create the need for new services to support them. Even fundamental services such as advertising, consulting, and food services are affected by shrinking development life cycles. Customers expect service entrepreneurs to provide new and innovative services more rapidly and at lower costs. As a result, the fast-food industry continues to grow; even grocery stores have gotten into the game with an increasing number of convenience food offerings, such as packaged salads and reheatable meals. In addition, with email and the Internet ubiquitous throughout the professional services industry, customers now expect much shorter response times on correspondence and document preparation.

Entrepreneurs quickly discover that it's not just about producing one product or service but rather managing an innovation pipeline that will keep their company competitive. A recent study of more than 400 product development executives and managers revealed some interesting facts about the challenges companies face when they try to manage their innovation and product development portfolio.[4] The executives in the study reported that their number one challenge was having too many projects for the amount of resources the company had. Another significant hurdle was meeting the window of opportunity for the new product. Missing it could mean delaying the product launch for several months or even a year or more, a significant problem in the apparel industry, for example. Missing a market window for a technology company might mean missing out on the first mover advantage, which could ultimately affect everything from pricing to gross profit margins.

How Entrepreneurs Develop Products and Services

A 2003 study of The Conference Board found that large companies had an increasing interest in innovation strategies. This study of 104 companies with sales over $1 billion in the United States and Europe found that 90 percent of the companies considered innovation "integral to current strategic goals," and 83 percent expected it to spur strong top-line growth for their companies. This is not innovation solely for innovation's sake, but innovation to produce new sources of revenues for the company.[5] What does this mean for these companies' smaller entrepreneurial counterparts? Entrepreneurial ventures typically don't like to play by other companies' rules, but if they are operating in a business environment where the major players are spending a large portion of their budgets on new product development, they will need to have a product development strategy in place to compete successfully in their own niches.

Most large corporations have separate departments responsible for research and development, engineering, and testing. In many cases, the budgets for these departments are astronomical, because new product development and the continual improvement of existing products and processes are among the most important and challenging, not to mention expensive, tasks of high-performing, world-class businesses. The high cost is due in large part to high-priced development staff, equipment, and, in some cases, regulatory requirements, such as those for medical devices. In the case of startup ventures, the task is equally challenging; however, most new ventures, unlike large corporations, have very limited or nonexistent budgets for product development. Investors frequently consider research and development, engineering, and testing to be the highest-risk stages for new companies, so funding for these activities is difficult, if not impossible, to secure. Entrepreneurs are left with a dilemma: how to perform the research and development (R&D) that will result in a high-quality, engineered prototype as quickly and as inexpensively as possible. A lack of sufficient new product development (NPD) resources has many unintended consequences. As illustrated in Figure 6.1, a lack of resources focused on NPD results in five common problems.[6]

1. *Poor execution.* The critical due diligence and market analysis required to ensure a successful product launch are often shortened or bypassed in favor of speed. Approximately 75 percent of NPD projects don't include vital market research.[7]

2. *Time-to-market increases.* When a new venture lacks sufficient resources, bottlenecks and backups tend to occur because there aren't enough people doing the work. When the work *is* completed, it must often be redone because it was done in haste. Overall execution is generally poor.

3. *First-to-market opportunities are missed.* Poor execution results in missed opportunities to enter the market at a quiet time without immediate competition. Also, because these "game changer" opportunities often require more resources than less risky initiatives, frequently they are bypassed in favor of incremental opportunities that are easier and can be done quickly at a much

---

FIGURE 6.1　　The Consequences of Resource Shortfalls for New Product Development

lower cost. Unfortunately, these kinds of opportunities provide little value or return to the company, and in fact, the returns continue to diminish until the company finally decides to change the game with a truly innovative project.

4. *Projects are made simpler so that more can be done with less.* The dumbing-down of projects is another consequence of resource scarcity. Where resources are limited, product features and customer benefits are often sacrificed in order to get more products out.

5. *Team morale declines.* The combination of a lack of resources and increasing time pressure causes morale problems on product development teams and a sense that the team must accomplish the impossible.[8] Although members of the team are often willing to get the job done, more frequently the stressful environment saps their morale.

Entrepreneurs can avoid a shortage of resources by carefully planning their product development strategy so as to focus on projects that are aligned with the company's core competency and will bring the company closer to its primary goal. Entrepreneurs also have to learn how to say no to an opportunity when it threatens to stretch the company's resources too thin and endanger other activities. Some resources should be dedicated to new product development to keep the company competitive; however, the mantra should be *fewer but better new product projects.*

New Product Failure

Despite all the benefits that have accrued to new product development with the advent of information and systems technologies, the probability of success at launch is still about 60 percent.[9] Figure 6.2 depicts the classic new product development process and illustrates the high failure rate of new product ideas as they move through the process.

A significant body of research has revealed that the principal reason for new product failure is lack of good market and industry analysis. Innovators can be successful at *creating* value but unless they have found a way to *capture* sufficient value, the returns from their innovation will be tapped by imitators, providers of complementary products, and others in the value chain.[10] When entrepreneurs consider the types of barriers they might erect to forestall the siphoning of innovation returns, they typically overlook the intellectual property environment (discussed later in the chapter) and industry architecture because they believe there is no way to control these environments.[11] To capture the full value from innovation requires that entrepreneurs invest in complementary products, technologies, and services. In other words, if the product is 3D digital television, the customer will expect original 3D content to support it. Electric cars require an infrastructure of charging stations. If entrepreneurs do not have control over complements, then strong intellectual property rights or trade secrets will be critical to making a product difficult to copy.[12]

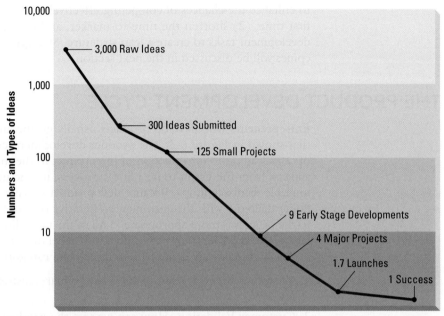

FIGURE 6.2

The New Product
Development Success
Curve

Source: Based on the research of Greg A. Stevens and James Burley in "Piloting the Rocket of Radical Innovation," *Research Technology Management*, March/April 2003. Reprinted with permission.

The industry architecture makes it easier or more difficult for entrepreneurs to succeed depending on whether they are producing a complete solution and control all the complements (a vertical architecture) or whether they are part of an industry where they are offering only part of the solution; that is, others in the industry produce parts that the entrepreneur needs. For example, independent film studios are essentially system integrators. They gather the resources they need to produce a film from a variety of different companies. Their position as the integrator is weak if they don't control any intellectual property, which explains why frequently a film will make money, but the studio that produced it will not.

Another significant cause of new product failure is technical problems. The path from laboratory to production is fraught with challenges and obstacles, often because the company has moved too rapidly through the design and early prototyping phase. Some recent research suggests that one overlooked cause of new product failure is the human factor.[13] The very early stages of the NPD process typically involve one person with an idea. If that person's level of creative thought, tolerance for risk, and commitment to doing thorough market research is not sufficient, a viable project may be doomed to failure. It is only in the later stages of development that teams typically form around new product projects that seem feasible.

There are ways for entrepreneurial firms to compete effectively in the area of product development. In fact, the new environment for product development is uniquely suited to smaller companies, which are often better able to adapt to change and move quickly in new directions. Three fundamental strategies should be incorporated into any entrepreneur's product development program to enhance the chances of competing effectively: (1) design products right the first time, (2) shorten the time-to-market, and (3) outsource some product development tasks to create a lean structure. Strategies that support these outcomes will be discussed in the next section.

THE PRODUCT DEVELOPMENT CYCLE

Entrepreneurs who develop products usually go through a process much like that shown in Figure 6.3. The product development cycle consists of a series of tasks leading to introduction of the product in the marketplace. Although it appears from the graph to be a linear process, it is actually quite iterative with multiple feedback loops. Because new product success usually requires an ongoing dialogue with the customer, an iterative or sense-and-respond approach to the process is more appropriate.[14] All of the tasks displayed in Figure 6.3 will take place; however, they occur often in parallel or out of order.

The eight tasks are grouped into three main categories:

1. Customer Identification. Who is the primary customer and what are their needs?
2. Customer Validation. How can we test the product, market, and business model?
3. Business Creation. What should the launch strategy be?

Opportunity Identification: Recall from Chapter 3 that the first stage in the development of a business concept is opportunity recognition: identifying a market

FIGURE 6.3   From Idea to Market

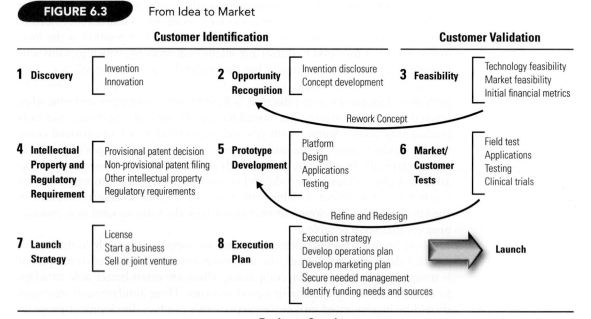

niche that has not yet been served, detecting a potential improvement in an existing product, or seeing an opportunity for a breakthrough product or process. At this point, the opportunity is simply an initial concept that must be validated.

Technical and Market Feasibility Analysis: Feasibility analysis is simply conducting preliminary research to determine whether the product or service idea currently exists, whether there is a potential application to solve a problem in a market, whether the product can be produced, whether it can be protected, how much it will cost to produce the product, and how much time it will take to produce it. This stage, known as customer validation, also involves considering some preliminary financial metrics based on the market research conducted. Table 6.1 provides a checklist for assessing the feasibility of new products.

Intellectual Property and Regulatory Requirements: Early in the product development process, it is important to determine the potential for intellectual property protections and to plan for filing for patent protection, if appropriate, at the optimal time. Regulatory requirements for many new technologies and products can be onerous, so it's also critical that entrepreneurs learn how their development process will be affected.

TABLE 6.1	New Product Checklist			
		YES	**NO**	**NEEDS MORE STUDY**
THE MARKET				
Is there an existing need for this product in the marketplace?		—	—	—
Will I be first in the marketplace with this product?		—	—	—
Can the product be protected through intellectual-property rights?		—	—	—
Can market entry barriers be erected?		—	—	—
SWOT ANALYSIS (STRENGTHS, WEAKNESSES, OPPORTUNITIES, AND THREATS)				
Do the strengths of this product exceed any weaknesses?		—	—	—
Are there various opportunities for commercializing this product?		—	—	—
Do any significant threats exist to the development of this product?		—	—	—
DESIGN/DEVELOPMENT/MANUFACTURING				
Is the product innovative?		—	—	—
Can it be developed quickly to market-ready state?		—	—	—
Can it be easily manufactured?		—	—	—
Do I have the resources to manufacture the product?		—	—	—
Is it more practical to subcontract the manufacturing?		—	—	—
Is there a possibility for spin-off products?		—	—	—
FINANCIAL				
Is the return on this investment sufficient to justify the effort?		—	—	—
Are the development costs within reason?		—	—	—
Will it be possible to minimize the manufacturing investment through outsourcing, while still maintaining quality and control?		—	—	—
Is money available to produce the product?		—	—	—

Prototype Development: The first stages of design preparation go hand in hand with concept investigation, because planners normally need some preliminary working drawings of the product to estimate costs and manufacturing processes. These preliminary drawings are also used to apply for a patent if the product is patentable. The platform is the core product or technology from which other products or applications can be developed. In an ideal situation, an entrepreneur will be working with a platform product that will provide many derivative products and services with corresponding revenue streams.

From the initial engineered drawings will come the prototype or model of the product. Often the first prototype does not closely resemble the final product in appearance, but it usually does in function. Physical prototypes are helpful in communicating the form, fit, and function of the device to customers; in providing an example to a vendor for quotation; in facilitating quick changes in a design; and in designing the correct tooling—those devices that hold a product component in place during manufacturing and assembly. Entrepreneurs often use small engineering firms or solo engineers with small job shops and machine shops to complete the prototype. These sources are normally quicker and less expensive than the larger, better-known firms. When seeking an engineer or a model builder, it is important to be cautious and check out their qualifications, experience, and references relative to the task required of them. A major university engineering department is a good source of referrals, as are other engineers.

Businesses that do not manufacture products—service, retail, wholesale, and so forth—still need to design a prototype, but the prototype in this case will not always be physical. Instead it will be a design or flowchart for how the business will provide a service or product to its customer. For example, a restaurant entrepreneur will design the layout of the restaurant and kitchen with an eye to how customers and servers move through the restaurant. The food preparation area will need to be laid out efficiently so that the chef and cooks can work quickly and not have to move great distances to retrieve cooking utensils and food items. Every activity the restaurant undertakes should be prototyped to ensure that there is no duplication of effort and that each task is performed as efficiently and effectively as possible.

Initial Market Tests: With a working prototype of near production quality, it is possible to field-test it with potential users in environments where the product will typically be used. For example, it would be important to put a new construction tool in the hands of construction workers on real jobs in the field. In this way, the company can collect feedback based on actual use in real-life situations. The number of prototypes used in the field-testing stage is normally limited, because the cost per unit is much higher (as much as ten times higher) than it will be when the startup is in normal production because the company will not yet be meeting its suppliers' volume levels for discounts. After conducting a small initial test production run in a limited market, the entrepreneur can go back and fine-tune the product and the process to completion and market-ready status. This is also the first opportunity to seriously test the manufacturing and assembly processes, particularly if these are outsourced to partners, and determine accurate costs of production at varying levels of volume.

Launch Strategy: The achievement of a production-quality prototype—one that has specifications that can be replicated in a manufacturing and assembly process—is a major milestone in the product development process, because the company now has a product that can be sold in the marketplace. During the final phases of developing this production-quality product, other aspects of the feasibility analysis have been completed. Now it will be important to consider manufacturing and assembly needs and whether to manufacture in-house or outsource. The final phase is business creation. From a business perspective, the entrepreneur will need to determine the launch strategy, whether to license the technology to another company to develop into applications, start a business to make and distribute the product, sell the technology, or joint venture with another company that has the resources the entrepreneur needs.

Execution Plan: Many of the activities that have to take place to move the product to market—the operations plan, the marketing plan, the funding plan, and so forth—have been taking place throughout the development process. It is at this stage that they are finalized and the company is preparing to ramp up manufacturing and launch the product.

Outsourcing Product Development

It is becoming more and more common for entrepreneurs with both large and small companies to outsource all or part of their product development to third parties. The decision is due in large part to today's requirements for fast-paced

GLOBAL INSIGHTS

Think Less to Tap Emerging Markets

The biggest markets for new products and services lie in developing countries, and they represent more than 80 percent of the world's population. Asia, Africa, and Latin America offer a wealth of new opportunity to entrepreneurs who can help customers in these regions become more productive and create wealth. But to do that, entrepreneurs need to leave their developed world perspective behind and look at these markets from a local perspective.

In India, for example, millions of consumers are getting around the crowded streets by means of unsafe scooters because they can't afford to purchase automobiles. Ratan Tata recognized the problem and challenged his company to come up with a car that would sell for under $2,500. Using the latest in innovative approaches to design and development, the team outsourced 70 percent of the components, stripped out a lot of unnecessary features that didn't matter to customers who simply wanted to get from point A to point B, and then distributed nearly completed kits for assembly by rural entrepreneurs. The Nano, as the vehicle is named, not only achieved its targeted price, but it created a number of opportunities for new entrepreneurs to start businesses.

Sources: Anthony, S. (June 1, 2009). "Loving the Low End: Innovation Inventory #8," *Harvard Business Review*, Blogs, http://blogs.hbr.org/anthony/2009/06/loving_the_low_end_innovation.html; and Christensen, C.M. Wunker, S. and Nair, H. (October 13, 2008). "Innovation Vs. Poverty," Forbes.com, www.forbes.com/forbes/2008/1013/101.html.

innovation with shorter windows of opportunity. Most startup companies don't have the resources to do adequate product development in-house. And there is no reason why it should be done this way when it is possible to reduce risk, lower costs, and decrease cycle times by factors of 60 to 90 percent by out-sourcing product development.[15] Outsourcing provides a young firm with a network of expertise that it couldn't afford to hire in-house. Some of the areas of product development that require engineering analysis, design, and expertise and are suitable for outsourcing are component design, materials specifications, machinery to process, ergonomic design, packaging design, assembly drawings and specifications, parts and material sourcing (suppliers), and operator's and owner's manuals.

When using other companies to do part or all of the product development, it is important to understand that these partners work with many other compa-nies, so no single company will be a high priority for them. That's why entre-preneurs must plan well in advance and allow extra time for delays that strategic partners might cause in the time-to-market plan. If time-to-market is the most critical factor in a business's success, entrepreneurs may want to consider do-ing tasks in-house that could delay the process rather than outsourcing them and being dependent on someone else's time schedule. It is also a good idea to help suppliers and original equipment manufacturers (OEMs) understand that the partnership will be a win-win relationship, so they have a vested interest in seeing it succeed. Contracts should be drawn up with every consultant, original equipment manufacturer, or vendor with whom the company does business so that there will be no confusion about what is expected and needed. During the process, it is vital to stay in touch with outsourced vendors and to be available to answer questions as they arise.

ACQUIRING INTELLECTUAL PROPERTY RIGHTS

Developing a new product creates an asset that must be protected. If the prod-uct is a unique device, a novel process or service, or other type of proprietary item, it may qualify for intellectual-property rights. These are the group of legal rights associated with patents, trademarks, copyrights, and trade secrets. Every business, no matter how small, has intellectual-property rights associated with it: a trademark on the name of the business or a product brand, copyrights on advertising design, patents on a device the entrepreneur has invented, or trade secrets such as the company's customer list.

In the growing knowledge economy, where intellectual assets are often more valuable than physical assets, the recognition and protection of intellectual-property rights are gaining increased importance. Beginning in the late 1990s, approximately 75 percent of the Fortune 100's market capitalization was based on intellectual property: patents, copyrights, trademarks, and trade secrets.[16] Every entrepreneur needs to understand what those rights are, not only to pro-tect his or her property but also to avoid infringing on the rights of others. Moreover, intellectual-property rights can provide a temporary monopoly, en-able the company to establish a standard, and protect its brands. Software is an example of a technology product that enjoys strong protection in the form of patents, copyrights, and the ability to safeguard the source code from users and competitors.[17]

The next four sections provide a brief overview of the various rights under intellectual-property law and how they can be used to protect the new venture's inventions and gain a competitive advantage.

PATENTS

If a new venture opportunity relies on a product or device of some sort, it is especially important that entrepreneurs investigate applying for a patent, which is the primary means of protecting an original invention. A patent gives the patent holder the right to defend the patent against others who would attempt to manufacture, use, or sell the invention during the period of the patent. At the end of the patent life, the invention is placed in public domain, which means that anyone can use any aspect of the device the inventor created without paying royalties to the inventor.

Today, although most inventors work in the research departments of large corporations and 80 percent of all patents come from large companies, the basic legal tenets of patent law still protect the interests of the independent inventor. And in cases where large corporations have infringed on those interests, the courts have generally sided with the independent inventor. In a further effort to support the small inventor, the Patent Office created the Office of the Independent Inventor to handle the 20 percent of patents submitted by these inventors.

One of the most common questions entrepreneurs have is "how do I know whether or not to patent my invention?" Answering positively to the following questions may suggest a need for patents:

- Does the invention solve a significant problem and change the way things are done?
- Does the invention fall under FDA regulations?
- Will the invention achieve revenues that exceed the potential cost of patent enforcement?
- Is there a plan to license?

On the other hand, if the field of use for the technology or product is changing rapidly, it may not make sense to spend the time and money to patent because the patent will outlive its economic life.

Is the Invention Patentable?

Before filing for a patent on an invention that an entrepreneur believes to be unique, he or she should consider the United States Patent and Trademark Office's (USPTO) four basic criteria that the invention must meet before it can be considered for a patent.

The invention must fit into one of five classes established by Congress:

1. Machine or something with moving parts or circuitry (fax, rocket, photo-copier, laser, electronic circuit)
2. Process or method for producing a useful and tangible result (chemical reaction, method for producing products, business method)
3. Article of manufacture (furniture, transistor, diskette, toy)
4. Composition of matter (gasoline, food additive, drug, genetically altered life form)
5. A new use or improvement for one of the above that does not infringe on the patents associated with them

The Supreme Court of the United States has stated that "anything under the sun that is made by man" falls into the statutory subject matter (*Diamond v. Chakrabarty,* 1980).[18] With this definition, it may appear that anything can receive a patent, but in fact, there are some exclusions. Laws and phenomena of nature, naturally occurring substances, abstract mathematical formulas, and mere ideas are not eligible to be patented. However, alterations to something found in nature, such as genetically enhanced corn, can be considered for a patent.

The invention must have utility; in other words, it must be useful: This is not usually a problem unless the invention is an unsafe drug or something purely "whimsical," although the USPTO has been known to issue patents on some fairly strange inventions, such as a laser beam to motivate cats to exercise (Patent No. 5,443,036, Aug. 22, 1995). However, the utility of the device must be a reality, not merely speculation, and must be described in the patent application.

The invention must not contain prior art; that is, it must be new or novel in some important way: Prior art is knowledge that is publicly available or was published prior to the date of the invention—that is, before the filing of the patent application. This means that an invention can't be patented if it was known or used by others, patented, or described in a printed publication before a patent was applied for. Accordingly, it is important to document everything that is done during the creation of the invention. Also, the invention must not have become public or available for sale more than one year prior to the inventor's filing the patent application. This rule is meant to ensure that the invention is still novel at the time of application. Novelty consists of physical differences, new combinations of components, or new uses. There are two levels of challenge to novelty: statutory and anticipatory. If the invention is published or used in an unconcealed manner either in the United States or in another country more than one year prior to the date of application, the inventor is statutorily barred from seeking a patent. Furthermore, if the patent is substantially similar to an existing patent, the inventor may not seek a patent because, in this case, the patent was anticipated.

The invention must not be obvious to someone with ordinary skills in the field: This is a tricky criterion, but it has been further explained by the USPTO as meaning that the invention must contain "new and unexpected results." That is, the invention should not be the next logical step for someone knowledgeable in the field. Obviousness is one of the most common reasons why patent applications are rejected.

Obviousness, however, did not keep Ron Lando from securing a patent on his CliC eyeware (www.clicgoggles.com). The "unique" aspect of his eyeware is that instead of hooking over the ears, the glasses wrap around the wearer's head and snap together between the lenses with a tiny but powerful neodymium magnet. The benefit? When you unhook them, they simply drop around the wearer's neck so they don't get lost. Lando knows that he will face copycats—it's a simple product, but he is counting on his brand and his strategy to supplement his patent protection.[19]

Patent Types

If all the requirements for patentability have been met, then the type of patent most appropriate for the invention should be considered. There are three major categories of patents: utility patents, design patents, and business method patents.

- **Utility patents:** Utility patents are the most common type of patent. They protect the functional part of machines or processes. Some examples are toys, film processing, protective coatings, tools, and cleaning implements. Software qualifies for patent protection if it produces a useful and tangible result. For example, the USPTO will not issue a utility patent on a mathematical formula used in space navigation, but it may on software that translates equations and makes a rocket take off.[20] (Copyrights, discussed in a later section, are commonly used for software programs that don't qualify for a patent.) A utility patent is valid for 20 years from the date of application.

- **Design patents:** Design patents protect new, original ornamental designs for manufactured articles. A design patent protects only the appearance of an article, not its structure or utilitarian features. The design must be non-functional and part of the tangible item for which it is designed. It cannot be hidden or offensive or simulate a well-known or naturally occurring object or person. Some examples of items that can receive design patents are gilding, an item of apparel, and jewelry. Inventors should be aware that although design patents are relatively easy to obtain, they are very hard to protect. It is not difficult to modify a design patent without infringing on the original patent. Design patents are valid for 14 years from date of issuance.

- **Business method patents:** The 1990s saw an exponential increase in the filing of business method patents, which arose out of Internet companies' desire to protect their ways of doing business. The rush to patent business methods all started with one click—that is, the single click of a mouse that enables a user to order a book from Amazon.com. That one click tells Amazon to charge the purchase, take the book from its warehouse shelves, and send it to the purchaser. Jeff Bezos, Amazon's founder, thought the concept was so original that he decided to patent it. And in September 1999, the PTO granted him U.S. Patent No. 5,960,411, "method and system for placing a purchase order via a communications network." Bezos followed that success with a lawsuit in U.S. District Court in Seattle for patent infringement against Barnes & Noble (*Amazon.com v. Barnesandnoble.com, 73F. Supp. 2 1228* [W.D. Wash. 1999]). In December 1999, a federal judge issued an injunction against Barnes & Noble to stop it from using its version of the "One-Click" process, but in February 2001, a federal appeals court overturned the lower court's ruling because it "raised substantial questions as to the validity" of Amazon.com's patent.[21] Barnes & Noble ended up designing around the Amazon patent with its double-click.[22]

Business method is actually a generic term to describe a variety of process claims, and as of this writing, the courts have not yet defined what differentiates a business method claim from a process claim. Thus business method claims are treated like any other process claim.[23] On March 29, 2000, the Patent Office issued a statement that the business method patent will cover only fundamentally different ways of doing business and that the embedded process must produce a useful, tangible, and concrete result.[24] The Supreme Court's most recent ruling in *Bilski v. Kappos* (Supreme Court 2010)(08-964) affirmed the unpatentability of "abstract ideas," but left open the possibility for the continuation of business method patents.

The process for applying for any of these patents is well defined by the USPTO and is discussed briefly in the next section.

The Patent Process

Although the USPTO has described the process clearly on its website (www .uspto.gov), it is always a good idea to seek the counsel of an intellectual-property attorney when considering filing a patent. An attorney who specializes in intellectual property can increase the chances of moving successfully through the USPTO application process. Figure 6.4 depicts the patent process for a utility patent.

U.S. or International Patents?

After determining which type of patent to file, the entrepreneur must determine the *filing strategy*, which means that the entrepreneur must decide if international patents are required or simply a U.S. patent. It is important to remember that the patent rights granted to an individual in the United States extend only to the borders of the United States. They have no effect in any foreign country. Because every country has different laws regarding intellectual property, patent attorneys face a real challenge when helping their clients apply for or defend foreign patents. Two important differences exist between international and U.S. procedures in the areas of first-to-file and novelty.[25] First, the European Patent Convention (EPC) grants patent rights to the first person to file for the patent, whether or not that person is the original inventor. By contrast, in the United States, only the original inventor has the first right to file an application.

FIGURE 6.4

The Utility Patent
Process

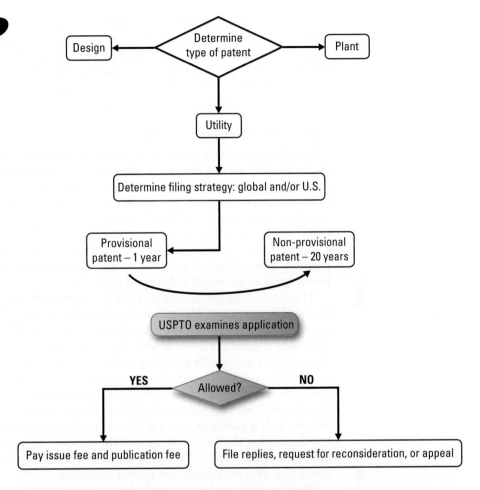

It should be noted that the U.S. Congress is considering changing to the European Convention, but for now, first-to-invent is still the rule.

Second, in the United States, an inventor can sell an invention up to one year before filing a patent application. That is not true in other countries, where publication of any kind before the date of filing will bar the right to a patent. Furthermore, most countries require that the invention be manufactured in the country within three years of the issuance of the foreign patent. In 1983, the Trilateral Co-operation was established between the European Patent Office (EPO), the Japan Patent Office (JPO), and the USPTO to process patent applications filed worldwide. The Patent Cooperation Treaty (PCT) allows inventors in any nation that signed on to the treaty to file a single international patent application covering all the countries under the treaty. That application is then subjected to an international search to determine the probability of a patent being issued. Subsequent to a positive finding, the applicant can begin to pursue the grant of patents directly from the countries or regions desired.

When considering foreign patents, be sure to consult an intellectual-property attorney who specializes in this area. Because of the high cost and effort involved in obtaining foreign patents, it is important to determine whether a reasonable profit can be made from them. Often, it's more valuable to seek solid strategic alliances in other countries, thus obtaining good distribution channels through which to export products, than to spend the time and money seeking patents in every country in which the entrepreneur will do business. Advice from a knowledgeable attorney can make this decision easier.

Provisional or Non-provisional?

A provisional patent is a way for inventors to undertake a first patent filing in the United States at a lower cost than a formal patent application. Legally, it permits the inventor to use the term *patent pending*, and is designed to protect small inventors while they speak with manufacturers about producing the invention. A provisional patent also puts U.S. applicants on par with international applicants under the General Agreement on Tariffs and Trade (GATT) Uruguay Round Agreements (see the discussion in the section on international patents). The provisional patent does not, however, take the place of a formal patent application, which is discussed next.

The term of the provisional patent is 12 months from the date of filing, and it cannot be extended. This means that the inventor must file a non-provisional (formal) patent application during that period. The 12-month period does not count toward the 20-year term for a non-provisional patent. Because the 20-year clock starts with the filing of the formal patent application, the provisional patent effectively extends patent protection by 1 year. The invention disclosure in the provisional patent application should clearly and completely describe the invention so that someone with knowledge of the invention could make and use it. If a earlier provisional date of application-provisional application is not filed within the 12-month period, the provisional application is considered abandoned, and the entrepreneur loses the ability to claim the earlier provisional date of application as the date of invention.

The *non-provisional patent application* is required for any patent, and it lasts for 20 years from the date of filing. The patent application contains a complete description of the invention, what it does, how it is uniquely different from anything currently existing (including prior art), and its scope. It also includes detailed drawings, explanations, and engineering specifications such that a person of ordinary skill in the same field could build the invention from the information provided.

The claims section of the application specifies the parts of the invention on which the inventor wants patents and must include at least one claim that attests to its novelty, utility, and nonobviousness. The claim serves to define the scope of patent protection; whether the USPTO grants the patent is largely determined by the wording of the claims. The claims must be specific enough to demonstrate the invention's uniqueness but broad enough to make it difficult for others to circumvent the patent—that is, to modify the invention slightly without violating the patent and then duplicate the product.

For example, suppose an entrepreneur attempts to patent a new type of rapid prototyping device. If the patent application defines the invention for use in prototyping of machine components, that would be a narrow definition. Another inventor could conceivably patent the invention for a new use, such as creating artificial bone, for example. That's why it is important to define the claims as broadly as possible to include as many potential applications as can be identified. Drafting a claim is an art, so it's a good idea to hire an intellectual-property attorney to craft the patent application.

What the USPTO Does

Once it has received the application, the USPTO will conduct a search of its patent records for prior art. The Patent Office then contacts the inventor to either accept or deny the application claims and, in the case of denial, gives the inventor a period of time to appeal or modify the claim. It is not uncommon for the original claims to be rejected in their entirety by the USPTO, usually due to the existence of prior art, but often because of lack of non-obviousness. It will then be the job of the inventor's attorney to rewrite the claims and resubmit the revised application for another review.

If and when the Patent Office accepts the modified claims, it issues a notice of allowance. Then all the inventor has to do is pay the required fees and wait for the patent to be issued. The inventor may market and sell the product during this period but must clearly label it "patent pending." Most patent applications will be published 18 months after the filing date of the application, but entrepreneurs should always be prepared for it to take longer. The USPTO maintains all patent applications in the strictest confidence until the patent is issued or the application is published. Once the patent has been issued, the original application and the patent itself become public record.

If the patent examiner rejects the modified claims again, the inventor has the right to appeal to a Board of Patent Appeals within the Patent Office. Failing to find agreement at this point, the inventor may appeal to the U.S. Court of Appeals for the Federal Circuit. This appeals process may take years.

One thing that many inventors fail to realize is that there are maintenance fees on patents to keep them in force. These fees are paid to the USPTO 3½, 7½, and 11½ years from the date the patent is granted. Failure to pay these fees can result in expiration of the patent. Entrepreneurs should check with the USPTO to determine if their company qualifies for Small Entity Status, which may lower their maintenance fees.

Patent Infringement

Once issued, a patent is a powerful document that gives the holder the right to enforce the patent in federal court. If such a lawsuit is successful, the court may issue an injunction preventing the infringer from making any further use of the invention and award the patent holder a reasonable royalty from the infringer; if the infringer refuses to pay, the patent holder can enjoin or close down the infringer's operation. Alternatively, the court may mediate an agreement between the parties under which the infringing party will pay royalties to the patent holder in exchange for permission to use the patented invention.

Infringement of patent rights occurs when someone other than the inventor (patent holder) or licensee makes and sells a product that contains every one of the elements of a claim. The Patent Office also protects inventors from infringers who would violate a patent by making small, insignificant changes in the claims. This policy is called the *doctrine of equivalents*. If, for example, an entrepreneur had a patent on a three-legged wooden chair, and the infringer produced and distributed the exact same chair but gave it three metal legs, that person would be violating the entrepreneur's patent under the doctrine of equivalents. Patent infringement actions are costly and difficult to prosecute. Many times, the alleged infringer will defend himself or herself by attempting to prove that the patent is invalid—that is, that the USPTO mistakenly issued the patent.

With infringement cases, the courts tend to favor the inventor and may issue injunctions against alleged infringers even before the case goes to trial. If the courts determine that infringement was willful, they can triple the damages.

TRADEMARKS

Trademarks have become nearly as popular as patents as intellectual-property assets. A trademark is a symbol, logo, word, sound, color, design, or other device that is used to identify a business or a product in commerce. The term *trademark* is regularly used to refer to both trademarks and service marks, which identify services or intangible activities "performed by one person for the benefit of a person or persons other than himself, either for pay or otherwise."[26] Other, less commonly used types of trademarks can be found at the USPTO website.

Here are some examples of trademarked items:

Logo: FedEx (www.fedex.com)

Slogan: L'Oreal: "Because you're worth it." (www.loreal.com)

Container shape: Coca-Cola's classic beverage bottle (www.coca-cola.com)

Colors can even be trademarked. In the 1995 Supreme Court case *Qualitex Co. v. Jacobson Products Co.*, 115 S.Ct. 1300 (1995), the Court held that the green-gold color of a dry-cleaning press pad could be trademarked. To do so, the applicant must be able to demonstrate that the color has a secondary meaning—that is, that people associate the color with the product. For example, pink has been associated with insulation, even though the color has nothing to do with the insulation's function. Colors that are functional in nature cannot be trademarked.

A trademark—with certain conditions—has a longer life than a patent. A business has the exclusive right to a trademark for as long as it is actively using it. However, if a trademark becomes part of the generic language, as have *aspirin* and *thermos*, it can no longer be trademarked. Furthermore, a trademark cannot be registered until it is actually in use. The symbol "®" means "registered trademark." Before a trademark is registered, the holder of the trademark should file an intent-to-use application with the USPTO and place ™ (or SM for services) after the name until the trademark has been registered. This is an important point, because trademarks cannot be stockpiled and then sold to potential users. They must be in use in the market to be protected.

Marks that cannot be trademarked include:

- Anything immoral or deceptive
- Anything that uses official symbols of the United States or any state or municipality, such as the flag
- Anything that uses a person's name or likeness without permission

Trademark Infringement, Counterfeiting, and Dilution

Like patents, trademarks can suffer from infringement, counterfeiting, or misappropriation. Infringement is found if a mark is likely to cause confusion with a trademark already existing in the marketplace. The deliberate copying of a mark (counterfeiting) is subject to civil and criminal penalties.

Trademarks are also subject to dilution, which occurs when the value of the mark is substantially reduced through competition or through the likelihood of confusion from another mark. For example, American Express was able to prove that it suffered dilution when a limousine service used the American Express trademark for its business, even though the two companies were in different industries.[27] In 2006, the Trademark Dilution Revision Act was signed into law to provide relief to owners of famous trademarks whose marks had been tarnished by third-party marks. The act says that the injured party can seek injunctive relief and monetary damages against a third party that adopts a trademark that will cause dilution of the famous mark even though it is a noncompeting use. It is difficult to say what the impact of the legislation will be until there are court rulings.

COPYRIGHTS

With the proliferation of digital content comes the difficult task of finding ways to protect all the intellectual property that is being accessed, duplicated, transmitted, and published in digital form. Copyrights protect original works of authors, composers, screenwriters, and computer programmers. A copyright does not protect the idea itself but only the form in which it appears, which cannot be copied without the express permission of the copyright holder. For example, a computer programmer can copyright the written program for a particular type of word processing software but cannot copyright the idea of word processing. This is why several companies can produce word processing software without violating a copyright. What they really are protecting is the unique programming code of their software. The First Sale Doctrine [Section 106 of the 1976 Copyright Act] grants a copyright owner six rights: reproduction, preparation of derivative works, distribution, public performance, public display, and digital transmission performance.[28]

Under the Copyright Extension Act of 1998, a copyright lasts for the life of the holder plus 70 years, after which the copyrighted material goes into public domain. Works for hire and works published anonymously now have copyrights of 95 years from the date of publication.

There is no question that copyright law is undergoing its most strenuous test in the knowledge economy. One of the areas of contention is the Doctrine of Fair Use, which has been codified in Section 107 of the copyright law. This section asserts that reproduction of a copyrighted work is "fair" when it is done for purposes such as criticism, comment, news reporting, teaching, scholarship, and research. There is no clear distinction between fair use and infringement; even acknowledging the source may not be sufficient, so the safest course is to secure permission from the original copyright holder.

The Digital Millennium Copyright Act

One of the problems associated with delivering products over the Internet is the ease with which a person can infringe on another's rights. In October 1998, President Clinton signed into law the Digital Millennium Copyright Act (DMCA), which prohibits the falsification, alteration, or removal of copyright management data on digital copies. In other words, it made it a crime to circumvent an encrypted work without authorization. The law also made it illegal to manufacture and distribute products that facilitate the circumvention of encrypted work.

John Lech Johansen was just 15 years old when, out of frustration with his MP3 player, he wrote a "fix it" program and posted it on the Web to help others who were having trouble playing some of their DVDs. Unfortunately, by removing the encryption code with his program, DVDs could now be copied. His ingenuity won him an award from the Electronic Frontier Foundation, a nonprofit organization that works to protect digital rights, but it also won him a visit from the Norwegian police in his hometown. He went on to figure out how to play legally acquired songs from distributors other than iTunes on the iPod, something Steven Jobs certainly did not want to happen. This involved circumventing Apple's FairPlay encryption program. According to Johansen, "If you legally acquire music, you need to have the right to manage it on all other devices that you own."[29] But under the First Sale Doctrine, when a digital file is transferred, there is no transfer of ownership. As a result, the First Sale Doctrine does not permit distribution of digital works.[30] The DMCA does contain a safe harbor clause to protect service providers from monetary damages if they unknowingly infringe on someone's rights, either by transmitting or storing infringing material or by linking users to websites containing infringing material. This law clears the way to licensing intellectual property for a fee over the Internet.

Obtaining Copyright Protection

To qualify for federal copyright protection, the work must be in a fixed and tangible form—that is, someone must be able to see or hear it. The law does not require that a copyright holder provide notice to a potential infringer; however, registering the copyright at the Copyright Office of the Library of Congress in Washington, DC, will ensure full protection under the law by creating a document trail. The notice should use the word *copyright* or the symbol © and should provide the year and the complete name of the person responsible for the work, as in © 2011 Stephen Barry.

Fortunately, copyright protection laws are fairly consistent across countries because of a number of international copyright treaties, the most important of which is the Berne Convention. Under this treaty, which includes more than 100 nations, a country must give copyright protection to authors who are nationals of any member country for at least the life of the author plus 50 years.

TRADE SECRETS

A trade secret consists of a formula, device, idea, process, pattern, or compilation of information that gives the owner a competitive advantage in the marketplace, is novel in the sense that it is not common knowledge, and is kept in a confidential state. Some examples of trade secrets are the recipe for Mrs. Field's cookies, survey methods used by professional pollsters, customer lists, source codes for computer chips, customer discounts, and inventions for which no patent will be applied.

Many companies, such as Hewlett-Packard (HP), choose not to patent some of their inventions but rather keep them for internal use only as trade secrets. The reason is that once a patent has been issued, anyone can look up the patent on the USPTO website and see how the device is made. Some of HP's inventions are devices and processes used in the manufacture of its computers and peripherals, and they give the firm a significant competitive advantage that it would lose if this information got into the hands of competitors. With the patent in hand, the competitor could build that device and use it to improve its own manufacturing processes. As long as the competitor is not selling the device in the market, it would require a court to decide whether the firm is actually infringing on HP's patent.

There are no legal means under patent and trademark law to protect trade secrets. The only way to protect them is through confidentiality agreements or contracts. An employer might have all employees sign an employment contract that specifically details what is considered trade secret information, both at the time the employee is hired and during his or her tenure as an employee. Then, should a current or former employee use or reveal a specified trade secret, the company can pursue legal remedies, such as an injunction or suing for damages.

There are risks and benefits associated with the products and services that entrepreneurs develop. Part of the goal of feasibility analysis is to address those risks and benefits so that informed decisions can be made about whether to go forward with the new business.

DRAWING CONCLUSIONS FROM PRODUCT/SERVICE ANALYSIS

Product/service analysis gives the entrepreneur a level of confidence about the ability to actually produce and protect the product or service being offered. The first conclusion to be drawn centers on the issue of whether it is possible to make the product in sufficient quantities to meet a market need. Are there methods of manufacture available globally that enable the product to be produced at a cost that yields a final price the customer is willing to pay? In the case of a service, how large an organization would be required to serve the size of the market identified? Are there efficient ways to deliver the service at a reasonable cost? Being able to patent a product or service affects the product development strategy as well as the market adoption strategy, so this test should answer the question *is a patent a feasible strategy?* Then conclusions should be drawn about any other forms of intellectual property that could become part of the bundle of competitive advantages the entrepreneur is developing. Finally, a timeline for the development of the product or service will prepare the entrepreneur for considering financial requirements.

New Venture Action Plan

- Find ways to incorporate customer input into the design of your products, processes, and services.

- Locate independent contractors who can help in the construction of a prototype.

- Identify intellectual-property rights appropriate to the business concept.

Questions on Key Issues

1. How has the environment for product development changed in the last decade, and what does this mean to entrepreneurs starting new businesses?

2. What are the principal reasons why new products fail?

3. Suppose you are going to develop and market a new device for tracking calories consumed during the day. What will your product development strategy be, and why?

4. In what ways should you protect an invention from the time of its earliest conception?

Experiencing Entrepreneurship

1. Visit an entrepreneurial company that is developing new products. What is the company's product development strategy, and how effective is that strategy? What criteria did you use to measure effectiveness? You may need to use outside sources to confirm what the company tells you.

2. Visit the U.S. Patent Office at www.uspto.gov. Pick a patented product that interests you and contact the inventor to determine whether the patent has ever been commercialized. If so, in what ways? If not, can the inventor provide a reason? What can you conclude about the potential for this patent?

Relevant Case Studies

Case 1 Command Audio

Case 6 Potion Inc.

BUILDING THE STARTUP TEAM

"Coming together is a beginning. Keeping together is progress. Working together is success."

—HENRY FORD

CHAPTER OBJECTIVES

- Explain how to effectively build a founding team.
- Understand how to work with professional advisers.
- Discuss when to add a board of directors.
- Compare and contrast the pros and cons of outsourcing with independent contractors versus hiring employees.

One would think that a founding team that consisted of two people with experience in startups and expertise in their new venture's domain might be a team made in heaven. However, it is rare for any founding team to have all the expertise and experience they need to grow their business, and the Green Sherpa team was no exception. Masen Yaffee, co-founder and CEO of Green Sherpa, a web-based financial tracking tool, had 15 years of experience developing web applications for diverse types of businesses including several Fortune 500 companies. His co-founder, Erin Lozano, COO of Sherpa, had dedicated her career to helping women become more effective at financial management.

Together they launched their business in 2007 with a very simple concept: they would provide their customers personal finance software that had the familiarity and functionality of a product like Intuit's Quicken, with the convenience and money-saving benefit of an online hosted service. They quickly discovered, however, that while they had a good share of the technical and business expertise, they knew nothing about raising capital or dealing with institutional investors, and these skills are critically important in a business that has to scale quickly. They tapped into the skills of the Guidewire Group, a global market intelligence firm based in Redwood City, CA, that works with early-stage technology companies to help them assess their market potential and prepare a funding package. Yaffee and Lozano's first attempt at an executive summary and pitch deck was met with a lot of comments and suggestions, further reinforcing the fact that this was an area of expertise the team was lacking. Then the team began presenting to Guidewire Group's network of contacts who were familiar with the financial services domain and the software-as-service business model. Every feedback session helped the team hone their message. The goal was to raise $5 million to build their development and marketing teams and to go global.

By the end of 2009, they were projected to have 7,500 users, but investors saw a rough road for the team to differentiate itself in a crowded market and to find a business model that customers would appreciate and be willing to pay for. In 2010, with no investor funding, they reported that they had secured an agreement with a new partner that serves 1,000 credit unions as customers, with a total potential user base of 38 million. This partner will sell Green Sherpa to those users and if successful, might position Green Sherpa to finally secure investor capital. Only time will tell if Yaffee and Lozano have closed the gap in their team's expertise.

Sources: "Green Sherpa," (May 26, 3010). *CrunchBase*, www.crunchbase.com/company/green-sherpa#src1; "Green Sherpa Case Study," Guidewire Group, http://guidewiregroup .com/clients/green-sherpa-case-study, accessed July 19, 2010; and Joyner, A. (November 1, 2009). "Elevator Pitch: Green Sherpa," *Inc Magazine.com*, www.inc.com/magazine/ 20091101/elevator-pitch-green-sherpa.html.

Historically, entrepreneurs, in their quest for independence, often have attempted a new venture as soloists. In this way they could retain individual ownership, make all the key decisions, and not have to share the profits. This approach to starting a business is still relatively common, but particularly in small lifestyle businesses and among craftspeople and artisans. The problem with the soloist approach is that in today's complex, global, and fast-changing environment, most entrepreneurs find it necessary to start their ventures with a team. In fact, a growing body of research supports a team approach to entrepreneurial startups.[1] Teams have a much greater chance for success than solo efforts for a variety of reasons:

- The intense effort required of a startup can be shared.
- Should any one team member leave, it is less likely to result in the abandonment of the startup.
- With a founding team whose expertise covers major functional areas—marketing, finance, operations—the new venture can proceed further before it will need to hire additional personnel.
- A skilled founding team lends legitimacy to the new venture in the eyes of lenders, investors, and others.
- The entrepreneur's ability to analyze information and make decisions is improved because he or she benefits from the diverse expertise of the team, and ideas may be viewed and analyzed from several perspectives.

When the startup effort is collective, with a team that displays diverse capabilities, the new venture is more likely to be innovative and carve out a unique niche for itself.[2] Furthermore, another body of empirical research has provided evidence that firms founded by heterogeneous teams are generally more successful than those founded by individuals.[3]

Despite the research support for team-based entrepreneurship, there is also evidence to support the role and importance of a lead entrepreneur—that is, a person who displays a higher level of entrepreneurial vision and self-efficacy than other members of the team.[4] Lead entrepreneurs drive the development of new ventures and serve as the guardians of the vision. They have the ability to see what others cannot see and to identify ways to change the marketplace rather than simply recognize an opportunity.

The reality is that entrepreneurs never really start businesses all on their own; rather, they are "embedded in a social context, channeled and facilitated, or constrained and inhibited, by their positions in social networks."[5] Successful entrepreneurs take advantage of social networks to grow and maintain loyal customers, seek and acquire resources, and eventually sell their companies. For example, building a community or social network was online auction company eBay's goal from the start, and its success in doing so has been one of the most important reasons why eBay has survived where others in the online space have failed. Its customers manage the site—rating the quality of trading experiences with buyers and sellers, forming neighborhood watch groups to protect users against fraud and abuse, and providing input to the company on website design.

The extended networks of entrepreneurs are critical to the entire entrepreneurial process.[6] When an entrepreneurial firm interacts with other firms in its industry, it creates additional extended networks. At the hub of these networks is the founding team that has the vision and dedication to coordinate the efforts of all the partners toward a common goal. See Figure 7.1 for a view of the entrepreneur's network.

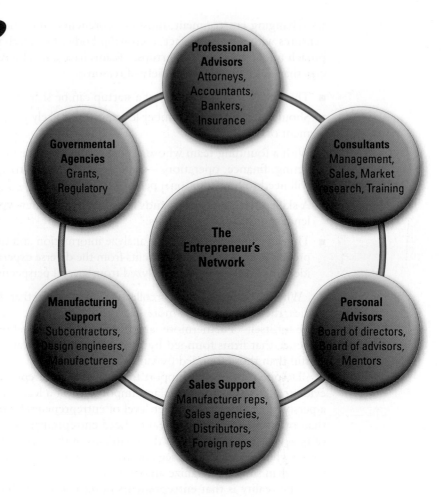

FIGURE 7.1

The Entrepreneur's
Network

It is also true that despite the type of venture or the network, some founders have an easier time acquiring resources than others, even when they don't have experience. For example, scientists who establish their legitimacy in their scientific field face less scrutiny when they launch a business requiring a completely different set of skills. The implication is that their ability to achieve success in one field will transfer to another.[7] In other words, investors will place their bets where the perceived probability of success is greater. This form of status or legitimacy for the entrepreneur is called *achieved status*, and it derives principally from the entrepreneur's education and experience.[8] Other types of status that entrepreneurs use to achieve legitimacy are *affiliation status*, the benefit of being associated with a prestigious institution, and *ascribed status*, which refers to unchangeable characteristics such as the gender and ethnicity of the entrepreneur.[9] Why is this important? It turns out that higher status founding teams receive preferential treatment from resource providers and that initial preferential treatment leads to a more rapid accumulation of subsequent resources.

CREATING THE FOUNDING TEAM

Choosing partners to start a new venture is one of the most critically important tasks that an entrepreneur must undertake. It is a difficult task because it's often not possible to understand a person's character until that person has spent some time working with the entrepreneur in the company. The stressful environment of a startup often reveals traits and responses that were not apparent when the person was originally selected. Everyone from investors to bankers to potential customers looks at the founding team of the new venture to determine whether its members have the ability to execute their plans. Therefore, it is vital to choose partners who have complementary skills and experience and who do not have a history that might be detrimental to the company.

Finding partners with complementary skills means making sure that the team is not overloaded with people who all have the same expertise. A team of three engineers or three finance analysts is less attractive than a team with more diverse skills. Research supports this argument saying that teams with diverse skills make better strategic choices that lead to higher performance.[10] In fact, some research has found team heterogeneity to be a significant predictor of long-term performance.[11] In terms of skill sets, heterogeneous teams also tend to handle the complexity of new ventures better than homogeneous teams.[12] Table 7.1 presents five factors that are significant in team composition: (1) homophily (similarity); (2) functionality (skill diversity); (3) status expectations (cultural bias); (4) network constraints (social contacts); and (5) ecological constraints (geographic distribution).

There is another advantage to forming a team. Because members of a startup team often invest not only their time but also their money, the burden of gathering resources is shared. The lead entrepreneur gains access to the network of contacts of the other members, which vastly increases the information and resources available to the new venture and enables it to grow more rapidly.

Of course, it isn't always possible or necessary to put together the "perfect" team from the start. The right person to fill a particular need may not have been determined, or the right person may be too expensive to bring on board during startup. In the latter situation, it is important to talk to that person about joining the team at a later date and to keep him or her apprised of the company's progress. Many an aggressive startup company has eventually wooed an experienced person away from a major corporation when it becomes apparent that the startup has a serious future.

Benchmarks for an Effective Team

Although there are no perfect founding teams and no fail-safe rules for forming them, effective founding teams tend to display the following characteristics:

- The lead entrepreneur and the team share the same vision for the new venture.
- The team members are passionate about the business concept and will work as hard as the lead entrepreneur to make it happen.

TABLE 7.1	Significant Factors for Founding Team Composition
Homophily (similarity)	The extent to which the characteristics of founding team members, such as gender, race, age, values, and beliefs, are similar. The benefit is that a high degree of similarity predisposes the team toward interpersonal attraction, trust, and understanding.
Functionality (skill diversity)	The degree of diversity among team members with respect to leadership skills and task expertise. Diversity of work experience and occupational background has been found to be linked to functional performance[*] and to communication and innovation.[†]
Status Expectations (cultural bias)	Widely held cultural biases regarding status (such as men having higher status than women) frequently affect the process of task group formation (although, in the case of gender, less so today). Those who perceive themselves to be in a higher-status group will tend to choose team members of the same status, however they define that status. Therefore, the entrepreneur who has lower status typically starts a venture as a soloist.
Network Constraint (social contacts)	The ability to choose members of a team is constrained by structural opportunities for social contact. For example, starting a business with only family members makes it more difficult to create a diverse team, because family members tend to be linked by strong ties and are in many respects an undesirably homogeneous group.[‡]
Ecological Constraint (geographic distribution)	The size of the population of potential team members and their geographic proximity is critical in the formation of founding teams.[§] The likelihood that different team members will associate is a function of their relative proportions in the population and their proximity to each other.[||]

[*]K. Eisenhardt and C.B. Schoonhoven (1990). "Organizational Growth: Linking Founding Team, Strategy, Environment, and Growth Among U.S. Semiconductor Ventures, 1978–1988." *Administrative Science Quarterly*, 35: 504–529.

[†]D. Ancona and D. Caldwell (1992). "Demography and Design: Predictors of New Product Team Performance." *Organization Science*, 3: 321–341.

[‡]H.E. Aldrich, A. Elam, and P.R. Reese (1996). "Strong Ties, Weak Ties, and Strangers: Do Women Business Owners Differ from Men in Their Use of Networking to Obtain Assistance?" in S. Birley and I. MacMillan (eds), *Entrepreneurship in a Global Context*. London: Routledge, pp. 1–25.

[§]G. Carroll and M. Hannan (2000). *The Demography of Corporations and Industries*. Princeton, NJ: Princeton University Press.

[||]P. Blau (1980). "A Fable About Social Structure." *Social Forces*, 58: 777–788.

Source: Based on Martin Ruef, Howard E. Aldrich, and Nancy M. Carter, "The Structure of Founding Teams: Homophily, Strong Ties, and Isolation Among U.S. Entrepreneurs," *American Sociological Review* (2003), 68(2): 195.

- One or more members of the founding team have experience in the industry in which the venture is being launched.

- The team has solid industry contacts with sources of capital.

- The team's expertise covers the key functional areas of the business: finance, marketing, and operations.

- The team members have good credit ratings; this will be important when the team seeks financing.

- The team is free to spend the time a startup demands and can endure the financial constraints of a typical startup.

Despite knowing a potential business partner as a friend or colleague for many years, the new venture scenario presents a different set of challenges that may reveal some negatives that were not apparent before. The founding team

TABLE 7.2	1. What are your core values?
	2. What is your goal for this business?
A Founding Team Quiz	3. What do you see as your role in the business? Why?
	4. What roles do you see the other team members playing and why?
	5. How should ownership of the business be divided?
	6. How should decisions be made?
	7. Do you enjoy business travel?
	8. What kinds of hours will you keep?
	9. What is your preferred mode of communication?
	10. What is your credit rating?
	11. How do you spend money?
	12. What is your lifestyle goal?

will need to agree on a number of important issues before launching a business together. One of the most effective ways to determine whether the team has the potential to work together successfully is to individually take a quiz that uncovers each person's values, goals, and expectations. Table 7.2 presents such a quiz. After each team member has taken the quiz independently of the others, the team should review the responses to learn if this team is rowing the same boat, heading in the same direction. It is not uncommon to find that one or more members of an otherwise cohesive team had different expectations for the outcomes of the business or their role in it. These differences must be discussed and agreed upon before moving further as a team. It will be far more costly in time and money, not to mention friendships, if these differences are ignored and cause problems later when the business is growing.

Special Issues for High-Tech Teams

High-tech teams suffer from a number of unique issues that can slow or derail startup and early growth processes. Some of these issues are the following:[13]

- **Putting structure on the organization before it's time**. Things never happen fast enough for entrepreneurs, but taking time to do sufficient market and competitor research may prevent entrepreneurs from creating the wrong type of organization for what they want to achieve. What this means is that entrepreneurial teams should operate as teams as long as possible, particularly through early product development, to avoid the weight of company bureaucracy and to assess whether the team is the right team to take this technology to market.

- **Pretending there are sales from beta customers**. While it's true that tech entrepreneurs often need to secure beta customers at no cost to the customer just to get their technology into the users' hands, entrepreneurs should not confuse these beta customers with actual customers. For beta customers, the value is "free." However, that value proposition is not going to build a company. The only bonafide customers are those who pay for entrepreneurs' products and services.

- **Suffocating under opportunity overload**. Entrepreneurs with new technologies rarely suffer from a lack of opportunities. In fact, quite the opposite is generally true: they have more opportunities than their resources can manage once they've established their businesses. That's why tech entrepreneurs must focus their efforts and stick to their strategy for growth so that the opportunities they do take advantage of have a greater chance for success.

- **Believing that engineers can do marketing**. Technology entrepreneurs must bring in critical business skills as early as possible to avoid slowing progress for lack of expertise. It takes both technical people and business people to successfully ramp up a technology startup, and it's rare to find an entrepreneur who is equally effective at both skills.

- **Licensing the technology too soon**. In an effort to speed the technology to market, entrepreneurs sometimes elect to enter into license agreements too soon and thereby give away significant upside potential or worse have to rely on a licensee that has chosen the wrong market or done a poor job of developing the market application. An alternative is to pay a strategic partner to develop the applications and retain the rights in-house.

New ventures in the high-tech arena are frequently funded by "angel," or venture capital, and these startups face different issues in the formation of their founding teams. Very often, the founding team consists of scientists and engineers with little market or business experience. Investors understand clearly that these kinds of teams are not the most effective for overseeing the rapid and successful execution of the business strategy. A high-tech venture with significant up-front funding and the potential for exponential growth early on requires a professional management team with experience and an excellent track record in the industry. Usually, investors will help entrepreneurs locate the right people for the job. Bringing on professional management soon after startup ensures that there will be no glitches when rapid growth begins, and it also leaves the creative founders the time they need to continue to develop and improve the product and/or service.

Unique Issues Surrounding Virtual Teams

Technology has made it possible for geographically dispersed teams to form and collaborate through synchronous and/or asynchronous communication media, relieving team members of the need to juggle global and local priorities.[14] Virtual teams are distinctly different from face-to-face teams in both spatial distance and communication. It is not the actual distance that matters but the effect that this distance has on how the team interacts. For example, suppose a startup team is located in Los Angeles and one team member lives in Pasadena, approximately 10 miles away. The spatial distance is not great, but given traffic and other challenges, the time distance may be 40 minutes or more. Therefore, technologies such as videoconferencing, phone, and email are used to mediate the distance. In addition, appropriate routines keep everyone connected and on track.[15]

Despite any disadvantages caused by distance, virtual teams have several advantages. They enable the entrepreneur to access the most qualified individuals for a particular position, regardless of location, and to create a more flexible organization. This will entail finding partners who will evolve into a coherent, seamless, and well-integrated team.[16] Trust, therefore, is a critical component of an effective virtual team.

Rob Bevis, president of Winspeer International Group Ltd., a Vancouver, Canada–based wine importer, has faced the challenges and advantages of working in a virtual environment. His company extends from Vancouver to Edmonton to Calgary and all roads in between. It is impossible for him to run his business in any other manner. In a rapidly growing global marketplace that is easily accessible via the Internet, an entrepreneur needs to expand into new markets. These new markets may not be geographically local, and therefore may create significant personnel challenges, complicating the task of getting people to work together. In his role as president of Winspeer, Bevis quickly realized that he needed to be able to coordinate the activities of his employees who were scattered throughout western Canada. His needs fell into three areas: (1) tactical collaboration to reach employees at their desks or on the road through email, instant messaging, and cell phone; (2) strategic collaboration that involved information sharing, file sharing, and message boards; and (3) task management using public calendars and checklists. His major concern was that all employees would be able to know what was going on at any given time. This required a central database, a virtual private network (VPN), and a common calendar. Today, with these collaboration tools in place, Bevis and his team can respond quickly to a marketplace that changes daily, and this has reduced costs and increased revenues—in short, it made all the difference for his winning team. In July of 2009, Winspeer completed a 3 year rebranding process and became Altovin International Ltd. now serving all of Canada.[17]

Founding Teams for International Ventures

Traditionally, entrepreneurs were advised to establish themselves in the domestic market before taking on the enormous challenge of a global market. Increasingly, however, we are seeing more and more firms going international from startup. And these international startups are generally being founded by teams.[18] Research indicates that whether these small firms succeed in the international market depends on the skills and knowledge of the entrepreneurial team.[19] The characteristics found to predict success in international ventures include the extent to which members of the founding team have traveled and/or worked abroad and the number of languages spoken.[20] Experienced founding teams are also more likely to form partnerships to facilitate their entering a foreign market.[21] Because international startups are relatively more vulnerable, due to their operations being at a distance, they usually seek partnerships to provide financial, political, and cultural resources and the contacts they will need to be successful. The topic of global entrepreneurial ventures is discussed in Chapter 17.

Rules for Friends and Families

Turning to friends and family members is certainly the easiest and quickest way to find partners to start a new venture, but it may not be the best decision for the business. If a small business has no intentions of seeking outside financing, having a founding team that consists entirely of family members may not be a problem if they are all compatible. But if the plan is to grow the venture significantly, seek outside investors, or potentially do a public offering, a founding team consisting of only family members may not be an attractive asset. Here are some things to think about before making the decision to take on a family member or close friend as a partner in a new venture:

- Friends or family members should possess real skills and expertise that the business needs to be successful.

- They should have the same work ethic as the entrepreneur. If the entrepreneur is a workaholic and loves it and a family member is a slacker, there will be problems.

- If there are family members on the startup team, there should be outsiders on the advisory board and/or board of directors so that the company will have the benefit of objective input to the business.

- The relationship with family and friends should be treated as a business relationship. The responsibilities and duties of all should be clearly spelled out, and everyone should understand how disagreements will be settled. As much as possible, the activities of the business should not be brought home at night.

SEEKING PROFESSIONAL ADVISERS

When a new venture is in its infancy, it generally doesn't have the resources to hire in-house professional help such as an attorney or accountant. Instead, it must rely on building relationships with professionals on an "as-needed" basis. These professionals provide information and services not normally within the scope of expertise of most entrepreneurs, and they can play devil's advocate for the entrepreneur, pointing out potential flaws in the business concept. They provide the new venture—and the entrepreneurial team in love with its own concept—an invaluable reality check. There are a number of these professional advisers that entrepreneurs rely on at various times in their venture's life.

Attorneys

There is hardly any aspect of starting a new venture that is not touched by the law. Unfortunately, entrepreneurs who have never had any education in the legal aspects of business often don't recognize that they need legal help until their business gets into trouble. Attorneys are professionals who typically specialize in one area of the law (such as taxes, real estate, business, or intellectual property) and can provide a wealth of support for the new venture. Within their particular area of expertise, attorneys can

- Advise the entrepreneur in selecting the correct organizational structure: sole proprietorship, partnership, LLC, or corporation.

- Advise about and prepare documents for acquisition of intellectual-property rights and for licensing agreements.

- Negotiate and prepare contracts for the entrepreneur, who may be buying, selling, contracting, or leasing.
- Advise the entrepreneur on compliance with regulations related to financing and credit.
- Keep the entrepreneur apprised of the latest tax reform legislation and help to minimize the venture's tax burden.
- Assist the entrepreneur in complying with federal, state, or local laws.
- Represent the entrepreneur in any legal actions as advocates.

Choosing a good attorney is a time-consuming but vital task that should be accomplished prior to startup. Decisions about such things as the legal form of the business or contracts made at inception may affect the venture for years to come—hence the need for good legal advice. To find the best attorney for the situation, entrepreneurs should

- Ask accountants, bankers, and other business people to recommend attorneys who are familiar with the challenges facing startup, particularly those in the entrepreneur's industry.
- Look for an attorney who is willing to listen, has time, and will be flexible about fees while the business is in the startup phase.
- Confirm that the attorney carries malpractice insurance.

Accountants

A lawyer is an advocate, but an accountant is bound by rules and ethics that do not permit advocacy. Whereas an attorney is bound to represent his or her client no matter what the client does, an accountant cannot defend a client who does something that violates the accounting industry's generally accepted accounting principles (GAAP).

Accounting is a fairly complex field that entrepreneurs need to understand at least at a basic level in order to communicate with accountants, auditors, lenders, bankers, and investors, in addition to internal and external stakeholders. In the beginning, the accountant may set up the company's books and maintain them on a periodic basis, or, as is often the case, the entrepreneur may hire a bookkeeper to perform the day-to-day recording of transactions. The accountant will also set up control systems for operations, as well as payroll. The entrepreneur then goes to the accountant during the tax season. Once the new venture is beyond the startup phase and is growing consistently, it's a good idea to do an annual audit to determine whether the company's accounting and control procedures are adequate. The auditors may also require a physical inventory. If everything is in order, they will issue a certified statement, which is important should the entrepreneur ever decide to take the company public.

Accountants are also a rich networking source in the entrepreneur's search for additional members of the new venture team. Like attorneys, accountants tend to specialize, so it is wise to find one who is used to working with young, growing businesses. Indeed, the accountant who takes a business through startup and early growth will probably not be the best person to take care of the company's needs when it reaches the next level of growth. As the financial and record-keeping needs of the business increase and become more complex, the entrepreneur may have to consider a larger firm with expertise in several areas.

Bankers

There is a saying that all banks are alike until you need a loan. Today this is truer than ever, so having a qualified banker on the advisory team will put the new venture in a better position to seek a line of credit for operating capital or a loan to purchase equipment. The firm's banker should be thought of as a business partner who can be a source of information and networking; help make decisions regarding capital needs; assist in preparing pro forma operations and cash-flow analyses and evaluate projections; and assist in all facets of financing.

To narrow the search for a banker, entrepreneurs should prepare a list of criteria that defines the banking needs of the new venture. They should also talk with other entrepreneurs in the same industry to identify a bank that works well with the type of venture they plan to launch. Another approach is to ask an accountant or attorney to suggest the best bank for a particular type of business.

When choosing a banker, seek out an officer with a rank of assistant vice president or higher, because these officers are trained to work with new and growing businesses and have enough authority to make decisions quickly. In particular, it is important to ensure that the lending officer can approve loans and lines of credit in the amounts needed. Today many of the largest banks have moved their lending facilities to a central location, so it is difficult to establish a relationship with the person who has responsibility for approving a request. That's why many entrepreneurs seek out community banks that have a vested interest in supporting local businesses.

Insurance Agents

Many entrepreneurs overlook the value of a relationship with a competent insurance agent, but a growing venture will require several types of insurance:

- Property and casualty
- Medical
- Errors and omissions
- Life (on key managers)
- Workers' compensation
- Directors and officers
- Unemployment
- Auto (on the firm's vehicles)
- Liability (product and personal)
- Bonding

Major insurance firms can handle all types of insurance vehicles, but specialists will be required for certain kinds of protection, such as bonding (which is common in the construction industry to protect against a contractor's not completing a project), product liability insurance, and errors and omissions (which protects the business against liability from unintentional mistakes in advertising). The new venture's insurance needs will change over its life, and a good insurance agent will help an entrepreneur determine the needed coverage at the appropriate times.

SEEKING PERSONAL ADVISORS

Personal advisors take on several forms, but they all have the purpose of supporting the founding team in their efforts to launch and grow the business. Here we discuss boards of directors, boards of advisors, and the mentor board.

Building a Board of Directors

Although the decision to have a board of directors is influenced by the legal form of the business, it is a long-held belief that establishing corporate governance early in the organization of a startup will enhance the quality of the company as it grows. If a new venture is a corporation, a board of directors is required and is elected by the shareholders. If the business needs venture capital, a board will be necessary, and the venture capitalist will probably demand a seat on it. Boards of directors serve a valuable purpose; if chosen correctly, they provide expertise that fills gaps in the founding team's knowledge. In that capacity they act as advisers. They also assist in establishing corporate strategy and philosophy. They do not have the power to sign contracts or commit the corporation legally; instead, they elect the officers of the corporation, who are responsible for its day-to-day operations. Board members assist with business development, act as arbitrators for dispute resolution, and give credibility to the new company's image.

It is important to distinguish between boards of privately owned corporations and those of publicly owned corporations. In a privately owned corporation, the entrepreneurial team owns all or the majority of the stock, so directors serve at the pleasure of the entrepreneur, who has effective control of the company. On the other hand, directors of publicly traded companies have legitimate power to control the activities of the company and liability for what they do or fail to do. They are elected by the shareholders and represent the shareholders' interests in the company.

Boards can be comprised of inside or outside members or a combination of the two. An inside board member is one who is a founder, employee, family member, or retired manager of the firm, whereas an outside board member is someone with no direct connection to the business. Which type of board member is better is a matter of opinion and circumstance; research has not provided any clear results on this issue. In general, however, outside directors are beneficial for succession planning and for raising capital. They can often bring a fresh point of view to the strategic planning process, along with expertise that the founders may not possess. Insiders have the advantage of complete knowledge about the business; they are generally more available and have demonstrated their effectiveness in the particular positions they occupy in the business. Typically where the entrepreneur/CEO has power to configure the board, the board will be small and comprised primarily of insiders, particularly family members.[22] Often the company chief executive officer (CEO), chief financial officer (CFO), and in-house attorney sit on the board. But there are political ramifications when the board members report to the CEO; insiders may not always be objective and independent. They also may not have the broad expertise from outside the company that is necessary to effectively guide the growth of the business.

Consider carefully whether the new venture requires a working board—that is, one that directs the strategy of the business. Most working boards are used for their expertise, for strategic planning, for auditing the actions of the firm, and for arbitrating differences. These activities are not as crucial in the startup phase, when the entrepreneurial team is gathering resources and raising capital. However, a board of directors can assist the entrepreneurial team in those functions and can network with key people who can help the new venture. Some stakeholders will ask to be included on the board so that they can monitor their investment in the company. This is common among significant private investors, venture capitalists, bankers, and even accountants. To be sure of getting only the best people on the board, entrepreneurs should set standards for membership in advance and should strictly adhere to them.

The size and complexity of an entrepreneur's business, as well as the legal requirements of the state in which the company operates, will determine how many directors serve on the board. There is no research consensus on the relationship between the size of the board and the performance of the company, although some research has found that a large board encourages laziness on the part of some members[23] and thus may undermine the board's ability to initiate strategic actions.[24] Moreover, larger boards tend to develop factions and coalitions that often lead to conflict. The general recommendation is to have no fewer than 5 and no more than 15 board members. In the earliest stages of a new venture, the board will often consist of the founders, though that should quickly change as the company begins to grow and needs to tap the expertise of people who have managed growth in their own companies.

When choosing people to serve on the board of directors, entrepreneurs should consider those who have

- The necessary technical skill related to the business.
- Significant, successful experience in the industry.
- Experience running a company at the level the entrepreneur wants to grow to next.
- Important contacts in the industry.
- Expertise in finance, capital acquisition, and possibly IPOs.
- A personality compatible with the rest of the board.

- Good problem-solving skills.
- Honesty and integrity, to engender a sense of mutual trust.

In addition, it is critically important to choose the right board members for the stage the company is in. Figure 7.2 displays the various stages of a company's growth, the status of the business during that stage, and the type of board member that may be most appropriate for the needs of the business at that point in time. Entrepreneurs must align their objectives with the venture's life cycle stage and then select the board members and advisers so that they are congruent with these objectives.

If the entrepreneurial team is not careful, it may learn too late that a director it has appointed to the board considers the position an appointment for life, much like being appointed to the Supreme Court. To prevent such a misunderstanding, and to bring a fresh point of view to the board, directors should be asked to serve on a rotating basis for a specified period of time.

The board is headed by the chairperson, who, in a new, private venture, is typically the lead entrepreneur. The entrepreneur is also likely to be the president and CEO. The current trend is for the CEO and perhaps the chief operating officer (COO) or CFO to be the only inside members on the board. Depending on the type of business, boards normally meet face-to-face an average of five times a year and through teleconferences as necessary. How often the board meets will be largely a function of how active it is at any given time. Directors typically spend about nine to ten days a year on duties related to the

FIGURE 7.2 Board Members and the Business Life Stage

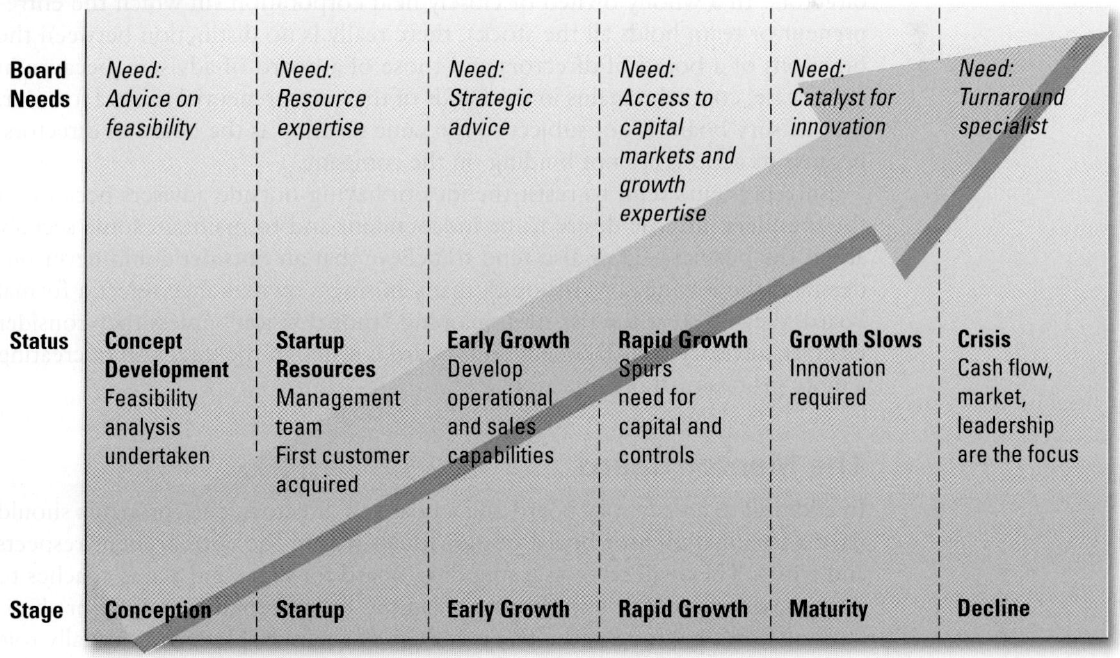

Board Needs	*Need: Advice on feasibility*	*Need: Resource expertise*	*Need: Strategic advice*	*Need: Access to capital markets and growth expertise*	*Need: Catalyst for innovation*	*Need: Turnaround specialist*
Status	**Concept Development** Feasibility analysis undertaken	**Startup Resources** Management team First customer acquired	**Early Growth** Develop operational and sales capabilities	**Rapid Growth** Spurs need for capital and controls	**Growth Slows** Innovation required	**Crisis** Cash flow, market, leadership are the focus
Stage	**Conception**	**Startup**	**Early Growth**	**Rapid Growth**	**Maturity**	**Decline**

business and are usually paid a retainer plus a per-meeting fee. Their expenses are also reimbursed. The compensation can take the form of cash, stock, or other perquisites.

Today it is more difficult to get people to serve as directors because in some cases they can be held personally liable for the actions of the firm, and the frequency with which boards are being sued is increasing. For this reason, potential directors will require that the business carry directors' and officers' (D&O) liability insurance to indemnify them. The expense of this insurance is often prohibitive for a growing company, but it is essential in getting good people to serve. Additional expenses related to the development of a board of directors include meeting rooms, travel, and food. Because of the expense of maintaining a formal board of directors, many entrepreneurs with new ventures maintain a small insider board of directors and rely heavily on their informal advisory board for objective perspectives.

Advisory Board

The advisory board is an informal panel of experts and other people who are interested in seeing the new venture succeed. They are a useful and less costly alternative to a formal board of directors. Advisory boards can range from those that meet once or twice a year and do not get paid to those that meet more regularly and are provided an equity stake in the company.

Advisory boards are often used when a board of directors is not required or in the startup phase when the board of directors consists of the founders only. An effective advisory board can provide the new venture with needed expertise without the significant costs and loss of control associated with a board of directors. In a wholly owned or closely held corporation (in which the entrepreneur or team holds all the stock), there really is no distinction between the functions of a board of directors and those of a board of advisers, because in either case, control remains in the hands of the entrepreneurial team. However, the advisory board is not subject to the same scrutiny as the board of directors, because its actions are not binding on the company.

Entrepreneurs tend to resist the idea of having outside advisers because of the founders' intense desire to be independent and to maintain some secrecy about the business. They also tend to believe that an outsider could never understand the business.[25] Although many business owners may reject a formal board, they do so at the risk of developing "tunnel vision" unless they consider using an advisory board. An advisory board is a step in the direction of creating a more professional organization.

The Mentor Board

In addition to an advisory board and a board of directors, entrepreneurs should have a personal mentor board of individuals whom the entrepreneur respects and trusts. They will serve as a sounding board for ideas and act as coaches to raise the entrepreneur's spirits and warn the entrepreneur when he or she is heading down a wrong path. The members of a personal board are usually role models and people who have businesses and lifestyles like the one the entrepreneur wants to create. Mentors also provide a safe place for entrepreneurs to air their fears and concerns and express their hopes and dreams.

Mistakes to Avoid with Teams and Boards

Assembling the extended founding team is a serious undertaking, and failure to put the team together effectively could have severe ramifications for the future of the business. It is important that all team members who are brought on board have the required experience and qualifications as well as the same goals for the business. The same is true of the board of directors. Appointing only friends and family members instead of the most qualified people will not result in the best advice for the entrepreneur. Due to limited resources, many entrepreneurs choose family members or friends to serve as professional advisers, such as an attorney or accountant, but it is often difficult for these advisers to be objective about the business, something that is necessary if the entrepreneur is to receive the best guidance.

One of the biggest mistakes cash-strapped entrepreneurs make is giving team members stock in lieu of salary or fees, for example, in the case of independent contractors. Once a person has stock in the company, it is much more difficult to terminate their position. It makes sense to wait to give stock until an individual has proven his or her worth to the company. Of course, the original founding team will want to split up the stock or ownership in the company, and it will be necessary to keep some stock available to offer to professional management personnel that must be hired.

Equity Distribution

One of the biggest incentives for taking on the risk of a startup venture is the opportunity to acquire an equity or ownership stake and participate in the potential upside if the startup is a success. Because equity is such an attractive incentive, it also causes untold problems for entrepreneurial teams. Essentially, the founders receive equity stakes based on what they're contributing to the business. Because equity equates with power, those founders who intend to remain with the business for the long term should have the most equity. Another indicator of a greater share of equity is whether a founder invested his or her personal capital in the business. While many entrepreneurs highly value their sweat equity, the investment of actual dollars trumps in-kind work. In addition to money, founders may contribute patents, vital connections, reputation, or unique business or technical expertise that is critical to the company. It is important to clearly understand what each team member is contributing and value it appropriately. If the team is three founders, it's probably not a wise idea to give equal stakes: first because founders are not all equal in what they contribute, and second, it creates the potential for an impasse with no one with enough power to make a decision.

Because companies often find that they need to tap some form of investor capital as they grow the business, it's important to keep the number of original founders at a manageable level so that when the company is sold or completes an IPO, the founders, who typically split 20 to 30 percent of the equity at that point, will still show a significant gain for their hard work.

The Buy-Sell Agreement

A buy-sell agreement is used to prevent an owner from selling his or her interests in the company to an outsider without consent of the other owners and to determine what happens to the business should the owner (or one of the partners in a partnership agreement) decide to leave the business. A properly written buy-sell agreement will also specify how an owner's interest will be valued. Jay Steinmetz learned the importance of buy-sell agreements the hard way when he started CaptureTech, a reseller of liquidated bar coding equipment in 1997. He brought in his unemployed friend to run the business and agreed to split ownership 50/50 even though the two strongly disagreed on many aspects of the business. One year into the business, the partners were completely at odds, but they had no agreement that spelled out how to deal with the situation. After the disgruntled friend stole the company laptop, changed the company's locks, and liquidated the joint bank account, he then filed assault charges against Steinmetz. Eventually, everything was resolved by the courts in Steinmetz's favor, but he had to close the business and start over again, this time without a partner. Today his new company, Barcoding, Inc., was named to the prestigious VAR500 as one of North America's top technology integrators, and buy-sell agreements are now standard practice.[26]

SOCIAL ENTREPRENEURSHIP: MAKING MEANING

Singing for Famine Relief

It was 1984 and British punk rocker Bob Geldof was facing the death of his band, the Boomtown Rats, who couldn't seem to make it past number 67 on the U.S. charts. They appeared to be doomed to being a regional band in the UK. One evening as he was watching television, the BBC aired a documentary about Ethiopia and its hundred-year drought; millions of Ethiopians were facing starvation. He couldn't just sit there and do nothing.

The very next day he was on the phone to his musician friends to suggest that as a group they cut a single to raise money to fight the famine. His friends agreed and in short order they had written and produced the single, raising hundreds of thousands of dollars for famine relief in the process.

Riding a wave of excitement, Geldof decided to go even further by developing the largest concert in history in just seven months. On July 13, 1985, Live Aid, a 16 hour extravaganza debuted to 1.5 billion viewers in 100 countries. Contributions exceeded $245 million. What was the secret to Geldof's success? He was solving a big problem that grabbed people's attention with a very grand solution that captured the imagination of everyone and gave them a way to be involved in something important. When you approach a problem in this manner, you don't have to sell people on it; they will be ready and willing to buy into your solution. A TV film of Geldof's story is in the works.

Sources: Smith, R. (Winter 2010). "The Big, Selfless, and Simple Leadership Platform," *Leader to Leader*, p. 7; and Mugan, C. (July 15, 2010). "Bob Geldof's Live Aid Vision Turned Into TV Film," *Spinner*, www.spinner.com/2010/07/15/bob-geldof-live-aid-tv-film.

There are two types of buy-sell agreements: a cross-purchase agreement and a stock redemption agreement. In the cross-purchase agreement each owner or shareholder purchases an insurance policy on the other shareholders and is named as the beneficiary on the policies. Proceeds received on the death of a shareholder are not taxable. This approach is complicated if there are several owners. In a stock redemption agreement, by contrast, the corporation owns the insurance policies on the lives of the owners. Upon an owner's death or departure for other reasons, the corporation purchases the owner's interest using the proceeds of the insurance policy. In either case, if an owner leaves the company, the owner is required to sell his or her interest back to the remaining owners.

OUTSOURCING WITH INDEPENDENT CONTRACTORS

A new business typically does not have the resources to pay for all the management and operational staff that may be necessary to keep it running. In fact, most entrepreneurs avoid hiring employees as long as possible, because employees are the single biggest expense in the business. But how does a new venture survive with as few employees as possible and still grow?

The solution lies in outsourcing, which means using independent contractors to undertake functions that the entrepreneur doesn't want to handle. Independent contractors (ICs) own their own businesses and are hired by the entrepreneur to do a specific job. They are under the control of the entrepreneur only for the results of the work they do, not for the means by which those results are accomplished. The independent contractors that entrepreneurs use on a regular basis include consultants, manufacturers, distributors, and employee leasing firms (note that professional advisers are also independent contractors). The popularity of outsourcing can be seen in the fact that Pricewaterhouse Coopers' Management Barometer Survey reports that 75 percent of multinational U.S. and European companies use outsourcing to support a significant portion of their financial activities.[27] However, the real growth in outsourcing has come from small and midsize companies. Computer Economics reported that of the 200 companies they surveyed, 14 percent went offshore in 2008, but that increased to 24 percent in 2009.[28] Other key areas for outsourcing are business processes and manufacturing. It is hard for most companies to keep up with changes in technology, and the vendors to which they outsource can provide the same service and better performance at a lower cost. Entrepreneurs seek out independent contractors for their expertise in specific areas. Using an independent contractor means that the new venture doesn't have to supply medical and retirement benefits, provide unemployment insurance, or withhold payroll taxes. These are costly benefits that can amount to more than 32 percent of an employee's base salary. But there are hidden costs to outsourcing whether domestically or globally that entrepreneurs should be aware of:[29]

- *The cost of searching for and contracting with an independent contractor (IC).* The best way to reduce this cost is for entrepreneurs to secure referrals from people they know who have had a successful experience with the IC.

- *Transferring activities to the IC.* Getting the IC "up to speed" on the business takes time and human resources. Transfer costs can be reduced if entrepreneurs identify up front what they want the IC to handle and lay out a plan for preparing the IC to do the work.

- *Managing the independent contractor.* This is one of those cases where experience counts. The first IC contract takes the longest and costs the most. The best IC relationships occur when communication is an ongoing process so that the IC becomes a real part of the business.

- *Bringing the activity in-house.* Many companies eventually bring in-house activities that they once outsourced. This may occur because the company has grown to the point where it needs and can afford in-house staff for the activity or because the company wants more control over the activity. One way to reduce the transition cost is to have the person who manages the IC relationship learn enough about the activity to be able to ease the company through the transition.

To reduce the hidden costs of using independent contractors, entrepreneurs should retain in house critical activities and core competencies that are idiosyncratic or unique to the business. They should also research vendors carefully and seek referrals. Above all, entrepreneurs must work with legal advisers who have experience with independent contractor law to draft binding contracts.

The IRS and Independent Contractors

The IRS has very strict rules for the use of independent contractors. The Law of Agency defines the terms *employee* and *independent contractor.* It states, "While an employee acts under the direction and control of the employer, an independent contractor contracts to produce a certain result and has full control over the means and methods that shall be used in producing the result."[30] If an employer doesn't follow the rules regulating classification of workers as independent contractors, they can be considered employees for tax purposes, and the employer can be held liable for all back taxes plus penalties and interest, which can amount to a substantial sum.

To ensure compliance with IRS regulations, entrepreneurs who use independent contractors should

- Consult an attorney.

- Draw up a contract with each independent contractor, specifying that the contractor will not be treated as an employee for state and federal tax purposes.

- Be careful not to indicate the means or methods of accomplishing the work, only the desired result.

- Verify that the independent contractor carries workers' compensation insurance.

- Verify that the independent contractor possesses the necessary licenses.

TABLE 7.3 The 20-Point Test for Independent Contractors	A worker is an employee if he or she 1. Must follow the employer's instructions about how to do the work. 2. Receives training from the employer. 3. Provides services that are integrated into the business. 4. Provides services that must be rendered personally. 5. Cannot hire, supervise, and pay his or her own assistants. 6. Has a continuing relationship with the employer. 7. Must follow set hours of work. 8. Works full-time for an employer. 9. Does the work on the employer's premises. 10. Must do the work in a sequence set by the employer. 11. Must submit regular reports to the employer. 12. Is paid regularly for time worked. 13. Receives reimbursements for expenses. 14. Relies on the tools and materials of the employer. 15. Has no major investment in facilities to perform the service. 16. Cannot make a profit or suffer a loss. 17. Works for one employer at a time. 18. Does not offer his or her services to the general public. 19. Can be fired at will by the employer. 20. May quit work at any time without incurring liability.

More specifically, the IRS uses a 20-point test for classifying workers (see Table 7.3). Even if an employer follows all the IRS rules, however, there is no guarantee that the IRS won't challenge its position. Therefore, it is important to document the relationship with an independent contractor through a legal agreement that explicitly demonstrates that the independent contractor owns his or her own business. The IRS can decide that an IC is an employee even if only one of the 20 points is true!

On the positive side, independent contractors can make the very small startup venture look like an established corporation to anyone on the outside. A large corporation will generally have vice presidents for departments of operations, sales, marketing, and finance. It is possible to replicate these functions by using independent contractors, thereby lowering costs and remaining more flexible.

Types of Independent Contractors

Many types of independent contractors operate behind the scenes of the new venture but make a valuable contribution nonetheless. Various independent contractors make up the entrepreneur's extended team. These include consultants, professional employer organizations (PEOs), manufacturing support, sales support, and government agencies.

Consultants

The consulting industry is one of the fastest-growing industries in the United States, and it can provide a variety of services for a new venture. Consultants can

- Train the sales staff and/or management.
- Conduct market research.
- Prepare policy manuals.
- Solve problems.
- Act as temporary key management.
- Recommend market strategy.
- Design and engineer products.
- Design a plant layout and equipment.
- Conduct research and development.
- Recommend operational and financial controls.

Because they tend to be fairly expensive, consultants are best used for critical one-time advising or problem-solving assignments. In that capacity, they are typically more cost-effective than employees because they are accustomed to working quickly within the constraints of a fixed budget. Consultants are generally paid in one of three ways: monthly retainer, which pays for a specified amount of time per month; hourly rate; or project fee. More recently, consultants have also been known to ask for some form of equity stake in the companies for which they consult. Some entrepreneurs have chosen to go this route when cash is in short supply. However, entrepreneurs should consult an attorney before giving up any equity in their company. It is much harder to dismiss an IC who is a shareholder in the company.

Professional Employer Organization (PEO)

Leasing staff is a way for a new business to enjoy the advantages of major corporations without incurring many of the expenses. A professional employer organization assumes the payroll and human resource functions for the business for a fee that generally ranges from 3 to 5 percent of gross payroll. Each pay period, the new venture pays the PEO a lump sum to cover payroll plus the fee. In addition to payroll processing and taxes, the services they provide include safety and risk management, benefits administration, and human resource management. PEOs and human resource business process outsourcing are growing rapidly as more companies take advantage of their services.

Manufacturing Support

Even those new ventures that involve manufacturing a product can avail themselves of the benefits of independent contractors. Because the cost of building and equipping a new manufacturing plant is immense by any standard, many entrepreneurs choose to contract the work with an established manufacturer domestically or in another country. In fact, it is possible for an entrepreneur who has a new product idea to subcontract the design of the product to an engineering firm, the production of components to various manufacturing firms, the assembly of the product to another firm, and the distribution to yet another. With the rapid rate of technological innovation, it is difficult for any one company to keep up, so remaining focused and profitable is critical to success.

Cooperative purchasing has become an important way for companies to be globally competitive and keep costs down. In addition to being able to take advantage of significant quantity discounts, companies who collaborate also reduce transaction costs with bundled orders.[31]

Sales Support

Hiring sales staff can be an expensive proposition for any new venture, not only from the standpoint of benefits but also because salespeople must be trained. As new high-growth ventures seek a geographically broad market, even a global one, it is vital to consider enlisting the aid of manufacturer's representatives (reps) and foreign reps who know those markets. Using distributors enables the entrepreneur to reach the target market without having to deal with the complex retail market. In addition, sales agencies can provide the new venture with fully trained salespeople—in much the same manner as temporary services supply clerical help. Some can also provide advertising and public relations.

DRAWING CONCLUSIONS FROM THE FOUNDING TEAM ASSESSMENT

It is rare for an entrepreneur to conclude that he or she has all the expertise and access to resources that are needed by the new venture. Gaps in the founding team are bound to exist; therefore, it is important to identify them and use the entrepreneur's social network to get recommendations on people who could fill those gaps. A complete team is not necessary to launch a business in its earliest stages. What *is* important is that entrepreneurs identify the essential participants for the initial launch. This decision is typically based on critical functions that the business will undertake immediately, whether that is a chef and personnel manager for a restaurant so that meals can be designed, produced, and distributed; or a sales manager and international sales partner for an import company so that sales outlets can be secured and the best suppliers located. The most important thing for entrepreneurs to remember is that not everyone involved with the new venture has to be an owner or an employee. Many other options are available.

New Venture Action Plan

- Identify the members of the founding team or at least the expertise needed to start the venture.
- Determine what expertise is missing from the management team and how you will supply it.

- Begin asking questions about potential professional advisers, such as an attorney or accountant.

- Determine whether you will need a board of directors, an advisory board, or a mentor board.

- Identify at least one type of independent contractor that the new venture could use.

Questions on Key Issues

1. For what kinds of businesses is starting as a solo entrepreneur sufficient? Are there advantages to starting even these types of businesses with a team?
2. What strategy should an entrepreneur employ when selecting a personal board, an advisory board, or a board of directors?
3. How might the need for an attorney differ for a service business and a high technology company?
4. How can you ensure that you are using independent contractors correctly and in accordance with the law?
5. Suppose you are starting an apparel company where you will design and manufacture a unique line of clothing. What kinds of independent contractors can help you start this venture?

Experiencing Entrepreneurship

1. Interview an entrepreneur who started a venture as a soloist, and then visit an entrepreneurial venture started by a team (two or more people). Based on your interviews, write a two-page report discussing the advantages and disadvantages of each approach.
2. Choose a lawyer, accountant, or banker to interview as a potential professional adviser to your business. What information will you need to secure from him or her to make your decision?

Relevant Case Studies

Case 4 The Crowne Inn
Case 6 Potion Inc.

CHAPTER

8

UNDERSTANDING THE NUMBERS

"Our greatest lack is not money for any undertaking, but rather ideas. If the ideas are good, cash will somehow flow to where it is needed."

—ROBERT H. SCHULLER

CHAPTER OBJECTIVES

- Demonstrate an understanding of entrepreneurial resource gathering.
- Explain the rationale for a business process map.
- Discuss the process for calculating startup requirements.
- Explain the role of pricing in forecasting sales.
- Identify typical startup financial metrics.
- Discuss the role of risk in the entrepreneur's assessment of financial needs.

What do you do when your dream business appears to be financially beyond your reach? You start getting creative and figure out a way to have what you want. That's precisely what Michael Brill did when, one day in 2002, he decided that he was tired of the high technology work life and wanted to pursue his dream of making wine. Isn't that many people's dream—to own a vineyard in Napa/Sonoma or Italy or France and live the idyllic life of a vintner? The problem is that the wine business requires a significant amount of capital. Brill's research figured the total cost of creating and maintaining the vineyard in Napa at $15 million, and he just didn't have access to that kind of money. Nevertheless, he wasn't about to give up, so he dug up his 625-square-foot lot in the Potrero Hill area of San Francisco and turned it into a tiny vineyard, planting some pinot noir and syrah vines. He also began immersing himself in the winemaking process, reading everything he could get his hands on. Although he remained at his software marketing job during the day, at night and on the weekends, he was a vintner.

Soon he became a curiosity in his neighborhood, and people would stop by and spend the day with him, helping him pick, crush, and process the grapes, so he didn't have to hire any help. But more importantly, the discussions and interest that he gained from his visitors gave him the confidence to start a business that would cater to wine enthusiasts who would typically pay $50 a bottle and up and who wanted to be part of the wine-making process. In 2004, he launched Crushpad as an online company that links vineyards with wine enthusiasts and cuts out the intermediaries. It provides customers with the opportunity to select a particular grape from a specific vineyard and have those grapes brought to Crushpad's 17,000-square-foot warehouse at the edge of the Mission District, where the grapes are then developed into a fine wine. The secret to his initial funding was his business model, which had customers fronting the cost of development by paying $6,000 to $9,000 to produce a barrel of wine (about 300 bottles) at a cost to customers that is about 40 to 50 percent of retail. Some customers grouped together via the Crushpad website to share the cost of a barrel. Customers who love working with the grapes under the guidance of professional winemakers can participate in the process and then either pick up the wine at the headquarters or have it shipped to them. Some of Brill's customers have looked at the experience as an apprenticeship that helped them make a decision about a career change. At least two of his customers have won gold medals in wine competitions, and many of the wines produced can be found in upscale restaurants in San Francisco. In February 2007, Brill succeeded in finalizing $3.5 million in debt and equity financing to double his production. As of 2010, Crushpad had more than 100 commerce clients, and more than 5,000 clients from 35 states and 8 countries making California wines.

In March 2010, Crushpad stunned the city of San Francisco by moving its winemaking operations to Napa Valley to establish a major presence on the Silverado Trail. This move gave commercial clients a tasting room, and larger clients access to larger ferment capabilities, which will reduce their costs. The company will maintain its warehouse and shipping operations in San Francisco. In 2009, Crushpad had opened additional operations in the Bordeaux region of France. Brill has not only succeeded in creating a successful entrepreneurial venture of his own, his business has spawned hundreds of boutique wine makers who are establishing their brands in the marketplace.

Sources: Quackenbush, J. (February 9, 2010). "Crushpad to Move to Napa Valley," *North Bay Business Journal*, www .northbaybusinessjournal.com/18269/crushpad-to-move-to-napa-valley; C. Rauber, "Crushpad Custom Winery Completes $3.5M Financing Round, Plans to

Expand," *San Francisco Business Times* (February 7, 2007), www.bizjournals.com/sanfrancisco; J.M. O'Brien, "In Vino Profitas," *Fortune* (December 22, 2006), p. 59; W. Reisman,

"Michael Brill: Virtual Winemaker Lets Vino Lovers Taste Their Dream," *The Examiner* (April 6, 2007), www.examiner.com; and Crushpad, www.crushpadwine.com.

Every business requires resources to start and grow. Resource gathering is one area where entrepreneurs demonstrate their unique capabilities to maximize the use of minimal resources, whether in the form of people, equipment, inventory, or cash. Up to this point, feasibility analysis has focused on testing the business model in the market to ensure that there are customers and sufficient demand, and on testing the product or service to gauge whether it can be produced at a cost that leaves room for overhead and profit. With a positive response from the market and a feasible product/service, it now becomes important to consider the financial conditions required for a successful launch and operation of the business to a positive cash flow generated through sales. No matter how many financial tools entrepreneurs use or how many complex analyses they construct, the bottom line for any new venture is cash. Income statements and balance sheets can make a company look good on paper—these are accounting tools—but cash pays the bills and enables the company to grow. A new venture's health is measured by its cash flow.

It makes no sense at the feasibility analysis stage to create a full set of pro forma financial statements. In the first place, because the business exists only on paper, there is no reliable way to forecast sales and expenses until the entrepreneur conducts proof of concept experiments in the market; therefore, any projections for sales and expenses will likely not approach reality. Nevertheless, entrepreneurs are still faced with having to paint a financial picture of their startup that is sufficiently supported by real data. They need this information so that they can achieve legitimacy in the eyes of investors, bankers, and others they will need to tap to make their business a success and, more importantly, to convince themselves that the venture has potential that can be achieved. Realistically, the only financing early stage companies without proof of concept are going to secure is seed capital from strategic investors who are not expecting to see detailed financial statements (and wouldn't believe them anyway), particularly when chances are the new venture is still in product development.

Second, investors will confirm that what is more important than the financial statements are the assumptions behind the numbers. For instance, how much money will it take for the company to support itself from its cash flows? And how long will that take? Generally speaking, investors focus on the first 18 months to 2 years of a startup because during that time, entrepreneurs are continually adjusting the business model as they respond to the market. The information they gain from this process will help them make decisions about how to grow the business from that point on. Third, absolutely no set of financial projections, no matter how elegant or detailed, survives first contact with customers. It's a simple fact that entrepreneurs do not control their customers' behaviors, and customers are fickle—they can change like chameleons based on new information. Therefore, at the feasibility stage, it is best to simply get a handle on whether this new business can make money (i.e., customers want what is being offered), whether overhead can be kept to a minimum for survival, and how long it will take for the company to be self sustaining. Once it has been determined that the business appears to be feasible, pro forma financials will be built as part of a business plan to support a pitch to investors, bankers, or other potential stakeholders. By then, the entrepreneur will have already launched the business and will have more real-life numbers to work with, so these financial statements will reflect how the financial side of the business will look after startup. It's important to keep in mind that at startup, the entrepreneur is testing and revising the business model to refine it based on customer feedback. Startup is an experimental stage, so focusing on a set of financial statements that portray numbers that are fluid is probably not very useful. Venture capitalist Steve Blank reminds entrepreneurs that they have to be actively involved not only in customer discovery but also in customer validation. This is too important a task to simply delegate to sales people.[1] Customer validation is the process of determining whether the business has a repeatable sales model: that is, can the entrepreneur demonstrate that multiple customers will buy the solution. The answer to this question will tell entrepreneurs when they can successfully execute the business model.

This chapter is structured to walk entrepreneurs through the process of determining the startup capital and other resource requirements to support the business model. It begins with looking at how the business will function at startup.

IDENTIFYING STARTUP RESOURCE REQUIREMENTS

Determining what resources are needed, when they are needed, and how to acquire them is a critical piece of the feasibility puzzle. Startup resources include (1) people, such as the founding team, employees, advisors, and independent contractors; (2) physical assets, such as equipment, inventory, and office or plant space; and (3) financial resources, such as cash, equity, and debt. At startup the goal is to create a mix of resources that will enable the new venture to start and operate until sales of the product or service produce a positive cash flow, that is, enough cash to cover all the cash outflows without investment capital.

One of the secrets to success in constructing this resource mix is to maintain flexibility by acquiring and owning only those resources that cannot be obtained by any other means because ownership reduces flexibility and mobility, two critical needs of a startup venture, and it increases startup capital requirements. A dynamic marketplace, coupled with the natural chaos inherent in startup ventures, requires that startups remain lean as long as possible so that their products, services, and strategies can be tested and modified quickly in response to customers' feedback. Consider the case of a software-as-service startup whose entrepreneur let his ego get the better of him. After signing a long-term lease on prime office space in an expensive section of Los Angeles, he expected potential customers to meet there, be impressed by his success, and decide to do business with him. Instead, he quickly discovered that his customers preferred that he meet them at their businesses or in restaurants, not in his office. Moreover, his software programmers did not require fancy offices; they preferred to work from home. As a result, this entrepreneur soon found himself saddled with expensive overhead that neither his customers nor his employees needed.

Bootstrapping is the term often applied to the minimizing of resources required to start and operate a business. It simply means that entrepreneurs beg, borrow, or lease resources whenever they can so they can keep their overhead, or fixed costs, as low as possible. A number of bootstrapping techniques will be discussed in Chapter 15 on funding a startup venture. New venture startup teams typically have no previous history, no track record with customers, and no evidence of performance, so their resource decision making is based solely on current information and advice from others.[2] Consequently, many new ventures fail because of poor decisions about resources and the management of those resources. To succeed, entrepreneurs must create innovative combinations of resources that will generate a competitive advantage and lead to the creation of wealth.[3] Research has also concluded that innovative entrepreneurial ventures require different types of resources than their small business counterparts, particularly due to their innovation and growth orientation.[4]

Figure 8.1 presents a plan for approaching the capital needs assessment for a new venture. The next sections will walk through those steps entrepreneurs need to take to have a clear picture of their resource needs.

Constructing a Business Process Map

Recall that resources can be divided into six categories: human, social, financial, physical, technological, and organizational. To identify accurately the resources required to start the venture, it's important to understand all the activities and

FIGURE 8.1   Steps in Calculating Startup Capital Requirements

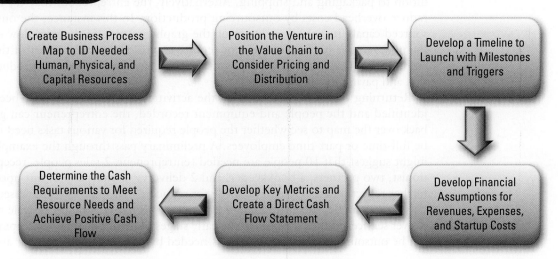

Create Business Process Map to ID Needed Human, Physical, and Capital Resources → Position the Venture in the Value Chain to Consider Pricing and Distribution → Develop a Timeline to Launch with Milestones and Triggers → Develop Financial Assumptions for Revenues, Expenses, and Startup Costs → Develop Key Metrics and Create a Direct Cash Flow Statement → Determine the Cash Requirements to Meet Resource Needs and Achieve Positive Cash Flow processes in the business—in other words, to know exactly how the business works. This is best accomplished by creating a process map that details how information flows through the business. Having such a map on hand makes it much easier to define the operations, information flow, and resource requirements of the business. To create a process map, take a virtual tour of the business during a single day, listing all the functions, people, equipment, supplies, and space required to run the business. Figuratively, begin at the front door of the business and ask the following questions:

1. Who does the work in this business?

2. Where do these people work?

3. What do they need to do the work (equipment, major supplies, space, etc.)?

4. What information is being generated (work orders, invoices, customer lists, etc.)?

5. Where does that information go?

Then begin making lists of tasks, equipment, and people needed to complete a particular process or activity. This information will be useful for figuring expenses for financial projections and for determining what kind of personnel will have to be hired to perform those tasks.

In a packaging solutions business, for example, what is the first thing a customer sees when he or she approaches the site? The sign for the business? A display window? When customers enter, is there a counter attended by someone who will answer their questions? What equipment does that person use to do his or her job? Note that without going beyond the customer's entry through the door of the business, a significant list of resources has already been amassed. The imaginary tour is one of the best ways to begin to detail the processes in the business. Figure 8.2 traces one such imaginary tour of a service business. Note that this process map also indicates outsourced functions that are another resource the company must pay for.

A product business may involve production and assembly processes in addition to packaging and shipping. Alternatively, the entrepreneur may try to reduce overhead costs by outsourcing production. In this instance, the outsourced capability could be shown on the graphic outside of the workflow of the new venture because it does not require any resources on the part of the entrepreneur beyond coordination with the company that is managing production and paying for their services.

Returning to Figure 8.2, once all the activities of the business have been identified and the people and equipment recorded, the entrepreneur can go back over the map to see whether the people required for various tasks need to be full-time or part-time employees. A preliminary pass through the example might suggest that 10 people are needed (entrepreneur, 2 sales people, receptionist, two partners, a bookkeeper, and 2 delivery/service people) but upon further reflection a case could be made for reducing that number to the essentials. For example, the entrepreneur and one of his partners might be able to deliver services to the customer in the early stages of the business. Bookkeeping can be outsourced on a part-time or as-needed basis and the entrepreneur and

FIGURE 8.2   A Virtual Tour of a Service Business

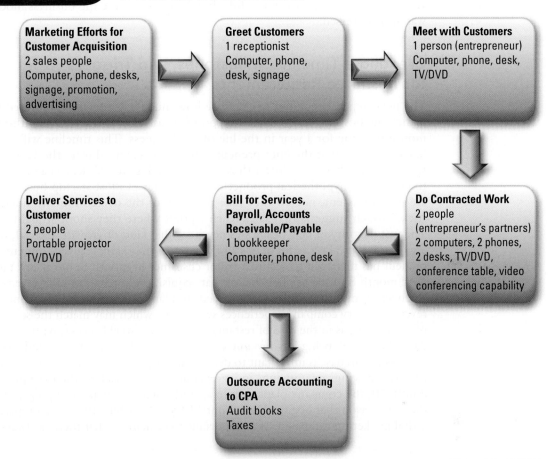

her partners can perform several of the other tasks to bring the total number of full-time employees down to four. Looking at the equipment required is also important. Capital expenditures, which are equipment expenses, can eat up a lot of startup capital, so it would make sense to consider whether any of this equipment could be leased.

Positioning the Venture in the Value Chain

Where the new venture lies in the value chain will determine what its margins are, who its customer is, and how much it can charge for its products and services—in short, what business the entrepreneur is in. In the case of a service business, the task is easy because services are delivered direct to the customer. But the case is much different with a product company. Where the company is positioned determines whether it is a manufacturer or producer, a wholesaler or distributor, or a retailer. Each position produces different margins, different ways of pricing, and different logistics requirements. The value chain was discussed more fully in Chapter 4, where the business model was also addressed.

Creating a Timeline, Milestones, and Triggers for Resource Requirements

The next step in preparing to calculate how much capital will be required to launch the business and operate to a positive cash flow is a typical month-by-month timeline for a year in the life of the business. This timeline will note key milestones that the entrepreneur expects to achieve during the year and trigger events that might affect those milestones. Figure 8.3 depicts a one-year timeline for a hypothetical product business. Sales of most startup businesses are not consistent, nor do they take the form of the overconfident "hockey stick," which suggests that sales reach a point where they shoot straight up. The vast majority of new businesses never see that kind of growth. Instead, the first year is typically a series of ups and downs. In the example given, this entrepreneur has managed to secure a major customer in month 5, but it will take until month 8 to see the benefits of that acquisition in terms of sales revenue. Then about month 9, the company needs to plan for a seasonal downswing of revenues. Every company experiences seasonality, which may match the seasons of the year or, as in the case of restaurants, may be a weekly event, with certain days of the week being low revenue days. Understanding the market and when customers purchase is important to determining when the company will experience downswings or upswings in its revenues. Going back to the example, in month 10, the company plans to hire an additional salesperson to prepare for the busy season that begins about month 12 and for which they have prepared a vital marketing campaign. It is important to remember that there is always a

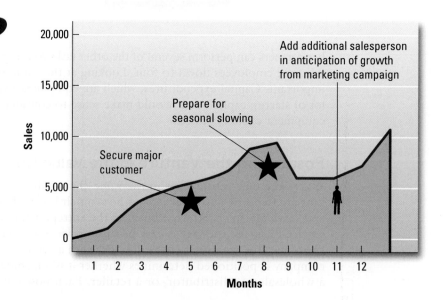

FIGURE 8.3

First Year Timeline, Milestones, and Triggers

lead time with respect to milestones. These lead times are known as triggers that indicate a change in the current revenue pattern. For example, the major customer was a trigger for an upswing in revenues.

Pricing for Feasibility Analysis

Pricing a product or service is as much a part of a marketing strategy as of the financial strategy. Unfortunately, entrepreneurs typically have to price their products and services long before they know the exact costs of producing the product and before they have a good handle on the price the customer will pay. Pricing is one of the many features associated with a product or service; it becomes the central selling point when the product or service is a commodity—that is, when the only feature differentiating the product or service from those offered by competitors is price. Some examples of commodities are basic food products, such as milk, and most electronics categories that have been in the market for some time, such as desktop computers and printers. Wherever there is competitive rivalry, prices will be driven down. Entrepreneurs can price new technology at a premium because it offers features and benefits not currently in the market, but technology quickly becomes a commodity as competitors introduce their versions, driving prices down.

Here we discuss pricing as it relates to the entrepreneur's attempt to calculate startup capital requirements. Pricing is addressed as part of the marketing mix in Chapter 14. How a product or service is priced is a function of a company's goals. If the goal is to *increase sales* or *market share*, prices may need to be lowered to raise the volume sold. If the goal is to *maximize cash flow*, raising prices and reducing direct costs and overhead may be the answer. *Maximizing profit* can be accomplished by raising prices, lowering prices and increasing volume, or decreasing overhead. If the goal is to *define an image*, setting a higher price based on higher perceived and/or actual quality is one way of establishing a particular image in a market. To *control demand* when a company doesn't have the resources to meet it may mean temporarily setting prices at a level that discourages sales to a particular degree. This approach also enables the company to recuperate its initial development costs through higher margins.

The Internet and search engines like Google have had a major impact on companies' pricing models because it is easy for customers to compare pricing across all competitors. Simple products, those whose price is transparent, or easily identified, are most subject to downward pricing pressure. Complex products (those that are bundled or modular) are more difficult to compare directly across companies, so they typically command a higher price.[5] An example is cell phone rates when they include a fixed monthly fee and a per-minute charge for options.

Customer goals also influence entrepreneurs' pricing strategies. Figure 8.4 depicts two scenarios for an entrepreneur who is offering a customer management software solution. In the first scenario, Customer A's goal is to keep operational costs low because their margins are thin. This type of customer focuses on price and makes purchasing decisions accordingly; consequently, the entrepreneur's margins will be small. This is a typical commodity situation. By

FIGURE 8.4

Customer Goals
and Price

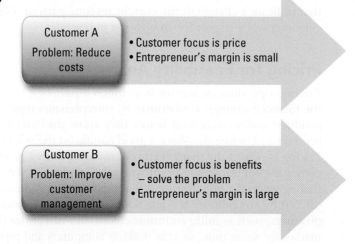

contrast, the second scenario depicts a customer whose goal is to improve the way the company manages its customers; in other words, this customer has a real problem that the entrepreneur can solve, so the entrepreneur's margins can be greater because a higher price can be charged. Entrepreneurs must decide which customer to target first so their company can enter the market and survive until it has a chance to grow. To accomplish that, it makes sense to target the customer who is in the most pain—who has a problem that the entrepreneur's product or service can solve. In this way, the entrepreneur can charge a premium and recoup development costs before competition enters the market and causes prices to decline.

There is a lot of evidence that customers will pay more for perceived superior benefits. Look no further than private labeled consumer products where the private label is always cheaper than the branded label for the same product; yet, customers are willing to pay more for the perceived benefit of getting a branded product.

Knowing what a pricing strategy is supposed to accomplish in advance of setting a price will ensure compatibility with company goals, both the entrepreneur's company and the customer's company. Table 8.1 presents the most common pricing strategies. For entrepreneurs, a combination of cost-based pricing and demand-based pricing with consideration for a premium based on the novelty of what is being offered can work well. For new products or services with no direct comparison, this approach is often used to arrive at a satisfactory price. In general, customers recognize several prices for any one product: the standard price, which is the price normally paid for the item; the sale price; the price paid for specials; and the relative price, which is the price of the item compared to the price of a substitute product. For some products, customers may have to add the normal cost of shipping, handling, or installation to their comparison with other like products.

TABLE 8.1	Premium Pricing	Uses a high price to reflect a unique product/service and a significant competitive advantage.
Common Pricing Strategies at Startup	Price Skimming	Starts with a high price to capture uniqueness and competitive advantage. Then as new competitors enter the market, drops the price to stay ahead of competition.
	Demand-based Pricing	Find out what customers are willing to pay for the product and price it accordingly.
	Captive Product Pricing	Where the entrepreneur's product has complements, charge a low price for source product (i.e., a printer) and a premium for consumables (i.e., ink cartridges).
	Psychological Pricing	To create a complex pricing structure by combining multiple products and services into one package.
	Product Bundle Pricing	In a channel with many intermediaries (distributors, retailers), the final price to the consumer or end-user must be tolerable, given all the markups along the value chain. Compare what the market will bear with the cost of getting a product to market.
	Geographical Pricing	Used where there are price variations in different geographical locations where the product is sold.

One mistake many entrepreneurs make is to set their prices so that they cover total costs plus a margin the entrepreneur is expecting to achieve. The problem with this approach is that pricing is not designed to cover *total* costs but "to maximize total contribution (i.e., unit price minus unit variable costs)."[6] What this means is that fixed costs (overhead) should not be apportioned within the price because these costs do not come into play when generating additional sales. It is the contribution margin that affects profitability. For example,

Unit price = $49.95

Variable costs (material costs, direct and indirect labor, factory overhead) = $35

Contribution margin = $49.95 − $35.00 = $14.95 or 30% of unit price

The contribution margin represents the amount available to pay for fixed costs and provide a profit to the business.

Entrepreneurs need to be aware that every industry has discounts associated with its various products and services. These include such things as cash and quantity discounts. Entrepreneurs should factor these discounts into their pricing models and into their cash needs for the business.

Converging on a Price

There are no formulas that will give a new venture with no track record a solution to the problem of pricing. Furthermore, getting answers from industry will not be an easy task; most companies do not want to talk about pricing because it is the cornerstone of their competitive strategy.[7] However, given the considerations discussed previously and triangulating by taking into account (1) costs, (2) any competitor pricing, and (3) feedback from customers and value chain partners, entrepreneurs can reach a number that can be tested in the market. The importance of understanding customer behavior cannot be stressed enough. If, for example, a product is complex and it is difficult for customers to judge quality, they will rely on price as a proxy for quality and therefore choose the higher-priced item. On the other hand, if the product bears a known brand, they might be willing to purchase the lower-priced item.

STARTUP FINANCIAL METRICS

The financial metrics that entrepreneurs employ at startup are very different from the metrics that established companies use to monitor their progress toward whatever goals they've set. Startup financial metrics must give entrepreneurs feedback on whether their business model is working and whether it's the business model the startup should keep as it grows. Some of the metrics that speak to the creation and capture of value are:

- **Customer acquisition costs (CAC).** In real dollars, how much did it cost the startup to acquire a customer? In figuring CAC, entrepreneurs must convert time to dollars, but the time it takes to secure a customer is time that could have been spent elsewhere, so there's an opportunity cost. Advertising expenses and promotional expenses must also be factored in as well as travel, food, trade shows, conferences, and so forth. Depending on the type of business, the CAC will be different, but there will always be a cost associated with securing customers.

- **Average order size, time to reorder, lifetime value per customer.** This entails tracking what each customer spends, how often they spend, and based on that data, projecting what the potential lifetime value of that customer is. At startup, with no customers, this metric will be based on market research with similar companies and be discounted to reflect the startup's inexperience in the market.

- **Revenues per salesperson and time to revenue for direct sales.** Entrepreneurs with businesses that sell directly to their customers may employ salespeople. The critical mistake that most entrepreneurs make is not factoring in the amount of time it takes for a new salesperson to get up to speed and begin generating revenue that exceeds their costs and their portion of the contribution margin or overhead. A salesperson selling a better, faster, cheaper type product or service will ramp up to revenue fairly quickly, but a salesperson who is selling something brand new or is developing new customer relationships is going to have a much longer ramp up period.

- **For Web 2.0 ventures: acquisition, retention, revenue, viral coefficient.** Internet ventures have unique metrics because they typically start with three types of "customers": (1) visitors or end users, (2) contributors, and (3) distributors, or people who share with or refer content to others helping to drive traffic to the site. Today many Internet ventures suffer from some of the same flaws in thinking that plagued the dotcom ventures. Much like

Munjal Shah, founder of Riya, a visual search photo service, they think that if they can get coverage by TechCrunch and benefit from a crush of users as a result, their site will go viral—that is, take on a life of its own. Shah succeeded in getting the TechCrunch effect from the blogging community, but his company's servers weren't prepared for the onslaught of users uploading photos to his site. Consequently, the user experience was unsatisfactory, and the initial benefit was lost. Ultimately, the company shut down.[8] This example speaks to the importance of understanding the viral coefficient, which is a measure of how many new users come to the site on referrals by existing users. It's used to track site growth, popularity, and level of engagement by users. As a formula, it is simply

Viral Coefficient = X (invited friends) * Y % (acceptance or conversion rate)

Practically speaking, if the coefficient is greater than 1.0, the site is growing, meaning that each user is bringing in at least one more user; if it's 1, the site is stagnant; and if it's less than 1, growth is slowing. The viral coefficient is simply one metric and it is hampered by the fact that it doesn't incorporate cycle time into the equation. Cycle time affects growth for more than the viral coefficient. The shorter the cycle time (visitor sees the application, tries it, invites friends, friends try application) the more dramatic the growth. Chapter 14 goes into tactics for decreasing viral cycle time. Table 8.2 presents some Internet metrics in each of the categories of visitor, contributor, and distributor.

- **Contribution Margin**. This figure, expressed as a percentage, is found by subtracting variable costs from revenues and dividing the difference by revenues to yield a percentage. That percentage expresses how much money remains to pay overhead and make a profit after the costs of producing the product are considered. This figure is important because it tells entrepreneurs how much room they have to make errors. If the contribution margin is very small, say 5 percent, there is very little room for error and the entrepreneur will need to plan for volume sales to generate enough money to cover overhead and make a profit.

TABLE 8.2	Metrics for Web 2.0 Ventures		
	Visitor	**Contributor**	**Distributor**
	Total unique visitors Total page views Total visits		Shares content with others
Acquisition (Registrations and activations)	Watch a video	Submit a video or other content	Shares a video with other users and other sites
Retention	Visit once a week for 3 months	Submits content once a month	Shares video that drives X visits a month for 3 months
Revenue	Click on an ad (qualified lead)	Pays for subscription or premium membership	Drives X number of premium users

■ **Monthly Burn Rate**. This figure represents how the startup uses its cash to cover its overhead before it generates a positive cash flow from operations. Burn rate signals to investors whether the company can sustain itself and how quickly it will need another infusion of capital.

DEVELOP FINANCIAL ASSUMPTIONS

With a good handle on how their business works and what specific resources are needed and when, entrepreneurs can attach some numbers to the timeline. To accomplish this, narrative assumptions about the numbers for demand, revenues, expenses, and startup costs must be developed.

One of the biggest problems that many entrepreneurs have when trying to present a case for the financial feasibility of their business models is that they can't justify the numbers they have put into their projections. Unfortunately, the business education courses they may have taken typically haven't prepared them to do this. Although they are wizards at creating spreadsheets with all sorts of what-if scenarios, they are rarely asked to explain where they found the actual numbers they entered into those spreadsheets. When asked, the response is typically "Well, I did best-case, worst-case, and most-likely-case scenarios and took the average." It is not likely that an investor or banker would accept that explanation.

The most important part of any analysis of financial feasibility is the assumptions on which the analysis is based. Every line item in the cash flow statement should be explained. Here is an example of how one entrepreneur explained customer acquisition costs.

Customer Acquisition Costs—The company will sell via a direct sales model, which requires regular client contact. In addition, the product plan calls for launching both the core product and the ancillaries at well-attended industry conferences to maximize the value of the presentations.

1. Customer site visits: 3–4 trips per month beginning Jul 07 @ $800 each
2. Booth price for Gartner-sponsored data mining conference: $3,000
3. Travel to/from conference for two attendees: 3 conferences, 2 people @ $2.2K each[9]

The narrative assumptions play a vital role in helping to explain the entrepreneur's rationale and establish his or her credibility. Therefore, the first step is to find good numbers and then justify them.

Estimate New Product/Service Demand

One of the most difficult tasks facing any entrepreneur is estimating the demand for a new product or service, particularly if that product or service has never existed previously in the marketplace. Much of this difficulty is due to a lack of historical data and to issues of seasonality and price discounts. Because entrepreneurs often overestimate the level of sales they will achieve in the early stages of the company, it is important to triangulate demand from at least three different points of view: (1) historical analogy with similar products/services;

(2) customer feedback, end-user and intermediary feedback; and (3) the entrepreneur's own perspective, gleaned from previous experience and from going into limited production or doing a test market. Calculating total demand is only part of the challenge, because every product or service is subject to adoption patterns and rates. Total demand is never achieved all at once but rather accumulates over time. Understanding the adoption patterns of similar products or services will be critical to forecasting sales revenues over the first couple years. Adoption patterns are discussed in Chapter 14.

Use Historical Analogy or Substitute Products

If the new product is an extension of a previously existing product, it may be possible to extrapolate from the existing product's adoption rate and demand to the new product. For example, the demand and adoption rate for compact disks was derived from the historical demand for cassette tapes and records. The adoption patterns did not match exactly but they certainly landed the entrepreneur in the ballpark. In other cases, it may be possible to turn to another product in the same industry for an indication of demand potential and the rate at which customers will purchase, assuming that the target markets are the same.

Talk to Customers

When attempting to gauge levels of demand, the customer is certainly the prime source of information, but many entrepreneurs fail to ask the right questions so that customers will give them honest answers. Asking "would you buy this product?" or "how much would you pay for this product?" is going about it the wrong way. This approach will overestimate the level of demand because customers have no reason to say no—no one is asking them to write a check, so they have nothing to lose by saying "yes." A better approach is to gauge demand from the customers' responses to the entrepreneur's solution to their problem. In other words, presenting potential customers with a solution in the form of a product or service and then monitoring the feedback and response to it will give the entrepreneur an honest estimate of whether this customer would purchase or not.

For example, suppose that 7 out of 10 potential customers respond positively to the entrepreneur's product. Given that these responses might be optimistic, the entrepreneur should consider reducing the ratio. The amount of reduction is purely arbitrary and is based on how confident the entrepreneur is in the responses received from research with the customer. Suppose the entrepreneur decides to reduce the estimate of demand to 6 out of 10, or 60 percent. Applying this percentage to the size of the niche market that the entrepreneur intends to enter can give a rough estimate of how many total customers might purchase. Then comparing these results with feedback from value chain partners might confirm the numbers or cause the entrepreneur to modify the estimate. Results of research on adoption patterns for similar products or services would then be applied to determine sales on a month-by-month basis. Of course it will also be important to factor in how quickly the entrepreneur can produce certain quantities of product or provide a particular service.

Interview Prospective End-Users and Intermediaries

No one knows the market better than the men and women who work in it every day. They are typically very astute at predicting trends and patterns of buyer behavior. Spending time in the field talking with intermediaries (distributors or wholesalers, sometimes referred to as "middlemen"), retailers, and the like can provide a fairly good estimate of demand or at least a range that would validate what the entrepreneur found when talking with customers. With a consumer product, observing the buying patterns of consumers for a similar product could be useful.

Use the Entrepreneur's Knowledge and Experience

The knowledge and experience an entrepreneur brings to the business will be helpful in forecasting sales, particularly if the entrepreneur has worked in the industry in which the business will be operating. However, it is important to remember that the entrepreneur's experience is anecdotal and should always be confirmed by other sources.

Go into Limited Production

The best way, and sometimes the only way, to accurately gauge customer demand is to go into business in a limited way—produce a small number of products and get them into the hands of people to use. If the business is an Internet business, put up a limited website to get feedback. Going into limited production is also an appropriate next step if the other two techniques have produced positive results. Limited testing of a product will not only gauge customer satisfaction in a very real way, but it may also suggest possible modifications to improve the product. This technique also works for service businesses and is excellent for testing procedures and for gauging the actual time it takes to provide a service, something that is difficult to do when the entrepreneur is not working with an actual customer.

Estimate Revenues, Expenses, and Startup Costs

Estimating revenues, expenses, and startup costs at the feasibility stage is a daunting task at best for entrepreneurs. At the nascent stage everything is fluid, so many of the numbers collected may change after the business is launched and factors entrepreneurs didn't consider come into play. There are many reasons why feasibility estimates of sales, expenses, and startup costs will probably change by the time the business plan is written.

1. If the entrepreneur's business is manufacturing or outsourcing to a manufacturer, it will be nearly impossible to estimate parts and manufacturing costs accurately without a production-quality product in place. For this reason, it is important to get to a physical prototype early, so as to have a better idea of the parts, components, and types of materials that will be needed, as well as what provision to make for labor.

2. For many new product companies, product development may take several months to several years, depending on the nature of the product—and the costs for prototyping are always substantially higher than the ultimate

GLOBAL INSIGHTS

Informal Investment Is Not a Global Phenomenon Yet

Informal investment (founders, friends, family, and risk-taking strangers) is a common phenomenon in the U.S. In fact, from the smallest mom-and-pop businesses to fast-growing, global companies like Google, all were funded initially by informal investment. The same is not true in the rest of the world where it is relatively rare by comparison. The *Global Entrepreneurship Monitor, 2009 Executive Report* details the prevalence of informal investment in 2009 among the adult population in 54 nations. In general, the majority of the 54 countries experienced less than 4 percent of the adult population serving as informal investors in new ventures. However, there are some signs that this pattern may be changing. Among the G7 nations, France and the United States exhibited the highest prevalence with just under 4 percent, which means that less than 4 percent of the population had invested in new ventures over the previous 3 years. This was down from the previous report. China had a higher rate of 6 percent, while Russia and Brazil were at 1 percent. The big surprise was an 18.6 percent prevalence rate in Uganda, which put that country at the top of the list.

Source: Bosma, N. and Levie, J. (2009). *Global Entrepreneurship Monitor, 2009 Executive Report*, www.gemconsortium .org/about.aspx?page=pub_gem_global_reports.

production costs will be. Therefore, it is difficult to determine true feasibility from an economic perspective before there is a physical prototype.

3. For service companies, the actual costs to deliver a service must be based initially on information gathered from other companies in the industry. This is tricky to achieve without "inside information"—that is, without knowing someone who works in that type of company. Estimates for the cost of delivery of the service will be more accurate if the service is prototyped under a variety of the most common scenarios. For example, a restaurant owner might want to calculate how long it takes to completely serve a customer, from arrival to departure. The owner needs to look at the number of tables planned, hours of operation, and the number of servers and cooks needed. Peak and slow periods and other aspects of serving customers are also factored in. The more variables that can be accounted for, the better the estimates will be.

4. As entrepreneurs grow in knowledge of their industry, they naturally gather better information because they know whom to talk with and where to find the best industry intelligence. Because getting inside an industry is difficult and time-consuming, many entrepreneurs choose to start ventures in industries with which they're familiar or in which they have experience.

Sales Forecast

The sales forecast should be calculated first because the volume of sales affects many business expenditures. Using the timeline, milestones, and triggers developed previously, and the demand and adoption rate estimates, the sales revenues can be laid out. An example of a forecast can be found in Figure 8.5 in the next section. In this example of a mobile peer-to-peer payment company, the 7,500 users per financial institution is an industry average number for online banking and bill pay usage for a bank with more than 12,000 total customers.[10] It is necessary to remember that any increase in sales will be influenced by the following factors:

- Growth rates in the market segment of the product or service
- The innovations offered that will make the product/service more attractive to the consumer, even at a higher price
- The technological innovations employed that enable the entrepreneur to produce the product or service at a lower cost than competitors, thus making it more accessible and enticing to the consumer

Expenses

Once sales have been forecast, predicting some expenditures becomes much easier, particularly for those expenditures that vary with the volume of sales, such as the direct costs of producing the product or service. In wholesale businesses, for example, after the sales forecast has been determined, the figures for inventory purchases can be applied as a percentage of sales and forecast from that. Therefore, if inventory cost is 25 percent of sales, one can apply that percentage to sales as they increase to forecast increases in the volume of inventory. Be aware, however, that in some industries, volume discounts on raw materials or inventory may actually reduce costs over time and should be factored into the expenditure forecast. Whether volume discounts will be available is an important piece of information that is gathered during field research.

In manufacturing businesses, forecasting expenditures is a bit more complex because cost of goods sold (COGS) must be derived first. COGS consists of direct labor, cost of materials, and direct factory overhead. Applying COGS as a percentage of sales will probably suffice for purposes of pro forma statements for the feasibility stage. Month-by-month analysis of outcomes and use of a cost accounting model that considers raw materials inventory, work-in-process inventory, finished-goods inventory, total inventory, factory overhead, work-in-process flow in units, and weighted-average cost per unit will give a more accurate estimate as the business grows.

In service businesses, the COGS is equivalent to the time expended to produce and deliver the service. The rate at which the service is billed, say $100 an hour, comprises the actual expenses incurred in providing the service, a contribution to overhead, and a reasonable profit. The actual expenses incurred are equivalent to the cost of goods sold.

The aggregate of all direct and indirect selling expenses and all general and administrative expenses is called SG&A (sales, general, and administrative expenses). To make the financial statements clearer and more concise, one can use only the totals of SG&A expenses for each month in the financial statements, with a footnote directing the reader to the SG&A breakout statement. Direct selling expenses, which include advertising costs, travel expenses, sales salaries, commissions, and the cost of promotional supplies; and indirect selling expenses, which are not linked to the sale of a specific product, but rather are proportionally distributed to all products sold during a particular period of time (telephone, interest, and postal charges), can be handled in the same manner, in a breakout statement, with only totals appearing in the financial statements. General and administrative expenses will include the salaries of nonsales person- nel and overhead such as rent, utilities, and equipment expenses.

Startup Costs

The bulk of expenses in the first year of a new business are probably incurred prior to the business opening its doors for the first time. The costs of purchas- ing furniture, equipment, startup inventory, and supplies can quickly add up to a substantial amount—and that doesn't include deposits for leases and utilities. A manufacturing startup might also include product development costs, a deposit on the lease for a plant, and raw materials costs. Startups with new products typically accrue heavy pre–startup development costs that include engineering, programming, prototyping, and patent assessment and application. These are one-time expenses to get the business started. In addition, entrepre- neurs must remember that employees may need training before the business opens, so that becomes part of the startup costs as well.

Keeping the Numbers Real

It's important for entrepreneurs to keep in mind that all of the numbers they come up with in their forecasts will be challenged and they must be prepared to defend them. It's difficult to do that if the number was simply pulled out of the air. "We assumed…" will not justify a number. There is a 100 percent chance that the numbers from the feasibility analysis will be wrong, but effort should be put into getting as close to the right number as possible. The founders of Redfin, an online real estate broker, shared their startup numbers against their numbers two years later and the difference was telling. Table 8.3 presents a summary of some of their expenses. It is instructive to note that many numbers worked in favor of the startup. This was due to the fact that the founders, while building their financial model, assumed the worst case scenario each month. Their goal was to outperform

TABLE 8.3 Redfin: How Startup Expense Estimates Change	Type of Expense	Redfin's Model	Actual Expenditures
	Rent per employee per month	$250	$336
	Initial per-employee equipment cost	$6,500	$5,700
	Annual payroll tax	12.5%	8.5%
	Monthly travel costs	$300	$369
	Monthly telephone costs per field employee	$125	$261
	Annual accounting costs	$45,000	$32,912

Source: Kelman, G. (October 1, 2007). "Financial Models for Underachievers: Two Years of the Real Numbers of a Startup," *How to Change the World*, http://blog.guykawasaki.com/2007/10/financial-model.html#axzz0uM3rRMgX.

their estimates, and in most cases they did. Founder Glenn Kelman had seen too many cases of venture funded Internet businesses that had burned through their money because they hadn't correctly or conservatively estimated their expenses.

Entrepreneurs need to remember that employee costs are the biggest costs the business will bear, so it's vital to track the number of employees needed and all costs associated with that employee and to keep in mind that employee costs go up every year.

Finally, it's important for entrepreneurs to compare their estimates to what other similar companies in the industry spend. It's not easy to get private company figures, but even public company numbers at least provide a sense of the upper limit of possibility. No startup is going to achieve anything close to the numbers for a public company, so those numbers are an important reality check.

CALCULATING A STARTUP'S CASH REQUIREMENTS

Developing the cash flow statement is the first step in arriving at startup cash requirements. For feasibility purposes a direct cash flow statement, essentially a cash budget or sources and uses statement, is used so that cash inflows and outflows are easy to identify and examine. Figure 8.5 displays a direct cash flow statement (also known as sources and uses) through month 14 for a mobile payment product company. The entrepreneur would support these numbers with narrative assumptions to explain how the figures were derived. The first section of the statement displays key milestones for the first 14 months of the business that will affect sales forecasts and expenses. The next section is cash inflows, which records all the inflows of cash into the business *when they are received*. Therefore, if a sale is made in March, for example, but payment is not received until April, the sale is counted in April on the cash flow statement because that's when it was received. Note that the income statement (discussed in Chapter 9) differs from the cash flow statement in this regard. Income is recorded when the transaction accrues, which may not be when the money is received, resulting in a receivable on the income statement.

The next section records cash outflows or disbursements. These are the expenses of the business and they are recorded when the company actually pays the bill. The final section of the cash flow statement provides crucial information about the net change in cash flow—in other words, whether the business had a positive or a negative cash flow in that month. Note that in each month, the net cash flow reflects only the cash inflows and outflows for that month, assuming no startup capital. Recall that the goal is to figure out how much startup capital is required. In the example in Figure 8.5, an additional line, the net cumulative cash flow, provides a critical piece of the cash needs requirements, which is the highest cumulative negative cash flow number. This figure ($564,374, which occurs in month 14), plus startup costs, is the minimum amount the entrepreneur needs to survive until a positive cash flow is generated from sales, which for this company occurs in month 18, supposing no investment capital.

Because this figure is an estimate based on a whole series of estimates, there is a very good chance that it is not entirely accurate, so entrepreneurs typically

FIGURE 8.5 Sample Direct Cash Flow Statement for Mobile Payment Product Company

Milestones	Mo. 1	2	3	4	5	6	7	8	9	10	11	12	13	14
New Financial Institutions (FI) on System	0	0	0	0	0	1	0	0	1	1	0	1	1	0
Cumulative Financial Institutions	0	0	0	0	0	1	1	1	2	3	3	4	5	5
Consumer Transactions	500	575	656	747	852	971	1,107	1,262	1,439	1,640	1,870	2,132	2,430	2,770
Salaried FTE	2	2	2	2	2	2	2	2	2	3	3	3	4	4
Lease Office Space	0	0	0	0	0	0	0	0	0	0	0	0	1	1
Cash Inflows	**Mo. 1**	**2**	**3**	**4**	**5**	**6**	**7**	**8**	**9**	**10**	**11**	**12**	**13**	**14**
Financial Institution (FI) Revenue														
FI Users (Net 30)	0	0	0	0	0	0	7,500	7,500	15,000	15,000	22,500	22,500	30,000	37,500
FI User Churn	0	0	0	0	0	0	0	0	−75	−75	−150	−150	−225	−225
Integration Fees (Net 30)	0	0	0	0	0	40,000	0	40,000	0	40,000	0	40,000	40,000	0
Total FI Revenue	0	0	0	0	0	40,000	7,500	47,500	14,925	54,925	22,350	62,350	69,775	37,275
Consumer Revenue Transactions (Net 30)	0	100	115	131	149	170	194	221	252	288	328	374	426	486
Total Consumer Revenue	0	100	115	131	149	170	194	221	252	288	328	374	426	486
Total Cash Inflows	**0**	**100**	**115**	**131**	**149**	**40,170**	**7,694**	**47,721**	**15,177**	**55,213**	**22,678**	**62,724**	**70,201**	**37,761**
Cash Outflows	**Mo. 1**	**2**	**3**	**4**	**5**	**6**	**7**	**8**	**9**	**10**	**11**	**12**	**13**	**14**
Fixed Costs														
Capex Equipment	50,000													
Salaries	10,000	10,000	10,000	10,000	10,000	10,000	10,000	10,000	10,000	15,000	15,000	15,000	20,000	20,000
Commissions	0	0	0	0	0	4,000	750	4,750	1,493	5,493	2,235	6,235	6,978	3,728
FTE Workstations	5,000	0	0	0	0	0	0	0	0	2,500	0	0	2,500	0
R&D Costs	250,000	0	0	0	0	0	0	0	0	0	0	0	100,000	0

(continued)

209

FIGURE 8.5 Sample Direct Cash Flow Statement for Mobile Payment Product Company (continued)

Cash Outflows		Mo. 1	2	3	4	5	6	7	8	9	10	11	12	13	14
	Office Space w/ Utilities	0	0	0	0	0	0	0	0	0	0	0	0	5,000	5,000
	Office Equipment	500	500	500	500	500	500	500	500	500	500	500	500	750	750
	Advertising	750	750	750	750	750	750	750	750	750	750	750	750	1,000	1,000
	Travel & Entertainment	1,000	1,000	1,000	1,000	1,000	1,000	2,000	2,000	2,000	2,000	2,000	2,000	2,000	2,000
	Accounting	1,000	1,000	1,000	1,000	1,000	1,000	1,000	1,000	1,000	1,000	1,000	1,000	1,000	1,000
	Legal	1,500	1,500	1,500	1,500	1,500	1,500	1,500	1,500	1,500	1,500	1,500	1,500	1,500	1,500
	Insurance	1,000	1,000	1,000	1,000	1,000	1,000	1,000	1,000	1,000	1,000	1,000	1,000	1,000	1,000
	FTE Load	3,500	3,500	3,500	3,500	3,500	3,500	3,500	3,500	3,500	5,250	5,250	5,250	7,000	7,000
Total Fixed Costs		324,250	19,250	19,250	19,250	19,250	23,250	21,000	25,000	21,743	34,993	29,235	33,235	148,728	42,978
Variable Costs	Server Lease	1,200	1,200	1,200	1,200	1,200	2,700	2,700	4,200	4,200	5,700	5,700	7,200	8,700	8,700
	Transportation	1,500	1,500	1,500	1,500	1,500	3,000	3,000	4,500	4,500	6,000	6,000	7,500	9,000	9,000
	Installation Costs	500	500	500	500	500	1,000	500	1,000	500	1,000	500	1,000	1,000	500
	Cell Phones	500	500	500	500	500	500	500	500	500	750	750	750	1,000	1,000
	Internet	500	500	500	500	500	500	500	500	500	750	750	750	1,000	1,000
Total Variable Costs		4,200	4,200	4,200	4,200	4,200	7,700	7,200	10,700	10,200	14,200	13,700	17,200	20,700	20,200
Total Cash Outflows		328,450	23,450	23,450	23,450	23,450	30,950	28,200	35,700	31,943	49,193	42,935	50,435	169,428	63,178
Net Cash In/Outflow		−328,450	−23,350	−23,335	−23,319	−23,301	9,220	−20,506	12,021	−16,765	6,020	−20,257	12,289	−99,226	−25,416
Cumulative Cash Flow		−328,450	−351,800	−375,135	−398,454	−421,754	−412,534	−433,040	−421,018	−437,783	−431,763	−452,020	−439,731	−538,957	−564,374

add a safety margin or contingency factor. The safety margin is an amount of cash that is often based on the sales and collection cycle of the business. If, for example, customers typically pay on a 60-day cycle, it will be important to be able to cover at least 60 days of fixed costs. The business used in this example is typical of most startup businesses in that it takes time to generate enough sales and other sources of cash to cover the costs of doing business, but it is important to calculate how much money is needed to start and operate the business to a positive cash flow, meaning the business is self sustaining, so that the entrepreneur can make a wise assessment of how much capital to raise.

Table 8.4 presents a breakout of the startup capital requirements for the mobile payment company. Note that the cash needs are separated into types of capital resources that will be required: capital expenditures, startup expenses, working capital, and a safety margin, which is a contingency amount based on the probability that the entrepreneur's estimates might be off (a fairly safe assumption). Breaking out the total funding requirements by types of capital helps an entrepreneur make decisions that might bring down the cost of starting the business. For example, it appears that this entrepreneur

TABLE 8.4			
Sample Cash Needs Table for the Mobile Payment Company	**Capital Expenditures (CE)**		
	Equipment	50,000	
	Pre-Operating Startup Costs (POSU)		
	R&D Costs	250,000	
	Salaries	10,000	
	FTE Workstations	5,000	
	Office Equipment	500	
	Advertising	750	
	Travel & Entertainment	1,000	
	Accounting	1,000	
	Legal	1,000	
	Insurance	1,000	
	FTE Load	3,500	
	Server Lease	1,200	
	Transportation	1,500	
	Installation Costs	500	
	Cell Phones	500	
	Internet	500	
	Total Pre-Op SU	277,950	
	Working Capital (WC)		
	Working Capital Needs	236,424	Difference between highest cumulative negative CF and CAPEX + Pre-Op SU
	Highest Cumulative Negative CF	564,374	
	Safety Factor (SF)		
	Safety Factor	77,000	120 days of fixed expenses
	Total Startup Capital	641,374	

requires a $50,000 piece of equipment. That is a significant expenditure at startup; the entrepreneur might want to investigate whether leasing the equipment might make sense. From this capital requirements analysis, it is clear that the entrepreneur will need a minimum of $641,374, including the safety margin, to start and operate this business until it generates a positive cash flow in month 18.

Assessing Risk

Many entrepreneurs make the mistake of thinking they have done a complete analysis of their startup financial requirements because they have generated pages of spreadsheets with numbers that, on the surface, appear to work. And if they have developed assumptions that justify their numbers, it is not irrational on their part to believe their work is done. But this would be a mistake. The true test of financial feasibility is whether the key financial figures are in line with the company's goals and are achievable. What would be the effect on the financials of a change in price, a decline in sales, or unexpected demand? What would be the effect on cash flow if the company grew at a more rapid pace than the predicted percentage a year? What if it grew more slowly? How sensitive to change are the cash flow numbers? And how will the company deal with these changes? Creating scenarios to consider the impact of these kinds of changes is called sensitivity analysis.

At the feasibility stage, it is important to consider the potential changes to the forecasts with the highest probability of occurrence and to factor in how the impact of these changes will be dealt with. Analyzing the financial risks and benefits of a new venture is a difficult and challenging exercise, but it must be done so that two fundamental questions can be answered: (1) Do the startup capital requirements make sense? In other words, is the business financially feasible? and (2) looking at the capital investment and the profit possibilities, is there enough money in this opportunity to make the effort worthwhile?

Unfortunately, many businesses are financially feasible—they can make a profit—but the return on the initial investment is so low that an entrepreneur would be better off putting that investment into real estate or some other vehicle. New businesses take an extraordinary amount of work, which entrepreneurs often fail to put a value on. All too often, the business is running and making a profit, but the entrepreneur is making less than he or she would have made working for someone else. The feasibility stage, when the investment has still been minimal, is the time to look seriously at financial feasibility and quantify the risks and potential benefits. Once the venture has been deemed feasible in all respects, a business plan with a full set of financial statements can be developed. That process will further reduce the uncertainty inherent in the startup process.

Figuring out how much money will be needed to launch and operate a new venture can be a daunting task for any entrepreneur, even one with a finance background, because there are so many unknowns and unknowables. Startup finances are based on best-guess projections for what the future might look like. That is why the entrepreneur's assumptions are so important; they serve to justify the numbers and provide a rationale for the thought process the entrepreneur followed to reach those numbers. A well-conceived financial plan will go a long way toward ensuring that the business is started with the appropriate amount of capital and for the right reasons.

New Venture Action Plan

- Determine the startup metrics for your company.
- Gather the numbers you need for performing your financial analysis.
- Gather sales forecast data through triangulation.
- Create a cash flow statement from startup until a positive cash flow is achieved.
- Perform a cash requirements assessment to determine how much capital you will need to start the business.
- Determine whether this venture is financially feasible.

Questions on Key Issues

1. Describe the typical metrics for a startup business.
2. What are the types of resources that entrepreneurs need to gather to start a new venture?
3. Why is the cash flow statement the most important statement for the entrepreneur?
4. What are some ways to forecast sales effectively for a retail business? For a manufacturer? For a service business?
5. What are the three categories of funds in the cash needs assessment, and how are they used to calculate how much money is needed to start the business?

Experiencing Entrepreneurship

1. Interview a banker and an investor about the key financial statements that entrepreneurs need to understand to launch their businesses. Ask about the biggest mistakes business owners make in preparing their financial models. Compare and contrast the responses of the banker and the investor. Are their views of the financials different? Why? Prepare your responses in a two-page report.

2. Interview an entrepreneur who has been in business no longer than five years to find out how he or she calculated how much money was needed to start the venture. Did it turn out to be enough? Why or why not? In a brief PowerPoint presentation, present what you would have advised the entrepreneur to do differently.

Relevant Case Studies

Appendix Currency13

HOMERUN.COM: BREAKING INTO A SATURATED MARKET*

"Business is terrific," reflected HomeRun.com CEO Jared Kopf, as he reviewed his first quarter profits. Kopf had just celebrated the opening of a satellite office in Phoenix, managed by former Go Daddy Vice-President of Business Operations Bob Olson. Hiring Olson was a coup for Kopf, who had spent several months hunting for the right executive to lead his sales organization.

The past several months had been a crucial time for HomeRun, an Internet business that had opened its doors in Fall 2009. The group buying market, which remained largely untapped in early 2009, was now erupting, with more than 200 copycat businesses offering daily deal emails and local discounts.[1] All of the companies were built around a similar model: a daily email to users with an offer that featured a deep discount on anything from a restaurant dinner to a series of yoga classes. As long as a certain number of people decided to opt in to buy the discounted item, the deal would "tip." This group dynamic ensured the product would go viral, as friends and family shared in the deal. "I think that the web today is very much about delivering personalized and relevant offers to people and helping people find the things that are actually meaningful to them," said Kopf, who believed that his business had huge potential to grow in a down market.

*This case was written by Jaime Ford as a basis for class discussion. Reprinted by permission.
[1]"Meet the Fastest Growing Company Ever." Forbes.com. August 17, 2010, www.forbes.com/forbes/2010/0830/entrepreneurs-groupon-facebook-twitter-next-web-phenom.html.

Company Background

HomeRun was the brainchild of Jared Kopf and Matt Humphrey, two entrepreneurs who met in San Francisco in October 2008. Kopf was the former co-founder of digital content publisher Slide, and chairman of the self-service advertising platform, AdRoll. Humphrey was a Carnegie Mellon prodigy (starting at the university at the age of 13) and founder of the social gaming company, Kickball Labs. Kopf and Humphrey became friends while working for Internet companies that shared office space in early 2008. The two met up again in November 2009, when both were looking for new ventures to launch. Over lunch, Kopf and Humphrey discovered their mutual interest in group buying. The net result? HomeRun.com.

Naming the company was no easy task, but in the end Kopf and Humphrey chose to go with HomeRun and acquired the domain name for $131,000. The team believed that the name immediately differentiated their venture from other group buying startups (or local e-commerce startups as they were also known) that were opting for more complicated monikers like GroupSwoop and Deals2Buy. HomeRun was "simple, memorable, and transmittable," noted Kopf. He also liked that the name didn't carry any money-saving connotations such as "deal" or "coupon" and promoted the ideals of teamwork and winning. Kopf wanted to "appeal to deeper emotions as a way to differentiate."

Initially, the company moved forward with Kopf, Humphrey, and two talented engineers who had previously worked with Humphrey. In December 2009, it became apparent that more help would be needed to hire and train a competent sales staff, so Kopf brought on Noah Lichtenstein, a business development executive from WeatherBill. With heavy personnel costs, Kopf needed to conserve capital, and he chose to farm out the initial content and graphic needs, keeping the full-time team as lean as possible.

HomeRun.com went live in late January 2010 in the local market of San Francisco and offered the following products:

> Daily Steal: One amazing thing to do in the city every day.
> Beginner's Luck: Great offers for members within their first thirty days of membership.
> Private Reserve: Unique experiences reserved for top point-earning members.

Most of the deals were given "avalanche pricing," which meant that the more inventory the customer bought, the lower the price fell. To keep other group buying sites from using "avalanche pricing," they had plans to trademark the name.

On the engineering side, Humphrey's team developed a versatile platform that worked not only for the HomeRun site, but also as a deal engine for other businesses. The team also worked diligently to make the daily offers available for redemption via mobile phones.

In June 2010, the team expanded to include account managers, sales representatives, content writers, and developers. Soon the demand for sales and customer service staff outweighed the existing manpower, so Kopf began searching for a customer service professional who could handle the rapidly expanding sales staff and customer base. His search brought him to Bob Olson, the legendary sales guru of GoDaddy.com. The problem? Olson was firmly rooted in Phoenix, Arizona, where he lived with his wife and children. Dedicated to making the situation work, Kopf met with his executive team and they decided that sales and customer service teams would relocate to Arizona where Olson would run the office and where the costs of doing business were considerably lower.

The Local E-Commerce Industry

The local e-commerce or group buying industry is based on a simple premise: businesses are always seeking new ways to connect with local consumers. At the same time, consumers are always searching for ways to save money. Companies involved in the local e-commerce space find local restaurants, spas, or other businesses that are willing to offer substantial discounts, as long as their brand is shared with a large number of new customers. The company offers the discount online to their user base and then takes a cut of the profits (often as much as 50 percent). As the company grows, it continually expands to new markets, offering duplicate services in major cities around the country and eventually the world.

The local e-commerce industry works particularly well in a down market. In late 2010, the recession was still going strong, with a 9.6 percent unemployment rate.[2] Consumers were opting to keep their cash in the bank, preferring to eat at home rather than eating out. The climate was ripe for the local e-commerce model, because people still wanted to enjoy their pre-recession lifestyles, as long as it was affordable.

Several key components of the local e-commerce industry set the successful companies apart from their competitors: socialization, technology, service, inventory, and pricing.

Socialization

Local e-commerce success relies on the power of group buying, which springs from the premise that people typically trust products recommended by friends and family. Coming together as a community means that consumer purchases garner more significance than items acquired by individuals. Successful group buying companies encourage social interaction on multiple platforms, including Twitter, Facebook, and mobile

---

[2]"United States Unemployment Rate." TradingEconomics.com. October 2010, www.tradingeconomics.com/Economics/Unemployment-Rate.aspx?Symbol=USD.

phone applications. They also incorporate social feeds on their websites that display what friends are buying and when. "It's addictive," claims Jay Gleason, a writer from San Francisco, who has spent more than $1,000 on dozens of daily deals in the past year.

Simply offering a daily deal isn't enough to capture the market at this level of market saturation, however. Companies need to add elements of serendipity to acquire a larger user base while also making the product more social. Free offers, VIP memberships, and website games are just some of the ways that group buying companies are staying competitive in the market.

Technology

Many local e-commerce sites offer real-time redemption through iPhone and Android applications. Most are integrated with Facebook and all employ a simple, deal-a-day email as their primary method of outreach. To stand out, a company must create proprietary technology that differs from the daily email standard that has become a norm in the industry. Local e-commerce company Tippr has gone so far as to secure ten patents for the technology its Seattle-based team has created to drive their site.

Successful local e-commerce companies must also develop and employ technologies that enable them to personalize their products. Generic deals geared for the masses result in a decline in memberships. By contrast, companies that engineer personalized alerts stay a step ahead of their competitors, cutting through the noise to deliver the offers that fit individual user needs.

Service

Anybody can start a local e-commerce company by sourcing merchant inventory and creating a simple redemption process. Success, however, lies in developing an effective customer service organization. At a minimum, companies must have one customer service person for every market, which creates an expansion problem for startups that want to compete against larger group buying

companies, such as Groupon and Living Social. In 2010, Groupon employed more than 300 customer service representatives and sales associates.

Focusing on service also helps to improve the company's customer retention. According to *The Wall Street Journal*, Groupon's research found that only 22 percent of Groupon buyers make a return visit to businesses that don't offer a second discount.[3] A business that can surpass that percentage stands to gain interest from merchants, who are losing faith in the ROI of the group buying model.

Inventory and Pricing

As the market becomes more saturated, diversity of inventory becomes increasingly important. For example, when a merchant is found on multiple deal sites, the deal site's brand becomes secondary to the discount offered. Some companies have overcome this challenge by creating exclusivity agreements with merchants. However, the merchants, seeing multiple deal platform opportunities available, rarely acquiesce to these agreements. Companies that choose to hire a telemarketing expert have the upper hand on companies that opt to learn the art of consumer telemarketing on the job. The pricing of the company's inventory is also a key differentiator. Most deal buying companies offer prices that are discounted by fifty percent or greater. This creates price sensitivity among consumers, who may use a new discounter once, but will not return until another similar discount is offered. This behavior may be due to the consumer's inability to afford full price merchandise or to a lack of desire to pay full price for anything.

The Opportunity

Although the market is over-saturated, there is still an opportunity for a strong group buying platform like HomeRun to earn substantial revenues if they closely examine their core markets:

[3]"Online Coupons Get Smarter." WallStreetJournal.com. August 25, 2010, http://online.wsj.com/article/SB100014 24052748703447004575449453225928136.html.

business owners and consumers. Struggling business owners are the bread and butter of the group buying industry because they are generally looking to unload excess inventory, and the opportunity to show that inventory to a large number of potential customers is very attractive. At the same time, the commission structure of the deal works in favor of the group buying company, which typically earns fifty percent of the proceeds from the inventory sold within a 24-hour period.

Struggling businesses are not the only beneficiaries of the group buying process. Given the high unemployment rate, it's no surprise that consumers are continually on the lookout for great deals and offers. In a saturated market, however, consumers trade brand loyalty for the largest discount they can find. If the group buying company can personalize the deal, it gains a chance to increase its customer retention rate.

If a company creates proprietary technology, potential B2B opportunities emerge. HomeRun's deal platform offered an opportunity for other companies to run offers to their customers under their proprietary branding without having to build their own ecommerce platform.

Successful companies create incentives for all their customers to share their offers. For example, Groupon encourages its customers to share news about deals through email, Facebook, and Twitter; it also promises that if one of its users sends a Groupon link to a friend, and the friend buys a Groupon item within 72 hours, the one who sent the link receives $10 worth of Groupon credits in their account.

Competition and Challenges

The biggest challenge in the group buying space is the ease with which these types of companies start up. There are no clear barriers to entry, and success lies in the ability to source deals and acquire consumer email addresses. For many deal companies, branding, coupled with massive email lists, is the only differentiator between success and failure.

In 2010, the most formidable competitor in the deal buying space was Groupon, with a valuation of more than $1 billion.[4] Besides offering a deal of the day email for more than 150 cities, Groupon sourced national deals accessible to all Groupon members. For example, a nationwide deal with Gap, Inc., offering $50 worth of clothing for $25 nabbed Groupon $11 million in revenue.[5] According to a report by Morgan Stanley, Groupon cleared more than $500 million in 2010. Following Groupon was Living Social, a company that in 2010 closed a $40 million round of funding to begin their international expansion.[6]

Although discounts for nationwide brands may work for all parties involved, they are not as ideal for local businesses. Platforms such as Facebook and Twitter provide a broader context for consumer engagement, branding, product introduction, and customer service. With group buying companies, it's not as clear what a local business would do to encourage deal-buyers to revisit their location.

As companies grow in popularity, they deal with an inevitable backlog of merchants who want to be featured but can't. In 2010, Groupon was struggling with a six-month backlog of eager merchants. HomeRun's opportunity to fill that void was clear, but the path to doing so was less obvious. The backlogged merchants at Groupon often sought refuge at smaller group buying companies that offered more advantageous margins and faster placement.

The Future of HomeRun

People will always buy things and there will always be interest in discounts. However, in a saturated market, consumers are less likely to be loyal

---

[4]"It's Official: Groupon Announces That $1.35 Billion Valuation Round." TechCrunch. April 18, 2010, http://techcrunch.com/2010/04/18/its-official-groupon-announces-that-1-35-billion-valuation-round.

[5]"Walmart Takes Page From Groupon." Chicago Business. October 27, 2010, www.chicagobusiness.com/article/20101027/NEWS07/101029899/walmart-takes-page-from-groupon.

[6]"Meet the Fastest Growing Company Ever." Forbes.com. August 17, 2010, www.forbes.com/forbes/2010/0830/entrepreneurs-groupon-facebook-twitter-next-web-phenom.html.

Relative Competitive
Market and Funding
for Group Buying

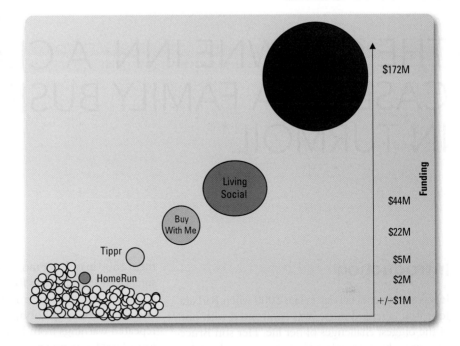

to a deal company and more likely to use an aggregator service to find the best deals.

To combat this, HomeRun competitor Groupon created a self-service platform known as Groupon Stores. The service enabled local businesses to create Facebook-like pages where fans could follow the company and access deals. The business customers were allowed to create their own deals, bypassing Groupon's average six-month waiting period. The catch? They were still required to pay Groupon's standard commission rate.

Similarly, HomeRun offered the HomeRun Merchant Scoreboard, which ranked local businesses in a city by how many potential "customers" they were able to reach through HomeRun. The customers counted as a composite score of followers and purchasers of that merchant's deals. The score produced the total number of new customers that the merchant could now access. Each merchant had a HomeRun page where fans could follow the brand and tap into new, special discounts.

To ensure a successful future for HomeRun, Kopf must examine several possibilities before

executing a strategy. He wonders if he has considered all the possibilities and debates with his team about the criteria they should use in making the decision.

Discussion Questions

1. What criteria should the HomeRun team use in selecting among the many strategic possibilities for the company?
2. Should HomeRun expand its merchant pages to allow merchants to run their own deals, similar to the Groupon Stores idea, or should the company differentiate itself by diving deeper into social gaming and membership rewards?
3. Should HomeRun continue to diversify by entering the global market or concentrate on national partnerships with large corporations?
4. Given the saturation in the market and difficulty maintaining brand equity, does it make sense to create a self-service platform that other companies can use to run their own proprietary deals?

THE CROWNE INN: A CLASSIC CASE OF A FAMILY BUSINESS IN TURMOIL*

Introduction

It was a clear, cool fall day in late 2000 when Barbara Johnston, a retired nurse, was confronted with one of the biggest challenges of her life. Her son Bruce had entered her dilapidated house, thrown down his keys, and blurted out the following:

> You are all plotting behind my back. You are trying to bankrupt and steal the bar away from me. Well, you can have the keys to my house, car, and the lousy bar. But you will lose your son and two grandchildren forever.
>
> No one wanted the bar. I made the bar what it is today. If I leave, the business will collapse and then you will have nothing. I have already talked to the employees and they will all walk out. After this is over, I am going to disown this whole family. I have had it with all of you!!

Barbara's family was on the verge of being torn apart over the family's largest asset, a bar called The Crowne Inn, located in Kansas City, Missouri. Since the death of her husband Harvey in 1997, Barbara had had problems with Bruce's inability to meet his previously agreed-upon oral agreement to take care of her. On the day of his father's retirement in 1995, Bruce had made an oral agreement to pay off the second mortgage of his parents' house ($23,500), give

them $500 in cash per month, and pay their health insurance and medical bills for the rest of their lives. He had made this oral agreement in front of his parents and their attorney, Bobby Free. However, despite repeated warnings from Free, Harvey had refused a formal written contract. As a result of the agreement, Bruce received all of the proceeds from the bar.

After five years, Bruce had not lived up to his agreement with his parents. The family was trying to work out a deal with Bruce's lawyer and accountant to sell him the business. The family's attorney, Bobby Free, devised three possible solutions to the problem: (1) have Bruce pay a lump sum, (2) have Bruce pay a smaller lump sum and $500 per month, or (3) sell the bar outright to an outside party.

Bruce stated that he would pay a lump sum of not more than $60,000 to his mother. The family was unsure whether this was a fair offer. If not, what was a fair offer? Also, was the lump sum method the best way to handle the problem? Furthermore, would Bruce be willing and/or able to pay a higher lump sum? Previously, he had told his older brother Karl that he refused to pay $75,000. He stated that he would be better off going into business with someone else rather than pay $75,000.

The real challenge was solving the family crisis without alienating Bruce and his family. Furthermore, Bruce had only one good relationship with his four brothers—Karl. Barbara was looking to her sons and her attorney for an answer to this complicated, nerve-racking, family crisis.

*This case was written by Todd A. Finkle, Director, Fitzgerald Institute for Entrepreneurial Studies, The University of Akron, as a basis for class discussion. Reprinted by permission.

The Johnston Family

Born in Kansas City in 1934, Barbara Johnston grew up in a lower-middle-class Lutheran family and was a by-product of the Depression. Despite her challenging upbringing, Barbara was a gregarious, warm, friendly, family-oriented woman.

During her junior year in high school, she fell in love with a senior named Harvey Johnston. Harvey married Barbara four years after she graduated from high school. The marriage proved to be very tumultuous, but produced five healthy boys and six grandchildren. Most of the boys had personality characteristics like their father, which included a very high need for independence, an extremely strong work ethic, and an entrepreneurial flair. The oldest son, Karl, a twice-divorced, 47-year-old, was currently married (Caren). Karl was a street-smart, successful entrepreneur who owned a 3M dealership in Seattle, Washington. He had grown the business to over $1.5 million in sales in four years. His salary, not including the profits from the business, was around $85,000 a year.

Her second son, Cal (Jessica), had been married for 22 years. His marriage produced three children: Jason, Jennifer, and Jim. Cal was a religious, optimistic, and successful 45-year-old cardiologist who lived in Kansas City. Of the five brothers, Cal was the most financially successful. His independent medical practice had sales of $1,000,000 with an annual net income of $250,000.

The middle child, Bruce (Sharon), had been married since 1985 and had two children, Albert and Bob. Bruce and Sharon were currently running the family business, The Crowne Inn.

Bruce enjoyed partying with his friends from the bar. Bruce and Sharon worked at the bar and made a combined salary of $84,000 (1999), not including the profits from the bar (see Exhibit 1).

The fourth son, Tyler, was a single (never married), 40-year-old dentist living in Las Vegas, Nevada. He was a hard-working free spirit who enjoyed his freedom and convertibles. His dental practice was very successful, and he made approximately $100,000 a year.

Danny, the last son, was also single (37 years old). He was extremely creative and enjoyed working with his hands. He had just started his own entertainment company that specialized in decorations for holidays and special events.

The Crowne Inn

Harvey and Barbara Johnston were married in 1952. Before their marriage, Johnston's father, Norm, realized that his son needed a profession to support his new wife. Norm approached his 22-year-old son and asked him what profession he wanted to enter. After some thought, Johnston stated that he wanted to start his own bar. The loose, free lifestyle appealed to him.

Before opening the bar, Johnston asked his best friend, Leo Smith, if he wanted to be his partner. Smith had been bartending with Johnston for the past two years and enjoyed it, so he agreed. Smith also had more experience in the bar business, so it was a good match. He was a warm, friendly man who was married and had one daughter.

In 1952, Johnston and Smith took out a $10,000 loan and started a bar called "Leo and Harvey's" in downtown Kansas City. The bar was structured as an S-corporation; both Johnston and Smith owned 50 percent of the stock in the company.

EXHIBIT 1			Bar's Net Income	
	Year	Bruce	Sharon	Pre Tax	Totals
Annual Salaries for Bruce and Sharon Johnston and The Crowne Inn's Net Income (Pre Tax) from 1997 to 2000	1997	53,500	20,000	(500)	73,000
	1998	60,000	20,000	3,440	83,440
	1999	62,000	22,000	6,450	90,450
	2000	64,000	24,000	6,500	94,500

After seven years of moderately successful business, they made a decision to move the business to the northeast part of Kansas City. The downtown area had become increasingly dangerous with an increase in crime and an increase in the number of homeless people. The new location had fewer competitors, less crime, and a better clientele. The partners purchased the land and building and moved into the new location in 1959, renaming the bar, "The Crowne Inn."

The Crowne Inn was unique because it was patterned after the Old West. Old wooden barrels lined the front of the building. The building itself was made of wood boards, and signs that ranged from "Dance Girls Wanted" to "Whisky Served Here" to "Coldest Beer in Town" were placed all over the front of the building. On the top of the building was a 7-Up sign.

At the entrance of the smoke-filled bar there was a shiny, dark-stained, wooden bar with 10 swinging stools for customers. A pair of small swinging doors led to the back of the bar where a small cooler held mugs, cans, and bottles of beer and wine. There were five taps: one for Champagne, Cold Duck, and Miller High Life, and two for Budweiser (their best-selling beer). On the other side of the bar were a small grill, refrigerator, office, and cooler for kegs and cases of beer. A limited supply of hard alcohol and food items were also for sale behind the bar.

The Crowne Inn differentiated itself from other bars in a number of ways. First, the bar had a very homey atmosphere with approximately 15 tables and a total capacity of 70 people. This gave customers the ability to converse without all the hassles (e.g., fights, loud music) of a typical bar. The bar also served lunch (hamburgers, hot dogs, chili dogs, and chips) and snacks (slim jims, beef jerky, bags of peanuts). The bar initially had a pool table and color TV; however, they dropped the pool table due to fights.

The ambiance of the bar was enhanced by the shellacked, historic newspaper clippings on the walls. Actual articles on the Japanese surprise attack at Pearl Harbor, the sinking of the Lusitania, and the D-Day invasion were all exhibited on the wall. The bar was also full of historic relics, which included old menus, beer trays, political buttons, and beer cans. Jim Beam bottles (novelty bottles filled with whiskey) were also located all over the bar.

The Crowne Inn's busiest times were weekdays for lunch (11 a.m.–1 p.m.), happy hour (5–7 p.m.), and weekend evenings (8 p.m.–1 a.m.). Business professionals made up the largest segment of customers at lunch. During the late afternoon and evenings, the customers were primarily local blue-collar workers.

Johnston and Smith worked alternating, two-week shifts: day (10 a.m.–6 p.m.) and evening (6 p.m.–2 a.m.). As their business slowly grew, so did their families. Smith eventually had four girls and moved into a beautiful four-bedroom house, while Johnston had five boys, moved into a small three-bedroom house, and struggled to pay his bills.

Transitional Years

In 1981, Harvey bought out Smith's stock in the company for $50,000 cash. At the age of 28, Karl joined the business full-time. Karl brought a new ambiance to the bar. He had a high level of energy, creativity, and numerous innovative ideas to enhance the sales of the bar. One of the first things that he did was add a large cooler that contained over 80 imported beers from all over the world. He also created an advertising campaign in the local entertainment papers, bought a popcorn machine, a stereo system, and a VCR to play movies. These ideas along with Karl's jovial personality bolstered sales and changed the culture of the bar from a primarily neighborhood blue-collar establishment to a younger, trendier 25- to 40-year-old crowd.

By late 1982, Karl had grown weary of the long hours, drunks, and low pay. Furthermore, he had recently been married and his wife, Jessica, wanted him to leave the bar business. Despite the rise in sales of the bar to $125,000, he was not making as much money as he had hoped. He quit the bar and moved to San Diego, California.

Turnaround

By late 1982, Johnston's middle son, Bruce, started working part-time for the bar; however, Harvey still worked the majority of the hours. In 1984, Karl returned from San Diego as a divorcee and started working at the bar again. Karl and Bruce came up with some innovative ideas to increase sales. They started selling warm, roasted peanuts at $.75 a bowl and ice-cold pints of imported beer on tap (e.g., Guinness, Heineken, Bass Ale). They also started selling pickles and added video games, a pinball machine, a jukebox CD player, and a big screen television.

After two years of working together, sales had increased to $185,000. Despite the increased success of the bar, Karl decided to quit. He had been robbed twice at gunpoint, including one time where the robbers took all of the money and jewelry from the customers. He also got remarried and his second wife, Judy, was pushing him to get out of the bar business. Karl and Judy moved to San Diego at the end of 1986.

By the end of 1986, Bruce was working full-time with his father. Bruce continued his entrepreneurial flair over the next 10 years. One of his most innovative moves was a strategic alliance with an Italian restaurant across the street, called Pappa's Pizza. This take-out or dine-in restaurant offered tasty Italian food. Because the bar did not serve food (besides snacks) in the evenings, it was an ideal strategy to allow people to order food from Pappa's Pizza and bring it into the bar. This strategy beefed up sales for both businesses.

Bruce also held promotional events where guest DJs would come in and play music. One of his most innovative special events was Crownewood. Crownewood was held every year on the night of the Oscars. Customers would vote on which stars would win. If they guessed correctly, they would win prizes. Other events focused on sporting events. For example, free chili was served during Monday Night Football.

These activities, combined with advertising in the local entertainment paper, *Rebel*, attracted two new market segments, the college crowd and young urban professionals. The Crowne Inn had transformed itself from a primarily blue-collar neighborhood bar into one of the most progressive bars in Kansas City. As a result, the Johnstons increased their prices and sales. Under Harvey and Bruce's tenure, the sales of the bar increased from $145,000 in 1984 to $200,000 in 1994 (4 percent increase in sales a year). See Exhibit 2.

EXHIBIT 2	The Crowne Inn Sales from 1982 to 2000

Year	Sales ($)
1982	125,000
1983	135,000
1984	145,000
1985	165,000
1986	185,000
1987	170,000
1988	175,000
1989	180,000
1990	185,000
1991	190,000
1992	192,500
1993	197,500
1994	200,000
1995	225,000
1996	250,000
1997	295,000
1998	326,000
1999	346,000
2000	366,000

One of the keys to Bruce's success in turning the bar around was his girlfriend, Sharon, whom he eventually married in 1985. Sharon was a very savvy businessperson with a very strict authoritarian management style with tight controls. This was in contrast to Harvey and Bruce's laid-back personalities, which led Sharon to take control the bar.

Failure of the Oral Agreement

In 1994, after 42 years of running the bar, Harvey was ready to retire. Harvey had emphysema, diabetes, and was obese. He approached his sons to see who wanted the bar. Bruce was the logical person to purchase the bar since he had been running it successfully for the past 11 years.

On the day of his father's retirement, Bruce entered into an oral agreement with his parents. In exchange for the future proceeds from the bar,

Bruce agreed to pay off the $23,500 left on the second mortgage of his parents' house, give them $500 in cash per month, and pay for their health insurance and medical costs for the rest of their lives. Harvey refused to have a written contract.

Harvey remained president of the company and owned all of the stock. If he passed away, the stock would move into his wife's name. After they both passed away, the stock would then pass on to Bruce. The remainder of the estate's assets would then be divided among the other four siblings. The estimated amount of the remainder of the estate in 2001 was $50,000 (house), $80,000 (cash and securities), automobile ($10,000), and miscellaneous ($5,000).

Bruce had paid his parents' health care premiums with the most inexpensive policy up until his father's death in 1997. By 1998, when Barbara was eligible for Medicare, Bruce did not pay for any of her health care costs, which included Medicare ($46 per month) and medications ($300 per month). Cal ended up paying for the medications, which caused resentment from Cal and his wife. Barbara paid for her Medicare.

From 1994 to 1998, Bruce paid his mother $500 per month; however, he treated her as an employee. Therefore, taxes were deducted from her paycheck of $500, which resulted in a final sum of approximately $400. Bruce did pay $500 cash for one year, but in 2000 he treated his mother as an employee again. Furthermore, Barbara often complained that Bruce missed paying her on time (the 5th of the month). However, Barbara stated that after a phone call to Bruce, he always paid her by the end of the month. She insisted that he never missed a payment. To make matters worse, the bar's accountant was also Bruce and Barbara's personal accountant.

In April 2000, Bruce told his mother that she owed $10,000 in taxes for the tax year 1999. He stated that she owed this because she cashed in $15,000 in stock (initial cost basis of $1,352 in 1965) to refurbish parts of her house. Barbara's total income and taxes paid for 1999 can be seen in Exhibit 3.

Bruce and Sharon recommended that Barbara take out a $10,000 loan for the taxes that she

| EXHIBIT 3 | Barbara Johnston's Sources of Income and Tax Summary for the Tax Year 1999 |

Source of Income	Amount ($)
Taxable Interest	2,294
Dividends	2,752
Cashed-in Stock (Capital Gain)	13,648
Taxable Pension	5,778
Taxable S-Corp Income (Bar)	2,299
Total Income	26,771
Adjusted Gross Income	26,771
Standard Deduction	5,350
Personal Exemptions	2,750
Taxable Income	18,671
Total Federal Tax	2,576
Total State Tax	942
Total Tax	3,518

owed. This was done within a 24-hour period of time. When Barbara informed her sons about this, they were suspicious. They decided to obtain a copy of the financial statements of the bar from 1997 to 1999. In October 2000, Danny requested a copy of the financial statements from Bruce. Bruce vehemently refused, stating that Danny was not a shareholder in the bar so he could not receive a copy of the financials. The next day Danny and Barbara visited Bruce's accountant and demanded a copy of the financial statements for the past three years. The accountant reluctantly gave copies to Barbara. See Exhibits 4, 5, and 6.

The next day the accountant called Barbara to tell her that she would be receiving a refund of approximately $6,482 from her taxes. Bruce and Sharon both went ballistic. They charged over to Barbara's house and threatened to disown her and the family:

> You have no right looking into our personal financial situation. You are trying to steal the bar away from us! You are taking away my kids' education money.

The following day Bruce and Sharon showed up unannounced at Barbara's house with an unsigned contract (see Exhibit 7). Under duress,

EXHIBIT 4	Income Statement for The Crowne Inn, 1997–1999					

	1997		1998		1999	
	$	%Sales	$	%Sales	$	%Sales
Sales	$295,621	100.00%	$326,352	100.00%	$345,669	100.00%
Cost of Goods Sold	$156,100	52.80%	$157,231	48.18%	$174,139	50.38%
Gross Profit	$139,521	47.20%	$169,121	51.82%	$171,530	49.62%
Operational Expenses						
Advertising	$8,318	2.81%	$8,277	2.54%	$5,777	1.67%
Bank Charges	$892	0.30%	$1,094	0.34%	$1,592	0.46%
Insurance—General	$9,762	3.30%	$7,024	2.15%	$11,555	3.34%
Payroll—General	$94,951	32.12%	$96,027	29.42%	$98,383	28.46%
Professional Expense	$1,083	0.37%	$1,424	0.44%	$2,341	0.68%
Repairs and Maintenance	$2,096	0.71%	$9,211	2.82%	$1,687	0.49%
Taxes—Other	$7,813	2.64%	$23,312	7.14%	$27,308	7.90%
Utilities	$7,011	2.37%	$7,689	2.36%	$6,883	1.99%
Other	$5,678	1.92%	$7,882	2.42%	$6,369	1.84%
Total SG&A Expense	$137,604	46.54%	$161,940	49.63%	$161,895	46.83%
Operating Profit	$1,917	0.65%	$7,181	2.43%	$9,635	2.79%
Depreciation Expense	$1,753	0.59%	$2,353	0.72%	$2,086	0.60%
Interest Expense	$664	0.22%	$1,387	0.43%	$1,096	0.32%
Pretax Profit (Loss)	($500)	–0.17%	$3,441	1.05%	$6,451	1.87%

EXHIBIT 5		1997	1998	1999
The Crowne Inn Balance Sheet, 1997–1999 (in Thousands)	Current Assets			
	Cash & Marketable Securities	$ 6,280	$ 5,359	$ 8,118
	Inventory	$ 6,250	$ 7,325	$ 6,785
	Total Current Assets	$12,530	$12,684	$14,903
	Property, Plant, & Equipment	$80,790	$82,315	$86,467
	Less: Accumulated Depreciation	$60,791	$63,144	$69,384
	Total Net Fixed Assets	$19,999	$19,171	$17,083
	Total Assets	$32,529	$31,855	$31,986
	Current Liabilities			
	Accounts Payable	$ 5,146	$ 3,183	$ 3,456
	Sales & Income Tax Payable	$ 1,460	$ 1,481	$ 1,827
	Total Current Liabilities	$ 6,606	$ 4,664	$ 5,283
	Long-Term Liabilities	$14,045	$11,872	$ 9,085
	Total Liabilities	$20,651	$16,536	$14,368
	Common Stock or Owners' Equity	$ 6,000	$ 6,000	$ 6,000
	Retained Earnings	$ 5,878	$ 9,319	$11,618
	Total Equity	$11,878	$15,319	$17,618
	Total Liabilities and Owners' Equity	$32,529	$31,855	$31,986

The Crowne Inn
Cash Flow Summary,
1997–1999

	1997	1998	1999
Total Sales	$295,621	$ 326,352	$ 345,669
Total Cash Available	**$295,621**	**$326,352**	**$345,669**
Total Purchases	$ 156,100	$ 157,231	$ 174,139
Increase (Decrease) in Inventory	$ 820	$ 1,075	($ 540)
Cash Available After Purchase	**$156,920**	**$158,306**	**$173,599**
Uses of Cash			
Operating Expenses			
Total per Income Statement	$ 137,604	$ 161,940	$ 161,896
Financing Activities			
Interest Expensew	$ 664	$ 1,387	$ 1,096
Principal Payments (Loan Additions)	($ 14,045)	$ 2,173	$ 2,787
Assets Additions	$ 16,917	$ 1,525	
Other Decreases (Increases)	$ 2,282	($ 1,942)	($ 3,532)
Cash Flow	**($ 157)**	**($ 921)**	**$ 2,759**
Beginning Cash	$ 6,437	$ 6,280	$ 5,359
Ending Cash	$ 6,280	$ 5,359	$ 8,118
Cash Flow Increase (Decrease)	($ 157)	($ 921)	$ 2,759

Contract Proposed by Bruce

AGREEMENT

This agreement made and entered into this 11th day of November 2000 by and between Barbara A. Johnston, hereinafter referred to as Seller, and Bruce S. Johnston, hereinafter referred to as Buyer:

WITNESSETH:

WHEREAS, Seller is the owner of a majority of the Stock in The Crowne Inn, Inc.; and

WHEREAS, Buyer desires to buy the Seller's stock, and to purchase all of the Seller's interest in the real and personal property where The Crowne Inn conducts business; and

WHEREAS, the parties had previously agreed to a monthly payment for the purchase of Seller's stock which agreement the parties wish to codify herein.

NOW THEREFORE, in consideration of the mutual promises and covenants contained herein, the parties agree as follows:

1. That seller shall sell to Buyer, and the Buyer shall buy from Seller, the real and personal property where The Crowne Inn, Inc., conducts its business. The parties agree that subsequent to this Agreement, all of the documents will be prepared, to effectuate said transfer, including a deed to the real property and billv of sale to all personal property and both parties shall execute such necessary documents. The consideration for this transfer shall be the sum of $50,000.00, which the Buyer shall pay forthwith even though the transfer documents shall not be prepared until after the date of this Agreement.

2. That Buyer shall continue to pay to Seller, the sum of $500.00 per month, for the remainder of her life, said payment being the consideration for the present transfer of all of the Seller's stock in The Crowne Inn, Inc. Seller shall, immediately upon receipt of said funds, execute any and all documents necessary to transfer all of Seller's interest in the stock in The Crowne Inn to Buyer.

IN WITNESS WHEREOF, the parties hereto have entered in this Agreement the day and date first above written.

_____
Barbara A. Johnston, Seller

_____
Bruce S. Johnston, Buyer

State of Missouri   :
                       : SS.
County of Jackson   :

(continued)

| EXHIBIT 7 | Contract Proposed by Bruce   (*continued*) |

On this ____ day of ____, 2000, before me, the undersigned, a notary public, duly commissioned and qualified for said state, personally came Barbara A. Johnston, to me known to be the identical person whose name is subscribed to the foregoing instrument, and acknowledged the execution thereof to be her voluntary act and deed.
WITNESS my hand and notarial seal the day and year last above written.

_____
Notary Public
State of Missouri   :
                                  : SS.
County of Jackson   :
On this ____ day of ____, 2000, before me, the undersigned, a notary public, duly commissioned and qualified for said state, personally came Bruce S. Johnston, to me known to be the identical person whose name is subscribed to the foregoing instrument, and acknowledged the execution thereof to be his voluntary act and deed.
WITNESS my hand and notarial seal the day and year last above written.

_____
Notary Public

they took Barbara to see their attorney and placed pressure on her to sign the contract. After this, they quickly went to see Barbara's attorney, Bobby Free. There was a sense of urgency on the part of Bruce and Sharon to get the contract signed immediately. Free could tell by the look on Barbara's face that she was under duress. Danny showed up at Free's office, and they stated that they needed time to examine the contract before they would allow her to sign anything.

Everyone left, but the turmoil continued. Danny updated the brothers and they determined that something had to be done about the situation. This had gone on for too long.

The Bar Industry in 2001

In 2001, the bar industry was in the mature stage of the industry life cycle. The sales of alcoholic beverages in the United States had increased from $90.5 billion in 1998 to $96.1 billion in 1999. Packaged alcohol consumption increased from $44.7 to $48.7 billion, while alcoholic drinks increased from $45.8 to $47.4 billion during the same time period. A survey of 434 colleges polled by the Higher Education Research Institute found that beer drinking in 2000 had decreased from the previous year by a half percentage point (Dees, 2001).

Over the past few years, the industry has seen numerous changes. One of the more popular trends was the increasing amount of imported liquor and beer. Another trend was the increase in sales of micro-brewed beer. Many bars have also increased the number of movies/videos, video games, and billiards available to customers.

Technology was also having an effect on the bar industry. Leisure time had been reduced 25 percent over the past 10 years due to the introduction of the Internet, digital television, and game consoles. Sixty percent of the bars in the United States currently have access to the Internet. Finally, there was the increasing liability associated with owning a bar due to the implementation of the .08 alcohol intoxication limit in most states.

Local Environment and Competition in 2001

Kansas City was the home of pro baseball's Kansas City Royals and pro football's Kansas City Chiefs. The city was split in two by the Missouri River. There was a Kansas City, Kansas, and a Kansas City, Missouri. Two million people currently live in the metropolitan Kansas City area.

The cost of living index for Kansas City was 98.6 on a U.S. scale of 100. This was significantly lower that other high-cost areas like San Francisco, which had an index of 179.8. Wages for most occupations were close to the national average in the United States. Furthermore, out of 180 metropolitan areas surveyed by the National Association of Home Builders, Kansas City ranked fourteenth in housing affordability during the fourth quarter of 2000.

The Crowne Inn was located on the northeast side of Kansas City (Clay County) about five miles from downtown. The surrounding area was a combination of both residential and commercial properties.

The total number of households in the surrounding area with the same zip code was 12,800, with a population of 31,500. The median age, household income, and household size were 43, $37,786, and 2.3, respectively. Most of the people owned their homes; only 30 percent of the households had children.

The primary competitive advantage for The Crowne Inn was its location. Several businesses, two major universities, a medical school, and two major hospitals were located within a five-mile radius. In addition to the local residential market, this added an additional 30,000 people.

Five competitors were located within a one-mile radius. However, The Crowne Inn had its niche. Its reputation was a homey place where you could relax, get good food and drinks, and have quiet conversations.

The Decision

Barbara and her sons had to come to a final resolution with Bruce. It was quite evident that Bruce was unable to meet his oral obligations. Their attorney came up with three alternatives. First, they could sell the bar outright to Bruce and receive a lump sum. This would allow Bruce to pay off all of his future financial obligations to his mother in one lump sum. Second, they could have Bruce pay a smaller sum and continue with payments of $500 per month. Or third, they could sell the bar to a third party.

Karl and Bruce discussed an appropriate way to deal with the problem. Karl communicated to his family that Bruce wanted to pay a lump sum of not more than $60,000. Furthermore, it became increasingly evident that Karl was now on Bruce's side. He was not looking at the situation from an objective viewpoint. Karl insinuated that Bruce had done nothing wrong. Bruce stated to Karl:

> I am not willing to go above $60,000. If you want me to pay more than that, I will go into business with the owner of Pappa's Pizza. We have been talking about opening a new pizza/bar in one of the fastest growing segments of the city, the East. This area is dangerous. We have been robbed three times in the last three years. If we move, this would put The Crowne Inn out of business.

The family, excluding Karl, Bruce, and Sharon, met over Christmas and discussed their next move. They were unsure whether or not the $60,000 was a fair offer. They were also uncertain as to how they would determine a fair lump sum. Bruce had previously sent Karl a letter outlining all of the money that he had spent on his parents over the years. In the letter he stated that he had given his parents $93,275 over the past five years. He insinuated that he had already paid for the bar. See Exhibit 8.

EXHIBIT 8	Money Bruce Spent on his Parents Since 1995

Type of Payment	Amount ($)
5 Years at $500/month	$25,000
Mortgage on House	23,500
Extra Money Given at X-Mas for 5 Years	4,000
Cost of Insurance	30,000
Lawn & Snow Care at House	3,000
Repair Bills Paid	2,000
New Furnace and Air Conditioner	4,800
Personal Tax CPA Costs	975
TOTALS	$93,275

Danny asserted that $60,000 was a ridiculously low offer. In 1999, the bar had sales of $346,000, and Bruce and Sharon made $84,000 plus the profits from the bar. Danny stated that they should pay $175,000. Danny also had a great idea:

> We need to determine the average life expectancy for a person in Barbara's age group. Once we do this we can determine a fair offer.

According to the tables, Barbara had a life expectancy of 17.5 years; however, her history of past health problems (e.g., heart condition) reduced her life expectancy to 14.5 years. See Exhibit 9.

As the holidays came to an end, Karl, Cal, Tyler, and Danny had a number of questions. Was the lump sum method the best way to handle the problem? If so, was the $60,000 offer fair? If this was not a fair offer, what was fair? Furthermore, would Bruce be willing and/or able to pay a higher lump sum? He had earlier told Karl that he was unwilling to pay $75,000. As they sat around pondering the situation, their mother was thinking,

> I do not want to lose my son and grandchildren over this bar. It is not worth it. However, Bruce made an oral agreement to take care of me.

Sources

Dees, J. (2001). "Fighting Back." *Nightclub & Bar*, www.nightclub.com/magazine/July01/fight.html; and Health Care Financing Administration (HCFA). *State Medical Manual 1999*, # 3258.9 (HCFA Transmittal No. 64).

Discussion Questions

1. Describe the historical progression of The Crowne Inn. What has made the business successful?
2. What mistakes did Harvey make during the succession process? As a result of having no written succession plan, what happened?
3. Why were the brothers so mad? Were they justified?
4. Bruce attempted to get his mother to sign a contract. Do you think this was a fair contract? If not, what was wrong with the contract?
5. Bruce gave the brothers a detailed analysis of all of the money that he had given to their mother since 1995. What role should this play in determining your final recommendation to the family?
6. Based on the financial information in the case, place a value on the business using the following methodologies: (a) balance sheet method, (b) income statement method, and (c) discounted cash flow method.
7. Based on the financial and statistical information in the case, what would you recommend to the Johnston family? Why?
8. How do you think the culture of the family will change in the future?

EXHIBIT 9	Life Expectancy Table for Females

Age	Life Expectancy (Years)
10	68.6
20	59.8
30	50.2
40	40.6
50	31.4
60	22.9
65	19.0
66	18.2
67	17.5
68	16.8
69	16.0
70	15.4
80	9.1
90	4.7
100	2.5
110	1.3
120	.6

Source: Health Care Financing Administration (HCFA). *State Medical Manual 1999*, # 3258.9 (HCFA Transmittal No. 64).

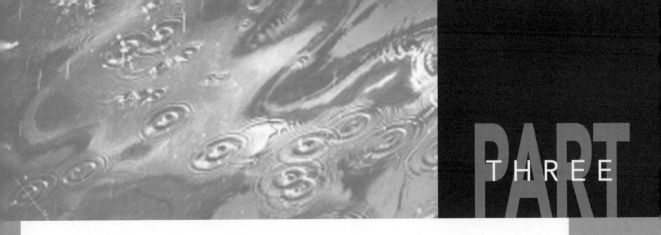

ORGANIZING THE VENTURE

CREATING THE BUSINESS PLAN

*"When all is said and done, the journey is the reward.
There is nothing else."*

—RANDY KOMISAR,
The Monk and the Riddle

CHAPTER OBJECTIVES

- Describe how to move from a feasible concept to a proof of concept.
- Identify stakeholder interests.
- Explain the components of a compelling executive summary.
- Discuss how to organize a business plan effectively.
- Describe how to successfully pitch a new business.

Stories of great successes can be inspiring, but entrepreneurs often learn much more and avoid fatal mistakes by doing a postmortem on a failed business. A good example of a business that seemed to have everything going for it and yet could not succeed is Future Beef, an Arkansas-based business founded in 2001.

The Opportunity

In today's world where genetic engineering is used to improve the quality, shelf life, and size of the foods we eat, Future Beef saw an opportunity to use genetic data and high-tech equipment to produce enormous amounts of superior meat. That was the company's primary product, but their plan also included providing its workers with the highest wages and benefits in the industry, as well as apartments and day-care centers as an additional benefit. Accomplishing these ambitious goals required a tremendous amount of investor capital. By late 1997, Future Beef had acquired its first round of capital, enough to enable the founders to quit their day jobs and recruit an experienced CEO (H. Russell Cross, former director of the Institute of Food Science and Engineering at Texas A&M) and two financial officers. A deal with grocery giant Safeway included a $15 million infusion of capital, and with the over $200 million total raised, the company was able to begin building plants.

Experience of the Founders

Rod Bowling and Rob Streight were the brains behind Future Beef. Bowling had a Ph.D. in meat and muscle biology from Texas A&M, and he had held the highest positions at some of the biggest plants in the industry. In 1996, frustrated by his inability to implement his innovative ideas inside a very traditional industry, Bowling sought the help of Streight in designing a very different kind of beef-producing company, one that integrated the value chain. Streight's role was to build the business's technology infrastructure.

How the Business Made Money

Not only did Future Beef want to control the entire value chain from the ranch to the packinghouse, it also wanted to use every bit of the steer to create value-added products and deliver those products through one grocery retailer, Safeway. Unfortunately, at that time prices for cattle that were fed and grown to certain specifications were soft, and the September 11 terrorist attacks followed by a foot-and-mouth disease rumor that drove down the futures market only served to worsen the situation. Future Beef found itself in trouble, with unexpected cost overruns, malfunctioning equipment, and even some lawsuits. It was losing money on every steer because it had purchased its cattle at market high prices and at lower weights than normal. Because Future Beef kept cattle in the grow yards longer than normal to control their nutrition, its holding costs were high. Only one month after it opened its first 450,000-square-foot plant in August 2001, the worst time of the year for any meat packer to source supply, its exclusive retail partner, Safeway, stopped paying on its contract. Safeway accounted for 51 percent of its sales, and it was an exclusive agreement that prevented Future Beef from developing other customers. Future Beef was selling to Safeway at rock-bottom prices, figuring to make up the difference in value-added product sales, but that never happened. Three months later, Future Beef was forced to declare Chapter 11 bankruptcy. Five months after the bankruptcy, it laid off all its workers and, in August 2002, liquidated its holdings. The postmortem revealed that the company was trying to implement too many expensive new systems simultaneously, largely because there was a lot of industry knowledge in the company but, unfortunately, no real business experience. It appears that the founders were visionaries and not execution people—a fatal flaw in many business plans. More importantly, a business model characterized by high costs and that relies on one customer is a dangerous position to be in.

Epilogue: In May 2003, just nine months after Future Beef closed its operations, the plant resumed cattle slaughter operations as Creekstone Farms Premium Beef. Creekstone Farms was the successful bidder for the plant and equipment at auction. It is estimated that 80 percent of Creekstone's employees are former Future Beef employees. Today Creekstone is a very successful company, leading the charge for beef products free of bovine spongiform encephalopathy (BSE), or "mad cow" disease. In May 2007, Creekstone

Farms won a decision in federal court to allow it to test for BSE. The USDA appealed and won the right to prohibit independent testing for BSE. Creekstone Farms is determined not to give up its fight to test animals for BSE because consumers want that assurance.

Sources: Adler, J. (August 29, 2008) *Creekstone Farms v. USDA,* http://volokh.com/posts/1220047130.shtml; www.creekstonefarms.com; J. McCuan, "Failure of Genius," *Inc. Magazine* (August 2003); "New Owners of Defunct Future Beef Plant Begin Operations," DodgeGlobe.com, accessed January 15, 2004; and Wes Ishmael, "Why Future Beef Went Under" (November 1, 2002), http://beefmagazine .com/mag/beef_why_future_beef, accessed June 24, 2004.

I t is an unfortunate fact that many universities and other institutions are perpetuating the myth that entrepreneurs must create business plans before they start businesses. Potential entrepreneurs are spending up to 200 hours of their valuable time in pursuit of the perfect plan to present at a competition or to an investor, only to discover that investors are more impressed by a founding team that has gotten the business up and running, even in a minimal way, to prove the concept.

Recall that feasibility analysis tests the business concept in the market to determine the conditions under which the entrepreneur is willing to move forward and start the business. Going through the process of feasibility analysis helps entrepreneurs learn about the business and prepare to launch. A business plan depends on a feasible business model that has been market-tested and is reliable, because a business plan is about building and growing a company. Business plans must be based on reality. In the wake of the recession that began in 2008, a lukewarm IPO market, and economic uncertainty, investors are now taking a far more conservative approach to both formal and informal investing. Nonetheless, there is plenty of investment capital available if entrepreneurs can convey a compelling story and deliver a management team that can execute the plan effectively.

For years, the traditional model of business planning involved carefully crafting a business plan and then sending it out to potential funders for consideration. Of course, much like a slush pile of manuscripts at a publishing house, these business plans sat stacked on the investor's desk, rarely seeing the light of day. Today, submitting a professionally crafted business plan is less important than making it clear what the entrepreneur has accomplished in the way of starting the business.[1] Investors want to see that the venture has customers and a track record, however brief. They want to see that the business model actually works. The new environment for business planning actually makes the case for the importance of a feasibility study and micro strategies to prove the concept and enable the founding team to launch the venture and test it before completing the formal business plan and seeking outside investment capital.

This chapter explores a new way to look at the business plan process that is not only more in alignment with investors but also makes sense in a changing business environment where speed, flexibility, and fast innovation are the new normal.

FROM FEASIBILITY TO PROOF OF CONCEPT

Chapters 1 through 8 focused on helping the reader design and analyze a business opportunity to determine if there was a market of sufficient size with customers who had a need the entrepreneur could fill. However, although feasibility analysis answers some vital questions, until the entrepreneur tests the business model in the market in a real way, there is no way to know if this business can succeed.

Proof of concept (POC) is simply evidence that a technology, product, business model, or idea is feasible. For entrepreneurs, the form that the evidence takes is critical because it will significantly influence the decision about whether to launch the business. Entrepreneurs typically face two types of POC: the technology or product POC, and the business model POC. The technology or product POC relates to whether the technology or product does what it's supposed to do and whether it can be manufactured or built in sufficient quantities at the right price to meet market needs. The business model POC proves that the there is a way to deliver value to the customer and make money with the venture.

Figure 9.1 depicts various types of POCs and the strength of the evidence they provide. Clearly having actual customer sales is the strongest proof. It is important to note that these POC tests all involve field work with the customer. Supporting evidence from secondary sources such as industry analysts and third party statistics providers are not POC, strictly speaking, because they don't directly address the specific product or technology the entrepreneur is offering. The next sections will discuss various approaches to developing a proof of concept beginning with a micro strategy approach.

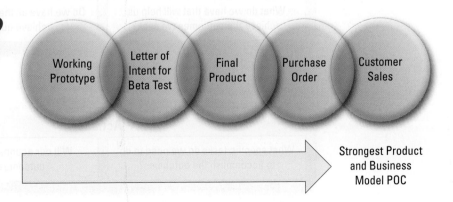

FIGURE 9.1

Proof of Concept Scale

Working Prototype

Letter of Intent for Beta Test

Final Product

Purchase Order

Customer Sales

Strongest Product and Business Model POC

The Micro Strategy Approach to Proof of Concept

The environment for entrepreneurs going forward will be characterized by an increase in uncertainty, fewer available resources, and a need for more innovation.[2] This type of environment calls for startups that can move and adapt quickly as they implement smaller strategies to accomplish near-term outcomes on the path to bigger, longer-term goals. Logan and Fischer-Wright have called this type of business planning *micro strategies*, and it is adapted from military science.[3] This text has taken micro strategies one step further to adapt the approach to an entrepreneur's need to prove a concept for a new venture quickly while avoiding the inertia of planning.

Figure 9.2 depicts the Entrepreneur's Micro Strategy for Proof of Concept. Like the Logan-Fischer-Wright model, it consists of three primary elements: (1) outcomes, which are the near-term goals that the entrepreneur is attempting to achieve; (2) assets, which are the human, social, physical, and financial assets needed to achieve the outcomes desired; and (3) actions, which are the tasks the entrepreneur must undertake to achieve the necessary outcomes.

The three elements interact and take the entrepreneur forward through much the same type of effectual process that was used to conduct feasibility analysis. What that means is the entrepreneur sets a specific outcome, then considers the assets currently available to achieve the outcome. If the entrepreneur

FIGURE 9.2

Entrepreneur's Micro Strategy for Proof of Concept

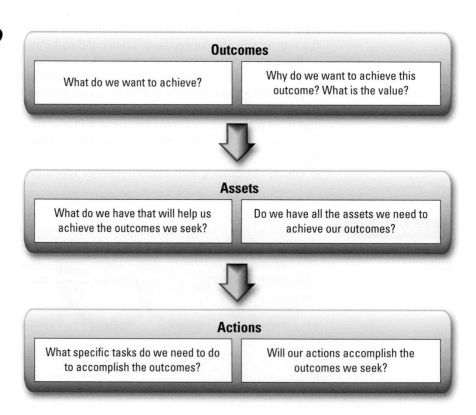

doesn't have the right assets or enough assets, the process doesn't stop, it simply shifts to an interim strategy designed to secure the needed assets. For example, the founders of one Internet company had set an outcome of proving their business model in two months. Unfortunately, along the way they discovered that their users were not willing to pay for their services. Instead of giving up, however, they devised an interim strategy to determine what their users valued so they would have a better understanding of what they were willing to pay for. Once they had that knowledge (the missing asset), they could go back to working on the original outcome.

The micro strategy process repeats itself over and over again and with each successful outcome, the new business is moved toward a complete proof of concept. Somewhere in the process, the business is actually launched in a small, controlled way, so that the feedback from the micro strategy process is real and meaningful. Assets are gathered, outcomes are determined, and when assets and outcomes are congruent, the entrepreneur sets up an action plan to achieve the outcome.

The Role of Intuitive Decision Making

The micro strategy approach to planning a business enables more flexibility and makes it possible for a startup to adapt and change quickly as new information is gathered. The problem with the traditional business plan is that it was always focused on the document, often a 50-page monstrosity that solidified the plan and made it more likely that the entrepreneur would not modify it in the face of new information. Entrepreneurs were expected to have everything resolved before they ever launched the business. In today's environment, no one is able to predict with any degree of certainty what the future holds. More and more, entrepreneurs have to rely on intuitive decision making, and the traditional business planning process is not conducive to this approach. Nobel Prize-winning psychologist Daniel Kahneman believes that there are some circumstances where intuition plays an important role in decision making. For example, when entrepreneurs are pressured by time, as occurs when there is a brief window of opportunity to launch, they may need to follow their intuition. This is particularly true where they have been able to create a clear and simple story around the business that gives them a high degree of confidence in their intuition whether or not that story is based in reality.[4] Intuition also works when a situation is defined by a certain structure or predictability; it is less reliable in a very uncertain environment or where the problem is unique with no precedent.

Unfortunately, entrepreneurs are typically very confident individuals, so they inspire confidence in others, even when there is no basis for that confidence. Entrepreneurs who are aware of this potential flaw in their objectivity would be well advised to consider the premortem, suggested by Gary Klein, senior scientist at MacroCognition.[5] The premortem has the entrepreneurial team assuming the new venture fails and then identifying all the reasons the business failed. This exercise is not designed to kill a new venture but to force the team to modify its thinking so as to avoid potential failure points.

Failure Points in Decision Making

One of the biggest failure points with a founding team is pattern-recognition bias. For example, where a team has deep experience in the industry in which they're starting the business, they tend to overweight the value of that experience: *we always do it that way.* By relying too heavily on previous experience, entrepreneurs are in danger of ignoring new information that might be important. To avoid pattern-recognition bias, the team needs to change its angle of vision by looking at the situation in a new way and then testing alternative hypotheses.[6]

Another failure point is forecasts of markets that are too optimistic. Anytime a member of the founding team is too confident in his or her projections, it raises a red flag that should warn the team to step back and reconsider the ways that forecast could miss the mark.

Business planning entails a series of decisions, many of which are intuitive. Each decision involves data gathering and analysis, conclusions and insights. In other words, business planning is a process, not an event or end document.

Proof of Concept with a Prototype

One of the biggest problems that technology or product entrepreneurs have is that until they actually build a POC prototype of what they're offering, it's difficult to gauge customer interest or demand. Even if the entrepreneur is solving a real problem customers have, they still will not make the commitment to purchase without the ability to try the product. The POC is usually developed quickly; it contains most of the key functionality, but it hasn't had a lot of testing. In that sense, it does not adequately represent the final product. Nevertheless, it does have a number of important benefits:

- The entrepreneur develops a clear understanding of customer needs
- Changes can be made early in the process when they are less costly
- The prototype reduces the risk of failure

Proof of Concept with a Website

Today when people hear about a new business or a new product or service, the first place they go for more information is the Internet. This makes sense, because the Internet is the perfect place to communicate a new venture's message and to get feedback. However, many new businesses make the mistake of simply slapping up a single page marked "under construction" or "coming soon" until they finish their due diligence and start the business. It is far better to wait to put up a website until the entrepreneur has something valuable for customers to see. On the Internet, a new business can look as successful and established as any large company for relatively few dollars invested in development of the site. A quick online demonstration can communicate to the visitor what the business does, who its customers are, and what its value proposition is.

The site can inform users about the founding team, the company's mission and goals, and disclose to potential investors, customers, and other interested parties how to contact the business. It can also communicate to customers/users the look and feel of the site without demonstrating the full functionality. But most importantly, this beta site will tell the entrepreneur whether people are interested, how much time they spend on the site, how often they come back, and whether they communicate with the company. In other words, it will prove that it's worth the time and money for the entrepreneur to build out a more elaborate site.

One word of caution about websites, particularly in the beta phase: Proprietary information that is not protected by patents or trademarks should not be put on the site, because companies regularly peruse the Internet for information on their competitors. In fact, entrepreneurs should definitely study the websites of their competitors for important clues about what features they should build into their own sites and how they might improve on what their competitors are doing. As with every promotional or informational piece about the business, differentiation is critical. It is not within the scope of this text to discuss website development; however, information on building an effective website is ubiquitous on the Internet and in every bookstore.

Proof of Concept with Purchase Orders and Customer Sales

Today most investors are seeking ventures that have the most powerful POC: a customer. For some types of products, securing a purchase order or actual sale is very possible. For example, Nordic Track, the successful supplier of workout equipment, started its business by getting customers to pay upfront to order one of its original skier machines. In this way, the company didn't have huge inventory costs and its customers were funding the manufacturing costs.

Proof of concept can take many forms, from the simple prototype to an actual sale. Figure 9.1 at the beginning of this section depicts the spectrum of POC approaches from weakest to strongest. The point is not to settle on one but to move through the entire spectrum with one POC building on the next until critical mass is achieved and the entrepreneur is confident that the business can survive.

STAKEHOLDER INTERESTS

Every new venture has stakeholders external to the founding team. These stakeholders view the new venture from different perspectives; consequently, entrepreneurs need to modify their executive summaries, pitches, and business plans to address the needs of these stakeholders. Here we discuss the interests of investors, bankers and lenders, and strategic partners.

Investor Interests

Anyone investing in a new venture has four principal concerns: rate of growth, return on investment, degree of risk, and protection. Investors are generally betting that the value of their ownership interest in the business will increase over time at a rate greater than that of another type of investment or of a bank account. They want to know how fast the business is projected to grow, when that growth will take place, and what will ensure that the growth actually occurs as predicted. For this reason, they tend to look for market-driven companies rather than product- or technology-driven companies. They expect that predictions will be based on solid evidence in the marketplace and on thorough knowledge of the target market.[7] Investors are naturally concerned about when and how the principal portion of their investment will be repaid and how much gain on that investment will accrue over the time they are invested in the company. The answers to these concerns are largely a function of the structure of the investment deal: whether it involves a limited or general partnership, or preferred or common stock, and so forth. Investors want to understand thoroughly the risks they face in investing in the new venture; principally, they want to know how their original equity will be protected. They expect the entrepreneur to present the potential challenges facing the new venture, along with a plan for mitigating or dealing with them to protect the investors against loss.

Although the business plan is vital to investment decision making, it is not the only piece of information considered. In one survey of 42 venture capitalists, 43 percent claimed to have invested in a venture in the previous three years without the benefit of a business plan.[8] Only 36 percent reported that the business plan was "very important" in their evaluation. And perhaps the most revealing statistic of all was that 96 percent preferred to learn about a potential investment through a referral from someone they trusted. Furthermore, investors found that the primary flaws in most business plans were overly optimistic financial projections, too much hype, poor explanation of the business model, and no demonstration of customer demand.

Bankers' and Lenders' Interests

Bankers and lenders are primarily interested in the company's margins and cash flow projections, because they are concerned about how their loans or credit lines to the business will be repaid. The margins indicate how much room there is for error between the cost to produce the product (or deliver the service) and the selling price. If margins are tight and the business has to lower prices to compete, the firm may not be able to pay off its loans as consistently and quickly as the bank would like. Similarly, bankers look at cash flow projections to see whether the business can pay all its expenses and still have money left over at the end of each month. Bankers also look at the qualifications and track record of the management team and may require personal guarantees of the principals. When considering a business plan and an entrepreneur for a loan, lenders have several concerns:

- *The amount of money the entrepreneur needs.* Lenders are looking for a specific amount that can be justified with accurate calculations and data.

- *The kind of positive impact the loan will have on the business.* Lenders would like to know that the money they are lending is not going to pay off old debt or to pay salaries, but rather will improve the business's financial position, particularly with regard to cash flow.

- *The kinds of assets the business has for collateral.* Not all assets are created equal. Some assets have no value outside the business, because they are custom-made or specific to that business and therefore cannot be sold on the open market. Lenders prefer to see industry-standard equipment and facilities that can easily be converted to another use.

- *How the business will repay the loan.* Lenders are interested in the earnings potential of the business over the life of the loan, but even more important, they want to know that the business generates sufficient cash flow to service the debt. Fixed expenses are fairly easy to predict, but variable expenses—those related to the production of the product or service—present a more difficult problem. In an attempt to avoid any long-term issues, lenders pay close attention to the market research section of the business plan, which highlights the demand for the product/service. They also focus on the marketing plan, which tells them how the entrepreneur intends to reach the customer.

- *How the bank will be protected if the business doesn't meet its projections.* Lenders want to know that the entrepreneur has a contingency plan for situations where major assumptions prove to be wrong. They want to ensure that they are paid out of cash flow, not by liquidating the assets of the business, which generally would only give them a small percentage of the value of the assets.

- *The entrepreneur's stake in the business.* Like investors, lenders feel more confident about lending to a business in which the entrepreneur has a substantial monetary investment. Such an investment reduces the likelihood that the entrepreneur will walk away from the business, leaving the lender stranded.

Strategic Partners' Interests

Some entrepreneurs, particularly those who intend to manufacture a product or bring a new drug or medical device to market, choose to form a strategic alliance with a larger company so that they don't have to incur the tremendous costs of purchasing equipment for a manufacturing plant or funding expensive clinical trials required by the FDA (Food and Drug Administration). They may, for example, license another firm to manufacture and assemble the product and supply it to the entrepreneur to market and distribute. Alternatively, an entrepreneur may enter into an agreement with a supplier to provide necessary raw materials in exchange for an equity interest in the startup venture.

Strategic alliances may take the form of formal partnership agreements with major corporations or may consist simply of an informal agreement such as a large purchase contract. In either case, the larger company that is allying itself with the new venture is usually looking for new products, processes, or technologies that complement its current line of products or services. Accordingly, it will seek a new venture management team that has some previous corporate experience so that the relationship will be smoother. Larger companies are also interested in strategic issues such as the marketing and growth strategies of the new venture.

Knowing in advance what these third parties are looking for will help entrepreneurs address their specific needs in the business plan, enhancing the partnership's ability to achieve the goals of the business.

CREATING A COMPELLING STORY IN AN EXECUTIVE SUMMARY

Today most investors want to see a well-written executive summary that tells a compelling story and grabs their interest. An important argument for developing an executive summary and pitch is that it forces entrepreneurs to identify and focus on the most persuasive aspects of the business. One of the biggest problems entrepreneurs have is developing and honing a convincing story about their new venture that creates excitement and interest and encourages the listener to want to know more. An effective executive summary and its associated pitch, which may be in the form of a PowerPoint deck or Prezi presentation, will do the following:

- Convey the compelling story quickly and memorably
- Highlight the critical elements of the business that provide a competitive advantage
- Highlight the various proofs of concept that have been achieved
- Present a coherent path to profitability and success that makes sense
- Demonstrate that the team can successfully execute the plan

With a highly focused executive summary and pitch presentation in hand, it will be easier to develop a full business plan, if required, without deviating from the essentials. In the next sections, essential questions are explored that must be answered by the executive summary. They are organized in an order that builds the compelling story.

What Is the Compelling Story?

It is vital to lead with the most persuasive reason for the existence of the business. Leading with the compelling reason solves the problem of grabbing attention in the first 15 seconds and makes sure that what investors need to hear is up front and obvious. Does the entrepreneur have a unique solution to a big

SOCIAL ENTREPRENEURSHIP: MAKING MEANING

The Little Schoolhouse That Could

Gifford Pinchot is best known for his classic 1985 book, *Intrapreneuring: Why You Don't Have to Leave the Corporation to Become an Entrepreneur*, but largely thanks to the influence of his grandfather, who founded the forest service in 1905, Pinchot has become an avid conservationist. In that capacity, he founded the Bainbridge Island Graduate Institute (BGI) near Seattle, Washington, in 2002. There, students are immersed in studies of environmental sustainability and social responsibility in the context of entrepreneurship and innovation.

BGI was launched in just six months with $120,000 of Pinchot's own money. Thereafter, he raised another $300,000 from Ben Cohen (Ben & Jerry's co-founder) and Wayne Silby (founder of the Calvert Fund). He recruited a president and together they worked to gain state authorization to award an MBA. The first class of 18 students enrolled in the fall of 2002. BGI is one of the first graduate schools in the United States to focus on sustainable business, to "create profit in ways that contribute to taking care of people and the planet." Pinchot is determined to make a mark on society by educating more people in how to be entrepreneurial while also being socially responsible. Today the school also prides itself on teaching its students how to find their "internal compass," which helps them figure out what they really want to do with their lives. Kelly Scott-Hanson, president of Co-Housing Resources, attended one of the entrepreneurial classes, where she learned how to write a business plan and present to local investors. Now her company is doing a better job of investing in projects that return their investment in five years while at the same time doing good for society.

Sources: BGI, www.bgi.edu, www.bgiedu.org "Green Curriculum," *Washington CEO* (January 12, 2006); BGI, http://www.bgiedu.org/index.htm; and E. Winninghoff, "The Little Green Schoolhouse," *Inc. Magazine* (July 2003), www.inc.com.

problem? Does the founding team include name brand people who have had previous successes? The compelling story needs to be the attention grabber so the listener will want to hear more.

What Pain Is Being Addressed?

Entrepreneurs need to emphasize that they are going to solve very big and very important problems. Note that big market was not included in that statement. This is because initial markets are always those in which the pain is greatest, so customers don't have to think about whether they want to buy, and that means that the initial market may be relatively small. As long as the market is growing, it is more important that the entrepreneur is solving a critical pain with a value proposition the customer quickly understands. For example, the new venture will reduce costs, increase speed, eliminate inefficiency, increase revenues, prolong life, or solve whatever the pain happens to be. Entrepreneurs need to demonstrate through their market research with potential customers that there is a growing market for their opportunity, which is based on solving a real need that customers possess.

How Is the Venture Solving the Problem?

Here the entrepreneur should demonstrate a clear link between the problem or pain and a solution. What is the new venture providing and how does it specifically solve the problem? What kind of business is this? Where does it fit in the value chain? If the entrepreneur currently has customers or any proof of concept, now is the time to emphasize these facts. It's important for entrepreneurs to be specific about who their first customer is and how they know that a customer exists. Getting the customer wrong means there is no business.

What Is This Venture's Competitive Advantage?

No venture can succeed in the long term without a sustainable competitive advantage—not a single competitive advantage, but a bundle of them encompassing every aspect of the business. The executive summary needs to address which advantages will enable this venture to create a unique unserved niche and to enter the market and secure customers with little or no competition in the beginning. The reality is that every new venture has competition, so it's important to recognize where competitive threats might occur. In the executive summary, entrepreneurs should be very specific about comparing their offering with a significant competitor. Given the competitor's established brand and position in the market, why would customers choose the entrepreneur's company?

Can This Venture Make Money?

Most executive summaries do not adequately address the business model. How will the business create and capture value that will enable it to make money over the long term? In general, value is created when the business is adequately capitalized and has highly regarded investors, an experienced management team, customers, a unique technology, product, or service, the ability to continually innovate, and a rapidly expanding market.[10] Once the new venture has passed the startup stage, additional value is created by its position in the market, significant customers, effective operating systems, a strong gross margin, positive cash flow, and a high return on equity. Entrepreneurs need to be able to identify the critical metrics on which the business will be judged and demonstrate that the business model can be leveraged to develop new revenue streams and is scalable as the market grows or new markets are added.

Because executive summaries are most often used to raise capital, the questions they answer are frequently of great interest to an investor or lender. How much money is needed to address this opportunity? How will capital be allocated (i.e., to increase sales, to boost profits, or to enhance the value of the company) and at which milestones? How will the business provide a superior return on investment (ROI)? Which exit strategies are possible?

In addition to explaining the business model, the entrepreneur needs to present a well-thought-out summary financial plan with 3 to 5 years of projected revenues, expenses, cash flow, and headcount or personnel requirements at various milestones. When will the company break even on cash? When will it make a profit? These numbers must be backed up with solid assumptions. In the executive summary, only the key numbers and their assumptions are presented.

Entrepreneurs also need to identify the critical success factors for the business as well as the critical risk factors and how they will mitigate them.

Can the Founding Team Serve That Need?

Why is this founding team the best team to execute this concept? Can it be demonstrated that the founding team has the experience and skills required by the various areas of the business? If the team has someone who accomplished something significant in the industry, it should be highlighted. Do the founders have their own money invested in this concept? It is easy to spend other people's money or to consider "sweat" equity as equivalent to cash—but it isn't equivalent in the eyes of investors, who figure that the founding team won't give up easily if they have invested their own money in the deal. Does the team have the passion and the drive to make this business a success? Passion and drive are difficult to measure but are reflected in the level of work that was put into the market research. How many people did the team talk to—industry experts, customers, and so forth? The bottom line is that entrepreneurs must prove that their team has relevant expertise and experience.

Why Is Now the Right Time to Launch This Venture?

What makes this concept so valuable right now? If this business is the only one of its kind, why is that so? Has anyone tried this before and failed? If so, why? What makes the current environment right for this venture? Timing is critical in the launch of any new venture, so it is important to explain why *now* is the right time and how long the window of opportunity will remain open.

What Is the Team Seeking from Investors?

A finely honed executive summary is needed whether or not the entrepreneur is seeking investor capital. If the new venture is self funded, this section would discuss the funding plan going forward. What will be the various sources of capital? If the entrepreneur is seeking investor capital, this section will specify the minimum amount of equity capital required to meet the next major milestone. If the entrepreneur expects to need several rounds of investment, the associated milestones and funding amounts should be projected.

Guidelines for Executive Summaries and Pitch Decks

Pulling the executive summary and the pitch into a coherent story is critical to persuading others to give the entrepreneur's business a chance. Here are some guidelines to consider when developing the executive summary and pitch deck.

- Keep the executive summary to no more than 3 to 5 pages, single spaced with white space and headers for easy reading.
- Read each sentence multiple times to prune unnecessary words and to make sure that the summary is focusing on the critical points. Each sentence should be clear and compelling.

- Include recognizable names if there is an established relationship.

- Avoid puff words and phrases such as "no one else is doing this" or "our financial projections are conservative." These types of words suggest that the entrepreneur hasn't done his or her homework.

- Avoid jargon and acronyms that might be foreign to the reader or listener.

- Explain the business, no matter how technical or complex, in words that anyone can understand.

- Use analogies if they help the reader or listener to quickly understand your business. For example, "we are the eBay for the auto parts industry."

- Keep the pitch deck to about 10 slides that contain only the key points. Graphics and high quality photos are generally more effective than text.

Entrepreneurs should keep in mind that the purpose for doing an executive summary or pitch is to sell the business. That means that entrepreneurs should not go deep into any one topic; they should hit only the most critical points. The problem or compelling pain statement should take no more than two sentences. If readers or listeners can't understand the pain immediately—if the entrepreneur has to explain it—then it's not a compelling pain. Explaining in excruciating detail how the product or technology works is not needed to sell the business. What is needed is an understanding of how the product or technology solves a problem.

THE FULL BUSINESS PLAN: STRATEGY AND STRUCTURE

Writing a business plan is a huge undertaking that should be planned in terms of tasks and timeline. If a new venture has already been launched in limited form to achieve proof of concept as suggested in previous sections—via a website or an actual startup based on a successful feasibility analysis—the writing of the business plan must now be sandwiched among all the day-to-day activities associated with an operating business. Even if a new venture has not yet been launched, an action plan for completing a business plan in a relatively short period of time will help accelerate the process. The following tasks are a guide to the founding team in preparing to write the business plan.

- *Identify who is responsible for what.* A lot of updated information must be gathered about industry, market, customer, and costs. Even though all of these data were gathered when the feasibility study was conducted, some time may have elapsed before the writing of the business plan, so it is important to make sure that all information is current. Make a list of everything that must be collected and how it needs to be collected (secondary research, talking to customers, etc.). Decide who will do what and by when it must be accomplished.

- *Develop a timeline based on tasks identified.* It is important to be realistic about how much time it will take to complete all the tasks associated with the business plan. The timeline is very likely to be too long, especially if the work is being done on evenings and weekends, so the next job will be to determine whether all of the tasks are critical to the business plan and to prune any that are not.

- *Hold the team to the timeline and work diligently to get the plan done.* Once the business plan is complete, it's a good idea to get a trusted third party to review the plan to catch anything the team may have missed.

Components of the Business Plan

All business plans have some major sections in common. The outline in Table 9.1 is a guide to the sections that are typically included and some of the areas that need to be covered in those sections. It is important that entrepreneurs customize their business plans to meet their specific needs and the needs of those who will read them. Table 9.1 notes the various chapters in this book where a particular section is discussed in detail. Here we will summarize only those sections that were not part of the feasibility analysis. The sections on "The Business," "Founding or Management Team," "Industry/Market Analysis," and "Product/Service Development" were discussed in detail in previous chapters as noted.

Operations Plan

This section of the business plan contains a detailed description of the business operations, including those processes that the new venture will own and undertake in-house, such as assembly, and those that will be outsourced to a strategic partner, such as manufacturing. A major portion of this section explains how the business will operate, where it will get its raw materials, how a product will be manufactured and/or assembled, and what type and quantity of labor will be required to operate the business. The location strategy for the business is also included in this section.

Organization Plan

This section discusses the legal form of organization that the venture will take, whether that be sole proprietorship, partnership, LLC, or corporation. It also deals with the entrepreneur's philosophy of management and company culture as these are significant competitive advantages if developed well. The section will include an organization chart showing key management, talk about personnel required for specific duties, employee incentives, and discuss the use of strategic partners.

Marketing Plan

The marketing plan is something quite distinct from market analysis. Market analysis gives the entrepreneur the information about the customer and market that will be used to create a marketing plan. The marketing plan, by contrast, is the strategy for communicating the company's message, developing awareness of the product or service (brand equity), and enticing the customer to purchase. The marketing plan includes a discussion of the plan's purpose, the market niche, the business's identity, tools that will be used to reach the customer, a media plan for specific marketing tools, and a marketing budget.

TABLE 9.1   Business Plan Outline

Executive Summary

Table of Contents

The Business—Chapter 4

What is the pain or problem the business is addressing?

Who is the customer and what is the value proposition (solution) being delivered?

How will the value be delivered (distribution) to the customer?

What is the differentiation strategy?

What is the business model?

What are the potential spin-offs from the original products/services, and what is the company's potential for growth?

Founding or Management Team—Chapter 7

Qualifications of the founding team

How critical tasks will be covered

Gap analysis, or what's missing (professional advisors, board of directors, independent contractors)

Industry/Market Analysis—Chapter 5

Industry analysis: demographics, opinion leaders, trends, etc.

Target market analysis: demographics, market segmentation, first customer profile, demand estimates

Competitor analysis and competitive advantages

Distribution channels (alternatives and risk/benefit)

Entry strategy (initial market penetration, first customer)

Product/Service Development Plan—Chapter 6

Detailed description and unique features/benefits of product/service

Technology assessment (if applicable)

Plan for prototyping and testing (all businesses require this)

Tasks and timeline to completion of product or service prototype (all businesses)

Acquisition of intellectual property

Operations Plan—Chapter 13

Facilities and location

Business processes including all functions (inventory, warehousing, etc.)

Plan for outsourcing

Plan for manufacturing and distribution

Organization Plan—Chapter 10, Chapter 12

Philosophy of management and company culture

Legal structure of the company and legal environment

Organizational chart and key management

Personnel required (headcount)

Strategic partners

Marketing Plan—Chapter 14

Purpose of marketing plan, business identity

Target market and unique market niche

Customer acquisition plan

Marketing strategy and tactics

Financial Plan—Chapter 8, Chapter 15, Chapter 16

Summary of key points and capital requirements

Risk factors and mediation

Break-even analysis and payback period

Narrative assumptions for financial statements

Full set of pro forma financial statements (cash flow, income, balance sheet) for three years

Plan for ongoing funding

Growth Plan—Chapter 17

Strategy for growth

Resources required (personnel, facilities, equipment, capital)

Infrastructure changes resulting from growth

Contingency Plan and Harvest Strategy—Chapter 18

Strategies for dealing with deviations from the plan

Strategies for harvesting the wealth created from the business

Timeline to Launch—Chapter 9

Graphic: Tasks that will need to be accomplished up to the date of launch of the business in the order of their completion. Also includes milestones: first customer, multiple customers, and multiple products.

Endnotes

Appendices (A, B, C, etc.)

Questionnaires, maps, forms, résumés, and the like

Financial Plan

This section demonstrates the financial viability of the venture and explains the assumptions made by the entrepreneur in doing the forecasts. It is designed to show that all the claims about the product, sales, marketing strategy, and operational strategy can work financially to create a business that can survive and grow over the long term. The financial plan begins with a summary of the key metrics for the business: time to positive cash flow, break-even, sales volume, and capital requirements to launch the business. Fundamentally, it presents a snapshot of the entrepreneur's predictions for the immediate future of the business. Generally, these forecasts are in the form of a complete set of pro forma financial statements broken out by month in the first year or two, and then annually for the next two to three years.

Statement of Cash Flows Many CEOs use a statement of cash flows from operations, which is a bit more complex than the simple direct cash flow statement used for feasibility analysis. It provides information on changes in the company's cash account through inflows and outflows of cash and cash equivalents associated with the daily operations of the business. Operating cash inflows include sales and accounts receivable that have been collected, whereas nonoperating cash inflows are comprised of loans, investments, or the sale of assets. Cash outflows consist of inventory payments, accounts payable payments, and payments associated with payroll taxes, rent, utilities, and so forth. Nonoperating cash outflows include such items as payments of principal or interest on debt, dividend distribution, and asset purchase. A financially healthy company will see its major source of cash inflows coming from operating sources, such as sales. In preparing this type of cash flow statement, the income statement items are linked with changes from normal operations in the balance sheet from one period to the next. These include sales, cost of sales, and operating expenses. It is not within the scope of this book to go into further detail on this statement.

Income Statement The income statement, also known as a profit and loss statement, gives information about the projected profit or loss status of the business for a specified period of time. It depicts when the new venture will cover its costs and begin to make a profit. It is important to note that revenues and expenses are recorded in the income statement when a transaction occurs in the case of sales, or when a debt is incurred in the case of expenses, whether or not money has been received or expended. The income statement is also important in determining the tax liability the company will have.

Balance Sheet The balance sheet, called a "statement of financial position," is different from the other financial statements in that it looks at the financial health of the business at a single point in time—a given date—whereas the cash flow and income statements review a period of time: month, quarter, or year. The balance sheet is divided into two parts that must balance; that is, be equal to each other based on the following formula:

$$\text{Assets} = \text{Liabilities} + \text{Shareholders' Equity}$$

In small businesses, shareholders' equity is often called "owners' equity." Decisions made by the entrepreneur have a direct affect on the balance sheet. For example, an increase in sales typically results in an increase on the asset side of the balance sheet because the entrepreneur has had to increase inventory or purchase equipment to meet demand. Likewise, an entrepreneur's decision to retain earnings for growth will increase the equity portion of the balance sheet. The balance sheet is an important tool for answering questions about the health of the business. For example,

- Did debt financing increase or decrease from period to period? It is important to match any changes in debt financing to a particular decision or event.
- Did the amounts of accounts receivable and inventory increase or decrease relative to sales in the same period? This is an important measure of how well the business is managing these items.

Examining changes from period to period on the balance sheet is one way to gauge business performance. Ratios are another.

Ratios Entrepreneurs have a number of ratios that can be used as gauges to analyze a company's performance. Ratios compare items in the financial statements and convert them to relative terms so they can be compared to ratios in other periods or in other companies. It is not within the scope of this text to present all of the possible ratios available, so we discuss here five of the most common ratios used to measure liquidity, debt, and profitability.

Current ratio The current ratio provides information on the company's ability to meet short-term obligations. It is found by

$$\text{Current ratio} = \text{Total current assets}/\text{Total current liabilities}$$

The higher the number, the more liquid the company is and the more easily these assets can be converted to cash to pay off short-term obligations.

Profit margin This is a profitability ratio that uses net income and net sales from the income statement to give the percentage of each dollar of sales remaining after all costs of normal operations are accounted for. It is found by

$$\text{Profit margin} = \text{Net income}/\text{Net sales}$$

The inverse of this percentage (100% − PM) equals the expense ratio, that is, the percentage of each sales dollar accounted for by operating expenses.

Return on Investment This ratio provides a measure of the amount of return on the shareholders' investment based on the earnings of the company. It is found by

$$\text{Return on investment (ROI)} = \text{Net income}/\text{Shareholders' equity}$$

Inventory turnover This ratio is a measure of the liquidity of inventory or the number of times it turns over in a year. It is found by

$$\text{Inventory turnover} = \text{Cost of goods sold}/\text{Average inventory}$$

This ratio helps the entrepreneur judge whether the business has too much capital tied up in inventory.

One other tool that is valuable to know is break-even analysis, which tells an entrepreneur how many units must be sold before the company can achieve a profit or the sales volume required to be profitable. The break-even point is that point at which the total variable and fixed expenses are covered and beyond which the company makes a profit. The formula to calculate breakeven is as follows:

$$BEQ = \frac{TFC}{SP - VC \text{ (unit)}}$$

Where
TFC = total fixed costs
SP = selling price
VC = variable costs

As an example, assume that total fixed costs are \$300,000; selling price per unit is \$95.00; and variable costs per unit are \$45.00. Then the number of units that must be produced and sold to breakeven is found by

$$B/E = \frac{\$300,000}{\$95 - \$45} = 6,000 \text{ units}$$

The dynamic nature of markets today makes it almost impossible to project out three to five years with any degree of certainty—hence, the need and importance of having detailed financial assumptions that explain the rationale for the numbers. Also important is sensitivity analysis to identify triggers that may change the financial forecasts and affect the business negatively. Finally, the financial plan includes a funding plan with a timeline and milestones to indicate when the new venture will need an infusion of investor or other capital.

Growth Plan

The growth plan discusses how the entrepreneur plans to take the business from startup through the various stages of growth and outlines the strategy that will be used to ensure that the business model is sustainable and continues to scale over its life. This may mean looking at new products and services or acquiring other businesses. It is important that this section reassure an investor or lender that the company has a future.

Contingency Plan and Harvest Strategy

The contingency plan is simply a way of recognizing that sometimes, even "the best laid plans" don't work the way they were intended to work. It presents potential risk scenarios, usually dealing with situations such as unexpected high or low growth or changing economic conditions, and then, for each situation, suggests a plan to minimize the impact on the new business. By contrast, the harvest or exit strategy is the plan for capturing the wealth of the business for the entrepreneur and any investors. It typically involves a liquidity event, such as an initial public offering, a merger, or a sale, among other options.

It is not normally a good idea to discuss deal structure in a business plan. Entrepreneurs rarely value their businesses correctly—typically, they are far too optimistic. Putting such optimistic statements into the business plan only alerts an investor or other interested party that the entrepreneur is naïve. Entrepreneurs who seek investment capital will find that it is a long process that evolves over many meetings with potential investors; the eventual deal structure will be reflected in a term sheet. Deal structure is discussed further in Chapter 16.

Timeline to Launch

The business plan should contain a graphic that depicts the timeline to launch and the critical milestones that take the business from its current status to first customer, multiple customers, and multiple products.

Appendices

Appendices are the appropriate place to put items that support the entrepreneur's claims in the main body of the report—things like résumés, calculations, surveys, spreadsheets, and so forth. A good rule of thumb is not to put in the appendix anything that it is vital for a reader to see. If the plan does have appendix items, a reference to those items should be made at the points in the body of the report where they are relevant.

Endnotes

Endnotes are simply the linked citations to material in the main body of the report that was gathered from sources other than the entrepreneur. Entrepreneurs must remember that when they are attempting to build a strong case for a new venture concept, they can't rely solely on their own opinions; they must support those opinions and arguments with solid evidence gathered from reliable sources.

Mistakes in Developing the Business Plan

Developing an effective business plan involves more than merely inserting information or data into the plan in an organized fashion. A persuasive plan requires that entrepreneurs weave a compelling story with supporting evidence so that readers can reasonably conclude that the business is viable. Unfortunately, many entrepreneurs make some common mistakes that could potentially cost them an investor or other interested party. The following sections present some of the common mistakes entrepreneurs make.

Rapid Growth That Requires Capabilities Beyond Those of the Founding Team

Examples of rapid growth include rapidly increasing demand, or sales doubling or tripling on an annual basis in the first few years. Entrepreneurs believe this will be very attractive to investors, but what they don't realize is that there is no evidence in the business plan that the founding team can manage and control this type of growth, which can cause great concern on the part of the investors who frequently have seen a business fail during rapid growth because management didn't have the systems in place to deal with it. It is far better to project controlled growth and exceed it with a plan for bringing on the necessary personnel when the company is ready for more rapid growth. The other danger in projecting too high a level of success is that doing so increases the chances that the new venture will not be able to live up to the projections; consequently, it is better to project more conservatively and try to exceed those projections.

One Ringleader in a Three-Ring Circus

Many entrepreneurs pride themselves on being generalists, claiming to have expertise in all the functional areas of the new venture. What they really have is general knowledge of all the functional areas and a real expertise in perhaps only one area. Investors are very nervous about relying on solo entrepreneurs to lead world-class ventures. They much prefer a team of founders with at least one person specializing in each of the functional areas.[11]

Performance That Exceeds Industry Averages

Entrepreneurs who report performance that is better than that of existing companies in the industry in some or all areas of the business is a serious red flag for investors. Although it is possible for a new venture to exceed industry averages in a particular area, it is not likely. Most averages, such as those for receivables turnover, manufacturing costs, and bad debt losses, have come about as a result of economies of scale, which the new venture is not likely to achieve for some time. An entrepreneurial business should report performance measures at or slightly below industry averages, with a credible plan for exceeding those averages at some time in the future.

Price as a Market Strategy

Using price as a strategy for a product or service suffers from the same problem as projecting performance above industry averages. It is rarely possible for a new venture with a product or service that currently exists in the marketplace to enter on the basis of a lower price than that of its competitors. Established companies have achieved economies of scale that the new venture usually cannot duplicate; moreover, they can no doubt easily match the price set by a new entrant into the market.

Not Investing Capital in Their Own Businesses

Investors are more comfortable investing in a new venture where the entrepreneur has contributed a significant amount of the startup capital. That signals to the investors a level of commitment necessary to achieve the goals of the company and gives them confidence that the entrepreneur will not easily walk away from the venture.

SUCCESSFULLY PITCHING THE BUSINESS

For entrepreneurs seeking outside investment capital, it is not uncommon to be asked to do a pitch or presentation designed to persuade or sell the value of the business. Usually the pitch occurs after potential funders have reviewed the executive summary and determine that it is worth their time to hear from the entrepreneur and the founding team to judge whether they measure up to expectations.

The pitch should answer the fundamental questions discussed in the section on creating a compelling executive summary. The pitch itself should take less than half an hour—usually about 15 to 20 minutes, though questions and discussion will probably follow. The pitch should catch the audience's attention in the first 15 to 30 seconds. This is usually accomplished by conveying the compelling story of the pain or problem in the market, the magnitude of the pain, and how the new venture will cure or solve that pain for the customer. Here are some additional guidelines to consider to ensure an effective pitch.

- Stand without using a podium. This enables a better command of the situation, enhances rapport with the audience, and makes it easier to use gestures and visual aids.

- Move around (but no pacing), because moving helps reduce stress and livens up the presentation.

- Maintain eye contact with everyone and talk to the audience. Do not talk over their heads to the back of the room—that technique only works in large auditoriums.

- Visual aids, such as colorful PowerPoint slides with high-resolution photos and minimal text keep the pitch on track and focused on key points. Entrepreneurs should avoid using too many slides and complex animations, or listeners may find themselves more interested in the rhythm of the slides' motion than in what the entrepreneur is attempting to convey.

- Slides should be kept simple (no more than three lines per slide), be big enough to read from a distance, and be professional-looking.

- If there is a service or product involved, a live demonstration helps to generate excitement about the business, but ensure in advance that the demonstration is flawless.

Typically, the CEO and chief technical person will do the pitch, although other members of the team may be drawn in during the question and answer period. Most important, the team should practice the pitch in advance for a small group of friends or colleagues who can critique it. Alternatively, a practice session can be videotaped so that the founding team can critique themselves.

Answering Questions

When the founding team has successfully made it through the pitch, it has cleared the first hurdle. The second hurdle, however, is harder: answering questions from investors. One thing to remember about investors is that they generally like to ask questions to which they already know the answers; this is a test to see whether the founding team knows what it's talking about or whether the team is making up answers spontaneously. Investors often ask questions that either require an impossibly precise answer or are so broad that it's hard to tell what they are looking for. In this instance, the presenter should repeat the question to ensure that it has been understood or ask for clarification.

The type of question that poses the most problems for the founding team is the inordinately complex one that contains several underlying assumptions. For example, "If I were to analyze your new venture in terms of its market share before and after this potential investment, how would the market strategy have changed and how much of the budget should be allotted to changing that strategy?" The first thing an entrepreneur should do when faced with such a question is to ask that the question be repeated, to ensure that she hasn't missed anything or made an incorrect assumption. Alternatively, the entrepreneur can restate the question and confirm that she has understood it correctly. She can then take a few seconds to formulate an answer. With the more complicated question, the entrepreneur may feel comfortable answering only part of it; for example, the entrepreneur may have evidence that could be presented to support a change in market share as a result of the capital infusion. On the other hand, it is critical not to commit the venture to any change in course of action or any budget amount without having had time to consider it further and gather more facts. Saying this to investors in response to the question will no doubt gain the entrepreneur a measure of respect for having demonstrated that she doesn't make important decisions precipitously, without considering all the facts.

If investors ask a factual question to which the entrepreneur does not know the answer (usually, such queries are tangential to the business plan and are asked to see how the entrepreneur will respond), the entrepreneur should admit that he doesn't have that answer off the top of his head but will be happy to find it after the meeting is over and get back to the questioner. Finally, if the pitch or anything the team has proposed is criticized by investors (a likely possibility), the entrepreneur should be careful not to be defensive or to turn the criticism in any way on the audience.

FINAL THOUGHTS ON BUSINESS PLANS

Preparing and pitching a business plan are the culmination of months of work and represent the heart and soul of the new venture. If the business idea has been researched thoroughly and the entrepreneur has proven the business model in the market, the chances of starting a successful venture are enhanced. Entrepreneurs should understand, however, that micro-strategy business plans are not just for those starting new businesses, but for growing companies as well that are moving into new areas. A well-conceived plan enables the benchmarking of progress toward the company's goals. It establishes the purpose, values, and goals of the company that will guide its decision making throughout its life. No entrepreneur plans to fail, but many fail to plan and thus end up reacting spontaneously to situations in the business environment instead of proactively dealing with changes.

Undertaking a micro strategy type business plan is certainly a daunting task, but it is an important exercise that helps entrepreneurs understand more clearly every aspect of a new venture and how all the pieces fit together to create a system. Even successful entrepreneurs who have started businesses without a written plan have had to write business plans when they needed growth capital, a government grant, or a credit line from the bank. The important thing to remember is that a business plan is a living document that will no doubt undergo numerous changes over the life of the business.

New Venture Action Plan

- Develop a micro strategy approach to achieving proof of concept.
- Identify the stakeholders in the business and their interests.
- Create a compelling executive summary and pitch.
- Plan the development of a full business plan.

Questions on Key Issues

1. What is the difference between a feasibility study and a business plan?
2. Why might it be better to start the business after completing the feasibility study and before completing a business plan?
3. What are the principles behind the micro-strategy approach to proof of concept?
4. How might the business plan change if the reader were an investor versus a potential management hire?
5. What are three key elements of a successful business plan pitch?

Experiencing Entrepreneurship

1. Interview someone who invests in small businesses about what he or she looks for in a business plan. On the basis of your discussion, what will you need to remember when you write your business plan?
2. Go to www.bplans.com and select a business plan to review. Using the guidelines for an effective plan given in this chapter, evaluate the plan in three to five pages. What are its strengths and weaknesses? How can it be improved?

Relevant Case Studies

Case 4 The Crowne Inn
Case 8 Demand Media

CHAPTER

10

SELECTING THE LEGAL ENTITY

"It will not injure you to know enough of law to keep out of it."

—*The Old Farmer's Almanac* (1851)

CHAPTER OBJECTIVES

- Distinguish between sole proprietorships and partnerships.
- Discuss the corporate form and its advantages and disadvantages.
- Explain the limited liability company.
- Define the nonprofit corporation.
- Make a decision about which legal form to use for which purpose.
- Discuss how a business entity can evolve from one legal form to another.

The path that partnerships take is rarely smooth; instead, it's often mired by disagreements, differing goals and expectations, and sometimes greed and fraud. Partnerships of family members are particularly difficult because if the partnership ends, the parties are still connected through their familial relationships. That certainly was the case with Heather Antonelli and her mother JoAnn when they co-founded Eminence Style, an Atlanta-based furniture wholesaler, in 1996. It was exciting to grow the business to $3 million by 2000 using a slow organic growth strategy that gave them a measure of control. But in 2001, an opportunity came along that would test the partnership and the survival of the business.

A $2 million order from a Sears buyer meant the company could jump to the next level, but the order also came with a problem—Antonelli didn't have the operating capital to pay her outsourced manufacturing partner to make the furniture that Sears required. Fortunately in 2002, bank financing was plentiful and Antonelli was able to borrow $200,000 from the U.S. Small Business Administration, and $700,000 from Bank of America in addition to $55,000 from friends and family. This meant that she was on track to produce $5.5 million in sales, so she went ahead and paid the Hungarian factory a deposit to begin production. Unfortunately, the dollar began to lose value against the Euro and what she now owed her manufacturer had increased by 30 percent. Then a series of events spelled the demise of her business. Her Sears buyer left the company and the new buyer no longer wanted to honor the order. Additionally, she was losing customers to competitors whose prices were lower because they manufactured in China.

In what only could be described as a moment of irrationality due to stress, Antonelli moved the company headquarters to Austin, Texas, where her boyfriend lived, leaving her mother behind in Atlanta to run the showroom. This shift put a tremendous strain on the partnership. Both Antonelli and her mother had personally guaranteed all the loans, which meant that their personal assets were at stake. With the guidance of an attorney, Antonelli considered their options. When it was determined that it would take 4 years for the company to recover, Antonelli decided that the only way out was bankruptcy. She filed Chapter 7 despite knowing that her mother would lose her home. In the end, her mother had to move into an apartment and take work as a freelance furniture merchandiser. Antonelli, meanwhile, went to China to design a line of bedding and potentially open a restaurant.

Partnerships between businesses can be just as challenging as those between individuals, particularly where one company is significantly larger than the other. Steve A. Stone was a product manager at Microsoft who had conceived an interesting way to track digital objects across the Web. With a few of his Microsoft colleagues, he launched a company, Infoflows, and partnered with the huge photo library and licensing company, Corbis, coincidently owned by Bill Gates, the co-founder of Microsoft. In 2006, the two companies signed a multimillion dollar agreement to develop the product. However, just four months into the partnership, things began to turn bad and Infoflows ended up suing Corbis for misappropriation of trade secrets, fraud, and breach of contract. The jury found in favor of Infoflows and awarded damages of over $20 million, although Corbis plans to appeal. In the meantime, the members of the Infoflows team have taken on jobs as consultants and contractors to cover their expenses.

Sources: Lohr, S. (July 18, 2010), "In a Partnership of Unequals, a Start-up Suffers," *The New York Times*, www .nytimes.com/2010/07/19/technology/19startup .html; Chard, T. (July 19, 2010) "Infoflows Wins $20M in Corbis Case," *Xconomy – Seattle*, www.xconomy.com/seattle/ 2010/07/19/infoflows-wins-20m-in-corbis-case; and Heintz, N. (December 1, 2005), "Case Study: Was Bankruptcy the Answer?" *Inc Magazine*, www.inc.com/magazine/ 20051201/handson-bankrupt.html.

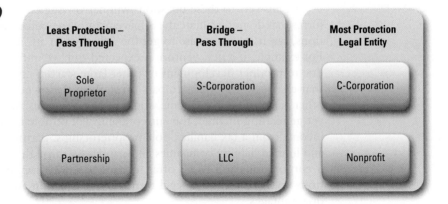

FIGURE 10.1

Legal Forms of Organization

The choice of legal structure is one of the most important decisions that entrepreneurs have to make because it will affect every aspect of the business, including tax planning and the cost of maintaining the legal structure. For example, if a business entails any degree of risk, such as product liability, then choosing a legal form that protects the entrepreneur's personal assets from being attached as the result of a lawsuit is just as important as carrying the appropriate insurance. The decision about the legal form of the business should reflect careful consideration about the type of business and the entrepreneur's personal goals for that business, and it should always be made under the guidance of a qualified attorney. To make an educated decision about the legal form of the business, it is imperative to understand all the risks and benefits associated with a chosen form. Figure 10.1 provides an overview of the various legal forms available to entrepreneurs according to the level of risk, with the sole proprietorship carrying the most risk.

MAKING THE DECISION ABOUT LEGAL FORM

Prior to making the decision on which type of legal form to choose, seven very important questions should be asked.

1. Does the founding team have all the skills needed to run this venture?
2. Do the founders have the capital required to start the business alone or must they raise it through cash or credit?
3. Will the founders be able to run the business and cover living expenses for the first year?
4. Are the founders willing and able to assume personal liability for any claims against the business?
5. Do the founders wish to have complete control over the operations of the business?
6. Do the founders expect to have initial losses or will the business be profitable almost from the beginning?
7. Do the founders expect to sell the business some day?

The answers to these questions will narrow the choices by eliminating legal forms that do not facilitate the achievement of the outcomes in these seven questions, but it is always wise to get the advice of an attorney and/or accountant. For example, if a new venture is expected to have initial losses in the first year due to product development or other large startup costs (question 6), a form that enables those losses to pass through to the owners to be applied against other personal taxable income would be advantageous. Since the company is not yet generating income, the entrepreneur will be able to shelter other personal income from a tax liability. Sole proprietorships, partnerships, S-corporations, and limited liability companies all permit pass-through earnings and losses, but S-corporations and LLCs offer more protection from liability. The next sections review the various legal forms of organization and their advantages and disadvantages.

SIMPLE FORMS: SOLE PROPRIETORSHIPS AND PARTNERSHIPS

All businesses operate under one of four broad legal structures—sole proprietorship, partnership, limited liability company, or corporation. Because the legal structure of a new venture has both legal and tax ramifications for the entrepreneur and any investors, entrepreneurs must carefully consider the advantages and disadvantages of each form. It is also quite possible that a business may decide to change its legal form sometime during its lifetime, usually for financial, tax, or liability reasons. These situations are discussed as each legal form is examined. Table 10.1 presents a summary comparison chart of all the structures.

Sole Proprietorship

More than 76 percent of all businesses in the United States are sole proprietorships, probably because the sole proprietorship is the easiest form to create. For the tax year 2006, the most current year for which numbers are reported, there were just over 22 million tax returns that reported sole proprietor income that was nonfarm in nature.[1] In a sole proprietorship, the owner is the only person responsible for the activities of the business and, therefore, is the only one to enjoy the profits and suffer the losses.

To operate as a sole proprietor requires very little—only a DBA, and not even that if the entrepreneur uses his or her name as the name for the business. In other words, a sole proprietorship called Jennifer Brooks Corporate Consultants does not require a DBA if the entrepreneur's name is Jennifer Brooks, but a sole proprietorship called Corporate Consultants does. A DBA, or Certificate of Doing Business Under an Assumed Name, can be obtained by filing an application with the appropriate local government agency. The certificate, sometimes referred to as a "fictitious business name statement," ensures that this is the only business in the area (usually a county) that is using the name the entrepreneur has chosen and provides a public record of business ownership for liability purposes.

TABLE 10.1   Comparison of Legal Forms

Issues	Sole Proprietorship	Partnership	Limited Liability Company	Subchapter S-Corporation	C-Corporation
Number of Owners	One	No limit	No limit. Most states require a minimum of two members.	100 shareholders or fewer	No limit on shareholders
Startup Costs	Filing fees for DBA and business license	Filing fees for DBA; attorney fees for partnership agreement	Attorney fees for organization, documents; filing fees	Attorney fees for incorporation documents; filing fees	Attorney fees for incorporation documents; filing fees
Liability	Owner liable for all claims against business, but with insurance can overcome liability	General partners liable for all claims; limited partners liable only to amount of investment	Members liable as in partnerships	Shareholders liable to amount invested	Shareholders liable to amount invested; officers may be personally liable
Taxation	Pass-through; taxed at individual level	Pass-through; taxed at individual level	Pass-through; taxed at individual level	Pass-through; taxed at individual level	Tax-paying entity; taxed on corporate income
Continuity of Life of Business	Dissolution on the death of the owner	Dissolution on the death or separation of a partner, unless otherwise specified in the agreement; not so in the case of limited partners	Most states allow perpetual existence. Unless otherwise stated in the Articles of Organization, existence terminates on death or withdrawal of any member.	Perpetual existence	Continuity of Life
Transferability of Interest	Owner free to sell; assets transferred to estate upon death with valid will	General partner requires consent of other generals to sell interest; limited partners' ability to transfer is subject to agreement	Permission of majority of members is required for any member to transfer interest	Shareholders free to sell unless restricted by agreement	Shareholders free to sell unless restricted by agreement
Distribution of Profits	Profits go to owner	Profits shared based on partnership agreement	Profits shared based on member agreement	Paid to shareholders as dividends according to agreement and shareholder status	Paid to shareholders as dividends according to agreement and shareholder status
Management Control	Owner has full control	Absent an agreement to the contrary, partners have equal voting rights	Rests with management committee	Rests with the board of directors appointed by the shareholders	Rests with the board of directors appointed by the shareholders

Advantages

A sole proprietorship has several advantages. First, it is easy and inexpensive to create. It gives the owner 100 percent of the company and 100 percent of the profits and losses. It also gives the owner complete authority to make decisions about the direction of the business. In addition, the income from the business is taxed only once, at the owner's personal income tax rate, and there are no major reporting requirements such as those imposed on corporations.

Disadvantages

There are, however, some distinct disadvantages that deserve serious consideration. The sole proprietor has unlimited liability for all claims against the business; that is, any debts incurred or judgments must be paid from the owner's assets. Therefore, the sole proprietor puts at risk his or her home, bank accounts, and any other assets. In today's litigious environment, exposure to lawsuits is substantial. To help mitigate this liability, a sole proprietor should obtain business liability insurance, including "errors and omissions coverage," which protects against unintentional negligence such as disseminating incorrect information in a company advertisement. Another disadvantage is that it is more difficult for sole proprietors to raise debt capital, because often the owner's financial statement does not qualify for the amount needed. The sole proprietor usually needs to rely on his or her skills alone to manage the business. Of course, employees with specific skills can be hired to complement those of the owner. Another complication associated with a sole proprietorship is that the business's ability to survive is dependent on the owner; therefore, the death or incapacitation of the owner can be catastrophic for the business if the owner did not transfer ownership through a will.

Often small businesses such as restaurants, boutiques, and consulting businesses are run as sole proprietorships. This is not to say that a high-growth venture cannot be started as a sole proprietorship—many are—but it will in all likelihood not remain a sole proprietorship for long, because the entrepreneur will typically want the protections and prestige that organizing as a corporation affords.

Jennifer Overholt, Anne Murguia, and A.C. Ross sought the freedom to work when they wanted and not have to worry about overhead and assets. They essentially wanted to be sole proprietors who partnered when it was expedient to do so. Indigo Partners, as their venture is called, is a loose association of seven partners who take on projects on their own or as a team. They all have the common bond of wanting to do what they want and spend a lot of time with family, friends, and traveling. As soloists, they partner to give themselves the freedom to control their time.

Partnership

When two or more people agree to share the assets, liabilities, and profits of a business, the legal structure is termed a partnership. The partnership form is an improvement over the sole proprietorship from the standpoint that the business can draw on the skills, knowledge, and financial resources of more than one person. This is an advantage not only in operating the business but also in seeking bank loans. Like the sole proprietorship, however, the partnership requires a DBA when the last names of the partners are not used in naming the business. Professionals such as lawyers, doctors, and accountants frequently employ this legal structure.

In terms of its treatment of income, expenses, and taxes, a general partnership is essentially a sole proprietorship consisting of more than one person so each partner pays taxes and receives income based on their proportionate interest in the partnership. However, where liability is concerned, there is a significant difference. In a partnership, each partner is liable for the obligations that any other partner incurs in the course of doing business. For example, if one partner signs a contract with a supplier in the name of the partnership, the other partners are also bound by the terms of the contract. This is known as the doctrine of ostensible authority. Creditors of an individual partner, on the other hand, can attach only the assets of that individual partner, including his or her interest in the partnership.

Partners also have specific property rights. For example, unless otherwise stated in the partnership agreement, each partner owns and has use of the property acquired by the partnership. Each partner has a right to share in the profits and losses, and each may participate in the management of the partnership. Furthermore, all choices related to elections such as depreciation and accounting method are made at the partnership level and apply to all partners.

Types of Partnerships

There are two types of partnerships: general and limited. In a general partnership, all the partners assume unlimited personal liability and responsibility for management of the business. In a limited partnership, by contrast, the general partners have unlimited liability, and they seek investors whose liability is limited to their monetary investment; that is, if such a limited partner invests $25,000 in the business, the most he or she can lose if the business fails is $25,000. It is important to note, however, that limited partners have no say in the management of the business. In fact, they are restricted by law from imposing their will on the business. The penalty for participating in the management of the business is the loss of their limited liability status. Other types of partnerships include (1) secret partners, who are active but not publicly known; (2) silent partners, who typically provide capital but do not actively participate in the management of the business; and (3) dormant partners, who are generally not known publicly and are not active, but still share in the profits and losses of the partnership.

Advantages

Partnerships have all the advantages of sole proprietorships plus the added advantage of sharing the risk of doing business. Partnerships enjoy the clout of more than one partner and, therefore, more than one financial statement. Partners can also share ideas, expertise, and decision making. Financially, partnerships enjoy pass-through earnings and losses to the individual partners, to be taxed at their personal tax rates.

Disadvantages

Partnerships also suffer from several disadvantages that entrepreneurs should consider carefully before choosing this form. Partners are personally liable for all business debts and obligations of the partnership, even when individual partners bind the partnership to a contract or other business deal. Unless otherwise stated in the partnership agreement, the partnership dissolves when a partner either leaves or dies. And finally, individual partners can be sued for the full amount of any partnership debt. If that happens, the partner who is sued, and loses, must then sue the other partners to recover their shares of the debt. It is important to understand that partnership litigation is expensive and time consuming, so having a solid partnership agreement that calls for arbitration may be the preferred way to go.[2]

Partnership Agreement

Although the law does not require it, it is extremely wise for a partnership to draw up a written partnership agreement, based on the Uniform Partnership Act, that spells out business responsibilities, profit sharing, and transfer of interest. This is advisable because partnerships are inherently fraught with problems that arise from the different personalities and goals of the people involved. A written document executed at the beginning of the partnership will mitigate eventual disagreements and provide for an orderly dissolution should irreconcilable differences arise. Many partnerships have minimized conflict by assigning specific responsibilities to each of the partners and detailing them in the partnership agreement. Additional issues arise when one or more of the partners in a partnership leaves, either voluntarily or through death. To protect the remaining partners, the partnership should have in place a buy-sell agreement and "key-person" life insurance.

A buy-sell agreement is a binding contract between the partners. It contains three primary clauses that govern the following issues:[3]

1. Who is entitled to purchase a departing partner's share of the business? May only another partner do so, or is an outsider permitted to buy in?
2. What events can trigger a buyout? Typically, those events include a death, disability, or other form of incapacity; a divorce; or an offer from the outside to buy the partner out.
3. What price will be paid for the partner's interest?

Having these issues decided from the beginning prevents disagreements and legal battles with the departing partner or with the estate of a deceased partner.

It is unfortunate that many entrepreneurs fail to take the precaution of creating a partnership agreement with a buy-sell clause. The consequences can be critical for the business. For example, say one partner dies, and the partnership, absent a buy-sell agreement, is forced to work with the spouse or a family member of the deceased, who may not be qualified to run the business. Yet another example is without a partnership agreement, one partner can potentially sell his or her interest to a stranger without the consent of the other partners, so it is critically important to have such an agreement.

"Key-person" life insurance is a policy on the life of principal members of the partnership, usually the senior partners. Upon the death of a partner, the insurance proceeds can be used to keep the business going or to buy out the deceased partner's interest under a buy-sell agreement. For more protection from liability than a partnership affords, organizing the business as a corporation or a limited liability company should be considered.

Any partnership should have an agreement to describe the structure of the partnership, who is entitled to what, and what happens if the partners disagree or leave the partnership. Table 10.2 presents some of the critical issues that should be addressed in the agreement. Because this is a legally binding contract, it should be reviewed by a qualified attorney.

GLOBAL INSIGHTS

China Espousing New Forms of Business Ownership

Since the 1970s, the Chinese economy has experienced exceptional growth, despite the fact that its transition from a centrally directed to a more open market economy has been relatively slow. China made a conscious decision to reform its state-owned enterprises gradually at the same time as it encouraged the development and growth of other forms of ownership, such as private, cooperative, and joint ventures. Today much of the success that China has experienced in the marketplace has been due to the rapid growth of entrepreneurial firms that are privately owned and market-driven. In China there are five types of entrepreneurial ventures: (1) state-owned businesses; (2) collective owned enterprises, which represent a defined group of people; (3) joint-stock companies, which are businesses that were previously state-owned but now have a majority of ownership shares held by private individuals; (4) sole proprietorships; and (5) foreign-invested ventures, which can be wholly owned by a foreign company or as a joint venture with a Chinese firm.

To continue its annual growth rate in GDP of approximately 8.7 percent, obstacles that the government has placed in the path of entrepreneurial ventures will need to be removed. These enterprises will have to be free to make production and business decisions, to set prices, market products, purchase materials, export and import, make investments, form partnerships, and set wages and bonuses, among many other activities common in a free enterprise system. In addition, the government will need to encourage foreign investment and increase the availability of low-cost borrowing and venture capital.

There is a long road ahead for China to become an efficient market economy where private ownership in the form of entrepreneurial firms drives technological change and economic growth and productivity. But the potential for positive effects domestically—and for the rest of the world—is there.

Sources: China Detail, www.chinadetail.com/Business/InvestmentChinaCompanyOwnership.php, accessed August 14, 2010; V. Hu, "The Chinese Economic Reform and Chinese Entrepreneurship," *Jornada d'Economia caixaManresa l'esperit emprenedor* (2005), http://unpan1.un.org/intradoc/groups/public/documents/APCITY/UNPAN023535.pdf; and A.M. Zapalska and W. Edwards, "Chinese Entrepreneurship in a Cultural and Economic Perspective," *Journal of Small Business Management*, 39(3) (2001): 286.

TABLE 10.2	**Critical Issues to Address with an Attorney Present**
Structuring an Effective Partnership Agreement	• The legal name of the partnership • The nature of the business • The duration of the partnership • Contributions of the partners • Sales, loans, and leases to the partnership • Withdrawals and salaries • Responsibility and authority of the partners • Dissolution of the partnership • Arbitration

CORPORATE FORMS

Only about 25 percent of all U.S. businesses are corporations, but they account for about 67 percent of all business receipts.[4] A corporation is different from the preceding two forms in that it is a legal entity in and of itself. The U.S. Supreme Court has defined the corporation as "an artificial being, invisible, intangible, and existing only in contemplation of the law." It is chartered or registered by a state and can survive the death of the owner(s) or the owner's separation from the business. Therefore, it can sue, be sued, acquire and sell real property, and lend money. The owners of the corporation are its shareholders, who invest capital in the corporation in exchange for shares of ownership. Like limited partners, shareholders are not liable for the debts of the corporation and can lose only the money they have invested.

Most new businesses form what is known as a closely held corporation; that is, the corporate stock is owned privately by a few individuals and is not traded publicly on a securities exchange such as the New York Stock Exchange. This chapter will focus on such private corporations. The issue of "going public" typically arises after the business is established and the entrepreneur wants to raise substantial capital for growth by issuing stock (shares of ownership in the corporation) through an initial public offering (IPO). The IPO and public corporations in general are the subject of Chapter 16.

A corporation is created by filing a certificate of incorporation with the state in which the company will do business and issue stock. This is called a domestic corporation. A foreign corporation, by contrast, is one that is chartered in a state other than in the one in which it will do business. A corporation requires the establishment of a board of directors, which meets periodically to make strategic policy decisions for the business. The regular documentation of these meetings is crucial to maintaining the corporation's limited liability status. The board also hires the officers who will run the business on a day-to-day basis.

There are two corporate forms from which to choose: the C-corporation and the S-corporation. Their purpose and advantages and disadvantages are discussed in the next sections.

C-Corporation

It would be difficult to claim that the Pennsylvania Railroad Corporation of the 1950s resembles in any way the General Electric Corporation of today, let alone the Business.com Corporation operating on the Internet. Even the most traditional of legal forms—the corporation—has evolved over time. Yet it remains the most commonly chosen legal structure for a growing company that seeks outside capital in the form of equity or debt.

Because it is a legal entity, the corporation can enter into contracts, sue, and be sued without the signature of the owners. In a startup or young company, however, bankers, creditors, and the like generally require that majority shareholders or officers personally guarantee loans to ensure that the lender is protected against the potential failure of the corporation by having the ability to pursue the assets of the owners. Personal guarantees should be avoided wherever possible, but the reality is that a young corporation has few assets, so its owners may not be able to avoid having to personally guarantee loans.

Advantages

The C-corporation offers several important advantages. It enjoys limited liability in that its owners are liable for its debts and obligations only to the limit of their investment. The only exception to this protection is payroll taxes that may have been withheld from employees' paychecks but not paid to the Internal Revenue Service. Capital can be raised through the sale of stock up to the amount authorized in the corporate charter; however, the sale of stock is heavily regulated by federal and state governments. A corporation can create different classes of stock to meet the various needs of its investors. For example, it may issue nonvoting preferred stock to conservative investors who, in the event that the corporation must liquidate its assets, will be first in line to recoup their investment. Common stock is more risky, because its holders are paid only after the preferred stockholders. Common stockholders are, however, entitled to vote at shareholders' meetings and to divide the profits remaining after the preferred holders are paid their dividends, assuming that these profits are not retained by the corporation to fund growth.

Ownership in a corporation is easily transferred. This is at once an advantage and a disadvantage, because entrepreneurs will want to be careful, particularly in the startup phase, to ensure that stock does not land in the hands of undesirable parties such as competitors. This problem is normally handled through a buy-sell clause in the shareholder's agreement that states that stock must first be offered to the corporation at a specified price before being offered to someone outside the corporation. Most entrepreneurs restrict the sale of their stock so that they can control who holds an ownership interest in the company.

Corporations typically enjoy more status and deference in business circles than do other legal forms, principally because they are a legal entity that cannot be destroyed by the death of one—or even all—of the principal shareholders. Moreover, to enter the public equity markets, a business must be incorporated, so it will be subjected to greater scrutiny from governmental agencies.

The reason for this scrutiny is the fact that the assets of the corporation are separate from the assets of the individual owner/shareholders. Therefore, the owners may take risks that they wouldn't take with their personal assets. Corporations can also take advantage of the benefits of retirement funds, Keogh and defined-contribution plans, profit-sharing arrangements, and stock option plans for their employees. These fringe benefits are deductible to the corporation as expenses and not taxable to the employee. Finally, the entrepreneur can hold certain assets (such as real estate) in his or her own name, lease the use of the assets to the corporation, and collect a lease fee.

Disadvantages

Corporations do, however, have disadvantages that must be carefully considered. They are certainly more complex to organize, are subject to more governmental regulation, and cost more to create than sole proprietorships or partnerships. Although it is possible to incorporate without the aid of an attorney, doing so is not recommended. In too many cases, businesses have failed or endured significant financial hardship because they did not incorporate properly at the start of the business or did not maintain the corporation according to the legal requirements.

A more cumbersome disadvantage derives from the fact that the corporation is literally a person for tax purposes. Consequently, if it makes a profit, it must pay a tax, whether or not those profits were distributed as dividends to the shareholders. And, unlike partners or sole proprietors, shareholders of C-corporations do not receive the pass-through benefit of losses (the S-corporation does enjoy these benefits). In a C-corporation, if losses can't be applied in the year they are incurred, they must be saved and applied against future profits. Accordingly, C-corporations pay taxes on the profits they earn, and their owners (shareholders) pay taxes on the dividends they receive; hence, the drawback of "double taxation." It is principally for this reason that many entrepreneurs who operate alone or with a partner do not employ this form. However, if an entrepreneur draws a salary from the corporation, that salary is expensed by the corporation, effectively reducing the company's net income subject to taxes. The entrepreneur will then be taxed at his or her personal income tax rate.

By creating a corporation and issuing stock, the entrepreneur is giving up a measure of control to the board of directors. Realistically however, in privately held corporations, the entrepreneur largely determines who will be on the board and will certainly seek people who support his or her vision. Entrepreneurs who seek outside venture funding in the very early stages of their venture where the risk is highest may find that they have to give up the majority of the stock to the investors. The choice is either to hang on to the equity and watch the business stall because funding can't be secured or to give up control so that the founder can own a smaller piece of something successful. It is not always necessary, however, that the founder retain 51 percent of the stock to maintain effective control. As long as the founder's skills and vision are vital to the success of the venture, and as long as the shareholders share that vision, the founder will have effective control of the organization, no matter how much stock she or he has given up. With a corporate form, unlike the sole proprietorship or partnership, the entrepreneur is accountable principally to the shareholders and secondarily to anyone else. If the corporation is privately held, the board usually serves at the pleasure of the entrepreneur, who is accountable to himself or herself and to any investors.

A corporation must endeavor in all ways to act as an entity separate from its owners. Entrepreneurs must keep personal finances completely separate from corporate finances, hold directors' meetings, maintain minutes, and not take on any financial liability without having sufficient resources to back it up. Failing to do any of these things can result in what is known as "piercing the corporate veil," which leaves the officers and owners open to personal liability.

Where to Incorporate

Apart from legal considerations, where to incorporate is also an important issue. It is normally advantageous to incorporate in the state in which the entrepreneur intends to locate the business, so that it will not be under the regulatory powers of two states (the state in which it is incorporated and the state in which it must file an application to do business as an out-of-state corporation). Normally, however, a corporation will not have to qualify as a "foreign" corporation doing business in another state if it is simply holding directors'/shareholders' meetings in the state, or holding bank accounts, using independent contractors, or marketing to potential customers whose transactions will be completed in the corporation's home state. It has often been said that incorporating in Delaware is wise because it has a large body of case law that makes it easier for a company to plan to avoid lawsuits, and Delaware's Chancery Court, which oversees corporate law, is reputed to be one of the finest in the United States. If neither seeking venture capital nor doing a substantial amount of business in Delaware is a goal of the company, however, the cost and hassle of qualifying in another state as well may outweigh the benefits of incorporating in Delaware. Moreover, today most states have modified their corporate laws to be in alignment with those in Delaware. Entrepreneurs should also consider the favorableness of the tax laws governing corporations in the state chosen. Some states, such as California, levy a required, minimum annual corporate income tax, whether the business has a taxable income or not.

S-Corporation

An S-corporation, unlike the C-corporation, is not a tax-paying entity. It is merely a financial vehicle that passes the profits and losses of the corporation to the shareholders. It is treated much like a sole proprietorship or a partnership in the sense that if the business earns a profit, that profit becomes the income of the owners/shareholders, and it is the owners who pay the tax on that profit at their individual tax rates. In this way, it avoids the double taxation found in the C-corporate structure. Approximately six states tax S-corporations like regular corporations, so it is important to check with the tax division of the state in which the entrepreneur will do business to find out if a tax will be imposed. S-corporation shareholders are not required to pay self-employment taxes (Social Security and Medicare), which can amount to more than 15 percent of income. In recent times, the S-corporation has largely been replaced by the limited liability company (LLC), which is a more flexible form.

Some of the key rules for election of the S-corporation option include the following: The S-corporation may have no more than 100 shareholders. These shareholders must be U.S. citizens or residents (partnerships and corporations cannot be shareholders). Profits and losses must be allocated in proportion to each shareholder's interest. An S-corporation shareholder may not deduct losses in an amount greater than the original investment. In addition, it is always wise to check with an attorney to make certain that the election of S-corporation status is valid. If a C-corporation elects to become an S-corporation and then reverts to C-corporation status, it cannot re-elect S-corporation status for five years.

Advantages

The S-corporation permits business losses to be passed through and taxed at the owner's personal tax rate. This offers a significant benefit to people who need to offset income from other sources. The businesses that benefit most from an S-corporation structure are those that don't have a need to retain earnings. In an S-corporation, if the entrepreneur decides to retain, say, $100,000 of profit to later invest in new equipment, the company must still pay taxes on that profit as though it had been distributed. The S-corporation is a valuable financial tool when personal tax rates are significantly lower than corporate rates. However, as top personal rates increase, a C-corporation might be preferable at higher profit levels. For some small businesses, however, the S-corporation may still be less costly in the long run because it avoids double taxation of income. A good tax attorney or certified public accountant (CPA) should advise the entrepreneur on the best course of action. Ventures that typically benefit from S-corporation status include service businesses with low capital asset requirements, real estate investment firms during times when property values are increasing, and startups that are projecting a loss in the early years.

Disadvantages

Entrepreneurs should probably not elect the S-corporation option if they want to retain earnings for expansion or diversification, or if there are significant passive losses from investments such as real estate. This is because unless the business has regular positive cash flow, it could face a situation in which profit is passed through to the owners to be taxed at their personal rate, but the firm has generated insufficient cash to pay those taxes, so they must come out of the pockets of the shareholders. Furthermore, although most deductions and expenses are allowed, S-corporations cannot take advantage of deductions based on medical reimbursements or health insurance plans.

Professional Corporations

Some state laws permit certain professionals, such as healthcare professionals, engineers, accountants, and lawyers, to form corporations called professional service corporations. Anyone who holds shares in the corporation must be licensed to provide the service it offers. The limited liability company (LLC) structure is also available to professionals, but in a special form known as a professional limited liability company (PLLC). Under this form, the member is liable only for his or her own malpractice, not that of other members. Some states also offer the limited liability partnership (LLP), which protects the owner from the malpractice claims of its partners but not from other partnership debts.

The Nonprofit Corporation

It is not outside the realm of possibility for a nonprofit corporation to be a high-growth, world-class company; however, it is not generally started with that goal in mind. A nonprofit corporation is a corporation established for charitable, public (scientific, literary, or educational), or religious purposes, or for mutual benefit (such as trade associations, tennis clubs), as recognized by federal and state laws. Some additional examples of nonprofits are child-care centers, schools, religious organizations, hospitals, museums, shelters, and community health care facilities. Like the C-corporation, the nonprofit corporation is a legal entity and offers its shareholders and officers the benefit of limited liability. There is a common misconception that nonprofit corporations are not allowed to make a profit. As long as the business is not set up to benefit a single person and is organized for a nonprofit purpose, it can still make a profit on which it is not taxed if it has also met the IRS test for tax-exempt status. However, income derived from for-profit activities is subject to income tax.

There are two distinct hurdles that a business must overcome if it wants to operate as a nonprofit corporation and enjoy tax-exempt status: The first is to meet the state requirements for being designated a nonprofit corporation and operating as such in a given state. The second is to meet the federal and state requirements for exemption from paying taxes [IRS 501(c)(3)] by forming a corporation that falls within the IRS's narrowly defined categories.

Advantages

Nonprofit organizations offer many advantages to entrepreneurs seeking to be socially responsible or just to start a business doing something they love that helps others. The nonprofit with tax-exempt status is attractive to corporate donors, who can deduct their donations as a business expense. The nonprofit can seek cash and in-kind contributions of equipment, supplies, and personnel. It can apply for grants from government agencies and private foundations. The nonprofit may qualify for tax-exempt status, which means that it is free from paying taxes on income generated from nonprofit activities.

Disadvantages

There are a few disadvantages to a nonprofit organization. For example, profits earned by the corporation cannot be distributed as dividends, and corporate money cannot be contributed to political campaigns or used to engage in lobbying. In forming the nonprofit corporation, the entrepreneur gives up proprietary interest in the corporation and dedicates all the assets and resources of the corporation to tax-exempt activities. If a nonprofit corporation is ever dissolved, its assets must be distributed to another tax-exempt organization. Finally, the nonprofit cannot make substantial profits from unrelated activities, and it must pay taxes on the profits it does make.

It is not uncommon for tax-exempt organizations to engage in activities that generate unrelated business income (UBI)—that is, income that is not related to the nonprofit's exempt purpose. For example, if a research institute were to operate a café on a regular basis, this would be considered a UBI activity. The institute would have to report it to the IRS and pay taxes on the income. If and when their UBI activities start to become significant, nonprofits often establish for-profit entities to run their UBI activities to protect the tax-exempt status of the parent organization.

Musical theatre companies are not the first type of company one thinks of when looking for examples of nonprofit organizations, but James Blackman had no doubt that this was the form of choice for the Civic Light Opera of South Bay Cities in California, one of the leading musical theatre companies on the West Coast. The nonprofit form would enable Blackman to receive donations from corporations and grants from foundations to support his efforts in the community with the physically challenged. It would also allow him to sell tickets to performances and make a profit, as long as that profit was not distributed but remained in the company. More important, he would meet the requirements for tax exemption, and that would enable him to keep more money in the business to help it grow.

LIMITED LIABILITY COMPANY

The limited liability company (LLC), like the S-corporation, enjoys the pass-through tax benefits of partnerships in addition to the limited liability of a C-corporation. It is, however, far more flexible in its treatment of certain ownership issues. Only privately held companies can become LLCs, and they must be formed in accordance with very strict guidelines. LLC statutes vary from state to state, so in addition to meeting the partnership requirements of the Internal Revenue Code, applicants must file with the state in which they intend to do business and follow its requirements as well.

An LLC is formed by filing articles of organization, which resemble articles of incorporation. There is no minimum number of people required to form an LLC, but if the entrepreneur is the only member, he or she must be very careful in both actions and how the activities of the LLC are documented so that the IRS or the state does not consider the LLC a sole proprietorship. The owners of an LLC are called members, and their shares of ownership are known as interests. The members can undertake the management of the company or hire other people to manage it. Managers, officers, and members are not personally liable for the company's debts or liabilities, except when they have personally guaranteed these debts or liabilities. The members create an "operating agreement," which is very similar to a partnership agreement that spells out rights and obligations of the members.

Advantages

Most LLCs will be organized for tax purposes like partnerships, so that income tax benefits and liabilities will pass through to the members. In New York and California, however, the LLCs will also be subject to state franchise taxes or fees. Under the Internal Revenue Code, an LLC exhibits all four characteristics of a corporation—limited liability, continuity of life, centralized management, and free transferability of interests—and can still be treated as a partnership for tax purposes without fear of being reclassified as a corporation. This enhances the attractiveness of the LLC, already the most rapidly growing legal form.

The LLC is often thought of as a combination of a limited partnership and an S-corporation. However, there are differences. In a limited partnership, one or more people (the general partners) agree to assume personal liability for the actions of the partnership, whereas the limited partners may not take part in the management of the partnership without losing their limited liability status. In an LLC, by contrast, a member does not have to forfeit the right to participate in the management of the organization in order to retain his or her limited liability status. Moreover, in an LLC, unlike in an S-corporation, there are no limitations on the number of members or on their status. Corporations, pension plans, and nonresident aliens can be members. Also, whereas S-corporations can't own 80 percent or more of the stock of another corporation, an LLC may actually possess wholly owned subsidiary corporations. LLCs are not limited to one class of stock, and in some ways they receive more favorable tax treatment. For example, unlike an S-corporation shareholder, the LLC member can deduct losses in amounts that reflect the member's allocable share of the debt of the company. If at a later date the entrepreneur decides to go public, the LLC can become a C-corporation by transferring the LLC assets to the new corporation. It is, however, a bit more difficult to go in the other direction, and capital gains tax must be paid on the appreciation.

Disadvantages

Clearly, the LLC offers more flexibility than other forms, but it does have a few disadvantages that should be considered. In contrast to the creation of a partnership or sole proprietorship, a filing fee must be paid when the LLC is formed. It is probably not a good form to choose if there will be a large number of members, because it will be difficult to reach consensus among the owners, who might also be the managers of the LLC. It is not a separate tax-paying entity. Earnings and losses are passed through to the members to be taxed at their individual tax rate, so members must make quarterly estimated tax payments to the IRS. If all the members do not elect to actively manage the LLC, the LLC ownership interests may be treated like securities by the state and the Securities and Exchange Commission (SEC). This means that if the company does not qualify for an exemption (most small LLCs do), it must register the sale of its member interests with the SEC.

LLCs are becoming a popular vehicle for companies that may have global investors because the S-corporation does not permit foreign ownership by non-legal residents. An attorney should be consulted to find out whether this form is available in a particular state. One ambitious entrepreneur knew that she wanted her furniture-importing business to be global in all respects. She even intended to bring in investors from among her business acquaintances around the world, because that would help her find the important contacts she needed to be successful. As an importer, she needed liability protection but did not want the high tax rates she would have with a corporation. Friends had told her that the S-corporation would solve the tax problem, but her attorney advised her to consider the LLC as her choice of legal form because it would allow her to have foreign investors.

CHOOSING THE RIGHT LEGAL FORM AT EACH MILESTONE

Having a strategic plan in place for the venture enables the entrepreneur to choose a legal form that won't have to be changed or one that can easily be shifted to when the time is right. For example, suppose an entrepreneur plans to offer shares of stock in the company at some point in the future to raise additional capital. To accomplish that, the company will need to become a corporation or LLC; so if the company began as a sole proprietorship, it would need to file incorporation or LLC papers in the state in which it would be doing business. Consider the following example of a married entrepreneur, Cheryl Kastner. Kastner's spouse is a highly paid executive for a major corporation, making it possible for her to devote herself full-time to developing a technology product she has been designing for some time. Kastner decides to set up a small business with a shop near their home. She is not worried about medical insurance because she is already covered by her spouse's company. However, she needs to limit liability, because they have acquired a number of valuable assets, such as their house and cars, and she doesn't want those assets to be in danger should things go badly. She realizes that in any business dealing with products, some liability issues might crop up and she wants to make sure they're covered. She also wants to ensure that she and her husband are protected from personal liability for things that happen at the business.

At startup, it is typical to experience losses as equipment is purchased, and prototypes are built and tested in the market. Once the product is launched, continuing losses will come from promoting the business, finding space outside the home to lease, and hiring new employees. Kastner has big plans for her business; in fact, within a year of introducing the product, she expects to need venture capital to be able to grow as fast as the market demands. She also sees an IPO in the future that will be the liquidity event that enables investors to cash out. Given these circumstances, she needs to consider which organization form is best at each milestone.

During product development, before the business is actually launched, it often doesn't make sense to use a more formal form such as a corporation, especially in a state where the entrepreneur has to pay minimum state franchise taxes. A simple sole proprietorship or partnership (if there's more than one person involved) will suffice. At this stage, the liability to family assets is negligible because only Kastner is involved with the technology. But the minute Kastner's business grows out of the home environment and takes on the responsibilities of a lease and employees, she must consider either being heavily insured or moving to a legal form with limited liability. Kastner plans to move the business to a leased location and hire employees. Since there would still be losses from product development and she would want to use them to shelter other income, she is also advised to consider either the S-corporation or the LLC, depending on the degree of flexibility she needs. She is also advised by her attorney that at the point at which she decides to seek venture capital and/or an IPO, she will need to convert to a C-corporation.

It is clear from this example that the legal form of an organization is not a static decision, but rather one based on the needs of the company at the time of formation and into the future. Choosing the legal structure of the new venture is one of the most important decisions an entrepreneur can make, because it affects the tax strategy of the company for years to come. The correct selection depends on the type of venture the entrepreneur is starting, the profits the venture generates, the personal tax bracket of the entrepreneur, the assets used by the business, the risk factors in the business, its potential for growth, and state laws. Again, particularly in the case of corporations and LLCs, it is important that an attorney who specializes in this area review the documents to ensure that all the rules have been followed and that the entrepreneur will receive all of the benefits to which the business is entitled.

New Venture Action Plan

- Answer the questions on page 259 before considering which legal form to choose.

- Consult with an appropriately qualified attorney to determine the best form to meet your business goals.

- Complete the necessary agreements for the legal form you have chosen (partnership agreement, articles of incorporation, and so forth).

- Determine if you meet the test for tax exemptions under IRC 501(c)(3) if you are founding a nonprofit corporation.

- Meet with a qualified attorney to determine what other legal issues might arise with your particular type of business.

Questions on Key Issues

1. Assuming that you were running a successful consulting practice as a sole proprietorship, what would induce you to change the legal form to a corporation?
2. Why would you choose an LLC form over a partnership or an S-corporation?
3. What kinds of businesses are well suited to the nonprofit legal structure?
4. What key factors determine the strategic plan for the legal organization of the business?

Experiencing Entrepreneurship

1. Employing this text and additional research on the Internet, acquire a basic understanding of the different legal forms of organization. Then, using a business that you are considering launching, discuss your initial strategic plan for the business with a qualified attorney to get his or her advice about the best form to use for that type of business. Write a two-page summary of your findings to justify the choice of legal form.
2. Visit an entrepreneur whose business is set up as a partnership. How do the partners describe the experience of setting up the business? How have they divided the duties and responsibilities? What key issues have they covered in their partnership agreement? Summarize your findings in a two- or three-page paper.

CHAPTER

11

ESTABLISHING AN ETHICAL AND SOCIALLY RESPONSIBLE BUSINESS

"… An ethic is not an ethic, and a value not a value without some sacrifice to it. Something given up, something not taken, something not gained."

—JEROME KOHLBERG, JR., KOHLBERG KRAVIS ROBERTS & CO.,
May 18, 1987

CHAPTER OBJECTIVES

- Explain the role of ethics in entrepreneurship.
- Discuss how entrepreneurs can demonstrate social responsibility.
- Describe how an entrepreneur's vision and values contribute to the culture of the new venture.
- Discuss the relationship of core values to success.

It is fairly commonplace for women to have financial power in developed countries, but it's the last thing you might expect to find in a developing country like Bangladesh. Nevertheless, thanks largely to one man's entrepreneurial genius, women are now gaining financial power in this impoverished country. In the 1980s, Muhammad Yunus, a Bangladeshi banker/economist, decided that traditional economic development programs would not bring about economic improvement fast enough in his home country of Bangladesh. A Fulbright scholar in classical economics, Yunus studied the challenges that the poorest people faced in attempting to secure capital to start even the smallest of businesses. They had no collateral and were generally illiterate, so he concluded that a traditional banking model was not appropriate for them. Instead, he began to work on a business model based on the concept of social collateral. He called it his "peer lending" model, wherein small groups of borrowers in the same village would take responsibility for repaying the loans of anyone in the group.

Founded in 1983, the Grameen Bank began lending to the poorest of the poor on a group liability basis with no collateral. Borrowers repay the loans in small weekly installments over one year. Because of peer pressure from the group to repay, the collection rate is about 98 percent, far higher than for traditional banking institutions. But what is most unusual about this entrepreneurial bank is that 95 percent of its borrowers are women. Traditionally, Bangladeshi women have had no employment opportunities and thus have lived far below the poverty line. With no other options, the women are inclined to try the Grameen loan system, which enables them to start micro-businesses such as making bamboo stools, weaving floor mats, and raising poultry. Borrowers are also required to save some of their money against potential natural disasters or sickness, which teaches them responsibility. From Grameen Bank's point of view, the return to them is infinite because, for example, a $100 donation to the nonprofit bank can be lent and repaid over and over again. The Grameen Foundation accepts donations, and the bank administers the loans. From the point of view of the Bangladeshi society, it has helped to create an entrepreneurial culture and raised the standard of living for those who have participated. The bank is owned by the borrowers, 97 percent of whom are women. Since its founding, the bank has disbursed over $9 billion with over $8 billion repaid to date.

Yunus built on the success of the micro credit effort by making mobile phone ownership possible as a business opportunity to Bangladeshis. Women have purchased phones and then provided services to other villagers who can't afford to own their own phones, creating new businesses and inter-village trade. Grameen Phone is a subsidiary of Grameen Bank and now has well over 23 million subscribers. Today communication between villages across Bangladesh is growing and is succeeding in reducing the gap between rich and poor. In 2006, Yanus and the Grameen Bank were jointly awarded the Nobel Peace Prize and in 2009 Yunus was awarded the Presidential Medal of Freedom.

Sources: Grameenphone, www.grameenphone.com, accessed August 15, 2010; Grameen Bank Monthly Update, www.grameen-info.org/index.php?option=com_content&task=view&id=453&Itemid=527, accessed August 15, 2010; "The Nobel Peace Prize 2006," www.nobelprize.org; "Motley Fool Selects Grameen Foundation USA for 2002 Foolanthropy Charity Drive," *PR Newswire* (December 3, 2002); "From Small Acorns," www.findarticles.com, August 2000; and Abu Wahid, "The Grameen Bank and Women in Bangladesh," *Challenge* (September–October 1999).

In a dynamic, global marketplace that places a premium on speed and quick returns, shareholder value is often considered more important than basic human values. The pressure to achieve unachievable goals and survive in such a chaotic environment causes stress; and when people suffer stress, they don't always make wise decisions. Moreover, the global economy, made more accessible than ever through the Internet, has juxtaposed U.S. businesses with cultures that may define morality in terms of very different contexts, values, and codes of ethics. Yes, it's a challenging environment, but those entrepreneurs who understand their value systems and create a code of ethics for their businesses can successfully maneuver through these challenges without forsaking their principles.

It takes great wisdom to build a world-class company. Ronald Cohen, the founder of the private-equity firm Apax Partners in the UK, and credited as the founder of the private equity industry in Europe, claimed, "Apax could only grow to the size it did in my time because we had an agreed-upon set of values: personal and corporate integrity; meritocracy; maintaining long-term relationships based on trust...leadership; and stewardship of the firm by each generation in turn." Cohen actually adopted the model used at U.S. consulting firm McKinsey & Co.[1]

This chapter looks at three key issues for entrepreneurial companies, issues that will become increasingly important as companies interact more frequently in the global marketplace: vision and values, ethics, and social responsibility. Profile 11.1 on Grameen Bank clearly demonstrates that every industry is looking for ways to reinvent itself and become more socially responsible. The chapter closes with a discussion of the components of success and how to make sure that a company's success is congruent with its vision and values.

ETHICS

Ethics, or the moral code by which we live and conduct business—essentially the concept of right and wrong—derives from the cultural, social, political, and ethnic norms with which we were raised as children. People don't often pause to reflect on their value system; instead, they merely act instinctively on the basis of it. It's only when they are faced with a dilemma that raises moral or ethical issues that they may consciously ask themselves what is the correct thing to do. Many people believe that if they follow the Golden Rule, the Judeo/Christian ethic that says "Do unto others as you would have them do unto you," they're safe from ethical dilemmas. Unfortunately, most ethical dilemmas in the business environment are complex and subject to "gray areas" that are troubling when one attempts to apply an ethical principle. One Oregon construction company hired a subcontractor to do a $15,000 concrete job. That particular subcontractor did not have solid bookkeeping practices and never submitted an invoice to the construction company for the work it did. The construction company could have kept quiet, but instead it sent the subcontractor a copy of the plans, specifications, and names of workers on the job, and told the subcontractor how much to bill it. The gray area here is the decision point—whether to notify the subcontractor of its failure to invoice. The construction company demonstrated its ethical values by contacting the subcontractor to ask for the invoice.

Another ethical decision had to be made by a marketing company that received two checks from a client for the same $50,000 project. There was no way the client would have easily discovered it, yet the marketing firm immediately sent the second check back. These kinds of ethical dilemmas occur every day in business. Although these two entrepreneurs did what they believed to be ethically correct, not everyone operates under the same standards of ethics. The employee who steals notepads, pens, and computer CDs because "the employer won't miss them," the executive who abuses his or her expense account, and the business owner who evades taxes by not reporting employee income demonstrate their lack of clear ethical standards. This kind of behavior is accepted too widely and costs entrepreneurs both time and money.

Entrepreneurs face special problems when it comes to ethical issues. Their small companies generally are more informal and often lack systems and controls. Entrepreneurs frequently don't have the time or resources to focus on ethics while they're struggling to keep their businesses alive, and they often take for granted that everyone in their organization and everyone with whom they do business shares their values. This is a mistake, because unethical behavior left undetected can contaminate a business for as long as it exists. Another very practical reason why small firms should pay attention to the ethics of employees concerns their ability to defend themselves against criminal action in a court of law. The U.S. Sentencing Commission's guidelines assert that a company needs an effective ethics program to protect it or lessen the impact of potential criminal penalties if an employee violates federal law.[2]

Recent research has identified four categories of ethical decision making that entrepreneurs face on a daily basis: (1) individual values, such as integrity and honesty, (2) organization values concerning employee well-being, (3) customer satisfaction, as reflected in the value provided to the customer, and (4) external accountability, or how the company relates to the community and the environment. The research further determined that in these four areas entrepreneurs do not differ in their ethical values from general societal norms.[3]

The work of Paul Adler has determined that awareness is a critical first step in identifying and assessing an ethical dilemma.[4] There are four components of awareness. The first component is identifying the issues. Entrepreneurs need to ask themselves if their conscience is bothered by the activity; does it violate any known laws or regulations; would they be OK if it were published on the front page of the newspaper? Does the activity harm anyone in some way? The second component of awareness is identifying the stakeholders affected by what the entrepreneur is proposing to do. Who exactly is affected by the entrepreneur's action or inaction? Third, how will the stakeholders perceive the action or inaction? Do these parties have any rights or legitimate concerns? Finally, what options are available to the entrepreneur? Is there anyone from whom the entrepreneur can seek advice?

Once the analysis of awareness of an ethical issue is complete, the entrepreneur has to make a decision and that decision is affected by the perspective of the entrepreneur. In ethics theory, there are generally three broad categories of perspectives about an ethical dilemma:

1. **Ideals.** This perspective is looking at the dilemma from an Aristotelian perspective about one's virtues, integrity, and values.

2. **Obligations.** This perspective is one's duty, rights, or what is lawful or just.

3. **Utility.** This perspective analyzes the costs and benefits of potential alternative consequences of action or inaction. Abuse of the utility perspective can be seen in business executives (and politicians) who believe that the end justifies the means. For many individuals accused of unethical behavior, taking the shortest path to wealth without regard for others who might be affected, generally ends badly—as seen in the cases of the CEOs of Enron, Arthur Andersen, and Worldcom.

In reality, most ethical dilemmas require balancing conflict among the three perspectives and acting with courage. This is no easy task; therefore, according to Alder, many people resort to avoiding ethical issues through one of four approaches, none of which is completely satisfactory:[5]

1. **Dogmatism:** "I simply will never lie or cheat or steal."

2. **Egoism:** "Everyone needs to look out for himself."

3. **Relativism or situational:** "When in Rome, do what the Romans do."

4. **Subjectivism:** "Ethics is a point of view."

Figure 11.1 depicts the relationship of these elements. Unfortunately, resolving ethical dilemmas is never simple. We will take an in-depth and pragmatic look at ethical dilemmas in business by considering the four most common types: conflicts of interest, survival tactics, stakeholder pressure, and pushing the legal limit.

FIGURE 11.1

The Elements of Ethical Action

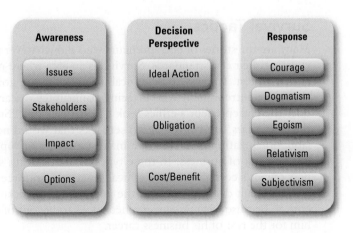

Conflicts of Interest

Conflict of interest is one of the most universal problems in business today. A conflict of interest occurs when a person's private or personal interests clash with his or her professional obligations such that an independent observer might reasonably question whether the individual's professional actions or decisions are influenced by personal gain, financial or otherwise. For example, a company may want to continue an important manufacturing process that provides many jobs and profit, even when the community claims that this same process is not good for the environment. Business owners have vested interests in many areas of their lives: careers, a business, family, community, and their investments, to name just a few. It is rare for all these interests to be in complete harmony with one another.

Conflict of interest has also found its way into Internet commerce. Today an online company can use its website to gather information about customers, profile them, and send the right message to the customer at the right moment. Through "cookie" technology, a company can track customers' movements on-line. Over time, the company will have compiled an enormous amount of data that it can use to better target its marketing messages. A company that uses cookie technology will usually offer a notice of privacy to its customers, promising not to sell the information it gathers to other companies. Unfortunately, many an Internet company has gone back on its promise to protect customers' privacy in the interest of making easy money. When Internet ad company DoubleClick (DCLK) was exposed for matching online and offline databases (essentially matching cookie data to real names, addresses, and phone numbers), it was hit with a Federal Trade Commission inquiry, investigations by the states of New York and Michigan, six lawsuits, and a lot of bad press.[6]

The healthcare community is not immune from conflict of interest issues. A recent study by the University of Michigan's Comprehensive Cancer Center found that a significant number of clinical cancer studies that have been published in highly regarded journals failed to disclose financial connections to major pharmaceutical companies, and that many of the results were biased to the benefit of big pharmas.[7]

Survival Tactics

Many are the stories of entrepreneurs who did whatever it took to survive, even violating their own standards. Survival is an area where most people's ethics really face a test. It's easy to be ethical when things are going your way, but what about the entrepreneur who is facing bankruptcy or can't make payroll? What does the entrepreneur's ethics look like at that point? Small firms, especially in the early years, are vulnerable to setbacks that would not significantly affect a large organization. The loss of a major customer or supplier could put a small business out of business. In these types of life-or-death situations, a small business owner's commitment to ethical practices can force the company to make some difficult decisions. Again, the importance of sticking to an ethical code is critical, because what an entrepreneur does today out of desperation will follow him for the rest of his business career.

One entrepreneur learned the hard way that one can't assume that everyone operates with the same value system and ethical code. This entrepreneur owns two successful bed and breakfast inns and, believing that she had reached the point where she could afford to cut back the time she spent managing them, she decided to rely on her general manager to run them while she took a two-year break to relax and travel; she even got married. She had the utmost confidence in her managers with whom she had been working for some time, but she continued to check in with them while she was on her self-imposed sabbatical. About 18 months into her retreat, she began to learn of problems at the B&Bs from the head housekeeper—reports of dishonesty on the part of the front-desk people, paying employees in cash, and not keeping records of guests' stays. In the end, the entrepreneur did an audit and discovered, to her dismay, that she was losing about $50,000 a year to internal theft. After firing her general manager, she returned to the B&Bs full-time, only to discover that the losses were much higher than expected. Not only did she not have solid procedures in place, but she also didn't have an effective way to monitor what was going on. Her general manager had actually been teaching employees how to cheat the company.[8] It is important to have high ethical standards in business, but it is also important to put procedures in place that make it difficult for employees to act in an unethical manner. Having more than one person sign checks and making sure that each person matches the check to an invoice or purchase order is one way to put a lid on those who might take more than they deserve.

Survival is not an excuse for poor ethical decisions. If the entrepreneur does pull the business back from the brink, those unethical actions will no doubt come back to bite.

Stakeholder Pressure

One area of research has focused on what the business ought to do in terms of the "ends it pursues and the means it utilizes."[9] There are many stakeholders in a business, and they all want what is owed them when it's owed them. Stakeholders include any person or organization that has an interest in seeing the company succeed—investors, shareholders, suppliers, customers, and employees, to name a few. Every business, no matter how small, has stakeholders. For many entrepreneurs, there are times when managing the demands of stakeholders becomes a real juggling act. For example, to grow a company to the next level, an entrepreneur may decide to consider an IPO. Once that issue is raised, the entrepreneur will find lots of stakeholders pressuring him to move forward, even when he is not sure it's the best thing to do. These stakeholders include investment bankers who get a fee for doing the deal, business partners who may be able to cash out of some of their holdings in the company, and lawyers who want the additional business. All these stakeholders want to be served, but research has revealed that the most healthy outcome is realized when an entrepreneur holds to his or her code of ethics and bases decisions on it, not on the personal agendas of stakeholders who may not have the best interests of the company at heart.

Pushing the Legal Limit

Some entrepreneurs look for ways to bend the law as much as possible without actually breaking it. They proudly claim, "We're entrepreneurs; we're supposed to break the rules." Entrepreneurs who regularly play too close to the edge of legality eventually get caught, and the price is high—often their businesses and their reputations. Ethical entrepreneurs don't play those games, but they're always on the alert for companies that might use quasi-legal practices against them to gain an edge in the market. These types of tactics must be dealt with decisively. For example, a large water-meter repair company that operated within the law was attacked by a competitor in collusion with a newspaper reporter. The competitor accused the repair company of bribing public officials. It was a false accusation, clearly unethical, but perhaps not illegal. It caused the innocent utility company a great many problems and cost it a lot of money defending itself, but the company had no choice because its reputation was at stake. An entrepreneur's reputation and that of his or her business must be protected at all costs, because without it, chances are there will be no business.

Learning from Real-Life Dilemmas

There is no better way to understand the role of ethics in any business than to encounter real-world dilemmas and think about how they might be dealt with. Here are some examples of real-life ethical dilemmas. Consider how they might be resolved.

1. A struggling Internet company is not producing revenues at the rate originally projected. At the same time, the burn rate (the rate at which cash is spent) is increasing as the company continually seeks new customers. The site claims to protect the privacy of visitors who purchase its products and services, and this is something the company takes pride in. However, the entrepreneur is concerned that if she doesn't find a quick source of income, the company may not survive. The entrepreneur learns that she can sell customer information lists to companies that will pay a lot of money for them. She has also heard that if she starts tracking which websites her customers visit, she can sell that information to major advertising firms for use in targeted advertising, another source of revenue. These tactics will violate customers' privacy, but if she doesn't do something quickly, she may have no business to offer them. What should she do?

2. One of a company's best customers has asked for a specific product. After telling the customer the price, the company learns from the customer that a competitor is selling the same item at the company's cost. It is well known that this competitor engages in unethical business practices. Should the company tell its customer about the competitor's practices or let the customer purchase where he can get the best price?

3. An employee confides to an entrepreneur that another employee is planning to leave the company in two months to start her own company as a

competitor. Armed with this knowledge, the entrepreneur is tempted to fire this employee immediately, but she is in the middle of a major project that is critical to the company, and it will be completed within two weeks. What should the entrepreneur do?

4. A retail company has hired a design firm as an independent contractor to design and build an e-commerce website. It paid a large portion of the fee, $25,000, up front to begin the work. The owner of the design company assures the customer that the work is on schedule to be completed on time; but as of a week before the due date, the company has yet to see any designs. A meeting is scheduled at the design office to check on the status of the project. While waiting at the office, the entrepreneur overhears employees talking about the impending closure of the business. She also hears that the programmer assigned to the project has not been paid and there is no money to pay him. The owner of the design firm says nothing about this during the meeting and instead assures the entrepreneur that the project will be completed as planned. The entrepreneur suspects that the owner is not being truthful and worries that if the business closes and she has not received the designs and software for the project, her company will be out $25,000 and will have to file a lawsuit. Should the entrepreneur talk to the programmer and reveal what she has heard? Should she confront the owner? Should she approach his disgruntled employees to find a way to gather the data she needs to win a lawsuit?

5. A company is about to begin doing business in another country where it is well known that paying cash to officials makes business transactions move more quickly. The entrepreneur knows that paying bribes is illegal in the United States, the home base for the business, but this contract will ensure that the company establishes a foothold in the global market before its competitors do. What should the entrepreneur do?

These are all difficult choices when the very survival of the business is at stake. Small businesses are as guilty as multinational corporations when it comes to ethical missteps. Paying personal expenses out of business funds and writing them off, not reporting all cash receipts, cheating customers on price, using misleading advertising, failing to pay bills on time, and lying to customers, employees, and suppliers are all examples of poor ethics. Aristotle, the Greek philosopher, said that courage is the first of the human virtues because without it, the others are not possible. How we make these difficult and courageous choices is the subject of the next section.

The Importance of Developing a Code of Ethics

Most of the research on ethics has been conducted in large organizations, so we have very little information about ethics in small businesses. Some studies have suggested that entrepreneurs are subject to compulsive behavior such as the need to be right and the need for an instant response. This tendency to make decisions under circumstances where there is little time for reflection and no

SOCIAL ENTREPRENEURSHIP: MAKING MEANING

Room to Read

Social entrepreneurs are on a mission. Their ventures often start as the result of an unusual experience that inspires them or simply as a passion to change the world. John Wood knew that being an executive at Microsoft was not going to be his life's work. He was successful, financially secure, and reasonably happy, but there was something missing, and he needed to get away from the rat race to find it. Wood found what was to be his life's mission while on a trek through the Himalayas. He discovered that in the villages of Nepal there were no libraries, and the schools had no books. He sent out an email to his friends back in the United States, telling about his adventure and the need for books. The next morning, his inbox was filled with 100 messages from people wanting to know how they could help. That told

him that he could do this. After many bumps in the road (which he recounts in his book, *Leaving Microsoft to Change the World*), in 2000 he made the decision to leave Microsoft and launch Room to Read as a nonprofit organization. Today his organization has established more than 10,000 libraries and 1,000 schools in the developing world and improved the lives of more than 1.2 million children. It has grown to 330 employees and 3,500 volunteers who do fundraising in 44 cities around the globe.

Sources: Whiting, S. (April 1, 2010), "Room to Read Sends Books Worldwide," *SFGate*, http://articles.sfgate.com/2010-04-01/entertainment/20830272_1_book-drive-empty-library-read; John Wood, *Leaving Microsoft to Change the World* (New York: HarperCollins, 2006); and www.roomtoread.org, accessed August 15, 2010.

one to advise can lead to ethical problems. Recent research notes that entrepreneurs have a "distinctive world-view" that is comprised of a "mosaic of virtue ethics, deontology, utilitarianism, and meta-ethical perspectives."[10] What this means is that it is simply impossible to stereotype entrepreneurs when it comes to decision making in ethical dilemmas.

The ethical behavior of employees is very much influenced by the code of ethics of the company.[11] When a code of ethics is spelled out and written down, people in the organization take it more seriously, so it's important for business owners to develop a formal code. After all, the best way to handle ethical dilemmas is to have in place a mechanism for avoiding them to begin with.

The Process of Developing a Code of Ethics

The process of developing a code of ethics begins with a company's self-examination to identify values held by individuals and alert everyone to inconsistencies in how people deal with particular issues. For a new company, this means getting the founding team together to discuss how certain issues should be dealt with. For a larger company, forming a committee to oversee the process may be appropriate.

The Josephson Institute of Ethics developed a list of ethical values that should be considered in any code of ethics,[12] and Table 11.1 presents a worksheet for employing these values to gauge how to respond in a particular ethical dilemma.

TABLE 11.1

Character Counts
Inventory

Michael Josephson, President of the Josephson Institute for Ethics, believes that entrepreneurs should consider how they incorporate the six pillars of character in their business and in their relationships with employees and others. List what you do to display each trait in your business environment.

Trustworthiness: Loyalty, honesty, integrity
Example: I always do what I say I will do.

_____

_____

_____

Respect: Privacy, dignity, courtesy
Example: I am courteous to everyone I meet.

_____

_____

_____

Responsibility: Accountability, pursuit of excellence
Example: I do not blame others for my failures.

_____

_____

_____

Fairness: Impartiality, consistency, equity, due process, equality
Example: I consider all the relevant facts carefully before making judgments.

_____

_____

_____

Caring: Compassion, kindness, giving, consideration
Example: I forgive the mistakes of my employees and guide them to do better.

_____

_____

_____

Citizenship: Abiding by laws, community service, protection of the environment
Example: I give my employees time off from work to do service in the community.

_____

_____

_____

Source: Based on Character Counts! National Office, www.josephsoninstitute.org.

A code of ethics should also outline behaviors that would enable the business to display these characteristics. This can be accomplished by using a Kantian[13] approach and asking four questions about any ethical decision to be made:[14]

1. Will the actions taken result in the "greatest good for all parties involved"?
2. Will the actions respect the rights of all parties?
3. Are the actions just? Will anyone be hurt by the actions?
4. Would I be proud if my actions were announced in my local newspaper?

The last question, in particular, gets to the heart of how one determines what is ethical in any situation, and most people can immediately and intuitively answer it.

Characteristics of an Effective Code

The most effective code of ethics will have the following characteristics. The code and its associated policies will be clear and easy to understand. Details about special situations that need further explanation will be included (for example, political factors in particular countries). In cases where employee judgment may be required, descriptions and examples will make it easier for the employee to make the decision.

Entrepreneurs should make sure that all employees are aware of and understand the code as well as the values and culture of the company. The following are some guidelines for ensuring that the code of ethics is implemented and maintained over time.

1. Entrepreneurs should model the behavior expected of others in the company. In some companies, the ethical behavior exhibited by managers and employees in tough situations can become legendary—a part of the company culture that people remember and speak about with pride over and over again.
2. Employees should be educated about ethics through workshops that put employees in hypothetical situations. For example, "What would you do if you found out that your best customer was harassing your administrative assistant?"
3. Entrepreneurs should demonstrate commitment to the ethics program by mentioning it on a regular basis and providing examples of appropriate behavior that employees display during the course of their work.

The code of ethics should be shared with customers so that they understand the company's commitment and are assured of its integrity. A clear channel for reporting and dealing with unethical behavior must exist, and there should be a means of rewarding ethical behavior through recognition, bonuses, raises, and so forth. Examples of Codes of Ethics can be found at http://yourcodeof ethics.com.

There is no way to avoid the ethical problems that business brings. But developing a strong ethical code and enlisting the cooperation of everyone in the business will go a long way toward making those challenges easier to deal with.

AN ETHICAL DILEMMA

Superior Machine Works had developed a new type of generator that was environmentally friendly and could be controlled from a distance. Superior's research had determined that the market was quite large and had the potential to be very profitable. Superior was marketing two models: a small, lightweight version for people who would use it to power small tools, and a bigger, heavier version used generally as backup power for an office or home, in addition to supplying power for a variety of electrical tools. The smaller version retailed for $895, and the larger version sold for $1,500. The larger version had a patented noise reduction feature that significantly reduced the sound the machine produced. Studies on similar equipment had shown that over a long period of time, the noise level of the small machine could actually produce hearing loss in the user.

At the same time, Superior's main competitor was also developing a generator very much like Superior's small version, and that company was also aware of the noise problem and the potential for deafness over time. Still, it was going ahead with the product. Superior was faced with a real dilemma. If it didn't move quickly to get its smaller version to market, it would lose its first-mover advantage to its competitor. At the same time, did Superior want to market a product that was known to cause deafness over time? If it marketed only the larger machine, it would quickly lose market share to its competitor's smaller, lighter machine. If Superior could not introduce a successful product quickly, it would have to lay off many of its workers. Considering the downward trend in its current sales, the company might fail if it couldn't introduce its product quickly.

1. What options does Superior have and what are the consequences of each?
2. What should Superior do and why?

SOCIAL RESPONSIBILITY

Today it's not enough to have a successful business and make a profit. The business must hold itself to a higher standard of social responsibility by giving something back to the community or communities in which it does business and, through them, to society as a whole. Social responsibility is operating a business in a way that exceeds the ethical, legal, commercial, and public expectations that society has of the business. This means obeying the law, respecting the environment, and being mindful of the impact the business has on its stakeholders, the industry, and the community in general. Socially responsible entrepreneurs, then, are distinct from other entrepreneurs in a number of ways. First and foremost, they start their businesses with a social mission, and they are faced with different challenges as they seek the resources to fund and sustain the business.[15] Their rewards derive not only from profits but also from the social value they create by being change agents for the betterment of society. This has been called a triple bottom line strategy: people, planet, profit.

There are many types of social ventures serving a variety of purposes. For example, Ten Thousand Villages is an international relief and development organization based in Winnepeg, Canada. It provides a way for artisans in underdeveloped countries to sell their handicrafts in North America, reducing unemployment.[16] Another example is The Nature Conservancy, which is a global organization based in Arlington, Virginia. With a mission of preserving plants, animals, and natural communities, it operates the largest private system of nature sanctuaries in the world.[17] The benefits to businesses that seek to become socially responsible are many. They include improved financial performance, reduced operating costs by cutting waste and inefficiencies, enhanced brand image and reputation, increased sales and customer loyalty, increased productivity and quality, increased ability to attract and retain employees, and reduced regulatory oversight.

The majority of social ventures are nonprofits that must seek their funding from philanthropists or grants. Jordan Kassalow, who is a practicing optometrist, founded VisionSpring to provide glasses to people in Asia, Latin America, and Africa. He also plans to train locals in how to sell the glasses, producing a new crop of entrepreneurs.[18]

Social entrepreneurs need to choose a mission that is achievable. Paul Brainerd founded a company, the Brainerd Foundation, in Seattle, Washington, for the purpose of helping entrepreneurs "give back" strategically to protect the region's air, land, and water. He suggests that entrepreneurs follow two simple rules:

1. Don't wait until later in life to begin giving back. Start when the business is young and giving can become part of the culture.
2. Don't go for something huge. Start at the grassroots level, where help is needed the most.

Three types of ventures typically engage in social entrepreneurship.[19] For-profit ventures in the private sector can have a socially oriented purpose, such as The Body Shop and Ben & Jerry's, whose missions are to respect the environment and to innovate ways to improve quality of life. The second type is social entrepreneurship ventures in the nonprofit sector conceived with a social purpose in mind and not constrained by the need to make and distribute a profit. The Brainerd Foundation and the Grameen Bank are two such ventures. The final type is social entrepreneurship in the public sector, which includes governmental agencies such as the Small Business Administration and community organizations like the Castleford Community Learning Centre of West Yorkshire in the United Kingdom, which works with adults with learning disorders.[20]

Effective Ways to Become Socially Responsible

A company does not have to be a large, multimillion-dollar firm to begin to give something back to society. Even a very small company can have an impact on its community if it does a few things by way of preparation. First, the company needs to set goals. What does it want to achieve with its social responsibility efforts? It should pick a single cause to focus on, rather than trying to support many different causes, and consider partnering with a nonprofit organization to make a great impact. The nonprofit contributes its expertise in the social issue, while the entrepreneurial company contributes its expertise and the time of its employees to the nonprofit. Next, it is vital that everyone in the organization be incentivized to get involved. There really is strength in numbers. In addition to getting employees involved, the company should also consider getting its customers involved, if appropriate. With goals in place and a cause that fits the company's core values, the new venture can do a number of things to establish positive relationships in the community. Here are just a few of them.

- *Donate products, services, or revenues.* Any company can donate the products or services it produces. However, Laura Scher takes it one step further and donates a portion of all the revenues of her company, Working Assets—a provider of long-distance, credit card, and wireless services—to nonprofit organizations to encourage "ordinary people to become activists." Since her company was founded in 1985, its members (customers) have donated over $65 million to nonprofit groups.[21]

- *Donate expertise.* Room to Read (see the "Social Entrepreneurship" box) donated its expertise in raising funding and starting libraries to teach students in Sri Lanka how to raise funding to rebuild the schools lost in the tsunami of 2004. They raised more than $400,000 and inspired a new student-led initiative to provide Room to Read programs around the world.

- *Contribute to the community.* Many entrepreneurs have found cost-effective ways to give back to their communities without breaking the bank. In fact, they have made social responsibility a regular part of their businesses. For example, one enterprising bagel store adopts a local nonprofit organization for a year. Customers vote for their favorite charity, and the winning choice receives a cash donation, bagels, meeting space, and a place to advertise its services in the store. They also get volunteer help from the bagel employees, who do their good deeds on company time.

Another entrepreneur shares the benefits of his success with his community by providing ski trips for underprivileged children, food drives for the hungry, highway cleanups, and the Easter Seals poster-child campaign, among many other things. There are numerous ways to demonstrate social responsibility through a business. It doesn't have to cost much time or money to make a significant difference as long as efforts are focused where they will count the most.

VISION AND VALUES

Every great company begins with the entrepreneur's vision of what that company will become. Just as top professional athletes envision every play of an upcoming game before they ever set foot on the playing field, so do entrepreneurs envision the kind of company they want to build. The company's "true north" acts like a beacon, guiding it and keeping it from straying when opportunities try to pull the company in a different direction. Although it is possible for a company to be successful without a vision, it is difficult, if not impossible, to become a *great* company without a vision. Researchers Jim Collins and Jerry Porras, authors of *Built to Last: Successful Habits of Visionary Companies* and *Good to Great,* back up this assertion.[22] Collins and Porras found that the number-one company in every industry it studied outperformed its number-two competitor by a significant amount in terms of revenues, profits, and return on investment. The primary reason was that each number-one company had a strong vision comprised of core values that it regarded as inviolable.

Core Values

Core values are the fundamental beliefs that a company holds about what is important in business and in life in general. They are based on the personal values and beliefs of the founder or the founding team; therefore, they are not something that can be created or invented for the company out of thin air. A company's core values tell the world who it is and what it stands for. Because they are so fundamental to the existence of a company, core values rarely change over time, and they endure beyond the tenure of the founder. For example, online shoe and apparel company Zappos.com's core values are:

- Deliver WOW Through Service
- Embrace and Drive Change
- Create Fun and A Little Weirdness
- Be Adventurous, Creative, and Open-Minded
- Pursue Growth and Learning
- Build Open and Honest Relationships With Communication
- Build a Positive Team and Family Spirit
- Do More With Less
- Be Passionate and Determined
- Be Humble

One way to test whether a value (for example, "The customer is always right") is a core value or not is to ask whether it would ever be relinquished if there were a penalty for holding it. If a company is willing to let go of the value, then it's not a core value.

Purpose

Purpose is the company's fundamental reason to be in business. It is the answer to the question "Why does the business exist?" It is not necessarily a unique characteristic of the business; in fact, more than one business may share the same purpose. What is crucial is that the purpose be authentic; that is, the company must mean what it says. "We are in the business of helping people" might be the purpose of a socially responsible business. Jordan Neuroscience, a company that provides patented brain nets to monitor a patient's brainwaves in the emergency room, is in the business of "saving brains." A properly conceived purpose will be broad, enduring, and inspiring, and it will allow the company to grow and diversify.[23]

Mission

A company's mission is what brings everyone together to achieve a common objective and is closely related to the company's purpose. According to Collins and Porras, a mission is a "Big Hairy Audacious Goal" (BHAG), designed to stimulate progress. All companies have goals, but a mission, or BHAG, is a daunting challenge, an overriding objective that mobilizes everyone to achieve it. The natural metaphor for a mission is mountain climbing. The mission is *to scale Mt. Everest,* a major challenge to be sure. To get there, however, will require smaller goals, such as *reaching base camp in one week.* The smaller wins motivate the team to achieve the more bold and compelling mission.

A company's mission is communicated through a mission statement. A mission statement precisely identifies the environment in which the company operates and communicates the company's fundamental philosophy.[24] Management guru Peter Drucker always asserted that a company's mission should "fit on a t-shirt."[25] The best mission statements are simple, precise, and use clear words.

Here are three examples of mission statements:

Starbucks: "Our mission: to inspire and nurture the human spirit – one person, one cup and one neighborhood at a time." (Source: www.starbucks.com/about-us/company-information/mission-statement.)

Facebook: "Giving people the power to share and make the world more open and connected." (Source: www.facebook.com/facebook.)

Leader to Leader Institute: "To strengthen the leadership of the social sector." (Source: www.leadertoleader.org/about/index.html.)

The mission statement should convey what the company wants to be remembered for; therefore, in writing a mission statement, it is important to gather the thoughts of everyone in the organization. The initial drafts should be evaluated against a set of criteria and should explain why the organization exists, indicate what the company wants to be remembered for, and be sufficiently broad in its scope. It should not prescribe means but should provide direction for doing the right things. Finally, the mission statement should address the company's opportunities, match the company's competence, and inspire the company's commitment.

Figure 11.2 presents a broad view of the components of a complete vision and their relationship to each other. To review, the vision for the company stems from the founder's core value system. It becomes the guideline for all the decisions made by the company as it grows and operates. The company then needs a compelling mission that is congruent with its core values—a BHAG to propel it forward—and goals or operating objectives, which are milestones along the way to achieving the mission.

FIGURE 11.2

The Components
of Vision

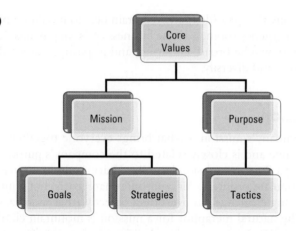

Strategies and Tactics

Once goals have been set, strategies should be developed. These are the plans for achieving those goals and, ultimately, accomplishing the mission. Tactics, which are the means to execute the strategies, should also be put in place. An example will make these points clearer. Suppose a company's mission is to be number one in its industry. Two goals or milestones it might set to help it accomplish the mission might be (1) to create an Internet presence and (2) to achieve brand recognition. Strategies for achieving these goals might include building a website to meet goal 1 and developing a marketing campaign to build the brand, goal 2. Then there must be a variety of tactics, or ways to implement the strategies. For example, to implement the strategy of building a website, a company might employ the following tactics: determine the purpose and focus of the website, hire a Web designer and developer, purchase a server, and plan the content.

Merely setting a goal is not enough. A plan for achieving the goal must be in place, and that is the role of strategy. But even strategy is not enough to achieve a company's goals; tactics, or action plans, will also be required.

CORE VALUES AND SUCCESS

Why are we talking about success in a chapter on ethics and social responsibility? Because an entrepreneur's personal definition of success—what it means to be successful—is really a function of the core values and vision that an entrepreneur has for his or her life. A business's success is easily measured in terms of total revenues, earnings, return on investment, and so forth, but entrepreneurs don't typically measure their personal success solely in these terms. In fact, research has shown that the personal rewards that motivate entrepreneurs to start businesses are independence and freedom.[26] Entrepreneurs tend to be goal-oriented, so being one's own boss, being in control of one's destiny, and having ultimate control of the success of the venture are reasons for going into business. They measure their personal success by their achievement of those goals.

Constants of Success

No matter how success is defined, there are some constants that seem to permeate everyone's definition. These constants are purpose, failure, a sense of satisfaction with what was accomplished, and having to pay for, or earn, success.

■ *Purpose.* To feel successful, entrepreneurs need to know that what they are doing is taking them in the direction of a goal they wish to achieve. True success is a journey, not a destination—even the achievement of a goal will be just a step on the way to the achievement of yet another goal.

■ *Failure.* The second constant is that life has its ups and downs. Failure is the other half of success, and most entrepreneurs have experienced several failures of one sort or another along the way. Still, they typically do not fear failure, because they know intuitively that those who obsessively avoid failure are doomed to mediocrity. To avoid failing, one has to virtually retreat from life, to never try anything that has any risk attached to it. Most entrepreneurs are calculated risk-takers, so they make sure that every time they come up to bat they give it their best; then, win or lose, they strive to learn from the experience and go on. Entrepreneurs are generally optimists who believe that failure is a normal part of the entrepreneurial process.

■ *Sense of satisfaction with work.* The most successful entrepreneurs are doing what they love, so their satisfaction level is usually very high. Does satisfaction with the work result in success, or does success bring satisfaction? Probably a little of both, so it's important to know what kinds of tasks and activities will return satisfaction in business.

■ *No free lunch.* Success rarely comes without work. Entrepreneurs do not have the luxury of a nine-to-five workday; they are usually married to their businesses twenty-four hours a day. It is not just the number of hours of work that distinguishes entrepreneurs, of course, but also the way they use their time. Entrepreneurs make productive use of odd moments in their day—while they're driving, on hold on the telephone, in the shower, or walking to a meeting. Because they love what they're doing, it doesn't feel like work, and that's probably why, wherever entrepreneurs are, they're always working on their businesses in one way or another.

Firm core values and ethics plus a socially responsible business can lead to the kind of success that is meaningful to most entrepreneurs: satisfaction in creating something and seeing it thrive. Today, more than ever before, the world is watching the way entrepreneurs run their businesses, so it is more critical than ever to design a new business on the basis of sound values and ethical practices.

New Venture Action Plan

■ Identify the core values held by the founding team.

■ Develop an initial code of ethics for the business.

■ List possible ways your business can be socially responsible.

■ Define what success means to you.

Questions on Key Issues

1. Do you believe that your code of ethics should remain firm in any situation? Why or why not?

2. Suppose you are doing business in a country where paying fees (bribes) to get through the process more quickly is standard practice. In the United States, bribery is against the law. How will you deal with this conflict taking into account your ethical standards when you're doing business in that country?

3. In addition to the suggestions given in the chapter, name two ways your company can demonstrate its social responsibility.

4. Would you require your employees to give back to the community as part of their work contract with your company? Why or why not? If yes, how could you implement this policy?

5. How do you define your personal success? How can your definition be applied to your business?

Experiencing Entrepreneurship

1. Choose an industry that interests you and interview a manufacturer, a distributor, and a retailer about the code of ethics in that industry. In a two-page report discuss whether the industry has ethical problems. If so, what are they and how are people responding? If not, how have they been avoided?

2. Choose two companies in different industries. Interview a manager in each company about how the company practices social responsibility. In a two-page paper, compare these managers' answers and account for any basic differences.

Relevant Case Studies

Case 2 MySpace

Case 7 1-800-Autopsy

CHAPTER 12

STRUCTURING AN ENTREPRENEURIAL VENTURE

"Nothing reveals more of what a company really cares about than its stories and legends . . . Listening to a company's stories is the surest route to determining its real priorities and who symbolizes them."

—**TOM PETERS and NANCY AUSTIN,**
A Passion for Excellence (Random House, 1985)

CHAPTER OBJECTIVES

- Describe how businesses are organized.
- Discuss the role of strategic alliances in a new organization.
- Explain how to identify the appropriate business site.
- Discuss the most critical issues related to organizing people.

The pizza business is nothing new; in fact, it's a very crowded industry with about 75,000 establishments in the United States alone. It's hard to find a town that doesn't have a pizza parlor and most have more than one. It's one of those businesses that hasn't seen a lot of innovation or creative thought since Dominos started the pizza delivery business, so it's ripe for something new and exciting.

Enter Nick Sarillo who grew up around pizza. His father owned a pizza restaurant in Carpentersville, Illinois, so it wasn't surprising when Nick opened his first restaurant in Crystal Lake in 1995. Although he did use his father's recipe, he decided early on that he was going to build a culture in his company that would set him apart from his competitors. One of the biggest problems in the pizza industry (and the fast food restaurant industry in general) is high employee turnover—about 200 percent annually. That means higher costs and time spent in training new workers. The industry also averages 6.6 percent net profit and most establishments find themselves competing on price. Sarillo was determined not to play that game.

Sarillo adopted a form of management known as "trust and track," which is essentially the opposite of command and control. In the typical pizza restaurant, the boss takes responsibility for success, tells the employees what to do, and then checks to make sure they did it. Sarillo wanted his employees to understand what had to happen for the business to be successful, and then he would

trust them to do what was necessary. That way the system would operate nearly flawlessly even if he weren't there. It seems to have worked because Sarillo's turnover rate is a mere 20 percent and his profit margins have reached 18 percent. One of the secrets to his success is his ability to understand the pain his community is experiencing. With an 11 percent unemployment rate in his community, he decided that people would pay half price in the dining room on Mondays and half price for carry outs on Tuesdays until the unemployment rate returns to normal. This approach benefitted the community and the business because the two slowest days of the week now became the most popular. Sarillo is also known for surprising his guests by picking up the check and hosting fundraisers nearly every week where his company donates 15 percent of the gross profit to a particular cause.

Sarillo hires only the best and they know that while they work for the company, they will have many opportunities to grow, learn, and increase their wages. Sarillo plans to grow the company, which in 2010 had locations in Crystal Lake and Elgin, but he's going to make sure that he has the right people managing his current restaurants—people who believe in "trust and track."

Sources: Nick's Pizza & Pub, www.nickspizzapub.com/home; Burlingham, B. (February 2010), "Lessons From a Blue-Collar Millionaire," *Inc Magazine*, p. 57; and Detwiler, M.W. (May 2006), "Field of Dreams," *Pizza Today*, www.pizzatoday.com.

Organizational design is a critical component of any business plan both at launch and as the company grows and faces challenges from an increasingly complex external environment. As the sources of competitive advantage at startup lose their power, while at the same time competition is intensifying, organizational design and capabilities become increasingly important to long-term success. Organizational design shapes the look and feel of the company and is a significant part of the company's strategy because it supports the achievement of the company's mission. Operations, which is covered in

Chapter 13, deals with the management of all the activities of the business and is more tactical. Superior organizational design begins with an understanding of how the business works—how information flows through the business. This understanding is critical to making decisions about business location, number of employees, management expertise required, and technology needed to facilitate business goals.

The principles that designers use to create successful products can also be applied to the creation of exceptional businesses.[1] For example, visualization, or finding ways to express the design of the business in a physical or visual form, is important to designers. In this chapter we deal with visualization as we look at the various business processes. And we look at those processes from the perspective of the customer who will have to interact with the business. That way, the various processes can be tested with actual users and the entrepreneur is encouraged to go beyond the first customers to consider other types of customers. Design thinking has entrepreneurs considering the entire organization and how the various components and activities are interconnected. It means, for example, bringing marketers and programmers into meetings about the design of an interface for a website or including manufacturing in a discussion about the development of a new product.

It's easy to understand the economic value of superior design on new products and services, but arguably its greatest value is applying design thinking to the business model and the business itself. Apple is a clear example of how a company designs its business to follow customers to new opportunities rather than sticking with the original business model. That ability to lead is how they diversified from a computer company to a social media company with iTunes, the iPod, the iPhone, and now the iPad.[2] This is also another example of designing and viewing the company through the lens of the customer.

Three broad components make up the entrepreneurial organization: processes, people, and culture. Formal processes include the planning system, control mechanisms, compensation and reward policies, and other processes that make the organization run more efficiently and effectively. These processes are not independent but, rather, are linked to all functions of the organization that require them. For example, quality control mechanisms are not solely the purview of a single department, but flow from product development through manufacturing, to distribution, and throughout all the support functions needed to get a product to the customer.

Teams are a common phenomenon in entrepreneurial ventures. People who work in entrepreneurial companies must have team-building skills as well as the ability to make decisions and implement them with very little input from top management or the CEO. In new ventures, those teams often consist of independent contractors whose skills are "rented" on an as-needed basis. Out of team building comes informal networks that create flexibility and speed up operations. Networks also facilitate the management of personal issues not easily handled through policies and structure. The entrepreneurial organization must be designed to facilitate collaboration both internally and externally.

Culture is the glue that binds people, processes, and structure. Culture is fundamentally the personality of the organization—the reflection of the company's vision and goals. It forms the basis for all the activities that the company undertakes. It is also the view of the company that customers see. An effective company culture enhances customer relationships, reduces employee turnover, and serves as a formidable competitive advantage for a company.

This chapter focuses on strategies for organizing the business and its many processes, finding a superior location, and putting together a team or work force that will implement the company's processes and build the company's culture. Operations related to the production of goods and services are discussed in Chapter 13.

DESIGN: UNDERSTANDING THE WAY THE BUSINESS WORKS

There probably is no single best organizational structure for all types of ventures in all situations. Rather, entrepreneurs must find the best fit, given the existing contextual factors (environment, technology, market), design factors (strategy and models), and structural factors (complexity, formalization).[3] A misalignment or misfit among these factors could result in an organizational structure that does not suit the particular market the company wishes to serve. For example, if an entrepreneur chose a low-cost strategy to compete but did not implement tight control systems, minimize overhead, and focus on achieving economies of scale, it would probably not succeed. Given that entrepreneurs at startup don't typically have the resources to implement control systems, minimize inventory, or achieve economies of scale, a low-cost entry strategy is rarely viable.

Firms in different industries tend also to differ in their administrative mechanisms and structures. Several studies have found that the design of the organizational structure—how business activities are grouped, divided, and coordinated—is a critical factor in business performance and as such a growing entrepreneurial firm must continually modify its structure to meet the demands of growth.[4] These findings reinforce the argument presented in Chapter 5 on the importance of conducting thorough industry and market analyses to understand the external conditions that will affect the business. Figure 12.1 depicts basic forms of organizational design and the devices used to link or connect different groups to share information or collaborate. Different types of groupings can utilize various kinds of linking methods depending on the types of people and the company culture. In general, liaison roles are trusted people who serve as brokers between groups. Cross-unit groups can often take the form of committees. Integrator roles make sure that the processes are functioning effectively, and matrix structures entail hierarchy and are complex to implement.

In the earliest stages of an entrepreneurial venture, the tendency is to group by output, that is, by the product or service that is being developed. This inclination for grouping is because startups have limited resources and most people on the founding team are serving in multiple capacities. It is also highly likely that the venture will be outsourcing some of the needed capability so liaison and integrator roles could come into play.

Building Blocks of
an Entrepreneurial
Organization

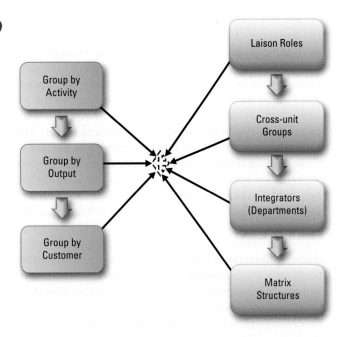

Ambiguity is a significant force in most entrepreneurial ventures. It derives from conflicting constituencies with different goals and needs, and from lack of immediate control over the external environment and resources. As a result, ambiguity often manifests itself in pressures on the new business for legitimacy and commitment.[5] Legitimacy is validation of the business by external constituencies such as suppliers, customers, distributors, and others in the value chain, while commitment is the binding of an individual to the goals of the business. Commitment and legitimacy are interdependent; specifically, legitimacy cannot exist without commitment. The success of an entrepreneurial organization is a function of its ability to secure commitment and legitimacy while operating in an ambiguous context. Suppliers and others in the value chain expect the firm to demonstrate legitimacy through formalized systems and controls, something that entrepreneurial ventures in the earliest stages typically don't have because the dynamic environment in which they operate predisposes them to develop structures that are flexible and loosely defined with informal and minimal management systems to better adapt to uncertain conditions.[6]

Information systems technology has facilitated various kinds of organizational structures that enable new businesses to compete more effectively in rapidly changing environments.[7] For example, the move from centralized structures to more decentralized or distributed structures is highly compatible with the mindset of the entrepreneur. Today, companies are increasingly operating at a global level and involve multiple partners on different continents working together. This more distributed form of organization requires new ways to coordinate activities, manage documents, and communicate. Companies are typically distributed on four levels: (1) geographically, whether it be locally or across continents; (2) organizationally by department or project group; (3) temporally by time zone; and (4) by stakeholder groups, which can include such stakeholders as customers, project managers, sales staff, and so forth.[8] Software companies are classic examples of distributed organizations where developers may be located in India, designers in Pakistan, corporate management and sales in the United States, and users around the globe. Despite geographic and organizational distances, the team must find a way to interact effectively to produce the best products and services it can. This is often accomplished through collaborative online work environments and videoconferencing.

Because of limited resources and a creative and opportunistic mindset, entrepreneurs are naturals at improvisation—they are the jazz musicians of the business world—they can find ways to work around even the most rigid structures. Because entrepreneurial organizations reflect a fine balance between structure and chaos, clarity and ambiguity, they must be innovative and creative. In this type of environment, entrepreneurs can give free rein to new ideas and create space to allow them to grow. They can retain internally what the company does best—its core competencies—and outsource the rest of the activities for which it doesn't have expertise. Limited resources also demand that entrepreneurs look for ways to keep overhead (non–revenue-producing plant and equipment) to a minimum, while spending precious capital on revenue-generating areas of the business like marketing and sales.

Identifying Business Processes

One of the most eye-opening experiences an entrepreneur can have is identifying all the processes (activities, tasks, etc.) that occur in the business. Even more revealing of how the business works is a process map or flowchart that traces how information flows through the business. Recall that in Chapter 8, a process flowchart was developed to understand the capital and other resource requirements of the startup. Designing the operations and organization of the business is not always within the entrepreneur's competence. Nevertheless, considering how the business will operate is crucial to figuring out how many people to hire, how much equipment to purchase, and what kind of facility will be needed. To create such a map of the business processes, take an imaginary tour of the business during a single day, listing all the tasks, people, equipment, supplies, and space required to run the business. Understanding how the business works makes it easier to determine how to organize the business. Refer to Chapter 8 for an example of a process map.

Making the Decision: Doing It All or Outsourcing

Today it is much more difficult for a new venture to achieve total in-house control of its value chain. The global marketplace is more complex, time-to-market has decreased, and it is difficult for any one company to have the broad expertise necessary to master all the functions of the distribution channel. At present, a growing company is more likely to increase its flexibility by choosing one function to concentrate on—its core competency—and subcontracting functions it does not want to handle. The general rule is that if the resources to manufacture, assemble, and distribute the product already exist efficiently in the market in which the entrepreneur wishes to do business, the process should be outsourced. Often a business whose competitive advantage lies in proprietary rights to its product will choose to maintain control of strategic functions and outsource such things as warehousing, transportation, and some aspects of marketing. Any business may choose to outsource administrative functions such as payroll, accounting, and inventory management and may even lease its employees from an employee-leasing company. In this way, the new venture is more innovative, stays closer to the customer, and responds more rapidly to the market. Today many companies outsource aspects of their business processes, but virtual organizations outsource everything except their core-management function. To their customers, they look like any other company, but behind the public image lies a very different kind of organization—one where the entrepreneur is basically a ringmaster in a three-ring circus.

The Virtual Enterprise: Getting Traction Quickly

The term *virtual enterprise* was borrowed from the science of virtual reality, which enables a person to become an integral part of a computer-generated, three-dimensional world. In business, a "virtual enterprise" has much the same purpose. The entrepreneur builds a company that to the rest of the world looks like any other company, but it's a business without walls where the entrepreneur does not incur the risk of acquiring employees, costly equipment, and enormous overhead. A virtual company makes it possible to operate the business from practically anywhere—a home, car, or vacation cabin. Research defines the virtual corporation as "a temporary network of independent companies, suppliers, customers, even erstwhile rivals—linked by information technology to share skills, cost, and access to one another's markets."[9] Today cloud computing has spawned a resurgence in virtual companies. Cloud computing is simply moving computing tasks and storage from local desktop PCs and business servers to remote servers across the Internet. It is analogous to the electricity grid: resources, software, and information are provided to the user on demand, saving them a significant amount of money. Some of the more popular applications of cloud computing are high definition VoIP phone services, teleconferencing, videoconferencing, email, customer relationship management, human resources, and executive search.[10]

The goal of the virtual enterprise is to deliver to the customer the highest-quality product at the lowest possible cost in a timely manner. To do this requires the participation and management of the entire distribution channel, from producer to customer, through a series of strategic alliances. Once the goal is achieved or a predetermined period of time is met, the virtual organization dissolves itself, or it grows to the point where it can afford to buy out its suppliers and/or distributors, giving the company more control over quality and delivery and becoming a more traditional company.[11] This strategy is known as vertical integration. Today, in a global business environment, this same goal can also be accomplished through strategic partnerships with other companies in the value chain, which is discussed in the next section.

Strategic Alliances

Another way in which startups become more flexible and responsive, as well as growing more rapidly, is by forming strategic alliances, or teams of businesses, to share resources and reduce costs. These alliances are more than sources of capability for the entrepreneurial venture; they are the glue that holds the venture together. Strategic alliances are more like true partnerships, but they take many forms. The two companies may purchase major equipment jointly or share the costs of research and development and of training. Particularly in the area of R&D, it is very difficult for any one small company to manage the expense alone. Networking and alliances enable smaller businesses to bid successfully against large companies. They offer the convenience and savings of access to one source for everything, shared quality standards, and coordination of vendors. The key to managing a small business alliance successfully is being willing to share internal information such as manufacturing processes, quality control practices, and product information for the good of all.

Building a virtual company and dealing with strategic alliances is not without problems. For the entrepreneurial team that wants to maintain control of every aspect of the growing venture, it is frustrating to have to give up some of that control to other companies. Getting virtual partners to meet entrepreneurs' demands for quality, timeliness, and efficiency can also be a long and difficult process. Shifts in economic conditions or customer demand can negatively affect one or more of the partners, making it difficult to achieve stated outcomes. Perhaps the biggest problem is the fact that new ventures don't have the experience or depth of resources to effectively manage their alliances. Unfortunately, large company partners know this and often take advantage by exerting their power to their own ends.

Consequently, it is important that the entrepreneur and the virtual partner come to written agreement on their duties and responsibilities and that they both enjoy the benefits of the relationship. The entrepreneurial firm should be represented by an attorney who can protect its interests and make sure that it can't be held hostage by its partner. Virtual organizations do have some challenges, namely, higher administrative costs, potential organizational culture differences among the partners, and ethical issues.[12] Many entrepreneurs have found that the benefits of virtual partners far outweigh the problems and that the virtual corporation is the most efficient and effective way to give the venture traction. However, there are management issues unique to this type of business, and they must be thoroughly understood. The next section describes what these management challenges are and how to solve them.

SOCIAL ENTREPRENEURSHIP: MAKING MEANING

When Sustainability Is the Culture

There's no telling Ken Grossman, an avid out-doorsman, that you can't have it all. From the day he founded Sierra Nevada Brewing Company (SNBC) in 1980, he was determined not only to produce the best beer he could, but he wanted his company to respect and honor the mountain range where he had spent so much of his life. Undaunted by a crowded market, he set out to prove that if you focus on people and the planet, not as a business strategy but because it's the right thing to do, you can create a highly profitable company.

Grossman's employees are incentivized to innovate in ways that make the business more sustainable, such as turning used vegetable oil from his restaurant into alternative fuel to power his trucks, and recycling spent hops and grains for cattle feed. An employee committee called Continuous Improvement Group (CIG) and pronounced "keg" meets on a monthly basis to identify problems or areas for improvement so that employees can begin thinking about how to solve them. The philosophy of sustainability even touches the lifestyles of the employees because the company provides organic-garden plots and teaches them how to grow organic fruits and vegetables. The new revenue streams and reduced costs that have derived from this effort have made Sierra Nevada the sixth largest brewery in the U.S.

Sources: Sierra Nevada Brewing Company, www.sierranevada .com/index2.html; and Casler, A., Gundlach, M.J., Persons, B. and Zivnuska, S. (2010), "Sierra Nevada Brewing Company's Thirty-Year Journey Toward Sustainability," *People and Strategy* 33(1): 45–51.

Keeping Distributed Employees and Strategic Partners Linked

One of the important challenges that virtual or distributed organizations with strategic partners face is keeping everyone connected and in touch even though they are geographically separated. A distributed company may be a great way to keep overhead down and flexibility up, but it is no substitute for human contact and face-to-face communication. Even in a virtual environment, it's important to conduct a face-to-face meeting at least once every three to six months and arrange for employees and partners in specific geographic regions to meet regularly in between company-wide meetings. It is also essential to create a discussion area on the company's Intranet and to encourage everyone to share important information and discussion points. A regular conference call should be set up once a week to stay in touch. With virtual companies growing by leaps and bounds, online companies have sprung up to provide services and products that these businesses may need. Here are some examples:

Management team: Many websites aggregate independent professional service providers and help small businesses find experienced financial management and other services on a limited budget.

Marketing: At several online sites, a company can accomplish its public relations, marketing, direct mail, customer relationship management, and even market research for far less than it would cost to hire a marketing firm.

Check out www.marketingprofs.com, one of the best sources for marketing help on the Internet.

Supply chain management: Online companies will do everything from order management to assembly, configuration, packaging, and e-commerce fulfillment and collaboration.

Virtual meetings: Some companies—IBM is one—are holding meetings in cyberspace through a virtual world known as "Second Life" (www .secondlife.com). Users (called residents) create avatars (animated characters) to represent themselves and through which they communicate via text messaging, IM, or voice. Other online collaboration services, such as Citrix, Google Groups, and Go to Meeting, help keep distributed organizations connected at a relatively low cost.

LOCATION STRATEGY: FINDING THE APPROPRIATE BUSINESS SITE

If the new venture cannot be operated as a virtual organization, a significant part of the organizing process will be finding an appropriate physical site for doing business. Most people are familiar with the three key factors for determining value in real estate: "location, location, location." Similarly, the location of the business has a serious impact on its success. Location determines who will see the business, how easily customers can find it and access it (Is the business at ground-floor level and easily seen? Or is it out of sight in a multistory building?), and whether or not they will want to access it (Is the neighborhood safe? Is parking available?). Even businesses such as manufacturing, where the customer doesn't come to the site, benefit from a location near major sources of transportation or supply. Because many business owners view their business site as permanent, selecting the best site becomes a crucial decision that will need to be justified to investors, lenders, and others. Site decisions generally begin at a macro level, considering first the state or region of the country, next the city, and then the parcel on which the facility will be located.

Choosing the Region, State, and Community

Locating a site for a new business normally begins with identifying the area of the country that seems best suited to the type of business being started. "Best suited" may mean that firms in a particular industry tend to congregate in a particular region, such as the high-tech firms that gravitate to Route 128 in Massachusetts or to the Silicon Valley in California. For some businesses, "best suited" may mean that a state is offering special financial and other incentives for businesses to locate there. In other cases, "best suited" means being located near major suppliers. Often an entrepreneur starts a business in a particular region because that's where he or she happens to live. This may be fine during the incubation period, but soon, what the area contributes to the potential success of the business over the long term must be considered.

The economic base of a region or community is simply the major source of income for the area. Communities are viewed as primarily industrial, agricultural, or service-oriented. In general, industrial communities export more goods than they import. For example, suppose the community's principal income is derived from farming and the associated products that it ships to other communities. This activity brings money into the community. Now suppose the citizens of the community must travel to another community to do major shopping. This activity takes money out of the community. An important thing to learn about any community being considered as the home base for the business is whether the money brought in from farming exceeds the money that leaves through shopping. If it does, the community appears to have a growing economic base, which is a favorable factor for new businesses. Entrepreneurs can learn more about the economic base of any community by contacting the state or regional economic development agency in the area. These organizations exist to bring new business into the region, so they have to stay on top of what is going on. They can provide all the statistics on the economic health of the region, as well as estimate the cost of doing business there. Another helpful site is the U.S. Department of Commerce website (www.commerce.gov).

Most community governments are faced with cash needs that go well beyond the tax tolerance level of their citizens; consequently, they work diligently with economic development agencies to attract new businesses—and the accompanying tax revenues—into the community. One of the ways they attract businesses is by offering incentives such as lower taxes, cheaper land, and employee training programs. Some communities have enterprise zones, which give the businesses that locate in them favorable tax treatment from the state on the basis of the number of jobs created, as well as lower land costs and rental rates. They also expedite permit processes and help in any way they can to make the move easier. It is important, however, to be wary of communities that offer up-front cash in compensation for the community's lack of up-to-date infrastructure. The community may be hiding a high corporate tax rate or some other disincentive that could hurt the new business's chances of success. In general, the larger the incentives, the more exacting the entrepreneur's homework must be.

Population Demographics

In addition to studying the economic base and the community's attitude toward new business, entrepreneurs, particularly those whose businesses deal with consumers, should carefully examine the population base. Is it growing or shrinking? Is it aging or getting younger? Is it culturally diverse? The level and quantity of disposable income in the community will indicate whether there is enough money to purchase what a new company is offering, and the skill level of workers in the community will need to meet the needs of the new venture.

Demographic information in the United States is usually based on the U.S. census, which tracks changes in population size and characteristics. The United States is divided into Standard Metropolitan Statistical Areas (SMSAs), which are geographic areas that include a major metropolitan area such as Los Angeles or Houston. These are further divided into census tracts, which contain approximately 4,000–5,000 people, and into neighborhood blocks. With this information, it is possible to determine, for example, whether the city in which an entrepreneur wants to locate a new software development firm has enough people with sufficient technical and educational skills to support it. Population data also indicate the number of people available to work. Demographic data are easily obtained from the economic development agency, the public library, the Internet, or the post office, which tracks populations by zip code. Population demographics for global communities can be found at a number of sites, such as GeoHive (www.geohive.com).

Choosing a Retail Site

With a retail business, the entrepreneur is dealing directly with the consumer, so naturally, one of the first considerations is locating near consumers. Because a retail business is unlikely to survive if not enough consumers have easy access to the business, it is imperative to locate where there are suitable concentrations of consumers. Understanding a trade area is one way to calculate the potential demand from consumers. The trade area is the region from which the entrepreneur expects to draw customers. The type of business will largely determine the size of the trade area. For example, if a business sells general merchandise that can be found almost anywhere, the trade area is much smaller; customers will not travel great distances to purchase common goods. Yet a specialty outlet— for example, a clothing boutique with unusual apparel—may draw people from other communities as well.

Once the location within the community is identified, the trade area can be calculated. With a map of the community, the business site is identified; then, the point of a compass can be placed on the proposed site and a circle can be drawn whose radius represents the distance people are willing to drive to reach the site. Within the circle is the trade area, which can now be studied in more detail. Using a census tract map, census tracts can be identified within the trade area, and the number of people who reside within the boundaries of the trade area can be calculated (see Figure 12.2). The demographic information will also describe these people in terms of level of education, income level, average number of children, and so forth.

Once the trade area is established, the competition can also be identified. One way to do this is to drive or walk through the area (assuming it is not too large) and spot competing businesses. Note their size and number, and gauge how busy they are at various times of the day by observing their parking lots or actually entering the business. If competitors are located in shopping malls or strip centers, look for clusters of stores that are similar to the new venture and have low vacancy rates. Then look at the stores near the proposed site to check for compatibility. Often, locating near a competitor is a wise choice because it encourages comparison shopping, which is a good thing if the entrepreneur's business has a competitive advantage. Observe the character of the area. Does

FIGURE 12.2 Sample of a Trade Area

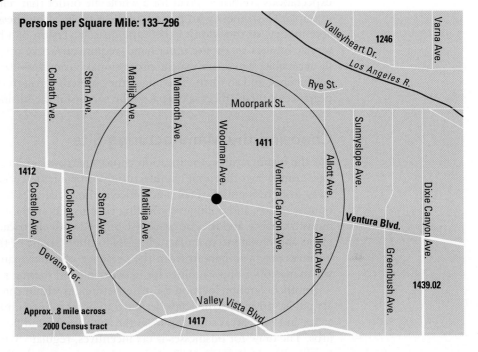

it appear to be successful and well maintained? Remember that the character of the area will have an important impact on the business. Online tools such as Google Earth (http://earth.google.com) are helpful for initial evaluation of a site that is not within driving distance.

It is important to identify the routes customers might take to reach a proposed site: highways, streets, and public transportation routes. If a site is difficult to locate and hard to reach, potential customers will not expend the effort to find it. The parking situation should also be checked. Most communities require provision of a sufficient amount of parking space for new construction, through either parking lots or garages; however, in some older areas, street parking is the only available option. If parking is hard to find or too expensive, customers will avoid going to that business. A foot and car traffic count for the proposed site will determine how busy the area is. Remember, retail businesses typically rely heavily on traffic for customers. A traffic count is easily accomplished by observing and tallying the customers going by and into the business. City planning departments and transportation departments maintain auto traffic counts for major arterials in the city.

Choosing the Service/Wholesale Site

If a service or wholesale business has customers who come to the place of business, an entrepreneur will need to find a site that offers some of the same attributes that a retailer looks for. Accessibility, attractiveness, and a trade area of sufficient size are all key factors in the selection of a site. There is no need to choose from among the more expensive commercial sites, because customer expectations are not as great for a wholesale outlet that sells to the public, for example. Customers who patronize these types of businesses usually want to save money, so they don't expect the upscale version of a business site. Some service businesses, on the other hand, require attractive office space that is easily accessible. These are usually professional businesses—lawyers, accountants, consultants, and so forth. The image they present through the location and appearance of their offices is crucial to the success of the business.

Choosing the Manufacturing Site

For the manufacturer, the location choices narrow significantly. Communities have zoning laws that limit manufacturing companies to certain designated areas away from residential, retail, and office commercial sites to reduce the chance of noise, odor, and pollutants affecting citizens. Often these areas are known as industrial parks, and they are usually equipped with electrical power and sewage plants appropriate to manufacturing. By locating in one of these parks, the new business may also benefit from the presence of other manufacturing nearby, which may offer opportunities for networking and sharing resources.

Another common location for manufacturing is within enterprise zones, which are public–private partnerships designed to bring jobs to inner cities, downtown areas, and rural areas suffering from the shift of jobs and population to the suburbs. The draw for businesses is tax incentives, regulatory relief, and employee training programs. Empowerment zones in any state can be found by going to the U.S. Housing and Urban Development Agency website (www.hud.gov). Entrepreneurs seeking manufacturing sites are concerned with four key factors: access to suppliers, cost of labor, access to transportation, and cost of utilities. These factors may not be weighted equally. Depending on the type of manufacturer, one or more factors may have greater importance in evaluating a site.

Manufacturers and processors usually try to locate within a reasonable distance of their major suppliers to cut shipping time and save transportation costs. Thus a company that processes food attempts to set up business near the growing fields, so that the food is as fresh as possible when it arrives at the processing plant. Similarly, a manufacturer that uses steel as one of its main raw materials might want to locate in the same region of the country as the steel mills to save the high costs of trucking heavy steel great distances.

Today, many manufacturers choose a location on the basis of the cost of labor, rather than proximity to suppliers, because labor is generally the single greatest cost in the production of goods. Wages and laws related to workers, such as workers' compensation, vary from state to state—and sometimes from city to city. For example, California laws and cost of living tend to make it a more expensive place to hire employees than, say, Missouri or North Dakota. Some labor-intensive businesses have found that the only way they can compete is by putting plants in Mexico or China, where labor costs are a fraction of those in the United States, and where regulations are less onerous. The bottom line is that the entrepreneur must carefully weigh the cost of labor when considering a particular location for a manufacturing plant.

Most manufacturers prefer to locate near major transportation networks: railways, major highways, airports, and ports of call. The reasoning is obvious: The greater the distance between the plant and a major transportation network, the higher the cost to the company and, ultimately, to the customer. Also, the more transportation people who handle the product, the greater the cost. Thus, in terms of simple economics, to remain competitive, manufacturers must conduct a cost-benefit analysis on any proposal to locate away from a major transportation network. Higher transportation costs will result in a smaller profit margin for the company or in higher costs for the customers. Either way, the company loses.

Utility rates vary from state to state, and usually from city to city within a given state. If the new venture is heavily dependent on electricity, gas, or coal, this factor could be a significant variable in the cost of producing a product and therefore should be carefully examined.

Land and location are only part of the equation. If the site contains an existing building, the question becomes whether to lease or to buy. If the site is bare land, building a facility is the only option. Because the facility accounts for a significant portion of a new venture's startup costs, it is important to consider these scenarios in more detail. See Table 12.1 for an overview of the broad criteria for the lease-build-buy decision and some of the important questions to ask.

Alternatives to Conventional Facilities

Today business owners have a variety of alternatives to conventional business locations. These alternatives lower the cost of overhead and make it easier for an entrepreneur to change her mind should the location not work out. We'll consider four of these alternative sites: incubators, shared space, mobile locations, and temporary tenant agreements.

Incubators

Some entrepreneurs find it helpful to start their new venture's life in a business incubator, which has the same purpose as an incubator for an infant—to create a controlled environment that will enhance the chances that the business will survive the startup phase. Private and state-sponsored incubators can be found in nearly every region of the country for almost any type of business. Incubators offer space at a lower-than-market rate to several businesses, which may then share common support functions, such as receptionist, copy machine, and conference room. The incubator may even offer business courses and training to help new entrepreneurs with the myriad details involved in running the business. After about three to five years, depending on the incubator, the young business is helped to move into its own site elsewhere in the community.

Some incubators cater only to high-tech firms or to service firms. Others, such as the Entrepreneur Partnership Program at the Mall of America in Bloomington, Minnesota, help entrepreneurs determine whether their retail or service businesses are suited to the demands of a major mall. This particular program helps the entrepreneur formulate a business plan and open a store. It also provides such incentives as waiving the costs of improving the store space and consulting in marketing and operations. When considering an incubator, it

TABLE 12.1		The Lease-Build-Buy Decision		
Stage of Business	**Lease**	**Build**	**Buy**	**Temporary Space**
Questions to Ask	Also ask the "buy" questions. Do you need to conserve capital for growth? Do you expect the company to grow rapidly and need to move? Can you include clauses that permit the option to renew the lease? Can you remodel to suit your needs? Which type of lease works best for the business: gross, net, or percentage? Do you have a choice?	Do you have the time to build? Is it important to show an asset on your balance sheet? Are your facility needs unique? Do you intend to remain in the facility for a long time?	Is the building of sufficient size to meet future needs? Is there sufficient parking? Is there space for customers, storage, inventory, offices, and restrooms? Is there curbside appeal and compatibility with surroundings? Is there sufficient lighting fixtures and outlets, and power to run equipment?	Do you need to keep overhead costs very low? Are you willing to share space? Is your product or service suitable to a mobile location such as a kiosk or pushcart? Do you need to test the product on customers in a real situation before committing to a building? Do you have a product that can be demonstrated?
Startup	A short-term lease gives the business the option to move and to gauge its long-term requirements.	At startup, use this approach only when there is no facility available to meet the needs of the business. It requires large amounts of capital and time.	Not recommended at startup unless it is the only option and the company is sufficiently capitalized.	Excellent for testing new products, services, and locations on customers. Low overhead.
Rapid Growth	A short-term lease will enable the business to move to larger facilities to meet growing demand without tying up a lot of precious capital.	Resist building during rapid growth as it will use up limited cash needed for growth. It is also a time-consuming process, and time is precious during rapid growth.	Rapid growth is not the time to buy a facility unless the company has received, from investors, a large infusion of cash that more than meets its operational needs.	During rapid growth, temporary locations make sense. This approach keeps the overhead low so that more cash can be directed toward satisfying demand.
Stable Growth	If the location is appropriate to the growth needs of the company, a long-term lease will provide more stability in cash flows.	With stable growth and positive cash flow, the company can afford to spend the time, effort, and capital to build a facility that specifically meets its needs.	Buying a building that allows for expansion is appropriate when company growth stabilizes and the company has a loyal customer base. It is also appropriate when the company needs to show a sizable asset on its balance sheet. If the company subsequently needs cash for a new period of growth, it can sell the building to an investor and lease it back, providing an instant infusion of capital.	Temporary space will typically be used to test new products and services before making a commitment.

is imperative to look at its track record and make sure it provides critical higher-order needs, such as a network of contacts, access to expertise and capital, professional resources, and access to customers.

Shared Space

Another choice is to locate the company within the facilities of a larger company. As the largest of the chain stores continue to downsize, opportunities to take excess space arise. A variation on this theme is to lease a location that has enough space to sublet to a complementary business. For example, a copy service might lease excess space to a new computer graphics company or one that is seeking a new location. A shared arrangement is an effective way to secure the best location at a reasonable price.

Mobile Locations

One of the more interesting ways to introduce new businesses and new products/services to the marketplace is through the use of pushcarts and kiosks. Pushcarts and their more fixed alternative, the kiosk (a small booth), also enable a company to expand so that they have many new locations without the high overhead of a conventional retail storefront. Mobile locations like these are often found in airports, malls, and other areas where consumers gather. Of the various areas where these types of mobile businesses can be found, airports pose perhaps the most difficult challenge to secure. They typically want an experienced business and the entrepreneur will often have to compete against companies that focus on airport locations.

Temporary Tenant Agreements

Some landlords have found that, rather than sitting on an empty space until the new tenant moves in, they can rent the space on a temporary basis so that their cash flow is not interrupted. In fact, the concept of the temporary tenant has grown so rapidly that there are now leasing agents who specialize in this area. The most successful of these temporary tenants possess the following characteristics that seem to draw customers to them: personalized merchandise, opportunities to sample the product, products that can be demonstrated, and products that can be used for entertaining the customers. For the temporary concept to work, significant foot traffic and high customer turnover are required. This is an excellent alternative for retail businesses that want to test a location before making a major commitment. Whichever choice is made, the location and type of facility need to be compatible with the business and its strategic goals.

PEOPLE STRATEGY: ORGANIZING STARTUP HUMAN RESOURCES

The organization of the business processes and the business location are critical aspects of the management and operational plan, but it is people who implement those processes and use the company facility on a daily basis. The

FIGURE 12.3

Simple Organizational
Chart for a Growing
Business

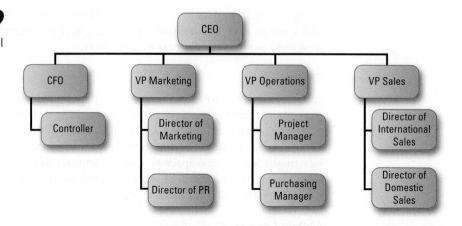

roles and responsibilities of people in the organization are typically displayed in an organizational chart like the one depicted in Figure 12.3. However, at startup, the organization chart is more likely to be flat, reflecting the fact that the entrepreneur and the founding team often perform all the functions when the business is starting, and much of the work is accomplished through an informal organization or network of relationships. Informal networks of people consist of those who tend to gravitate toward each other in an effort to accomplish tasks in a more efficient and effective manner than may be dictated by the organizational chart. These networks form the "shadow" organizational structure that often brings the business through an unexpected crisis, an impossible deadline, or a formidable impasse. They are social links that constitute the real power base in the organization. Metaphorically speaking, the organizational chart is the skeleton of the body, while the informal networks are the arteries and veins that push information and activity throughout the organization—in other words, they are the lifeblood of the organization.

Entrepreneurs seem to recognize intuitively the value of informal networks in the organizational structure, and often the most successful new ventures adopt a team-based approach with a flatter structure. The lead entrepreneur is the driving force for the entrepreneurial team, which normally consists of people with expertise in at least one of the three functional areas of a new venture: marketing, operations, and finance. The organization consists of interactive, integrated teams. In the new venture, these are rarely "departments" in the traditional sense, but rather functions, tasks, or activities. What is the explanation for this? For one thing, entrepreneurs are usually too creative and flexible to be bound by the strictures of a formal organizational structure. They are more comfortable bringing together resources and people as a team and making decisions on the spot without having to go through layers of management. Another reason is that new, growing ventures must be able to adapt quickly as they muscle their way into the market. Uncertainty and instability are a way of life for young ventures, and a rigid, formalized, bureaucratic structure would unduly burden a new venture both financially and operationally.

What makes the entrepreneur's situation unique is that—at least when the venture is in the startup phase or the initial growing phase and capital resources are limited—the team the entrepreneur develops will probably include several people from outside the organization: independent contractors. For example, an entrepreneur may decide to subcontract the manufacturing of a product to an established company. The subcontractor will then, of necessity, become a part of that company's team in the production of the product. Marketing, sales, operations, and finance people must also be able to work with the manufacturing subcontractor to ensure that the goals of the new venture are met with the timeliness and level of quality desired. This requires the team to have skills not normally learned in school, skills such as diplomacy in the management of intra- and inter-team relationships, problem-solving skills, and the ability to take responsibility for innovative changes on the spot, often without direct approval.

At no time is the entrepreneur's role as leader of the organization more critical or more vulnerable than in the first year of the business. If entrepreneurs are not able to gain traction and build momentum to propel the new venture forward, the new business will remain in a constant state of struggle. To build an effective organization, entrepreneurs must avoid some common leadership traps:[13]

- Isolating themselves from the rest of the startup team and failing to keep the lines of communication open
- Always having the one "right" answer instead of looking for the best solution
- Keeping people on board who are not up to the needs of the company
- Taking on too much too soon
- Setting unrealistic expectations based on inadequate information
- Not building support

Creating the Company Culture

Researchers actually disagree as to exactly what culture is. Some believe it is the reflection of the core values of the company, which stem from the firm's history.[14] Others believe culture is changeable, that it really reflects the behaviors and attitudes of those in the company at the time.[15] In their 1982 book *Corporate Cultures: The Rites and Rituals of Corporate Life*, Terrence Deal and Allan Kennedy coined the term *corporate culture* to describe the organization's tendency to develop its own characteristic way of doing things.[16] In very simplistic terms, organizational culture is the personality of the company, that intangible set of values that determines how and why the people in the organization respond to their business environment as they do.[17] A description of the company culture may be spelled out in the company handbook, but the real culture is found within the attitudes and actions of the organization's people as they interact on a daily basis.

It is often said that entrepreneurial companies—startups in particular—have a distinct culture, one much different from that of large, established corporations. This is misleading, because not all startups are alike. If the founders came from the big corporate environment or from a traditional business school education, they are very likely to think in terms of elaborate organization charts and multiple levels of management that look much like those of GE or Procter & Gamble. Often it is the founders, who don't have these experiences and basically organize to make the business happen, who end up with the "just do it," fast and flexible culture generally associated with startups.

The culture of a startup generally derives from the vision and values of the founder or founding team and that vision and those values produce behaviors or ways of doing things. The advantage of startups is that the founder has the opportunity to hire only people who fit with the culture; this is a much easier task than trying to re-engineer the ingrained culture of an existing company. For culture to create a competitive advantage for a startup, however, the values, practices, and behaviors need to align with the goals, processes, and tasks that the business engages in.[18] Figure 12.4 depicts this relationship. For example, the processes and activities a company undertakes are reflected in the practices or the way those processes are implemented. In the figure, the right side of the circle reflects people while the left side represents organizational issues.

In organizing the business to reflect its culture, the founding team would identify its core values and the overriding mission of the company. Then the team would specify the outcomes it's trying to achieve. Suppose an outcome is developing a loyal customer base. It would be important to do significant market research with customers to determine what's important to them. The

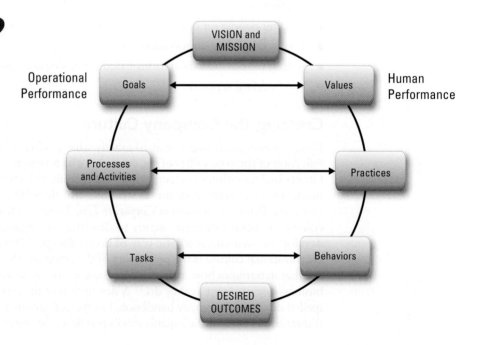

FIGURE 12.4

Aligning Culture and Strategy

results of this research would tell the team what they would have to do to get the result they want. This would lead to practices such as giving customers an easy way to provide feedback to the company and behaviors such as always being honest with customers. On the operational side, this might mean setting up an interactive website as a process with all its associated tasks.

Aligning the operational and organizational performance of the company with its beliefs and behaviors is only the start. In some manner, this all has to be conveyed to the market in the form of a story—not a dry, factual statement, but a story that gives customers a sense of what this culture feels like. Stories are much stickier than business statements because they contain people that customers can relate to and they provide rich context that gives customers a lot of information.[19] Saying, "we help people find the best prices" is less effective than telling a story about a customer who was able to save a lot of money using the company's product. A great story will provide context, characters, content, and takeaway lessons that the customer can extrapolate to their own situation.

Some of the questions that lead to a definition of a company's culture are the following:

1. Do the organization's people work in teams or individually?
2. How does the organization deal with change?
3. How does the company deal with failure?
4. How are decisions made? Who makes the critical decisions?
5. How is work prioritized?
6. How is information shared within and outside the organization?
7. Does the company take a long-term or short-term focus on decision making?
8. How does the company ensure employee competence?
9. Does the company encourage diversity?
10. How are employees treated, and what is their role in the company's vision?

Hiring the Right People

Today, with more and more employees suing their bosses for wrongful termination, sexual harassment, and racial/gender/age discrimination, it is increasingly important that an entrepreneur understand how to hire. Hiring is not a simple matter of placing a help-wanted ad in the newspaper, receiving résumés, and then holding interviews to select the best candidate. The bulk of the work of hiring comes before the person is actually needed.

Part of organizing the business is determining what positions are needed for the required tasks of the business. This is a wise practice, because employees are generally the largest expense of the business and therefore should be hired only when necessary. Nevertheless, it is important to develop job descriptions to prepare for the eventuality of hiring employees. Typically, when entrepreneurs (and managers) develop job descriptions, they focus entirely on the duties and responsibilities of a particular job. Although this is important, it is equally important to develop behavioral profiles of these jobs. Even though a job candidate may have the education and experience required by the job description and may display some of the behavioral traits necessary for success in the position, the candidate's personality and values may not fit in well with the culture of the organization. This is an important distinction, because education and experience can be acquired and behaviors can in most cases be taught, but the right values—which enable compatibility with the company culture—must already be present. In today's business environment, a company's culture is a competitive advantage, so hiring people whose attitudes and values are consistent with it becomes an important goal in hiring.

The first and best place to look for an employee is among current employees, subcontractors, or professional advisers. Referrals from trusted people who know the business have a greater likelihood of yielding a successful hire. Even during startup, it is important to be constantly on the lookout for good people who might come on board as the business grows. Executive search firms are good sources for management positions, and online resources have become an effective starting place for hiring, particularly with technically oriented positions. Companies such as Monster (www.monster.com), Guru.com (www.guru.com), and Craigslist (www.craigslist.com) are places where qualified people post their résumés, and it's easy for an employer to search for the particular skills required. But to save time and avoid interviewing the wrong people, it's always wise to follow up with references before calling the candidate in for an interview.

Most entrepreneurs dread interviewing job candidates, primarily because they don't know what to say and don't understand that their questions should be designed to reveal the individual's personality and behavior—how he or she might react in certain situations. This is because a resume simply reveals what the candidate sees as their relevant experience and that's only part of the total picture. How the candidate behaves during the interview and particularly what their nonverbal communication tells the interviewer is far more revealing of the candidate's character. Understanding who the candidate is can be effectively accomplished in part by asking open-ended questions, questions that call for more than "yes–no" answers. For example, ask, "What is your greatest strength?" or "How would you handle the following hypothetical situation?" While the person is answering the questions, the interviewer should be careful to note the nonverbal communication being expressed through body language.

Entrepreneurs must be aware that certain questions should never be asked in an interview situation because they are illegal and leave the entrepreneur open to potential lawsuits. Under the laws administered by the Equal Employment Opportunity Commission (EEOC), before the point of hire a person may *not* be asked about religion or religious background, nation of origin, living arrangements or lifestyle choices, plans for pregnancy, age (to avoid discrimination against people over 40 or under 21), criminal arrest record ("Have you ever been convicted of a crime?" may be asked), or military record.

Human Resource Leasing

Entrepreneurs who are not ready to hire permanent employees or who need to remain flexible because the business environment is volatile and unpredictable may want to consider leasing employees or employing temporary services.

A leased employee is not legally the entrepreneur's employee but is, rather, the employee of the lessor organization. That firm is responsible for all employment taxes and benefits. The entrepreneur simply receives a bill for the person's services. Employee leasing is a rapidly growing industry now known as the professional employer organization (PEO) industry (www.peo.com). More and more business owners are finding it advantageous to have a third party manage their human resources. In effect, the PEO becomes a co-employer, taking on the responsibility of payroll, taxes, benefits, workers' compensation insurance, labor law compliance, and risk management. Elizabeth Bradt is an accomplished veterinarian, but like many professional service providers, she did not have the skills or the patience to handle human resource issues, such as hiring interviews, regulatory compliance, and benefits. She couldn't offer the types of benefits that large employers offer, such as 401(k) plans and dental insurance. As a result, her business, All Creatures Veterinary Hospital in Salem, Massachusetts, lost half its employees in the first year. Bradt had not realized how much she would have to deal with when it came to hiring and supporting her staff. To solve the problem, she made Integrated Staffing, a professional employer organization, the legal employer of her staff. The PEO gave her peace of mind and provided her employees with benefits that she alone could not have provided. As a result, in 2006, she had zero turnover.[20]

Managing Employee Risk

Risk management is a set of policies and their associated decision-making processes that reduce or eliminate risks associated with having employees. For example, one entrepreneurial service company with 120 employees was suffering from a high turnover rate of new hires during the first 90 days of employment. Although the company's overall turnover rate was in line with the industry average, its turnover rate for new hires was about double that of its competitors. This turnover was costing the company more than $10,000 per employee, which was a significant financial risk for the company and raised its cost of doing business substantially. To solve the problem and reduce the risk, the company realized that it needed to implement some new procedures, so it improved its interviewing skills and instituted an orientation program for new employees.

Financial risks are one type of employee risk. In Chapter 10 the legal issues related to the formation of the business were discussed, but the law affects every aspect of business operations as well, especially the way employees are treated. The federal government and state governments have enacted a number of laws and regulations to protect employees from unhygienic or dangerous work environments, discrimination during hiring, and payment of substandard wages. One of the critical tasks of the person in charge of human resources is to make certain that the business is obeying all the laws and regulations to which it is subject. Failure to do so could result in severe penalties for the business and its owners. It is not within the scope of this text to address these laws in depth; however, Table 12.2 presents some of the major employment laws that affect small businesses. More information about these laws can be found on the Internet and through the federal and state agencies.

TABLE 12.2   Important Employment Laws

Law	Type of Business It Applies to
Age Discrimination in Employment Act	
Prohibits discrimination against people age 40 to 70, including discrimination in advertising for jobs	All companies with 20 or more employees
Americans with Disabilities Act	
Prohibits discrimination on the basis of disability	All companies with 15 or more employees
Civil Rights Act	
Guarantees the rights of all citizens to freedom from discrimination on the basis of race, religion, color, national origin, and sex	All companies with 15 or more employees
Equal Pay Act	
Requires equal pay for equal work	All companies with 15 or more employees
Family and Medical Leave Act	
Provides for up to 12 weeks of unpaid leave for employees who are dealing with family issues	Companies with 50 or more employees
Immigration Reform and Control Act and the Immigration Act of 1990	
Designed to prevent undocumented aliens from working in the United States. Companies must complete an Employment Eligibility Verification Form (I-9) for each employee.	All companies of any size
National Labor Relations Act and Taft-Hartley Act	
Requires employers to bargain in good faith with union representatives and forbids unfair labor practices by unions	All companies of any size
Occupational Safety and Health Act (OSHA)	
Designed to ensure safety and health in the work environment	All companies of any size
Title VII of the Civil Rights Act	
The original was amended to include discrimination against pregnant women; people with AIDS, cancer, or physical and mental disabilities; and people who are recovering from, or being treated for, substance abuse. Victims of discrimination may sue for punitive damages and back pay.	Companies with 15 or more employees for 20 weeks in the current or preceding year
Workers' Compensation	
Each state has enacted a law to compensate employees for medical costs and lost wages due to job-related injuries.	Requirements vary by state

Planning for Ownership and Compensation

Two of the most perplexing management issues faced by an entrepreneur heading a new company are how much of the company to sell to potential stockholders and how much to pay key managers. Whatever route is ultimately chosen, it should reflect the goals of the company and reward the contributions of the participants. There is a tendency on the part of small, privately held companies to use minority shares as an incentive to entice investors and to pay key managers, primarily because new companies do not have the cash flow to provide attractive compensation packages. The prevailing wisdom is that providing stock in the new company will increase commitment, cause management to be more cost-conscious, reduce cash outlay for salaries, and induce loyalty to the company in the long term. But studies have found that this is not always the case.[21] More often than not, the person who has been given stock in good faith will ultimately leave the company, possibly taking the stock with her or him (absent an agreement prohibiting this), and this action creates the potential for future harm to the business. During the dot com boom of the late 1990s and into 2000, stock options were the most attractive benefit to potential employees, and many candidates would forgo large salaries in favor of more stock options. But after the dot com crash in April 2000 and the subsequent decline in valuation of technology stocks in general, stock options took second place to salaries in the minds of many employees.

In the initial growth stage of a new venture, it is difficult to determine with any degree of accuracy what long-term role a particular person may play in the organization. As a consequence of their limited resources, entrepreneurs typically are not able to attract the best people to take the company beyond the startup phase, so they often hire a person with lesser qualifications for little salary plus a minority ownership in the company. In this scenario, the entrepreneur is literally betting on the potential contribution of this person—and it's a gamble that frequently doesn't pay off. Later, when the company can afford to hire the person it needs, it will have to deal with a minority shareholder who has developed territorial "rights." Therefore, when minority ownership is an important issue to a potential employee, it is imperative to make clear to that person exactly what it means. There are few legal and managerial rights associated with a minority position; thus, for all practical purposes, minority ownership is simply the unmarketable right to appreciated stock value that has no defined payoff period and certainly no guarantee of value. Using a stock-vesting agreement is one way to make sure that only stock that has been earned will be distributed. With a stock-vesting agreement, stock purchased by the team is placed in escrow and released over a three- to five-year period. A buyback provision in the stockholders agreement is another way to ensure that stock remains in the company even if a member of the team leaves in the early days of the new venture.

Worse than giving stock to an employee who is new to the company with no track record is giving an equity stake to an independent contractor who is providing a service. For example, one entrepreneur who was short on cash wanted to give a programmer equity in lieu of paying him for building the website. The amount agreed upon was 3 percent of the company for a job that would have cost $3,000. The problem with this scenario is that if at some point the company is worth $1 million, the entrepreneur would now have paid that programmer $30,000 for a $3,000 website. Giving someone ownership rights in the company is a serious decision that should receive very careful consideration. There are several things to contemplate before taking on an equity partner, be it an investor, independent contractor, or key employee. Anyone brought in as an investor/shareholder or partner with the entrepreneur does not have to be an equal partner. An investor can hold whatever share of stock is negotiated on the basis of what is contributed to the business. In general, one should never bring someone in as a partner/investor if that person can be hired to provide the same service, no matter how urgent the situation. In addition, the company should not be locked into future compensation promises such as stock options, and cash for bonuses should be used whenever possible. It is important that the company be established as the founder's company before any partners are taken on—unless, of course, the company has been founded by a team. Finally, employees should typically work for the company at least two years before they are given stock or stock options. In this way, the entrepreneur learns if this employee is someone they want to keep.

Founder's Stock, Dilution, and Alternatives to Equity

Founder's stock (144 stock) is stock issued to the first shareholders of the corporation or assigned to key managers as part of a compensation package at startup. The payoff on this stock comes when the company experiences a liquidity event such as an IPO or an acquisition by another company. Assuming that the company is successful, founder's stock at issuance is valued at probably the lowest it will ever be, relative to an investor's stock value. Consequently, a tax problem can arise when private investors provide seed capital to the new venture. Often the value of the stock the investors hold makes it very obvious that the founder's stock was a bargain and that its price did not represent the true value of the stock. According to Internal Revenue Code (IRC) §83, the amount of the difference between the founder's price and the investor's price is taxable as compensation income. One way to avoid this problem is to issue common stock to founders and key managers and to issue convertible preferred stock to investors. The preference upon liquidation should be high enough to cover the book value of the corporation, so the common stockholders would essentially receive nothing. This action would effectively decrease the value of the common stock so that it would no longer appear to be a bargain for tax purposes and subject the founders to an immediate tax liability.

Founder's stock is restricted, and the SEC rules (Rule 144) state that the restriction refers to stock that has not been registered with the SEC (private placement) and stock owned by the controlling officers and shareholders of the company (those with at least 10 percent ownership). If a stockholder has owned the stock for at least three years and public information about the company exists, Rule 144 can be avoided in the sale of the stock. If the stockholder has held the stock for less than three years, the rules must be strictly complied with. It is not the intent of this chapter to discuss the details of Rule 144. Suffice it to say that the rule is complex and that the appropriate attorney or tax specialist should be consulted.

Issuing Stock When the Company Is Capitalized

The number of shares authorized when a corporation is formed is purely arbitrary. Suppose a new venture, NewCorp, authorizes one million shares of stock. This means that NewCorp has one million shares available to be issued to potential stockholders. If each share of stock is valued at $1 and $100,000 is capitalized, the company will have 100,000 issued shares; if each share is valued at $10, the company will have 10,000 issued shares. The value placed on each share is arbitrary. For psychological reasons, however, it is customary to value a share at $1, so a shareholder who contributes $10,000 to the business can say that he or she owns 10,000 shares of stock (as opposed to 1,000 shares at $10/share). In short, the number of shares issued depends on the initial capitalization and the price per share.

Now suppose that the founder of NewCorp initially contributes $250,000 in cash and $300,000 in assets (equipment, furniture, etc.) to fund the company. At $1 a share, the company issues the founder 550,000 shares of stock; this constitutes a 100 percent interest in the company, because only 550,000 shares have been issued. At a later date, the company issues 29,000 additional shares at $5 a share to an investor. This minority shareholder has therefore contributed $145,000 (29,000 shares at $5/share) to the company and owns a 5 percent (29,000/579,000) interest in the company (that is, 29,000 of the 579,000 shares of stock that have been issued). The investor will require that the current value or future additional income of the company be sufficient to justify the increase in price per share. As additional shares are issued, the original investor's percentage ownership in the company declines or is diluted. However, the founder's shares will not go below 55 percent (550,000/1,000,000) unless the company authorizes additional shares and issues a portion or all of those additional shares.

The type of stock issued is common stock, which is a basic ownership interest in the company. This means that holders of common stock share in both the successes and the failures of the business and benefit through dividends and the appreciating value of the company. Once common stock is issued, a company can then issue preferred stock to holders who are paid first if the company is liquidated. Preferred stockholders must accept a fixed dividend amount, no matter how much profit the company makes. Recall that if the company were a sub-chapter S-corporation, it could issue only one class of stock.

Alternatives to Equity Incentives

There are other ways to compensate key managers that do not require the founder to give up equity in the company. The following are a few of these alternatives. In choosing among them, consider the advice of an accountant, who can recommend the most appropriate structure for the business.

Deferred Compensation Plans

In a deferred compensation plan, the entrepreneur can specify that awards and bonuses be linked to profits and performance of both the individual and the company, with the lion's share depending on the individual's performance. The employee does not pay taxes on this award until it is actually paid out at some specified date.

Bonus Plans

With a bonus plan, a series of goals are set by the company with input from the employee, and as the employee reaches each goal, the bonus is given. This method is often used with sales personnel and others who have a direct impact on the profitability of the company. The key to success with bonus plans is to specify measurable objectives.

Capital Appreciation Rights

Capital appreciation rights give employees the right to participate in the profits of the company at a specified percentage, even though they are not full shareholders with voting rights. Capital appreciation rights, or "phantom stock," provide long-term compensation incentives whose value is based on the increase in the value of the business. The phantom stock will look, act, and reward like real stock, but it will have no voting rights and will limit the employee's obligation should the business fail. Typically, the employee has to be with the company for a period of three to five years to be considered vested in capital appreciation rights, but otherwise employees do not have to pay for these rights.

Profit-Sharing Plans

Profit-sharing plans are distinct from the previously discussed plans in that they are subject to the ERISA rules for employee retirement programs. These plans must include all employees, without regard to individual contribution to profit or performance. They are different from pensions in that owners are not required to contribute in any year and employees are not "entitled" to them.

Organizing business processes, location, and people is an important and difficult task that requires considerable thought and planning. Decisions made in the earliest stages of the new venture can seriously—and often negatively—affect the new firm's ability to grow and be successful in the future. This chapter highlighted many critical organizational considerations and offered suggestions for addressing them. However, it is important to consult with people who specialize in these functions to be sure that the right decisions are made.

New Venture Action Plan

- Identify the processes and information flow in your business.
- Identify ways to operate like a virtual enterprise or at least to outsource some aspects of the business.
- Locate a site for the business.
- Decide whether to lease, buy, or build a facility.
- Determine the personnel required to run the business at startup and over the next three to five years.
- Create job profiles for positions in the business.
- Determine the ownership and compensation requirements of the business. Formulate a plan to find the best candidates for positions in the company.

Questions on Key Issues

1. What are the advantages and the disadvantages of a virtual company?
2. What is the purpose of the imaginary tour of the business?
3. Which factors important in choosing a retail site would not be relevant to a manufacturing site—and vice versa?
4. What are the advantages and disadvantages of using stock as compensation and incentives?
5. How can the entrepreneur improve the chances of choosing the best job candidate?
6. List three alternatives to equity incentives for key managers.

Experiencing Entrepreneurship

1. Choose an industry in which you have an interest. Find a business in that industry; arrange to visit the site and talk with key personnel, and do a flowchart of the business processes that reflects what you learned about it on your visit. Did you find any inefficiencies that if corrected could improve the process flow?
2. Interview an entrepreneur about his or her hiring practices. How successful have those practices been in getting and retaining good employees?

Relevant Case Studies

Case 6 Potion Inc.
Case 9 The Case of Google, Inc.

UNDERSTANDING PRODUCTION AND OPERATIONS

"One way to increase productivity is to do whatever we are doing now, but faster. . . . There is a second way. We can change the nature of the work we do, not how fast we do it."

—ANDREW S. GROVE,
CEO, Intel Corporation

CHAPTER OBJECTIVES

- Identify the components of the production process for products and services.

- Explain the critical aspects of supply-chain management.

- Discuss how to manage quality.

- Explain how outsourcing can benefit an entrepreneurial venture.

FINDING GOLD IN SOMEONE ELSE'S GARBAGE

Imagine generating $40 million in revenues from an opportunity someone else didn't want. That's exactly what Thomas Mackie and Paul Reckwerdt did when, in 1997, GE Medical, which had been funding their research, decided that it wouldn't amount to a substantial business. Mackie and Reckwerdt were working on a machine that would make a radiation beam lock onto a tumor so that a doctor could clearly see it and, at the same time, zap it with radiation with amazing accuracy. GE Medical had been providing the duo with approximately $700,000 annually, so losing that funding was a major crisis. But since both men had lost close relatives to cancer, they were not about to give up. Using $1.5 million that they had received for selling a medical software program, they launched TomoTherapy to develop and market the Hi-Art, a combination CT scan and radiation gun. They received FDA approval in 2002 and in 2003 began installing eight of the $3.2-million machines.

Yet as positive as that was, there was danger on the horizon. Large medical device companies such as Siemens Medical Solutions and Varian Medical Systems had also recognized the opportunity and were hastening to bring their own versions of the Hi-Art to market. It is not easy for a small, entrepreneurial company spun out from a university lab to compete with the manufacturing and marketing resources of a public company. But Mackie and Reckwerdt were innovators who were able to look at a problem from hundreds of angles. They also knew that they didn't possess the business smarts to compete in the volatile medical device industry. So they brought on John Barni, a 28-year veteran of Marconi Medical, who was experienced in both manufacturing and marketing. Still, the road ahead was rocky. Despite patents on aspects of its machine, TomoTherapy can't prevent competitors from building machines that also combine high-quality imaging with radiation treatment. Varian and Elektra were both introducing machines that competed directly with TomoTherapy, but Barni was convinced that Tomo could preserve its advantage by constantly innovating at a faster pace than its much larger competitors. As of 2010, TomoTherapy Inc. has more than 200 installations in more than 16 countries. In 2007, the company successfully completed an initial public offering and now holds exclusive licenses on more than 100 issued patents globally. The benefits of its TomoTherapy® Radiation Therapy are presented in 82 research studies examining its use for tumors in the head, neck, prostate, breast, and lung, as well as for treating blood cancers, mesothelioma, and pediatrics.

Sources: TomoTherapy, www.tomotherapy.com, accessed September 29, 2010; J. Martin, "Finding Gold in GE's Garbage," *Fortune Small Business* (April 25, 2004), www.fortune.com; and "TomoTherapy Inc. Gains FDA 510(k) Clearance for New Radiation Therapy System," eReleases, www.ereleases.com/pr/2002-02-01b.html, accessed July 20, 2004.

I n today's fast-moving, uncertain global environment, operations management has become a critical success factor for any business wanting to increase profits and particularly startups that need to get up to speed quickly or risk losing customers. It is important to remember that startups are not simply smaller versions of large companies. For one thing, entrepreneurs don't generally operate their startups with a well-tested and proven business model, so they're constantly sensing and responding to their customers and then revising and refining the business model. Large companies typically have a proven business model in place that they execute with experienced management through the formal operations of their company. By their very nature, startups don't have formal systems and controls in place and they often rely on partnerships or outsourced capability to fill the gaps in their operations expertise and experience. When it comes to operations management, large companies are chiefly dealing with variables that are known and predictable while startups are dealing with unknowns and uncertainty. And that is precisely why so many large, established companies have missed game-changing transformations in industries from computers (mainframes to PCs) to journalism (newspapers to digital news to user-generated content), and telephone (landline to mobile).[1] The inertia of their hierarchical operational and product development structures have made it difficult to spot opportunities that didn't fit those structures. Bringing these same corporate types into a startup will burden the new venture with structure that it can neither afford nor needs. Although the formal operations of a large company can be a competitive advantage in terms of achieving economies of scale efficiencies, startups need to create operational competitive advantages in very different ways.

Operations management covers activities and processes such as new product development, purchasing, inventory, production, manufacturing, distribution, and logistics that are necessary to produce and distribute products and services. The manner in which operations are managed is dependent on the type of organization, whether that be retail, wholesale, manufacturing, or service. The ability to innovate in the operations of the business can be a superior competitive advantage for any startup. Operational innovation is about "fundamentally changing how [the] work gets accomplished."[2] This means finding new ways to fill customer orders, create new products and services, and deal with customer service. Wal-Mart is the largest company in the world because of operational innovation. Its cross-docking strategy for moving goods from the supplier directly to its trucks going to the various Wal-Mart stores has resulted in substantially lower operating costs that it has passed on to its customers in the form of lower prices. Zappos.com, the highly successful online shoe company, now owned by Amazon.com, has turned the entire notion of customer service on its head to create a game-changing opportunity and competitive advantage. Where most companies think of customer service as a cost center, Zappos CEO Tony Hsieh understands that his customers are taking a huge risk buying online something as difficult to fit as shoes. So Zappos decided to take a risk and make customer service an investment rather than an expense. Not only were they going to spend more on customer service than the average company, they would make it easy for customers to "try on" shoes by offering free shipping and returns. In fact, Zappos has built its entire company culture around understanding the mind of the customer and being viewed as a customer service company.

Very few business owners think about the cost of operations until their products and services have become commoditized—that is, they find themselves competing on price rather than on value. It is only then that they begin to look for ways to improve operations and cut costs to maintain or improve their profit margins. Entrepreneurs with startup ventures have an advantage in this regard, because they can more easily implement process innovations without having to overcome the challenge of existing structures. In this chapter we look at the major areas of operations that entrepreneurs need to understand and which areas offer opportunities for both process innovation and operational excellence.

PRODUCING PRODUCTS AND SERVICES

In simple terms, production is managing the flow of material and information from raw materials to finished goods. Think of manufacturing equipment as hardware, and of the people and information needed to run the machines as software, and it's easy to see why it's possible for two companies to have the same equipment and yet produce significantly different products. The difference lies in the software driving the machinery—in other words, information and people.

Many high-growth ventures market innovative new products. The operational plan for the business consists of a fairly complex product development analysis that includes prototyping, production processes, supply chain, distribution, and inventory control mechanisms. The depth of analysis is a function of the type of product offered, the technological newness of the product, and the number of different ways the product can be produced. The more complex the product, the deeper the analysis needs to be.

Building a complex production system while the company is in startup or even later when it is rapidly growing is a recipe for disaster. Not having a reliable fulfillment process in place prior to launch has cost many a company customer loyalty and significant revenues because the company was unable to produce and deliver products to customers in a timely fashion. Once lost, that customer base is nearly impossible to regain in time to fend off competing firms and save the company from failure. As noted in Chapter 12, the virtual enterprise, consisting of strategic alliances among all links in the value chain, is one way to achieve control of the entire process from raw materials to distribution, while still keeping the firm small and flexible enough to meet changing needs and demands. With the exception of ownership, this model is similar to the Japanese *keiretsu* in the automobile industry, which links banks, suppliers, electronics firms, and auto companies through a series of cross-ownerships. The U.S. model leaves ownership in the hands of the individual owners but links the organizations into a virtual entity that acts as a team with a common goal. Wal-Mart is probably the best example of this type of partnership and integration in the United States. It has established point-of-sale linkups with its suppliers and has given its manufacturers the responsibility for handling inventory. The ultimate goal is to construct one organization with a common purpose that encompasses the entire supply chain from raw materials supplier to retailer, with each link along the chain performing the task that it does best. Establishing this type of network takes time. A startup can't expect to achieve quickly the level of integration and control that a Wal-Mart has taken years to accomplish. Instead, startup companies need to build relationships slowly, beginning with key independent contractors to whom they may be outsourcing some tasks.

One of the best ways to understand how the production process touches customers and affects the bottom line is to follow an order through the company and document where the order flow gets bogged down, is duplicated, or is hindered in some manner. Any slowdown or duplication of effort means higher production costs and slower response to the customer. Consider a market research firm that provides customized reports to companies to enable them to judge their markets for new products and services. This is an example of what would typically be called a service firm, yet note that this service firm produces a product—a market research report. Now suppose that in the process of gathering the research and analyzing it, there is no plan for who should do a particular aspect of the research. Duplication of effort could easily occur, and it's possible that something important, such as an emerging competitor, might be overlooked. Both duplication of effort and the need to go back and cover something that has been overlooked are costly and delay the production process, potentially causing the company to miss a customer deadline.

SUPPLY CHAIN MANAGEMENT

In an increasingly complex and global environment where outsourcing, off-shoring, and insourcing are common activities, supply chain management (SCM) has become a mission-critical position for most companies.[3] At the same time, global competitiveness has forced most companies to do more with fewer resources. Because effective supply chain performance is now critical to a company's success, entrepreneurs must have ways to measure that performance, especially in terms of customer satisfaction. Entrepreneurs must have a clear understanding of what is important to their customers—what is the level of service they are expecting and what performance level are they willing to pay a premium for. For example, one company judged its performance by the percentage of orders received in any one day that were filled on time. This metric indicated that the company was performing at over 98 percent effectiveness. However, when the company tracked how long it took for the customer to receive the order from the time they placed it, their performance level dropped dramatically. In examining what was causing the delay, the company found that their system for tracking orders was often sending orders to the wrong distribution center. The goal in supply chain management is to provide the exact service the customer wants at minimal cost. In SCM terms, it's the *efficient frontier* and it's not easy to achieve. To do so, entrepreneurs need to use current technology that provides superior data analysis, ensure that the warehouses and distribution centers they use are efficiently located, and they should look at every aspect of the supply chain to see if there are ways to reduce costs.

Any business that purchases raw materials or parts for production of goods for resale must carefully consider the quality, quantity, and timing of those purchases. Quality goods are those that meet specific needs. Quality varies considerably among vendors, so if a company has established certain quality standards for its products, it must find vendors who will consistently supply that precise level of quality, because customers will expect it. The quantity of raw materials or parts that are purchased is a function of (1) demand by the customer,

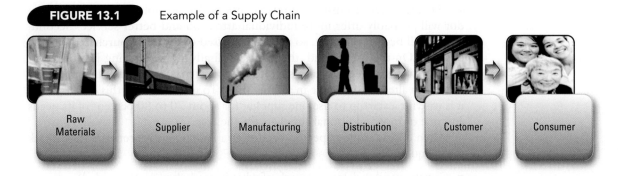

FIGURE 13.1 Example of a Supply Chain

Raw Materials → Supplier → Manufacturing → Distribution → Customer → Consumer

(2) manufacturing capability, and (3) a company's storage capability; consequently, timing of purchases is very important. Purchases must be planned so that capital and warehouse space are not tied up any longer than necessary. Because materials account for approximately 50 percent of total production cost, it is crucial to balance these three factors carefully.

Figure 13.1 depicts a generic supply chain for a good that is being produced. Within the major supply chain functions as displayed are many activities that must be planned for and coordinated. They include such things as

- Purchasing for profitability.
- Reducing inventories.
- Tighter supplier integration.
- More frequent and smaller customer orders and receipts.
- Faster time from source to stock.

We will look at some of the important functions of the supply chain here.

Purchasing

Locating vendors to provide raw materials or goods for resale is not difficult, but finding the best vendors is another matter entirely. The issue of vendor relationships has become increasingly important in markets that demand that companies reduce costs and maintain effective relationships. Research has found that these vendor relationships reflect factors such as trust or commitment,[4] uncertainty and dependence, and how these factors affect performance.[5]

Furthermore, buyers and sellers are connected in an increasing number of ways: through information sharing that improves the quality of the product produced or brings about new product development; operational linkages such as computerized inventory, order replenishment systems, and just-in-time delivery; legal bonds such as binding contractual agreements; cooperative norms; and relationship adaptations wherein vendors modify their products to meet the needs of the customer.

Given the importance of the vendor–customer relationship, should a startup buy from one vendor or from more than one? Obviously, if a single vendor cannot supply all the startup's needs, that decision is made. However, there are several advantages to using a single vendor where possible. First, a single vendor will probably offer more individual attention and better service. Second, orders will be consolidated, so a discount based on quantity purchased may be possible. On the other hand, the principal disadvantage of using just one vendor is that if that vendor suffers a catastrophe, it may be difficult or impossible to find an alternative source in a short time. To guard against this contingency, it is wise for a startup to use one supplier for about 70 to 80 percent of its needs and one or more additional suppliers for the rest.

When considering a specific vendor as a source, entrepreneurs should ask several questions:

- Can the vendor deliver enough of what is needed *when* it's needed?
- What is the cost of transportation using a particular vendor? If the vendor is located far away, costs will be higher and it may be more difficult to get the service required.
- What services is the vendor offering? For example, how often will sales representatives call?
- Is the vendor knowledgeable about the product line?
- What are the vendor's maintenance and return policies?

It is also important to "shop around," compare vendors' prices, and check for trade discounts and quantity discounts that may make a particular vendor's deal more enticing. Computer technology has made materials planning more of a science than ever before. Information systems can now provide a purchaser with detailed feedback on supplier performance, reliability of delivery, and quality control results. Comparing results across suppliers provides more leverage when it's time to renegotiate the annual contracts with suppliers. It is, however, important to keep in mind that sourcing materials and supplies is a time-consuming process that can often slow the startup's ability to launch on schedule.

Inventory Management

Inventory is defined as the stocks of items used to support production, associated activities, and customer service.[6] Whether entrepreneurs start small manufacturing enterprise, retail businesses, or restaurants, they will frequently hold an inventory of materials or goods. Today, businesses that hold inventories of raw materials or goods for resale have found that they must reduce these inventories significantly to remain competitive. Instead of purchasing large quantities and receiving them on a monthly basis, businesses are purchasing daily or weekly in an effort to avoid costly inventories. Of course, some inventory of finished goods must be maintained to meet delivery deadlines; therefore, a delicate balance must be achieved among goods coming into the business, work in progress, and goods leaving the business to be sold.

The problem that entrepreneurs face relative to inventories is that once they get beyond early startup and begin growing, most still do not have the resources to purchase raw materials and goods for sale in sufficient quantities to trigger significant industry discounts, often ranging from 30 to 50 percent. Even if entrepreneurs could purchase the required quantities, they typically don't have the space to store the inventory. As a result, today many entrepreneurs are taking advantage of inventory management companies that oversee storage, track inventory numbers, and fill and ship orders, among many other services. There are many advantages to this approach. It saves the entrepreneur time and the cost of hiring employees to manage the inventory. It frees up space at the entrepreneur's place of business and the need to purchase special equipment. In addition, because most inventory management companies have information technology for tracking and providing detailed data on the inventory, entrepreneurs can inspect and control their inventory from any computer with Internet access.

In general, the entrepreneur orders the goods or raw materials direct from the manufacturer and they are delivered to the inventory management company, which immediately pays the entrepreneur under due-on-receipt terms. This means that the entrepreneur now has cash flow to use until the OEM must be paid, typically in three to six weeks. Meanwhile, the entrepreneur accesses the raw materials or goods as needed, paying the inventory management company as they're purchased, depending on the terms of the agreement.

Businesses such as UPS help startups that need to ship to retailers. They stock merchandise in their warehouses, process orders, make deliveries, and handle billing. In that way, retailers don't incur the costs associated with maintaining a backup supply of items from the entrepreneur. Avoiding too much inventory is a trend that is expected to continue for the foreseeable future. However, working effectively requires careful coordination and cooperation of all members of the supply chain.

Production and Manufacturing

Production is the actual manufacturing and assembly of the product. Today manufacturers tend to produce one unit at a time serially in manufacturing cells—also called flexible manufacturing cells (FMCs) or work cells. What that means is that the product moves from raw materials through a series of tasks and processes in a continuous flow to complete the product while remaining inside the manufacturing cell. The benefits of cell manufacturing are reduced lead times, improved costs, quality, and timing in addition to giving employees more involvement in the production of the entire product rather than simply one component of a product. This means that workers need to be cross-trained in all the required tasks to produce the product, but it also means that when a worker is out sick, another is there to immediately fill the gap.

The production process—as depicted in Figure 13.2—consists of a series of inputs, such as raw materials, labor, and machinery, which are then transformed through a series of processes into new products and services. Each component of the process must be managed, measured, and tested for efficiency and effectiveness.

FIGURE 13.2

The Production
Process

Transformation

Inputs
Raw materials
Labor
Machinery
Facility

Materials management
Production scheduling
Manufacturing
Assembly
Quality control
Packaging

Output
New products
and services

In general, manufacturing and production firms are organized as product-focused or process-focused organizations. Product- or project-focused organizations normally are highly decentralized or distributed so that they can respond better to market demands. Each product or project group acts essentially as a separate company or profit center. This type of organization is well suited to products and projects that don't require huge economies of scale or capital-intensive technologies. Process-focused organizations, on the other hand, are common among manufacturers with capital-intensive processes (such as those in the semiconductor industry) and among service companies (such as advertising firms). These organizations are highly centralized in order to control all the functions of the organization.

Production Scheduling

The lifeblood of any business is its production function. Decisions made about production directly affect output level, product quality, and costs. Planning for production, therefore, is critical to manufacturing efficiency and effectiveness. Most manufacturers and producers begin by scheduling—that is, by identifying and describing each activity that must be completed to produce the product and indicating the amount of time it takes to complete each activity. Two methods traditionally used in the scheduling process are Gantt Charts and PERT Diagrams.

Gantt Charts are a way to depict the tasks to be performed and the time required for each. Consider Figure 13.3. The tasks to be completed (in this case, filling customer orders) are listed in the first column, and the time to completion is traced in horizontal rows. Note that the solid line represents the plan for completion, whereas the dashed line depicts where the product is in the process. Gantt Charts work best for simple projects that are independent of each other.

PERT is an acronym for Program Evaluation and Review Technique. This method is helpful when the production being scheduled is more complex and is subject to the interdependence of several activities going on either simultaneously or in sequence. In other words, some tasks cannot be started until others have been completed. To begin, the major activities involved in producing the product must be identified and arranged in the order in which they will occur. Any activities that must occur in sequence should be identified—that is, cases where one activity cannot occur until another is finished.

FIGURE 13.3 Sample Gantt Chart

—— Scheduled time - - - - Actual progress

Order Number	Order Quantity	September				October				November			
		6–9	12–16	19–23	26–30	3–7	10–14	17–21	24–28	1–5	7–11	14–18	21–25
5348	1,000												
5349	1,500												
5350	500												

A pictorial network that describes the process is then constructed. The time to complete each activity is estimated and noted on the chart. This is usually done three times, and the answers are given as most optimistic, most likely, and most pessimistic. The statistics of analyzing the network are beyond the scope of this book, but the process consists essentially of (1) identifying the critical path, which is the longest path and is important because a delay in any of the activities along the critical path can delay the entire project; (2) computing slack time on all events and activities (the difference between latest and earliest times); and (3) calculating the probability of completion within the time allotted. The numbered nodes on Figure 13.4 refer to the start and completion points for each event. The dummy line was placed in the diagram to account for the completion of event *e* being preceded by events *b* and *d*. Both must be completed before event *g* can start. There are several popular software products on the market, such Microsoft Project, that can help entrepreneurs schedule

FIGURE 13.4

Sample PERT Chart

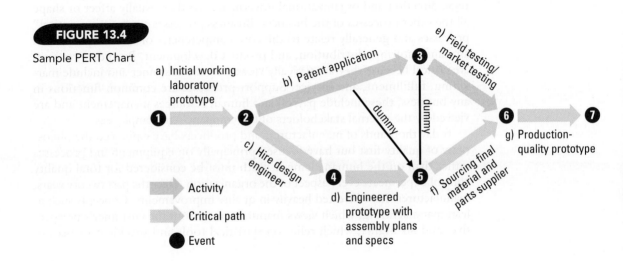

a) Initial working laboratory prototype

b) Patent application

c) Hire design engineer

d) Engineered prototype with assembly plans and specs

e) Field testing/ market testing

f) Sourcing final material and parts supplier

g) Production-quality prototype

dummy

Activity

Critical path

Event

their production capacity. Like any new technique, it takes time to learn the PERT system, but it is time well spent. Tracking production from the outset of the business permits more realistic strategic decisions about growth and expansion.

Identifying all the tasks in the production process makes it easier to determine what equipment and supplies are needed for completing the tasks. If, for example, the equipment necessary to produce the product is beyond a startup's resources, it may be necessary to outsource part or all of production to a manufacturer that has excess capacity with the needed equipment and workers. This topic is discussed in a later section in this chapter. After the production tasks have been identified, a preliminary layout of the plant can be undertaken to estimate floor space requirements for production, offices, and services. It may be beneficial to consult an expert in plant layout to ensure that the layout makes the most efficient use of available space.

Quality

Quality control is the process of reconciling product or project output with the standards set for that product or project. More specifically, it is "an effective system for integrating the quality-development, quality-maintenance, and quality-improvement efforts of the various groups in an organization so as to enable marketing, engineering, production, and service at the most economical levels, which allow for full customer satisfaction."[7] In this sense, quality does not necessarily mean "best"; rather, it means "best for certain customer requirements," which consist of the features and benefits of the product or service and its selling price.[8]

Quality is a strategic issue that is designed to bring about business profitability and positive cash flow. Effective total quality programs result in customer satisfaction, lower operating costs, and better utilization of company resources. There are three major processes in any company that must be aligned if quality is going to be the outcome. They are management processes, business processes, and support processes.[9] Management processes are the source of strategic direction and organizational governance, so they usually affect or shape all the other processes of the business. Business processes are "mission-critical" processes and generally relate to the core competencies of the company, such as manufacturing, distribution, and product development. Business processes are critical because they are typically viewed by the customer and include marketing, fulfillment, and service. Support processes are common functions in any business; these include payroll and human resources management and are viewed by the internal stakeholders of the company—the employees.

Today thousands of manufacturers and producers have embraced the philosophy of quality first but have focused principally on equipment and processes rather than on the human element. Both must be considered for total quality control to permeate every aspect of the organization. Over the past twenty years, manufacturers have invested heavily in quality improvements. Concepts such as lean manufacturing, which views manufacturing from the customer's perspective, and Six Sigma, which relies on statistical tools and specific processes to achieve the measurable goals of fewer defects, increased productivity, reduced waste, and superior products and processes,[10] have helped companies lower production costs, produce less scrap, allow fewer defects, and reduce warranty expense.[11] Even though the highest probability is that entrepreneurs will not manufacture their own products, they still need to select a quality manufacturer that practices these concepts.

One way manufacturers and producers control quality is through a regular inspection process that takes place during several stages of the production process. Often, primarily to reduce cost, a random sample of products or project outcomes is chosen for the inspection. This method catches potential defects early in the process, before the products become finished goods. Whether each item produced is checked or a random sampling is conducted depends on what is being produced, on its cost, and on whether the inspection process will destroy the item. For example, when a company is producing an expensive piece of machinery, it may be prudent to subject each item to the inspection process, because the cost of inspection is more than offset by the price of the item. But compare the situation when a food is being produced. Once such a product is inspected, it cannot be sold, so it is not feasible to inspect more than a representative random sample of each batch.

Today, technology has made it possible to error-proof processes using sensors, thereby eliminating traditional quality checks and guaranteeing that what is being produced meets the customer's specifications. Entrepreneurs who want to achieve total quality will probably set a no-defect goal for product manufacturing. Pelco Inc., a leader in the video surveillance industry, has designed quality control into every process in its company. Any worker can stop production for a defect, so by the time the product reaches the end of the production line, it is defect-free. Pelco would rather take the time to look for errors before the product reaches the customer than have the customer find defects. Contrast this approach with that of the software industry, which regularly launches products with "bugs" that they expect their customers to find and report.

The real success or failure of the quality control effort is dependent on the human element in the process: customers, employees, and management. Quality begins with satisfying the needs of the customers, and that cannot be accomplished unless those needs and requirements are communicated to managers and employees. An entrepreneur with a new venture has a unique opportunity to create a philosophy of quality from the very birth of the business, in the way the business is run and in the employees hired. Startups have the advantage of creating new habits and patterns of behavior instead of having to change old ones.

Many quality programs exist to help companies better meet the needs of their customers. Table 13.1 lists several of them.

Logistics

Logistics is the management and control of the flow of goods and resources from the source of production to the marketplace. Every business is affected by logistics to some degree, even service businesses that rely on logistics to

TABLE 13.1	Quality Management Programs
Benchmarking	Involves the use of criteria or standards that can be employed to compare one company with another to better understand organizational performance
Continuous Improvement	A program that focuses on undertaking incremental improvements in processes to increase customer satisfaction
Failure Mode and Effects Analysis	A way to identify and rank potential equipment and process failures
ISO 9000	An internationally recognized quality set of standards with a certification process
Total Quality Improvement	A set of management practices designed to meet customer requirements through process measurement and controls
Six Sigma	A data-driven approach to eliminating defects with a goal of 3.4 defects per million

receive their supplies. Logistics is a fundamental part of supply chain management and can make the difference between success and failure, profit and loss in a growing company. South West Trading (http://soysilk.com) had the pleasant problem of more demand for its yarns made from bamboo, corn, and soy fibers than it could handle. The problem was not with its manufacturing operation in China, which churned out 800 metric tons of yarn every month, but rather with the logistics of getting the yarn from China to the warehouse in Phoenix, Arizona. Because founder Jonelle Raffing was concerned about meeting the needs of her customers, she maintained a $1 million excess inventory, which increased her operating costs. She was unable to combine orders from different factories into one container so she incurred a charge of $1,000 to $2,000 for each separate shipment. She also paid a customs agent $17,000 a year to move the products through the various ports. In all, her annual logistics costs amounted to over $100,000.[12] Raffing was able to reduce her costs by turning to UPS and its Shanghai facility, which combines orders into one container, handles the paperwork, and delivers the products all the way to Phoenix, Arizona. Raffing's logistical problems are not solely because her business is small; even multinational companies experience them.

Small companies that sell to large discount retailers like Wal-Mart are subject to strict requirements for packing, shipping, and tagging for RFID tracking. Most small companies don't have the people resources to meet these requirements so they outsource to third-party logistics providers who can move packages by air, land, and sea from the factory to the customer without stopping at the entrepreneur's business. Although a majority of the major logistics providers service large companies, today many of those providers have begun offering services to entrepreneurs. Among the most aggressive is UPS Supply Chain Solutions, which uses its own aircraft to handle shipping of products that meet the weight requirement and do not need to go by sea. For heavier products, Seattle-based Expeditors provides services. Global logistics is discussed in more detail in Chapter 17.

GLOBAL INSIGHTS

Emerging Players in Outsourcing

Although China and India are the acknowledged leaders in the outsourcing world, other countries are scrambling to enter the race and reap the rewards of partnering with developed countries. But companies that outsource are also looking for new regions to improve their cost structure and seek the same or better engagement relationships.

Three recent additions to the race include Brazil, Nicaragua, and Botswana. After visiting places like India to learn how they set up call centers, fulfillment operations, and support services, these countries have developed economic reforms that will make them more attractive to the outsourcers. Some of these improvements include major infrastructure like highways, airports, and telecommunications systems. But infrastructure is not enough to lure outsourcing companies away from China and India; they must be able to provide reliable, trained workers who speak English.

Nicaragua has completed an infrastructure that supports the call centers designed to serve Spanish-speaking customers in North and South America. Nicaragua benefits from being in the same time zone as the United States, which is very appealing to companies such as IBM and Russell

Athletic that use them. Botswana, the South African nation, is considered to be the most advanced and politically stable nation in sub-Saharan Africa. It has decided to make training of its workers an incentive for outsourcing companies by paying the companies $2 for every $1 the company spends in training the Botswanan workers for call centers or other outsourced work. Despite Russia's supply of highly trained engineers and scientists, this country did not focus on outsourcing until recently. Now it is in the process of building technoparks to support companies that provide IT services and software programming contract work and offering favorable tax incentives to the outsourcers.

Sources: Durant, J. (April, 2010). "Emerging Nations: Locating the Sweet Spots," *The International Institute for Outsource Management*, www.the-outsourcing.com; D. Harman, "Outsourcing Gets Closer to Home," *USA Today* (November 7, 2005), www.usatoday.com/money/companies/management/2005-11-07-nearsourcing-usat_x.htm; "Up-and-Comers in the Outsourcing Race," Special Report: Outsourcing, *BusinessWeek Online*, www.businessweek.com/magazine/content/06_05/b3969423.htm, accessed April 22, 2007; and "Profiting from Contact Center Outsourcing in Botswana," *Datamonitor*, www.datamonitor.com, accessed April 22, 2007.

Warranting the Product

Entrepreneurs who subscribe to total quality management will probably wish to provide warranties with products and services, both in order to protect their companies from potential liability and to demonstrate that they stand behind what they produce and the work that they do. Today, product/service warranties have also become a competitive marketing tool.

A number of decisions must be made about warranties. Although the length of the warranty depends on industry standards, the components of the product, or what aspects of the service to cover, depend on the situation. Some components may come from other manufacturers who have their own warranties. In this case, it is important to have use of that component on the product certified by the original equipment manufacturers (OEM) so that the warranty isn't inadvertently invalidated. Then, if a warranted component from that manufacturer becomes defective, it can be returned to the OEM. However, it is probably good business practice to have customers return the product directly to the entrepreneur's company or its distributors for service, repair, or exchange under the warranty, which covers the whole product. Warranties on services cover satisfaction with work completed. For example, a company may conduct ISO 9000 certification workshops for companies and may warrant that if a client's company attends the workshops and implements the suggestions, it will receive certification. If, for some reason, the client does not receive certification, there is no way to "return" a workshop in the way that a product could be returned, but the entrepreneur can offer the client a fact-finding audit to discover what went wrong or can simply refund the client's money (a less satisfactory solution for the client).

The product/process scope should also be considered. Will the warranty cover one or all products in a line or will there be separate warranties? Generally, for services, a warranty covers the service as a whole, unless there are products involved as well. In addition to the product scope, the market scope is a factor. Will the same warranty apply in all markets? This will depend on local laws. Another consideration involves the conditions of the warranty that the customer must fulfill. Is there anything the customer must do to keep the warranty in force, such as servicing or replacing disposable parts? These conditions should not include registering the product via a postcard. Today a product is covered by warranty from the moment it is purchased, whether or not the purchaser returns a postcard stating when and where it was purchased and answering a short, informational questionnaire. What many companies now do is offer update notification and potential discounts on future products in exchange for the information the postcard solicits or the option to register online.

Yet another consideration is who executes the warranty. The entrepreneur must decide who will handle warranty claims (manufacturer, dealers, distributors, the entrepreneur's company), recognizing that customers do not like to mail products back to the manufacturer. It is also necessary to decide how the public will be educated about the warranty. What are the plans for advertising and promotion relative to the warranty? Finally, the policies for refunds and returns, and who will pay shipping and handling costs, need to be considered. A return policy is a function of the entrepreneur's philosophy about doing business. A customer-oriented company is likely to offer a generous return policy and pay for the cost of returns.

The manufacturer who provides a warranty incurs a cost, but that cost must be weighed against the potential loss of business if no warranty is provided. In the case of a new business with a new product or service, it is difficult to anticipate the number of problems that might occur as the product or service gets into the marketplace. Careful and adequate field-testing prior to market entry will go a long way toward eliminating many potential problems and the possibility of a recall (in the case of a product), which is very costly for any firm, let alone a growing new business.

OUTSOURCING TO REDUCE COSTS

Calculation of the up-front investment in plant, office, and equipment, coupled with the high per-unit cost of production, has convinced many entrepreneurs to outsource manufacturing to an established manufacturing firm, particularly one overseas, where labor costs are much less. Some products that consist of off-the-shelf components from original equipment manufacturers can give the entrepreneur the option to set up an assembly operation, which is far less costly than a manufacturing plant. In any case, the process of outlining all the costs of setting up a product company is invaluable in making the final decisions about how the business will operate.

Entrepreneurs who wish to manufacture products have many options today. It is still possible, in many industries, to manufacture domestically and to compete successfully if processes are refined and quality is built into every step. If it is too costly to do all the manufacturing in-house, outsourcing non-core capabilities is one possibility; another is outsourcing everything and playing the role of coordinator until the company is producing a healthy cash flow.

Manufacturing Overseas

In some industries, particularly labor-intensive ones, the only way to achieve competitive costs is to manufacture in a country where labor costs are low; Mexico, India, and China are examples. Entrepreneurs should look at what other firms in their industry are doing. Barry-Wehmiller Cos., a St. Louis–based holding company that acquired Paper Converting Machine Company in an industry consolidation strategy and laid off half the company's workforce, was able to turn the company around by sending some of its design work to an engineer center in Chennai, India. Now its U.S. and Indian designers can collaborate 24/7, reducing development costs and speeding service to customers.[13] Tiny Crimson Consulting Group now competes with the likes of market research firms McKinsey and Bain by outsourcing its research to companies in China, the Czech Republic, and South Africa. However, outsourcing is not always the wisest choice. One Tampa, Florida, manufacturing company moved some of its manufacturing operations to China several years ago and achieved real cost savings by doing so. Today, however, it is re-evaluating that decision for several of its products. These products are too heavy to ship by air, and shipping by sea is costly because the company loses the advantage it has in schedule flexibility. Schedule flexibility is an example of an opportunity cost—that is, forgoing an important competitive advantage in order to save on production costs.

The truth is that many companies have not been able to leverage the benefits of outsourcing to create real impact in their companies in the areas of pricing at a premium, entering new markets, and creating entry barriers for competition.[14] That is why entrepreneurs need to work backwards from customer needs and align their workflows appropriately. Not all products are appropriate for offshore manufacturing. For example, a business that uses expensive equipment to produce its products may not achieve enough cost savings to overcome the problems associated with offshore manufacturing, such as difficulties in communication and degradation in quality control. By contrast, a manual-labor-intensive business such as apparel manufacture can often achieve significant cost savings by moving overseas.

The weight of the product is also a factor in the decision whether to manufacture overseas. Heavy products with large "footprints" must be shipped by sea, which typically takes four to six weeks. That represents an inventory issue for the entrepreneur and added cost for the customer. Some entrepreneurs have calculated that it takes a 15 to 20 percent cost savings to justify manufacturing offshore and to balance the added costs of freight, customs, security, logistics, and inventory carrying cost. It is also important to remember that customers are not always looking for the lowest price; rather, they're looking for the highest quality at a competitive price. If products are innovative and meet the specific needs of target customers, a company may be able to manufacture domestically in a successful way.

Some important considerations that entrepreneurs should look at before deciding to leap offshore are the following:[15]

1. Go offshore when all efforts to boost efficiency and innovation at home have been exhausted. Don't do it just because everyone else is doing it.
2. Consider whether to set up a captive operation (the entrepreneur owns it) or to contract with a local specialist.
3. Management and employees must both believe in going offshore and must be in the loop during transition.
4. Don't do it if management does not have the time and willingness to put a lot of effort into the process. Savings are in direct proportion to the effort exerted to train and prepare offshore workers in the company's processes.
5. Entrepreneurs must be willing to treat their outsourcing partners as equals, not as subservient workers, and make them part of the project design process.
6. The supply chain needs to be flexible to avoid disruption, particularly through natural and man-made disasters.

Lessons From Outsourcing Overseas

Whether entrepreneurs are looking to ship manufacturing overseas or outsource their back office functions to firms in China and India, successful outsourcers point to several critical lessons they have learned from the experience.[16]

1. It is important to start small and gradually build the overseas capability because there will always be problems in the beginning that will slow the process. The most common problem is a technical workforce that doesn't understand the industry in which the entrepreneur is doing business.
2. Communicating by email and fax is not enough. Most projects require a company expert who can guide the technical workers in person.

3. Often it is best to use a combination of an offshore captive operation and a local contract firm to supplement critical needs. In this way the entrepreneur has more control over outcomes.

4. Outsourced staff typically have a high turnover rate because the average age is 25 and they are constantly looking to move up. Therefore, it is important that the entrepreneur create a culture that encourages the staff to stay with the business long term.

5. It is important to outsource only those tasks that have a high probability of going smoothly and making the customer happy. Problematic projects are better handled domestically.

Operations is not the glamorous side of an entrepreneurial startup, but it *is* a critical aspect of any business because the activities associated with operations are increasingly becoming a source of opportunities for innovation that will give a growing company a significant competitive edge.

New Venture Action Plan

- Source suppliers for your materials and supply requirements.
- Determine how inventory will be handled.
- Develop quality control metrics.
- Itemize and calculate production costs and determine whether to outsource.
- Determine warranty service requirements.
- Identify a third-party logistics provider.

Questions on Key Issues

1. Why is it important to consider your manufacturing plan in the earliest stages of a new venture?

2. What are three factors that an entrepreneur must take into consideration when choosing vendors to meet materials requirements?

3. Suppose you had a new advertising firm. How could you schedule activities to create more efficiencies in your operations?

4. What are some of the key factors that must be considered when setting up a quality control system?

5. Characterize the critical aspects of an effective supply chain for any business.

Experiencing Entrepreneurship

1. Visit a manufacturing facility that is using technology to facilitate its processes. Develop a flowchart of the manufacturing process. Can you see any ways to improve the process?
2. Interview an entrepreneur with a product company about his or her views on quality. How is this entrepreneur implementing quality control in his or her organization?
3. Choose a young company that has a global supply chain. Develop a process flowchart depicting the supply chain and analyze it for efficiency and flexibility based on information provided in the chapter.

Relevant Case Studies

Case 5 B2P

Case 6 Potion Inc.

MARKETING

"Don't forget that it [your product or service] is not differentiated until the customer understands the difference."

—TOM PETERS,
Thriving on Chaos

CHAPTER OBJECTIVES

- Discuss the role of the product adoption/diffusion curve for marketing strategy.

- Explain how to create an effective marketing plan.

- Discuss the forms of advertising and promotion that entrepreneurs can tap.

- Describe the role of publicity in a marketing strategy.

- Explain how entrepreneurs can employ new media to their advantage.

- Discuss the role of personal selling in a marketing strategy.

"The Search is Over." That was the slogan that peppered every page of Ty Simpson's website as he sought to create brand equity with his primary customers—shoppers who were looking for scarce licensed products that originally sold in big box stores but now had disappeared from the shopping scene because the big box stores don't keep new products on the shelf very long. The problem was that kids hadn't forgotten these toys, so parents were left scrambling to find them without much luck. In fact, Simpson himself was one of those parents. His daughter absolutely had to have Wiggles toys, a licensed product from Australia that could not be found in U.S. stores. When he finally tracked down the manufacturer, he bought more than he needed and decided to sell the rest on eBay to see if there were other consumers looking for them.

Within just a year, selling on eBay became a full-time job and he decided to build a website as a companion to his eBay auction pages. The only problem was that now he was essentially running two businesses, two processes, and two sets of customers. His now 12-employee company in Erlanger, Kentucky, was under stress. That's when he decided that he needed to bring in the professionals to help him manage all his back-end activities that support the marketing, selling, and distribution of his products. He hired Truition, a Canadian company that specialized in integrating a company's primary online storefront with all its other selling sites (eBay U.S., eBay UK, and eBay Australia) and supplying all the functionality for processing payments, managing orders, and fulfillment. That left Simpson free to focus on finding new products and marketing them. It turned out to be a fortuitous decision because he saw his average sale amount rise 15 percent due to more effective cross selling.

He has also seen the number of customers coming to the site through referrals rise, and this has produced an increase in return customers from 45 percent to 57 percent of all his shoppers. Originally the model was to offer all the licensed character products that the big box stores no longer offered, but that model has evolved to where he hopes to actually debut new products from manufacturers on the Internet where he can create a huge online display that would be too expensive to do in the offline world. Another value he offers customers is bundling different items with the same licensed character, such as Strawberry Shortcake Too Cute Swim Sets with sandals, a beach towel, and a raft. He has also incorporated a blog where he talks about the latest things happening in the toy industry.

Where many traditional toy companies have failed, Simpson's sales volume keeps increasing, and that gives toy manufacturers hope that their licensed products will have a longer economic life.

Sources: Ty's Toy Box, www.tystoybox.com, accessed September 29, 2010; and McKinley, E. (October 2006), "Tying e-Commerce Efforts Together," *Stores Magazine*, www.nxtbook.com/nxtbooks/nrfe/stores1006/index.php.

In today's digital world, launching a business can be as easy as putting up a simple website, but that doesn't guarantee that the business will be sustainable. To create a sustainable business requires a plan for winning market share; to accomplish that, entrepreneurs need to understand thoroughly customer needs, preferences, channel demands, and competition. Marketing includes all the strategies, tactics, and techniques used to raise customer awareness; to promote a product, service, or business; and to build and manage long-term customer relationships. Marketing can be thought of as a bundle of intangible benefits a company is providing to its customers, and these benefits reflect the company's core values. Traditionally, marketing has been described in terms of the "5 P's"—people, which is customers; product or what is being offered to the customer; price or what the customer is willing to pay; place, which is the channel through which customers can find the product or service; and promotion, which involves the strategies for creating awareness and reaching the customer. Most entrepreneurs understand that a business cannot exist without customers, so pushing a marketing strategy on potential customers— a very costly approach—does not make sense to entrepreneurs, who typically have limited resources at startup. Rather, they prefer to invest in building relationships with customers and designing their products or services with the customers' needs in mind. In that way, much of the "selling" that would otherwise have to be done has been taken care of by giving customers what they want, when they want it, and in the way they want it.

Marketing in times of global change means that traditional methods may no longer work. Indeed, given much shorter competitive and economic lives for products and services and the impact of Internet search capability on price transparency, price dispersion, market entry, and product variety, the real challenge is how to rise above the crowd and build a competitive brand that is sustainable. It is estimated that about 30,000 new consumer products launch each year and 90 percent of them fail, primarily because they don't meet customer needs.[1] Too many entrepreneurs also underestimate the strength of their competitors, discount the impact of the global market, and develop products for a broad market rather than a specific and unique niche market.

Because entrepreneurs can now reach millions of potential customers for very little cost via the Internet, a disruptive paradigm has emerged—the "long tail." Chris Anderson, in his best-selling book, *The Long Tail*, adopted the term to describe a probabilistic statistical phenomenon (also known as power laws or Pareto distributions) where niche markets, when aggregated, account for a significant portion of total sales in some consumer sectors.[2] Figure 14.1 depicts

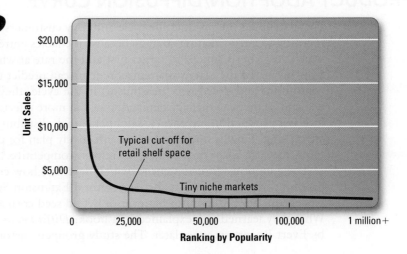

FIGURE 14.1

The Long Tail Phenomenon

a hypothetical long-tail distribution that could describe record sales, book sales, or anything else that is typically sold through brick-and-mortar retail outlets. The vertical axis represents the number of unit sales while the horizontal axis depicts the ranking of those sales from most popular item to least popular. As is the case in many consumer markets, a very tiny percentage of all sales do really well while the vast majority of items in a particular category, like books, sell very few or none. In the traditional retail world, this matters because of the problem of limited shelf space. Barnes and Noble, for example, carries multiple volumes of only the top sellers and perhaps one of each of those books not listed on *The New York Times* Bestseller list; the rest have to be ordered by special request from the customer. In general, they carry about 100,000 titles, but Barnes and Noble's online store carries everything the customer wants including the most obscure books for the tiniest niche markets. In other words, they believe in the theory that there is someone out there somewhere who will buy any book that was ever written. At least one quarter of all Amazon's book sales come from books that are not included in the top 100,000 bestselling titles, and that number is growing. Furthermore, when you consider that most Internet businesses today are aggregators of niche markets (eBay is a good example), the concept of the long tail has huge implications for marketing, and this is good news for entrepreneurs who are accustomed to operating in the niche world.

The intent of this chapter is not to review marketing fundamentals, which are best left to textbooks focused on this subject or to excellent websites like www.marketingprofs.com where professionals gather to discuss the subject. The purpose is to explore marketing from an entrepreneurial perspective in an age of new media and to look at how to create a marketing plan that will enable a startup to develop a successful brand and build long-term relationships with its customers. This chapter builds on the feasibility analysis and market research strategies and tactics discussed in Chapter 5. The market/customer information gathered during market research can now be applied to a marketing plan.

THE PRODUCT ADOPTION/DIFFUSION CURVE

Understanding the product life cycle and how customers adopt new products is critical to any marketing strategy because it enables entrepreneurs to plan for which customer segment to target first and the rate at which sales can potentially occur. To the extent that entrepreneurs can predict the points of takeoff (optimism) and slowdown (pessimism) in the cycle, they can better manage demand. If they can manage demand, they can more effectively plan for varying levels of production, inventory, sales personnel, distribution, marketing, and advertising. Finally, if they can more effectively plan for changes in sales patterns, they can adapt their strategy to remain competitive.[3]

The adoption/diffusion curve, which describes how customers adopt new products, was developed at the Agricultural Extension Service at Iowa State College in 1957 to monitor patterns of hybrid seed corn adoption by farmers. What they learned was explained in a book, *Diffusion of Innovation*, written by Evert Rogers six years later. The study grouped customers into categories based on how quickly they adopted a new product, ranging from those who adopted immediately to those who were the last to adopt.[4] Critics of Rogers's model claim that it is simplistic and doesn't take into account the evolution of the product in terms of improvements as it moves from the first customer to the last customer. Another criticism is that disruptive technologies, those that make previous technology in the area obsolete, tend to follow a different diffusion pattern than the one Rogers described; this pattern will be explained later in the chapter. Despite these challenges, the adoption/diffusion curve is still employed to explain customer adoption behavior. Figure 14.2 presents a depiction of the new product adoption/diffusion curve. What the Iowa agricultural agency found over time was that not all farmers would adopt new technology at the same time; only those most comfortable with new methods would adopt in the earliest stages. Everyone else would wait to see what the outcome of the first trials would be before taking on the risk.

Referring to Figure 14.2, the innovators are the visionaries; they are a very tiny customer base that is always interested in trying the latest, greatest thing. These innovators, who are typically younger in age, represent the gatekeepers, the group that is instrumental in deciding whether a new product will go forward to ultimately achieve mass adoption. They will typically follow the development of the technology or product over a long period and often become beta version testers. The early adopters, by contrast, are the true first customers. They are eager to adopt new products to solve problems and create a competitive advantage for themselves. An optimistic group, they usually have money to spend, and they only require that the product be able to solve about 80 percent of their problem. For that reason, they are not good reference points for the mass market because they tend to understand the need for the product better, and they don't expect productivity improvements and ease of use like the early majority does.

The early majority comprises the more pragmatic customers who tend to wait until a new product is proven and plenty of people are using it. They need

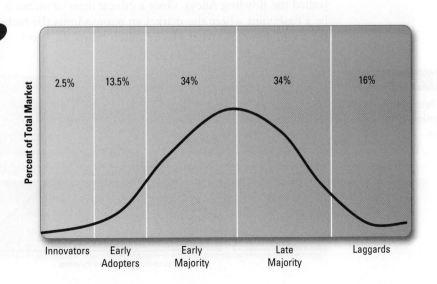

FIGURE 14.2

New Product Adoption/Diffusion Curve

to know that a product actually works before they adopt it because they don't want to make bad decisions. They tend to watch the early adopters to see how they fare before leaping into a purchase. The late majority tends to be an older group who typically buys only proven products with good price points. This group waits for the price to come down, which means that for the entrepreneur the product has become a commodity. The final group is the laggards who tend to only purchase the product if they absolutely have to; in other words, they are skeptical that the product is necessary to solve their problem at any price. For the entrepreneur, this group is the non customers. To entice them to buy will mean making the product significantly cheaper, easier to use, and with no switching costs.

For technology products, the adoption/diffusion cycle has a twist. Figure 14.3 presents a modification of the adoption/diffusion curve showing what Geoffrey Moore has called the "chasm."[5] The chasm is a period when the early adopters have been exhausted and the technology stops selling. The reason is that only the innovators and the early adopters had an interest in the technology, while the rest of the potential market, which was far more pragmatic, was not experiencing any "pain" or problem that the technology would solve. Moore believes that to cross the chasm, the customer has to have a compelling reason to buy. For the entrepreneur, this means identifying niche markets where the technology can produce a pragmatic application that solves a real problem. For example, GPS (global positioning satellite) technology was available long before there was an actual pain in the market that it could alleviate. When GPS began to be used in luxury automobiles, early-adopter customers liked that it could help them find where they needed to go. Eventually, as the price came down and the technology became more user-friendly, it was adopted by the early majority in less expensive automobiles. It is still in the process of "crossing the chasm."

Moore suggests that to cross the chasm, entrepreneurs must find multiple niche market applications that get the technology into many different customer sectors (called the Bowling Alley). Once a critical mass of niches is acquired, there may be a flashpoint where the market *en masse* adopts the technology. That throws the technology into what Moore calls a "tornado," with year-over-year growth

FIGURE 14.3

The Technology Adoption-Diffusion Curve

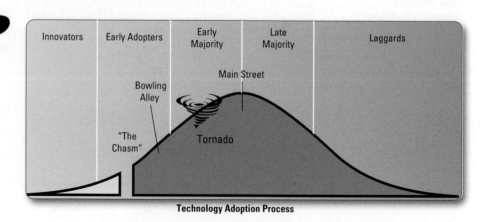

Technology Adoption Process

of 100 percent or more and where the most important job of the entrepreneur is to focus on producing and distributing the product. Customer demand is not an issue, because there is more demand than the company can manage. That is why having good systems and controls in place prior to attempting to achieve a tornado is critical. A recent example was the market share battle between high definition DVD formats Sony Blu-ray and Toshiba's HD DVD. After a protracted battle, Toshiba abandoned its format, paving the way for Blu-ray to cross the chasm and become the standard. Once the tornado has passed, the entrepreneurial venture has arrived at "main street," which is a period of aftermarket development where the company is attempting to sell more to its current customers. This can be a very difficult period for a young venture because it must now learn how to be a large company with operational excellence. Crossing the chasm is a critical achievement for technology companies that want to set a new standard in the industry and keep competitors from doing the same.

What is important to take away from the discussion of adoption/diffusion cycles is that the rate at which a new product is adopted across the various customer segments is a function of several factors that include perceived benefit, price and total product costs, usability, acceptance of promotional efforts, distribution intensity, switching costs, learning curve, and the ability to test the product before purchase. Not all customers will respond the same way to a new product introduction.

THE MARKETING PLAN

For any company, an effective marketing strategy begins with a marketing plan. The marketing plan for a startup is a living guide to how the company plans to build customer relationships over its life in order to fulfill the company's mission statement. It details the strategies and tactics that will create awareness on the part of the customer and build a brand and a loyal customer base. Furthermore, an effective marketing plan develops a consistent message to the customer and creates an opportunity for the entrepreneur to make a sale. Marketing plans are written at many points in the ongoing life of a business. The original plan will contain a strategy for introducing the company and its products and services to the marketplace. Later a marketing plan may be used to launch new products and services and/or to grow the business, perhaps in a new direction.

A few important steps taken before the actual writing of the marketing plan ensure that the plan is on target and is one the company can live with for a long time. Living with a plan for a long time may sound inconsistent with an entrepreneur's need to remain flexible and adapt to change in the marketplace, but one of the biggest problems with most marketing plans is that they are not followed long enough to achieve the desired results. Typically, when business owners do not see immediate results from their marketing effort, they decide that it must not be working—so they change it and start the cycle all over again. Changing the plan on impulse is the wrong thing to do. It takes time to make customers aware of a product or service. Furthermore, it takes time for a particular marketing strategy to take hold and secure trust on the part of the customer. For example, from the first time a customer sees an ad to the point at which the customer actually buys the product, weeks or even months may pass. In fact, on average, the customer will see an ad 15 to 20 times before actually purchasing the product. This pattern speaks to the importance of providing a product or service that meets a compelling need so that the time to purchase can be shortened. Just like a successful stock market investor, an entrepreneur must think of the marketing plan as an investment in the future of the business and must remember that any investment takes time to mature. Reaping the benefits of a well-structured marketing plan requires persistence and unwavering dedication until the plan has an opportunity to perform.

Creating Customer Value

A company's mission and core values will set the tone for the marketing plan and inform the initial steps in writing the plan. First, the approach to the market, or the bridge between strategy and execution, must be defined. The approach to the market includes such things as the message, differentiation tactics, channel strategies, and performance goals. Choosing the wrong approach can result in customers not understanding the benefits being provided. Choosing the same approach for all customers will ensure that not everyone will be satisfied. Selecting an approach is based on a thorough understanding of customers—what they need, when they need it, and where they want to find it. That understanding should have been acquired during the market research phase of the feasibility analysis. Next, it is important to identify a niche that the entrepreneur can dominate. Typically, this is a segment of the market that is not being served. To capture customers, entrepreneurs need to create value, which is a central aspect of marketing activity.[6] It is the principal way that entrepreneurs differentiate themselves[7] and is essential for customer satisfaction.[8] Customer value has been defined as "a customer's perceived preference for, and evaluation of, those product attributes, attribute performances, and consequences arising from use that facilitates (or blocks) achieving the customer's goals and purposes in use situations."[9] More simply, it is seen as intangible benefits, such as quality, worth, and utility, that customers receive from the product as measured against what they paid for it.[10] Recall the discussion of the development of the business model in Chapter 4. Intangible benefits that customers appreciate include such things as access, saving money, saving time, convenience, health, and so forth.

Developing the Pitch

Once the value proposition has been defined, it's time to develop the marketing message or pitch, which is based on presenting a solution to the problem the customer is experiencing in such a way as to highlight the benefits or value. This is followed by a list of all the marketing options or means to communicate that message. To begin to understand which options should be considered, it is important to talk to other business owners, customers, and suppliers and to read books and articles on marketing strategies for entrepreneurs such as those found at MarketingProfs.com. This process will generate a list of possibilities to consider, which may range from sponsoring a business conference to advertising in a national trade publication to developing a social media approach. Determining which strategies are the most effective, or even feasible, can be left for later. It is important for the entrepreneur to think like a customer and imagine the business from the customer's point of view. What would entice a customer to enter that store, buy that product online, or avail himself or herself of that service? An entrepreneur should study the competition and take a look at competing businesses to determine what makes them successful or unsuccessful. What marketing strategies do competitors seem to employ, and are they effective? What improvements could be made on what competitors are doing? Finally, an entrepreneur must analyze the marketing options and rank them by first eliminating those that either don't meet the needs of the target market or simply are not feasible at the time (usually for budgetary reasons). A ranking of the top ten choices should suffice.

Setting Sales and Marketing Goals

Once the methods to reach the customer have been determined, sales and marketing goals need to be established. These goals should follow the SMART rule; they must be sensible, measurable, achievable, realistic, and time specific.[11] Measurable means that there must be financial metrics associated with the goals, such as gross profit, sales revenue, and amount of sales per salesperson, as well as customer acquisition costs and number of customers acquired. These metrics are discussed further in a later section.

Many experienced marketers suggest that the first step in creating the marketing plan is to condense all the ideas about marketing strategy into a single paragraph. Impossible? Not at all. Crafting a single well-written paragraph forces an entrepreneur to focus carefully on the central point of the overall marketing strategy. This paragraph should include the purpose of the marketing plan (*What will the marketing plan accomplish?*), the benefits of the product/service (*How will the product/service help the customer or satisfy a need?*), the target market (*Who is the primary buyer or first customer?*), the market niche (*Where does the concept fit in the industry or market? How does the company differentiate itself?*), the marketing tactics to be used (*What specific marketing tools will be employed?*), the company's convictions and identity (*How will the customers define the company?*), and the percentage of sales that the marketing budget will represent (*How much money will be allocated to the marketing plan?*). Here is an example of an effective one-paragraph statement of the marketing plan for a product/service business.

> TradePartners enables qualified importers and exporters from a variety of countries to find trading partners through an Internet-based, business-to-business network. The purpose of the marketing plan is to create awareness and name recognition for TradePartners in the market space. The target customer or first customer is the small exporter who needs to find buyers for excess inventory in another country; the secondary customer is the importer who wants to find new sources for products to import to the U.S. Customers will enjoy the benefits of reduced time and risk

in finding new customers or suppliers. TradePartners has defined a niche targeting small companies that want access to the same opportunities as large companies worldwide. Customers will view TradePartners as a professional, innovative, and customer-focused company. Initial marketing tactics include personal selling at industry events, strategic alliances with complementary companies, and providing free workshops on import/export. TradePartners will spend an average of 40 percent of sales to implement the marketing strategy in the initial stages.

The next section outlines the major issues that should be addressed in the full marketing plan.

Launch Objectives and Milestones

Launch objectives are the key goals for the marketing campaign. What needs to be accomplished, when, and how does the company intend to do it? For a startup venture, two important objectives are (1) to create awareness for the company and its brand, and (2) to reach target customers to produce sales quickly. As the company begins to grow, it will add other objectives such as reaching out to non-customers in the current market or diversifying the product line to attract a new market. Objectives need to be matched to a timeline for achieving them. Marking on a timeline the major milestones for advertising and promotional events, trade shows, and social media events gives some direction to the marketing plan.

Brand Strategy

Brand building is a critical part of any marketing strategy, but what is a brand? The American Marketing Association defines the term as a "name, term, design, symbol, or any other feature that identifies one seller's good or service as distinct" from other sellers. This definition is distinguished from "brand image," which is how the customer perceives the brand.[12] Brand strategy is "a set of decisions about the brand's positioning in a marketplace."[13] These decisions can include developing the brand concept (BMW's "the ultimate driving machine"), building brand extensions to take the brand into new product areas, licensing the brand to third parties to expand opportunities, or co-branding with another company, such as Godiva chocolate did when it partnered with SlimFast to co-brand a new diet drink. "Brand equity," another often-used term, conveys the effectiveness of the brand in the market, often in terms of financial metrics such as return on marketing costs. These metrics are important because entrepreneurs are typically dealing with limited resources and they want to ensure that the dollars they spend will produce the results they want.

Building brand equity requires that customers form an emotional attachment to the brand. To accomplish that, everything associated with the entrepreneur's company—products, services, signage, location, and so forth—must convey the overall value message that the entrepreneur wants to project. So, if the company is in the educational software business with a focus on children, for example, it may need to create a brand image that suggests expertise, integrity, fun, perhaps a sense of adventure, and trust. The company's location, color scheme, product packaging, and advertising must all be aligned in a consistent message. Customers should have no doubt about what the brand stands for because that clarity and consistency serve to engender trust on the part of the customer.

To ensure that a new brand and the branding strategies used to build the brand image have a chance to achieve a high level of brand equity, an entrepreneur should test the brand against the following three questions:[14]

1. Is everyone in the company in agreement as to what the brand stands for?
2. Is there consistency between the brand image the company is projecting and the perceptions of customers?
3. Do customers describe the brand in ways that could inspire loyalty and evangelism?

It's also important to understand that branding strategies that take advantage of "word-of-mouth endorsements" through social networks, enabling endorsers to gain recognition by their peers is a powerful way to sustain the brand. Consumers also enjoy bragging about their achievements relative to what the entrepreneur is offering. For example, Bodybuilding.com finds that members like to tell the world when they achieve their target weight and this serves as essentially no-cost promotion for the company.[15] Connecting the company website to Facebook and Twitter enables these endorsements for the entrepreneur's brand to reach a much wider audience.

Strategic Alignment

Strategies deal with the needs of the customer and what is being offered to satisfy those needs. Tactics are the media, channels, and delivery mechanisms used to reach the customer and create brand awareness. To be effective, goals, strategies, and tactics must be in alignment. If an entrepreneur's goal is to emphasize reliability and customer satisfaction, for example, the marketing plan should spell out strategies and tactics for achieving that goal. Some examples of tactics might be customer feedback mechanisms and training in the use of the products. Because the brand is such a critical part of any company's success, overall company strategy should be informed by the branding strategy; that includes pricing, distribution, sales, and any activity or process in the company that touches the customer. Everything the company does must be consistent in the message it sends.

Assessing Effectiveness

Measuring the effectiveness of marketing efforts is critical to avoid wasting precious company resources. For example, matching sales forecasts to specific marketing tactics and assigning a specific person responsible for measuring the outcome is important to assessing the effectiveness of the marketing plan. Another way in which entrepreneurs measure success in a marketing effort is to ask customers how they heard about the company or the product/service.

Tracking specific marketing efforts, advertising, and promotion, and matching specific performance outcomes to each effort is vital to understanding where to focus resources. Sales reports alone will not provide the required information to make a decision about customer value.[16] For example, consider a situation where annual sales are increasing, the number of orders is increasing, and the number of customers is increasing. This all sounds promising; however, looking closer reveals that the number of orders per customer is declining significantly, which means that more customers are ordering less frequently. That translates to higher marketing costs (to keep attracting more customers) and reduced lifetime customer value (the goal is to sell more to existing customers).

It is not within the scope of this text to go into detail on marketing metrics, but Figure 14.4 provides some key performance indicators that should help entrepreneurs understand how successful they are in acquiring customers, maintaining customers, and building brand equity. It is important to note that entrepreneurs should also consider any additional metrics that might be appropriate to their specific business. We will talk about metrics used in Internet businesses in a later section.

Advertising and Promotion

Advertising and promotion are both used to create awareness for a company's products and services and influence customers to buy; but they are not interchangeable terms because they have different objectives. Advertising generally focuses on non-price benefits and targets end-users. It can also have some influence on the channels of distribution through which the customer will seek a product or service. In that sense, advertising is employed to pull the product through the distribution channel—called a pull strategy. By contrast, promotion tends to be more price-focused or incentive-focused and therefore is usually

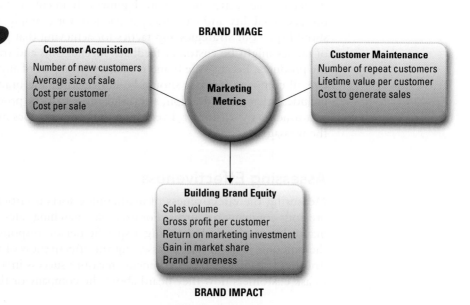

FIGURE 14.4

Some Marketing Metrics for Entrepreneurs

BRAND IMAGE

Customer Acquisition
Number of new customers
Average size of sale
Cost per customer
Cost per sale

Marketing Metrics

Customer Maintenance
Number of repeat customers
Lifetime value per customer
Cost to generate sales

Building Brand Equity
Sales volume
Gross profit per customer
Return on marketing investment
Gain in market share
Brand awareness

BRAND IMPACT

SOCIAL ENTREPRENEURSHIP: MAKING MEANING

Fabio Rosa: Bringing Energy to Rural Brazil

To the people in Encruzihada do Sul, Brazil, part of the two billion people who have no access to electricity, Fabio Rosa is a hero. The remoteness of their village made it very unlikely they would ever be connected to the electricity grid because companies in the energy business typically have no experience with supplying power to the developing world. However, through Rosa's nonprofit organization, The Institute for Development of Natural Energy and Sustainability (IDEAAS), he developed the idea of renting solar equipment to rural Brazilian villages so that the people could avoid having to purchase expensive solar panels and also avoid paying Brazil's harsh sales taxes of more than 50 percent. The biggest challenge he had to overcome was the villagers' belief that they couldn't afford the system and that it was unreliable. For more than a year he worked with community leaders to understand the needs of the people and was finally able to convince the villagers that they would pay no more than they were already paying for candles and lamp oil. Where it might cost at least $3,000 to have a house hooked up to the grid, Rosa could rent his solar energy to the villagers for less than $24 a month. In 2010 he had more than 600 families in the Encruzihada region on his program, well on his way to serving this community of 1,000.

Sources: "The New Heroes," PBS, www.pbs.org/opb/thenewheroes/meet/rosa.html, accessed September 27, 2010; and "Fabio Rosa – Making the Sun Shine for All," *MercyCorps, Global Envision*, February 7, 2006, www.globalenvision.org/library/10/954.

considered a push strategy. Table 14.1 depicts a matrix of factors that affect whether a push or a pull strategy should be used and under what conditions.

For many entrepreneurs, putting a great deal of money into advertising and promotion doesn't make sense. They simply don't have the resources and budgets of a Starbucks, so their money is better spent on more effective ways of reaching very specific customers. Today entrepreneurs can sometimes achieve phenomenal speed in awareness for a new product by turning it into a fad through the speed and reach of social networking. For example, Crocs, the plastic shoes that are a combination of clog and sandal, achieved explosive

TABLE 14.1	Factors to Consider	Use Advertising (Pull)	Use Promotion (Push)
Push or Pull Strategy?	Price sensitivity	Not effective	Effective
	Brand loyalty	High loyalty	Low loyalty
	Need for information	High need	Low need
	Risk—switching costs, learning curve	High risk for customer	Low risk for customer
	Product life cycle stage	Growing or mature	New product or declining product
	Market status	High market share	Low market share
	Purchasing pattern	Predictable	Unpredictable
	Contribution to profit	Above average	Below average
	Differentiation	Strong differentiation	Little differentiation

growth from 2005 to 2007, when consumers were seeing them everywhere. But then the fad was over, sales dropped precipitously, and the company had to scramble to sustain itself as a much smaller company.[17] So, the cautionary note is that entrepreneurs who want to use the Internet to create a viral effect and speed the adoption of their product need to have a plan for what they will do when the fad dies.

ENTREPRENEURIAL MARKET STRATEGIES

Entrepreneurs approach marketing from a point of view distinctly different from that of the traditional marketer. Although they may employ some of the same techniques as a large corporate marketer, they also take advantage of many other marketing opportunities that the corporate marketer may ignore. Jay Conrad Levinson has called the entrepreneurial marketing approach *guerrilla marketing*, an alternative to traditional, expensive marketing tactics.[18] Because entrepreneurs don't have the time or money for elaborate, high-profile marketing strategies, they essentially mimic what the big companies do, but they do it for much less money, in more creative ways, and for a shorter period of time. There are many ways to promote a company and its products and services effectively. The next sections consider a variety of entrepreneurial marketing tactics.

Traditional Advertising

Traditional advertising—a pull strategy—consists of print and broadcast media. It is not the purpose of this book to provide all the information entrepreneurs need to use each medium presented, but only to create awareness of how and when each is used. Table 14.2 presents some of the traditional print and broadcast media options available to entrepreneurs with some hints for how to use them most effectively. Internet advertising and promotion will be the subject of a later section.

Publicity and Referrals

Publicity and word-of-mouth (referrals) are two of the most effective entrepreneurial marketing tools around because they don't cost the company any money. What they do require is a compelling story that will attract attention. If a business or product is newsworthy, there are several ways to get some publicity. Contacting newspapers, magazines, or online reporters, editors, and bloggers to pitch them with an idea and then following up with a phone call often works. Whenever possible, it's a good idea to get to know people in the media on a first-name basis. Taking a reporter to lunch before there is a need for free publicity will help to cement a relationship that can be accessed when the time is right. When it comes time to seek publicity, entrepreneurs who already have a contact can simply issue a press release answering the who, what, where, when, and why of the business.

| TABLE 14.2 | Traditional Media Comparison Chart | | |

Media	Advantages	Disadvantages	Hints
Print Media			
Newspapers	Broad coverage in a selected geographic area Flexibility and speed in bringing to print and modifying Generates sales quickly Costs relatively little	May reach more than target market Difficult to attract reader attention Short life	Look for specialized newspapers for better targeting Include a coupon or 800 number Locate ad on right-hand page above the fold
Magazines	Can target special interests More credible than newspapers	Expensive to design, produce, and place	Look for regional editions Use a media-buying service Use color effectively Check on "remnant space," leftover space that must be filled before magazine goes to print
Direct marketing (direct mail, mail order, coupons, telemarketing)	Lets you close the sale when the advertising takes place Coverage of wide geographic area Targets specific customers More sales with fewer dollars More information provided Highest response rate	Not all products suitable Need consumable products for repeat orders Response rate on new catalogs is very low, about 2%	Create a personalized mailing list and database from responses Use several repeat mailings to increase the response rate Entice customers to open the envelope
Yellow pages	Good in the early stages for awareness Good for retail/service	Relatively expensive Targets only local market	Create ad that stands out on the page
Signs	Inexpensive Encourage impulse buying	Outlive their usefulness fairly quickly	Don't leave sale signs in windows too long; people will no longer see them
Broadcast Media			
Radio	Good for local or regional advertising	Can't be a one-shot ad, must do several	Advertise on more than one station to saturate market Sponsor a national radio program Provide the station with finished recorded commercials Stick to 30-second ads with music

(continued)

TABLE 14.2	(continued)		

Media	Advantages	Disadvantages	Hints
Television	Second most popular form of advertising People can see and hear about product/service Can target at national, regional, or local level	Very expensive for both production and on-air time Must be repeated frequently	Time based on GRP (gross rating points). Range is $5-$500 per GRP. Use only if you can purchase 150 GRPs per month for three months. Seek help of media-buying service
Cable TV shopping	Good for new customer products Targets the consumer Good products sell out in minutes	Not a long-term strategy Good only for products between $15 and $50 Product must be demonstrable	Call network for vendor information kit Contact buyer for your product category Be prepared to fill an initial order of between 1,000 and 5,000 units
Infomercial	Good for consumer items that can't be explained quickly	Very expensive to produce Hit rate is about 10%	Most profitable times are late nights, mornings, and Saturday and Sunday during the day Test time slots and markets to confirm effectiveness
Miscellaneous			
Affinity items (T-shirts, caps, mugs), Searchlights, Couponing, In-store demonstrations, Videotapes, Free seminars	Good for grabbing consumer's attention Effective, yet inexpensive, way to showcase the company	Value varies significantly with type of business and product or service	Every company should make use of affinity items to create free publicity

It is also important to understand that seasonality affects publicity just like it does sales in a business. New stories or product introductions receive the most notice when they are placed near an event that normally gets a lot of attention, such as a presidential election or tax season. Summertime is when many journalists are looking for interesting stories because not much is happening, so summer is a better time to get out a story about the company in general. When contacting the press, a good approach is to include a press kit containing the press release, bios, and photos of the key people in the story, any necessary background information, and copies of any other articles written about the company. The idea is to make it as easy as possible for the reporter to write or tell the story. The media are always looking for news and appreciate the effort to give them something newsworthy. When an article is written about the business, reprints can be used in future advertising and brochures, and thus the company gains even more value for the effort.

Constructing an Effective Press Release

Although some have argued that the traditional press release is dead in the age of new media, the fact is that it is alive and well. Press releases are certainly important for investor relations and they help to tell the marketplace the ongoing story of a company. An effective news release should contain the date, the name of the person to contact for more information, and a phone number; the release date (for immediate release or for release after a certain date); an appropriate, descriptive headline; the release information typed double-spaced with wide margins; the who, what, where, when, and why at the very beginning of the press release; a photo, if appropriate; and a note explaining briefly why the release was sent. There are also several publishing services that can be used to gather and distribute information about the business. For example, PR Newswire is a leading source for press releases on companies (www.prnewswire.com).

Getting Customer Referrals

The best customers are those acquired through referrals from current satisfied customers. A study conducted over 3 years by a team at Goethe-University in Frankfurt, Germany, looked at the customer referral program of a leading German Bank. The researchers wanted to learn if social capital converts to economic capital. What they found was very encouraging. Referred customers generate higher profit margins than other customers, are 18 percent more likely to stay with the bank, and to produce a significantly higher customer lifetime value.[19]

Unfortunately, most entrepreneurs don't understand how to get customers to refer others to their business and become their company evangelists. The process is actually quite simple. Entrepreneurs should begin by getting critical information that will clarify customers' motivations for buying and referring. Talking with current customers who have provided referrals is an excellent way to find out what they really like about the company, how they describe it to others, and what they value most about it. Specific ways to gather this information include taking a customer to lunch at least once a week and encouraging him or her to do the talking. Another approach is doing a global Internet search on a search engine like Google to find out what is being said about the company. Companies frequently don't know that some customers set up personal websites to either praise or criticize a company they have strong feelings about. Other options include having a qualified third party conduct in-depth interviews with customers, administering an open-ended online survey that's easy to complete, and hosting an online discussion. Finally, another great way to gather customer feedback is to create a customer advisory board to advise the company on everything from what products to carry to how best to market them.[20]

When It Makes Sense to Give It Away

Although it seems contrary to what is taught in business schools, more and more entrepreneurs are using the tactic that Netscape and Microsoft used when they gave their browsers away in order to grow their markets rapidly. Giving customers something for nothing makes sense in an environment where it's hard to get the customer's attention. But it is important to know whether giving something away will help the business or simply cost money that it can't afford to lose. Entrepreneurs should consider giving away information, consulting, or samples of a product when the customer is likely to return; when the cost for each additional item is low and margins are high; when customers need to try the product or service in order to risk the money to buy it, especially if it's unproven technology (consider offering the product or service to a well-known customer who will testify to his or her satisfaction with it); or when samples of the product or service can be offered at a large event such as a conference or trade show. On the other hand, it's important not to give away a service such as financial expertise that relies on credibility, because doing so may cause customers to question its value. Similarly, expensive items and commodity items, which customers buy on the basis of price, should not be given away, especially when the probability of retaining those customers is low.

INTERNET MARKETING AND NEW MEDIA

The United States' online advertising industry was $300 billion in 2009 with advertising and marketing revenues comprising $85 billion, according to a recent IAB/Harvard study.[21] Industry experts see traditional media boundaries disappearing while information floods markets, producing commodity pricing. Information erupting from a multitude of sources and not controlled by any one organization has the potential to overwhelm decision makers or at the very least distract them or prevent them from making effective decisions. Moreover, with everyone having access to the means to produce highly targeted messages to reach customer niches, the competitive advantage of Internet marketing disappears. With video and content production technology now priced within the reach of individuals and small businesses, the barriers to content creation have been breached so that anyone can produce a broadcast-quality commercial or magazine-quality advertisement and distribute it to a very targeted audience. Customers, who are being deluged with these targeted ads, however, have become jaded and can now use the same technologies the marketers use to opt out of receiving promotions and advertising. Customers also find themselves with the power to control when, where, and how they view ads. These and other media trends discussed later in this section present huge challenges to entrepreneurs but also new opportunities for those seeking to market their products and services.

Any marketing strategy should be anticipated, personal, and relevant. Potential customers don't want to be surprised by marketing tactics. They want to know that marketing is about them, and they want to know that it's about things they're interested in. The reason why most online marketing campaigns (and offline ones, as well) are unsuccessful is that they are unanticipated, impersonal, and irrelevant. Today entrepreneurs must find ways to give their customers more control over the purchase experience and engage them using new media tools, a topic for discussion in the next section.

In addition, there must be an effective way to measure advertising performance that is interactive, capable of being updated quickly, and minimally intrusive, so that customers don't opt out. There is a misconception that advertising on the

Internet is cheap and/or free. Actually, any method of acquiring new customers on the Internet carries an acquisition cost that can often be quite high. For example, suppose a company spends $150 on pay-per-click Google ads to attract 25 people to its site, which equates to $6 per lead. Now suppose that 3 of these people actually buy something. That means that the conversion rate is 12 percent and the cost of acquiring those 3 customers is $50 per customer ($150/3 conversions). If each customer only spends $25 on the site, the company has a problem.

Social Media

Viral marketing and crowdsourcing emerged as a direct result of the Internet's ability to replicate and distribute information quickly and efficiently. Its offline counterparts are "word-of-mouth" and "network marketing." Even though the term *viral marketing* has negative connotations, it is widely used to describe a marketing strategy that entices customers to pass on the marketing message to others. For example, Adobe, the successful software company, gives away its proprietary software that lets people share documents across multiple platforms in a form called PDF, which retains the original formatting and can't be manipulated. Adobe puts a link in the document that sends the person to the Adobe website to download the required Adobe Reader. That gives Adobe an opportunity to let the user know about its other software products available for sale. The strategy has been so successful that Adobe is now the de facto standard for sending corporate documents. Dell, the computer manufacturer, used crowdsourcing to improve its customer service reputation by developing user forums so that users could help each other as well as interact with Dell technical people.

Today, social media tools have taken the concept of viral marketing to a new level. Social media tools include Facebook, Twitter, YouTube, blogs, podcasts, RSS Readers, and wikis. Each has a specific purpose and each is more or less effective depending on what the entrepreneur is attempting to promote and to whom.

- **Blogs, Twitter, email, and e-newsletters** are generally a way for entrepreneurs to communicate the expertise of their company or opinions on relevant issues of the day and to generate interest and excitement. In the case of blogs, the communication is typically bi-directional so that customers can respond or add to the discussion. Email opt-in subscriptions, such as newsletters, can be an effective way to keep the message in front of the customer. Giving customers the ability to receive a targeted message on their mobile device or place the message on their Facebook page or LinkedIn site, send a Tweet, or forward the email to their network increases the company reach dramatically and also increases the entrepreneur's subscriber list.

- **Podcasts and vodcasts** are ways to bring the human element into communications with customers by adding voice and video. They are often used for "how to" information on new products or to provide advice. Podcasts, which can be either video or audio, can be downloaded from the company's site as well as iTunes where the company can achieve a broader reach. YouTube has become a huge source of viral videos on the Internet. Entrepreneurs can use YouTube as a hosting platform to embed or link content to other sites, to build and support the company's brand by creating a profile or channel, and to create a group and invite others to join and participate.

- **RSS Readers (Really Simple Syndication)** provide a way to find out what others are saying about an entrepreneur's company by enabling the entrepreneur to subscribe to blogs and podcasts. RSS is also used to add targeted news, blogs, or podcasts to the entrepreneur's website, usually by using an RSS aggregator, a software that locates all the news of interest to the entrepreneur.

- **Wikis** are editable websites that let multiple users create content and then edit it. Typically they provide information, such as the most popular wiki, Wikipedia, does.

- **Facebook and YouTube** are social networking sites that are effective at reaching a broad market, particularly if the target demographic is young consumers who are interested in new types of advertising that can't be found on traditional broadcast TV.

Although there is no single best way to craft a viral strategy using new media, most successful marketers:

- **Provide free products and services.** Good marketers know that "free" is the most powerful word in any language, and online marketers know that if they generate enough "eyeballs" through an effective viral marketing campaign, somewhere down the road, they will also achieve their desired level of revenues.

- **Make it easy to pass on the message.** There is nothing easier than clicking on a button and forwarding an email to someone. For example, online magazines and newspapers have made it easy to forward an article to someone by simply clicking on a button that brings up an email message into which the person's address is entered.

- **Make sure that the mail server can handle the traffic.** There is nothing worse than starting a viral campaign that ultimately annihilates its host. Viral marketing spreads a message extremely rapidly, so it is important to plan ahead for additional server capacity.

- **Take advantage of existing social networks.** Just as in the offline world, people in cyberspace create networks of people and information that they tap into regularly. Placing an interesting message into one of those networks can accelerate its diffusion exponentially.

- **Use other people's websites.** Finding compatible websites and arranging to place a message on them works because the company is tapping into another network and increasing the scope of its own.

Social Media Metrics

Over time, those who use social media tools have developed ways to measure the effectiveness of those tools. In general, there are three major categories of metrics that entrepreneurs should be aware of.[22]

1. **Registration.** This is a measure of how many people come to the entrepreneur's site and are willing to register and provide their email address in

addition to other information that might assist the entrepreneur in developing a customer profile. Making it easy for users to register will increase the performance level of the registration process.

2. **Sharing.** Giving users the ability to share content, ratings, and other information dramatically increases the traffic on the site. It is estimated that the average user on Facebook or Twitter has approximately 120 "friends." Enabling those friends to share with their friends increases the network effects exponentially. Entrepreneurs should examine the number of shares per day into social networks and study how those shares are distributed among the many social networking sites to optimize how content is delivered and displayed. In addition, it's important to monitor how many clicks return to the company's site from the shared content.

3. **Traffic.** Entrepreneurs need to track the percentage of traffic that is coming from social network sites. Some experts suggest that this traffic should be about 15 percent of total traffic to the site.[23] Examining the mix of traffic will help the entrepreneur prioritize their effort and their resources.

To stay on top of metrics, entrepreneurs will need to bring on board talent with experience in Internet analytics.

Search Engine Marketing

Search engine marketing (SEM) and search engine optimization (SEO) are simply tools for increasing the level of visibility of a website when customers search. Visibility is critical for businesses that sell products and services online or generate leads from their websites. Today, branding a company online means that entrepreneurs must be aware of their company's positioning in the Google search engine. Although there are a number of search engines available, when customers hear about a company, they immediately Google the name. Therefore, it is critical to have a website that conveys what the entrepreneur wants the customer to learn about the company. Optimizing a site with appropriate keywords can help customers find a company much faster, but it is important to note that major search engines such as Google have very specific rules regarding how keywords are used. Failing to follow those rules could get a website "Google-sacked," which means that the site is not assigned a PageRank (used for parsing sites) and therefore simply disappears from a user's search. It is wise to get referrals for third-party optimization specialists because there are many such companies that do not deliver what they promise.

A number of new terms have emerged out of keyword search marketing, and they represent ways to capture value for an advertiser and measure how effective that advertising is. They also serve as a means for entrepreneurs to create revenue streams on their sites. Here are a few of them.

- *Conversion rate:* The number of customers who take a particular action such as register on the site, subscribe to a newsletter, download software, or purchase a product.
- *Cost-per-action:* A payment model where the advertiser pays based on some manner of conversion such as a sale or site registration. In this model, the

entrepreneur, or publisher, is taking the risk because they receive a commission based on leads generated.

- *Cost-per-click:* The cost of a paid click-through.
- *Cost-per-impression:* Cost per 1,000 advertising impressions, with an impression being a single instance of an online advertisement being displayed. This form of advertising is not dependent on a click-through type of activity.
- *Pay per lead:* A model where payment is based on qualified leads.

Affiliate Programs

One way to increase the traffic on a website is to use affiliate programs, which are basically strategic partnerships with other companies that offer complementary products and services. Banner exchange programs are one example of an affiliate program. The banner company posts the entrepreneur's banner on other compatible Internet sites. Costs may be associated with posting a banner, or it may be possible to negotiate a barter exchange if the company's website is compatible with the website on which it wants to place a banner. Getting a banner on a website may be the easiest part of the challenge. Convincing people to click through and buy a product or service is quite another thing. There are many effective ways to attract customers to a website. These include assuring them that their private information will not be sold; giving them something free to entice them to discover more; offering them more, beyond the free information, that they will have to pay for; using electronic gift certificates as a way of getting customers to try products or services; providing a toll-free number for people who need to hear a human voice to overcome resistance; and offering to accept payment for items in as many ways as possible: credit cards, checks, debit cards, and so on.

Lobster Gram, the creation of Chicago-based Dan Zawacki, who sends out fresh lobsters through overnight mail services, relies on more than 2,000 affiliate sites that in 2006 generated about 6 percent of its online sales. To set up the program, Zawacki paid a one-time fee of $1,800 plus a 13 percent commission on every sale to affiliate marketer Commission Junction, which found and negotiated the appropriate affiliates for Lobster Gram. In addition to the affiliate program, Zawacki spent money on radio ads to drive customers directly to his site without going through an affiliate. However, because affiliate marketing works, many customers hit the affiliate's site first, which generated a commission for Commission Junction that Zawacki had to pay on top of his regular marketing costs. Nevertheless, according to Zawacki, his customer acquisition costs have actually gone down as a direct result of affiliate marketing.[24] Like everything else, it's important to get a recommendation from a satisfied user of an affiliate marketing program. Banner ads on affiliate sites should never be the primary source of advertising for any company; rather, they should be one tool in an arsenal of tools designed to create awareness and give customers a reason to think of the brand the next time they want to purchase something.

Content Strategy

One of the effective ways that entrepreneurs generate leads for their businesses is through a well-conceived content strategy that addresses the needs of customers at every stage of the buying process. Content tactics typically include research, eBooks, Webinars, white papers, and social media. MarketingSherpa's *2008-2009 Business Technology Marketing Benchmark Guide* reports that only about 38 percent of B2B marketers tailor content to specific stages of the buy cycle.[25] This means that entrepreneurs have an opportunity to secure a competitive advantage by addressing the needs of business customers at the various stages. Figure 14.5 depicts the major stages of a typical buy cycle for a typical manufactured product.

At the awareness stage, the goal is to capture attention and demonstrate that what is being offered meets the precise needs of the potential customer. Seeds of awareness can be planted in social media sites such as Facebook and YouTube or even by speaking at conferences or to targeted organizations. In the search stage, customers are seeking more information about the entrepreneur's offering and other similar offerings from competitors. At this stage it's important that customers see a sufficient amount of informational and positive content around what is being offered so they will be incentivized to move to the evaluation stage. The evaluation stage is where the unique value proposition the entrepreneur has created by meeting specific customer needs should be apparent because the customer will be comparing the entrepreneur's product with competitors. The ability to provide user testimonials, supporting research, and other relevant information through a variety of media will serve to strengthen the entrepreneur's case. Offering something for free (a report, white paper, or video) or a limited time discount may be the incentive that gets the customer

FIGURE 14.5

A Typical Buy Cycle

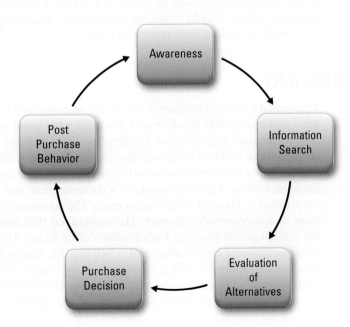

to decide to purchase. Once the purchase has been completed, maintaining contact and developing the customer relationship should be an important part of the ongoing content strategy.

Privacy Issues

Although companies have collected consumer information for years and used it to target customers and sell more products and services, the advent of online commerce has made consumers more aware of privacy issues. When Jane Consumer goes online to purchase a handmade doll for her collection, she soon finds that she is inundated with advertisements for gifts, collectibles, and anything else remotely related to her doll collection. This is the power of the Internet at work, as it magnifies anything done in the offline world. The retailer who sold her the doll collected demographic and contact information about her and then probably also sold her email address and other information to catalog companies and others looking to target the same customer. Amazon.com ran afoul of the Federal Trade Commission (FTC), which claimed that the company's practices were deceptive. Amazon did not make it clear to customers that it was selling their information to other companies. In fact, an FTC survey estimates that 97 percent of all e-commerce websites collect information that is personally identifiable. Therefore, companies must now do more to ensure that their customers' privacy is respected. Customer-focused companies inform their customers how the information collected will be used. The most successful companies maintain policies against selling customer information. Other firms seek seals of approval from online auditing companies such as TrustE and PricewaterhouseCoopers LLP, but these audits can cost up to tens of thousands of dollars. The best practice is to get a customer's permission before using his or her information for any purpose. Any effective marketing strategy, whether online or offline, should target the appropriate customers and address their specific needs, including their need for privacy.

PERSONAL SELLING

Traditional selling techniques don't always meet the needs of today's customers, who expect a quality product at a fair price with good service. Today, a business distinguishes itself in the marketplace by identifying and meeting specific customer needs. Therefore, even if entrepreneurs are selling a commodity, they need to figure out some way to add value to the product, and one way is through personal selling. A good example of a company that adds value to a commodity product is Danny O'Neill, who owns The Roasterie, a coffee roaster company in a very crowded market. He recognized that recently Africa has been the "in" place for growing high quality coffee beans. He buys his beans from small agricultural cooperatives and is helping the African farmers improve their production capability. "We get involved in the community; we have long-term relationships."[26] In this way he can distinguish his brand from others in the market and command a premium to serve the ever-increasing upscale coffee market.

Becoming a value-added company by tailoring products to meet customers' needs requires that everyone in the company become service-oriented, a time-consuming task that necessitates training and educating employees. It also demands an opportunity mindset, rather than a selling mindset. It is a lengthier process, but the returns are potentially greater. Working more closely with customers can translate into reduced selling and marketing costs.

Improving Personal Selling Skills

Personal selling is an important talent that entrepreneurs should possess and continue to hone throughout their careers. To improve upon personal selling skills, entrepreneurs need to do some research before attempting to sell, whether it's their product, their company, or themselves. It is important to learn what customers want from the sale and give them what they want. The following are some suggestions:

- The first meeting with the customer is typically designed to gather as much information as possible about the customer's needs and build credibility with the customer before trying to sell anything.

- Next, the entrepreneur must position the company as a solution provider in the mind of the customer, making sure to grab the customer's interest immediately. Whenever possible, the customer should be able to actually use the product in order to understand and appreciate it. During demonstrations and conversations, the entrepreneur should stand in front of the customer, not to the side, paying close attention to the customer's facial expressions as the benefits are being explained. The major benefits of the product or service should be explained to facilitate speedy decision making.

- If the customer declines the offer, the entrepreneur should maintain a sense of composure, then inquire why, and follow up by repeating the value the company is providing.

- As a final touch, the entrepreneur could invite the prospect to contact two existing customers and ask them about their experience working with the entrepreneur.

Selling at Trade Shows and Exhibits

For entrepreneurs in many industries—electronics, industrial equipment, and gift items, for example—trade shows, fairs, and exhibits are a primary way to expose their products and do some personal selling. Attending trade shows is an effective way to find out who the competitors are and what marketing techniques they are using. A trade show is one of the best places to meet and negotiate with sales representatives and to gather contact information for a mailing list. But the primary reason to display products at a trade show is to eventually sell more product. To accomplish this, entrepreneurs should consider renting booth space and hiring a display designer to produce a quality display booth that will attract attention. Visiting several trade shows before setting up a booth will clarify what works and what doesn't. It may also be possible to work out a deal with a company that has compatible products to share a booth and combine resources. Entrepreneurs should save the expensive brochures to hand out to potential customers who actually come to the booth and provide their business cards. It is important to have enough knowledgeable, personable people in the booth at all times so that potential customers are not kept waiting to talk with someone. Another good idea is to offer something free at the booth, such as a sample or a raffle. Finally, it is vital to follow up with letters to anyone whose business card was collected and to call all serious prospects.

MANAGING CUSTOMER RELATIONSHIPS (CRM)

One of the most rapidly growing areas of marketing is customer relationship management, or CRM. Customer relationship management (CRM) is a combination of technology, training, and business strategy that results in a system for gathering and using information on current and prospective customers, with the goal of increasing profitability. This critical component of any successful marketing strategy has long been a mainstay of large corporations, but until only a few years ago it was too costly for smaller companies. Today, however, affordable database software with sample templates makes it easy to set up a CRM system in a relatively short period of time. A good CRM system can generate better sales leads, allow rapid responses to changing customer needs, and ensure that all employees who need customer information have it when they need it in the form they need. A well-constructed CRM system contains the names, addresses, and attributes of people who are likely to purchase what the company has to offer. It will help the entrepreneur define a trading area, reach new customers in the marketplace, select specific target audiences, and survey current customers.

CRM is not merely a way to reach customers by mail more easily. Today, retaining and maintaining current customers is more important than spending money to find new customers. It has been reported that 65 percent of a company's business comes from current customers. In fact, it costs five to ten times more to go after a new customer than to serve an existing one. Furthermore, with good customer profiles, an entrepreneur can match demographic information about current customers with demographic data in the geographic area of interest to find prospects more effectively. Information contained in the database can be used in advertising, sales promotion, public relations, direct mail, and personal selling.

CRM is really an overall approach to doing business, an approach that requires the total commitment of everyone in the organization. As in any marketing effort, the payoff to this approach takes time, and many frustrated entrepreneurs give up before seeing the results of their efforts. To achieve satisfied, life-long customers, a learning environment must be developed where customer and company learn from each other with the goal of achieving a mutually beneficial lifelong relationship.

There is another benefit to building relationships with customers. If a problem occurs, a customer who has a relationship with the company won't automatically shift their loyalty to a competitor. Often their loyalty is actually *strengthened* when a problem-solving session with the company results in a satisfying conclusion. All too often, however, customers have had negative experiences with companies, where the problem has not been resolved satisfactorily. In those situations, the customer never forgets. Today, customers have a multitude of platforms from which to publicize their grievances, and one problem aired on national television or on YouTube or Facebook can cause a public relations nightmare from which the company may never recover. A classic case in point was the Cunard cruise line's public relations disaster during the launch of its expensive 2001 Christmas cruise on the renovated Queen Elizabeth II. Despite a ship full of builders still working to complete construction, management decided to sail the ship. Apparently Cunard believed the customers would overlook the mess! They did not and complained bitterly. This is clearly not the way to build long-term customer relationships.

Perhaps the most important benefit of establishing lifelong customer relationships is that over time, the full value of customers is revealed. Customers are no longer viewed as a series of transactions but as bona fide, contributing members of the team who bring value to the bottom line. The more the company learns from its customers, the better the company becomes, and the more difficult it will be for a competitor to attract these customers.

Identifying and Rewarding the Best Customers

It is not uncommon for a company to find that as few as 24 percent of its customers account for 95 percent of its revenues. Those 24 percent are the customers the company needs to know well and to keep happy, because these are the customers who will readily try new products and services and refer the company to others. After a company has been in business for a while, it becomes easier to identify the most valuable customers. One way to do this is to calculate the lifetime customer value as a series of transactions over the life of the relationship. A statistical method for doing this calculates the present value of future purchases, using an appropriate discount rate and period of time for the relationship. Add to that the value of customer referrals, and subtract the cost of maintaining the relationship (advertising, promotions, letters, questionnaires, 800 numbers). The result will be the customer's lifetime value.

Complaint Marketing

A dissatisfied customer will probably tell at least nine other people about the problem he or she faced with a company. (And those nine people will tell their friends as well!) It's easy to see how quickly even one unhappy customer can damage a company's reputation. Consequently, complaints should be viewed as opportunities for continual improvement. Making it easy for a customer to register a complaint and carry on a dialogue with a human being who listens and attempts to understand is an important way to learn from the customer. Nothing is more frustrating than to have to leave a complaint on a voice mail message. Some companies have used bulletin board type services on the Internet to let customers communicate complaints, but this method, though effective, attracts more complaints than any other method. Companies using these methods have found, in fact, that this system works almost too well, because customers feel free to vent their frustrations more angrily online than when they are hearing a soothing, caring voice at the other end of a phone line. Moreover, because anyone with access to the Internet can read the angry messages, a strong complaint can build momentum and create more problems than necessary.

One way to stem complaints at the source is to provide satisfaction surveys at every point of contact with the customer so that problems can be coped with quickly, at the outset, before the customer becomes so angry that resolution and satisfaction are nearly impossible. Effective handling of complaints can be accomplished by understanding that the customer is a human being and should be treated as such—never as a number or as someone without a name or feelings. The customer should be allowed to explain the complaint completely, without interruption. Extending this courtesy acknowledges that the complaint is important and worthy of attention. Customers should always be asked the most important question: "What is one thing we can do to make this better?" A customer's anger should be defused by sincerely taking his or her side on the issue; then the customer should be moved from a problem focus to a solution focus. Finally, the customer should be contacted one week after the complaint to find out whether he or she is still satisfied with the solution and to express the company's desire for a continued relationship.

The most important message that can be sent to customers through a company's marketing effort is that the customer is the most important part of the organization and the company will do whatever it takes to keep good customers satisfied. While it's certainly true that a young, growing company needs to build a customer base by continually adding new customers, it will reap the greatest returns from investing in the customers it currently has.

New Venture Action Plan

- Determine your business's compelling story.
- Analyze your marketing options and rank them.
- Write a clear, concise, one-paragraph statement of the marketing plan.
- Develop an advertising, publicity, and promotion strategy incorporating social media.

Questions on Key Issues

1. What are the differences between an entrepreneurial marketing strategy and a large corporation's marketing strategy?
2. Is it important to stick with your marketing plan even if it isn't returning immediate results? Why or why not?
3. What role should new media play in your marketing strategy?
4. What are the critical factors that should be considered in building a brand?
5. How can personal selling be used to build long-term customer relationships?

Experiencing Entrepreneurship

1. Compare and contrast the marketing strategies of two companies in the same industry in terms of the points in the marketing plan on page 353.
2. Find an Internet company that interests you. Contact the entrepreneur or the person in charge of implementing their marketing strategy to discuss their plan for building a brand. Are they undertaking any of the strategies or tactics discussed in this chapter? What is working and what is not? Present your findings in a brief PowerPoint presentation.

Relevant Case Studies

Case 1 Command Audio
Case 3 HomeRun.com

CHAPTER
15

UNDERSTANDING FINANCING

"Money is the seed of money, and the first guinea is sometimes more difficult to acquire than the second million."

—JEAN JACQUES ROUSSEAU

CHAPTER OBJECTIVES

- Develop a resource strategy.
- Understand the importance of a financial plan.
- Explain methods of funding with equity.
- Discuss how to finance with debt.
- Explore non-dilutive funding sources.

NOTHING HAPPENS UNTIL SOMEONE SELLS SOMETHING

Greg Gianforte's motto "Nothing happens until someone sells something" is the essence of what he believes bootstrapping is—focusing entirely on the customer to figure out whether you have a business that will work. With bootstrapping, if you fail, all you've lost is time, according to Gianforte. At the age of 33, after selling a successful venture for over $10 million, Gianforte moved to Bozeman, Montana, to raise a family. But it wasn't long before he had the urge to start another business. It was 1997, and an Internet software business seemed to make sense. By searching the Internet, he learned that there was no one helping companies respond to email from their customers. To determine whether he could "sell" his fantasy product that didn't yet exist, he began cold-calling companies, talking to them about whether a product like this might be useful if it were available within 90 days. If they said no, he would ask why and then build their response into his product design as long as he could do it within the 90 days he had specified. It took Gianforte only a couple of weeks of cold calls to learn exactly what his potential customers wanted. Then he spent two months developing a rough prototype that potential customers could test and report back to him the benefits they still needed. Because he wasn't incurring any overhead working out of his house, he decided to give the product away just to get people using it. Within three months he was able to price his RightNow software at a very low license fee. By early 1998, he was bringing in revenues of $30,000 a month and was ready to hire his first three employees, all

of them for sales positions. He didn't create sales materials but, rather, prepared a demonstration website built by students at Montana State University that showed customers how their websites would work with the RightNow software loaded.

In late 1998, Gianforte hired his first technical person, which represented his first investment in real overhead. Nevertheless, he stayed in bootstrap mode until he was confident that he understood the business model. By that time, he also had several large competitors, so it was the right moment to seek some outside funding to open offices in Dallas, London, and Sydney, Australia. He knew he could have grown with internal cash flows, but it would have taken a lot longer.

Gianforte is perhaps an extreme example of a bootstrapper. He housed his business in his home, then in a room at the back of a real estate agency, and then in a former elementary school. It was only when he began to hire experienced managers that he decided it was time to think about the company's image. In 2010, RightNow was still headquartered in Bozeman, Montana, employing more than 800 people and serving more than 2,000 organizations worldwide. Nevertheless, Gianforte stands by bootstrapping; he still makes sure that money is spent to *make* money not just to spend money.

Sources: RightNow Technologies, www.rightnow.com, accessed October 10, 2010; E. Barker, "Start with Nothing," *Inc. Magazine* (February 2002), www.inc.com; and M. Middlewood, "RightNow Technologies Jumps on the IPO Bandwagon," *TechNews World*, www.technewsworld .com/story/33730.html.

"How can I fund my new business?" Probably no question is more on the minds of first-time entrepreneurs with new venture ideas; and it's no wonder when they hear about huge transactions like Google's acquisition of YouTube for $1.65 billion in a stock-for-stock transaction on October 9, 2006, or Amazon's acquisition of online shoe company

Zappos.com for $928 million. Money seems to be the topic that always draws a crowd, whether it's for a university course on venture capital investment or a conference hosted by Donald Trump teaching investor wannabes how to become rich in real estate. Budding entrepreneurs suppose that if they have enough money they can make any business concept a success. Unfortunately, that reasoning is faulty. In fact, throwing money at a bad idea won't change it into a good idea; it just delays the inevitable failure. Putting a lot of money into the hands of an inept team is essentially throwing it away. Moreover, a team that has more money than it needs often makes poor decisions because there's plenty of money to pay for mistakes. The truth is that it is much more challenging (and rewarding) to figure out how to launch without outside capital than it is to raise money. In addition to placing too much value on money as a critical success factor, inexperienced entrepreneurs typically identify venture capital as their first and primary source of funding at startup, but this mistake springs from a misconception about the needs of startup ventures, the requirements of venture capitalists, and the nature of financial markets. In general, the vast majority of startup ventures do not meet the criteria that venture capitalists use to define high-growth, high-return companies. The reality is that money is only one of the resources needed to start a successful business, and it may not even be the most important resource at startup.

Securing resources for a new venture is a time-consuming and difficult process made more challenging by the issue of information asymmetry; that is, entrepreneurs have more information about themselves and their ventures than do the people from whom they seek resources.[1] In other words, the value proposition may be very clear to the entrepreneur but if it can't successfully be conveyed to a potential investor, supplier, customer, or partner, that value is lost. How does an entrepreneur improve his or her chances of securing required resources from sources available at startup? Research points to the importance of the entrepreneur's social network and reputation in increasing the chances of securing funding. But that is only the beginning. This chapter will discuss the financial resources that startups require and strategies for securing the right resources from the right sources at the appropriate time. Because venture capital is typically sought as growth capital, it will be dealt with in Chapter 16. Not all of the sources and strategies discussed in this chapter will be suitable for every business, but it's important that entrepreneurs understand a variety of options so they can make wiser choices.

STARTUP RESOURCE STRATEGY

The resources necessary to launch a new venture fall into four broad categories: human capital, social capital, physical capital, and financial capital. Although this chapter focuses on financial capital, it is important to understand its role relative to the other resources. All of these resources have significant implications for the survival and growth of a venture. Determining which activities require which resources and in what quantities is part of putting together a carefully conceived financial plan. Creating a unique bundle of resources that

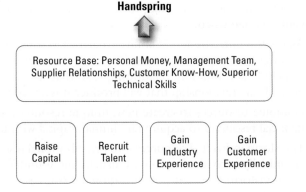

FIGURE 15.1

An Entrepreneur's
Resource Strategy

is rare, valuable, and inimitable becomes a core competency for the business as well as a competitive advantage.[2] The primary resource is the entrepreneur, who brings his or her experience, expertise, personal assets, and vision to the new venture. Many entrepreneurs find themselves in a position much like that of Jeff Hawkins, who founded Palm Computing in 1992. A highly regarded neurobiologist, Hawkins had developed a handwriting algorithm on which he received a patent. He had his reputation and the patent, but no money, no business plan, and no know-how to start a business.[3] Figure 15.1 depicts Hawkin's resource strategy. Using his social (reputational) capital and his technical skills, he was able to raise $2 million from two venture capitalists whom he had met through one of his work associations. Then he executed a deal with Tandy Computer Corporation, his former employer, for that firm to invest $300,000, sit on the board of directors, and have nonexclusive distribution rights to his new products and cross-license technology.[4] With these pieces in place, he was able to recruit the engineers he needed and an experienced executive to fill the role of president and CEO. Starting with only his social capital and his technical expertise, Hawkins was able to build the beginnings of a complex bundle of resources. Years later, when Hawkins left Palm to start Handspring, he started off with a strong resource base of personal money, a core management team, supplier relationships, customer know-how, and superior technical skills. This time, he was able to launch without the aid of outside investors.

The work of Brush and associates[5] suggests a process for constructing a resource base that will support the development of the business. It consists of five steps:

1. Identify and specify required resources at various milestones in the company's growth: human, social, financial, physical, technological, and organizational. Recall that in Chapter 8 the idea of taking an imaginary tour of the business was discussed as a way to identify resource needs.

2. Identify potential suppliers of those resources. Finding the best resources is a long and time-consuming process, so it is important to do this before the venture is launched.

3. Assess the entrepreneur's ability to attract resources. To attract the right resources, entrepreneurs must be out in the industry and market, talking to people and building relationships, so that when a particular resource is needed, the relationship that will produce it is already there.

4. Combine resources to create new, unique resources. One example is using financial resources to acquire rare human capital with unique technical skills.

5. Transform individual resources into organizational resources. Most resources are initially individual resources, usually the founder's. If the entrepreneur can transform these into organizational resources, they can become a core competency and competitive advantage for the company.

THE FINANCIAL PLAN

Knowing whom to tap for startup capital is only half the battle. The other half is having a strategic plan for funding the startup and growth of the company with the right kind of money from the right sources at the right milestones. Entrepreneurs should raise only what is actually needed, not whatever is possible in the prevailing economic environment. At the same time, planning carefully will avoid the need to seek financing too often, which can be costly both in time and money. It is important at the outset to approach the search for money armed with accurate information. The fact is that relatively few investment sources for startup companies exist outside of the three F's: friends, family, and fools. That fact is particularly important in the current economic times when third party investment and debt capital availability have declined substantially.

The Global Entrepreneurship Monitor (GEM) 2008 survey found that about 5 percent of U.S. adults invest informally in new ventures with the average amount of investment being $17,000. This investment represented about 1.4 percent of GDP in 2008.[6] These figures don't take into account investments by the founders of these new ventures. It should be noted that this survey was taken on the eve of the banking industry collapse in 2008, so these numbers have likely declined. Total first-time investment in startups and early-stage companies declined by about 14 percent in 2008. Dow Jones VentureSource's research found a 50 percent drop in investment in 2009 as compared to 2008.[7] The MoneyTree Report, put out by PricewaterhouseCoopers, reported that venture capital deals had declined by 47 percent in the first quarter of 2009 over the previous quarter.[8] On a global basis, informal investment is relatively a rare phenomenon, with most investment coming from professional funding sources or the government.

It should be clear from these findings that, in general, entrepreneurs should not start their ventures with the firm expectation that they will find investor capital outside their personal network. For this reason, they need a plan, and the following sections review three important considerations in developing that plan.

Growth Stage Identification

The starting point for planning is identifying the stages of growth that a business will experience. Every business is different, but in general, each will reach certain milestones that suggest the time has come to grow to the next level. Figure 15.2 indicates the typical funding stages. In the first stage, where the business model is being developed and tested with the first customers, seed funding is usually needed. This type of funding will normally come from the founders and other sources of "friendly money." In general, these "investors" are individuals who believe in the entrepreneur and want to support the earliest stages of startup.

By the second stage, transition, the business is requiring capital to grow on the basis of a proven business model. In fact, customer demand may require that the company grow, but it may be unable to grow rapidly enough solely using internal cash flows. The entrepreneur may need outside capital from a private investor, early-stage venture capitalist (VC), or debt source. Taking on outside investment capital means that the entrepreneur must plan for some type of liquidity event so that investors can cash out of the business and receive a return on their investment at some defined point in the future. That liquidity event may be in the form of an initial public offering (IPO) or an acquisition. At this stage, more types of capital are available than at startup because the venture has survived and appears to be growing.

If the new venture has been successful moving through the first two stages, it is likely that the company will begin to experience rapid growth that calls for large sums of capital and perhaps a different type of money, termed *mezzanine financing* or *bridge financing*, to provide the entrepreneur with the funds required to get through an initial public offering. This phase of rapid growth can come relatively early in a startup's life cycle or very late depending on the type of business and the industry in which the company operates. For some businesses, particularly lifestyle businesses, rapid growth may never be part of their

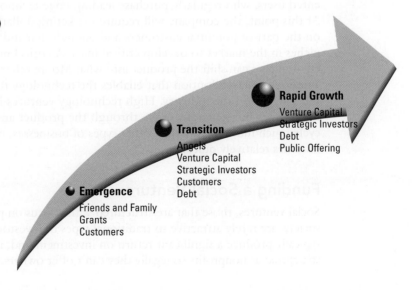

FIGURE 15.2

Stages of Investment

Emergence
Friends and Family
Grants
Customers

Transition
Angels
Venture Capital
Strategic Investors
Customers
Debt

Rapid Growth
Venture Capital
Strategic Investors
Debt
Public Offering

evolution. They may instead enjoy slow, steady growth. If a business survives over the long term, it will probably reach a relatively mature phase in which it ideally maintains a stable revenue stream with a loyal customer base. In today's dynamic environment, however, stability is rarely an enduring state. To continue to be profitable, a mature business must punctuate its equilibrium with new products and services and new markets so that it can remain competitive.

What is clear from this discussion is that there are different types of money for different stages of the venture. In general, each milestone a business achieves creates more value for the company and enables it to seek greater amounts of capital in the form of equity or debt. The issue of growth capital is taken up in Chapter 16.

The Unique Funding Issues of High-Tech Ventures

High-tech ventures that introduce breakthrough or disruptive technologies, such as a new drug, device, or process that changes the way we do things, tend to follow a pattern discussed in the works of Geoffrey Moore.[9] Recall that the adoption/diffusion curve was discussed at length in Chapter 14. In technology ventures, early seed funding and grants support a long period of product development. Often this early-stage money comes from government grants or foundations. It is a rare venture capital firm that will invest during the earliest product development phase of a high-tech venture because the risk is too high. The time from idea generation through product development, market testing, and product launch is often referred to as the "valley of death," because the failure rate is high due to the lack of identifiable markets, poor product design, and lack of funding. The valley of death is similar to the "chasm" referred to by Moore where a new technology languishes because no practical or useful applications have been found. Once the technology approaches market readiness—in other words, it has successfully traversed the valley of death—it moves into a phase known as the "early adopter" stage where technically oriented users, who regularly purchase leading-edge technology, begin to use it. At this point, the company will require marketing dollars to create awareness on the part of potential customers and enough demand to capture sufficient niches in the market to develop critical mass. A critical mass of users in a variety of niches can shift the product into what Moore refers to as the "tornado," a period of mass adoption that enables the technology to potentially become the standard in the industry. High technology ventures have longer development times but generally move through the product and business evolution cycle much more rapidly than other types of businesses, often becoming commodities relatively quickly.

Funding a Social Venture

Social ventures, those that are structured with a focus on providing a benefit to society, are rarely attractive to traditional types of investors because they don't typically produce a significant return on investment and, in most cases, they're structured as nonprofits so legally they can't offer ownership stakes.

VisionSpring, a nonprofit based in New York that sells affordable reading glasses to the poor in Asia, Latin America, and Africa, faced the problem that all social ventures face: how to scale the venture so that it can achieve its goals in a big way. Founder Dr. Jordan Kassalow decided to try the "Business in a Bag" approach by providing entrepreneurs in the communities he wanted to serve with a kit containing all the products and materials they would need to sell eyeglasses in their community. They would pay the company back as the eyeglasses sold.[10] The creative approach enabled the company to grow much more rapidly.

A new type of investing in social ventures, called "impact investing," is emerging. For example, major insurance companies and pension funds make equity investments and cash deposits into community banks that then lend to social ventures to help them grow. The investors are able to receive a return on their investment in the bank and do good at the same time.[11] The social entrepreneurs then get access to capital they need to scale.

Social investment funds are another example of creative ways to finance social ventures. These funds pool various sources of funding (donations, foundations, financial institutions, and corporations) and then lend to social ventures for lower-than-market rates of return, but significant social impact. An example of such a fund is the Nonprofit Finance Fund with offices in a number of U.S. cities (www.nonprofitfinancefund.org).[12]

In addition, several foundations, such as Ashoka and Skoll Foundation, offer seed-stage and growth-stage grants to social ventures, and these grants do not need to be repaid. As an increasing number of entrepreneurs choose to start social ventures, more creative ways to fund those ventures are emerging to meet the need.

FUNDING STARTUPS THROUGH BOOTSTRAPPING

Most startup ventures begin with a patchwork of funding sources that include credit cards, savings, friends, family members, borrowing, and bartering or trading products and services. The term *bootstrapping* refers to techniques for getting by on as few resources as possible and using other people's resources whenever feasible. It involves begging, borrowing, or leasing everything needed to start a venture and is the antithesis of the "big-money model" espoused by many when they talk about entrepreneurial ventures.[13] More often than not, bootstrapping is a model for starting a business without money—or at least without any money beyond that provided by the entrepreneur's personal resources.

The capital structure of startup ventures depends heavily on the entrepreneur's personal resources: savings, credit cards, mortgages, stock market accounts, vendor credit, customer financing, and loans. According to a Wells Fargo/Gallup study,[14] most new ventures are started with less than $10,000. RightNow Technologies was started in a spare bedroom of Greg Gianforte's home in Montana and is now a public company with 2009 revenues at just over $152 million. He started by getting customers to pay him to finish the software he would ultimately sell them to solve the problem of responding to email inquiries. (See Profile 15.1.) San Francisco-based TechCrunch, the highly regarded technology

GLOBAL INSIGHTS

Think Small to Grow Big in Istanbul

In 2003, Bülent Celebi had just left his Silicon Valley CEO position with Ubicom, a microprocessor company. He had dreams of starting a global business in his native Turkey, but with a twist—it would operate like an American company. The company, AirTies, would manufacture wireless routers in Asia using American chips and sell into developing countries where broadband was still emerging. Celebi figured that in Istanbul he could bootstrap the operation and take advantage of the many new incentives being offered by the Turkish government as a component of its bid to become part of the European Union. For example, his company does not have to pay corporate income tax for ten years because it developed a product inside one of the many "technoparks" set up by the Turkish government as economic zones. However, there were some negatives to Celebi's plan. Turkey is still trying to overcome problems with bribery and corruption, and it suffers from oppressive regulations that make it difficult to launch a business there. Celebi deals with the red tape, but he refuses to pay bribes, so things sometimes take longer. For example, at one point he had $400,000 worth of inventory that remained in customs for six months because he didn't bribe the officials. Nevertheless, for AirTies, Istanbul was ideally located to sell into Europe, Africa, and the Middle East, so with $300,000 that he raised from Silicon Valley

investors, Celebi and his family made the decision to change their life and settle in Istanbul. Immediately he began laying the groundwork for an American-style culture in his company; he encouraged his employees to take initiative and to set their own goals and deadlines, and he hired as many Turkish citizens who had been educated in the United States as possible. However, when he and his employees went outside the office, they did business Turkish style. By 2006, his company was enjoying $24 million in revenues, and he was having a positive impact on the creation of an entrepreneurial environment in Turkey. As a successful R&D company entrepreneur, something that is rarely found in Turkey, Celebi has become somewhat of a celebrity and can now influence the decisions of high-profile government officials through his many discussions with them.

The company has increased its market share in Turkey to 60 percent with over 4 million customers. In 2009, AirTies was ranked number 4 of 75 communications and networking vendors by Deloitte's Technology Fast 500. It has expanded its operations to Greece, Russia, and Ukraine.

Sources: "AirTies Rated in Top Four Fastest Growing Communications and Networking Vendors in Deloitte Technology Fast 500 EMEA," (December 9, 2009), *IT Backbones Innovation News*, www.itbinnovation.com/pr/34476; AirTies, www.airties.com; and S. Clifford, "Fully Committed," *Inc. Magazine* (April 2007).

blog, was started in 2005 by Michael Arrington, who set up a simple blog site to satisfy his need to talk about technology ventures and Internet startups. As of 2010, the company had 25 employees with annual revenues of $10 million and was about to be acquired by AOL.[15]

These entrepreneurs are the rule, not the exception; typically, personal resources are the most reliable, and sometimes the only, source of startup funding. This is because new ventures suffer from the liability of newness. By definition they have no track record, so all their estimates of sales and profits are pure speculation. A large number of new ventures fail, so the risk for an outside investor is usually high. Many new ventures have no proprietary rights that would give them a competitive advantage and a temporary monopoly in the market they enter. The founders often do not have a significant track record of success. And too many new ventures are "me too" versions of something that already exists, so they have no competitive advantages. Consequently, pre-launch preparation in the form of feasibility analysis and business planning is critical to optimizing the firm's use of the options available at startup. Poor planning can result in less than advantageous financial choices and a poor return on investment.

Although there are thousands of ways entrepreneurs can bootstrap, the following are some of the most common tried-and-true methods.

Get Traction as Quickly as Possible

Getting traction, or getting into business in some form, is a step that many entrepreneurs overlook, yet it is one of the most important steps entrepreneurs can take if they want to build credibility so they can eventually raise outside capital. Getting traction means launching the business in the quickest manner possible to start receiving real feedback from customers and to test the business model. This may mean putting up a website, opening a kiosk location, or putting product in an existing store on consignment to test the retail potential for a new product. Potential investors, and that includes friendly money, will be much more likely to consider an investment if they can see the business in operation and attracting customers.

Hire as Few Employees as Possible

Hiring as few employees as possible runs counter to the economic development efforts of most communities that are looking at job creation, but the goal of the entrepreneur at startup is survival. Typically, the greatest single expense a business has is its payroll (including taxes and benefits). Subcontracting work to other firms domestically or offshore, using temporary help, and hiring independent contractors can keep the number of employees and their associated costs down. However, it is important to follow IRS regulations carefully. One California company, a maker of heart catheters, found out the hard way that failing to follow the rules can cost the company a lot. Several of this company's "independent contractors" were working 40 hours a week exclusively for the high-tech company and were being paid by the hour, all of which suggested to the IRS that they were really employees. This misclassification cost the company $25,000 in penalties and interest. The rules for using independent contractors and leasing employees were discussed in Chapter 7.

Lease or Share Everything

At some point, virtually all new ventures need to acquire equipment, furnishings, and facilities. By leasing rather than purchasing major equipment and facilities, entrepreneurs can avoid tying up precious capital at a time when it is badly needed to keep the venture afloat. With a lease, there usually is no down payment, and the payments are spread over time. A word of caution, however. Be careful about leasing new, rapidly changing technology for long periods of time to avoid saddling the company with obsolete equipment. Some entrepreneurs have also shared space with established companies not only to save money on overhead but also to give their fledgling ventures the aura of a successful, established company.

Use Other People's Money

Another key to bootstrapping success is getting customers to pay quickly and suppliers to allow more time for payment. To accomplish this, entrepreneurs must be willing to continually manage receivables. Sometimes that means walking an invoice through the channels of a major corporation in person or locating the individual who can adjust the computer code that determines when a government agency pays its bills.

Suppliers are an important asset of the business and should be taken care of. Establishing a good relationship with major suppliers can result in more favorable payment terms. After all, the supplier has an interest in seeing the new venture succeed as well. Often a young company can't get sufficient credit from one supplier, so it is a good idea to seek smaller amounts of credit from several reputable suppliers. In this way, the firm can establish its creditworthiness, and when it qualifies for a larger credit line, the entrepreneur will know which supplier is the best source. Where possible, it's preferable to sell wholesale rather than retail. Dealing with wholesale distributors makes life easier because they are the experts at working with customers. They have already set up the consumer and industrial channels needed to expand a company's markets. Nevertheless, using a wholesaler (the entrepreneur's customer) does not alleviate the entrepreneur of the responsibility for understanding the needs of the end-user—the wholesaler's customer. No one knows the product better than the entrepreneur, and the relationship with a wholesaler must be a coordinated team effort. More bootstrapping techniques can be found in Table 15.1.

TABLE 15.1 Some Great Bootstrapping Techniques	• Use student interns, who will often work free just to get the experience. • Barter for media time. • Seek ways to motivate employees without money. • Manage receivables weekly. • Leverage purchasing discounts. • Put resources into things that make money rather than use money. • Work from home as long as possible. • Seek referrals from loyal customers. • Use independent contractors whenever possible. • Seek vendor credit. • Get customers involved in the business. • Keep operating expenses as low as possible. • Use email; it's essentially free. • Network to find complementary resources that can be shared or leveraged.

Bootstrapping Ethics

No discussion of bootstrapping would be complete without dealing with the ethical issues that arise whenever bootstrapping tactics are employed to enable a new venture to survive at startup. When entrepreneurs bootstrap, by definition they are making a new venture appear much more successful than it is to gain credibility in the market. But they must be careful not to cultivate that image at all costs, because those costs can be too great. Lying to survive by misrepresenting who the entrepreneur is or by misrepresenting how long the company has been in business is not an acceptable business practice. Intuit, a very successful software manufacturer, spent several startup years bootstrapping, during which time it became clear to the company that earning the customer's trust is essential to long-term success. It had been a common practice in the software industry to use promotional schemes to load dealers with excess product in the belief that the dealer would then push that product to get rid of it before taking on a competitor's product. Intuit refused to participate in this behavior scheme and unfailingly communicated honestly its expectations for sales to the dealers. Thus, the dealers were not burdened with excess inventory, and Intuit kept its manufacturing facilities operating on an even keel rather than experiencing costly boom-and-bust cycles.

FUNDING WITH EQUITY

When someone invests money in a venture, it is normally done to gain an ownership share in the business. This ownership share is termed *equity*. It is distinguished from debt in that equity investors put their capital at risk; typically there is no guaranteed return and no absolute protection against loss. For this reason, most entrepreneurs with startup ventures seek investment capital from people they know who believe in them. There are a variety of sources of equity financing, including informal capital, such as personal resources, "angels," private placement, and formal sources such as venture capital. This chapter focuses on informal capital. Venture capital is discussed in Chapter 16.

Friends and Family

Entrepreneurs need to think very carefully about accepting money in the form of loans or equity investment from family members and friends. This type of money is often called the most expensive money around because the entrepreneur pays for it for the rest of his or her life. Chris Baggott knows that all too well. In 1992, he quit his job and bought a local dry-cleaning business, eventually building it into a seven-store chain. To fund the business, Baggott borrowed $45,000 from his father-in-law, who also co-signed on a $600,000 bank loan. Things were going well until the "business casual" trend happened, and people stopped wearing suits and clothes that needed dry cleaning. The unfortunate end to the story was that Baggott had to sell the business, pay his debts, and live with the very uncomfortable knowledge that his father-in-law had lost tens of thousands of dollars on the deal.[16] Because of the difficulties associated with equity investments from friends and family, many entrepreneurs prefer debt, because it is cheaper and lets the entrepreneur retain control of the business. Debt is discussed in a later section. However, at times, friendly money is the only money available. In that case, it is important to treat the deal as a business deal and put everything in writing so there is no question about who gets what and what happens if there's a disagreement or the business fails.

Many investors suggest structuring a convertible debt deal for friends and family because this tactic avoids having to place a valuation on the company that is likely to be wrong. If the entrepreneur overvalues the company, friends and family will see their shares diluted in the next round of financing. With convertible debt, the issue of valuation is deferred and the entrepreneur essentially gets a loan that can be exchanged for equity in the next round of financing.

Private Investors—Angels

The most popular follow-up source of capital for new ventures is private investors, typically people the entrepreneur knows or has met through business acquaintances. These investors, who are called "angels," are part of the informal risk-capital market, the largest pool of risk capital in the United States. They can't be found in a phone book, and they don't advertise. In fact, their intentions as investors are often well hidden until they decide to make themselves known. They do, however, have several definable characteristics. Angels normally invest between $10,000 and $500,000 and usually focus on first-stage financing—that is, startup funding or funding of firms younger than five years. They are generally well educated, are often entrepreneurs themselves, and tend to invest within a relatively short distance from home, because they like to be actively involved in their investment. They tend to prefer technology ventures, manufacturing, energy and resources, and service businesses. Retail ventures are less desirable because of their inordinately high rate of failure, but angels with restaurant experience can often be found. They typically look to reap the rewards of their investment within three to seven years, but the risk/reward ratio is a function of the age of the firm at the time of investment. Angels may want to earn as much as ten times their original investment if the venture is a startup, and as much as five times their investment if the venture has been up and running for a couple of years. They find their deals principally through referrals from business associates and tend to make investment decisions more quickly than other sources of capital. Their requirements in terms of documentation, business plan, and due diligence may be lower than venture capitalists, but they are still onerous.

Today, many angels have joined forces to create larger pools of capital. These "bands" of angels have strict rules about how much their members must invest each year and how much time they must spend in exercising due diligence over other members' deals. In some cases, these angel groups look and act like professional venture capitalists. As venture capital pools have grown in size to the point where the deals they engage in are much larger, angels have stepped in to take the deals formerly funded by VCs. The largest angel network in the United States is the Tech Coast Angels, which spans the area from Santa Barbara to San Diego and has hundreds of members. They fund startups and early-stage ventures, primarily in high-tech areas like life sciences and information systems, but more recently, they are funding retail and other types of ventures that have high growth potential.

In general, angels are an excellent source of seed or startup capital. The secret to finding these elusive investors is networking—getting involved in the business community and speaking with those who regularly come into contact with sources of private capital: lawyers, bankers, accountants, and other businesspeople. Developing these contacts takes time, so it is important not to wait until the capital is needed before beginning to look for them. Of course, taking on an investor will mean giving up some of the ownership of the company; therefore, it is probably wise to plan at the outset for a way to let the investor exit. Including a buyout provision with a no-fault separation agreement in the investment contract will ensure that the entrepreneur doesn't have to wait for a criminal act such as fraud to end the relationship. Structuring the buyout to be paid out of earnings over time will avoid jeopardizing the financial health of the business. Above all, it is vital to avoid using personal assets as collateral to protect an angel's investment.

The bottom line on an angel investment is that the angel is investing in the entrepreneur, and it's a very personal investment. Angels often want to experience again the excitement of starting a new venture, but they want to do it vicariously through the entrepreneur. That is why they often fund young entrepreneurs with a lot of enthusiasm, a great idea, and the energy to make it happen. They want to be involved and to mentor the entrepreneur. Like the venture capitalist, they want to make money, but the real payback is in doing good and helping a novice entrepreneur get his or her start.

Private Placement Memorandum

A private placement memorandum (PPM) is a way of raising capital from private investors by selling securities in a private corporation or partnership. Securities include common stock, preferred stock, notes, bonds, debentures, voting-trust certificates, certificates of deposit, warrants, options, subscription rights, limited partnership shares, and undivided oil or gas interests. PPM provides many benefits over venture capital. Entrepreneurs can raise an unlimited amount of capital, and, typically, investors are willing to stay in longer for returns of 10 to 20 percent on their investment. PPM costs less than either a public offering or venture capital and the money can often be raised more quickly. The best type of business for private placement is one that is seeking some growth funding, but startups that have proven their concept and have a first customer may also be able to tap this source.

The investors solicited via a PPM must meet the rules of private placement, which are stated in the Securities and Exchange Commission's Regulation D. Regulation D was designed to simplify the private offering process and enable entrepreneurs to seek funding from private investors who meet the rule's requirements. Doing a PPM requires first completing a business plan and a prospectus detailing the risks of the investment. Just as in the drafting of any complex legal document, it is crucial that entrepreneurs consult an attorney well versed in the preparation of the PPM and in the disclosure of information about the company and its principals. Problems don't usually arise if the business is successful; however, if the venture fails and the investors uncover a security violation, the entrepreneur and other principal equity holders may lose their protection under the corporate shield and become personally liable in the event of a lawsuit. Security violations have been dealt with severely by the courts, and there is no statute of limitations on the filing of such a suit.

Many states now offer standardized, easy-to-fill-out disclosure statements and offering documents. However, entrepreneurs should never undertake a private placement offering without the guidance of a qualified attorney. The advantages of a private offering are many. The growing venture is not required to have a great many assets or credit references, which it would need for bank financing, nor does it need a lengthy track record. The entrepreneurs also don't have to file with the Securities and Exchange Commission (SEC). They do, however, have to qualify under the strict rules of Regulation D, which makes it easier and less expensive for smaller companies to sell stock. Not all states recognize the exemptions under Regulation D in their "Blue Sky" laws (laws that protect investors from fraud), so the issuer of a private placement memorandum may have to register with the state.

The burden is on the issuer to document that the exemption from registration requirements has been met. Therefore, the "sophistication" of all offerees should be examined closely, and the reasons why they qualify should be carefully documented. A sophisticated investor is one who has a net worth of at least $2.5 million, has earned more than $250,000 per year during the previous two years, and has taken investment risk in the past. Entrepreneurs should number each private placement memorandum and keep a record of who has looked at the memorandum or discussed the offering with the issuer. The memorandum should include a qualifying statement that the contents must not be copied or disclosed to anyone other than the offeree. If an offeree becomes an investor, the issuer should document when and where the offeree examined the books and records of the company. When the offering is complete, the issuer should place in the offering log a memo stating that only those persons listed in the log have been approached about the offering.

Even if the offering qualifies as exempt from registration, it is still subject to the antifraud and civil liability provisions of federal securities laws and state Blue Sky securities laws. Many states have adopted the Small Corporate Offering Registration Form, also called SCOR U-7, which makes the registration process much simpler by providing 50 fill-in-the-blank questions that ask for the basic financial, management, and marketing information for the company. A lawyer should be consulted, because some of the adopting states restrict who can use Form SCOR U-7.

Venture Capital Institutes and Networks

Many areas of the country offer access to venture capital networks through institutes established on the campuses of major universities. The university acts as a conduit through which the entrepreneurs and investors are matched; it neither assumes any liability for nor has any ownership interest in either the new venture or the investor's company. The entrepreneur typically pays a fee, in the range of $200 to $500, and submits a business plan to the institute. The plan is then matched to the needs of private investors in the database who subscribe to the service. If an investor is interested in the business concept, he or she contacts the entrepreneur. In general, venture capital networks are a way for entrepreneurs to gain access to investors whom they may not be able to find through other channels. Furthermore, the investors have chosen to place their names in the database, so they are actively looking for potential investments.

Small Business Investment Companies

Small business investment companies (SBICs) are actually privately managed venture capital firms licensed by the Small Business Administration. They receive financing at very favorable rates, in partnership with the federal government, to invest in small and growing businesses through equity (generally preferred stock or debt with warrants) and long-term debt. Companies that qualify for SBIC financing must have a net worth under $18 million and average after-tax earnings of less than $6 million during the previous two years. In addition, at least 51 percent of assets and employees must reside in the United States. The typical deal involves a loan with options to buy equity, a convertible debenture (debt that can be converted to equity). Preferred stock, which pays the investor back first in the event of a failure, is sometimes used for first-round financing.

FINANCING WITH DEBT

When entrepreneurs choose a debt instrument to finance a portion of startup expenses, they typically provide a business or personal asset as collateral in exchange for a loan bearing a market rate of interest. The asset could be equipment, inventory, real estate, or the entrepreneur's house or car. Although it is best to avoid pledging personal assets as collateral for a loan, it's sometimes unavoidable, because banks generally require first-time entrepreneurs to guarantee loans personally. There are several sources of debt financing.

Commercial Banks

Banks are not normally a readily available source of either working capital or seed capital to fund a startup venture. Banks are highly regulated; their loan portfolios are scrutinized carefully, so they generally do not make loans that have any significant degree of risk. To mitigate risk, banks like to see a track record of positive cash flow, because it is out of this cash flow that their loan will be repaid. Unfortunately, new ventures don't *have* a track record, so an unsecured loan is probably not possible.

Generally, banks make loans on the basis of what are termed the five C's: character, capacity, capital, collateral, and condition. In the case of entrepreneurs, the first two—character and capacity—become the leading consideration, because the new business's performance estimates are based purely on forecasts. Therefore, the bank will probably consider an entrepreneur's personal history carefully. However difficult, it is important for an entrepreneur with a new venture to establish a lending relationship with a bank. This may mean starting with a very small, secured loan and demonstrating the ability to repay in a timely fashion. Bankers also look more favorably on ventures with hard assets that are readily convertible to cash.

Commercial Finance Companies

As banks have tightened their lending requirements, commercial finance companies have stepped in to fill the gap. Often called "hard asset" lenders, they are able to do this because they are not so heavily regulated, and they base their decisions on the quality of the assets of the business. They do, however, charge more than banks, as much as 5 percent or more over prime, at rates more similar to those charged by credit card companies. Therefore, an entrepreneur must weigh the costs and benefits of taking on such an expensive loan. Of course, in cases where starting the business or not starting it, or surviving in the short term or failing to survive, depends on that loan, the cost may not seem so great.

Factoring, one of the oldest forms of banking, accounts for more than $1 trillion a year in credit. Factoring is a particular type of receivable financing wherein the lender, called the factor, takes ownership of a receivable at a discount and then collects against it. When the U.S. military needed machinery to create the infrastructure in Afghanistan after the initial invasion, it turned to one of its major contractors, IAP Worldwide Services, which specializes in logistics. But IAP had to purchase the goods the government needed and meet payroll before it would be paid from the order. IAP turned to a factor to get the cash it needed to serve its customer.[17] Factoring has become a popular form of cash management in smaller businesses that sell to big companies. Large companies are notorious for paying extremely slowly, which can wreak havoc with an entrepreneur's cash flow. But a small business that sells to Wal-Mart must be patient with the giant, because that account is probably very important to the entrepreneur. Therefore, the entrepreneur sells some of those receivables to a factor so as to not disrupt its cash flow. Factors know that Wal-Mart will eventually pay, so there is little risk to them of taking on the receivable. In fact, Wal-Mart has helped to grow the factor industry significantly. Entrepreneurs should make sure that any factor they use is a member of the Commercial Finance Association, which is the major trade group for the industry. They should also have an attorney verify the authenticity and background of the factor. In general, taking out a bank loan is less expensive than using a factor, but in hard times, bank loans for startups are difficult to secure.

Small Business Administration Loan

When a conventional bank loan does not appear to be a viable option, entrepreneurs may want to consider an SBA-guaranteed loan. With an SBA-guaranteed loan, an entrepreneur applies for a loan of up to $2 million from his or her bank, and the SBA guarantees that it will repay up to 90 percent of the loan to the commercial lender (generally a bank) should the business default. This guarantee increases the borrower's chances of getting a loan. A further incentive to banks is that SBA-funded ventures tend to be growth-oriented and have a higher survival rate than other startups. Of course, because the government backs these loans, the documentation and paperwork are extensive, and interest rates are usually no different from those paid on a conventional loan. Entrepreneurs should be aware that it's difficult to secure an SBA loan at startup. The SBA requires a track record of at least a couple of years before they're willing to step in.

The Small Business Administration also has a program called the micro loan that makes it easier for entrepreneurs with limited access to capital to borrow small amounts (up to $35,000) with the average loan about $13,000. Instead of using banks, as in the guarantee program, the SBA uses nonprofit community development corporations. In addition to the money, entrepreneurs are usually required to participate in business training and technical assistance.

OTHER NON-DILUTIVE FUNDING SOURCES

Entrepreneurs who need funding but don't want to dilute their ownership in their company choose debt if it's available and other sources where the return to the source is not based on ownership. Some examples are strategic alliances, grants, state-funded incentives, and incubators, which are discussed in the next several sections.

Strategic Alliances

A partnership with another business—whether formal or informal—is a strategic alliance. Through strategic alliances, entrepreneurs can structure deals with suppliers, manufacturers, distributors, or customers that will help reduce expenditures for marketing, raw materials, production, or research and development (R&D). Reducing expenditures increases cash flow, providing capital that wouldn't otherwise have been available. One type of strategic alliance is the R&D limited partnership. This vehicle is useful for entrepreneurs starting high-tech ventures that carry significant risk due to the expense of research and development. Through a limited partnership agreement, the strategic partner contracts with the entrepreneur to provide funding for the development of a technology that will ultimately be profitable to the partnership. This is advantageous for both the limited partner and the new venture. Limited partners are able to deduct their investment in the R&D contract and enjoy the tax advantages of losses in the early years on their personal tax returns; they also share in any future profits. In the R&D limited partnership, the startup acts as a general partner to develop the technology and then structures a license agreement with the R&D partner whereby the entrepreneur can use the technology to develop other products. Often the limited partnership's interest becomes stock in a new corporation formed to commercialize the new technology. An alternative to this arrangement is an agreement to pay royalties to the partnership.

Yet another vehicle to secure resources for the startup is the formation of a joint venture, which enables the entrepreneur to buy back the joint venture interest after a specific period of time or when the company reaches a certain volume in sales. As in a private placement, it is important to work through an attorney. The startup may incur significant costs in creating the partnership, a process that could take up to a year. In addition, giving up sole ownership of the technology may be too high a price to pay if the partnership does not survive. Strategic alliances are discussed further in Chapter 16, where growing a company is considered.

Many entrepreneurs neglect to consider one of the largest and most accessible sources of funding—their customers and suppliers. The reason why these two groups are more accessible than many other types of financing is that they are colleagues in the same industry; they understand the entrepreneur's business and have a vested interest in seeing the entrepreneur succeed. Suppliers and customers can grant extended payment terms or offer special terms favorable to the business. In return, the entrepreneur's business can provide such things as faster delivery, price breaks, and other benefits. Customer financing is not easy to achieve, but definitely possible under the right circumstances. In general, those circumstances include such things as offering higher returns than more traditional investments or getting in on the ground floor of a potentially high-growth business. When Randi Payton started the first weekly magazine dedicated to African-American consumers, *On Wheels Media*, he managed to secure advance payments from advertisers such as BMW and General Motors who wanted to market to this ethic group.[18]

Grants

The Small Business Innovation Development Act of 1982 was designed to stimulate technological innovation by small businesses in the United States. It requires that all federal agencies with research and development budgets in excess of $100 million give a portion of their budgets to technology-based small businesses in the form of Small Business Innovative Research (SBIR) grants. Small businesses find out about these grants by checking the published solicitations by the agencies to see whether they can qualify by providing what the agency needs. Grants have three phases. Phase I is the concept stage and feasibility phase, which provides up to $150,000 for an initial feasibility study to determine the scientific and technical merit of the proposed idea. This amount is made available for six months. If results are promising, the company is eligible for Phase II funding. Phase II provides up to an additional $1 million for two years, for the firm to pursue the innovation and develop a well-defined product or process. Phase III requires the entrepreneur to access private sector funds to commercialize the new technology but may also include government contracts for products, processes or services that might be used by the U.S. government.[22]

To qualify for an SBIR grant, the company must employ fewer than 500 people, be at least 51 percent independently owned by a U.S. citizen, be technology-based, be organized for profit, and not be dominant in its field. The grant holder must perform two-thirds of the Phase I effort and one-half of the Phase II effort. At least half of the principal investigator's time must be spent working in the small business.

The STTR program fosters partnerships between small businesses and universities or research labs. Unlike the SBIR program, the small business must conduct only 40 percent of the grant activities. STTR Phase I provides $100,000 total costs for 12 months and $750,000 total costs for Phase II.

State-Funded Incentives

Many states provide a range of services to help new and growing ventures. From venture capital funds to tax incentives, states such as Massachusetts, New Jersey, and Oregon are seeing the value of establishing business development programs. New and growing ventures usually receive their funding from the state government, which enables them to seek larger investment amounts from private sources. In states where equity funding is not available, there is typically a loan program aimed at new ventures. In Massachusetts, for example, favorable debt financing is often exchanged for warrants to purchase stock in the new company. Pennsylvania was the first to create a funding program aimed at minority-owned businesses. South Dakota has recently implemented a seed grant program to encourage commercialization of research from its universities.

Incubators

There is no doubt that after the dot com crash of 2000 and the subsequent drop in the valuation of technology stocks, the incubators that spawned a rash of Internet businesses fell on hard times. But today incubators are enjoying a resurgence of interest. Incubators are places where startup ventures can get space and support for the early stages of startup. Incubators are typically nonprofit organizations designed to help nascent businesses get up and running to improve their chances of survival in the marketplace. Chapter 12 provided some suggestions on what to look for in an incubator.

Starting a business takes preparation, particularly when outside capital is required. However, careful planning and a successful launch can also lead to additional sources of funding for growth, the subject of Chapter 16.

New Venture Action Plan

- Calculate how many personal resources you have to help fund a new venture.

- Determine ways to bootstrap the startup of the new venture.

- Network to come in contact with potential "angels."

- Identify an attorney who can help structure any legal documents.

- Investigate the sources of debt financing in the community.

- Determine if any of the non-dilutive sources of funding are appropriate for your business.

Questions on Key Issues

1. How does bootstrap financing fit into the strategic plan of a new venture?
2. What is the role of angels as a source of new venture funding?
3. Contrast funding with equity and funding with debt or non-dilutive sources.

4. Why are commercial banks not usually a reliable source of new venture financing?
5. What are the benefits of a private offering as compared to a public offering?

Experiencing Entrepreneurship

1. Make a list of all the sources of friendly money, including your personal resources, that you can tap to start a new business. How much startup money could you reasonably raise?
2. Interview an angel and a banker to learn what his or her expectations are when reviewing business plans for new ventures. In a two-page report, compare their criteria for choosing to fund or not fund the new business.

Relevant Case Studies

Case 2 MySpace

Case 7 1-800-Autopsy

B2P: MICRO-BIOINFORMATICS TECHNOLOGY AND GLOBAL EXPANSION*

"That's fantastic," Dr. Rosemary Sharpin said as she hung up the phone. Dr. Sharpin was ecstatic and could not wait to share the news with the researchers. She had just found out that her company, B2P, which makes bacteria testing systems for water and food, had been selected as one of the finalists in the New Zealand Focus on Health Challenge, a contest for companies specializing in innovative health technology. Because the challenge focused on helping New Zealand based companies commercialize their products in the United States, Dr. Sharpin knew that expanding outside of New Zealand—something that she has always wanted B2P to do—was eminent.

The international opportunities for B2P had grown in recent years as stories of contaminated food and drinking water had become more and more common. Outbreaks of disease traced to tainted supply chains and careless agricultural practices had caused panics among consumers and led the government to crack down on the industries that controlled the nation's food supply. With thousands of illnesses or deaths and millions of dollars in losses associated with food recalls, insurance claims, and lawsuits every year, the problem had reached critical mass.

A potential solution for the problem lay in the process used to test food and water for contaminants. Current methods of testing for E. coli and related bacteria required a professional laboratory, skilled staff, and up to three days for results to be received. These limitations slowed down the testing process and could contribute to outbreaks. However, B2P Micro-Bioinformatics Technology (B2P), Dr. Sharpin's company, had developed a portable, one-time use, self-contained testing device that enabled almost immediate detection of bacteria present in or on anything.

Before taking advantage of the opportunity, Dr. Sharpin had to answer a number of questions. Although the publicity from the New Zealand Health Challenge might help her gain a foothold in the international market, she had to decide whether to expand her efforts in Australasia, where she had already made some progress, concentrate on the more lucrative European and North American markets, or look for opportunities in the third world market. Dr. Sharpin had to identify which industries had the greatest need for B2P's products and where the barriers to entry might cause problems. And most importantly, Dr. Sharpin had to develop a strategy for entry to these new markets that maximized her chances for success while minimizing the risk to her young company.

Company Background

In 1983, Dr. Rosemary Sharpin formed ICPbio International Ltd., New Zealand's first biotech company. ICP developed and marketed products

*This case was written by Melissa Wu, a graduate of the Marshall MBA program at the University of Southern California, as a basis for class discussion. Reprinted by permission.

related to embryo transfer in animals, bio-chemical extraction from animal blood, and quality assurance testing for the dairy industry. It was at ICP that Dr. Sharpin learned of the need for better E. coli and coliform testing. As a result, in conjunction with NZDRI (the New Zealand Dairy Research Institute), ICP began to research and develop the innovative biotechnology that would become the foundation for B2P's testing products.

After 20 years with the company as the Joint Managing Director responsible for product development, international sales, and marketing, Dr. Sharpin was ready to begin another startup. In 2002, she bought the intellectual property that was the basis of the B2P product suite from ICP, and she and business partner Maxine Simmonds "spun off" B2P Ltd. from the successful bio-tech manufacturing company. Wanting to focus fulltime on B2P, Dr. Sharpin also sold her shares in ICP.

As the sole owner of B2P technology and products, Dr. Sharpin had several different options for setting up the company. One of her goals in organizing was to not over extend the company too much in the initial stages. As a result, B2P's structure was straightforward and leveraged outsourced resources including contract manufacturing, marketing, and non-essential design and development. While the company had initially been headquartered in Auckland, New Zealand, B2P expected to eventually move its corporate headquarters to Europe to be closer to larger markets.

Due to her experience at ICP, Dr. Sharpin knew what the market needed: a fast, simple, portable bacteria testing system. B2P's solution—essentially a large bottle in which the contents turn either pink or white, depending on the bacteria present—effectively filled that need and quickly became popular in the New Zealand dairy and shellfish industries. As a result of this success, B2P developed multiple products varieties and complementary products, all with the same testing concept. The products included:

- B2P WaterCheck™: Tests for E. coli and coliforms in water. Requires 100ml of water sample for testing in a self-contained unit.

- B2P FoodCheck™: Tests for E. coli and coliforms in solids, including whole shellfish, meat, chicken, yogurt, and leafy greens. Similar to WaterCheck but features wide neck opening to easily add 10g of sample food.
- B2P DairyCheck™: Tests for E. coli and coliforms in dairy liquids.
- B2P COLIQUIK™: Tests for E. coli and coliforms in salt water, chemically-treated water, wash from food products, and any other sample with a matrix which may interfere with growth of bacteria or which could spontaneously cause oxidation or reduction in the system (e.g. lemon juice, vitamin C, etc.).
- B2P Swab-It™: Tests for E. coli and coliforms on surfaces. Features a moist swab to wipe sample and test for bacteria.
- B2P MicroMagic (rental-financed): Test reader and analyzer. Incubates up to four COLIQUIK samples and illuminates the sample every minute, measures the light responses, plots the readings, and calculates all changes. The system features optional GPS and GPRS technology and battery unit for remote messaging to a central location. Can transmit compressed, encrypted data to nominated personnel (via SMS text message) and/or to a data management system (the Micro Wizard™).
- B2P MicroWizard: An on-line interface used to track and verify results.

The Food and Water Testing Industry

Consumer concern and government involvement have caused an increased opportunity within the testing industry as demand for safer products grows.[1] Two ongoing developments that affect E. coli and coliform testing are the growth

---

[1]The testing may occur in a laboratory or on-site. Research and testing can be carried out within the laboratory environment or it may involve field studies. Much of the testing in this sector involves the maintenance of utility, agricultural, food, and industry/product standards. The research is carried out and used by industry, government, universities, colleges, individuals, and non-profit organizations.

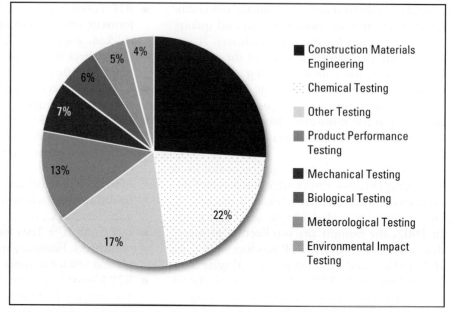

EXHIBIT 1

U.S. Laboratory Testing Services by Product/Service

Legend:
- Construction Materials Engineering
- Chemical Testing
- Other Testing
- Product Performance Testing
- Mechanical Testing
- Biological Testing
- Meteorological Testing
- Environmental Impact Testing

Pie chart values: 4%, 5%, 6%, 7%, 13%, 17%, 22%

E. coli and coliform testing falls within the Product Performance Testing and Environmental Impact Testing categories (depending on the product on which the tests are being conducted).

Source: Adapted from data found in Laboratory Testing Services in the U.S., IBISWorld Industry Report, August 19, 2009.

in the environmental testing activities industry (Exhibit 1) and an increase in agricultural testing, with both areas benefiting from additional government funding and increased competition. Overall, it is estimated that the general testing industry grew 2.6 percent from 2004 to 2009, despite the recession.[2]

The U.S. E. coli and coliform testing space is segmented, with laboratory services divided by size and industry focus (Exhibit 2). There are no large companies that dominate the industry; instead, the industry is comprised of many small players (nearly 70 percent of laboratories have fewer than 10 people).[3] Much of the industry is comprised of regional and national companies that require samples from around the country to be shipped to central laboratories. Many of the smaller labs will employ a few staff members who perform industry-specific tests of water, beef, leafy greens, or dairy products. The larger labs also tend to be industry focused but many have multiple products capable of testing additional contaminants besides E. coli and coliform. It is worth noting that several of the larger labs will outsource specific tests to smaller facilities. IBIS World predicts that existing companies will expand their operations, either by the acquisition of a complementary or rival business or by entering into joint ventures.[4] As such, industry concentration is likely to increase in the future.

Within the E. coli and colioform testing industry there are several "areas of pain." Overcoming them can place an organization ahead of the other testing outlets. They include:

Breadth of services: A testing laboratory that can provide a broad array of services often

[2]Laboratory Testing Services in the U.S., IBISWorld Industry Report, August 19, 2009.
[3]Laboratory Testing Services in the U.S., IBISWorld Industry Report, August 19, 2009.
[4]Laboratory Testing Services in the U.S., IBISWorld Industry Report, August 19, 2009.

EXHIBIT 2

U.S. Market Segments for Testing Services

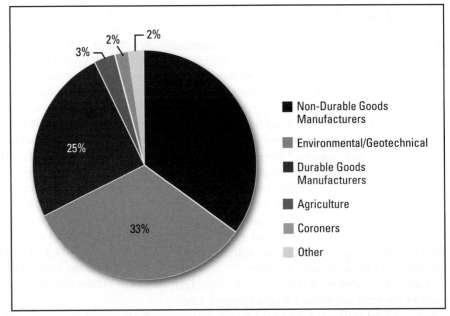

- ■ Non-Durable Goods Manufacturers
- ▨ Environmental/Geotechnical
- ■ Durable Goods Manufacturers
- ■ Agriculture
- ▨ Coroners
- ▨ Other

Markets for E. coli and coliform testing would fall within the Durable Goods Manufacturers, Agriculture, and other categories (depending on the product on which the tests are being conducted).

Source: Adapted from data found in Laboratory Testing Services in the U.S., IBISWorld Industry Report, August 19, 2009.

has a competitive advantage over smaller labs. This flexibility enables customers that require a range of different tests to get them all performed at one laboratory.

Reliability: Reputation and reliability are extremely important within the testing world.[5] According to Eric Gorman, a Senior Geologist with GSI/water, laboratory reputation is so important that he will frequently test labs with "blanks" of a known contaminant in order to cross reference the final lab results for validity.[6] Because many tests require skilled, knowledgeable technicians, labs that have more highly skilled technical teams may have the advantage.

Technology: Not surprisingly, proprietary technology can also be an advantage in the testing world. New discoveries and testing methodologies can help save time and money, and improve the accuracy of results. Patents can protect the intellectual property and provide an added competitive advantage to the testing organization.

Time: Slow turnaround time has plagued laboratories for years. While many labs can complete tests within 24 hours, transportation time and/or backlog can result in delays of more than 72 hours. In 2007 it was estimated that only 8 percent of the entire testing industry's tests were performed onsite.[7]

Price: While the price charged for services can be a critical point of competition, many clients are more concerned with accuracy and timeliness. They are often inclined to pay a premium to feel certain that their testing will be reliable and prompt.

[5]Laboratory Testing Services in the U.S., IBISWorld Industry Report, August 19, 2009.

[6]Gorman, Eric. "follow up questions. Re: question about water." Email to Melissa Wu, 13 January 2010.

[7]Laboratory Testing Services in the U.S., IBISWorld Industry Report, August 19, 2009.

The Opportunity

As a result of continuing outbreaks and extensive media coverage, E. coli in food and water remained at the top of mind for many Americans. In a 2007 survey funded by *The Beef Check-Off* and managed by the National Cattlemen's Beef Association, E. coli was the food borne pathogen with the highest consumer recognition and the highest consumer concern.[8] Every new incident and media report raised consumer fears, which in turn resulted in consumer demand that the government and food industry ensure the safety and quality of their products. In fact, government entities such as the CDC, EPA, and FDA had all indicated that clean drinking water and safe recreational water were ongoing priorities.[9]

Current methods of testing for E. coli and related bacteria required a well-equipped laboratory, skilled staff, and 22 to 72 hours for results to be received. Sending samples to the lab meant that production managers lost control of the testing process, and the ability to make rapid responses to problems that invariably arose might compromise the product and cause health issues. Sample integrity was also frequently compromised. These obstacles could force companies such as fresh food suppliers, who must ship their products out immediately, to bypass key steps in the testing process or even to move on without waiting for results. There was an opportunity in the marketplace, therefore, for a company and product that could avoid these pitfalls entirely by producing results quickly, on site, and without a trained staff.

Dr. Sharpin believed that B2P's simple, electronic, and field-ready automated bacterial testing systems were perfectly suited to solve the current global crisis. The self-contained units could be used in any environment to detect, count, and report E. coli and related bacteria. The products did not require the presence of a skilled technician and reduced the results delivery time to fewer than 2 hours for highly contaminated material and 12 to14 hours for a confirmed negative test. According to Dr. Sharpin, "There is no user-friendly product on the global market that operates with this speed, specificity, sensitivity and reporting immediacy. This has a huge impact on marketability into existing and new markets in the hospitality and pre-prepared/fast food markets, as well as Third World and 'aid' markets and emergency management."

Any area that could be affected by E. coli could be considered a potential market. Based on consumer demand and government intervention, the two markets with significant opportunities were within the water and food industries' supply chains. These included:

- Water testing for:
  - Drinking/ground water
  - Private wells
  - Oceans, lakes, rivers, etc.
  - Amusement parks
  - Hotels, cruise ships
  - Post-disaster

- Food testing:
  - Suppliers of products related to:
    - Beef
    - Dairy
    - Leafy greens
    - Chicken, other meats
  - Restaurants
  - Hotels, convention centers, etc.

Within the larger markets were a number of different opportunities, each with a different business model based on audience type. On a high level, they included:

Suppliers: For suppliers, time is money. Waiting for test results means holding back inventory and adding delays to their operations. The USDA did not require certain tests to be conducted and as a result, much of the industry was self-regulated.[10] Many suppliers were hesitant to perform non-required tests due to fear of being "found out" and losing potential revenue. Additionally,

---

[8]Food poisoning from *E. coli* and vegetables most concerning by Rick McCarty, Executive Director, Issues Management – NCBA accessed via web www.beef.org/uDocs/foodpoisoning fromecoliandvegetablesmostconcerning631.pdf.

[9]http://ucce.ucdavis.edu/files/filelibrary/1598/34148.pdf, 9 January 2010.

[10]Moss, M. (2009, November 12). E. Coli Outbreak Traced to Company That Halted Testing of Ground Beef Trimmings. *The New York Times.* Retrieved from www.nytimes.com/2009/11/13/us/13ecoli.html?_r=2.

because tracking E. coli contamination could be time consuming and difficult, it was easier for suppliers to "play the blame game" when outbreaks occurred. While most did not want to self-test, more and more companies, such as Tyson Chicken, were taking the initiative. Making it easier for suppliers to test their products and reducing the test result time could only help this audience.

Commercial Retail Outlets: If contaminated food makes its way through the supply chain to retail outlets (hotels, stores, fast food restaurants) or commercial recreational water becomes contaminated, companies' reputations can be seriously damaged. While many outlets preferred to rely on heath inspectors to regulate their facilities, a growing number were taking control of the situation. Companies such as Costco, Nestle, and Trader Joe's had taken an active and public stance regarding self-testing and/or only working with suppliers who tested their products. For these outlets, the B2P web connected RFID/bar code product tracking tags found in the MicroMagic device would help reassure the outlet and the consumer that the product had sufficiently passed E. coli tests.

Cities, Towns, Utilities: In general, the testing of drinking water was heavily regulated and a number of tests had to be passed before the water was considered potable. Because of these requirements, using B2P's products alone would not be sufficient. However, B2P's kits could still act as a vital step in the testing process. For example, Mr. Gorman was required to send water samples to a specialized lab for final testing. However, he also wanted the convenience of being able to test the water for contamination and treat it accordingly before sending in the sample. In essence, he could use the kit to determine whether or not to disinfect a well before taking the final sample, possibly saving additional money and time. B2P products, such as the MicroMagic and testing containers, could be used to regularly monitor city water supplies and conduct "pre-tests" before sending the water to a lab for a final

report. Additional revenue could be generated by charging for data management and the sale of additional containers.

Beaches, Lakes, Rivers: Testing for E. coli in beaches, lakes, and rivers can be challenging due to their distance from water testing facilities. This causes delays in results and increases the possibility of contamination. The B2P product was ideal for this situation as local organizations could easily test the water and obtain the necessary results quickly. Dr Sharpin, keen to enter the recreational water market, noted that "If every lifeguard did a test at night, then in the morning they would know whether the water was safe for swimming, right then and there." As with testing for drinking water sources, revenue could be generated by charging for data management and the sale of additional containers.

Testing Laboratories: With the consolidation of labs within the industry, partnerships with local and regional laboratories will create an advantage to those labs that want to expand their product line. While there may be some issue with IP, a joint venture or license agreement may be a good short-term advantage to introducing the product to the U.S. market.

Consumers: Americans are increasingly concerned about food and water safety and there is a growing market within the U.S. for do-it-yourself water and food testing kits. Consumers are familiar with the Brita model of purchasing a primary water filtration unit and additional filters. This model could work well for B2P with the sale of kits that include an incubator and testing containers and subsequent sales in containers. Because B2P did not have established operation and distribution systems within the U.S., a practical option would be for the company to establish a joint venture with a consumer water filtration company. These agreements could be entered exclusively or openly. Some water options included: Culligan International Co; RainSoft Water Conditioning Co; EcoWater Systems, LLC; Kinetico, INC; Brita; Everpure; William R. Hague, INC; Atlantic

Ultraviolet Corp; CUNO; and GE Water and Process Technologies. Food partnerships could also be explored.

Competition and Challenges: The E. coli testing market had a mixture of company types, from large laboratories to consumer-oriented products, and no single company dominated the industry.[11] The majority of these organizations had aligned themselves with one industry or another. Competitive product in the existing market was in the form of test kits which had to be used in some form of laboratory with significant additional equipment and skilled personnel. While there was no direct competitor that offered B2P's combination of self-contained, reliable, do-it-yourself, fast result tests, there were organizations that did offer similar products. Bluewater Biosciences in Canada offered a do-it-yourself kit that did not require incubation. It differed from the B2P product because it took 2–3 days to obtain results and could be hazardous due to the lack of protection against breakage and spillage. Colitag, a product from CPI International was another similar product. It had been on the market for several years and featured a do-it-yourself test with results in 2–24 hours. This product required an incubator and did not offer a solution to dispose of the billions of dangerous bacteria that could be found in the test solution.

When considering the testing market, and specifically the U.S. testing market, there were several key challenges that had to be considered. They included:

- **Breadth of Services.** Many labs offered multiple types of testing. By sending samples to a lab of this kind, a company could obtain lab results for more than one contaminant.

- **Reputation.** Without a proven American track record, entering the testing market could be a challenge.
- **Regulation.** The U.S. was a highly regulated market and obtaining government approvals was expensive.[12]
- **Requirement.**[13] When possible, companies sometimes chose not to test their products at all. If testing was not required and its cost exceeded the cost of a product recall, many—especially in the meat industry—chose not to test their products.

The Future of B2P

The frightening threat of E. coli contamination in food and water will always be a problem. Fortunately, serious outbreaks can easily be prevented if the contamination is caught quickly and dealt with immediately. Thus, the need for a reliable, convenient, quick method of testing food and water provides an ample opportunity for B2P to expand its business. Their E. coli and coliform testing kits are more reliable, more efficient, and more convenient than any other product on the market, and the company has made successful inroads in Australasia. However, breaking into the lucrative European and American markets will likely take a serious commitment of both time and resources.

To maximize its chances for success, Dr. Sharpin knows B2P must answer a number of questions before moving forward. Specifically, what industries should they focus on and is the U.S. the best place to start? What kinds of challenges will the company face and how are they best overcome? And which of the many opportunities the company has available should it pursue first?

---

[11]Laboratory Testing Services in the U.S., IBISWorld Industry Report, August 19, 2009.

[12]Generally speaking, the Testing Services industry is subject to regulation by numerous government agencies and international groups. The major regulating bodies affecting the industry include: American National Standards Institute (ANSI); National Institute of Standards and Technology (NIST); U.S. Food and Drug Administration (FDA); Occupational Safety and Health Administration (OSHA); Environmental Protection Agency (EPA); and the U.S. Department of Agriculture (USDA).

[13]Laboratory Testing Services in the U.S., IBISWorld Industry Report, August 19, 2009.

POTION INC.: OUTSOURCING FOR THE FUTURE*

It had been a long month at the Internet startup. Every day for the past two weeks, Victor had spent the mornings and part of the evenings interviewing overseas companies, hoping to find a group to synthesize and organize data from the thousands of surveys that the company had collected. But time and again he had been frustrated by poor execution on the sample projects he had sent out, and he was tired of working around the local hours many international companies kept. Victor shared his frustrations with a fellow coworker, Andrew, and together the two theorized that there had to be a better way to manage outsourcing projects and to get the needed work done accurately and efficiently.

Despite more research, the two budding entrepreneurs were unable to find an existing solution to their project challenge. Frustrated, they decided that if no answer could be found, the two of them would leave their jobs and create a new solution by founding their own outsourcing company. The result was Potion Inc., a company built on the idea that outsourcing could overcome challenges without creating new ones.

Four years later, Victor and Andrew had grown Potion into a small, successful multinational organization with over 50 employees working out of management offices in New York and California and with production facilities in Delhi, India. The company relied heavily on technology of all kinds to collaborate, communicate, and manage its geographically distributed teams and clients. Based on Andrew and Victor's observation of the market place, Potion initially chose to offer high quality services in data and information management, technology development, and graphics and design to small and midsized clients.

After years of hard work, the two company leaders finally had some time to evaluate their organization and they now believed it was necessary to make another important decision. The management team had spent the last year building the company, obtaining new clients, and combating the negative stereotypes associated with off-shoring. With limited management and financial resources, Andrew and Victor needed to decide if they wanted to continue to invest time and money into obtaining new graphics and small business customers and advocate for off-shoring, or if they should use the core competencies and technology they had built to start another business that used the same backend technology and labor team. A third option would require concentrating on marketing and networking techniques to develop the company in a way that would make it more attractive for acquisition. They believed that each opportunity was doable but they wanted to make a concerted effort to focus their efforts to maximize their chances of success.

Company Background

In 2005, Andrew and Victor were working together at a small Internet startup that was working on several projects—data entry, website design,

*This case was written by Melissa Wu, a graduate of the Marshall MBA program at the University of Southern California, as a basis for class discussion. Reprinted by permission.

and market research—that could not be accomplished in a cost-effective manner internally or by a local team. The few American contractors they had found who seemed capable of doing the work were significantly outside their price range. They needed to complete these projects and add several others but did not want to expand the business too quickly or add significant overhead.

Andrew and Victor immediately considered off-shoring as a potential solution. Unfortunately, they soon discovered the pitfalls of dealing with foreign companies. Many companies they explored had problems with quality control, showed poor execution in trial runs, and had serious communication issues due to language barriers and time zone differences. Further research exposed the fact that these experiences were industry wide and that other companies had experienced similar difficulties.

Long days and late night discussions led to Andrew and Victor determining that an acceptable solution simply wasn't available. After conducting some initial research and speaking to contacts in India, the two entrepreneurs believed they could create a company that could meet the needs of their own Internet startup as well as those of other similar organizations. Needing a change and wanting to avoid any conflict of interest issues, they quit their jobs at the startup and launched their own company, Potion Inc. As the new senior management of Potion and its only two employees, Andrew and Victor believed that their business-process outsourcing company could overcome the traditional challenges of using offshore labor.

During the development of the concept behind Potion, Andrew and Victor noticed a gap in the market. Many off-shoring companies served large corporate clients but very few offered comprehensive services for startups and small to midsized companies. As a result, Andrew and Victor decided that this would be their niche, and they would focus on bringing rapid, accurate, cost-effective technology development and support to small and midsized companies. They hoped that in doing so they could provide these smaller sized companies with the labor, cost, and technical support to solve issues that arise when these companies do not have the manpower, budgets, or knowhow to organize and input data, build web-based systems, and/or manage technology projects.

Andrew and Victor also realized that the outsourcing techniques and resources they had developed could be applied outside of small and midsized company technology development. They took special notice of the graphic design industry and the magazine and publishing sector. Their analysis of these industries indicated that magazines and newspapers were suffering because of decreasing print circulation, declining advertising revenue, and other macro issues.

Although offshore production of books had become quite common, the same services were not leveraged by magazine and newspaper publishers because of those companies' need for tighter production turnarounds. The team also realized that a large portion of magazine and newspaper publishers were smaller operations and did not have the resources to access cheaper production sources overseas that would have been beneficial to their bottom line. These factors presented a clear need for a cost effective, on-demand graphics and digital production solution for the industry, so Andrew and Victor took the opportunity to move Potion into the market.

The Development of OPUS

As the company grew and expanded its capabilities and more clients came on board, Andrew and Victor faced two significant challenges. First, with more clients and projects, data management was becoming increasingly more difficult. Huge amounts of data (40–60 GB every day) were being generated by the designers in India, which then had to be organized and relayed to clients in the U.S. for approvals. Multiple rounds of notes and revisions only complicated the process. Second, potential clients were sometimes deterred by negative stereotypes associated with outsourcing. The poor work done by some overseas companies had created a negative image for outsourcing. Weak project execution and unsatisfactory results (missed deadlines, obvious errors, and incomplete final products) created the impression that overseas outsourcing resulted in lower quality.

Potion management knew that to succeed they would need to overcome these obstacles. After all, without the ability to manage more projects or bring on new clients, the company would not grow. Their solution was to create a new system that would give Potion a competitive advantage over the rest of their competition and build trust and peace of mind with new clients. This system would address their issues by making project management more efficient, accountable, and precise for customers and Potion alike, while working with existing technologies to make data management automatic.

The result of Potion's search for a technology solution was the creation of OPUS, a project management platform that uses an online interface to streamline the outsourcing process. Potion's entrepreneurial team built OPUS from the ground up by leveraging cutting edge research and open source technologies. OPUS was designed to provide transparency into the project development process for both the client and the production team. Specific OPUS features enabled clients to:

- **Create a Project.** In a few minutes, clients could create a new project on OPUS by inputting instructions, uploading documents, and generating deadlines. This enabled the project to get off to a fast, client-directed start, which ultimately sped up the entire process and increased the customer's sense of control.
- **Define Quality Parameters.** OPUS had an extensive Quality Assurance (QA) system intended to guarantee client satisfaction. Criteria lists developed by experts in various fields enabled the client to specify exactly what they would require from a finished project. While a preset list of criteria existed, the QA criteria for projects were customizable and new standards could be added to the standard QA checklists anytime.
- **Track a Project.** Project status was available for the client at all times. The client could login

to OPUS to see the status of each item in a project and to check completed items. Detailed billing data was also available.
- **Track Quality Assurance.** After work was complete, the production team was required to do a first level QA check of the project directly through the OPUS platform. This created greater accountability throughout the project's lifetime.

Giving transparency and control to the client were not the only benefits of the OPUS system. The online platform also enabled Potion clients, production teams, quality assurance teams, and management to interact efficiently, track project status, and obtain up-to-date detailed information on productivity and quality. Creating OPUS helped the Potion team and the company's clients focus on a simple workflow that held all parties accountable. For example:

- **Production Teams** received instant notification when projects were created. Team members could immediately download the project information and begin work, tracking project process on OPUS.
- **Team Leaders** used OPUS to determine the optimal allocation of work to their team members, using the skills and capacity data on OPUS. For each team member, OPUS stores detailed skill level data, as well as previous project experience. OPUS also tracked available capacity for each team member to ensure maximum schedule efficiency.
- **QA Teams** received a notification each time the Product Team completed an item, and were then required to perform at least two QA checks—one established for all Potion clients and others that were customized for the project.
- **Managers** could continually assess productivity and performance through OPUS and ensure that final delivery of each product was on time and done to perfection.

Implementing the OPUS platform had immediate benefits for Potion. By standardizing the work flow and placing clients and production teams on the same platform interface, consistency and quality improved. Clients and management were now able to monitor projects more efficiently and status updates were available at every point. Clients were no longer left wondering at what stage their projects were in the process or when they would be completed. For the Potion management team, this ability to make the client feel comfortable with the ongoing production steps was an extremely important factor in increasing customer loyalty and satisfaction. The success of OPUS even led Andrew and Victor to create a new service offering the company's unique expertise in modular technology development and aggregative design to other entrepreneurs. However, while the initial implementation of OPUS was successful, there were still improvements to be made.

Improving Communication

Communication problems are often the Achilles' heel of outsourcing companies, and despite the success of the OPUS platform, Andrew and Victor were still having trouble communicating with their offshore team. While Potion tried many technologies for daily staff interaction, such as Skype and Vonage for international calling, Webex for conference calls, and instant messaging for quick conversations, the management team found that the sheer number of emails, project tracking messages, and file transfers were overwhelming for the team in India. Managing messages was time consuming and reduced productivity. Emails were not being read and deadlines were missed, which created additional client issues, reduced the reliability of the company's product, and reinforced the negative stereotypes of overseas outsourcing. The Potion management team knew that despite having a successful project tracking system, they would need an effective communication platform as well. They hoped that by keeping messages organized and manageable, they could increase productivity and efficiency and reduce the number of mistakes being made as a result of communication issues.

The team decided that the best way to improve communication was to add functionality to OPUS itself. Revisions to OPUS were immediately implemented and a portion of OPUS was designed to enable online collaboration, message boards, data sharing, instant feedback, and knowledge management. Messages were posted on a common message board and subscribers (managers, production, clients, etc.) were notified of messages via email. These message boards helped keep message streams intact and enabled newcomers to get an overview of the project without causing delays. Additionally, the improved platform enabled clients and managers to notify the production floor of any changes in real time, reducing the likelihood of work being done on outdated assignments or specifications. All team members were trained on the new communication platform and bonuses were tied to efficiency and the amount of relevant detail provided.

Implementing the communication platform enabled the Potion team to quickly and easily organize messages and improve communication with the overseas team. Productivity increased because team members no longer needed to spend time searching through email messages or bringing new teammates up to speed. Less time spent on administrative work meant more time spent on projects and a quicker turnaround. All the data and messaging were stored in one place and maintained for the next project; and because deadlines were clear to all the members of the production team, project completion was timelier.

Marketing

With OPUS in place and communication problems minimized, Andrew and Victor were now able to increase their marketing efforts. Stereotypes about the outsourcing industry, which held that off-shoring was complicated and led to inferior quality, were limiting the number of companies that participated in the market and prevented new ones from trying it. The Potion team combated these stereotypes through a targeted marketing strategy that utilized email marketing campaigns, direct mail, and in-person meetings. The goal was to educate companies on the OPUS system and highlight the benefits of outsourcing.

Potion also positioned itself as an authority on the offshore labor industry through a public relations campaign. This effort focused on the company's experiences through traditional forums such as tradeshows and seminars, as well as guerilla marketing venues such as blogs. As a side benefit, this marketing and public relations strategy also created a passive lead source because executives discovered international outsourcing as a positive solution to corporate growth and began to inquire about Potion's services.

To further tempt customers to try off-shoring and experience the OPUS process, Potion offered a free opportunity for clients to send in samples for the Potion team to work on. By offering complimentary samples to prospective clients, Potion was able to reveal to clients the quality of work, quick turnaround time, and the system's ease of use, which had proven to be extremely successful in securing and keeping new customers.

The Future

Potion's future success will be affected by trends in the larger outsourcing industry. Off-shoring has become increasingly competitive and vendors like Potion are continually redesigning business models and service offerings to adapt to the changing market. Among the changes has been an increase in competition with the emergence of industry-specific vendors that focus on narrow fields and strive for higher quality levels. These vendors have responded to clients' calls for superior performance by implementing better planning and execution strategies. The result has been a move away from the "do-it-all" approach and toward industry specialization. Price has become less of an area of competition, allowing the evolution of more focused client-vendor relationships that can even mature into partnerships.

In terms of sheer volume, the outlook is good for companies that specialize in offshore labor. According to a study by Michael F. Corbett & Associates 2008,[1] one in four organizations plans

to increase its outsourcing spending by 25 percent or more in the near future. This translates into U.S. organizations expanding their outsourced business services from $100 billion to $318 billion. While Potion currently occupies a very small space within the outsourcing market, it provides an important and potentially lucrative service— enabling small companies and entrepreneurial startups access to affordable outsourcing. If the company can capture just 1 percent of the revenue in areas in which it is strongest (Information Technology and Sales and Marketing), Potion can anticipate over $1.3 billion in revenue.

Potion has a number of advantages in the current market. Most importantly, the OPUS interface is unique to the industry. While some competitors have elements of the system in place, none have all the pieces integrated into one platform. This gives Potion a distinct advantage when competing for clients, as they can generate successful projects and boost its reputation while competitors are still improving their systems. Another key selling point for Potion is its physical presence in the U.S. With offices in New York and Los Angeles, the company provides clients with a sense of comfort and security that other outsourcing companies do not. Customers like the ease of working with an American company with convenient business hours and no language barrier and still benefit from the cost savings provided by foreign labor.

While the outsourcing industry continues to grow and Potion is well positioned within it, there are ongoing challenges that still must be overcome. Poor project execution and unsatisfactory results continue to cause problems throughout the industry. Although Potion's implementation of OPUS has streamlined project management and largely eliminated communication woes, the company must still combat the image that outsourcing can lead to quality problems. Stereotypes continue to persist, suggesting that outsourcing is only for large organizations and is best suited to low-level non-core tasks, cost cutting, and reduction of domestic work force. As a result, there are still a number of companies that are hesitant to begin the outsourcing process. The industry

[1]Michael F. Corbett & Associates, Ltd. conducted research in 2008 with more than 500 executives.

as a whole must continue taking positive steps to overcome these negative stereotypes to ensure that opportunities within the global outsourcing marketplace continue to increase.

Within this global context, Andrew and Victor must decide what to do about the future of their company. They have spent the last few years building up the company's technology and reputation. Referrals are strong, but the negative stereotypes regarding outsourcing persist. With this background and the limited management resources, should Potion use the infrastructure and core competencies that they've set up to continue on the graphics and small business path? Should they use the core competencies to start other businesses that utilize the same backend technology and labor; or should they position their company for sale?

Relevant Chapters

Chapters 3, 6, 17

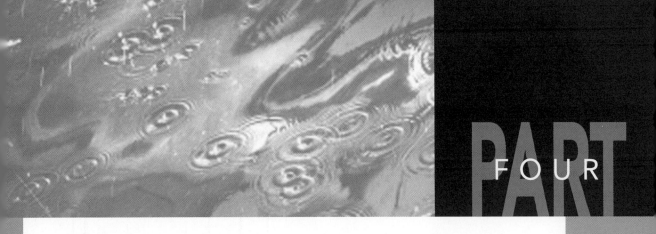

EVOLVING THE BUSINESS

UNDERSTANDING CAPITAL

"Growth is directly proportionate to promises made: Profit is inversely proportionate to promises kept."

—JOHN PEERS,
President, Logical Machine Corporation, 1979

CHAPTER OBJECTIVES

- Discuss the cost and process of raising capital.
- Explain the role of the venture capital market.
- Describe the process associated with the initial public offering.
- Discuss how to grow with strategic alliances.
- Explain ways to value a business.

It's a common phenomenon that even the savviest entrepreneurs can stumble trying to take their businesses to the next level. Marco Giannini wasn't new to entrepreneurship and he wasn't new to failure. While an MBA student at the University of Southern California, he launched Clear Day, a natural beverage company designed to take advantage of consumers' desire for functional beverages. Due to too much money spent on product development and not enough customer validation, that business failed in 2003. Not one to dwell on failure, however, Giannini decided to use his experience in functional beverages to deal with health problems in the pet industry. His childhood dog had suffered from arthritis and hip dysplasia, so he began to study how supplements in dog treats might help. After finding a manufacturer to produce his first product—Happy Hips—Giannini began driving all around California visiting pet store owners to convince them to try his product. He also handed out samples at sporting events. When a customer wrote to him to tell him that her aging dog was now able to walk normally after two years of Dogswell treats, he knew he had a hit on his hands.

In 2004, the first year of the business, revenues came in at $500,000. By 2008, the company was on the Inc. 500 list of fastest growing private companies at position 101, sporting 21 employees, an annual growth rate of 1,800 percent, and $17 million in revenues. Dogswell went from being carried by 4,000 independent pet stores to being picked up by Whole Foods Market and Target. It was now a national brand. That's when Giannini began feeling the pressure to grow the company and start competing with the large established pet food companies. To do so, he would need to develop a line of dog food. Giannini determined that he had enough cash to go ahead with the product development, and the result was a kibble that was preferred 15 to 1 over the leading brands by dog focus groups.

Because he had a brand to protect, Giannini knew he couldn't bootstrap this launch. He invested in an East Coast warehouse, hired 15 more employees, and in September of 2008, he shipped his first bags of dry dog food. But all did not go well because Giannini had used an expensive approach to get customers to try this new line. He offered a free bag of kibble with every purchase of a 15-ounce bag of Dogswell treats. At $10.99 a bag, it was costing the company $100,000 a month in rebates, and his employees were having trouble keeping up with all the incoming coupons. At the same time, Giannini and his chief financial officer were out trying to raise money from the private equity market, which was taking them away from the business for long periods at a time when they were sorely needed. Giannini managed to close a deal for investment capital with San Francisco-based TSG Consumer Partners and came back to Los Angeles, only to discover that the coupons from the new dog food line were eating up all the company's profits. The company's focus on the new product meant that they were no longer providing samples of their core product—the healthy treats—so their sales were declining.

Now Giannini had to use TSG for more than just money. Daily conversations with his TSG partner, Jenny Baxter, gave him help in analyzing Dogswell's market data and provided lessons learned from other products in TSG's portfolio of companies. Giannini quickly learned that no matter how much it was important to grow Dogswell, it was even more important to take care of the core business that had made them a success. "With all the success, I had gotten cocky...," claimed Giannini. However, now that his investors had given Dogswell a new lease on life, this time he was going to make it last.

Sources: Tiku, N. (December 2009/January 2010), "Dogswell's Ambitious Expansion Had Flopped. Would Its New

Investors Give the Company Another Chance?" *Inc Magazine*, p. 56-58; Flandez, R. (July 21, 2009), "Entrepreneurs Strive to Turn Buzz Into Loyalty," *The Wall Street Journal*, *Marketplace*, B4; and Phillips, T. (June 2008). "Functional Treats Take Off," *Petfood Industry*, p. 20–23.

The natural by-product of a successful startup is growth. But growth is costly and often puts an enormous strain on the already sparse resources of a young venture. Typically, to meet significant demand, a new company will need additional capital beyond any internal cash flows it may be generating. Growth capital, or second-round financing, consists of those funds needed to take a venture out of the startup phase and move it toward securing a market presence. To the extent that the entrepreneur has met the sales and earnings targets estimated in the startup business plan, available financing choices increase substantially when growth financing, or second-round financing, is sought. The fact that more choices are available is important because, normally, the amount of money needed to grow a business is significantly greater than that required to start a business. One exception is high-tech companies that incur considerable research and development costs prior to startup. This type of company may spend millions of dollars and accrue several years of losses before its first sale. It may also go through several rounds of financing and grants before it has something to sell to customers.

Most venture funding today is still going to biotechnology, software, and other high technology ventures, but in general, the best companies in any industry have the easiest time finding capital from any source. Being one of the "best" companies requires having an excellent track record (however short), a sound management team, a potential for high growth, and a plan for investor exit with an excellent rate of return on the money invested. Investors in growth companies typically will not go into a situation where their new money is paying off old debt or where cash flow is poor. They want to know that the infrastructure is in place, sales are increasing, and the growing venture needs capital only to take it to the next stage. This chapter looks at some of the sources of growth capital available to entrepreneurs and how to value a business to prepare for funding.

THE COST AND PROCESS OF RAISING CAPITAL

Make no mistake about it, raising growth capital is a time-consuming and costly process. For this reason, many entrepreneurs choose to grow slowly instead, depending exclusively on internal cash flows to fund growth. They have a basic fear of debt and of giving up to investors any control of or equity in the company. Unfortunately, they may act so conservatively that they actually stifle any growth. Entrepreneurs must understand the nature of raising money so that their expectations will not be unreasonable. The first thing to understand about raising growth capital (or any capital, for that matter) is that it will invariably take at least twice as long as expected before the money is actually in the company's bank account. Consider the task of raising a substantial amount of money—several million dollars, for instance. It can take several months to find the financing, several more months for the potential investor or lender to do "due diligence" and say yes, and then up to six more months to receive the money. In other words, if entrepreneurs don't look for funding until it's needed, it will be too late. Moreover, because this search for capital takes entrepreneurs away from their business just when they're needed most, it is helpful to use financial advisers who have experience in raising money, and it is vital to have a good management team in place.

The second thing to understand about raising growth capital is that the chosen financial source may not complete the deal, even after months of courting and negotiations. It's essential, therefore, to continue to look for backup investors in case the original investor backs out. If they do complete the deal, second-round investors will often request a buyout of the first-round investors, who typically are friends and family. The rationale is that these early investors have nothing more to contribute to the business and the second-round funders no longer want to deal with them. This can be a very awkward situation, because the second-round funder has nothing to lose by demanding the buyout and can easily walk away from the deal; there are thousands more out there.

It Takes Money to Make Money

It is a fact of life that it takes money to make money. The costs incurred before investor or bank money is received must be paid by the entrepreneur, whereas the costs of maintaining the capital (accounting and legal expenses) can often be paid from the proceeds of the loan or (in the case of investment capital) from the proceeds of a sale or internally generated cash flow. If the business plan and financial statements have been kept up-to-date since the start of the business, a lot of money can be saved during the search for growth capital. When large amounts of capital are sought, however, growth capital funding sources prefer that financials have the approval of a financial consultant or investment banker, someone who regularly works with investors. This person is an expert in preparing loan and investment packages that are attractive to potential funding sources. A CPA will prepare the business's financial statements and work closely with the financial consultant. All these activities result in costs to the entrepreneur. In addition, when equity capital is sought, a prospectus or offering document will be required, and preparing it calls for legal expertise and often has significant printing costs. Then there are the expenses of marketing the offering; such things as advertising, travel, and brochures can become quite costly.

In addition to the up-front costs of seeking growth capital, there are "back-end" costs when an entrepreneur seeks capital by selling securities (shares of stock in the corporation). These costs can include investment banking fees, legal fees, marketing costs, brokerage fees, and various other fees charged by state and federal authorities. The cost of raising equity capital can go as high as 25 percent of the total amount of money sought. Add to that the interest or return on investment paid to the funding source(s), and it's easy to see why it costs money to raise money.

SOCIAL ENTREPRENEURSHIP: MAKING MEANING

Investing in Ocean Power

To become a success in ocean power technology, you have to have a lot of patience and wait for just the right moment to launch a serious business and tap the investor market. Back in 1970, George Taylor and his partner Joseph Burns founded a company to design flat-panel liquid-crystal displays and sold it five years later to Fairchild Semiconductor. It was the basis for the technology used in television and computer displays today. Not satisfied to rest on their success, they looked for a technology in the energy arena. After dismissing wind technologies because of the unpredictability of wind, they settled on ocean waves. Taylor, a former surfer, invented a buoy that could convert a wave's up-and-down movement to electricity, which could then be transported via undersea cables to shore to connect with the national power grid. Scientists at Oregon State University predict that approximately 0.2 percent of the ocean's wave energy could satisfy the entire world's need for electricity. Taylor saw a perfect storm of factors creating the window of opportunity for his technology: high oil prices, climate change, unstable relationships in the Middle East, and a growing interest by investors in environmentally responsible companies.

Taylor avoided the venture capital route, preferring to seek funding from private investors who had a long-term vision. Two of his first investors were an electrical-components manufacturer and a small Australian energy company. He then took the company public on the London Stock Exchange AIM market (international market for smaller growing companies and with more flexibility in requirements than U.S. stock exchanges) and was able to raise $40 million. His goal was to create an array of 40 buoys that, linked together, could generate clean electricity at rates significantly less than coal-burning plants, which are currently the cheapest form of electricity. However, the U.S. investor market did not appear to be as enthusiastic as the international market as witnessed by Ocean Power Technologies' IPO on NASDAQ in April 2007 (NASDAQ OPTT), which was tepid at best. However, by 2010, revenues had grown to $5.1 million, up 26 percent from the previous year due to a project off the coast of Oregon and U.S. Navy projects in Spain and Hawaii. They are still considered a product-development company and they fund their research and development from external sources. The company has been on a slow growth path, but still has hopes of providing significant sources of alternative power with its PowerBuoy system.

Sources: D. Drollette, "Electricity from Wave Power," *Fortune Small Business* (December 2006/January 2007), p. 26; Ocean Power Technologies, www.oceanpowertechnologies.com, accessed October 15, 2010; and OPT Annual Report for the year ended April 30, 2010.

THE VENTURE CAPITAL MARKET

Private venture capital companies have been the bedrock of many high-growth ventures, particularly in the computer, software, biotechnology, and telecommunications industries. Venture capital is, quite simply, a pool of money managed by professionals. These professionals usually assume the role of general partner and are paid a management fee plus a percentage of the gain from any investments. The venture capital (VC) firm takes an equity position through ownership of stock in the company, and normally requires a seat on the board of directors and often brings their professional management skills to the new venture in an advisory capacity. Because traditionally venture capitalists rarely invest in startup ventures outside the high-tech arena, the growth stage of a new venture is where most entrepreneurs consider approaching them. Waiting until this stage is advantageous to entrepreneurs, because using venture capital in the startup phase can mean giving up significant control. Today, however we are seeing VCs investing in nontechnology-based deals that are located outside their immediate geographic region. The pressure to find great investments for their portfolio investors has caused them to expand the scope of the types of deals they are willing to consider.

The ability to secure classic venture capital funding depends not only on what an entrepreneur brings to the table but also on the climate in the venture capital industry. PricewaterhouseCoopers, Thomson Venture Economics, and the National Venture Capital Association have joined forces to track total venture capital investing in the United States. They report that at the historical peak in 2000, the height of the dot com/technology boom, VC investing was at $105 billion. By the end of 2003, that amount had plunged to approximately $20 billion (see Figure 16.1) and as of the end of 2009, it was at just over $18 billion. Although that is certainly a drastic decline in investment activity, it is closer to the historical norm for venture capital investment, so it may be considered a return to normal from an aberrant period.[1] Many would say that the recent trend is a healthy return to investment rates that prevailed before the dot com boom and bust. Fewer deals are being made, but those that are made are likely to fund well-conceived business concepts with solid business models. In fact, historically, difficult economic times have spawned great companies such as Compaq Computer (now owned by Hewlett Packard) in the early 1980s and Palm Computing and Starbucks in the early 1990s. Table 16.1 presents venture capital investments by industry for 2009. Clearly, biotechnology and software dominated the investment focus, followed by energy and medical devices.

FIGURE 16.1 Total Venture Capital Investing in the United States from 1995–2009

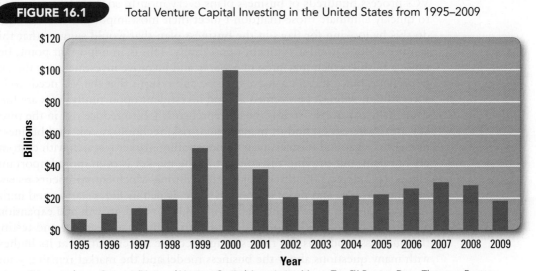

Source: PricewaterhouseCoopers/National Venture Capital Association MoneyTree™ Report, Data: Thomson Reuters.

TABLE 16.1	Industry	Amount Invested
Venture Capital Investment by Industry	Biotechnology	$3,625,730,400
	Software	$3,272,928,200
	Medical Devices and Equipment	$2,563,508,000
	Industrial/Energy	$2,339,005,500
	Media and Entertainment	$1,204,594,300
	IT Services	$1,105,848,200
	Semiconductors	$863,827,500
	Networking and Equipment	$752,079,400
	Telecommunications	$583,149,400
	Consumer Products and Services	$372,440,400
	Financial Services	$371,569,400
	Computers and Peripherals	$336,383,800
	Electronics/Instrumentation	$312,991,500
	Business Products and Services	$242,484,800
	Retailing/Distribution	$186,231,100
	Healthcare Services	$108,442,800
	Other	$9,172,800
	Total	$18,250,387,500

Source: PricewaterhouseCoopers/National Venture Capital Association MoneyTree™ Report, Data: Thomson Reuters.

The Sequence of Events in Securing Venture Capital

To determine whether venture capital is the right type of funding for a growing venture, entrepreneurs must understand the goals and motivations of venture capitalists, for they dictate the potential success or failure of the attempt. VCs process hundreds of business plans every month, so their first priority is to quickly eliminate those that don't meet their most important criteria. They do this by looking for flaws in the business plan that would suggest that this venture is not a good investment opportunity. This is an important point, because a business plan may present a viable and lucrative investment for the entrepreneur, but if it can't achieve the size and returns that the VC needs to be successful, it will not be deemed a good investment opportunity. VCs are fundamentally risk averse, so it is the entrepreneur's job to reduce risk in the three key areas where VCs find it: management risk, technology risk, and business-model risk. A sound business plan demonstrating market research with customers can help, but proving the concept in the market is even more important. Figure 16.2 depicts the three major stages during which entrepreneurs receive funding: (1) idea and proof of concept stage, which includes startup and initial survival; (2) early growth and transition; and (3) rapid growth and expansion. The first stage, identification and validation of the first customer and testing the business model, is the riskiest stage because uncertainty is at its highest with many questions about the business model and the market remaining unanswered until the second stage. VCs rarely invest at this stage even though the

FIGURE 16.2

Funding Stages
and Risk

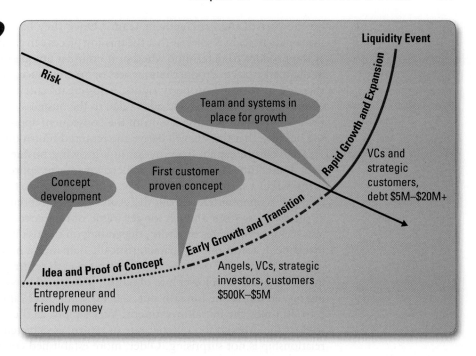

returns will be higher because the probability of not achieving those returns is also at its highest. The early growth and transition stage sees the business in operation, having proven the business model in the market, so a significant amount of risk has been reduced. VCs will enter at this stage if the potential to move into rapid growth is imminent. The third stage, rapid growth, is where most VCs invest because this stage is more likely to bring them to the liquidity event they need in three to five years to make the investment worthwhile. Most of the critical questions have been answered, the team has been proven, and now it's a matter of funding rapid growth and preparing the venture for an IPO, acquisition, or other liquidity event. At this point, funding is used to finance several stages: scale-up of manufacturing and sales, working capital for expanding inventories, receivables and payables, funding for new products, and bridge financing to prepare for an initial public offering.

When venture capitalists scrutinize a new opportunity, they typically evaluate the market, management, and technology, in that order. Market is usually first because it serves to weed out opportunities that don't solve a serious problem or don't have large markets in a fast-growing industry sector that will enable the business to do an IPO in three to five years. If the market is great (year-over-year growth of at least 25 percent and no domination by other companies), the management team does not have to be complete at the time the VC considers investing in the venture. The team does need to have technical skills, industry experience, and a track record that suggests that they could take the company to the next level of growth.[2] In addition to experience, VCs are looking for founding team commitment to the company and to growth because they recognize that growing a company requires an enormous amount of time and effort on the part of the management team.[3] Once they have determined that the management team is solid or that the missing pieces can easily be found, they look at the product to determine whether it enjoys a unique or innovative position in the marketplace. Product uniqueness or "secret sauce," especially if protected through intellectual-property rights, helps create entry barriers in the market, commands higher prices, and adds value to the business. All of these characteristics are important because it is from the consequent appreciation in the value of the business that the VC will derive the required return on investment.

The venture capital firm invests in a growing business through the use of debt and equity instruments to achieve long-term appreciation on the investment within a specified period of time, typically three to five years. By definition, this goal is often different from the goals of the entrepreneur, who usually looks at the business from a much longer frame of reference. The venture capitalist also seeks varying rates of return, depending on the risk involved. An early-stage investment, for example, characteristically demands a higher rate of return, as much as 50 percent or more annual cash-on-cash return, whereas a later-stage investment calls for a lower rate of return, perhaps 30 percent annually. Depending on the timeframe for cash-out, the VC will expect capital gains multiples of 5 to 20 times the initial investment. Very simply, as the level of risk increases, so does the demand for a higher rate of return, as depicted in Figure 16.2. This relationship is not surprising. Older, more established companies have a longer track record on which to base predictions about the future, so normal business cycles and sales patterns have been identified, and the company is usually in a better position to respond through experience to a dynamic environment. Consequently, investing in a mature firm does not command the high rate of return that investing in a high-growth startup does.

Armed with an understanding of what VCs are looking for, an entrepreneur is prepared to begin the search for a company that meets his or her needs. Because the venture capital community is fairly close-knit, at least within regions of the country, it is wise not to "shop" the business plan around looking for the best deal. It is important to do some research on the local venture capital firms to determine whether any specialize in the particular industry or type of business that the entrepreneur is growing. Getting recommendations from attorneys and accountants who regularly deal with business investments is an excellent way to find these VC firms. In fact, the best way to approach venture capitalists is through a referral from someone who knows the VC. Because VC funding is usually later-stage funding, it is likely that entrepreneurs seeking this type of funding have already tapped the angel investor network (see Chapter 15). In fact, new ventures that have successfully navigated through angel investor screenings and mentoring are typically in a more valuable position when they are introduced to the VC firm that can provide them their next round of capital. Angel networks work closely with the VC firms in their region, so they understand their strict requirements and can help prepare the new venture to meet those requirements.

The venture capital firm will no doubt ask for a copy of the entrepreneur's brief business plan with an executive summary. The executive summary is a screening device. If it can't be immediately determined that the entrepreneurial team's qualifications are outstanding, the product concept innovative, and the projections for growth realistic, the VCs will not bother to read the rest of the business plan. On the other hand, if they like what they see in the plan, they will probably request a meeting to determine whether the management team can deliver what they project. This may or may not call for a formal presentation of the business by the entrepreneur. During this meeting, the initial terms of an agreement may be discussed in a general sense, but it will probably take several meetings before a term sheet is delivered. The term sheet is essentially a letter of intent and it spells out the terms that the VC is prepared to accept. Term sheets are discussed in the next section. If the meeting goes well, the next step is due diligence—that is, the VC firm has its own team of experts check out the entrepreneurial team and the business thoroughly. If after exhaustive due diligence the VCs are still sold on the business, they draw up the term sheet, which signals the start of a negotiation. Entrepreneurs should not expect to receive funding immediately, however. Some venture capitalists wait until they know they have a satisfactory investment before putting out a call to their investors to fund the investment. Others just have a lengthy process for releasing money from the firm. The money is typically released in stages linked to agreed-upon milestones. Also, the venture capital firm will continue to monitor the progress of the new venture and probably will want a seat or several seats on the board of directors, depending on its equity stake in the company, to ensure that it has a say in the direction the new venture takes.

Getting to a Term Sheet

Getting to a term sheet is a sign that the VC firm is serious, but it does not guarantee a "done deal." The term sheet lays out the amount of investment the VC firm is willing to consider and the conditions under which it is willing to consider the funding. The entrepreneur is not required to accept the term sheet as is; it simply represents the start of a negotiating process. At the top of the term sheet will be the actual dollar amount the firm is offering and the form that those funds will take, whether that be common stock, preferred stock, a bond, promissory note, or some combination of the aforementioned. It will also set a price, usually per $1,000 unit of debt or share of stock, which represents the cost basis for investors to get into the deal. The term sheet will also refer to the "post-closing capitalization" or post-money valuation, which is the projected value of the company on the day the terms are agreed upon and accepted by all parties. For example, the VCs might offer $3 million in Series B preferred stock at $.50/share (6 million shares with a post-closing capitalization of $16 million, the VC's estimate of value; see the section on valuation). The VC firm then owns 18.7 percent of the company ($3M divided by $16M). The rest of the term sheet outlines the capital structure for the company and is discussed in the next section.

Capital Structure

It may seem that entrepreneurs are totally at the mercy of venture capitalists when it comes to the negotiation of a deal. That, unfortunately, is true if they enter a negotiation from a weak position, desperately needing the money to keep the business alive. A better approach is to go into the negotiation from a position of strength. True, venture capitalists have hundreds of deals presented to them on a regular basis, but most of those deals are not big hits; in other words, the return on the investment is not worth their effort. VCs are always looking for that one business that will achieve high growth and will return enough on their investment to make up for all the average- or mediocre-performing investments in their portfolio. If entrepreneurs enter a negotiation with a business that has a solid record of growth and performance, they are in a good position to call at least some of the shots.

Any investment deal is comprised of four components:

1. The amount of money to be invested
2. The timing and use of the investment moneys
3. The return on investment to investors
4. The level of risk involved

The way these components are defined will affect the new venture for a long time, not only in constructing its growth strategy but also in formulating an exit strategy for the investors. VCs often want both equity and debt—equity because it gives them an ownership interest in the business, and debt because they will be repaid more quickly. Consequently, they tend to want redeemable preferred stock or debentures so that if the company does well, they can convert to common stock, usually at a 1:1 ratio at the investor's option. Alternatively, if the company does poorly or fails, they will be the first to be repaid their investment. In another scenario, the VCs may want a combination of debentures (debt) and warrants, which enables them to purchase common stock at a nominal rate later on. If this strategy is implemented correctly, they may be able to get their entire investment back when the debt portion is repaid and still enjoy the appreciation in the value of the business as stockholders.

There are several other provisions that venture capitalists often request to protect their investment. One is an antidilution provision, which ensures that the selling of stock at a later date will not decrease the economic value of the VC's investment. In other words, the price of stock sold at a later date must be equal to or greater than the price at which the VC could buy the common stock on a conversion from a warrant or debenture. In addition, to guard against having paid too much for an interest in the company, the VC may request a forfeiture provision. This means that if the company does not achieve its projected performance goals, the founders may be required to give up some of their stock to the VC as a penalty. The forfeited stock increases the VC's equity in the company and may even be given to new management that the VC brings on board to steer the company in a new direction. Entrepreneurs should never accept these terms unless they are confident of their abilities and commitment to the venture. One way to mitigate this situation is for the entrepreneur to request stock bonuses as a reward for meeting or exceeding performance projections.

Venture capital is certainly an important source of funding for an entrepreneur with a high-growth venture. It is, however, only one source, and with the advice of experts, entrepreneurs should consider all other possible avenues. Clearly, the best choice is one that gives the new venture the chance to reach its potential and the investors or financial backers an excellent return on investment.

THE SUPER ANGEL MARKET

As VCs have moved farther up the business life cycle, seeking investments that are less risky and more certain of providing a liquidity event, a new group of investors has moved in to fill the gap between the traditional angel market and the VCs. These investors are known as "super angels" and they're essentially the type of investor that VC firms used to be when they were younger. A number of these super angels come out of extraordinarily successful entrepreneurial ventures such as Google, Paypal, and eBay. Although they are not professionally organized in the same manner as the VCs and some angel networks, they are commonly found using Twitter and blogging about their exploits. Unlike traditional angels who invest their own money, super angels do that and also manage the investments of friends and family. The size of their funds is definitely different from VCs, generally in the $10 million or less range, and any investment is normally in the $500,000 to $2 million range.[4]

Super angels tend to favor the types of businesses where the investment required is relatively small and it's easy to determine whether the business will be a success within six months to a year. They also prefer companies that can tolerate a slow burn rate so they can tweak the business model until they get it right. As a result, super angels seem to have a lower rate of failures than VCs. Unlike traditional angel investors who often have to stay in the venture until the VCs cash out, super angels typically exit in about four years. Many of their portfolio companies are attractive to industry leaders such as News Corp, Amazon, Google, and Microsoft because these companies can acquire them for a relatively small amount of money. For example, Invite Media, an advertising technology company, was launched in 2007, received two rounds of money from First Round Capital for less than $5 million, and was then sold to Google for $80 million.[5] For the super angels, it's a good return on investment.

THE INITIAL PUBLIC OFFERING (IPO)

Undertaking the initial public offering, or "going public," is the goal of many companies because it is an exciting way to raise large amounts of money for growth that probably couldn't be raised from other sources. However, deciding whether to do a public offering is difficult at best, because doing so sets in motion a series of events that will change the business and the relationship of the entrepreneur to that business forever. Moreover, returning to private status once the company has been a public company is an almost insurmountable task. An initial public offering (IPO) is just a more complex version of a private offering, in which the founders and equity shareholders of the company agree to sell a portion of the company (via previously unissued stocks and bonds) to the public by filing with the Securities and Exchange Commission and listing their stock on one of the stock exchanges. All the proceeds of the IPO go to the company in a primary offering. If the owners of the company subsequently sell their shares of stock, the proceeds go to the owners in what is termed a secondary distribution. Often the two events occur in combination, but an offering is far less attractive when a large percentage of the proceeds is destined for the owners, because that clearly signals a lack of commitment on the part of the owners to the future success of the business. For IPOs, market timing is critical because not every year or portion of a year is favorable for an IPO. Research suggests that the value of the stock at the time of issuance is an important determinant in the ultimate decision to issue stock.[6] The bottom line is that an IPO is never a sure thing, either for the entrepreneur or the investor. Recall what happened to Vonage, the voice-over-IP company, which debuted on the New York Stock Exchange on May 24, 2006, and within the first seven days lost approximately 30 percent of its value, precipitating a class-action lawsuit claiming that shareholders were misled.[7] This is not an uncommon occurrence, however, because historically IPOs have underperformed the broader market. One exception in recent times was the class of 2004, which performed better than any group of IPOs since 1999, with the first day jump averaging 11 percent and total return to shareholders of 34 percent on 216 companies.[8]

Recently, many smaller companies that have not found the U.S. IPO market very inviting have looked to the European and Asian markets to find money. These markets have less stringent capitalization requirements and reporting rules, and investors there are eagerly looking for technology companies in which to invest.[9] With small valuations of $10 to $60 million, these companies are very attractive to Japanese investors, for example, who typically only see later-stage Japanese companies on the Nikkei exchange. They would prefer to get in at an earlier stage where there is greater potential for larger gains. The trend of companies looking for money in foreign markets will only increase due to the global economy and the relative ease with which these markets can be tapped.

Advantages and Disadvantages of Going Public

The principal advantage of a public offering is that it provides the offering company with a tremendous source of interest-free capital for growth and expansion, paying off debt, or product development. With the IPO comes the future option of additional offerings once the company is well known and has a positive track record. A public company has more prestige and clout in the marketplace, so it becomes easier to form alliances and negotiate deals with suppliers, customers, and creditors. In addition, restricted stock and stock options can be used to attract new employees and reward existing employees. It is also easier for the founders to harvest the rewards of their efforts by selling off a portion of their stock or borrowing against it. In fact, research reveals that the median ownership percentage of officers and directors in public companies actually declines in the decade following an IPO, from about 68 percent to 18 percent, and this decline holds true not only for U.S. markets, but also for markets in Malaysia and China.[10]

Public offerings do display some serious disadvantages, however. Since 1980, more than 9,000 companies have completed initial public offerings, raising a total of $450 billion. However, research conducted in 2004 by Peristiani and Hong for the Federal Reserve Bank of New York found that in the two-decade period from 1980 to 2000, there was a dramatic decline in the pre-IPO financial condition of issuers, as well as a significant rise in the failure rate of issuers after the offering.[11] In general, those firms that undertook an IPO with negative earnings (many such cases occurred in the later part of the 1990s) were three times more likely to be dropped from a stock exchange than their profitable counterparts. In fact, 2001 saw an unprecedented 3.8 percent of all publicly traded stocks dropped from the major stock exchanges.[12] A 2010 study by the Center for Effective organizations at the University of Southern California found that investment in human resources is the most positive predictor of 90 day, 1 year, 3 year, and 5 year stock price and earnings growth for companies that survive the IPO past 5 years.[13] Those firms that scored highest on human resource factors had a 92 percent chance of survival five years after the IPO, while those firms that scored low had only a 34 percent chance of survival. What this means is that those companies that value their employees and create team cohesion in a risk-taking environment will generally outperform their less employee-oriented counterparts by a significant amount.

A public offering is a very expensive process. Whereas a private offering can cost about $100,000, a public offering can run well over $750,000, a figure that does not include a 7 to 10 percent commission to the underwriter, which compensates the investment bank that sells the securities. An IPO failure can be a financial disaster for a young company. One way to prevent such a disaster is to ask for stop-loss statements from lawyers, accountants, consultants, and investment bankers. The stop-loss statement is essentially a promise not to charge the full fee if the offering fails.

In addition to the expense, going public is enormously time-consuming. Entrepreneurs report that they spend the better part of every week on issues related to the offering over a four- to six-month period.[14] Part of this time is devoted to learning about the process, which is much more complex than this chapter can express. One way many entrepreneurs deal with the knowledge gap about the process is by spending the year prior to the offering preparing for it by talking with others who have gone through the process, reading, and putting together the team that will see the company through it. Another way to speed up the process is to start running the private corporation like a public corporation from the beginning—that is, doing audited financial statements and keeping good records.

A public offering means that everything the company does or has becomes public information subject to the scrutiny of anyone interested in the company. A shift in company control makes the CEO of a public company responsible primarily to the shareholders and only secondarily to anyone else. The entrepreneur/CEO, who before the offering probably owned the lion's share of the stock, may no longer have a controlling portion of the outstanding stock (if he or she agreed to an offering that resulted in the loss of control), and the stock that he or she does own can lose value if the company's value on the stock exchange drops, an event that can occur through no fault of the company's performance. Macroeconomic conditions, such as world events and domestic economic policy, can adversely (or positively) affect a company's stock, regardless of what the company does.

Public companies are also subject to the stringent disclosure rules under the Sarbanes-Oxley Act. This act was passed in response to accounting scandals that started with Enron Corp. and to improve the accuracy and reliability of corporate disclosures. Sarbanes-Oxley covers such issues as establishing a public company accounting oversight board, auditor independence, corporate responsibility, and enhanced financial disclosure.[15] Financial Executives International surveyed 185 companies and found that the costs to comply with Section 404 (internal controls audit requirements) had declined 5.4 percent at the same time that total audit costs were up 2 percent. That brings total audit costs on average to $3,400,000.[16]

Finally, a public company faces intense pressure to perform in the short term. An entrepreneur in a wholly owned corporation can afford the luxury of long-term goals and controlled growth, but the CEO of a public company is pressured by shareholders and analysts to show gains in revenues and earnings on a quarterly basis that will translate into higher stock prices and dividends to the stockholders.

The Public Offering Process

There are several steps in the IPO process, as depicted in Figure 16.3. The first is to choose an underwriter, or investment banker, which is the firm that sells the securities and guides the corporation through the IPO process. Often called "the beauty contest," investment banking firms parade before the company's board of directors proclaiming their strengths after which the entrepreneur chooses one or more to co-manage the IPO. Some of the most prestigious

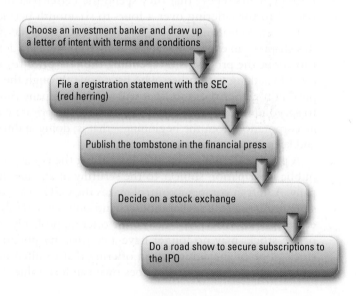

FIGURE 16.3

The IPO Process Simplified

Choose an investment banker and draw up a letter of intent with terms and conditions

File a registration statement with the SEC (red herring)

Publish the tombstone in the financial press

Decide on a stock exchange

Do a road show to secure subscriptions to the IPO

investment banking firms handle only well-established companies because they believe that smaller companies will not attract sufficient attention among major institutional investors. Getting a referral to a competent investment banking firm is a first step in the process. Investment banks underwrite the IPO based on either a firm commitment or a best efforts basis. Best effort suggests that this will not be a strong IPO and should serve as a warning to investors. A commitment, by contrast, means that the investment bank will purchase shares at a discount (typically 7 percent) and resell them at full price to institutional investors primarily, but also to individuals.[17]

The importance of investigating the reputation and track record of any underwriter cannot be overemphasized. Investment banking has become a very competitive industry, and the lure of large fees from IPOs has attracted some firms of questionable character. The entrepreneur should also examine the investment mix of the bank. Some underwriters focus solely on institutional investors; others, on retail customers or private investors. It is often useful to have a mix of shareholders; private investors tend to be less fickle than institutional investors, so their presence contributes more stability to the stock price in the market. The investment bank should also be able to support the IPO after the offering by giving financial advice, aid in buying and selling stock, and assistance in creating and maintaining interest in the stock over the long term.

Once chosen, the underwriter draws up a letter of intent, which outlines the terms and conditions of the agreement between the underwriter and the entrepreneur/selling stockholder. It normally specifies a price range for the stock, which is a tricky issue at best. Typically, underwriters estimate the price at which the stock will be sold by using a price/earnings multiple that is common for companies within the same industry as the IPO. That multiple is then applied to the IPO's earnings per share. This is only a rough estimate; the actual going-out price will not be determined until the night before the offering. If the entrepreneur is unhappy with the final price, the only choice is to cancel the offering, an action that is highly unattractive after months of work and expense.

A registration statement must be filed with the SEC. This document is known as a "red herring," or prospectus, because it discusses all the potential risks of investing in the IPO. This prospectus is given to anyone interested in investing in the IPO. It is a critical document because the SEC will render a decision on the IPO based on this statement. After filing the registration statement, an advertisement called a "tombstone" announces the offering in the financial press. The prospectus is valid for nine months; after that, the information becomes outdated and cannot be used without officially amending the registration statement. Another major decision is where to list the offering—that is, on which exchange. In the past, smaller IPOs automatically listed on the American Stock Exchange (AMEX) or the National Association of Securities Dealers Automated Quotation (NASDAQ) because they couldn't meet the qualifications of the New York Stock Exchange (NYSE). Today, with technology companies such as Amazon.com and Qualcomm listed on NASDAQ, it is the fastest-growing exchange in the nation. NASDAQ operates differently from the other exchanges. The NYSE and AMEX are auction markets with securities traded on the floor of the exchange, enabling investors to trade directly with one another. NASDAQ, by contrast, is a floorless exchange that trades on the National Market System through a network of broker–dealers from respected securities firms that compete for orders. In addition to these three, there are regional exchanges (such as the Boston stock exchange) that are less costly alternatives for a small, growing company.

The high point of the IPO process is the road show, generally a two-week whirlwind tour of all the major institutional investors by the entrepreneur and the IPO team to market the offering. This is done so that once the registration statement has met all the SEC requirements and the stock has been priced, the offering can be sold virtually in a day, before its value has a chance to fluctuate in the market. The coming-out price determines the amount of proceeds to the IPO company, but those holding stock prior to the IPO often see the value of their stock increase substantially immediately after the IPO. The final price is typically agreed upon by the company and its underwriters the day before the offering. In some cases, IPOs reach the final stage only to be withdrawn at the last minute. After the dot com bust, many companies had to pull their plans for an initial public offering because institutional investors were backing away from the public markets. More recently, in August 2006, The Go Daddy Group Inc., a prominent Internet domain registrar, pulled its IPO filing after the SEC had declared it a go. CEO/founder Bob Parsons explained that there were three reasons for the decision: (1) IPO market conditions were not favorable due to volatile global conditions such as the Iraq War, rising oil prices, and poor performance by tech stocks in general; (2) the quiet period (required from the time a filing is made until one month after the stock is available in the market) posed a significant problem for the CEO, who had a regular radio show that would have to be discontinued; and (3) the company really didn't have to go public because the sole investor was Bob Parsons. At the start of the process, it looked like a good thing to do, but by the time the IPO was to occur, the environment had changed.[18] An entrepreneur who is considering doing an IPO should look at the condition of the market and very carefully weigh the pros and cons of becoming a public company at that time.

An Easier IPO

Despite the value of being a public company in terms of accessing large amounts of capital relatively easily, it is still beyond the reach of many small companies. Martin Lightsey's company, Specialty Blades, a medical and industrial blade manufacturer with 100 shareholders and $6 million in annual sales in 2006, was faced with shareholders who wanted to cash in some of their earnings. Lightsey learned of a little-known exemption in the SEC regulations that permitted an intrastate offering so that Lightsey could sell stock to Virginia residents without having to register with the SEC. Intrastate offerings give entrepreneurs the right to create small local stock exchanges through investment banking firms with shareholders in a single state. Not all businesses can apply, however; the requirements are that the company hold less than $10 million in assets and have fewer than 500 shareholders.[19] The company must also earn more than half of its revenue from operations within the state in which it filed. The reason that not too many offerings of this type have occurred is because of the strict residency requirements. If even a single share of stock is sold to a nonresident or traded to someone in another state within nine months of the offering, the entire offering will be declared void and the entrepreneur will have to buy back all the stock.

GROWING VIA STRATEGIC ALLIANCES

Strategic alliances with larger companies are also an excellent source of growth capital for young companies. A strategic alliance is defined as "a close collaborative relationship between two or more firms with the intent of accomplishing mutually compatible goals that would be difficult for each to accomplish alone."[20] Sometimes the partnership results in major financial and equity investments in the growing venture. Such was the case for United Parcel Service of America, which acquired Mail Boxes Etc. (MBE) for $191 million in 2001 after that company had become the industry leader. Growing companies that link with established companies usually get a better deal than they would have gotten from a venture capitalist. In addition, they derive some associated benefits that give them more credibility in the marketplace. Recent research suggests that in a global economy a significant portion of entrepreneurial success is the result of the ability to access formal and informal business networks.[21] In particular, ventures with new inventions but no expertise in commercialization and no social capital are more inclined to seek out partnerships, particularly for manufacturing and distribution.[22] Furthermore, where the environment is characterized by high levels of uncertainty, small businesses use a network of partners as a hedge against the risks associated with this type of environment.[23] The large investing partner is looking for a return of the cost of capital and, in general, for a return of at least 10 percent on the investment.

Strategic alliances are every bit as tricky as partnerships, so the potential partner must be evaluated carefully, and due diligence must be conducted on the company to make sure that it is everything it claims to be. The entrepreneur should examine the potential partner's business practices, talk to its customers and value chain members, and make sure that this company will make the entrepreneur's company look good. It is also crucial not to focus on one potential partner but, instead, to consider several before making a final decision. It probably is wise not to form a partnership that makes one of the partners (usually the smaller company) too heavily dependent on the other for a substantial portion of its revenue-generating capability. This is a dangerous position to be in and can spell disaster if the partnership dissolves for any reason. For the partnership to work best, the benefits should flow in both directions; that is, both partners should derive cost savings and/or revenue enhancement from the relationship. Strategic partnerships are a natural offshoot of a global economy that has been flattened by the Internet. Entrepreneurs should view these partnerships as one effective alternative to grow their ventures.

VALUING THE BUSINESS

A key component of any financial strategy is determining the value of the company, because a realistic value figure is needed no matter which avenue is taken to raise growth capital. However, valuation of early-stage private companies is typically a very subjective process fraught with the challenge of predicting future earnings in a highly uncertain environment and with no track record on which to base these projections. Moreover, the already difficult task of valuation is exacerbated by the fact that most of the valuable assets that companies hold are intangible. That is, they consist of patents, knowledge, and people instead of plant and equipment.[24] Calculating value is fundamentally challenging because *value* is a subjective term with many meanings. In fact, at least six different definitions of value are in common use. They can be summarized as follows:

Fair market value—the price at which a willing seller would sell and a willing buyer would buy in an arm's-length transaction. By this definition, every sale would ultimately constitute a fair market value sale.

Intrinsic value—the perceived value arrived at by interpreting balance sheet and income statements through the use of ratios, discounting cash-flow projections, and calculating liquidated asset value.

Investment value—the worth of the business to an investor based on his or her individual requirements in terms of risk, return, tax benefits, and so forth.

Going-concern value—the current financial status of the business as measured by financial statements, debt load, and economic environmental factors (such as government regulation) that may affect its long-term continuation.

Liquidation value—the amount that could be recovered by selling off all the company's assets.

Book value—an accounting measure of value that reflects the difference between total assets and total liability. It is essentially equivalent to shareholders' or owners' equity.

In today's economy, those who finance ventures also use some new, nonfinancial yardsticks to measure value. These include:

- The experience level of the management team
- The innovative level of the firm's distribution channels
- The nature of the company's relationships in the industry and with customers
- The company's ability to be fast and flexible
- The company's amount and kind of intellectual property

In January 2007, *Inc. Magazine* conducted a study of private business valuation to learn which types of businesses command a premium against their earnings when they're sold. What they found was that companies doing business in the life sciences, energy, financial services, and technology sectors commanded high sales multiples with median sales prices of $100 million, while day-care centers, plumbers, and retailers produced very modest multiples, with median sales prices of $100,000. The most valuable types of companies were garnering 16:1 ratios of their sale price to their annual revenue while the discount zone businesses commanded 8:10 ratios and worse.[25]

The following sections examine some financial measures for business valuation. The first thing to know about valuation is that nearly all techniques rely on the analysis of the future market for the company's products. This is why neither book value nor liquidation value is a satisfactory method, except to establish a residual value to use in a discounted cash flow method. Further, with more businesses—and more new businesses—relying on intangible assets, book value does not make sense. Market multiples such as price/earnings (P/E) ratios are often used by venture capitalists, but their use is speculative because they are based on public companies in the industry and on the bet that the new company will go public in three to five years. The discounted cash flow (DCF) method is probably the technique most commonly used to account for the going-concern value of a business, but it has problems as well. In the following sections, we look at several of the more commonly used methods for applying a value to a business. In general, a combination of methods will help the entrepreneur arrive at a range of possible values. Negotiation between buyer and seller will ultimately determine the real value of the business.

Comparables

Comparables are a common way to get a fix on the value of a new venture. Comparable companies are those that have similar value characteristics to the new venture, such as risk, rate of growth, capital structure, and the size and timing of cash flows.[26] The most challenging aspect of using comparables is the ability to find actual valuation numbers on other privately held firms to use as comparables. When numbers are found, they may not be accurate or the assumptions used to make the valuation may not be known. To successfully use comparables, nonfinancial measures also need to be used to gauge the value of the new venture. For example, a technology firm can be assessed based on the number of patents it holds and compared against other similar firms in that manner. Simply comparing a new venture to a public company is specious at best because the shares of a private company do not have the marketability of public stock, so an arbitrary discount rate must be applied. In general, comparables should be used only to validate or support findings arrived at by more appropriate means.

Multiple of Earnings

A multiple of earnings is frequently used to value publicly owned companies because the technique is simple and direct. The first step is to figure normal earnings and then capitalize them at some rate of return or at a multiple of earnings. The rate of return or multiple used is based on assumptions about the company's risk level and projected future earnings, so the greater the potential

TABLE 16.2		
	Net income plus depreciation	$ 2,425,000
Using Multiples to Calculate Value	Earnings multiple	6X
	Company value including long-term debt	$17,953,410
	Less outstanding debt	$1,500,000
	Company value	$16,453,410

earnings, the higher the multiple will be. Similarly, the greater the risk, the lower the multiple. Table 16.2 presents some information used to calculate the value of a hypothetical company.

A variation of this method, which typically results in a higher valuation, is multiplying a year's worth of after-tax earnings by an industry average multiple based on the P/E ratio of public companies in the industry. This method must be used with care. To say that a young private company with earnings of $250,000 in an industry where the average P/E is 12 should be valued at $3 million is probably overstating the case. It has been suggested that public firms have a premium value of about 25 to 35 percent over closely held companies because they are more highly regarded by the financial community. It is also important to remember that public companies are subjected to greater scrutiny than private companies, so any P/E multiple that is used should be discounted to reflect that premium.[27] Even with discounting, the variation in the ways in which a company can calculate earnings, and the difficulty in finding a public company that is comparable, make multiple of earnings a dubious measure for purposes of valuation. Nevertheless, many venture capital firms use one or another version of industry multiples.

Discounting Cash Flows

If valuing the business by its potential earning power is the goal, the most common measure—and the one that gives the most accurate results (assuming forecasts are correct)—is discounted future cash flows, because only cash or cash equivalents are used in the calculations. The method is called discounted cash flow analysis, or capitalization of future cash flows to the present value. This simply means calculating how much an investor would pay today to have a cash flow stream of X dollars for X number of years into the future.

There are four components of the DCF that must be addressed:

1. *The assumptions.* Assumptions define the model for conducting the business and take into account sales, R&D, manufacturing costs, selling costs, and general and administrative costs. These should be benchmarked against the growth of other successful companies in the industry.

2. *Forecast period.* Typically, the forecast period is three to five years and reflects the length of time that investors intend to have a stake in the venture.

3. *Terminal value.* Terminal value is the going-concern value at the end of the projection period, assuming that the company will continue in operation into the foreseeable future (in perpetuity). It may be thought of as a perpetuity, which assumes no growth and constant earnings (annual payment

divided by the cost of money), or as a growth in perpetuity, which estimates a growth rate and profitability. The estimate of terminal value is significant because most of the company's value in the early stages lies in the terminal value. The terminal value is found by the following formula:

$$TV_t = [CF_t * (1 + g)] / (r - g)$$

where t is time, r is the discount rate, and g is the growth rate in perpetuity. Although price/earnings ratios and market-to-book value multiples are sometimes used to calculate terminal value, they are simply shortcuts so the outcomes produced from using them are frequently suspect.[28]

4. *Discount rate.* The discount rate determines the present value of the projected cash flows and is, in reality, the expected rate of return for the investor.

For this analysis, pro forma cash flow statements for the business are used and a forecast period is determined. (Refer to Chapter 8 for a discussion of pro forma cash flows and methods for forecasting sales and expenses.) The length and nature of business cycles in the industry must be understood to decide whether the forecast period goes from trough to trough or from peak to peak. In other words, the forecast period must include at least one complete business cycle in order to give a fair representation of the effect of that cycle on cash flow.

Once the forecast period has been defined and the cash flow projections prepared, a discount rate must be chosen. This is not a purely arbitrary exercise. The buyer's or investor's point of view must be considered, and that viewpoint will often include the opportunity cost of investing in or buying this business. Table 16.3 lists the main categories of factors that influence the discount rate and examples of each. It should be observed that these factors are highly subjective and difficult to quantify; yet, they must be considered when making

TABLE 16.3	Factor Categories	Factors That Affect Risk
Risk Adjustment Factors	External Environmental Factors	Economic expectations
		Current status of the economy
		Current status of the industry
		Trends in the industry
		Competitive environment
	Firm Factors	Expectations for the success of the business
		Current financial condition
		Competitive position
		Business size and type
		Management team quality
		Reliability of financial forecasts
	Investment Factors	Amount of capital to be invested
		Risk of this investment relative to others
		Probability of a liquidity event
		Amount of management team support required
		Expectations for capital appreciation

Source: Adapted from J.H. Schilt (1991), www.nacva.com/FTT_PDF/Chapter5+.pdf, p. 51.

a decision about how to discount the cash-flow projections based on risk. In general, three broad factors should be considered.

1. *The rate achievable in a risk-free investment such as U.S. Treasury notes over a comparable time period.* For example, for a five-year forecast, the current rate on a five-year note is appropriate.

2. *A risk factor based on the type of business and the industry, which should be added to the interest rate.* Several precedents for determining what these factors are have been established over years of study. One accepted standard is that offered by James H. Schilt[29] in the form of five categories of business. Note that even within each category, there is room for degrees of risk. The percentages given should be considered for their relative value rather than as absolute values. For example, Category 5 businesses are perhaps the most risky in terms of investment and, therefore, experience the biggest percentage reduction in value.

   a. Category 1: Established businesses with good market share, excellent management, and a stable history of earnings: 6–10 percent
   b. Category 2: Established businesses in more competitive industries, still with good market share, excellent management, and a stable earnings history: 11–15 percent
   c. Category 3: Growing businesses in very competitive industries, with little capital investment, an average management team, and a stable earnings history: 16–20 percent
   d. Category 4: Small businesses dependent on the entrepreneur or larger businesses in very volatile industries; also the lack of a predictable earnings picture: 21–25 percent
   e. Category 5: Small service businesses operating as sole proprietorships: 26–30 percent

   It is important to note that the risk premium chosen from this list is then added to the risk-free rate, producing the risk-adjusted capitalization rate that is used to discount the projected cash flow stream.[30]

3. *The life expectancy of the business.* Discounting is typically based on this factor. The example in Table 16.4 illustrates this valuation method. Assuming

Assume: 6% risk-free rate
+14% risk factor (Category 2 business)
20% discount rate

Discount the Cash Flow

End of Year	Cash Flow ($000)	Factor (20%)	Present Value
1	200	.8333	166.7
2	250	.6944	173.6
3	300	.5787	173.6
4	375	.4823	180.9
5	450	.4019	180.9
Totals	$1,575		$875.7

that the current rate on a ten-year Treasury note is 6 percent and that the business is a Category 2 business with a 14 percent risk factor, the adjusted discount rate becomes 20 percent. Using a calculator or a present value table, one can calculate the present value of the five-year cash flow stream. The hypothetical business in this example will generate $1,575,000 of positive cash flow over five years. Hence, a buyer would be willing to pay $875,700 today for that business, given the discount rate.

It is possible to estimate different cash flow scenarios based on best-case, most-likely case, and worst-case assumptions, which will provide a range of values for the business. Then a probability can be assigned to each scenario based on the likelihood that the scenario will occur, and the discounted cash flow can be multiplied by that probability to arrive at an adjusted present value. Once a mathematical estimate of value has been achieved, other factors will come into play that are difficult to put into the equation and are more rightly points of negotiation. All the projections used in the valuation of the business are based on assumptions, and the buyer/investor is likely to question them and perhaps to discount the value of the business even further.

Another factor affecting the final valuation is the degree of legitimate control the owner has over the business. This is typically measured by the amount of stock the owner holds. Buying out an owner who holds the majority of the stock is more valuable than buying out one who does not hold a majority interest. A company in which the entrepreneur can control the majority of the stock is more valuable than one in which the entrepreneur holds only a minority interest. Finally, marketability of the company and intangibles such as a loyal customer list, intellectual property, and the like create additional value. The "real" value or market value of the business will ultimately be determined through negotiation with investors, lenders, or underwriters. However, doing the calculations just discussed provides an excellent point of departure for those negotiations.

The Real Options Model

Where an investor has the ability to make decisions about whether to invest now or at some milestone in the future, whether to invest for a particular outcome from many possible outcomes or not, or decide not to go forward with a deal, discounted cash flow models do not accurately measure the value of the company involved in the investment decision. Furthermore, given that VCs typically fund a company in stages based on achieving performance milestones, it makes more sense to use an option-pricing technique that is derived from financial options applied to securities, currencies, and commodities. In a new venture, this technique is applied to the entrepreneur's options under changing circumstances.[31] They are called real options, as opposed to options as used with financial instruments, because they refer to tangible choices such as—in the case of a new venture—investing in research and development of a new technology. The investor calculates the probability that specific events will occur and how they will affect the investment in a new venture. Recall that investors are always attempting to reduce their risk, so a real options method enables them to consider the best time to invest for the least risk. For example, suppose that an investor is looking at a company that requires a $10,000 investment today to generate revenues from one of three projected revenue scenarios in the next year. Discounted to today's dollars, those projected revenues could turn out to be $15,000, $12,000, or $5,000 and so the net present value of the investment would be $5,000, 2,000, or –$5,000. Traditional discounted cash flow analysis often yields a negative net present value for many scenarios, and the potential investor who relied on it would decide not to invest in the new venture. However, if the investor were allowed to delay his investment one year, he would gain additional information and may be able to avoid the scenario of investing when the revenues are negative $5,000. In other words, the investor would have reduced his risk to $5,000 and $2,000 because the risk of the third scenario (–$5,000) is now zero. Under a real options approach, the question is whether the future earnings of the company are greater than the cost to grow the business to the level where it can achieve those earnings. In other words, is the return on investment greater than the cost of the investment? Using real options as a valuation method is more complicated than can be presented here, and it is not yet in common use within the private equity community despite its benefits for early-stage investments.

The Venture Capital Model

Often employed in the private equity arena to value investments with negative cash flows and earnings but with future promise, the VC firm determines what return on investment is required during the holding period it desires. It then applies a P/E ratio or multiple of earnings to the estimated future value of the venture at the end of that period, which is equivalent to its terminal value. The terminal value is then discounted based on the targeted rate of return the investor is seeking.

Discounted TV = TV / (1 + Target Return)$^{\#years}$

Percentage ownership is then calculated using the following formula:

Required Ownership Percent = Investment Amount / Discounted Terminal Value

For example, suppose a company required an investment of $5 million over three years. Considering the high risk of an early-stage venture, the VC wants a 50 percent return on the initial investment and forecasts that the company's after-tax earnings in the third year will be $10 million. The investor sets the P/E ratio at 8 on the basis of comparables in the public market and multiplies that times the $10 million to get the terminal value in year three. Using the formulas shown previously, the investor would expect to receive a 21 percent ownership stake in the company assuming no additional capital was raised during that time that might dilute the VC's interest:

Discounted TV = ($10M × 8) / (1 + .50)^3 = $23.7 million
Required Percent of Ownership = $5M/$23.7M = 21%

Valuation is by its very nature an incremental process of bringing together key pieces of information that give some insight into the health and future of the business. In all discussions of value, the entrepreneur should be clear about whose definition of value is being used. In general, what a willing buyer and seller can agree on under normal market conditions is the real value of the company at a particular point in time. With a new venture, there are many financing options. However, creating a capital structure that works depends in large part on creativity and persistence in securing, at the right price, the capital needed to launch the venture successfully. Growing a venture requires substantial resources, but if the company has established a healthy track record and has good potential for growth, the number of resources available to the business increases substantially. Preparing for growth is the subject of Chapter 17.

New Venture Action Plan

- Determine how much growth capital will be needed and at what stages.
- Develop a strategy for seeking growth capital.
- Consider whether and, if so, when to proceed with an IPO.
- Establish a value for the business.

Questions on Key Issues

1. At what stage of venture development do venture capitalists typically become involved, and why?
2. For what kind of business would soliciting private venture capital be a logical financial strategy for growth? Why?
3. How can strategic alliances be used to help grow the business?
4. What are some things that an entrepreneur should do to prepare for a public offering before the year of "going public"?
5. In approaching a venture capitalist, how can the entrepreneurial team deal from a position of strength?
6. What are the key components in valuing a new or growing venture?

Experiencing Entrepreneurship

1. Interview a partner in a venture capital firm. Ask the partner to describe a recent investment that the firm completed. What were the critical factors that made the firm decide to invest? Discuss your findings in a two-page report.
2. Locate a business that was recently sold or had an initial public offering. Talk to a principal and, if possible, to the buyer or investment banker to learn what was considered when they valued the company. How much of the decision on valuation was based on negotiation and nonmonetary factors?

Relevant Case Studies

Case 8 Demand Media
Case 9 The Case of Google, Inc.

MANAGING GROWTH

"No great thing is created suddenly."

—EPICTETUS,
c. 60–120, Roman Stoic philosopher

CHAPTER OBJECTIVES

- Explore strategic innovation as a growth strategy.
- Discuss intensive growth strategies—growing within the current market.
- Explain integrative growth strategies—growing within the industry.
- Examine diversification growth strategies—growing outside the industry.
- Consider growing by going global.

The Dead Sea, bordering Jordan and Israel, is known for containing the highest concentration of minerals in the world, about 32 percent, and those minerals are purportedly important to the maintenance of healthy, supple skin. Bathers in the Dead Sea float rather than sink because of the healthy salts it contains. Moreover, because this body of water is at the lowest point on earth—1,300 feet below sea level—it has natural filters that act like sunscreen. For hundreds of years, a variety of dermatological diseases, rheumatic ailments, and respiratory problems have been treated with the natural ingredients found in the Dead Sea.

In 1988, spa technician Ziva Gilad began noticing that tourists coming to the Dead Sea were bottling up the mud and taking it home. This sparked an opportunity that led to the launching of Ahava, a venture to sell bottles of mud and salt crystals in stores throughout Israel. In its first year, the company took in $1 million in revenues. However, Gilad and her partners realized that they ultimately needed to become a global company if they wanted to achieve sustainable success because the market in Israel was only 7 million total. Ahava was the sole company with a license to mine the minerals in the Dead Sea, so that gave the company a serious competitive advantage. In addition, rather than selling in an ad hoc fashion, the company wisely concentrated on high-end chains such as Nordstrom and Sephora. Capitalizing on the trend toward natural ingredients in cosmetics, Ahava also opened retail stores in Berlin, London, Singapore, and Israel, with plans to open additional stores in the U.S.

Despite early success, the skin care market is not an easy one to penetrate because women generally experiment less in this area than they do with makeup. In addition, there are political issues facing the company that could hurt its efforts to grow. In some countries, Israeli products have been banned or have elicited protests. More than politics, ecology may be the biggest challenge to Ahava's growth. The fact is that the Dead Sea is dying because the majority of its water comes from Jordan and Israel, and both countries have diverted large quantities of this water for irrigation and drinking. Ahava is doing its best to restore the water levels in the Dead Sea by collaborating with Jordan and an organization that is working to make the Dead Sea one of the new seven wonders of the world, right alongside the Grand Canyon and the Great Barrier Reef.

Sources: Lev-Ram, M. and Shalem, M. (December 2009/January 2010) "Money From Mud," *Fortune Small Business*, p. 69; and "The Earth's Precious Wellspring of Vitality," www.ahavaus.com, accessed October 17, 2010.

Expansion is a natural by-product of a successful startup. Growth helps a new business secure or maintain its competitive advantage and establish a firm foothold in the market. It is the result of a strong vision on the part of the entrepreneur and the founding team that guides decision making and ensures that the company stays on course and meets its goals. Some entrepreneurs shy away from growth because they're afraid of losing control. That fear is not unfounded; many businesses falter during rapid growth because of the enormous demands placed on the company's resources. In fact, it is unlikely that a business can consistently grow over its life without ever faltering.[1] Of the original Forbes 100 list of most powerful companies in 1917, only

18 companies remained in the top 100 by 1987, and 61 had ceased to exist. Of the remaining group, only General Electric Co. and Eastman Kodak Co. outperformed the S&P 500's 7.5 percent average return over the 70-year period, and they surpassed it by only 0.3 percent.[2] A pretty dismal record overall, but it is similar to the records of companies that have fallen off the New York Stock Exchange and the NASDAQ since their inception. The truth is that all companies have periods in which they appear to stall, but the larger a company gets the more its growth rate slows.[3] What this means to the entrepreneur is that sustaining double-digit growth over the long term is probably not possible. But with solid planning in place before growth occurs, many of the pitfalls of rapid growth can be avoided, and growth can continue for a longer time than otherwise would be possible.

The Inc. 500 companies are representative of rapidly growing private ventures, and the statistics about them reveal some interesting patterns. It is particularly relevant to view the 2010 crop of companies that have over the past decade seen two wars, the September 11, 2001, tragedy at the World Trade Center in New York, a financial disaster, and two recessions. According to *Inc. Magazine's* annual survey for 2010, the highest rates of growth were sustained in environmental services and consumer products companies. The top five growth companies were found in the following industries: energy, online retailing, staffing, consulting, and advertising. Table 17.1 displays the top 10 companies by growth rate, and it provides a sense of the diversity in types of companies that grow rapidly. It also reflects the trend in the U.S. of moving away from production to service.

High-growth companies stand out from the crowd because they display some very distinct characteristics. Typically, they are early leaders in a niche

TABLE 17.1	Top 10 Inc. 500 Companies by Growth Rate		
Company	**Location**	**3-Year Growth Rate**	**What the Company Does**
Ambit Energy	Dallas, TX	20,369.42%	Electricity and natural gas provider
ModCloth	Pittsburgh, PA	17,190.98%	Vintage clothing online retailer
Luke & Associates	Merritt Island, FL	16,636.55%	Provides medical staffing and military contracting services
Lexicon Consulting	El Cajon, CA	14,017.74%	Linguistic and cultural training to U.S. troops deploying to Iraq and Afghanistan
WDFA Marketing	San Francisco, CA	13,969.46%	Advertising agency
Coyote Logistics	Lake Forest, IL	13,846.79%	Helps companies coordinate truck and train shipments for environmental and economic efficiency
Debt Free Associates	Oklahoma City, OK	12,376.19%	Debt consolidation company
LifeLock	Tempe, AZ	11,474.27%	Identity theft protection
Carbonite	Boston, MA	11,207.60%	Online backup software
KPaul	Indianapolis, IN	10,925.57%	Government contractor

Source: Based on the 2010 Inc. 500 Fastest Growing Private Companies, www.inc.com.

market that they created to serve an unmet need. They are often better at what they do than their competitors, leaner in their operations, and unique in what they offer. Being early in the market with a new product or service, if executed effectively, is one of the strongest competitive advantages. It provides a chance to establish brand recognition so that customers immediately think of the company when they contemplate a particular product or service. This strategy has the potential to enable entrepreneurial ventures to set the standards for those who follow. This was certainly the strategy of Samuel Adams in the microbrewed beer industry, Amazon.com in the online book industry, and Microsoft in the operations and applications software industry. By combining an entrepreneurial strategy with solid resources, innovative processes, leaner operations, and a unique, innovative product or service, companies can create formidable barriers to competition.

However, being first mover is also a risky strategy for most entrepreneurs because they may not fully understand customer needs or the best features and benefits to meet those needs. The new venture business model is generally untested and it either burns out or creates enough hype that the company is acquired. With the exception of the life sciences where, because of huge development costs and intellectual property protections, it is critical that new drugs and the like be first to market. The reality is that none of the technology market leaders were first movers. Even Google, arguably one of the most successful technology companies, was not the first mover when it introduced Google AdWords, the hugely successful pay-per-click search and advertising engine. A little company called Goto.com (which later became Overture) actually introduced the concept behind pay-per-click advertising in 1998, two years before Google AdWorks was launched. Goto.com was ultimately acquired by Yahoo for $1.6 billion, but Google went on to be worth more than $25 billion. Being number two or three in a market can be a winning strategy, primarily because pioneers usually haven't perfected the product or service, so the number two or three entrepreneur can learn from number one's mistakes and better serve customers' needs. It is also a fact that the failure rate for first movers is high, by some estimates 47 percent, while a fast follower who enters early but not first has a failure rate of about 8 percent.[4] Given that markets tend to evolve over many years, there are many opportunities to enter a market and become successful often long after the pioneer has entered.

TO GROW OR NOT TO GROW

Some entrepreneurs make a conscious choice to control growth even in the face of extraordinary market demand. This is not to say that growth is slowed to single digits. Instead, an entrepreneur may choose to maintain a relatively rapid growth rate of 25 to 45 percent per year in the early years rather than subject the young venture to a roller-coaster ride in the triple digits. In general, entrepreneurs who restrain growth do so because they are in business for the long term; in other words, they're not in a hurry to harvest their newly created wealth by selling the business or doing a public offering. They also typically don't like to take on a lot of debt or give up equity to grow. Consequently, they don't advertise heavily, and they don't aggressively seek new customers beyond their capabilities. They also diversify their product or service line from the beginning to make themselves independent of problems that may face their customers or their industries. By offering a diversified product/service line, slow-growth entrepreneurs maintain multiple streams of revenue that protect them from the loss of any one customer or market.

Nevertheless, it is intoxicating for an entrepreneur with a new venture to realize that potential demand for its product or service is enormous and that the company could grow well beyond industry averages. But "hyper-growth" has destroyed many companies that did not have the capacity, skills, people, or systems in place to meet demand. For example, the failure of American Home Mortgage Investment, a victim of the subprime mortgage collapse of 2007, suggests that even traditional businesses that grow too fast without having a plan in place to deal with the inevitable economic downturns will collapse. The growth phase of a new business can be one of the most exciting times for entrepreneurs. However, if they have not prepared for growth with a coherent plan and a budget to match, it can be disastrous.

How, then, do entrepreneurs decide whether to grow or not to grow? In many cases, it may not be the entrepreneur's decision at all; demand for the product or service may compel the entrepreneur to keep up to survive, or, by contrast, the market may not be big enough to enable the company to grow much at all. Making the decision about the strategy and timing of growth requires leadership. When entrepreneurs start businesses, they are involved in every one of the business's activities, but as the company begins to grow, they find it necessary to delegate tasks to others. The more they delegate, the more they realize that their job has suddenly changed. Now they're not needed to do the fundamental tasks of the business; they are needed to lead the business—to make sure that the original vision becomes reality. Everyone looks to the entrepreneur to ensure that the company survives. Because leadership involves guiding the company and its people to achieve the company's goals, entrepreneurs must have the ability to inspire people to action to accomplish those goals. Employees must be given opportunities to learn and develop their skills because a company can't successfully grow and change if its people don't grow and change with it. Employees should be encouraged to stretch beyond what they knew when they were hired in the early days of the company to learn more aspects of the business, and to offer input into how the business is run.

Everyone in the organization must be responsible and accountable for the success of the company. Everyone should understand what he or she contributes to the financial success of the company, and everyone should have a stake in that financial success. Rapid growth requires teamwork, and for teams to operate effectively, they must be given responsibility and accountability for what they do. There are times, however, when saying no to growth makes sense for a business. For example, Cardinal Partners' managers learned early on to say no to clients who pulled their small executive search firm away from its core values and mission. Even though the company was growing quickly, Jayne Cardinal, its founder, noticed that its profit margin remained low and that, even as it took on more clients, the company's earnings remained flat. Cardinal pulled her team together and started asking questions. To her amazement, she discovered that everyone had a different vision of the company and where it was going. No wonder they had problems defining the right customer for the company. Once Cardinal conveyed her vision to the employees, they worked together to define their customers and say no to those who didn't match their model. In the end, the company grew faster and remained healthy with a more focused strategy.

STAGES OF GROWTH IN A NEW VENTURE

Rates and stages of growth in a new venture vary by industry and business type; however, there appear to be some common issues that arise during growth that suggest areas of strategic, administrative, and managerial problems. The importance of knowing when these issues will surface cannot be overstated, for it should be part of the entrepreneur's well-orchestrated plan to anticipate events and requirements before they occur. Research results suggest that organizations progress sequentially through major stages in their life and development.[5] Still other studies have noted that at each stage of development, the business faces a unique set of problems.[6] The stages of growth (see Figure 17.1) can be described as four phases through which the business must pass. (1) Startup is characterized by concerns about capital, customers, and distribution; (2) initial growth, by concerns about cash flow and marketing; (3) rapid growth, by concerns about resources, capital, and management; and (4) stable growth, by concerns about innovation and maintaining success.

Startup Success

During startup, the first stage, the entrepreneur's main concerns are to ensure sufficient startup capital, seek customers, and design a way to deliver the product or service. At this point, the entrepreneur is a jack-of-all-trades, doing everything that needs to be done to get the business up and running. This includes securing suppliers, distributors, facilities, equipment, and labor. The very complexity of startup is one reason why many new ventures fail. Complexity also suggests that a team-based venture is better equipped to achieve a successful launch than a solo effort. If the company survives to achieve a positive cash flow from the revenues it generates, it is in a good position to grow and expand its market.

FIGURE 17.1

Stages of Growth and Company Focus

Startup	Early Growth	High Growth	Stable Growth
Capital Customers Distribution	Cash flow Marketing	Resources Capital Management	Innovation Maintaining success

If, however, revenues generated fail to cover company expenses, it will not be possible to grow without seeking outside capital in the form of equity or debt.

Initial Growth

If a new venture makes it through the first phase, it enters the second level of activity with a viable business that has enough customers to keep it running on the revenues it generates. Now the entrepreneur's concerns become more focused on the issue of cash flow. Can the business generate sufficient cash flow to pay all its expenses and at the same time support the growth of the company? At this point, the venture is usually relatively small, there are few employees, and the entrepreneur is still playing an integral role. This is a crucial stage, for the decisions made here will determine whether the business will remain small or move into a period of rapid growth, which entails some significant changes in organization and strategy. The entrepreneur and the team need to decide whether they are going to grow the business to a much larger revenue level or remain stable yet profitable.

Rapid Growth

If the decision is to grow, all the resources of the business have to be gathered together to finance the growth of the company. This is a very risky stage because growth is expensive, and there are no guarantees that the entrepreneur will be successful in the attempt to reach the next level. Planning and control systems must be in place and professional management hired because there will be no time to do that during the period of rapid growth. The problems during this stage center on maintaining control of rapid growth. They are solved by delegating control and accountability at various levels; failure is usually due to uncontrolled growth, lack of cash, and insufficient management expertise to deal with the situation. If growth is accomplished, it is at this stage that entrepreneurs often sell the company at a substantial profit. It is also at this stage that some entrepreneurs are displaced by their boards of directors, investors, or creditors because the skills that made them so important at startup are not the same skills the company needs to grow to the next level. As a result, many entrepreneurial ventures reach their pinnacle of growth with a management team entirely different from the one that founded the company. To the extent that the entrepreneur is a vital part of the vision of the company and can identify an appropriate new role in the now larger company, he or she will remain the primary driver of the business. Bill Gates, Microsoft's co-founder, is one example of an entrepreneur who stayed at the helm and took his company from startup to global corporate giant. Only in the past several years has he stepped out of the CEO position in favor of one of the founding team members, Steve Ballmer.

Stable Growth and Maintenance

Once the business has successfully passed through the phase of rapid growth and is able to effectively manage the financial gains of growth, it has reached Phase 4, stable growth and maintenance of market share. Here the business, which is usually large at this point, can remain in a fairly stable condition as long as it continues to be innovative, competitive, and flexible. If it does not, sooner or later it will begin to lose market share and could ultimately fail or become a much smaller business. High-tech companies seem to be an exception to traditional growth patterns. Because they typically start with solid venture capital funding and a strong management team (dictated by the venture capitalists), they move out of Phases 1 and 2 very rapidly. During Phases 3 and 4, if the structure is effective and their technology is adopted in the mainstream market, they can become hugely successful. If, on the other hand, the structure is weak and the technology is not readily adopted, they can fail quickly.

FACTORS THAT AFFECT GROWTH

To comprehend the role of growth in a company's evolution, it is important to understand the factors that affect growth: market factors, management factors, and scale factors.

Market Factors

The degree of growth and the rate at which a new venture grows are dependent on market strategy. If the niche market that a company is entering is by nature small and relatively stable in terms of growth, it will of course be more difficult to achieve the spectacular growth and size of the most rapidly growing companies. On the other hand, if the product or service can expand to a global market, growth and size are more likely to be attained.

Entering a market dominated by large companies is not in and of itself an automatic deterrent to growth. A small, well-organized company is often able to produce its product or service at a very competitive price while maintaining high quality standards, because it doesn't have the enormous overhead of the larger companies. Moreover, if an industry is an old, established one, a firm entering with an innovative product in a niche market in that industry can experience rapid rates of growth. In some industries, such as the wireless industry, innovation is a given, so merely offering an innovative product is not enough. In highly innovative industries such as this, the key to rapid growth is the ability to design and produce a product more quickly than competitors do. By contrast, in an industry that is stable and offers commodity products and services, entering with an innovative product or process will provide a significant competitive advantage.

Intellectual-property rights, like patents, copyrights, trademarks, and trade secrets, offer a competitive advantage to a new venture because they provide a grace period in which to introduce the product or service before anyone else can copy it. However, relying on proprietary rights alone is not wise. It is important to have a comprehensive marketing plan that enables the new business to secure a strong foothold in the market before someone attempts to reproduce the product and compete with it. True, an owner of intellectual property has the right to take someone who infringes on those proprietary rights to court, but the typical small company can ill afford this time-consuming and costly process when it needs all its excess capital for growth. See Chapter 6 for a more in-depth discussion of intellectual property.

Some industries are by their very nature volatile; that is, it is difficult to predict what will happen for any length of time and with any degree of accuracy. The computer industry in the 1980s was such an industry; it has since become more predictable with dominant players. The nanotechnology industry, however, is very volatile at this time. Consequently, there are opportunities for extraordinary growth of new ventures in the industry and, at the same time, a higher risk of failure. A new entry into such an industry needs to maintain a constant awareness of potential government regulations, directions the industry is taking, and emerging competitors.

Some industries, simply by virtue of their size and maturity, are difficult for a new venture to enter and impossible to penetrate with sufficient market share to make a profit. Other industries prohibit new entries because the cost of participating (plant and equipment, fees, and/or compliance with regulations) is so high. Yet in the right industry, a new venture can erect barriers of its own to slow down the entry of competing companies. Patent rights on products, designs, or processes, for example, can effectively erect a temporary barrier to permit a window of opportunity to gain market share.

Management Factors

Along with market factors, management factors influence a company's growth. When the new company has survived and is successful, even as a small business, there is a tendency to believe that it must be doing everything right and should continue in the same manner. That is a fatal error on the part of many entrepreneurs who don't recognize that change is a by-product of success. Many times it isn't until the venture is in crisis that an entrepreneur realizes the time has come to make a transition to professional management, a step that requires of the entrepreneur a fundamental change in attitudes and behaviors.[7] Rapid growth requires skills that are very different from startup skills. In the beginning of a new venture, the entrepreneur has more time to take part in and even control all aspects of the business. But when rapid growth begins to occur, systems must be in place to handle the increased demand without sacrificing quality and service. Unless an entrepreneur is able to bring in key professional management with experience in high-growth companies, chances are good that growth will falter, the window of opportunity will be lost, and the business may even fail.

It is an unfortunate fact that with very few exceptions, most entrepreneurs do not scale—meaning, they have a difficult time moving from the entrepreneur role to the executive role, which requires adapting their leadership capabilities to the needs of the growing company. Four leadership tendencies seem to be a problem for entrepreneurs attempting to manage growing organizations.[8]

- *Loyalty to the original founding team.* While this trait may appear to be admirable and is necessary in the earliest stages of a new venture, it can become a problem in a larger organization if the leader doesn't see the weaknesses in those people that might prevent the company from achieving its growth goals.

- *Task orientation—Focus.* In an entrepreneurial venture, driving forward with single-minded focus is an advantage, but in a large, growing company, excessive focus on details can result in losing the big picture. A good example is Dogswell (see Profile 16.1), a company whose CEO focused so much on raising money to fund growth and the launch of a new product that he didn't see that the company's coupon campaign to get customers to try the new product was eating up the profits in the core business.

- *Single-mindedness of vision—Discipline.* A new venture needs the strong vision of its entrepreneur to enable it to survive all the challenges of startup; however, the entrepreneur needs to make sure that he or she is not plagued by tunnel vision and unable to clearly see what's coming. An effective CEO needs to listen to and communicate with employees in all areas of the company to insure their loyalty and productivity.

- *Working in isolation.* Entrepreneurs have to be careful not to isolate themselves and their business from all the stakeholders in the business. Cutting themselves off from the external stakeholders is often a way to stay in the more comfortable planning mode. It takes courage to face analysts, media people, and most importantly customers. Entrepreneurs must learn to communicate and work with a diverse group of interests beyond those with which they're most comfortable.

Entrepreneurs who grow into leaders do so because they're open to the feedback of board members, mentors, investors, employees, and customers; and they're eager to address their weaknesses, leave behind the skills that are no longer needed, and develop new skills that will facilitate the growth the company.

Not all entrepreneurs are capable of becoming leaders of their growing company. Many have found that at some point in the business's growth, they must step down and allow experienced management to take over. However, growing the business does not have to mean that the spirit the entrepreneur brought to the startup is lost, only that the entrepreneur must become very creative about maintaining that sense of smallness and flexibility while the business is growing. Subcontracting some aspects of the business is one way to keep the number of employees down and retain team spirit.

Re-evaluation of key metrics is another significant management factor that affects growth. The research of McGrath and MacMillan[9] has uncovered some critical metrics that should not be overlooked. Most businesses are selling a unit of something, whether it be hours of time or boxes of widgets, and those units have some metrics associated with them that enable an entrepreneur to determine whether the business is doing well: inventory turnover, working capital ratios, average gross margins, and so forth. Sometimes, simply changing the business unit so that it more closely represents the value customers want is enough to make a significant difference in the business. For example, Cemex, a Mexican cement company, decided to change how it charged customers for cement. Traditionally, cement had been sold by the cubic yard, but over time the company found that what customers really valued was delivery—anytime, anyplace. On balance, concrete is a commodity product, so customers were not going to pay a premium for it. Cemex decided that its ability to grow depended on finding

TABLE 17.2	Change the business unit.	Align the way customers are billed with what they value most.
Profit Driver Strategies	Improve productivity by an order of magnitude.	Use the latest technology to create efficiencies that competitors do not have.
	Increase the speed at which cash flow is captured.	Make it easy for customers to pay quickly.
	Increase asset utilization.	Reduce the number of assets the business requires to operate.
	Find ways to help customers improve their performance.	Study where customers can improve their workflow and find ways to contribute to that improvement.
	Find ways to help customers save time.	Make the company's customer processes as easy and effortless as possible.
	Help improve customers' cash flow.	Demonstrate how what the company does improves the customer's bottom line.
	Help customers improve their asset utilization.	Know the customer's balance sheet and find ways to help the customer remove hard assets from its balance sheet.

Source: Based on the work of R. Gunther McGrath and I. C. MacMillan, "MarketBusting: Strategies for Exceptional Business Growth," *Harvard Business Review* (March 2005), p. 4.

a way to create new value, so it focused on delivery and decided to become the FedEx of cement companies, delivering cement in a just-in-time fashion. With that change, it became the third largest concrete business in the world.[10]

McGrath and MacMillan further suggest eight strategies for growth in addition to the traditional methods discussed in the remainder of the chapter. These strategies are found in Table 17.2.

Scaling Factors

It is a sad fact that many entrepreneurial ventures that start with great concepts and experience early success eventually hit a wall. Growth stalls and the firm flounders. Studies have found that among all the factors affecting growth, the most critical in a slowdown or failure appears to be inability to understand and respond to the business's environment.[11] That is, the entrepreneur did not recognize the opportunities and challenges developing outside the company and their potential to harm it. For example, in its first 8 years, one manufacturer's representative firm with 30 highly trained salespeople grew to $20 million in sales and came to dominate its Midwestern market. But at the 8-year point, the firm stopped growing and sales hit a plateau. Its founder thought the problem was an internal one, sales effectiveness. What really happened, however, was that the firm's competitors had changed their marketing and distribution strategies. One competitor had moved into direct sales; another developed a strong telemarketing capability. The effect of these changes was to depress the sales of the entrepreneur's company in a matter of just months. This entrepreneur had failed to recognize the changes in the environment and respond rapidly to them. What this suggests is that entrepreneurs must continually scan their environment and assess it for changes and emerging competitors. They must also plan for growth and hire for growth. Most important, growth must become part of the company culture.

Table 17.3 provides a framework for planning the growth of a business. Today we can identify at least five general categories of growth strategies: (1) strategic innovation strategies that change the game in an industry or market;

TABLE 17.3	Strategies	Tactics

A Framework for Growth	Scan and assess the environment.	1. Analyze the environment.
		  a. Is the customer base growing or shrinking? Why?
		  b. How are competitors doing?
		  c. Is the market growing?
		  d. How does your company compare technologically with others in the industry?
		2. Do a SWOT analysis (strengths, weaknesses, opportunities, threats).

	Plan the growth strategy.	3. Determine the problem to be solved. Where is the pain?
		4. Brainstorm solutions.
		  a. Don't limit yourself to what you know and have done in the past.
		  b. Think about how you can innovate strategically.
		  c. Choose two or three solutions to test.
		5. Set a major goal for significant change in the organization.
		6. Set smaller, achievable goals that will put you on the path to achieve the major goal.
		7. Dedicate resources (funding and staff) toward the achievement of these goals.

	Hire for growth.	8. Put someone in charge of the growth plan. 9. Bring in key professional management with experience in growing companies. 10. Provide education and training for employees to prepare them for growth and change.
	Create a growth culture.	11. Involve everyone in the organization in the growth plan. 12. Reward achievement of interim goals.
	Build a strategy advisory board.	13. Invite key people from the industry who can keep you apprised of changes. 14. Make industry partners and customers part of the planning process. 15. Invite more outsiders than insiders onto the advisory board.

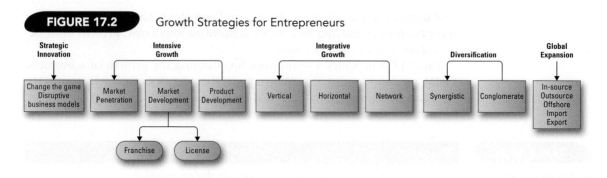

| FIGURE 17.2 | Growth Strategies for Entrepreneurs |

(2) growing within the current market; (3) taking advantage of growth within the industry as a whole; (4) diversifying to exploit opportunities outside the current market or industry; and (5) taking the business into the international arena. See Figure 17.2 for an overview of these strategies.

STRATEGIC INNOVATION—CHANGING THE GAME

When upstart company Amazon began selling books online, it changed the playing field and disrupted the rules for retailers in general. When Ryanair began offering no-frills, low-cost airline service that bypassed the major airline hubs in 1991, it changed the game for the major airlines in Europe and eventually in the United States. And when First Direct in the United Kingdom introduced telephone banking in 1989, PC banking in 1996, and online banking in 1997, it forced traditional banking institutions to change their centuries-old business model.[12]

The reason that small businesses can succeed with an innovation strategy is that new concepts are not generally attractive to established companies in the early stages because (1) they break the mold, which would mean significant change for the large company and possibly pull the company from its core competency; (2) the early markets are generally small with low margins; and (3) large companies typically wait to see how the new model fares in the market and then they either change their model or attempt to acquire the entrepreneur's company.

Effective strategic innovation is about finding ways to innovate in every activity the business undertakes, from customer acquisition to after-sales service. To be clear, achieving operational effectiveness, which is essentially doing what competitors do only better, is not strategic innovation. With strategic innovation, entrepreneurs create a unique and sustainable competitive advantage by doing things differently for a different purpose.[13] That purpose typically relates to the specific needs of their customers. For example, IKEA, the Swedish furniture company, is focused on young, first-time buyers who want style at a low price point. To distinguish itself from other furniture retailers while addressing the specific needs of its customers, IKEA provides modular, easily assembled designs that are on display in its warehouse stores. They are open long hours, provide child care, and even offer inexpensive onsite restaurants to encourage customers to spend time. In this way, IKEA demonstrates that it understands the critical success factors for its business, the core competencies it has that it can leverage, and the key resources it will need to deploy to meet the customers' needs.

GROWING WITHIN THE CURRENT MARKET

Intensive growth strategies focus on exploiting the current market fully—that is, expanding the category to the greatest extent possible. This is accomplished by increasing the volume of sales to current customers and increase the number of customers in the target market. There are generally three methods for implementing growth within the current market: market penetration, market development, and product development.

Market Penetration

With market penetration, entrepreneurs attempt to increase sales by using more effective marketing strategies within the current target market. This is a common growth strategy for new ventures because it enables entrepreneurs to work in familiar territory and grow their businesses while they're getting their systems and controls firmly in place. Under this strategy, the company would expand gradually from the initial target market, whether it is a geographic area or a customer base. For example, the initial target market for a portable electronic travel guide might be travel agencies. Efforts and resources would be focused on getting those customers solidified and then gradually moving on to other target customers, such as hotels and convention bureaus. Promoting additional uses for the product persuades customers to buy more, as Arm & Hammer experienced when its customers began buying baking soda not only for cooking but also for brushing their teeth and deodorizing their refrigerators. Yet another way to employ market penetration is to attract customers from competitors by advertising product qualities, service, or price that distinguishes the entrepreneur's product from others. A fourth way is to go after noncustomers who typically have not purchased because the product or service was too costly, had too steep a learning curve, or had high switching costs. Once the entrepreneur's first product is firmly established in its market, the entrepreneur can think about how to now meet the needs of noncustomers with a less costly version that might be simpler and easier to adopt.

Market Development

Market development consists of taking the product or service to a broader geographic area. For example, a company that has been marketing on the East Coast may decide to expand across the rest of the United States. One of the most popular ways to expand a market geographically is to franchise, because this approach is generally less costly than setting up a national distribution system. The next section explores franchising in more detail and the succeeding section deals with licensing.

Franchising

Franchising enables a business to grow quickly into several geographic markets at once. The franchiser sells to the franchisee the right to do business under a particular name; the right to a product, process, or service; training and assistance in setting up the business; and ongoing marketing and quality control support once the business is established. The franchisee pays a fee and a royalty on sales, typically 3–8 percent. For this fee, the franchisee may get

- A product or service that has a proven market
- Trade names and/or trademarks
- A patented design, process, or formula
- An accounting and financial control system
- A marketing plan
- The benefit of volume purchasing and advertising

Franchises generally come in three types: dealerships, service franchises, and product franchises. Dealerships enable manufacturers to distribute products without having to do the day-to-day work of retailing. Dealers benefit from combined marketing strength but are often required to meet quotas. Service franchises provide customers with services such as tax preparation, temporary employees, payroll preparation, and real estate services. Often the business is already in operation independently before it applies to become a franchise member. The most popular type of franchise is one that offers a product, a brand name, and an operating model. Examples include LA Boxing, Great Harvest Bread Company, and Golf USA. Although it is a popular vehicle for growth, franchising a business is not without its risks. It is much like creating a whole new business, because the entrepreneur (franchiser) must carefully document all processes and procedures in a manual that will be used to train the franchisees. Potential franchisees need to be scrutinized to ensure that they are qualified to assume the responsibilities of operating a franchise. Moreover, the cost of preparing a business to franchise is considerable and includes legal, accounting, consulting, and training expenses. Then, too, it may take as long as three to five years to show a profit.

The risk to franchisees who may have purchased the franchise as an entry into business ownership is also great. Franchisees typically pay the franchiser 2–10 percent of gross sales in monthly royalties and marketing fees, which means that it is a tremendous challenge for the franchisees to control costs and achieve a return on their investment. One reason why some franchises fail is that they are typically found in retail industries, primarily eating and drinking establishments, which have a pattern of high risk and low return. However, other types of franchises in the recent past have been successful. For example, Minuteman Press International, Inc. has grown into one of the top full-service printing franchises, with nearly 1,000 locations in several countries. And Snap-on Tools, now a public company, is the leading global developer, manufacturer, and marketer of tool and equipment solutions.

Although the Small Business Administration found that only 5 percent of franchises fail as compared to 30 percent of non-franchise businesses,[14] bankruptcy of the parent company—the franchiser—should be a concern for potential franchisees; it is not uncommon. In the past decade, dozens of franchises, including 7-Eleven, NutriSystem, American Speedy Printing, Church's Chicken, and Day's Inn, have experienced Chapter 11 bankruptcy. Most have emerged intact, but not without some harm to the franchisees. During the bankruptcy, the franchisees are left in limbo, without support or information, wondering whether they'll have a viable business when it's all done. The association of the franchisee with the bankrupt parent is also likely to have a negative effect, because customers assume that if the parent has financial problems, so does the offspring. Furthermore, most franchisees have invested their life's savings in their businesses. Under the arbitration clauses in most franchise agreements, franchisees don't have the option of going to court to recoup their losses. Even if the company comes out of Chapter 11, its image is tarnished. It will have to cut back somewhere, and savvy consumers know this to be true. There are several reasons why franchises might fail; they include ineffective systems, bad location, lack of sufficient marketing, too much competition, and insufficient startup capital.

Not all businesses should use franchising as a means for growth. A successful franchise system will need to have the following characteristics:

- A successful prototype store (or preferably stores) with proven profitability and a good reputation so that the potential franchisee will begin with instant recognition
- A registered trademark and a consistent image and appearance for all outlets
- A business that can be systematized and easily replicated many times
- A product that can be sold in a variety of geographic regions
- Adequate funding, because establishing a successful franchise program can cost upwards of $150,000
- A well-documented prospectus that spells out the franchisee's rights, responsibilities, and risks
- An operations manual that details every aspect of running the business
- A training and support system for franchisees, both before they start the business and ongoing after startup
- Site selection criteria and architectural standards

Some examples of successful franchises that can be studied as models include Curves for Women (fitness), Supercuts (salon), and Jackson Hewitt Tax Service.

Developing a franchise program requires the assistance of an attorney and an accountant, both of whose advice should be carefully considered before undertaking the effort. One of the things that will be developed with the aid of an attorney is a franchise agreement. This document is often 40–60 pages in length and deals with a variety of legal issues. The franchise agreement should include the following:

- Rules by which the franchisor and franchisee will have to abide during the term of the franchise
- The term of the agreement (a franchise is like a lease where the franchisee is merely renting the business for the period of the franchise)
- Renewal provisions that include when notice must be given that the franchisee wishes to renew the agreement and what fees are to be paid
- First right of refusal or option to take on additional franchises offered by the franchisor
- Costs associated with purchasing the franchise (these may include an up-front fee, regular meeting expenses, and a percentage of the gross revenues to cover marketing and promotion costs)
- Rules related to the premises on which the franchise will be located (the franchisor may pay some of the costs of renovation and will often lease the property and grant a sublease to the franchisee)
- The stock of goods and materials needed to open the business and maintain a proper level of inventory
- Intellectual-property rights and who owns them
- Whether the contract gives the franchisee the right to sell the franchise
- How the franchise agreement can be terminated and what to do in case of disputes

It should be very clear why it's important to engage an attorney when structuring a franchise offering.

Licensing

Like franchising, licensing is a way to grow a company without investing large amounts of capital in plant, equipment, and employees. A license agreement is a grant to someone else to use the company's intellectual property and exploit it in the marketplace by manufacturing, distributing, or using it to create a new product. For example, a company may have developed a new patented process for taking rust off machinery. That process could be licensed to other companies to use on their equipment in return for paying a royalty back to the company. Conversely, an entrepreneur may have an idea for a new line of promotional products and want to license a famous name and likeness to use on them, to make them more attractive to consumers. This would entail seeking a license agreement from the owner of the trademarked name and likeness to use it commercially. An example is seeking a license from the Walt Disney Company to use Mickey Mouse on a line of products.

But licensing is much more than this, and entrepreneurs need to understand fully the value of intellectual property and how it can provide income in a variety of different ways. For the purposes of this discussion, anything that can be patented, copyrighted, or trademarked, and anything that is a trade secret, has the potential to be licensed. Many entrepreneurs don't realize that frequently in the conduct of their business, they gather valuable data on customers, markets, methods, and processes, but rarely do they package that data as intellectual property for sale. Restaurant Technologies, based in Eagan, Minnesota, is a supplier of cooking oil to restaurant and fast-food chains and grocery stores. To better understand when a customer needed to be restocked, the company installed sensors that tracked oil usage. Over time, the company realized that it had amassed valuable data—intellectual property—that its customers might appreciate having. Using password-protected websites for each customer, it began posting the information. Then the company sold solutions to the customer to fix problems their telemetry had detected; in this way, the company was helping its customers become more efficient.[15] If a company has intellectual property that someone else might pay to use or commercialize in some way, certain steps should be taken to ensure that both parties to the transaction win. Licensor and licensee depend very much on each other for the success of the agreement, so the outcomes must be worthwhile at both ends of the deal.

The following are steps that licensors should take to ensure a successful transaction:

Step 1: Decide exactly what will be licensed. The license agreement can be for a product, the design for a product, a process, the right to market and distribute, the right to manufacture, or the right to use the licensed product in the production of yet another product. It will also be important to decide whether the licensee may only license the product as is or may modify it.

Step 2: Understand and define the benefits the buyer (licensee) will receive from the transaction. Why should the licensee license from the company? What makes the product, process, or right covered by the license unique and valuable? The licensee should be convinced that dealing with the licensor offers many advantages and will be much more profitable than dealing with someone else.

Step 3: Conduct thorough market research to make certain that the potential customer base is sufficient to ensure a good profit from the effort. Of course, the licensee will also have done market research, particularly if he or she approaches a company with a proposal for a licensing agreement. But the latter situation is typical only with intellectual property that is well recognized in the marketplace—characters, for instance (Batman, Harry Potter). A company with a new intellectual property that is unproven in the marketplace may need to seek out licensing agreements to get the product commercialized.

Step 4: Conduct due diligence on potential licensees. It's important to make certain that any potential licensee has the resources to fulfill the terms and conditions of the license agreement, can properly commercialize the intellectual property, and has a sound reputation in the market. A license agreement is essentially a partnership, and choosing partners carefully is vital.

Step 5: Determine the value of the license agreement. The value of a license agreement is determined by several factors: (1) the economic life of the intellectual property—that is, how long it will remain viable as a marketable product, process, or right; (2) the potential that someone could design around the intellectual property and compete directly; (3) the potential for government legislation or regulation that could damage the marketability of the IP; (4) any changes in market conditions that could render the IP valueless. Once the monetary value of the license has been calculated on the basis of these four factors, the license becomes negotiable. Generally, the licensor wants some money up front, as a sign of good faith, and then a running royalty for the life of the license agreement. The amount of this royalty will vary by industry and by how much the licensee must invest in terms of plant, equipment, and marketing to commercialize the license.

Step 6: Create a license agreement. With the help of an attorney who specializes in licenses, draw up a license agreement or contract that defines the terms and conditions of the agreement between licensor and licensee.

Product Development

The third way to exploit the current market is to develop new products and services for existing customers or offer new versions of existing products. That is the tactic employed by software companies, which are constantly updating software with new versions their customers must buy if they want to enjoy all the latest features. Savvy businesses get their best ideas for new products from their customers. These new ideas usually come in one of two forms: incremental changes in existing products or totally new products. Incremental products often come about serendipitously when engineers, sales personnel, and management spend time out in the marketplace with customers, learning more about their needs. Bringing all these team members together on a weekly basis to discuss ideas helps the business zero in quickly on those incremental products based on needs that are possible within the current operating structure and budget. The advantage of incremental products is that, because they are based on existing products, they can usually be designed and manufactured quite rapidly, and the marketing costs are less because customers are already familiar with the core product.

Brand-new or breakthrough products, on the other hand, have a much longer product development cycle and are therefore more costly to undertake. Breakthrough products cannot be planned for; instead, they usually come about through brainstorming, exercises in creativity, and problem-solving sessions. In other words, if an entrepreneur creates a business environment that encourages creative, "off-the-wall" thinking, the chances are greater that his or her company will eventually come up with breakthrough products. The breakthrough environment, out of necessity, has no budget or time constraints and does not run on a schedule. Offering a combination of incremental and breakthrough products is probably the most effective approach. The speed and cost efficiency of the incremental products keep cash flowing into the business to help fund the more costly breakthrough products.

GROWING WITHIN THE INDUSTRY

There are many opportunities for entrepreneurs to pursue integrative growth strategies—to grow their ventures through acquisition. Acquisition is in many respects less about the financial ability of the entrepreneur to purchase another company and more about the ability to negotiate a good deal. With several research studies reporting that upwards of 75 percent of all acquisitions damage shareholder value, it is clear that this approach to growth must be taken very carefully.[16] In general, successful acquisitions target opportunities that integrate well with the core business, that can be implemented quickly, and that ensure the continuation of smooth operating processes.[17] Traditionally, when entrepreneurs have wanted to grow their businesses within their industries, they have looked to vertical and horizontal integration strategies, but now that it is important to run leaner operations, they have been looking, more often than not, to a modular or network strategy. This section examines all three strategies—vertical, horizontal, and modular.

Vertical Integration Strategies

An entrepreneurial venture can grow by moving backward or forward within the distribution channel. This is called *vertical integration*. With a backward strategy, either the company gains control of some or all of its suppliers or it becomes its own supplier by starting another business from scratch or acquiring an existing supplier that has a successful operation. This is a common strategy for businesses that have instituted a just-in-time inventory control system. By acquiring the core supplier(s), an entrepreneur can streamline the production process and cut costs. With a forward strategy, the company attempts to control the distribution of its products by either selling directly to the customer (that is, acquiring a retail outlet) or acquiring the distributors of its products. This strategy gives the business more control over how its products are marketed. Surface Technology, Inc. (STI) is a Trenton, New Jersey–based nickel-plating shop working in a very competitive business. To continue to grow, STI had to find broader uses for its customers' parts, so it talked to customers to find out exactly what the various processes are that their parts go through before coming to STI for coating, and then where they go after leaving the STI plant. For example, STI found that before certain steel parts came to its shop, they were hardened in a process conducted by another vendor. STI saw a value in developing its own trademarked process and eliminating one vendor from the customer's process. A side benefit was that quality for the customer went up because STI now controlled how the two processes worked together. Similarly, STI developed downstream processes so that eventually it became more of a one-stop shop for the customer.[18]

Horizontal Integration Strategies

Another way to grow the business within the current industry is to buy up competitors or start a competing business (sell the same product under another label). This is *horizontal integration*. For example, an entrepreneur who owns a chain of sporting goods outlets could purchase a business that has complementary products, such as a batting cage business, so that customers can buy their bats, balls, helmets, and the like from the retail store and use them at the batting cage. Another example of growing horizontally is agreeing to manufacture a product under a different label. This strategy has been used frequently in the major-appliance and grocery industries. Whirlpool, for example, produced the Sears Kenmore washers and dryers for years. Likewise, many major food producers put their brand name food items into packaging labeled with the name of a major grocery store.

Modular or Network Strategies

Another way for a company to grow within an industry is for entrepreneurs to focus on what they do best and let others do the rest. If the core activities of the business include designing and developing new products for the consumer market, other companies can make the parts, assemble the products, and market and deliver them. In essence, the entrepreneur's company and its core activities become the hub of the wheel, with the best suppliers and distributors as the spokes. This *modular strategy*, or *network strategy*, helps the business grow more rapidly, keep unit costs down, and turn out new products more quickly. In addition, the capital saved by not having to invest in fixed assets can be directed to those activities that provide a competitive advantage. The electronics and apparel industries used this growth strategy long before it became trendy. Today many other industries are beginning to see the advantages of a modular approach. Even service businesses can benefit from outsourcing functions such as accounting, payroll, and data processing, which require costly labor.

Outsourcing non-core functions to strategic partners can often help a company get products to market faster and in greater quantities, while at the same time spreading risk and delivering the capabilities of a much larger company without the expense. Finding key capabilities that will help the venture grow more rapidly is another use of outsourcing. The cost to the entrepreneur is perhaps the same as that of performing the task in-house, but the company acquires access to key processes and expertise that will speed its growth.

As with anything else, there are some drawbacks to outsourcing. If most functions are outsourced, it becomes difficult to develop any kind of corporate culture that will bind workers together and make them loyal to the company. When "employees" are no longer employees, they may find it easier to leave on a moment's notice. They also will tend to be less committed to the company's goals because they don't see a long-term role for themselves. These problems also apply to suppliers and distributors to whom an entrepreneur may outsource a capability. They must understand how they can also benefit from this relationship. That way, when the business begins to grow rapidly, they will be willing to ramp up to meet demand.

DIVERSIFICATION GROWTH STRATEGIES—GROWING OUTSIDE THE INDUSTRY

When entrepreneurs expand their businesses by investing in or acquiring products or businesses outside their core competencies and industries, they are employing a diversification growth strategy. Generally, but not always, this strategy is used when the entrepreneur has exhausted all growth strategies within the

GLOBAL INSIGHTS

Africa Focuses on Startups

It might surprise most people to learn that between 2001 and 2008, Africa was one of the fastest growing regions in the world at about 5.6 percent per year. This growth is attributed in large part to the wealth of commodities in the country, but also to the privatization of state-owned enterprises and the lowering of barriers to competition. The African Development Bank, as well as other multinational financial institutions, has worked to improve the business climate by financing private businesses and public–private partnerships. The strongest economies in Africa are found in Botswana, Mauritius, Morocco, South Africa, and Tunisia where the average per capital GDP of $10,000 exceeds the combined per capital GDP of Brazil, Russia, India, and China. In these areas, entrepreneurs are creating wealth and jobs that are lifting these economies out of poverty.

However, not all of Africa is well suited to startups. On the "Ten Worst Countries for Startups" list compiled by the World Bank, most are located on the African continent. The main problems in places such as the Republic of Congo and Chad are extremely high costs, lack of access to financing, and lack of protections for investors and lenders, in addition to the daunting political and economic challenges.

Sources: Kaberuka, D. (2010). "Capturing Africa's Business Opportunity," *McKinsey Quarterly*, June, 2010, 1–4; and *Doing Business: Measuring Business Regulations*, 2010, www.doingbusiness.org/Rankings.

current market and industry and now wants to make use of excess capacity or spare resources, adapt to the needs of customers, or change the direction of the company because of impending changes in the market or economy. One way to diversify is to use a synergistic strategy in which the entrepreneur attempts to locate new products or businesses that are technologically complementary. For example, a food processor may acquire a restaurant chain that can serve as a showcase for the food. Another way to diversify is to acquire products or services unrelated to the company's core products or services. For example, a manufacturer of bicycle helmets may acquire an apparel manufacturer to make clothing with the company logo on it to sell to helmet customers. A final strategy for diversifying, conglomerate diversification, entails acquiring businesses that are not related in any way to what the company is currently doing. An entrepreneur might use this strategy to gain control of a related function of doing business—for example, purchasing the building in which the business is housed and then leasing out excess space to other businesses to produce additional income and gain a depreciable asset. Many entrepreneurs whose work causes them to travel extensively find it advantageous to acquire a travel agency to reduce costs and provide greater convenience.

A diversification strategy for growth is not something to undertake without careful consideration of all the factors and potential outcomes, and this is particularly true of acquisition. Entrepreneurs can find consultants who are experts in mergers and acquisitions to help smooth the path financially and operationally, but it is extremely difficult to predict with any degree of confidence how the cultures of the two businesses will merge. Acquisitions and mergers cannot be successful on the basis of financial and operational synergy alone. Organizational styles and the individual personalities of key managers all come into play when an acquisition or a merger takes place. As a result, the human side of the two businesses must be analyzed and a plan developed for merging two potentially distinct cultures into one that can work effectively.

Many researchers have attempted to determine the most effective growth strategy for a new venture. In general, it has been found that horizontal integration, vertical integration, and synergistic diversification have been more successful than unrelated diversification. This is true whether the entrepreneur acquires an existing company or starts another company to achieve the goal. That is not to say that unrelated diversification should never be chosen as a growth strategy. If the potential gains are extraordinarily high, the risk may be worth taking. It is also generally true that an acquired business has a better chance of success than a brand-new venture, for the obvious reason that it usually has already passed the crucial startup and survival stages and is more likely to be poised to grow.

Growing by Going Global

Today the question for a growth-oriented company is not "Should we go global?" but "When should we go global?" There are many reasons why entrepreneurs must consider the global market even as early as the development of their original business plan. Some entrepreneurs will launch companies that are born global. The term *born global* usually denotes a company that generates at least 25 percent of its sales in the first three years from the international marketplace and that derives a competitive advantage from outsourcing and selling in several countries.[19] Entrepreneurs who attend world trade shows know that their strongest competition may as easily come from a country in the Pacific Rim as from the company next door. Entrepreneurs also know they may have to rely on other countries for supplies, parts, and even fabrication to keep costs down and remain competitive.

Furthermore, with increasing competition and saturated markets in some industries, looking to global markets can add a new dimension to an entrepreneur's business. Many entrepreneurs have found new applications for their products in other countries or complementary products that help increase the sales of their products domestically. Although a global strategy should be contemplated in any business planning, a new venture may not be able to export until it is somewhat established and is offering a high-quality product or service at a competitive price. Nevertheless, more and more "global startups"—an example is Logitech, the Swiss manufacturer of computer mouses—take a global strategy from their very inception. Oviatt and McDougall studied a dozen global startups and followed them over time. Four failed, for a variety of reasons, but those that failed tended to exhibit fewer of the "success characteristics" that the researchers found in those that survived. Those success characteristics included:[20]

1. A global vision from the start

2. Internationally experienced managers

3. Strong international business networks

4. Preemptive technology

5. A unique intangible asset, such as know-how

6. Closely linked product or service extensions (i.e. the company derives new and innovative products and services from its core technology)

7. A closely coordinated organization on a worldwide basis

However, going global is also a risky proposition. Building a customer base and a distribution network is difficult in the domestic market; it is a colossal challenge in foreign markets. Moreover, financing is more difficult in global markets because of currency fluctuations, communication problems, and regulations that vary from country to country, to name just a few. Many small entrepreneurial companies have made their first foray into the global marketplace via a single order from a potential customer in another country. If that one transaction goes smoothly, the entrepreneur may forge ahead under the mistaken impression that doing business in another country is easy.

Exporting is a long-term commitment that may not pay off for some time. In the meantime, it may be necessary to adapt the product or service somewhat to meet the requirements of the importing country and develop good relationships with agents in the country. If the entrepreneur is dealing in consumer products, it's a good idea to target countries that have disposable income and like U.S. products. If, however, the entrepreneur is dealing in basic or industrial products, it might be wise to look to developing countries that need equipment and services for building infrastructures and systems. One example is Mexico, which is taking on the enormous task of building bridges and roads as it positions itself as a major player in the world market. Savvy entrepreneurs understand that they can't simply land in a country and immediately do business. It takes time to establish relationships and build trust before a sale can be made. Developing a network of resources that include the following will help the entrepreneur get to the right people who can make things happen.[21]

- The U.S. Commerce Department Commercial Service
- U.S. Chambers of Commerce
- International law firm
- Big four accounting firm
- Large institutional investment bank
- International trade representative

Finding the Best Global Market

Finding the best market for a product or service can be a daunting task, but consulting certain sources of information can make the job easier. A good place to start is the *International Trade Statistics Yearbook of the United States*, which is available in any major library or online at http://unstats.un.org/unsd/trade/default.htm. With the United Nations Standard Industrial Trade Classification (SITC) codes found in this reference book, it is possible to locate information about international demand for a product or service in specific countries. The SITC system is a way of classifying commodities used in international trade. Entrepreneurs should also be familiar with the Harmonized System (HS) of classification, which is a ten-digit system that puts the United States "in harmony" with most of the world in terms of commodity-tracking systems. If an international shipment exceeds $2,500, it must have an HS number for documentation. The district office and the Washington, DC, office of the International Trade Administration are also excellent sources, as is the Department of Commerce (DOC). The commerce department's online database links all the DOC International Trade Administration offices and provides a wealth of valuable research information.

The World Bank does an annual survey of the world's friendliest regulatory environments for startups and small companies, and for 2010, the top three countries in order were Singapore, New Zealand, and Hong Kong SAR China.[22] See Table 17.4.

The successful launch of a program of global growth should include a marketing plan and a budget directed toward that goal. It is also important to bring onto the team someone who has international management experience or export experience. Depending on the budget, a consultant who specializes in this area can be hired. It is also a good idea to attend foreign trade shows to learn how businesses in countries of interest conduct business, who the major players are, and who the competition is. Entrepreneurs seeking to do business in politically closed countries like China, South Korea, and Pakistan must be vigilant to the potential for political instability and the impact that could have on their business. Entrepreneurs should develop risk-management practices and make sure they have a solid "in-country" network.

Export Financing

To make a sale in the global market, a company needs funds to purchase the raw materials or inventory to fill the order. Unfortunately, many entrepreneurs assume that if they have a large enough order, getting financing to fill the order will be no problem. Nothing could be further from the truth. Export lenders,

TABLE 17.4 Friendliest Countries for Startups	
Singapore	Start a business in 4 days
New Zealand	24 hours to set up a business
Hong Kong, China	Low importing and exporting costs
United States	Ease of hiring and firing labor
United Kingdom	Access to credit and strong legal rights
Denmark	Strong legal rights for borrowers and lenders
Ireland	Bankruptcy in 5 months
Canada	Foreclosure, reorganization, and liquidation procedures are quick
Australia	Easy access to credit, strong legal rights
Norway	Registering property takes 1 procedure and 3 days. Lowest costs for resolving insolvency
Georgia	Low cost and rapid property transfer

Source: Based on data collected by World Bank's Annual "Doing Business" Report 2010.

like traditional lending sources, want to know that the entrepreneur has a sound business plan and the resources to fill the orders. Entrepreneurs who want to export can look for capital from several sources, including bank financing, internal cash flow from the business, venture capital or private investor capital, and prepayment, down payment, or progress payments from the foreign company placing the order. A commercial bank is more interested in lending money to a small exporter if the entrepreneur has secured a guarantee of payment from a governmental agency such as the Export-Import Bank of the United States, because such a guarantee limits the risk undertaken by the commercial bank. It is very similar to an SBA loan guarantee. Asking buyers to pay a deposit up-front, enough to cover the purchase of raw materials, can also be a real asset to a young company with limited cash flow.

Another financial issue that plagues companies doing business overseas is currency fluctuation. In a very short time frame, as little as a couple months, currency in a country can move up or down 5 to 10 percent, which is challenging for entrepreneurs who don't have margins that can withstand that kind of volatility. An international bank can help an entrepreneur find ways to mitigate the risk of currency fluctuation. For example, an entrepreneur may be able to take advantage of a forward contract that will lock in the price at which the foreign currency will be converted to U.S. dollars. Some entrepreneurs choose to use local banks and collect and spend the money they earn in the country in which they earn it to avoid having to convert it.

Foreign Agents, Distributors, and Trading Companies

Every country has a number of sales representatives, agents, and distributors who specialize in importing U.S. goods. It is possible to find one agent who can handle an entire country or region, but if a country has several economic centers, it may be more effective to have a different agent for each center. Sales representatives work on commission; they do not buy and hold products. Consequently, the entrepreneur is still responsible for collecting receivables, which, particularly when one is dealing with a foreign country, can be costly and time-consuming.

Using agents is a way to circumvent this problem. Agents purchase a product at a discount (generally very large) off list and then sell it and handle collections themselves. They solve the problem of cultural differences and the related difficulties inherent in these transactions. Of course, using an agent means losing control over what happens to the product once it leaves the entrepreneur's hands. The entrepreneur has no say over what the agent actually charges customers in his or her own country. If the agent charges too much in an effort to make more money for himself or herself, the entrepreneur may lose a customer.

Entrepreneurs who are just starting to export or are exporting to areas not large enough to warrant an agent should consider putting an ad in U.S. trade journals that showcase U.S. products internationally. For products an entrepreneur is manufacturing, it may be possible to find a manufacturer in the international region being targeted that will let the entrepreneur sell his or her products through its company, thus providing instant recognition in the foreign country. Ultimately, that manufacturer could also become a source of financing for the entrepreneur's company. Another option is to use an export trading company (ETC) that specializes in certain countries or regions where it has established a network of sales representatives. ETCs often specialize in certain types of products. What typically happens is that a sales representative may report to the ETC that a particular country is interested in a certain product. The ETC then locates a manufacturer, buys the product, and sells it in the foreign country. Trading companies are a particularly popular vehicle when a company is dealing with Japan.

Choosing an Intermediary

Before deciding on an intermediary to handle the exporting of products, entrepreneurs should undertake some due diligence. Specifically, they should check the intermediary's current listing of products to see whether there is a good match, understand the competition and question whether the intermediary also handles these competitors, and find out whether the intermediary has enough representatives in the foreign country to handle the market. They should also look at the sales volume of the intermediary, which should show a rather consistent level of growth. And they should make sure the intermediary has sufficient warehouse space and up-to-date communication systems, examine the intermediary's marketing plan, and make sure the intermediary can handle servicing of the product.

Once a decision has been made, an agreement detailing the terms and conditions of the relationship should be drafted. This is very much like a partnership agreement, so it is important to consult an attorney who specializes in overseas contracts. The most important thing to remember about the contract is that it must be based on performance, so that if the intermediary is not moving enough product, the contract can be terminated. It is best to negotiate a one- or two-year contract with an option to renew should performance goals be met. This will probably not please the intermediary, because most want a five- to ten-year contract, but it is in the best interests of the entrepreneur to avoid a longer-term contract until the intermediary proves that he or she is loyal and can perform. Other issues should be addressed in the agreement. Retaining the ability to use another distributor is important. An entrepreneur should negotiate for a nonexclusive contract to have some flexibility and control over distribution. Another issue concerns the specific products the agent or distributor will represent. As the company grows, an entrepreneur may add or develop additional products and may not want this agent to sell those products. Specific geographic territories for which the agent or distributor will be responsible should be outlined, as well as the specific duties and responsibilities of the agent or distributor. Finally, the agreement should include a statement of agreed-upon sales quotas and should indicate the jurisdiction in which any dispute would be litigated. This will protect an entrepreneur from having to go to a foreign country to handle a dispute.

Choosing a Freight Forwarder

The job of the freight forwarder is to handle all aspects of delivering the product to the customer. The method by which a product is shipped has a significant impact on the product's cost or on the price to the customer, depending on how the deal is structured, so the choice of a freight forwarder should be carefully considered. Filling shipping containers to capacity is crucial to reducing costs. Freight forwarders can present shipping documents to a bank for collection. They can also prepare the shipping documents, which include a bill of lading (the contract between the shipper and the carrier) and an exporter declaration form detailing the contents of the shipment. The entrepreneur, however, is responsible for knowing whether any items being shipped require special licenses or certificates, as in the case of hazardous materials and certain food substances.

Growth can be an exciting time. And although a company's growth rate won't resemble a hockey stick for long (if ever), strong growth can be sustained over time if entrepreneurs plan for it and keep scanning the horizon for changes.

New Venture Action Plan

- Identify market, management, and scale factors that may affect the growth of the business.
- Determine which growth strategy is most appropriate for the business.
- Identify potential international markets for the product or service.
- Develop a plan for globalization of the company at some point in the future.

Questions on Key Issues

1. What are four characteristics of high-growth companies?
2. How can both market and management factors affect the growth of a new venture?
3. What questions should you ask at each level of the new venture's growth?
4. What advantages do growing within the current market have over integrative and diversification strategies?
5. Why is it important to start a growth-oriented business with a plan for globalization from the beginning?
6. How do foreign agents, distributors, and export trading companies differ in the services they provide?

Experiencing Entrepreneurship

1. Visit an export center in your area and talk to a Department of Commerce trade specialist who can advise you on how to become prepared to export. What did you learn that you hadn't learned from reading this text?
2. Interview an entrepreneur whose new venture is in its early stages, and question him or her about the growth strategy for the business. Can you identify the type of strategy being used?

Relevant Case Studies

Case 8 Demand Media
Case 9 The Case of Google, Inc.

18

MANAGING CHANGE

"We know not yet what we have done, still less what we are doing. Wait till evening and other parts of our day's work will shine than we had thought at noon, and we shall discover the real purport of our toil."

—HENRY DAVID THOREAU

CHAPTER OBJECTIVES

- Discuss the role of risk management in the entrepreneur's growth planning.
- Explain the various risks that affect startups during early growth.
- Discuss the importance of succession planning for entrepreneurs.
- Describe the various ways that entrepreneurs can exit and harvest the wealth created by the business.
- Describe the role of bankruptcy in business failure.

In July 2009, Bob King took the reins from CEO Steve Savage of Colorado-based Eco-Products, and as he faced the employees, he wondered how he would be received. After all, the company had been a family-owned business run by the son of the founder for the past 10 years. King was charged with growing the business, and he knew that he could do it: he had already taken Corporate Express, a $50 million office products company, to a $4.5 billion business. The question was, would the employees accept a non-family CEO?

It was 1990 when Kent Savage decided to pitch a business idea he had been mulling over to his son Steven, who had just graduated from college. He wanted to provide eco-friendly products to businesses located in central Colorado, particularly those that used large volumes of paper products such as office paper and paper towels. The two started the business in 1990 and by 1993 they had a lot of competitors, so they made a shift to focus on food service disposables and janitorial supplies to differentiate themselves. The company continued to grow at a relatively slow pace for the next 15 years and eventually became one of the leading distributors of environmentally-friendly products in the U.S. Kent Savage retired in 1999 leaving his son in charge. Steve Savage began to notice that they were having particularly good success in restaurant supplies, but if they really wanted to grow the business to the next level, the company would need to start manufacturing its own products. Consequently, in 2005, Savage began the process of transforming the company from a distributor to a manufacturing wholesaler. He also believed that he needed to move into new markets such as office supplies, to acquire some businesses in those areas as well.

It was at this point that Savage began to realize that maybe he wasn't the best person to grow the company to the next level. It was an emotional decision because he and his father had started the company and now someone outside the family would be driving its success. To help him make the decision, he talked with Aaron Kennedy, founder of Noodles & Company, the fast food chain. Kennedy advised Savage that stepping down from his business was the best decision he had ever made. Today that company has 230 company and franchise-owned restaurants in 18 states. Savage listened and finally decided that it was in the best interests of the company that he take on a different role.

As it turned out, Savage was right about hiring Bob King as the new CEO and right about the positive impact of shifting to wholesale manufacturing. Since 2005, the company has grown to 50 employees, started Ellie's Eco Home Center to retail sustainable home products, and in 2009 introduced its first product made from recycled content: a paper hot cup made from 24 percent post consumer recycled fiber, the first step on the road to 100 percent recycled products. Savage now serves as chairman of the board and splits his time among Eco-Products, National Eco Wholesale (the distribution company), and the retail store. Savage is certain he made the right decision.

Sources: Eco Products, www.ecoproducts.com, accessed October 27, 2010; Del Rey, J. (September 1, 2010). "Why I Stepped Down," *Inc.com*, www.inc.com/magazine/20100901/why-i-stepped-down.html; and Kurtz, R. (February 1, 2004), "To Franchise, or not To Franchise," *Inc. com*, www.inc.com/magazine/20040201/casestudy.html.

Change is a certainty that every entrepreneur can count on. There is no way to avoid it in today's global environment; therefore, entrepreneurs must be ready and willing to adapt to new conditions, new threats, and new opportunities. Many entrepreneurs have started a business with a vision and a plan for where that business would go but quickly have found that things change along the way. Forces beyond the control of the entrepreneur push the venture in new directions, and a new set of plans has to be constructed. Consider the highly volatile technology market during the first two years of the new millennium. How many entrepreneurs who had developed business plans for new e-commerce ventures and were seeking capital in early 2000 knew that their window of opportunity to secure those investments was about to close? In April of that year, the stock market plummeted, foreshadowing an enormous shakeout in the dot com world and the end of "money for nothing." In a matter of months, hundreds of potential new e-commerce ventures failed to make it to the marketplace because they had no backup plan in place. Some would argue that the signs were there all along, but the easy availability of venture capital inspired the notion that all an entrepreneur needed was a great idea that could scale out to a huge market. In any case, most entrepreneurs were not prepared for the change and had no contingency plans in place.

One of the events for which entrepreneurs often fail to plan is the harvest or exit from the business. Knowing in what manner the entrepreneur wants to realize the benefits of having created a successful business guides decision making throughout the life of the business. Moreover, if an entrepreneur has taken investment capital during the growth of the business, the investors will be looking for an exit strategy that involves some type of liquidity event. This chapter looks at contingency planning, alternatives for harvesting the wealth of the venture, and alternatives to consider if the venture should fail.

PREPARING FOR CONTINGENCIES: RISK MANAGEMENT

It is important to distinguish between risk and uncertainty. The difference between the two is very clear in the economics literature dating back to the work of Frank H. Knight in 1921 who said that we have risk when future events occur with measurable probability and we have uncertainty when the likelihood of future events is unknown, indefinite, incalculable.[1] In other words, risk refers to situations where a probability of the risk occurring and its potential impact can be calculated because at least some of the variables involved in the decision can be controlled. Uncertainty, on the other hand, is unpredictable and not subject to probability. Entrepreneurs engage in risk management, but they also know that their ventures are faced from time to time with uncertainty that cannot be controlled, such as the economic and political environment that evolved at the end of the first decade of the new century.

The ability to assess risk is an important skill for any business owner, but it is rarely accomplished in the most effective manner. Traditional risk management proponents have typically adopted an objectivist—or frequentist—view that sees risk as a physical property that has associated probabilities of occurrence. These probabilities come from repetitive historical evidence, such as coin flips and weather patterns that assume a normal distribution. According to researchers Borison and Hamm, this approach doesn't take into account human judgment or the observation process (called the Bayesian or subjectivist view), but relies simply on the physical world.[2] The Bayesian view takes into account the motives, trustworthiness, and process of the people involved in the risk assessment and for this reason generally gives a better result. This approach has not been widely employed in business risk management, which explains why so many attempts to manage risk fail. The Bayesian approach considers the possibility that even if the entrepreneur's business has had successful growth with its current strategy over several years, an unexpected event or series of events could disrupt the pattern. Many businesses saw that happen after the financial crisis in 2008. Their financial models, based on unrealistic assumptions about the strength of the economy, did not take into account the forces converging to create an environment of no access to credit because the models were based on historical data over a relatively long period of easy credit.

Entrepreneurs, by the very nature of what they do, are compelled to consider risks that their businesses face, along with multiple outcomes and possibilities as a result of that risk. Contingency plans help a growing business deal with downturns and upturns in the economy, new regulations, changes in customer tastes and preferences, and many other events that regularly—and often without much warning—disrupt the equilibrium of the firm. For example, the 2001 recession revealed how many businesses fail to understand business cycles. Recessions in general are actually quite normal in the U.S. economy, but the 2001 recession displayed distinct characteristics resulting from the fact that it occurred in the middle of an industrial revolution.[3] American icons such as Bethlehem Steel, Burlington, Kmart, and United Airlines all faced bankruptcies. Even the housing collapse of 2007 and subsequent recession were entirely predictable. Recessions do not happen overnight. There are signs, even within specific industries, that signal a slowdown or potential bursting of an economic bubble, as in the case of the housing bubble in 2007. Since the government began compiling indices on the economy after World War II, some consistent trends have emerged. For example, the Leading Index of Economic Indicators, which consists of such items as the Producer Price Index, the Consumer Confidence Index, and the Manufacturers' Orders for Durable Goods, typically declines for 9 months prior to the onset of a recession. The coincident-lagging index, which is a ratio of the coincident index (employment, personal income, industrial production) to the lagging index (consumer price index, interest rates, unemployment), declines for 13 months prior to the onset of a recession. Recognizing the signs of recession before they affect a business gives the entrepreneur a chance to prepare in many ways, including maintaining a higher degree of liquidity. In recessionary times, it is more difficult to raise capital from either bankers or private sources, so liquidity opens up opportunities that become available only during recessions. For example, an entrepreneur may be able to purchase a building that in good economic times was beyond reach, or he or she may be able to negotiate more favorable terms from suppliers just to keep the business moving forward.

An effective contingency plan will answer several important questions:

1. In the event of a problem, which suppliers will be willing to extend the entrepreneur's repayment time and for how much?

2. What nonessential assets does the business have that can be turned into cash quickly?

3. Is there additional investment capital that can be tapped?

4. Does the business have customers who might be willing to prepay or purchase earlier than planned?

5. Has a good relationship with a banker and accountant been established? How can they help the business get through the crunch?

After answering these questions, entrepreneurs can (1) identify the potential risks associated with their venture, (2) calculate the probability that those identified risks will in fact occur, (3) assign a level of importance to the losses, and (4) calculate the overall loss risk. In the next section we consider some of the major categories of risk that entrepreneurs face. Figure 18.1 summarizes the process for addressing risk.

Identifying Potential Risks

Risk is a fact of business life, and a company's exposure to risk increases as the venture grows. Understanding where the risk lies enables entrepreneurs to respond effectively through process improvement strategies and buffer strategies. *Process improvement strategies* involve reducing the probability that the risk will occur by forming strategic alliances with strong partners[4] or by developing backup suppliers and better communication with suppliers.[5] However, even with process improvement strategies in place, it is impossible to eliminate risk completely. *Buffer strategies* are used to protect a company against potential risk that can't be prevented. Maintaining sufficient inventory and alternative sources of supply are two examples of buffer strategies.

Supply Chain Risks

The common practice of outsourcing the upstream activities of the business—raw materials, manufacturing, assembly, inventory—presents advantages and risks to the entrepreneur. The advantages of outsourcing include the sharing of risk, expertise, and resources, but the risks are many and significant. The financial health of the supplier is critical to the stability of the entrepreneur's business. When a supplier faces financial hardships and cannot provide supplies, raw materials, and so forth in a timely manner and the entrepreneur has no backup, the results can be loss of customers and, in some cases, the failure of the entrepreneur's business. Supplier capacity constraints are another source of risk for an entrepreneur. When demand fluctuates or increases precipitously, suppliers may not be able to ramp up quickly enough to meet the demand.[6] Quality-related risks and the inability of suppliers to keep up with technological change can have ramifications throughout the entire value chain, including raising the

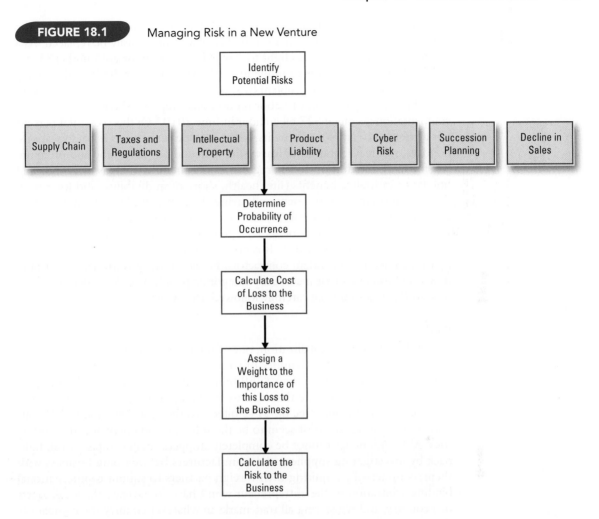

FIGURE 18.1   Managing Risk in a New Venture

cost of producing a product.[7] Changes in customer needs can affect product design and, by extension, the types and quantities of supplies needed. When suppliers are unable to make required changes in product design, entrepreneurs incur a risk. Finally, risks in the form of disasters—floods, fire, earthquakes—can disrupt supply chains and affect an entrepreneur's ability to manufacture and distribute products.

Taxes and Regulations

During the life of every business, new laws, regulations, and rules will be enacted, and frequently there is no way to prepare for them. Government regulations and regulatory paperwork are severe problems for growing ventures, and the cost of compliance is rising to the point where entrepreneurs are looking for ways to avoid coming under the purview of some of these regulations. For example, the Family and Medical Leave Act has a threshold firm size of

50 employees, which means that very small businesses are now faced with the possible protracted absence of an employee who cannot easily be replaced. As a result, many small businesses fight to stay below that important number.

The cost of employing an individual is becoming so prohibitive that many companies are solving the problem by subcontracting work and leasing employees. The U.S Department of Labor reports that employers' costs for employee compensation averaged $27.64 an hour in June 2010.[8] Of this cost, 29.4 percent was attributed to employee benefits, which include such things as paid vacations, holidays, sick leave, and other leave; supplemental pay (overtime and premium pay for work in addition to the regular work schedule, such as weekends and holidays); insurance benefits (life, health, short-term disability, and long-term disability insurance); retirement and savings benefits; and legally required benefits (Social Security, Medicare, federal and state unemployment insurance, and workers' compensation). Benefits, as a percentage of total compensation, have increased every year since 2001. It is no wonder that many business owners prefer to work with independent contractors. However, the government is cracking down on businesses that incorrectly categorize people as independent contractors, so IRS rules must be carefully followed. (See Chapter 7.)

Intellectual Piracy

For all the benefits of globalization, one of the biggest negatives has been intellectual piracy. The U.S. Chamber of Commerce reports that piracy costs the United States alone more than $250 billion annually and 750,000 lost jobs every year.[9] Some estimate that if software piracy could be cut by 10 percent over four years, it would free up $142 billion to the global economy.[10] The industries that suffer the most seem to be the software and pharmaceutical industries. Although piracy cannot be completely stopped, small companies can fight back by investigating suppliers and manufacturers before doing business with them, contractually requiring their foreign partners to submit to international binding arbitration so the entrepreneur won't have to navigate the local courts of a country, and registering all trademarks in whatever country the company is doing business in.

Product Liability

The chances are fairly good that any company that manufactures products will face a product liability suit at some point. More and more of the risk of product-related injuries has been shifted to manufacturers, creating a legal minefield that could prove disastrous to a growing company. Even if a company carefully designs and manufactures a product and covers it with warnings and detailed instructions, that company may still be vulnerable if misuse of the product results in injury. For a company to be legally liable, the product must be defective and an injury must have occurred. But in a litigious society, those requirements don't stop people from initiating lawsuits even when there are no grounds. Most product liability insurance covers the costs of defense, personal injury, or property damage, but not lost sales and the cost of product redesign. Moreover, if the insurance company must pay on a claim, the entrepreneur's premiums will no doubt increase.

A growing company must plan for potential litigation from the very inception of the business. One proven method is to establish a formal safety panel that includes people from all the major functional areas of the business. During the startup phase, that panel may consist of only the entrepreneur and one or two outside advisers with experience in the area. It is the job of the panel to review safety requirements on a regular basis, establish new ones when necessary, and document any injuries or claims made against the product. Prior to product introduction in the marketplace, the panel should see that careful records are maintained of all decisions regarding final product design, testing, and evaluation procedures. Advertising of the product should contain no exaggerated claims or implied promises that may give customers the impression that the company is claiming more safety features than the product actually possesses. Implied promises can be used against the entrepreneur in a court of law.

Early in the operation of the business, it is important to identify a qualified attorney familiar with the industry to handle any potential product liability claims. This attorney should handle the first case that confronts the business. Thereafter, if other suits arise in various parts of the country, the entrepreneur can save money by hiring a "local attorney" in the jurisdiction of the claim. Then the primary attorney can brief the local attorney on the precedent-setting cases related to the claim and assist while the local attorney carries the case to court. In this way, the entrepreneur does not have to send the primary attorney on the road, incurring significant travel and time expenses.

Cyber Risk

One of the more recent and insidious risks a company that is doing business online faces is cyber risk: hacker attacks that could bring the business network down, phishing attacks (acquiring sensitive information such as user names and passwords), spybots, and the ever-present viruses and worms. More recently, cyber militias have emerged—groups of hackers that act in the national interests of the country that sponsors them to provide nearly constant attacks on the national security infrastructure of countries like the United States. The 2008 CSI/FBI Computer Crime and Security Survey found that 49 percent of all U.S. companies surveyed had suffered virus attacks. However, attacks of all types, ranging from denial of service to unauthorized access and system penetration have declined steadily since 2004. The area that has seen an increase is financial fraud.[11]

Many businesses have secured cyber insurance policies to attempt to mitigate the risk. However, these policies are often difficult to understand and contain so many exclusions that one company figured that the insurance policy price was close to what it would cost them to do what they could to reduce their cyber risk on their own. However, entrepreneurs with companies that rely heavily on Internet-based systems will want to get advice about securing a policy that protects the company against liability for security breaches, crisis management (notifying customers about the theft of information), business interruption, and the cost associated with restoring information that has been corrupted.

Decline in Sales

When sales decline and positive cash flow starts looking like a memory, entre-preneurs often go into a period of denial. They start paying their suppliers more slowly to preserve cash, they lay people off, they stop answering the phone, and they insulate themselves against the demands of their creditors. Their panic frequently causes them to make poor decisions about how to spend the pre-cious cash they do have. They figure that if they can just hold on long enough, things will turn around. Unfortunately, this attitude only makes the problem worse, effectively propelling the business toward its ultimate demise. How can an entrepreneur lose touch with the business and the market so much that he or she puts the business at risk? What often happens is that entrepreneurs get so wrapped up in the day-to-day operations of the business that they don't have time to contemplate the "big picture" or stay in tune with their customers. Consequently, all too often they don't see a potential crisis coming until it's too late. Beloit Corp., a manufacturer of paper mill machinery, went out of business in 2001 and the ripple effect on small businesses in Beloit, Wisconsin, was enor-mous. Barker Rockford, a hydraulic systems manufacturer, had depended on Beloit for 75 percent of its sales revenues. When Beloit closed, Barker Rockford dropped from 51 employees to 11. In an effort to turn around the company, Pierce Barker III, the company's vice president, took an innovative approach to create customers. With two partners he founded ProStuff, which invented a new kind of starting gate for the BMX bike-racing industry. Now Barker Rock-ford manufactures the gates for ProStuff, which sells them worldwide with high margins.[12]

When sales decline, lowering prices isn't necessarily the solution. If the company's customers understand the value of the product or service, any such sudden discounting will confuse them. When there is a decline in sales, it is especially important to look at all possible sources, not just the economy. The entrepreneur may have been lax about checking the credit status of customers and distributors, or the inventory turnover rate may have changed. He or she may have failed to notice an emerging competitor offering a product or service more in line with current tastes and preferences. When a growing business first notices a dip in sales, it is time to find the cause and make the necessary changes. This will be easier if the business has a contingency plan in place. If, however, those changes cannot be made in time to forestall a cash flow problem, it is time to consult a debt negotiation company, a crisis management consultant, or a bankruptcy attorney who is willing to work through the problem without go-ing to court. These experts can help an entrepreneur work with creditors until the problem is resolved. To prepare the best defense against a cash flow crisis, entrepreneurs must remain committed to producing exceptional-quality prod-ucts; controlling the cost of overhead, particularly where that overhead does not contribute directly to revenue generation (expensive cars, travel, excessive commissions); controlling production costs through subcontracting and being frugal about facilities; making liquidity and positive cash flow the prime direc-tive, so that the company can ride out temporary periods of declining demand; and having a contingency plan in place.

Calculating the Risk Probability and Cost to the Business

It is extremely difficult to calculate the probability that a given risk will occur with any degree of accuracy. Consequently, any cost-benefit analysis conducted will probably contain flaws and may even cause the company to decide that the cost of protecting itself is nearly equal to the cost of the loss.[13] Nonetheless, it is important to gauge, based on industry and customer knowledge, the chance that a particular risk will occur and what the impact of that occurrence will be on the company. For example, an entrepreneur might want to know how many widgets to order for the summer season. He knows he can sell 50 in a day and that he makes a profit of $10 each. The average number of days in the season is 95. Thus he multiplies 4,750 widgets times $10 to get the average profit for the season. He has just committed a common error that has been called the "flaw of averages."[14] The problem with averages is that they mask risk. Average inputs don't always produce average outputs. For example, if a lower-than-average demand produces lower-than-average revenues, then a higher-than-average demand is not possible because the company would have made only enough product to satisfy an average demand. This kind of error is quickly exposed when doing probability modeling such as Monte Carlo simulation, which models behaviors under multiple uncertainties within a specified period. It is often used in the insurance industry to model accident risk. Working with this type of modeling software is an effective way to get a feel for the risk inherent in any business. Understanding the magnitude of a potential loss is important in deciding where to devote limited resources to protecting against a particular loss. Assigning a level of significance is again an arbitrary exercise, because the weight given to any risk impact is based on the company's goals, core competencies, and focus.

The overall risk of loss is simply the product of the probability of occurrence times the cost of the impact to the business times the level of significance of that impact:

$$\text{Risk of Loss} = (P \times C \times S)$$

For example, suppose an entrepreneur determines that there is a 40 percent chance that she will lose a key manager to a competitor. The financial cost of that loss is the cost of doing a search for a new manager, which she estimates at $10,000 (this does not include the nonfinancial costs, such as loss of tacit knowledge). She assigns a weight of 80 percent, on a scale of 1 percent to 100 percent, to reflect the importance of this risk to the company. Thus, the overall risk of loss is approximately

$$\text{Risk of Loss} = (\$10,000 \times 0.40 \times 0.80) = \$3,200$$

If this calculation is done for all the identified risks, it will be easier to decide on which risks to concentrate efforts and focus resources, remembering at all times that the risk-of-loss numbers are merely educated guesses.

SOCIAL ENTREPRENEURSHIP: MAKING MEANING

The Social Venture Network

What happens when a group of visionary leaders comes together to make a difference in the world of entrepreneurship and investment? What happens is a nonprofit network, the Social Venture Network (SVN), whose mission is to promote "models and leadership for socially and environmentally sustainable business." SVN has created a community of practice that provides information and community forums to empower their members to achieve the vision collectively. Founded in 1987, SVN's membership stands at over 420 business leaders, investors, and nonprofit leaders who are dedicated to making the business world a better place. One of SVN's passionate members is Tom Szaky, the founder and CEO of TerraCycle, Inc.

His company produced the first fertilizer made entirely from organic waste fed to millions of worms that produce worm poop, which is then packaged in recycled plastic bottles. His eco-friendly product is sold at Home Depot and has led to partnerships with many big companies such as Kraft and Frito Lay to collect "post-consumer" packaging, which is used to create eco-friendly products.

An immigrant from Hungary, Szaky's built his company to 45 workers housed in a 20,000 square foot facility in Trenton, New Jersey. TerraCycle is an excellent example of the triple bottom line: profit, people, and planet. Find out more about SVN at www.svn.org and TerraCycle at www.terracycle.net.

LEADERSHIP SUCCESSION

No company can count on keeping the same management team over the life of the business—or even after the startup phase. The demand for top-notch management personnel (particularly in some industries, such as high-tech) means that other companies will constantly be trying to woo the best people away from the best firms. Losing a CEO in times of high turnover is not uncommon. In 2006 alone, 15 percent of the world's largest companies changed their CEOs,[15] including public giants such as Hewlett-Packard as well as private companies like Bio-Micro Systems. But key employees are often lost for other unpredictable reasons like death or illness. In fact, some estimates suggest that the chances of losing a key executive to death are significantly greater than losing a business to fire.

Succession planning—identifying people who can take over key company positions in an emergency or in a change of ownership—is an important part of contingency planning. Ideally that person or persons will come from within the company, but in the case of a growing entrepreneurial company that has been operating in a "lean and mean" mode, promoting from within may not be possible, so outsiders must be found. The process of succession planning is a long one.[16] Consequently, it is not surprising that research has found that about 49 percent of companies do not have a succession plan in place, despite believing that it's very important. If you exclude public companies, a study conducted by the American Institute of CPAs (AICPA) in 2008 found that only 9 percent of sole proprietorships had succession plans.

Succession planning for small enterprises and for the unique issues of family businesses is the subject of the next two sections.

Change of Ownership in Small Enterprises

Employing a simple process for succession planning will increase the likelihood that the process will actually result in an effective succession plan. One such simple process was advanced by the research of Pasmore and Torres.[17] It calls for a four-step plan:

1. *Situation assessment.* Here the company determines the timing of succession, the criteria for selection, the likely internal candidates, a plan for identifying possible external candidates, and plans for engaging the appropriate stakeholders in the process.

2. *Announcement of the process.* Once the company's situation is assessed, the CEO needs to announce the plans and process to relevant stakeholders such as board members, advisors, and employees. Making people aware of how the selection will be made will go a long way toward preventing unsubstantiated rumors and misunderstandings.

3. *Execution of the search.* At this stage, management moves forward to search and select either an internal or external candidate.

4. *Transition.* Once the selection has been made, the current CEO needs to help the new leader during the transfer of power, smooth the transition with important stakeholders, and make a graceful exit at the appropriate time.

To prepare for the possible loss of a key employee, it is a good idea to purchase "key-person insurance," which will cover the costs associated with abruptly having to replace someone. Bringing in a consultant to guide the management team in succession planning is a valuable exercise for any growing venture. Often consultants are hired temporarily to take over a vacant position for a specified period, during which they train a permanent successor. Another solution is to cross-train people in key positions so that someone can step in, at least for the short term, in the event of an emergency. Cross-training is generally an integral part of a team-based approach to organizational management.

Succession Planning in Family-Owned Businesses

Entrepreneurs who head family-owned companies face special problems because they tend to look to a son, daughter, or other family member to succeed them. Succession in a family-owned business will not happen unless it is planned for, however. In fact, the Family Firm Institute of Boston reports that less than a third of all family businesses survive the transition from first to second generation ownership.[18] This is partly because the owner must deal not only with business issues related to succession—ownership, management, strategic planning—but also with the unexpected, such as a death or relationship issues with family members, a much more difficult task. Succession planning tends to expose family issues that may have been kept in the background but have been building over time. For example, the daughter who the entrepreneur assumed would take over the business may have no interest in doing so but may never have told her entrepreneur father. Or, a child may believe himself or herself capable of simply stepping into a managerial role with no previous experience. If an entrepreneur has created a plan for succession, a problem like this may be solved by making it a requirement that a child or potential successor work for another company for several years to gain some business savvy and to decide whether he or she wants to take over the family business. Many sports enterprises are family businesses that face these same issues. When the iconic George Steinbrenner, owner of the New York Yankees baseball team died in July 2010, he left the ownership of the team to his two sons. He began planning for succession and preparing his sons starting in 1973.[19] Although the family business could look outside the family for their next leader, they are not likely to do that as research has found that most family businesses want to retain control within the family.[20]

Entrepreneur/owners leave their family businesses for a variety of reasons that go beyond retirement. These reasons include change in interests, the desire to start a different business, change in the family situation (divorce, illness, death), or change in the competitive environment that signals new leadership is required to carry the business forward. Research has learned that in first-generation family businesses, the issues of business survival and growth take precedence over family concerns; while in second-generation businesses and beyond, the need to take care of family members seems to come to the forefront in the priorities of management.[21]

It is very important to think about succession planning very early in the growth of the business, because finding the right person to succeed the entrepreneur parent in the business is not an easy task. Unfortunately, most family businesses wait too long to put a plan in place. Because CEOs act as visionaries and also play functional roles, balancing finance, marketing, and operations, a person whom an entrepreneur has chosen to succeed him or her must be given the time to understand the role; it's not something that will happen overnight.

Succession planning in family businesses takes a long time due to three key issues:

- Physiological and emotional issues that stem from the interrelations of family members[22]
- The complexity of succession, particularly since the owner typically has no experience in this area[23]
- Relevant laws and taxation that impact the financial status of the company[24]

To start the process of succession planning, all the active family members should participate on a committee to explore the options. Some of the questions to examine are the following:

- Is the next generation being sufficiently prepared to take over the business when the time comes?
- What is the second generation's expectation for the future of the business, and is it congruent with the company's vision?
- What skills and experience does the second generation need to acquire?
- What would the ideal succession plan look like?

Then, with the help of an attorney, buy-sell agreements should be developed to ensure that heirs receive a fair price for their interest in the business upon an owner's death and to protect against irreparable damage in the event of a shareholder's permanent disability by outlining provisions for buying out the disabled shareholder's interest. An estate planning professional can help evaluate the impact of any changes in the business on the entrepreneur's personal assets. Given that most privately owned businesses in the United States are family-owned businesses, this succession planning strategy is useful for any business that wants to be prepared for the loss or retirement of its leader.

PLANNING FOR HARVEST AND EXIT

Many first-time entrepreneurs have questioned the need for an exit plan, or harvest plan, because they are more concerned with launching the business and making it a success than with thinking about how they're going to get out. But even though some entrepreneurs stay with their new ventures for the long term, the majority enjoy the challenge of startup and the excitement of growth and abhor the custodial role of managing a stable, mature company. Consequently, exiting the business does not necessarily mean exiting the role of entrepreneur. It may in fact mean taking the financial rewards of having grown a successful business and investing them in a new venture. And there are serial entrepreneurs who do that very thing over and over again throughout their lives, starting businesses and then selling them or letting others run them. Whether or not an entrepreneur intends to exit a business at any point, there should be a plan for harvesting the rewards of having started the business in the first place. There is another important reason why a harvest plan is essential. Many entrepreneurs take investor capital at some point in the growth of their companies, and investors require a liquidity event so that they can exit the business with their principal and any return on investment they have accrued.

Entrepreneurs need to think of their companies as part of an ongoing career path. So says Jerome Katz, professor of management at St. Louis University. He studied the career paths of entrepreneurs and finds that there are four major types:

1. *Growth entrepreneurs.* These are entrepreneurs who measure their success by the size of their company. They tend not to have an exit plan because they're always striving for bigger, better, faster.

2. *Habitual entrepreneurs.* These are people who love to start businesses and may start and run several at once. They are probably even less likely to have an exit plan because there are always new opportunities out there.

3. *Harvest entrepreneurs.* These entrepreneurs start and build a venture for the purpose of selling it. Some of these owners will start, build, and harvest many companies during a career.

4. *Spiral, or helical, entrepreneurs.* Women entrepreneurs often fall into this category. These entrepreneurs are driven by what is going on in their personal lives, so their entrepreneurial tendencies emerge in spurts. At times they may appear oblivious to the business as they deal with family issues.

Katz believes it is never too early to begin to think about an endgame strategy, so that the exit will be graceful rather than "feet first."[25] The following paragraphs examine several methods by which an entrepreneur can achieve a rewarding harvest.

Selling the Business

Selling the business outright to another company or to an individual may be the goal if an entrepreneur is ready to move on to something else and wants to be financially and mentally free to do so. Unfortunately, however, selling a business is a life-changing event because for several years, the entrepreneur has probably devoted the majority of his or her time and attention to growing the business, and it played an important role in structuring the entrepreneur's life. Although the market may be good for selling the particular type of business an entrepreneur owns, he or she may not be ready to "retire" or may not have identified what to do next. Consequently, after the business has been sold, its owner may experience a sense of loss, much like what accompanies the death of a loved one; without preparation, emotional stress could be the consequence. Therefore, planning for this enormous change will be vital.

The best way to sell a business is for entrepreneurs to know almost from the beginning that selling is what they eventually want to do, so that they will make decisions for the business that will place it in the best position for a sale several years later. For one thing, the business will need audited financial statements that lend the business forecasts more credibility. The tax strategy will not be to minimize taxes by showing low profits but, rather, to show actual profits and pay the taxes on them, because that will provide a higher valuation for the business. Throughout the time that the entrepreneur owns the business, its expenses and activity should be kept totally separate from the owner's personal expenses. It will also be important to plan for the amount of time it will take to sell the business and wait to sell until the right window of opportunity has opened.

Smaller businesses for sale often use the services of business brokers; however, a high-growth venture is more likely to employ the services of an investment banking firm that has experience with the industry. Investment banks normally want a retainer to ensure the seriousness of the commitment to sell, but that retainer will be applied against the final fee on the sale, which could average about 5 percent of the purchase price. It is recommended, however, that a third party with no vested interest in the sale be enlisted to judge the fair market value of the business. This "appraiser" can also prepare financial projections based on the history of the company and the appraiser's independent market research. When a business is sold, the entrepreneur does not have to sell all the assets. For example, the building could be held out of the sale and leased back to the business purchaser, with the original owner staying on as landlord.

While the potential purchaser is conducting due diligence on the entrepreneur and the business, the entrepreneur needs to do the same with the purchaser. The purchasing firm or individual should be thoroughly checked out against a list of criteria the entrepreneur has developed. The purchaser should have the resources necessary to continue the growth of the business, be familiar with the industry and with the type of business being purchased, have a good reputation in the industry, and offer skills and contacts that will ensure that the business continues in a positive direction. In order to compare one buyer with another fairly, it is often helpful to make a complete list of criteria and then weight them to reflect their relative importance.

Cashing Out but Staying In

Sometimes entrepreneurs reach the point where they would like to take the bulk of their investment and gain out of the business but are not yet ready to cut the cord entirely. They may want to continue to run the business or at least retain a minority interest. There are several ways this can be accomplished. If the company is still privately owned, the remaining shareholders may want to purchase the entrepreneur's stock at current market rates so that control doesn't end up in other hands. In fact, the shareholders' agreement that was drafted when the entrepreneur set up the corporation may have specified that shareholders must offer the stock to the company before offering it to anyone else.

If the company is publicly traded, the task of selling the stock is much simpler; however, if the entrepreneur owns a substantial portion of the issued stock, strict guidelines set out by the SEC must be followed when liquidating the shareholders' interests. If the company had a successful IPO, founders' stock will have increased substantially in value, which presents a tax liability that should not be ignored. That is why many entrepreneurs in such situations cash out only what they need to support whatever goals they have. This strategy, of course, is based on the presumption that the company stock will continue its upward trend for the foreseeable future.

Entrepreneurs who want to cash out a significant portion of their investment and turn over the reins to a son, daughter, or other individual can do so by splitting the business into two firms, with the entrepreneur owning the firm that has all the assets (plant, equipment, vehicles) and the other person owning the operating aspect of the business while leasing the assets from the entrepreneur's company. See Figure 18.2.

A Phased Sale

Some entrepreneurs want to soften the emotional blow of selling the business, not to mention softening the tax consequences, by agreeing with the buyer—an individual or another firm—to sell in two phases. During the first phase, the

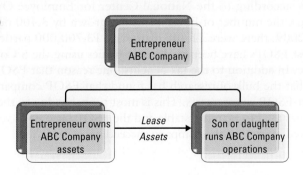

FIGURE 18.2

Restructuring the
Family Business

entrepreneur sells a percentage of the company but remains in control of operations and can continue to grow the company to the point at which the buyer has agreed to complete the purchase. This approach gives the entrepreneur the ability to cash out a portion of his or her investment and still manage the business for an agreed-upon time, during which the new owner will probably be learning the business and phasing in. In the second phase, the business is sold at a prearranged price, usually a multiple of earnings.

This approach is fairly complex and should always be guided by an attorney experienced in acquisitions and buy-sell agreements. The buy-sell agreement, which spells out the terms of the purchase, specifies the amount of control the new owner can exert over the business before the sale has been completed and the amount of proprietary information that will be shared with the buyer between Phases 1 and 2.

In recent times, the consolidation play has become a way for many small business owners to realize the wealth they have created in their businesses. This is how it works. A large, established company finds a fragmented industry with a lot of mom-and-pop–type businesses. The consolidator buys them up and puts them under one umbrella to create economies of scale in the industry. The local management team often stays in power, while the parent company begins to build a national brand presence. The payoff for the entrepreneur comes when the consolidator takes the company public and buys out all the independent owners. It is important to conduct due diligence on any consolidator, because one's ability to cash out will be a function of the consolidator's ability to grow the company and take it public.

The ESOP

Entrepreneurs frequently find themselves in situations where succession is not a clear path. Suppose one member of the founding team wants to leave the business and there is not enough cash to buy him or her out. Employees become concerned that the business might be sold and begin looking for alternative employment. Combine internal uncertainty with economic uncertainty and baby boomer CEOs and company founders looking to retirement, and we see the makings of a perfect environment for the Employee Stock Ownership Plan (ESOP). An ESOP is an employee benefit plan that buys and holds company stock in special employee trust accounts that qualify as retirement accounts for tax purposes. Therefore, the employees don't actually own the stock and they receive the benefits of it when they either retire or leave the company.[26] In fact, according to the National Center for Employee Ownership (www.nceo .org), the number of ESOP plans has grown by 3,400 percent since 1980. As of 2009, there were 11,400 plans with 13,700,000 participants.[27] Since 1996, most ESOPs have been private companies using the S Corporation legal structure. In addition to the tax benefits, one reason that ESOPs have been popular is that the bulk of research has found that ESOP companies outperform their non-ESOP counterparts. This is most probably due to the fact that these companies tend to be more stable and the ESOP becomes a willing buyer that has a vested interest in the company succeeding.

It is very important to consult ESOP experts and to implement an ESOP plan as part of the company's succession planning so that when the owners are ready to exit the business, they can do so smoothly.

Dealing with Failure: Bankruptcy

Death is certainly part of any business life cycle, and, therefore, some entrepreneurs must exit their businesses through liquidation. For whatever reasons, the business could not manage a down sales cycle, find new sources of revenue, pay its obligations, or secure capital to float the business until conditions improved. Certainly no entrepreneur starts a high-growth venture with liquidation in mind as the exit strategy, but sometimes the forces working against the business are so great that the entrepreneur must have an exit vehicle so he or she can move on to do something else. What forces a company into bankruptcy is difficult to pinpoint. The immediately precipitating cause is the failure to pay debt; however, myriad other events contributed to that cause. They include a lack of understanding of economic and business cycles, excessive debt, surplus overhead, shifts in demand, excessive expenses, poor dividend policies, union problems, supplier problems, and poor financial management. Of course, the common denominator for all these factors is poor management.

Not all businesses can file for bankruptcy protection, however. Those that are exempt include savings and loan associations, banks, insurance companies, and foreign companies. Furthermore, a bankruptcy filing cannot occur where the intent has been to defraud, and a company may file only once every six years. The Bankruptcy Reform Act of 1978 and Public Law 95–958 provide for more than just liquidation of the business, so that businesses owners might be able to save their businesses through a process of restructuring. Therefore, it is important to have a clear understanding of the bankruptcy mechanisms available if the entrepreneur is faced with financial adversity. The bankruptcy code consists of several chapters, but two chapters are relevant to an entrepreneurial business: Chapter 7 discusses liquidation, and Chapter 11 is about reorganization of businesses.

Chapter 11

Chapter 11 reorganization under the bankruptcy code is really not a bankruptcy in the commonly used sense of the word. It is simply a reorganization of the finances of the business so that it can continue to operate and begin to pay its debts. Only in the case where the creditors believe the management is unable to carry out the terms of the reorganization plan is a trustee appointed to run the company until the debt has been repaid. Otherwise, the entrepreneur remains in control of the business while in a Chapter 11 position. If the entrepreneur has aggregate non-contingent liquidated secured and unsecured debts that do not exceed $2 million (11 U.S.C. Sec. §101 [51C]), then she or he qualifies to be considered a small business owner, which puts the case on a fast track and doesn't require a creditors' committee. After filing a petition for reorganization, the entrepreneur and the creditors must meet within 30 days to discuss the status and organization of the business. The court then appoints a committee, which usually consists of the seven largest unsecured creditors, to develop a plan for the business with the entrepreneur. Of the total number of creditors affected by the plan, representing at least two-thirds of the total dollar amount, at least one-half must accept the plan. Once the court has approved the reorganization plan, the entrepreneur is relieved of any debts except those specified in the plan.

Entrepreneurs can take advantage of a vehicle under Chapter 11 known as a "prepackaged bankruptcy." It requires an entrepreneur to present the creditors and equity owners with a reorganization plan before the bankruptcy filing actually goes to court. If an entrepreneur can achieve the required number of votes agreeing to the plan (more than half the total creditors and two-thirds within each class of creditors), the prepackaged plan can then go forward expeditiously. This process generally takes just four to nine months to complete, rather than the typical nine months to two years. An entrepreneur gains an obvious advantage from using this approach. Under the traditional Chapter 11 process, the creditors and everyone else learn of the company's problems only at the filing. With a prepackaged plan, by contrast, an approved plan is already in place at the point at which the public becomes aware of the problem, and the creditors thus may experience a greater sense of confidence in the entrepreneur. Moreover, the prepackaged plan ties up far less time in legal processes. For this approach to succeed, however, the statement of disclosure about the positive and negative aspects of the business must be carefully constructed to give the creditors all the information they need in order to consider the plan and protect their interests.

Chapter 7

The filing of a petition under Chapter 7 of the bankruptcy code constitutes an Order for Relief and is usually chosen when the business does not have sufficient resources to pay creditors while continuing to operate. It is essentially the liquidation of the assets of the business and the discharge of most types of debt. The debtor files a petition and several required schedules of assets and liabilities with the bankruptcy court serving the area in which he or she lives. A trustee is appointed to manage the disposition of the business, and a meeting of the creditors is held after the petition is filed. The goal of the bankruptcy is to reduce the business to cash and distribute the cash to the creditors where authorized. After exemptions, the monies derived from liquidation go first to secured creditors and then to priority claimants, such as those owed wages, salaries, and contributions to employee benefit plans. Any surplus funds remaining after this distribution go to the entrepreneur. Prior to distribution, the entrepreneur has the right to certain exempt property. If the business is a corporation, those exemptions are minimal. They include interest in any accrued dividends up to a specified maximum; the right to social security benefits, unemployment compensation, public assistance, veterans' benefits, and disability benefits; and the right to stock bonuses, pensions, profit sharing, or a similar plan. Lest it seem as though the entrepreneur is at the mercy of the creditors in a bankruptcy situation, it should be made clear that in either type of bankruptcy petition, Chapter 7 or Chapter 11, the business owner has a great deal of power and control over the process. This power comes from the natural desire of the creditors for a quick and equitable resolution to the problem and from the protections inherent in the bankruptcy law. Often the creditors are better served by negotiating a restructuring of debt while the company is still operating and prior to Chapter 7 liquidation, where they are likely to receive a lesser portion of what is owed them, if anything. There are, however, certain things the entrepreneur will not be permitted to do within a certain period of time before the filing of a bankruptcy petition. These prohibited acts include hiding assets or liabilities, giving preferential treatment to certain creditors up to 90 days prior to the filing of the petition, and making any potentially fraudulent conveyances up to one year prior to the filing. Also the court may nullify any of these transactions during the bankruptcy proceedings.

Before considering bankruptcy as an option to either exit a troubled business or restructure the business in an effort to survive, entrepreneurs should seek advice from an attorney and/or a specialist in turnarounds in the industry. Turnaround consultants are good at putting an unhealthy business on a diet; setting small, achievable goals; and making sure the business stays on track until its finances are in the black. Even when the business cannot be turned around, a bad situation can still be turned into a more positive one by heeding the following advice:

- Entrepreneurs should talk to other entrepreneurs who have been in a similar situation and listen carefully to what they learned.

- If the business is going to fail, end the business quickly before it affects an entrepreneur's personal life. The business may have failed, but the entrepreneur did not. A hard deadline should be set for when the business must be profitable or generate a positive cash flow; if it doesn't, the business should be closed. When the numbers don't add up, an entrepreneur should limit the time devoted to making the business work.

- Under no circumstances should a business owner commingle personal and business funds or other assets. If an entrepreneur lends money to the corporation, she or he will simply be another creditor in line to receive funds from the bankruptcy. And, in fact, the owner may be required to return any funds received in repayment of the loan during the year prior to filing of the bankruptcy petition.

- It is important not to ignore the government. The entrepreneur may risk personal assets and accrue a debt for life if he or she borrows funds from payroll-tax and sales-tax accounts.

- The entrepreneur should begin looking for opportunity. It is important not to wallow in failure. Sometimes the best opportunities are found when an entrepreneur is willing to leave a failing business behind.

- The entrepreneur should do whatever possible to pay back investors. Although it is true that they took a calculated risk investing in the business, if there is a way to pay them back—even if it takes a long time—they will respect the entrepreneur and be there when that next opportunity comes along.

In the end, for entrepreneurs, knowing how to harvest the wealth the business has created can help in structuring a growth plan that will get the entrepreneur where he or she wants to go. Preparing for the unexpected—contingency planning—will go a long way toward ensuring that the business stays on the path to achieving its goals.

SOME FINAL THOUGHTS

Entrepreneurship as a field of study has been in vogue for more than 30 years. There is hardly a media source today that does not talk about entrepreneurs. In fact, the term is in real danger of becoming a cliché and losing its value because it is used to describe all kinds of ventures, from the small "mom-and-pop" to the Fortune 500 conglomerate. It has been used to define successful artists, scientists, and journalists whether or not they start a business. This book has focused on the birth and early growth of innovative, growth-oriented new ventures and has used a classic definition of the term *entrepreneurship*: the discovery, evaluation, and exploitation of opportunities that are innovative, growth oriented, and that create new value for customers. These ventures face unique opportunities and challenges, but their relatively small size and lean structure also make them particularly adaptable to an uncertain and rapidly changing environment. Entrepreneurs are the source of breakthrough innovation, economic growth, and job creation. Startups and the entrepreneurs who create them stand out from the crowd. However, entrepreneurship is more than just new venture creation; it is a mindset, a way of viewing the world, and a skill set that can be learned. Adopting an entrepreneurial mindset is valuable for corporate venturers, small business owners, and those who want to take charge of their lives, their careers, and their businesses and differentiate themselves in a way that enables them to realize their dreams. In that sense, entrepreneurship is for everyone who wants to experience the freedom and independence that come from knowing that opportunities and the resources to make those opportunities a reality are within their grasp.

New Venture Action Plan

- Identify the risks that could affect the business at various points in the future.
- Develop a contingency plan for all the high-probability/high-impact scenarios that may affect the business in the future.
- Set goals for the business that will enable the appropriate exit or harvest strategy.

Questions on Key Issues

1. Contingency planning is not foolproof. How can an entrepreneur ensure that the contingency plans he or she has devised will keep the business on the path to its goals?
2. How can the entrepreneur prepare for potential product liability litigation, both to minimize the chance that such lawsuits will be brought and to give the company the best chance of prevailing against a product liability claim?
3. How can an entrepreneur prepare for a potential decline in sales?

4. Suppose an entrepreneur has built a successful business over several years and now has the opportunity to start another business compatible with the current one. How can the entrepreneur leave the original business and yet stay involved in it?

5. If an entrepreneur's business finds itself in trouble, what are the options available to the entrepreneur to attempt to remedy the situation?

Experiencing Entrepreneurship

1. Interview an entrepreneur in an industry of your choice to learn what his or her harvest strategy is. What is this entrepreneur doing to ensure that the harvest strategy will be achieved?
2. Interview a turnaround consultant about some ways to recognize problems that could lead to business failure. From this interview, devise a list of do's and don'ts that will help an entrepreneur avoid business failure.

Relevant Case Studies

Case 4 The Crowne Inn

Case 9 The Case of Google, Inc.

1-800-AUTOPSY: GIVING THE DEAD A VOICE

Vidal Herrera's motto is "mortis praesdium eet vocem dare necesee est," which translates to "the deceased must be protected and given a voice." El Muerto (the dead one), as he's called in the Latino community of East Los Angeles where he grew up, has spent more than 38 years of his life living with death, and it's still taking its toll. "Death maimed me, death sustained me, and death motivates me," responds Herrera to yet another reporter eager to understand the man behind the enigmatic smile who is on a mission to make sure that the dead have a voice in a world where too often that voice is never heard.

1-800-Autopsy, a company that pioneered the private autopsy business, is now a franchisor with new sites opening around the U.S.; and Vidal Herrera, the founder, has gone from autopsy assistant to deputy medical investigator (CSI) and expert in training pathology residents to serial entrepreneur and industry icon. He cannot believe how fortunate he has been because nothing in his early childhood would have predicted this version of his future.

Background and the Opportunity

Vidal Herrera began his life in a way that could quite easily have taken him on a very different path from the one he ultimately took. Born one of seven boys, Herrera spent his early childhood in a foster home; his mother was suffering from tuberculosis and unable to take care of her brood.

To survive, Herrera legally began working at the age of 12, doing everything from shining shoes, making pizza, and selling newspapers to landscape maintenance and selling maps to movie stars' homes in nearby Hollywood. Barely graduating from high school, he found it hard to secure a full-time job; no one wanted to hire this imposing man in black with the tattoos and a background they didn't understand.

Death had always been part of Herrera's life on the tough streets of Los Angeles. In 1974, Vidal Herrera decided that he had to find a career with a future. He began volunteering as a diener (the person who cleans up after an autopsy) 20 hours a week for two and a half years, simultaneously working full-time as a morgue attendant at the Los Angeles County General Hospital while attending community college part time. Somehow, in the midst of all this work, he also found time to train to become a qualified autopsy technician. At long last, he was given a job at the morgue as a way to earn a living while continuing to attend school. It was on-the-job training with the LA County Chief Medical Examiner/Coroner, from transporting bodies to assisting pathologists at autopsies. He learned about medical photography, how to eviscerate, excise, and dissect tissue. He also learned how to harvest tissue for research and clean crime scenes. He worked on such high-profile cases as the Hillside Strangler and the Nightstalker; at the crime scene of the latter, he discovered a fingerprint that ultimately led to the identification of Richard Ramirez as the Nightstalker. He worked his way up from a diener to autopsy technician, forensic photographer, and then coroner's investigator or what is popularly called today a crime scene investigator (CSI).

However, August 28, 1984, while removing a 284-pound cadaver from a crime scene, he suffered a back injury that put him out of business for over four years. During that time he underwent multiple surgeries and rehabilitation that made it impossible for him to sit or stand for more than 15 minutes at a time. As a result, he had trouble finding another job—he sent out over 2,000 applications and no one would hire him, not even to work in a fast-food restaurant. By then he was married with children and had to find a way to support them. Finally, in 1988, his former boss, onetime Los Angeles County Coroner Ronald Kornblum, who by then was in private practice, hired Herrera to help with an autopsy and passed the word of Herrera's skills to others in the industry. As a result, the VA Medical Center in West Los Angeles hired him as an autopsy technician on a contract basis to fill the gap in the availability of trained technicians. Herrera soon discovered that other hospitals and mortuaries were experiencing the same problem: too many autopsies and not enough technicians or a budget big enough to support them. He began to explore the idea for a private autopsy service that could serve the unmet need. With more than 2.4 million deaths each year in the U.S. alone and only 2 percent of those deaths autopsied by pathologists, the opportunity appeared to be huge. Doctors were generally hesitant to suggest autopsies to the families of their patients out of fear of litigation, even though the Archives of Pathology and Laboratory Medicine found in 2002 that autopsy findings are rarely the source of medical liability decisions. As a consequence, families had to request autopsies and rely on private services to secure them.

In late 1988, Herrera launched Autopsy-Post Services as a subcontractor to hospitals. In the beginning, the company grew through referrals, world of mouth, and the support of funeral directors and the medical and legal communities. Because autopsies must be supervised by an MD, Herrera contacted board-certified pathologists

with whom he had worked to bring them on board in their off-hours. It wasn't until 1993 that the business really began to take off. One day as he was watching TV, he noticed ads for 1-800-DENTIST and 1-800-FLOWERS. Herrera remembered a *Forbes* article he had read about the growing popularity of 1-800 numbers, and he thought, "Why not 1-800-Autopsy?" He quickly checked with the telephone company to see if 1-800-AUTOPSY was available, and it was. He now had the hook for his business. He purchased a van and painted 1-800-AUTOPSY on the side panels. This attracted a lot of attention for his growing business. Soon families began calling him for second opinions on suspicious deaths or to exhume bodies for re-autopsy. The majority of his customers were families and medical malpractice and criminal defense attorneys. Whereas a coroner's office would charge $2,854 for a private autopsy (if they even had the time to perform it), Herrera charged $2,000 and produced in 10 days the results that the coroner's office took nearly 120 days to provide. Today, to discourage requests for autopsies, most coroners' offices charge at least $7,000 per autopsy.

With the Internet becoming the place to be for businesses, Herrera created his website www.1800autopsy.com to serve as a way to educate his customers about the positive side of the death business and to sell t-shirts and unusual items like a brain gelatin mold and a coffin purse. While most pathologists don't seek publicity, Herrera decided that a more high profile approach was the way to create more awareness for the field and the benefits of autopsies. He was not at all bashful about claiming that he was the autopsy technician for all of iconic lawyer Johnnie Cochran's cases before his death. He also did the autopsy on Coretta Scott King's daughter. A man of integrity, however, he would never take on a case for publicity's sake. In that regard, he turned down a request to do a second autopsy on pop icon Michael Jackson because it wasn't needed.

By 2010, Herrera had a staff of four full-time employees and two part-timers that performed more than 700 procedures a year costing from

$1,500 to $3,200. In addition, the company offered:

- Exhumation and disinterment autopsies
- Toxicology analysis
- Tissue procurement
- Post-mortem neurological diagnosis
- Post-mortem asbestos procurement
- Post-mortem DNA (paternity) analysis
- Hospital services support
- Medical photography services
- TV and movie consulting

The Industry

The anatomical pathology testing sector of the Diagnostic & Medical Laboratories industry in the U.S. represents about 12 percent of this $47.5 billion industry, which is experiencing an annual growth rate of about 3.4 percent. But the reality is that the practice of autopsy in some respects is a dying science. Thirty years ago, hospitals performed autopsies on about 50 percent of hospital deaths. Today only about 2 percent of all deaths in the U.S. are autopsied, with most occurring in academic hospitals. The *Journal of the American Medical Association (JAMA)* reports that this is a disturbing trend to medical practitioners who believe that autopsy "is the one place where truth can be sought, found, and told without conflicts of interest." It is the unequivocal source of the cause of death. Only 5.4 percent of all services in the diagnostic testing industry are paid by the patient out of pocket, which is the segment in which private autopsy services lies.

Several reasons have been proposed for the current demand for private autopsy services: (1) Many hospitals don't have autopsy suites and can't provide the service; (2) city and county governments have cut budgets to coroners' offices; (3) many hospitals don't have trained technicians because there are no schools that teach them how to perform autopsies; (4) insurance companies don't cover them; (5) many doctors are concerned that autopsy results could be used against them or the hospital in malpractice suits; and (6) most hospitals will perform autopsies only

for deaths under suspicious circumstances, not to determine such conditions as Alzheimer's disease, because the Joint Commission on Accreditation of Health Care organizations no longer requires hospitals to maintain a minimum autopsy rate.

Nevertheless, autopsies are recognized as an important epidemiologic tool for establishing risk factors for various diseases as well as identifying potential disease outbreaks. Many studies have found that about 20 to 30 percent of autopsies will uncover a significant medical condition that was not previously known. It is also an important tool for educating physicians because it gives them a way to point out discrepancies in clinical diagnoses that might have implications for patient care.

The critical success factors for businesses in this industry are:

- Reputation
- Economies of scale
- Proximity to hospitals and doctors
- Appropriate price structure
- Rapid adoption of new technology
- Understanding of government policies and regulations

The drivers of costs in this industry include pressure on profit margins as costs of laboratory-related supplies increase, and a shortage of skilled technicians.

Currently, there are no certification bodies for autopsy technicians, and the industry is fragmented with a growing number of small service companies. Barriers to entry for those trained in pathology are relatively moderate, and the only requirement is that an MD supervise the autopsy. However, the capital investment is intensive, depending on the scope of services being provided. The need for specialist pathologists is decreasing as trained technicians under the supervision of a qualified pathologist can perform most tests and maintain quality control.

Growing the Business

In 1995 alone, Herrera turned away 9,000 autopsy cases while doing about 900 cases a year without advertising. By 1998, he and his team were performing five or more autopsies a day, generating more than $1 million for the business. The demand for his services led to the idea to franchise the business so that it could grow more quickly. Autopsy/Post-Services could be duplicated relatively easily; the demand was worldwide, and the franchise would probably face less competition because, according to Herrera, most franchisees "would rather open a restaurant or a yogurt shop than a dead body." The typical franchisee candidates would be certified pathology assistants, autopsy technicians, embalmers, and doctors.

He also knew that autopsy technicians, embalmers, pathologists, or pathology assistants were always looking for ways to grow their own businesses and increase their income. He would build a model franchise and provide franchisees with thorough training, materials, techniques, and guidance. His manual would provide checklists for every type of procedure possible. In 2005, he began his franchise effort, training his franchisees at his Los Angeles headquarters. By 2010, he had four franchises in Florida, Northern California, and Nevada, with several more in the planning stages. The franchising strategy took far longer than he thought it would when he first conceived it in 1999. However, without all the right systems and controls in place, he risked putting franchises out in the market that didn't meet his high standards for quality and performance.

To overcome the negative perception that many people had of the business and to find another way to grow it, Herrera began promoting the donation of tissues and organs for research. He firmly believed that all human tissue could be used for transplants or research to save lives and bring the cost of medical care down. Two particular areas of interest for Herrera were AIDS research and Alzheimer's disease. The tissue research and organ donation side of his business was his way of demonstrating that death is not necessarily bad, but merely a part of the cycle of life; when someone dies, someone else's life can be saved or otherwise helped by organ donation or tissue research. Herrera always tried to balance death with life-affirming activities, so he

also started a rather whimsical business building couches out of coffins in his spare time as a way to turn something morbid into something useful: www.Coffincouches.com.

Not everyone was enthusiastic about Herrera's plans for his business. In October 2000, the city of Tujunga revoked his permit to operate a laboratory in a business district where his neighbors were restaurants and retail establishments. The Planning Department had decided it had made a mistake six months after Herrera had spent thousands of dollars remodeling the facility. While appealing the decision, Herrera refurbished the space into a replica morgue and began renting it to film studios for shooting TV shows and movies. A collector of antique morgue and mortuary equipment, he soon discovered that there was a demand for such properties from film studios. When the CSI franchise on television took hold, he created a rental business, MorguePropRentals .com, to serve TV shows like CSI (Las Vegas, the original), CSI Miami, and CSI New York, as well as other top shows such as House and Law and Order. He rented his replica autopsy room and all the accessories that were typically found in an autopsy suite.

In 2010, Herrera stopped doing autopsies himself and concentrated his time speaking around the country and doing sales and marketing for his franchises. However, he didn't stop launching businesses. In November 2010, with two friends from grammar school, he started 1-800-Tamales to respond to the growing demand for his "Truly the Best!" tamales (www.1800tamales.com) packaged in miniature coffins. Once again he recognized a need because his clients, who had received tamales as Christmas gifts, asked him to start the business.

"Death is, in fact, a recession-proof business— it just never stops," quips Herrera. And he may just be right on that point because the death rate is expected to double as the baby boom generation ages. Nevertheless, Herrera, who was a pioneer in this market, is now seeing new competition every day trying to take advantage of the markets he opened up. A business never remains exactly the way it started, and Vidal Herrera is conscious of the fact that he has to stay ahead of the game. Are there ways to change the game to make the entry barriers higher for new entrants? Is his diversification play a wise one and will franchising take off and make him the next Ray Kroc of McDonald's fame in the world of private autopsies?

Sources

Interview with Vidal Herrera, Los Angeles, October 19, 2010; "Demand Breathes life into Private Autopsy Companies." *The Wall Street Journal*, October 14, 2010; "Small Business Carves Up Autopsy Trade." MSNBC, October 28, 2008; Snyder, S. (October 2010). "Diagnostic & Medical Laboratories in the U.S." *IBIS World*, www.ibisworld.com/industry/default .aspx?indid=1575; Burton, E.C. (April 8, 2010). "Autopsy Rate and Physician Attitudes Toward Autopsy." *eMedicine*, http://emedicine.medscape.com/article/1705948-overview; "Pathologists Request Autopsy Revival." Medical News & Perspectives, *JAMA*, June 28, 1995, Vol. 273, No. 24, p. 1989; Howard, Robert E. "Autopsy/Post-Services—A Sure Thing!" *The Stakeholder*, September 1995; and "Breathing New Life into Autopsies." American Medical News, *AMA*, March 9, 1998, Vol.41 No.10.

Discussion Questions

1. What were the precipitating factors that play in the role of Herrera becoming an entrepreneur?
2. What was the source of the original opportunity and how did Herrera position himself to take advantage of it?
3. Does his growth strategy make sense for the type of business he operates? Why? Why not?
4. What conclusions can you draw about serial entrepreneurship from Vidal Herrera's journey?

DEMAND MEDIA: CREATING A TRANSFORMATIVE BUSINESS

In 2005, the editor of *Wired Magazine*, Chris Anderson, published a highly regarded book called *The Long Tail*. In it, he proposed that culture and the consumer economy were quickly moving away from a focus on a few big hits (the top artists, the top brands, and so forth) and toward a huge number of tiny niches that met very specific needs, for example, finding a favorite B horror film that never made it to the big screen. The cost of reaching all these interest niches has been declining rapidly. Couple that with the fact that society is relying more and more on systems where no one's in charge, and where intelligence is simply emergent, and you have what is called the "long-tail phenomenon."

Chris Anderson didn't know how prophetic his words were when he wrote his book or that by May 2006, less than a year later, a serial entrepreneur named Richard Rosenblatt would put the long-tail theory to the test with extraordinary success and become one of the earliest major players in the New Media Industry. In the short space of about 4.5 years, Demand Media has grown to over 600 employees with locations in North America and Europe, and Rosenblatt has managed to raise $355 million in investor capital to fund Demand's growth. He is that rare entrepreneur who has the ability to envision not just a new company but a new industry.

The Mind of a Serial Entrepreneur

Forbes Magazine once wrote that if you attached a cable to Richard Rosenblatt, you could power a small town.[1] He is a multi-tasker of the highest order with the ability to juggle several phone calls and text messages while carrying on a coherent conversation. A graduate of UCLA with a degree in political science ("Which means you're not sure what you want to do or you want to go to law school"), he decided to attend law school at UCLA's cross-town rival, the University of Southern California (USC).

> Back then, you only had two choices being a Jewish kid growing up in the [San Fernando] Valley, either a doctor or a lawyer; there really wasn't anything else. There was nothing else you could do. I hated blood, so I decided I was going to be a lawyer. What I also liked about law was the fact that you had to argue two sides. And I think as a good entrepreneur you have to look at both sides of everything; and in particular as a CEO, you're going to find yourself in-between two very smart people that see things completely differently, and you in the end have to decide which one you want to select without bruising the ego of another person so they're afraid to ever give you that feedback again.[2]

[1]Brown, E. (September 26, 2007). "The Mixologist," Forbes.com, www.forbes.com/2007/09/26/myspace-online-media-tech-cz_eb_0926demandmedia.html.
[2]Interview with Richard Rosenblatt, November, 2009.

In 1994, Rosenblatt and his wife started a small business called R & R advertising.

> We had this crazy concept that we were going to put a bunch of small businesses in newspapers all around the country. Whatever people wanted to sell, we wanted to advertise. We'd buy lots and lots of newspapers; chop them up into small pieces, and our guarantee was that you'll never pay more by coming through us. Anyhow, the way it works with the rate cards and newspapers, if you buy a full page, you can chop it up into little 16ths and make huge margins on those. The only reason I'm telling you this is because it grew to be a pretty big business. We were making millions of dollars a year at 24 and 25, selling advertising, not net to us, but gross dollars.[3]

Rosenblatt's father was a computer scientist who introduced him to the World Wide Web. In 1994, there were no websites and the interface for users at the time was Mosaic. His father suggested that Rosenblatt could put his clients on the Web at no cost. Lured by the possibilities, Rosenblatt began acquiring domains and putting his clients on the Web, from the local dry cleaner to Big Dog sportswear and eventually the Super Bowl at imall.com. The early days of the Web were much like the wild West, but Rosenblatt began to notice that small sites weren't able to attract a lot of visitors. It occurred to him that if he aggregated all his clients into one central place, he could create the equivalent of a shopping mall, and they would all benefit from the aggregation of traffic. And in fact, in 1994, Rosenblatt's mall, later named iMALL, became the first shopping mall on the Web. The revenue model for iMALL included website development, hosting, and related services, and eventually included expansive ecommerce services. iMALL was one of a very few Internet companies in 1996 that even had a valuation. Amazon was valued at $500 million, Yahoo! at $300 million, and iMALL at $50 million. By then Netscape, the first commercial browser, had gone public.

iMALL was a powerful business model in 1996, but the company was running out of money and Rosenblatt had never raised capital or knew anything about finance. He was introduced to a potential investor whose investment bank was willing to put in $250,000 and sent Rosenblatt on the road to pitch his business and raise an additional $3 to $5 million. Apparently, his hastily put together pitch was effective because Rosenblatt raised $20 million in 5 days. Flush with capital, he became Chairman and CEO and began reducing costs, changing the business model, and recruiting a new board of directors. In 1997, he pitched the idea of credit card processing online to First Data Corporation, then a Fortune 100 company. First Data bought 10 percent of iMALL, and Rosenblatt was on his way to building a serious company. Armed with this partnership, iMALL morphed its value proposition and became the first ecommerce enabler of small merchants. The customer could pay $30 a month for iMALL's ecommerce tools, snap them into their website, and generate traffic from the aggregated mall. In 1999, he sold the company to Excite Home for $565 million, taking advantage of the irrational exuberance over ecommerce; at the time, iMall was generating about a $1.5 million in revenue with no profits. Timing is everything; the dot com bubble hit, and two years later Excite Home was bankrupt.

After the sale of iMALL, Rosenblatt was approached by a small startup called Great Domains, an Internet domain reseller. Rosenblatt invested $1 million in the business, reasoning that they could create an exchange where domain names could be resold. Starting with three founders and no employees, he became vice-chairman and helped them build the business and sell it one year later to Verisign for $100 million. During that same year, he was approached by the entrepreneurs of a startup called Web Million. Rosenblatt leaped in again and within six months, they sold the company for $20 million. "So, it was a great streak. That is about as good as it gets . . . We sold $700 million worth of companies in a year. I know it's silly to even say it."[4]

For the next few years following the dot com crash, money dried up, and Rosenblatt started a small venture fund to do some investments of his

---

[3]Ibid.

[4]Ibid.

own. His original investors in iMALL, who by now had made multiple millions on companies Rosenblatt had built and sold, told him that he wasn't going to invest anymore until Rosenblatt had experienced a failure. "You won't be a great executive until you actually learn from a failure." He also warned Rosenblatt to only have one failure, because at two failures, investors begin to believe that maybe "you don't learn from your mistake." That advice stayed with Rosenblatt, but he didn't realize that his very next venture would be the one that would fail.

Dr. C. Everett Koop, Surgeon General of the United States under President Ronald Reagan from 1982 to 1989, had built a website and company worth a billion dollars on the idea of a Web portal dedicated to health issues. After the dot com crash, the company was on the verge of bankruptcy, and Rosenblatt was once again called in to turn the company around. His team flew to Austin, Texas, and raised $20 million on the strength of Dr. Koop's brand. At the time, the company had no revenue, was losing $10 million a month, and was supporting 300 employees. Once again Rosenblatt began the turnaround by laying off 280 employees. Then he discovered that he hadn't done sufficient diligence. The company was selling advertising, but the online advertising market had dried up. It was also licensing health content to NBC, but after the crash, the content licensing model ended. Rosenblatt decided it was time to get creative and suggested a line of supplements branded with Dr. Koop's name. He succeeded in getting distribution in Wal-Mart and was ready to launch when September 11, 2001, hit, and the capital markets simply went away. The company was public but had no access to capital. Although Rosenblatt's investors were willing to put some investment money into the venture, he was reluctant to risk their capital, so the company went back into bankruptcy in 2002.

> We were proud that we went from losing $10 million a month to near profitability in a year. We tripled the market cap. We did all these good things, but in the end we failed and we lost everybody's money. And that was probably the worst feeling I ever had. And nobody was even upset. The most amazing part was

that you had this giant flameout, and we didn't have one lawsuit from the invenstors . . . that doesn't happen. They [investors and shareholders] even sue you when you do everything right. So for us not to get sued with this just shows how honest and straight-forward we were during pretty tough times.[5]

After this experience, Rosenblatt didn't want to raise money from anyone. In 2002, he opened the first of what was to be four nightclubs named Air Conditioned. Then, in 2003, he and two partners started an online company called Super-dudes. The concept was pre-MySpace, and it enabled kids to create a persona online through an avatar—"You could be a superhero, and if you're really into this superhero, you can help people." This site was one of the first on the Internet to use avatar technology and it quickly grew to 1 million registered members in the first year. It was during this time that Rosenblatt received the phone call that would change his life.

The Rise of Demand Media

In 2004, Rosenblatt left Superdudes to become the CEO of eUniverse, concluding that this move was either going to make his career or he'd have to go back to doing small deals for the rest of his life.

> I came in as the CEO of eUniverse, which had to be the most challenged company on the Internet; it made Dr. Koop look good. It was just delisted from NASDAQ, the founder and CEO was removed by the Board, it had an accounting restatement, and just completed a bitter proxy battle. It was even being investigated by the FDA for some of its products that were burning people's skin, and it was losing $4 million a quarter. And I took the job. Why did I take the job? I told everybody I knew that after the failure at Dr. Koop, I believed that I was capable of doing much more than running a fifteen person company called Superdudes.[6]

Rosenblatt immediately made personnel cuts, brought in a new team, and got eUniverse (Rosenblatt changed the name to Intermix) to break even

5Ibid.
6Ibid.

in the first quarter of 2004. At that time, the market cap for the company was about $65 million. He quickly took the stock from $1.83 a share to $10 a share. He put the bulk of the resources into MySpace and let them increase their staff because he was convinced that giving "creative power to the people . . . is the greatest revenue model in the world." MySpace grew from 1 million members to 24 million by the time the company was sold. As the company was building momentum, Rosenblatt was completely blindsided by New York State Attorney General Elliot Spitzer who wanted to prosecute the company based for violations committed under former eUniverse CEO Brad Greenspan. Rosenblatt signed a non-binding letter of intent to pay $7.5 million over three years. The moment he signed the letter, the stock went up 300 percent because the market now knew the exact amount of the liability and it stopped the rumor mills. Then Rosenblatt and the board decided it was time to sell the company. MySpace needed further investment and the fee to Spitzer had tapped their cash reserves. At the time, everyone was claiming that Intermix was worth $4 to $5 a share, but the board authorized Rosenblatt to sell at $8 a share. When News Corp and its Fox Interactive Division expressed interest, Rosenblatt boldly claimed that the stock was worth $12 a share.

In a 20 minute meeting with just Rosenblatt and Chairman/CEO Rupert Murdoch, Intermix was sold. During the meeting, Murdoch asked Rosenblatt why he should buy this business Rosenblatt responded:

> It's the perfect business model. The users create their own content, and drive their traffic by inviting their friends, which means you have no distribution or traffic acquisition costs and all you have to do is sell the ads . . . And I said, Mr. Murdoch that's $12 a share, that's the price. If not . . . its going to be a long process and maybe you'll get it, but it's possible that someone else will get it. And he [Rupert Murdoch] said if I get it done for $12 a share, can I have it this weekend. And it was Tuesday night, and this was a very large transaction. I mean, if you deal with lawyers, they can't do a contract in 4 weeks. And I said yes, subject to

my fiduciary duties as a public company I will have it delivered to you by Sunday. So we shook hands, we left there, and over the next two days, they [News Corp] did a couple days of diligence, we got in a room from Friday to Sunday, and we negotiated this deal that I'm really proud of, that really changed the landscape of the internet.[7]

Reports vary on the actual price, but the reported price was $650 million. Rosenblatt considered running the Internet side of News Corp for a while, but the former CEO of E-Trade and Newscorp advisor told him it would never work because Rosenblatt was too much of an entrepreneur. So, Rosenblatt consulted to News Corp for six months while he built his next venture, Demand Media. Immediately, he was able to raise $120 million without hiring an investment banker because he had experienced so many previous successes and had built a loyal base of investors. His goal was to raise as much money as possible while it was available as part of his overall strategy to acquire a number of companies and build a fast growing organic business. As of 2010, he had raised $355 million.

Demand Media: Transforming the Long Tail into a Sustainable Business

In June, 2006, Rosenblatt and co-founder, Shawn Colo, launched Santa Monica-based Demand Media. They immediately bought eHOW .com and soon thereafter the core social networking platform they had sold with Intermix to News Corp. That became the foundation for a diverse portfolio of companies and websites. Demand Media is "a leader in a new Internet-based model for the professional creation of high-quality, commercially valuable content at scale."[8] Demand

---

[7]Ibid.
[8]United States Securities and Exchange Commission, Form S-1 Registration Statement for Demand Media, Inc. August 6, 2010, www.sec.gov/Archives/edgar/data/1365038/000104746910007151/a2199583zs-1.htm#ca40301_prospectus_summary.

Media identifies, creates, distributes, and monetizes in-demand content through two distinct offerings: content and media, and domain registrar. The competitive advantages that they claim are (1) proprietary technologies and processes, (2) the freelance content creator community, (3) rapidly growing content library of more than 3 million articles and 200,000 videos, (4) more than 94 million unique visitors a month, (5) the second largest domain registrar, and (6) a highly scalable operating platform.[9]

In content and media, Demand Media exploits both the demand and the supply side of the equation when it comes to economic efficiencies. The company creates content based on *demand* from the market, which it determines through a proprietary algorithm that tells the company what people are searching for on the Internet. On the *supply* side, the content business, which is arguably the largest on the Internet, takes advantage of the millions of "experts" who write well, and are looking for additional opportunities to create an online presence.[10] Given that the median price of content on the Internet (blogs, Wikis, tweeting, Q & A websites) is zero, Demand Media can pay this untapped supply anything beyond zero and capture top-notch writers who can research and write quickly. The best of the more than 10,000 freelance content creators in Demand Media's stable earn $80 for a premium article instead of the $15 that most writers get. These content creators produce a daily average of 5,700 text articles and videos. Taking advantage of untapped talent means that Demand Media is putting itself in a position to arbitrage the value. Some estimates place the value of this opportunity at $30 billion, and currently Demand Media owns the niche. In the S-1 filling for their IPO, Demand revealed its return on new articles.

> We base our capital allocation decisions primarily on our analysis of a predicted internal rate of return and have generally observed favorable historical returns on

content. For example, our article content published on eHow in the third quarter of 2008, or Q308 cohort, generated a 76% internal rate of return. This internal rate of return measure does not account for any revenue after September 30, 2010, although we anticipate that our Q308 cohort will continue to general revenue for the foreseeable future and, therefore, achieve a higher internal rate of return.[11]

Also included within the content and media portion of the business are enterprise-class social media applications that bring user profiles, comments, forums, reviews, blogs, and photo/video sharing to websites within the Demand Media portfolio and to the more than 375 websites owned by customers such as USATODAY.com and the National Football League (NFL.com). The company's owned and operated websites attract more than 94 million unique visitors and 621 million page views per month. Moreover, Demand Media matches targeted advertisements with content to optimize advertising revenue from those long-tail sites.

The registrar side of the business, eNom, holds more than 10 million Internet domain names and is now the largest wholesale registrar in the world and the second largest registrar overall after GoDaddy.com. eNom was the first business that Demand Media purchased in 2006 when the company launched and it provided Demand Media with very important generic domain names such as gardening.com, map.com, and trails.com. eNom now generates approximately 41 percent of Demand Media's revenue. Exhibit 1 from the Form S-1 SEC filing displays the consolidated statements of Operations from 2007 through June 30, 2010.

As of September 30, 2010, Demand Media employed 600 people in three primary locations—Santa Monica, CA, Bellevue, WA, and Austin, Texas—as well as sales offices, support facilities, and data centers in various locations in North America and Europe. In addition, the company hires about 10,000 freelance writers and 650 copy editors.

---

[9]Ibid. p. 19.
[10]Hobart, B. (August 12, 2010). "Demand Media's IPO: Everything You Need to Know." *Business Insider,* www.businessinsider.com/author/byrne-hobart.

[11]Op.cit United States Securities and Exchange Commission, p. 15.

EXHIBIT 1 Demand Media Statement of Operations 2007–2010

	Nine Months Ended December 31	Year Ended December 31		Six Months Ended June 30	
	2007	2008	2009	2009	2010
Consolidated Statements of Operations:					
Revenue	$102,295	$170,250	$198,452	$91,273	$114,002
Operating expenses(1)(2)					
Service costs (exclusive of amortization of intangible assets)	57,833	98,238	114,482	53,309	61,735
Sales and marketing	3,601	15,360	19,994	9,181	10,396
Product development	10,965	14,407	21,502	9,775	12,514
General and administrative	19,584	28,191	28,358	13,994	17,440
Amortization of intangible assets	17,393	33,204	32,152	16,429	16,173
Total operating expenses	109,376	189,400	216,488	102,688	118,258
Loss from operations	(7,081)	(19,150)	(18,036)	(11,415)	(4,256)
Other income (expense)					
Interest income	1,415	1,636	494	223	11
Interest expense	(1,245)	(2,131)	(1,759)	(1,139)	(349)
Other income (expense), net	(999)	(250)	(19)	—	(128)
Total other expense	(829)	(745)	(1,284)	(916)	(466)
Loss before income taxes	(7,910)	(19,895)	(19,320)	(12,331)	(4,722)
Income tax (benefit) provision	(2,293)	(5,736)	2,663	1,596	1,327
Net loss	(5,617)	(14,159)	(21,983)	(13,927)	(6,049)
Cumulative preferred stock dividends	(14,059)	(28,209)	(30,848)	(15,015)	(16,206)
Net loss attributable to common stockholders	$(19,676)	$(42,368)	$(52,831)	$(28,942)	$(22,255)
Net loss per share: Basic and diluted(3)	$ (2.12)	$ (2.59)	$ (2.37)	$ (1.38)	$ (0.84)
Weighted average number of shares	9,262	16,367	22,318	20,961	26,347
Pro forma net loss per share Basic and diluted(4)			$ (0.15)		$ (0.04)
Weighted average number of shares used in computing pro forma net loss per share Basic and diluted(4)			145,662		149,691

(continued)

EXHIBIT 1   Demand Media Statement of Operations 2007–2010 (continued)

	Nine Months Ended December 31	Year Ended December 31		Six Months Ended June 30	
	2007	2008	2009	2009	2010
(1) Depreciation expense included in the above line items:					
Service costs	$ 2,581	$ 8,158	$ 11,882	$ 5,391	$ 6,826
Sales and marketing	42	94	184	90	82
Product development	509	1,094	1,434	675	659
General and administrative	458	1,160	1,463	668	921
Total depreciation expense	$ 3,590	$ 10,506	$ 14,963	$ 6,824	$ 8,488
(2) Stock-based compensation included in the above line items:					
Service costs	$ 52	$ 586	$ 473	$ 202	$ 428
Sales and marketing	241	1,576	1,561	613	968
Product development	504	1,030	1,349	463	775
General and administrative	2,873	3,158	3,973	1,923	2,600
Total stock-based compensation	$ 3,670	$ 6,350	$ 7,356	$ 3,201	$ 4,771

(3) Basic loss per share is computed by dividing the net loss attributable to common stockholders by the weighted average number of common shares outstanding during the period. Net loss attributable to common stockholders is increased for cumulative preferred stock dividends earned during the period. For the periods where we presented losses, all potentially dilutive common shares comprising of stock options, restricted stock purchase rights, or RSPRs, warrants and convertible preferred stock are antidilutive.

RSPRs are considered outstanding common shares and included in the computation of basic earnings per share as of the date that all necessary conditions of vesting are satisfied. RSPRs are excluded from the dilutive earnings per share calculation when their impact is antidilutive. Prior to satisfaction of all conditions of vesting, unvested RSPRs are considered contingently issuable shares and are excluded from weighted average common shares outstanding.

(4) Unaudited pro forma basic and diluted net loss per common share have been computed to give effect to the conversion of our convertible preferred stock (using the if-converted method) into an aggregate of 123,344,512 shares of our common stock on a one-for-one basis as though the conversion had occurred at January 1, 2009.

Source: Op.cit United States Securities and Exchange Commission, p. 25.

Competitive Challenges Going Forward

Demand Media operates in a highly competitive market competing with social media platforms such as Jive Software and KickApps, specialty websites in niche interest areas such as golf and humor, and online marketing, content, and media companies such as AOL, About.com, and Yahoo! that also own proprietary search data and algorithms. The biggest potential competitor is Google who could decide to compete directly in the content creation area and terminate commercial agreements with Demand Media. To date, Demand Media has not sought brand recognition in the way that Google, Yahoo!, and AOL have, so its name does not enjoy the recognition of the more established brands. However, in 2010, AOL and Yahoo began developing a studio model much like Demand Media's successful model.

As arguably the largest SEO (search engine optimization) company on the Internet, Demand Media depends on major Internet search engines (Google, Bing, Yahoo!) to direct a significant amount of traffic to its websites. The company reports that about 40 percent of its page view traffic comes from these large search engines. Moreover, Demand Media generates approximately 18 percent of its annual revenue from cost-per-click advertising provided by Google. Relying on advertising revenues makes the company vulnerable to a variety of factors that it can't control such as reduced ad spending by advertisers, project delays, economic conditions, and unpredictable events. Demand Media's advertising contracts with Google for cost-per-click expire in the second quarter of 2012 and will be an important factor in determining Demand Media's revenue mix going forward. In 2010, the company began moving into branded sales in a big way, hiring Yahoo's head of sales Joanne Bradford as CRO.

Demand Media has been granted five U.S. patents with 19 applications pending in the U.S. Patent and Trademark office as well as other jurisdictions. Although patents are important proprietary assets, most of the company's IP is held as trade secrets. The considerable funding they've raised from the likes of Goldman Sachs, 3i Group, Generation Partners, Oak Investment Partners, and Spectrum Equity Investors has helped to build a proprietary back-end system that is a significant competitive advantage. That system enables the company to calculate the average cost per click on any search query and multiply that times the projected traffic to figure out how much money would be generated over five years in the form of revenue. Those who develop, edit, and fact check the content pieces share in that revenue. The amount of revenue generated also is an important indicator of what kind of content to produce in the future. "Did you know that every month, 50,000 people search on ways to make detergent at home?" reports Rosenblatt.[12] That's important information about what people are looking for.

In December of 2010, Demand Media was preparing to do an IPO. It had originally been slated for early fall 2010, but as often happens, IPOs get delayed. On October 29, 2010, the company filed an amended version of its August S-1 regulatory filing with updated financials reflecting the third quarter. Once the SEC approves the filing, the company can do its road show for several weeks to persuade investors to commit. In its initial filing, Demand Media was trying to raise $125 million on a $1.5 billion valuation. Its revenues were expected to top $230 million in 2010 and profit had grown from $18.9 million to $41.9 million using less stringent non-GAAP financial rules. Under GAAP rules, the company had a net loss for the first 9 months of 2010 of $6.4 million. With a long dry spell for big brand IPOs and no billion dollar IPOs since 2004 when Google went public, the tech world was hungry for Demand Media to pull the trigger.

Discussion Questions

1. What do you believe led to Richard Rosenblatt becoming a serial entrepreneur?
2. Would you have made the decision Rosenblatt made to take Dr. Koop into bankruptcy?
3. What is Demand Media's business model and competitive advantage?
4. How does Demand Media justify doing a public offering when it is not yet profitable under GAAP rules?

---

[12]Malik, O. (February 5, 2010). "Inside the Mind of Demand Media's Richard Rosenblatt," Gigaom.com.

CORPORATE ENTREPRENEURSHIP AND INNOVATION IN SILICON VALLEY: THE CASE OF GOOGLE, INC.*

Introduction

In May 2009, Sergey Brin and Larry Page, co-founders of Google, Inc., watched Green Day in concert at the famous Shoreline Amphitheatre in Mountain View, California. The brilliant young entrepreneurs had many things on their minds. They tried to determine how they were going to navigate Google during the worst recession the United States had seen since the Great Depression (Willis, 2009). The Standard and Poor's 500 (S&P 500), one of the most popular indicators of the U.S. economy, had dropped to an intra-day low of 666.79 on March 6, 2009, from an intra-day high of 1576.09 on October 11, 2007, for a collapse of 57.7 percent (S&P 500 Index, 2009). World-wide stocks had decreased on average by approximately 60 percent.

Warren Buffett, Chairman of Berkshire Hathaway and one of the most prolific investors of all time, foresaw the current economic turmoil in early 2008. Buffett stated, "Even though the numbers

do not state it, the United States was in for a deep long-lasting recession" (*USA Today*, 2008).

By early 2009, U.S. retirement accounts also dropped by an average of 40 percent or $3.4 trillion (Brandon, 2009). Many U.S. retirees saw their pensions cut in half and many were forced to go back to work or rely on their families to support them.

Brin and Page had never witnessed anything like this in their young lives. Even the ever successful company they created in 1998, Google, Inc., was feeling the effects of the crisis. At its low point, Google's stock price dropped 51.35 percent from an intra-day high of $713.58 on November 2, 2007, to an intra-day low of $259.56 on November 20, 2008. The stock price picked up momentum recently and traded at $410 as of May 28, 2009.

As the young entrepreneurs listened to the Bay Area band Green Day, they pondered their next moves. Google had problems. The company's primary problem was how to maintain the culture of corporate entrepreneurship and innovation in the face of flat net profits from 2007 to 2008. As a result of this, the firm had to fire several employees for the first time in the company's history and eliminate products that made no money (Blodget, 2009). Furthermore, employees left for a variety of reasons (e.g., lack of mentoring and formal career planning, too much bureaucracy, low pay and benefits, high cost of living in the area, desire to start their own business, etc.).

| **EXHIBIT 1** | Google Income Statements 2004–2008 (in millions) |

	2008	2007	2006	2005	2004
Period End Date	12/31/2008	12/31/2007	12/31/2006	12/31/2005	12/31/2004
Period Length	12 Months	12 Months	12 Months	12 Months	12 Months
Revenue	21,795.55	16,593.99	10,604.92	6,138.56	3,189.22
Total Revenue	**21,795.55**	**16,593.99**	**10,604.92**	**6,138.56**	**3,189.22**
Cost of Revenue, Total	8,621.51	6,649.09	4,225.03	2,577.09	1,468.97
Gross Profit	**13,174.04**	**9,944.9**	**6,379.89**	**3,561.47**	**1,720.26**
Selling/General/Administrative Expenses, Total	3,748.88	2,740.52	1,601.31	854.68	483.9
Research & Development	2,793.19	2,119.99	1,228.59	599.51	395.16
Depreciation/Amortization	0.0	0.0	0.0	0.0	0.0
Interest Expense (Income), Net Operating	0.0	0.0	0.0	0.0	0.0
Unusual Expense (Income)	1,094.76	0.0	0.0	90.0	201.0
Other Operating Expenses, Total	0.0	0.0	0.0	0.0	0.0
Operating Income	**5,537.21**	**5,084.4**	**3,550.0**	**2,017.28**	**640.19**
Interest Income (Expense), Net Non-Operating	0.0	0.0	0.0	0.0	0.0
Gain (Loss) on Sale of Assets	0.0	0.0	0.0	0.0	0.0
Other, Net	4.52	−4.65	3.46	4.14	−5.09
Income Before Tax	**5,853.6**	**5,673.98**	**4,011.04**	**2,141.68**	**650.23**
Income Tax – Total	1,626.74	1,470.26	933.59	676.28	251.12
Income After Tax	**4,226.86**	**4,203.72**	**3,077.45**	**1,465.4**	**399.12**
Minority Interest	0.0	0.0	0.0	0.0	0.0
Equity In Affiliates	0.0	0.0	0.0	0.0	0.0
U.S. GAAP Adjustment	0.0	0.0	0.0	0.0	0.0
Net Income Before Extra. Items	**4,226.86**	**4,203.72**	**3,077.45**	**1,465.4**	**399.12**
Total Extraordinary Items	0.0	0.0	0.0	0.0	0.0
Net Income	**4,226.86**	**4,203.72**	**3,077.45**	**1,465.4**	**399.12**

Source: www.google.com/finance?fstype=bi&cid=694653.

EXHIBIT 2   Google Cash Flow 2004–2008 (in millions)

	2008	2007	2006	2005	2004
Period End Date	12/31/2008	12/31/2007	12/31/2006	12/31/2005	12/31/2004
Net Income/Starting Line	4,226.86	4,203.72	3,077.45	1,465.4	399.12
Depreciation/Depletion	1,212.24	807.74	494.43	256.81	128.52
Amortization	287.65	159.92	77.51	37.0	19.95
Deferred Taxes	−224.65	−164.21	0.0	0.0	0.0
Non-Cash Items	2,055.44	489.44	−112.83	656.47	682.66
Changes in Working Capital	295.32	278.8	43.96	43.74	−253.21
Cash from Operating Activities	**7,852.86**	**5,775.41**	**3,580.51**	**2,459.42**	**977.04**
Capital Expenditures	−2,358.46	−2,402.84	−1,902.8	−853.04	−355.9
Other Investing Cash Flow Items, Total	−2,960.96	−1,278.75	−4,996.35	−2,505.16	−1,545.46
Cash from Investing Activities	**−5,319.42**	**−3,681.59**	**−6,899.15**	**−3,358.19**	**−1,901.36**
Financing Cash Flow Items	159.09	379.21	581.73	0.0	4.3
Total Cash Dividends Paid	0.0	0.0	0.0	0.0	0.0
Issuance (Retirement) of Stock, Net	−71.52	23.86	2,384.67	4,372.26	1,195.03
Issuance (Retirement) of Debt, Net	0.0	0.0	0.0	−1.43	−4.71
Cash from Financing Activities	**87.57**	**403.07**	**2,966.4**	**4,370.83**	**1,194.62**
Foreign Exchange Effects	−45.92	40.03	19.74	−21.76	7.57
Net Change in Cash	**2,575.08**	**2,536.92**	**−332.5**	**3,450.3**	**277.88**
Net Cash - Beginning Balance	6,081.59	3,544.67	3,877.17	426.87	149.0
Net Cash - Ending Balance	8,656.67	6,081.59	3,544.67	3,877.17	426.87

Source: www.google.com/finance?fstype=bi&cid=694653.

In a little over 10 years, Google had grown to a company with over 20,000 employees. If Google wanted to continue its main strategy of growth through innovation, it would have to find a way to recruit the best employees and retain them.

Background of Founders

Google was founded by Larry Page and Sergei Brin who met in 1995 while they were Ph.D. students in computer engineering at Stanford University. Page was born in Lansing, Michigan, on March 26, 1973, and was the son of a computer science professor at Michigan State University who specialized in artificial intelligence. Page's mother also taught computer programming at the Michigan State University (Thompson, 2001, page 50).

Page spent his youth learning about computers and immersed himself into multiple technology journals that his parents read. Page had a very impressive educational background. He attended a Montessori school initially, and then went to a public high school. He later went on to earn a Bachelor of Science Degree (with honors) in computer engineering from the University of Michigan. Page was then accepted to graduate school at Stanford where he met Brin and began his study of website linkages. Nicola Tesla, a Serbian inventor who was a contemporary of Thomas Edison, was Page's inspiration. Tesla was superior to Edison in some respects; however,

| EXHIBIT 3 | Google Balance Sheet 2004–2008 (in millions) |

	2008	2007	2006	2005	2004
Period End Date	12/31/2008	12/31/2007	12/31/2006	12/31/2005	12/31/2004
Assets					
Cash & Short Term Investments	15,845.77	14,218.61	11,243.91	8,034.25	2,132.3
Total Receivables, Net	2,642.19	2,307.77	1,322.34	687.98	382.35
Total Inventory	0.0	0.0	0.0	0.0	0.0
Prepaid Expenses	1,404.11	694.21	443.88	229.51	159.36
Other Current Assets, Total	286.11	68.54	29.71	49.34	19.46
Total Current Assets	**20,178.18**	**17,289.14**	**13,039.85**	**9,001.07**	**2,693.47**
Property/Plant/Equipment, Total - Net	5,233.84	4,039.26	2,395.24	961.75	378.92
Goodwill, Net	4,839.85	2,299.37	1,545.12	194.9	122.82
Intangibles, Net	996.69	446.6	346.84	82.78	71.07
Long Term Investments	85.16	1,059.69	1,031.85	0.0	0.0
Note Receivable - Long Term	0.0	0.0	0.0	0.0	0.0
Other Long Term Assets, Total	433.85	201.75	114.46	31.31	47.08
Total Assets	**31,767.58**	**25,335.81**	**18,473.35**	**10,271.81**	**3,313.35**
Liabilities and Shareholders' Equity					
Accounts Payable	178.0	282.11	211.17	115.58	32.67
Payable/Accrued	0.0	0.0	0.0	0.0	0.0
Accrued Expenses	1,824.45	1,575.42	987.91	528.94	269.29
Notes Payable/Short Term Debt	0.0	0.0	0.0	0.0	0.0
Current Port. of LT Debt/Capital Leases	0.0	0.0	0.0	0.0	1.9
Other Current Liabilities, Total	299.63	178.07	105.51	100.87	36.51
Total Current Liabilities	**2,302.09**	**2,035.6**	**1,304.59**	**745.38**	**340.37**
Total Long Term Debt	0.0	0.0	0.0	0.0	0.0
Deferred Income Tax	12.52	0.0	40.42	35.42	0.0
Other Liabilities, Total	1,214.11	610.53	88.5	72.05	43.93
Total Liabilities	**3,528.71**	**2,646.13**	**1,433.51**	**852.86**	**384.3**
Common Stock	0.32	0.31	0.31	0.29	0.27
Additional Paid-In Capital	14,450.34	13,241.22	11,882.91	7,477.79	2,582.35
Retained Earnings (Accumulated Deficit)	13,561.63	9,334.77	5,133.31	2,055.87	590.47
Other Equity, Total	226.58	113.37	23.31	−115.0	−244.03
Total Equity	**28,238.86**	**22,689.68**	**17,039.84**	**9,418.96**	**2,929.06**
Total Liabilities & Shareholders' Equity	**31,767.58**	**25,335.81**	**18,473.35**	**10,271.81**	**3,313.35**
Total Common Shares Outstanding	315.11	313.28	309.0	293.03	266.92

Source: www.google.com/finance?fstype=bi&cid=694653.

EXHIBIT 4 Google's Stock Price from IPO through May 28, 2009

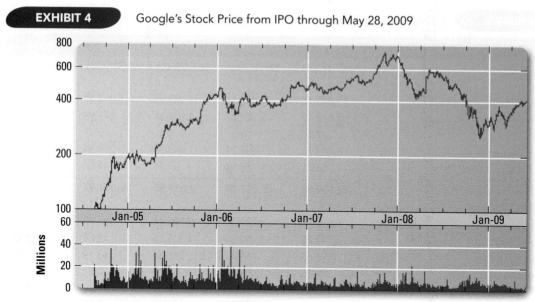

Source: finance.yahoo.com, Copyright 2009 Yahoo! Inc.

he failed at commercializing his inventions. Page wanted to do both.

In 1973, Sergey Brin was born in Moscow Russia. At age six, Brin and his family who were Jewish, fled Russia to the United States to escape anti-Semitism. Brin's father was a mathematics professor at the University of Maryland and his mother was a research scientist at NASA's Goddard Space Flight Center. Brin attended a Montessori high school and graduated with a degree in computer science and mathematics with honors from the University of Maryland. He then began to study computer science at Stanford University until he dropped out to form Google with Page. Brin was the more gregarious; however, both were strong willed and opinionated.

At Stanford they began their quest to "organize the world's information and make it universally accessible" (Miller, 2006, page 10). Google began as a research project at Stanford University in January, 1995.

Page started his research under the tutelage of Dr. Terry Winograd, a computer science professor at Stanford. His research focused on which web pages linked to a given page. His initial problem was trying to determine the number of citations in academic publishing. He called his research project "BackRub." Brin soon joined Page on the project. Page began exploring the web in March 1996 by using Page's Stanford home page. It was at this point that Page and Brin developed PageRank, an algorithm that ranked the importance of the sites that were relevant to the entry.

Page and Brin did not create the algorithm with the intention of making money, but they wanted to have a significant impact on the world. As time went on they decided that they did not want to create their own company, but they wanted to sell their invention to one of the existing search companies (e.g., WebCrawler, AltaVista, Yahoo!, etc.). However, all of these companies stated that there was no money in search and rejected them.

By 1996, Brin and Page had servers and computers stacked in their dorm room. Initially targeted at Stanford students, the two consulted with two former Stanford students that started Yahoo!, Jerry Yang and David Filo. They encouraged Brin and Page to create their own company. So the two decided to drop out of school and start their own business. In 1998, Sun Microsystems co-founder Andy Bechtolsheim, who also dropped out of Stanford to become a successful entrepreneur, wrote a check for $100,000 to Brin and Page and they formed a new company called Google, Inc.

Growth of Google

Since its founding in 1998, Google was one of the most innovative companies in the world. The company ranked at the top with other leading companies like Apple in the development of innovative products and technologies. Corporate entrepreneurship and innovation was the heart and soul of the company's success.

Google initially set up its business in a garage at 232 Santa Margarita, Menlo Park, California in 1998. Later that year, Google was named Search Engine of Choice by *PC Magazine* in the Top 100 Sites of 1998 (Lowe, 2009, page 282). In 1999, Google moved to a new office space in Palo Alto to make room for several new employees. Palo Alto was the location of Stanford University. The city was in the heart of Silicon Valley and was the location where the first semiconductor chip was created in 1956 by Fairchild Semiconductor.

In 1999, Google received its first significant influx of capital, $25 million in venture capital financing from Sequoia Capital and Kleiner, Perkins, Caufield, and Byers, both located in Silicon Valley. Members of both firms sat on the board of directors of Google.

In 1999, the term "googler" was termed for "people who used Google." In August, 1999 Google moved to Mountain View, just south of Palo Alto. Google moved into an empty building next door to Silicon Graphics, a firm that was founded by a former Stanford electrical engineering professor, Dr. James Clark and seven graduate students and staff from Stanford. Clark would go on to found Netscape Communications, myCFO, and Healtheon. A review of the history of Google can be seen below.

Stages of Growth

Hamel and Breen (2007) described the growth of Google into five stages:

Google 1.0: Brin and Page invented a search engine that searched the Web, won millions of eyeballs, but generated no real revenue.

Google 2.0: Google sold its search capacity to AOL, Yahoo!, and other major portals. These partnerships generated revenue and sparked a surge in search requests. Suddenly, Google started to look like a business.

Google 3.0: Google crafted a clever model for selling ads alongside search results called AdWords. Unlike Yahoo! and others, it eschewed banner ads, and took a newspaper's "church-and-state" view of advertising and content by clearly differentiating between ads and search results. Moreover, advertisers paid only when users actually clicked on a link. Google was well on its way to becoming the Internet's leading retailer of ad space.

Google 4.0: Google's initially controversial Gmail service, which served up ads based on a computer analysis of each incoming message,

---

⬤ EXHIBIT 5 Google's Corporate History

Aug-98	Sun co-founder Andy Bechtolsheim writes a check for $100,000 to an entity that doesn't exist yet: a company called Google, Inc.
Sep-98	Google files for incorporation in California on September 4. Larry and Sergey open a bank account in Google's name and deposit check.
Dec-98	"PC Magazine" reports that Google "has an uncanny knack for returning extremely relevant results" and names it the search engine of choice.

(continued)

EXHIBIT 5   Google's Corporate History (*continued*)

Jun-99	Google's first press release announces a $25 million round from Sequoia Capital and Kleiner Perkins.
May-00	The first 10 language versions of Google.com are released targeting the Western European market from Spain up to Denmark. (New Market)
Jun-00	We forge a partnership with Yahoo! to become their default search provider. (Partnership)
Sep-00	We start offering search in Chinese, Japanese and Korean, bringing our total number of supported languages to 15. (New Market)
Oct-00	Google AdWords, the self-service ad program with keyword targeting, launches with 350 customers - revenue stream. (New Product)
Dec-00	Google Toolbar is released. It's a browser plug-in that makes it possible to search without visiting the Google homepage. (Innovation)
Feb-01	Acquires Deja.com's Usenet Discussion Service, adds search and browse features, and launches it as Google Groups. (Acquisition)
Mar-01	Google.com is available in 26 languages. (Foreign)
Jul-01	Image Search launches, offering access to 250 million images. (New Product)
Aug-01	Google opens its first international office, in Tokyo. (International)
Aug-01	Eric Schmidt becomes CEO, and Larry and Sergey are named presidents of products and technology, respectively.
Oct-01	A new partnership with Universo Online (UOL) makes Google the major search service for millions of Latin Americans. (Partnership)
Feb-02	The first Google hardware is released, the Google Search Appliance. (Related Diversification - Hardware)
Feb-02	Google releases a major overhaul for AdWords, including new cost-per-click pricing. (Innovation)
May-02	Partnership with AOL to offer Google search and sponsored links to customers using CompuServe, Netscape, and AOL.com. (Partnership)
Sep-02	Google News launches with 4000 news sources. (New Product)
Oct-02	Google opens its first Australian office in Sydney. (International)
Dec-02	Google launches Froogle to buy stuff (later called Google Product Search). (New Product)
Feb-03	Acquires Pyra Labs, the creators of Blogger. (Acquisition)
Mar-03	We announce a new content-targeted advertising service called AdSense. (New Product)
Apr-03	Acquires Applied Semantics, whose technology bolsters AdSense. (Acquisition)
Apr-03	Google launches Google Grants, an advertising program for nonprofit organizations to run ad campaigns for their cause. (New Product)
Dec-03	Google launches Google Print (later renamed Google Book Search), indexing small excerpts from searched for books. (New Product)
Jan-04	Google launches Orkut as a way to tap into the sphere of social networking. (New Product)
Mar-04	Google formalizes its enterprise unit with the hire of Dave Girouard to run the enterprise search business. (Related Diversification)
Mar-04	Google introduces Google Local (later part of Google Maps), offering business listings, maps, and directions. (New Product - Maps)
Jul-04	Acquires Picasa, a digital photography company. (Acquisition)
Aug-04	Google's Initial Public Offering of 19,605,052 shares of Class A common stock with opening price of $85 per share. (IPO)
Oct-04	Google opens an office in Dublin, Ireland. (International)
Oct-04	Google launches SMS (short message service) to send search queries to GOOGL or on a mobile device. (Related Diversification - Phone)

(*continued*)

EXHIBIT 5	Google's Corporate History (*continued*)

Oct-04	Google opens new engineering offices in Bangalore and Hyderabad, India. (International - Outsourcing)
Oct-04	Google Desktop Search is introduced so users can search for files and documents stored on their own hard drive. (New Product)
Oct-04	Acquires Keyhole, a digital mapping company whose technology will later become Google Earth. (Acquisition - Maps)
Dec-04	Google opens an R&D center in Tokyo, Japan, to attract bright Asian engineers. (International - Outsourcing)
Feb-05	Google Maps goes live. (New Product - Innovation - Maps)
Mar-05	Google launches code.google.com, a new place for developer-oriented resources, including all of our APIs. (New Product)
Mar-05	Acquires Urchin, a web analytics company whose technology is used to create Google Analytics. (Acquisition)
Apr-05	Google Maps features satellite views and directions. (Innovation - Maps)
Apr-05	Google Local goes mobile, and includes SMS driving directions. (Related Diversification - Phone)
May-05	Google releases Blogger Mobile, enabling mobile phone users to post and send photos to their blogs. (Related Diversification - Phone)
May-05	Google launches Personalized Homepage (now iGoogle) enabling users to customize their own Google homepage. (New Product)
Jun-05	Google Mobile Web Search is released, specially formulated for viewing search results on mobile phones. (Related Diversification - Phone)
Jun-05	Google launches Google Earth: a satellite imagery-based mapping service. (New Product - Innovation - Maps)
Aug-05	Google launches Google Talk, which enables Gmail users to talk or IM over the Internet for free. (New Product)
Sep-05	Google opens new R&D center in China. (International - Outsourcing)
Sep-05	Google Blog Search goes live to facilitate finding current and relevant blog postings. (New Product)
Oct-05	Google launches Google.org, a philanthropic arm of the firm, to address energy and environmental issues. (Diversification - Charity)
Oct-05	Google introduces Google Reader, a feed reader. (New Product)
Nov-05	Google release Google Analytics, formerly Urchin, for measuring the impact of websites and marketing campaigns. (Innovation)
Nov-05	Google opens our first offices in São Paulo, Brazil, and Mexico City, Mexico. (International)
Dec-05	Gmail for mobile launches in the United States. (Innovation - Phone)
Jan-06	Acquires dMarc, a digital radio advertising company. (Acquisition - Unrelated Diversification)
Jan-06	Google launches Google.cn, a local domain version of Google in China. (International – Multi-domestic Competition)
Jan-06	Google introduces Picasa in 25 more languages. (New Market)
Feb-06	Google releases Chat in Gmail, using the instant messaging tools from Google Talk. (New Product)
Feb-06	Google launches Google News for mobile launchers. (New Product - Phone)
Mar-06	Acquires Writely, a web-based word processing application that subsequently becomes the basis for Google Docs. (Acquisition)
Mar-06	Google launches Google Finance, our approach to an improved search experience for financial information. (New Product)
Apr-06	Google launches Google Calendar, complete with sharing and group features. (New Product)
Apr-06	Google releases Maps for France, Germany, Italy and Spain. (New Market)

(continued)

| EXHIBIT 5 | Google's Corporate History (*continued*) |

May-06	Google releases Google Trends, a way to visualize the popularity of searches over time. (New Product)
Jun-06	Google announces Picasa Web Albums, allowing Picasa users to upload and share their photos online. (Innovation)
Jun-06	Google announces Google Checkout, a fast and easy way to pay for online purchases. (New Product)
Jun-06	Gmail, Google News and iGoogle become available on mobile phones in eight more languages. (New Markets - Phone)
Aug-06	Google releases Apps for Your Domain, a suite of applications including Gmail and Calendar for any size organization. (New Product)
Aug-06	Google Book Search begins offering free PDF downloads of books in the public domain. (Innovation)
Oct-06	Acquires YouTube. (Acquisition)
Oct-06	Acquires JotSpot, a collaborative wiki platform, which later becomes Google Sites. (Acquisition)
Dec-06	Google releases Patent Search in the U.S., indexing more than 7 million patents dating back to 1790. (New Product)
Jan-07	Google partners with China Mobile, world's largest mobile telecom carrier, to provide mobile searches in China. (International - Partnership)
Feb-07	Gmail is opened up to everyone, no longer by invitation only. (New Market)
Feb-07	Google launches Google Apps Premier Edition, bringing cloud computing to businesses. (Innovation)
Feb-07	We introduce traffic information to Google Maps for more than 30 cities around the U.S. (Innovation- Maps)
Jun-07	Google partners with Salesforce.com, combining that company's on-demand CRM applications with AdWords. (Partnership)
Jul-07	Acquires Postini. (Acquisition)
Aug-07	Google launches Sky inside Google Earth, including layers for constellation information and virtual tours of galaxies. (New Product - Maps)
Sep-07	Google introduces AdSense for Mobile, giving sites for mobile browsers the ability to host same ads as on computers. (Innovation - Phone)
Sep-07	Google adds Presently, a new application for making slide presentations, to Google Docs. (New Product)
Nov-07	Google (with Open Handset Alliance) announces Android, first open platform for mobile devices. (Related Diversification - Phone)
Nov-07	Google.org announces RE<C, an initiative designed to create electricity from renewable sources. (Unrelated Diversification - Energy)
Mar-08	Acquires DoubleClick, which provides internet ad services. (Acquisition)
May-08	Google releases Google Health to the public, allowing people to manage their medical records and health information online. (New Product)
Jul-08	Google releases first downloadable iPhone app. (Related Diversification - Phone)
Sep-08	Unveils G1, the Google Phone on the Android operating system, available through T-Mobile. (Forward Vertical integration - Hardware)
Oct-08	Google introduces Google Earth for the iPhone and iPod touch. (New Market)
Jan-09	Google launches of Picasa for Mac. (New Market)
Feb-09	Google introduces Google Latitude, that lets users share their location with friends. (New Product - Maps)
Feb-09	Adding new languages enables Google Translate to accommodate 41 languages, covering 98% of Internet users. (Innovation - New Markets)

Source: Google Milestones (2009). Retrieved on March 31, 2009, www.google.com/corporate/history.html.

provoked a serendipitous bit of learning that led to the creation of AdSense. This breakthrough gave Google the ability to link its ads to virtually any sort of Web content, not just its own search results. AdSense gave webmasters a new way of monetizing content and vastly expand the scope of Google's business model.

Google 5.0: Google used its windfall from advertising to fund a flock of new services, including Google Desktop (a cluster of information utilities accessible directly from a user's PC screen), Google Book Search (an ambitious plan to digitize the books from the world's greatest libraries), Google Scholar (a tool for searching academic papers), and Google Chrome, a new Internet search browser.

The company also purchased a number of other firms over the years including, Keyhole (which became Google Earth), Writely (which became Google Docs), YouTube, and Android (which went on to become the Android Operating System for Google's new phone launch called the Android in 2008).

In 2008, Google had more than $4 billion in revenues with the majority of it coming from the company's AdWords business model or click through advertising. AdWords was one of the most revolutionary developments in the media world since television itself, said author John Battelle (2009): "AdWords was what made Google . . . Google." AdWords was what generated the ads—or "Sponsored Links," you see on a Google results page. You only have to pay for the link when someone actually clicks on the link and goes to the advertiser's web site. It was called "pay-per-click."

Strategies at Google

Google's primary corporate strategy was related diversification. Google achieved its diversification strategy through corporate entrepreneurship and innovation and acquisitions. This enabled Google to increase its offerings and decrease its competition. As the industry leader, Google used offensive strategies by constant innovation of its product lines and expansion into other industries

like mobile phones, maps, blogging, news, health, etc.

Google provided internet users with the most relevant search results on as many topics as possible. This included going international to outsource and expand markets by providing its products in foreign languages. Google's business level strategy was a broad differentiation strategy, because it offered features that other search engines did not, such as translating from one language into another, while still providing the most relevant search results.

Philanthropy at Google

Philanthropy was widespread at Google. The company gave 1 percent of its equity and yearly profits to philanthropy. Google's five primary areas that it focused on were: (1) Google.org which used Google's information and technology to build products and advocate for policies that address global challenges; (2) Engineering Awards and Programs that supported the next generation of engineers and maintained strong ties with academic institutions worldwide pursuing innovative research in core areas relevant to its mission; (3) Information and Tools to Help You Change the World that were used to promote causes, raise money, and operate more efficiently; (4) Charitable Giving that supported efforts in the local communities and around the globe; and (5) Google Green Initiatives where Google gave back to the community through financing humanitarian efforts in Africa and research on alternative fuels and global warming (Google.org, 2010).

Competition

Google operated in markets that changed rapidly. Google faced the possibility of new and disruptive technologies and faced formidable competition in every aspect of their business, particularly from companies that sought to connect people with information on the web. The company considered Microsoft Corporation and Yahoo! Inc. to be their primary competitors.

Google faced competition from other web search providers, including start-ups as well as developed companies that were enhancing or developing search technologies. Google competed with internet advertising companies, particularly in the areas of pay-for-performance and keyword-targeted internet advertising. The company also competed with companies that sold products and services online because these companies were trying to attract users to their web sites to search for information about products and services. Google also provided a number of online products and services, including

---

EXHIBIT 6   Google Philanthropic Initiatives

Google.org

Google.org used Google's strengths in information and technology to build products and advocate for policies that address global challenges.

Google Flu Trends - A tool that uses aggregated Google search data to estimate flu activity in near real-time for 20 countries.

Google PowerMeter - A home energy monitoring tool that gives you the information you need to use less electricity and save money.

Earth Engine - A computational platform for global-scale analysis of satellite imagery to monitor changes in key environmental indicators like forest coverage.

RE<C - An effort to develop utility-scale renewable energy at a price cheaper than that of coal.

Google Crisis Response - A team that provides updated imagery, outreach through our web properties, and engineering tools such as the Person Finder application, in the wake of natural and humanitarian crises.

All For Good - A service, developed by Google and other technology companies, that helps people find volunteer opportunities in their community and share them with their friends. All for Good provides a single search interface for volunteer activities across many major volunteering sites and organizations.

Engineering Awards and Programs

Google supported the next generation of engineers and maintained strong ties with academic institutions worldwide pursuing innovative research in core areas relevant to its mission.

Google Research - Awards for world-class, full-time faculty pursuing research in areas of mutual interest.

BOLD Scholarships - Diversity internships to encourage those who are historically under-represented in the technology industry to explore a new career opportunity.

Google Code University - Tutorials and sample course content so computer science students and educators can learn more about current computing technologies and paradigms.

Google PhD Fellowship Program - Recognition for outstanding graduate students doing exceptional work in computer science, related disciplines, or promising research areas.

Google RISE Awards (Roots in Science and Engineering) - Awards to promote and support science, technology, engineering, mathematics (STEM) and computer science (CS) education initiatives.

Google Scholarships - Scholarships to encourage students to excel in their studies and become active role models and leaders.

Summer of Code - Stipends to student developers to write code for various open source software projects.

Information and Tools to Help You Change the World

Google tools were used to promote causes, raise money, and operate more efficiently.

Google for Non-Profits - Information on free Google tools for creating awareness, fundraising, and operating more efficiently.

(continued)

| **EXHIBIT 6** | Google Philanthropic Initiatives (*continued*) |

Google Grants - In-kind online advertising for non-profit organizations.

Apps for EDU/Non-Profits - Free communication, collaboration and publishing tools, including email accounts, for qualifying non-profits.

Checkout for Non-Profits - A tool to increase online donations for non-profit organizations.

Custom Search for Non-Profits - A customized search experience for non-profit organizations.

Sketchup for EDU - A product allowing educators to create, modify, and share 3D models.

YouTube for EDU - An educational channel for two- and four-year degree granting public and private colleges and universities.

YouTube for Non-Profits - A designated channel, premium branding, and additional free features to drive non-profit fundraising and awareness.

YouTube Video Volunteers - A platform to connect non-profit organizations with volunteers who can help them to create videos.

Google Earth Outreach - Resources to help non-profits visualize their cause and tell their story in Google Earth and Maps.

Google MapMaker - A tool that allows users to contribute, share and edit map information for 174 countries and territories around the world.

Charitable Giving

Googler-led giving to support efforts in our local communities and around the globe.

Corporate Giving Council - A cross-Google team that coordinates support for Googler-led partnerships on causes such as K-12 science/math/technology education and expanding access to information.

Holiday gift - A $22 million donation in 2009 to a couple dozen deserving charities from around the globe in order to help organizations who have been stretched thin by increasing requests for help at a time of lower donations. Gift was in lieu of giving holiday gifts to clients and partners.

Community Affairs-Investments in local communities where Google has a presence, creating opportunities for Googlers to invest their time and expertise in their communities, engage in community grant making, and build partnerships with stakeholders in the community.

Google employee matching - Up to $6,000 company match for each employee's annual charitable contributions and $50 donation for every 5 hours an employee volunteers through the "Dollars for Doers" program.

Google Green Initiatives

Google implemented innovative and responsible environmental practices across the company to reduce its carbon footprint, to ensure efficient computing, and to help its employees be green.

Source: Philanthropy at Google. Accessed May 18, 2010, www.google.org/googlers.html.

Gmail, YouTube, and Google Docs, which competed directly with new and established companies offering communication, information, and entertainment services integrated into products or media properties.

Google competed to attract and retain relationships with users, advertisers and Google Network members and other content providers in different ways (see below, Google's 2008 Annual Report):

- *Users.* Competed to attract and retain users of their search and communication products and services. Most of the products and services Google offered to users were free, so the company did not compete on price. Instead, the

EXHIBIT 7	Yahoo! Financial Ratios 2004–2008

Liquidity Ratios

Liquidity Indicators	2008	2007	2006	2005	2004
Quick Ratio	1.97	1.12	1.7	1.79	1.1
Current Ratio	2.78	1.41	2.54	2.86	3.46
Operating Cash Flow Ratio	.007	.302	.638	.919	.583
Debt to Equity	.217	283	.257	.265	.295

Profitability Ratios

Profitability Indicators	2008	2007	2006	2005	2004
ROA	3.27	5.56	6.73	18.95	11.08
ROE	4.07	7.06	8.48	24.21	14.61
ROI	0.12	7.15	9.79	12.9	10.59
EBITDA Margin	12.29	21.64	25.49	50.46	37.24
Revenue per employee	528,589	487,362	563,656	536,497	469,046
Net Profit Margin After Tax	(2.31)	7.35	9.96	36.1	20.9

Asset Management Ratios

Asset Management	2008	2007	2006	2005	2004
Total Asset Turnover	0.55	0.59	0.58	0.53	0.47
Receivables Turnover	6.79	7.02	7.78	8.75	9.35
Accounts Payable Turnover	43.83	48.86	71.63	88.74	89.01

company competed in this area on the basis of the relevance and usefulness of search results, features, availability, and ease of use of products and services.

- *Advertisers.* Google competed to attract and retain advertisers. Google competed in this area principally on the basis of the return on investment realized by advertisers using the company's AdWords and AdSense programs. Google also competed based on the quality of customer service, features and ease of use of its products and services.

- *Google Network members and other content providers.* Google competed to attract and retain content providers (Google Network members, as well as other content providers for whom the company distributed or licensed content) primarily based on the size and quality of its

advertiser base, and its ability to help these partners generate revenues from advertising and the terms of the agreements.

Silicon Valley

Culture and Location

Google was located in the heart of Silicon Valley, Mountain View, California. According to Randy Komisar, an entrepreneur-turned-venture capitalist at Kleiner, Perkins, Caufield, and Byers, "In Silicon Valley we have created a culture that attracts the sort of people who prosper in ambiguity, innovation, and risk taking" (Harris, 2009). Other parts of the U.S. have also been successful at building innovative technology corridors like Boston, Massachusetts, and Austin, Texas.

Silicon Valley was often called South San Francisco, but was really comprised of about 60 miles of suburbs immediately to the south of the city of San Francisco. Some of the more prominent cities and companies included (North to South) South San Francisco (Amgen and Genentech), San Mateo (YouTube), Redwood Shores (Oracle Corporation, Electronic Arts, and Sun Microsystems), Menlo Park (most venture capital firms), Palo Alto (Hewlett-Packard and Facebook), Mountain View (AOL, Intuit, RedHat, Symantec, and VeriSign), Sunnyvale (Yahoo!, Ariba, NetApp, and Advanced Micro Devices), Santa Clara (Applied Materials and Nvidia Corporation), Cupertino (Apple, Inc.), San Jose (McAfee, eBay, Adobe Systems, and Cisco Systems), and Los Gatos. Hundreds of prestigious high technology companies were located here.

Cost of Living

Silicon Valley was one of the most expensive places to live in the U.S. During the recent housing boom, the average house in the region sold for $800,000. Prices differed depending on the city. For example, during the height of the housing boom an average house in San Jose sold for $710,000. However, by 2009, the price had fallen to $475,000 or a 33 percent plunge. Real estate in Palo Alto held up better than other parts of Silicon Valley. The average price of a home at the housing peak was $1.2 million versus $1.1 million in early 2009. Several factors contributed to Palo Alto's resilience: (1) The city was sunny and beautiful; (2) its proximity to Stanford; (3) the limited amount of housing available (no space for new homes); (4) its proximity to all of the top high-tech companies in the region (Google and Apple were 15 minutes away), and (5) the prestigious K-12 school system. Steve Jobs, CEO of Apple Inc., Steve Young, former star quarterback of the San Francisco 49ers, and Page all lived in Palo Alto.

The average per capita personal income in the U.S. was $39,751; however, in Silicon Valley salaries were 30 percent above the average. While this may sound encouraging, the cost of living in Silicon Valley was significantly higher than most places in the U.S. For example, if you made $100,000 a year in Dallas, Texas, and took a job at Google and moved to Palo Alto you would have to make a salary of $252,226 to afford the same lifestyle. The high cost of living was a barrier that the company had to overcome when recruiting employees.

Education and Employees

There were a number of universities and colleges in the San Francisco area; however, there were only two world class research universities; Stanford University and the University of California at Berkeley. Some of the brightest minds from all over the world came to Silicon Valley to work and/or attend these schools. San Jose State University, which was also located in Silicon Valley, was also a major feeder of engineers to high tech companies in the region. Furthermore, several of these engineers went on to become leaders in their respective companies (e.g., Gordon Moore, founder of Intel Corporation in 1968).

The region was a breeding ground for some of the brightest minds in the world. The area had a forward looking energy. People were more entrepreneurial because they had witnessed great wealth creation. According to Bill Powar, one of the founders of VeriSign, "I worked at Visa for 30 years, but when the internet was created we saw an opportunity to create the first internet security system that is still used today." Powar made millions on the initial public offering and retired.

Access to Capital and Legal Infrastructure

Money was another key variable for the success of Silicon Valley. Sand Hill Road in Menlo Park was famous for the large number of venture capital firms in a very small area. During the dot.com boom, real estate there was the most expensive in the world. A small number of employees worked in

EXHIBIT 8   Map of Silicon Valley

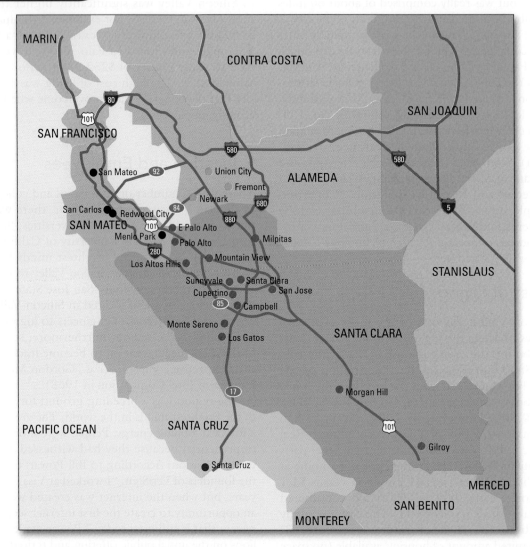

Source: Silicon Valley Cities and Counties. Retrieved May 19, 2009, www.siliconvalleyonline.org/cities.

very small office buildings that were often hidden by trees and brushes. At Kleiner, Perkins, Caufield, and Byers, one of the premier venture capital firms in the world, bottlebrush trees hid the name of the firm. Other prestigious venture capital firms there were Sequoia Capital, Interwest Partners, Kohlberg Kravis Roberts, Draper Fisher Jurveston, etc. This proximity to venture capital gave Google a competitive advantage since venture capital firms liked to be close to their investments and sit on their boards.

As Silicon Valley grew, the number of law firms specializing in funding, litigation, resolving disputes, high tech companies, and intellectual property grew enormously. Many of these firms were located in San Francisco and Palo Alto.

| EXHIBIT 9 | | Leading Public Companies in Silicon Valley |

Company	Symbol	Company	Symbol
Agilent Technologies, Inc.	A	Ipass	IPAS
Apple	AAPL	Intersil-A	ISIL
Actel	ACTL	Intuitive Surgical	ISRG
Adobe Systems	ADBE	Integr Silicon Sol	ISSI
Adaptec	ADPT	Intevac	IVAC
Affymetrix	AFFX	Interwoven, Inc.	IWOV
Align Technology	ALGN	Sun Microsystems	JAVA
Altera Corp	ALTR	JDS Uniphase	JDSU
Applied Materials	AMAT	Juniper Networks	JNPR
Applied Micro	AMCC	KLA-Tencor	KLAC
Advanced Micro Devices	AMD	Linear Technology	LLTC
Applied Signal Tech	APSG	Lam Research Corp	LRCX
Ariba	ARBA	LSI Corporation	LSI
Aruba Networks	ARUN	Micrel	MCRL
Atheros Comms	ATHR	Mcafee, Inc.	MFE
Bigband Networks	BBND	Monolithic Power	MPWR
Brocade Comm	BRCD	Macrovision Solns	MVSN
Cadence Design	CDNS	Nanometrics Inc	NANO
Chordiant Software	CHRD	Netflix	NFLX
Credence Systems Corp	CMOS	Nektar Therapeutics	NKTR
Coherent	COHR	National Semiconductor	NSM
Cisco Systems	CSCO	Netapp	NTAP
Cypress Semiconductor	CY	Netgear	NTGR
Cybersource	CYBS	Nvidia	NVDA
Data Domain	DDUP	Novellus Systems	NVLS
DSP Group	DSPG	Omnicell	OMCL
Ebay	EBAY	Oplink Comms	OPLK
Electrs For Imaging	EFII	Openwave Systems	OPWV
Echelon	ELON	Oracle	ORCL
Equinix	EQIX	Omnivision Tech	OVTI
Electronic Arts	ERTS	Palm	PALM
Extreme Networks	EXTR	Verifone Holdings, Inc.	PAY
Foundry Networks, Inc.	FDRY	PDL Biopharma	PDLI
Finisar	FNSR	PMC-Sierra	PMCS
Gilead Sciences	GILD	Power Integrations	POWI
Google-A	GOOG	Pericom Semicondctr	PSEM
Granite Construction, Inc.	GVA	Quantum Corporation	QTM
Harmonic	HLIT	Rackable Systems	RACK
Hewlett-Packard Company	HPQ	Robert Half International, Inc.	RHI
Integr Device Tech	IDTI	Rambus	RMBS
Informatica	INFA	Silicon Graphics, Inc.	SGIC
Intel	INTC	Silicon Image	SIMG
Intuit	INTU	Symyx Technologies	SMMX

(continued)

| EXHIBIT 9 | | Leading Public Companies in Silicon Valley (*continued*) | |

Company	Symbol	Company	Symbol
Sandisk	SNDK	Trident Microsystem	TRID
Synopsys	SNPS	Trimble Navigation	TRMB
Synnex Corporation	SNX	Tessera Tech	TSRA
Sunpower-A	SPWR	Varian Medical Systems, Inc.	VAR
Silicon Storge Tech	SSTI	Varian	VARI
Symantec	SYMC	Vmware, Inc.	VMW
Symmetricom	SYMM	Verisign	VRSN
Synaptics	SYNA	Xilinx	XLNX
Tivo	TIVO	Yahoo	YHOO

Corporate Entrepreneurship and Innovation

Corporate entrepreneurship (Guth & Ginsberg, 1990) is a term used to describe entrepreneurial behavior inside established mid-sized and large organizations. Corporate entrepreneurship can be formal or informal activities aimed at creating new businesses in established companies through product and process innovations and market developments (Zahra, 1991). Innovation is a key ingredient of corporate entrepreneurship where one can take an idea or invention and create something new of value. For example, an innovation of the toothbrush is the electric toothbrush.

Rule and Irwin (1988) stated that companies established a culture of innovation through: the formation of teams and task forces; recruitment of new staff with new ideas; application of strategic plans that focused on achieving innovation; and the establishment of internal research and development programs that were likely to see tangible results.

The roots of corporate entrepreneurship proliferated at 3M Corporation. 3M was the first company that introduced "organizational slack" as a key factor enabling their engineers and scientists to spend 15 percent of their time on projects of their own design. As a result of this many inventions came out of 3M (e.g., Post-it Notes and Scotch Tape).

Corporate Entrepreneurship and Innovation at Google

Google's mission was not based on money alone; rather it was to improve the world. The heart and soul of Google was based on entrepreneurship and innovation. The philosophy of the company started at Stanford University. Stanford had a program dedicated to the formation of technology oriented ventures called the STVP or the Stanford Technology Ventures Program in the School of Engineering. The school had a rich 100 year history of students and faculty that created fledging organizations like Federal Telegraph and Telephone, Hewlett-Packard, Varian Associates, SRI International, Yahoo!, Cisco, Sun Microsystems, Silicon Graphics, Varian Medical Systems, and VMware.

Stanford encouraged their professors to create companies based on their research. According to Dr. Thomas Lee, the founder of Stanford's Integrated Circuits Laboratory, "Entrepreneurship is built into the DNA of Stanford." When Lee arrived, he said that colleagues told him that he would have to do a startup. He said there was a kind of peer pressure on campus to start a business. The President, John L. Hennessey, had prospered as an entrepreneur in MIPS Computer Systems (now MIPS Technologies) and Silicon

Graphics (Harris 2009). Stanford also encouraged their professors to take equity stakes in companies. This culture fostered entrepreneurial ventures throughout the region. In the 2009 student business plan competition there were 235 entries, double the amount during the dot.com boom.

Google's management model was similar to other high-tech companies like Microsoft, Apple, and Cisco. Google bought many of the buildings around its original office. The make-up, location, and culture of the company were similar to that of a college or university. It was not uncommon to see many bicycles around the campus traveling from building to building along with people playing volleyball outdoors.

According to current CEO Eric Schmidt (2009), "I looked at Google as an extension of graduate school; similar kinds of people, similar kinds of crazy behavior, but people who were incredibly smart and who were highly motivated and had a sense of change, a sense of optimism. It was a culture of people who felt that they could build things; they could actually accomplish what they wanted and ultimately people stay in companies because they can achieve something."

Brin and Page created a company that had some of the brightest minds in the world. Similar to a top flight university, they hired the brightest minds, worked in small teams, received feedback, and their mission was to improve the world. The culture of Google had similar values as academia in the sense that everything was questioned. Ideas were critiqued by your peers not just your managers. At Google, position and hierarchy seldom won an argument, and the founders wanted to keep it that way (Hamel and Breen, 2007).

Another factor that contributed to the success of Google was their flat, open organizational structure. Typical corporate models had many layers of management and strategy was driven top down. However at Google, the company was highly democratic and employees were encouraged to question anyone. Strategy tended to come from bottom up. Company President, Eric Schmidt, stated that he talked with many employees every day about their various projects. The culture and structure of Google initiated from Brin and Page's attitude, "We do not like authority and we do not like being told what to do." Brin and Page understood that breakthroughs come from questioning assumptions and smashing paradigms (Hamel and Breen, 2007).

In order to increase the effectiveness of communication, the company developed an intranet, called "MOMA," or "Message Oriented Middleware Application." MOMA was a Web page and threaded conversation for each of the company's several hundred internal projects, making it easy for teams to communicate their progress, garner feedback, and solicit help. The company also created a program called Snippets; a site where all Google engineers could post a summary of their activities. Any Googler could search the Snippets list to locate individuals working on similar projects, or to simply stay abreast of what was happening (Hamel and Breen, 2007).

Google also had a policy of giving outsized rewards to people who came up with outsized ideas, a team-focused approach to product development, and a corporate credo that challenged every employee to put the user first (Hamel and Breen, 2007).

Support from Top Management

Google sought out the best and brightest from all over the world. Google was committed to having one of the most open and entrepreneurial environments in the world. Evidence of this could be seen in a recent study of MBA graduates who were interviewed about which company they wanted to work for and Google was number one, where 20 percent of all MBA graduates said they wanted to work for Google after graduation (CNNMoney.com, 2009).

Corporate Culture and Employees

The most critical factor in stimulating entrepreneurship within Google was the culture. Keys to success included forming an innovative and loose structure with quality employees. It was also essential to reward entrepreneurship and innovation.

Google's hiring process was based upon the belief of Brin and Page that A-level talent wanted to work with A-level talent and B-level talent tended to hire B-level talent or lower. This can ruin an organization. As a result, Google's hiring process could be painful to applicants. Interviews often extended several weeks and potential employees were often given scientists, Mensa-level problems to solve on the spot. Decisions on candidates were made by veteran associates and executives. It was an admittedly brutal process, but it weeded out anyone who was merely average (Hamel and Breen, 2007).

Brin and Page tried to keep the layers of management to a minimum. They also tried to keep the communication channels narrow so people could act quickly. They disliked taking orders from people and hated being managed. According to Brin and Page, "Our management philosophy amplified that quality employees who are motivated do not need to be managed." Similar to academia, Google gave their employees a lot of freedom.

Google's web site stated that its philosophy was, "Never Settle for the Best." Google's persistence, along with enormous amounts of energy and ambition brought about its success. The company's website listed "Ten Things Google Has Found to be True:"

1. Focus on the user and all else will follow.
2. It is best to do one thing really, really well.
3. Fast is better than slow.
4. Democracy on the web works.
5. You do not need to be at your desk to need an answer.
6. You can make money without doing evil.
7. There is always more information out there.
8. The need for information crosses all borders.
9. You can be serious without a suit.
10. Great is not good enough.

(Source: www.google.com/corporate/tenthings. html, accessed May 17, 2009.)

Page and Brin placed heavy emphasis on providing a relaxed and fun work environment. They believed that employees should create their own hours and work them as they felt they were most productive. Google's staff worked 80 percent of their hours on regular work and the other 20 percent on noncore projects (organizational slack). The company estimated that it developed 10-12 new service offerings every quarter. According to Marisa Mayer (2009), Vice President of Search Product and User Experience and the first female engineer hired at Google, "The 20% was one of the keys to our success. It gave the engineers the ability to work on whatever they were passionate about. You never know when you are going to create great products. That was why we gave them the opportunity to be creative. That was how Google News and Gmail were born. You have to try a number of different things. Certainly we are in the business of searching and advertising, but basically we are in the business of innovation. Our innovation strategy has been three fold: (1) allow small teams to work together, (2) allow ideas to come from everywhere, and (3) give employees 20% free time to work on any projects they have a passion for. These have all contributed to our success."

Google prided itself on its open, social environment but many people felt that Google had turned increasingly "corporate". The environment in which engineers were able to create their own products and services was decreasing since it had to go through a full review process that could take months before the product was released to market. Although engineers enjoyed being creative, they might as well create a product/service that they can monetize on their own.

Despite these factors, Google had problems related to the rapid growth of the company. As of May, 2009 Google had over 20,000 employees. This had a negative effect on the company's ability to maintain an entrepreneurial culture. The most often heard complaint was that the employees' skills were not being utilized. As one Ivy League graduate stated, "I have an Ivy League education and I was hired to shuffle papers in Human Resources. I quit after six months."

Small, Self-Managed Teams

The majority of Google's employees worked in teams of three engineers when working on product development. Big products like Gmail could have 30 or more teams with three to four people on a team. Each team had a specific assignment (e.g., building spam filters or improving the forwarding feature). Each team had a leader; however, leaders rotated on teams. Engineers often worked on more than one project and were free to switch teams. According to Shona Brown, Google's VP for operations, "If at all possible, we want people to commit to things, rather than be assigned to things" (Hamel and Breen, 2007).

Reward Structure

Google was called a playground on steroids where there were 18 cafes staffed with 7 executive chefs. Google was known for offering its staff incredible free perks: volleyball court, gyms, gourmet lunches and dinners (although leaving after eating dinner was frowned upon), Ben & Jerry's Ice Cream, yoga classes, employees could bring their dogs to work, onsite masseuse, office physician, laundry service, travel back and forth to work, etc. This made Google one of the most sought after companies to work for. Google offered great perks to their employees because they wanted the brightest and most qualified employees focusing their attention on their jobs all of the time.

Google employees earned a base salary that was on par with, or slightly lower than the industry average, however the standard deviation around that average was higher at Google than it was at most other companies. At Google, annual bonuses amounted to 30 to 60 percent of base salary, but the financial upside could be much, much bigger for those that came up with a profit-pumping idea (Hamel and Breen, 2007).

Google understood that entrepreneurs were motivated by money. Therefore in 2004, they created the "Founders Awards." These were restricted stock options (sometimes worth millions) that were given quarterly to teams that came up with the best ideas to increase the profitability of the company. The largest such award to date went to a team led by Eric Veach. His team created a new advertising algorithm, dubbed "SmartAds" and won $10 million (Hamel and Breen, 2007).

Decision Point

As Brin and Page sat through the concert they thought, "Look at Green Day. These guys have been successful for years and they still ROCK!! If Green Day can do it, so can Google." But Brin and Page realized that in order to accomplish their goals they would need to figure out how to solve their corporate problems. Their primary problem was how to maintain their culture of corporate entrepreneurship and innovation in the face of flat net profits from 2007 to 2008. Additionally, a multitude of other issues faced the company: (1) a decrease in advertising revenue, (2) the firing of several employees for the first time in the company's history and the elimination of products that made no money, and (3) the loss of employees for a variety of reasons (e.g., lack of mentoring and formal career planning, too much bureaucracy, low pay and benefits, high cost of living in the area, desire to start their own business, etc.). If Google wanted to continue its main strategy of growth through innovation, it would have to find a way to recruit and retain the best employees.

Google had to figure out how to maintain its culture of corporate entrepreneurship and innovation in an era of stagnant profitability. Furthermore, the company had grown to over 20,000 employees. How could it maintain its culture with so large an organization?

Discussion Questions

1. What are the major problems facing Google in 2009?
2. Given the economic environment in 2009 as described in the case, what implications, opportunities, and threats does this context pose for Google currently? What about in 2012?
3. Based on the content of the case, what was the primary Strategic Inflection Point for Google? Why did you select this point?
4. A. Calculate the key profitability, liquidity, and asset management ratios for Google over the past five year period and compare them with Yahoo! Based on the financial ratios, what advantages does Google have over Yahoo!? What vulnerabilities does Google have versus Yahoo!?

   B. Is Google financially healthy? Why or why not?
5. What were Google's keys to success?
6. What recommendations would you make to Google? Why?

References

100 Top MBA Employers. CNNMoney.com. Accessed May 28, 2009, http://money.cnn.com/magazines/fortune/mba100/2009/full_list.

Battelle, J. (2009). Inside the Mind of Google. CNBC Interview. December 3, 2009.

Blodget, H. (2009). Google Announces Layoffs (GOOG). *Silicon Valley Insider.* Accessed May 15, 2009, www.businessinsider.com/2009/1/google-announces-layoffs-goog.

Brandon, E. (2009). Retirement Accounts Have Lost $3.4 Trillion. USNews.com. Accessed May 28, 2009, www.usnews.com/blogs/planning-to-retire/2009/03/13/retirement-accounts-have-now-lost-34-trillion.html.

Buffett: Economy in a Recession Will Be Worse Than Feared. USAToday.com, April 4, 2008. Accessed May 15, www.usatoday.com/money/economy/2008-04-28-buffett-recession_N.htm.

Christie, L. (2009). Homes Almost 20% Cheaper. CNNMoney.com. Accessed May 24, 2009, http://money.cnn.com/2009/05/26/real_estate/CaseShiller_home_prices_Q1/index.htm?cnn=yes.

Google Milestones (2009). Accessed on March 31, 2009, www.google.com/corporate/history.html.

Google.org (2010). Philanthropy at Google. Accessed May 18, 2010, www.google.org/googlers.html.

Guth, W., and Ginsberg, A. (1990). "Guest Editors' Introduction: Corporate Entrepreneurship." *Strategic Management Journal*, 11, 297–308.

Hamel, G., and Breen, B. (2007). Aiming for an Evolutionary Advantage. *Harvard Business Review.* Harvard Business School Press, Boston, MA.

Harris, S. (2009) Stanford's Rich Entrepreneurial Culture Still Bursting with Ideas, Nurturing Minds. *San Jose Mercury News*, May 10, pages 1, 19.

Lowe, (2009). *Google Speaks: Secrets of the World's Greatest Billionaire Entrepreneurs.* John Wiley & Sons. Page 282.

Miller, M. (2006). *Googlepedia: The Ultimate Google Resource.* Que. Page 10.

Pinchot, G., and Pellman, R. (1999) *Intrapreneuring in Action: A Handbook for Business Innovation.* Berrett-Koehler.

Pohle, G., and Chapman, M. (2006). IBM Global CEO Study 2006: Business Model Innovation Matters. *Strategy and Leadership*, 34, 5, 34–40.

Rule, E., and Irwin, D. (1988). Fostering Intrapreneurship: The New Competitive Edge. *Journal of Business Strategy.* 9, 3, 44–47.

S&P 500 Index (2009). Accessed October 24, 2009, http://finance.yahoo.com/q/hp?s=^GSPC&a=0&b=3&c=1950&d=9&e=25&f=2009&g=d&z=66&y=132.

Schmidt, E. (2009). Inside the Mind of Google. CNBC Interview. December 3, 2009.

Thompson, C. (2001). *Current Biography Yearbook.* H.W. Wilson Co. Page 50.

Willis, B. (2009). U.S. Recession Worst Since Great Depression, Revised Data Show. Accessed November 27, 2009, www.bloomberg.com/apps/news?pid=20601087&sid=aNivTjr852TI.

Wolcott, R., and Lippitz, M. (2007). The Four Models of Corporate Entrepreneurship. *MIT Sloan Management Review.* Fall, 49, 1, 74–82.

Zahra, S. (1991). Predictors and Financial Outcomes of Corporate Entrepreneurship: An Exploratory Study. *Journal of Business Venturing*, 6, 4, 259–285.

¢URRENCY13*

Enabling Bank Trusted
Peer-to-Peer Payments

Whitney Kalscheur

Bryan T. Walley

*The Currency13 feasibility study was completed to meet, in part, the requirements for a graduate level course. It is intended for discussion purposes only and should not be considered a "model" for how to do feasibility analysis. Rather, it offers the opportunity to discuss various elements of a new venture prior to launch.

Source: Reprinted by permission of the authors.

By the year 2016, peer-to-peer payments are expected to reach $1.6 trillion, and global mobile payments are expected to reach $600 billion by 2011. However, with this growth comes an increase in fraud.[1] The solution is Currency13, a proprietary payments platform that issues unique, one-time use codes through its closed system to enable safe and easy payments. This patent-pending technology can be white labeled by small and medium-sized financial institutions to offer peer-to-peer payments to end users while continuing to enjoy use of funds. It's a winning scenario for banks, bank customers, and consumers.

Market Pain and Currency13 Opportunity

Peer-to-peer payments are a burgeoning industry; however, it is imperfect and poses problems for both consumers and banks. Rapid expansion has shown that current service providers have focused on convenience as the key benefit for the consumer while other very real concerns still persist.[2] When making online payments, consumers still have the very real threat of identity theft. The Federal Trade Commission has stated that is identify theft is the fastest growing crime, with 10 million people becoming victims each year. That equates to approximately 19 people per minute.[3] Additionally, consumers are charged almost 3 percent per transaction for exchanges under $3,000 by the most dominant players such as PayPal. This decreases the appeal of online shopping and electronic payments.[4]

Not only are peer-to-peer payments problematic for consumers, they are also cumbersome for financial institutions. Currently, when a transaction is in progress using some of the current popular systems, banks lose the opportunity to use member funds for lending and investment. The challenge is that many banks do not have a method for creating a network that allows consumers to make funds transfers with people who are not members of the consumer's institution.

Currency13 Solution

While these very real concerns may seem insurmountable, there is a solution: Currency13. Currency13 is a proprietary online software that issues unique one-time use codes per transaction. The process is simple. Consumers authenticate a bank account through their online banking interface. If a consumer's bank does not currently use Currency13, an account can be set up directly through the system's website. Once authenticated, a consumer can begin issuing codes to other consumers within the Currency13 system. The payee enters the amount of the transaction and is issued a code. The receiver of funds inserts the code received from the payee into their Currency13 account and enters the amount of the transaction. The money is then transferred.

Currency 13 completely eliminates the security threat to consumers. By having to enter both a code and the dollar amount, the system guarantees the authenticity of the receiver. Additionally,

---

[1] "Alternative Payment Schemes: Leveraging ACH" The Santa Fe Group. April 7, 2009.
[2] Agrawal, Mohit. "Mobile Payments: Will the Consumers Adopt?" Telecom World. Accessed 18 November 2009, www.mohitagrawal.com/2009/04/mobile-payments-will-consumers-adopt.html.
[3] "Chilling Facts About Identity Threats." Identity Theft Information Center. Accessed 03 October 2009, www.scambusters.org/identitytheft.html.
[4] "Transaction Fees For Domestic Payments." PayPal.com. Accessed 3 November 2009, www.paypal.com/cgi-bin/webscr?cmd=_display-receiving-fees-outside.

in order to receive payment, one must be a member of the Currency13 system. Therefore, the company is able to track where money is sent. Lastly, should a consumer lose the unique code, the threat is mitigated because the code has an expiration date. Once a code expires and cannot be used, a new code can be issued for payment.

Consumers also have the benefit of making payments without charge. This is because banks will pay one dollar per member using Currency13 through their online banking interface. In return, financial institutions will be provided access to their members' Currency13 account funds and also have a large network of banks that have been interconnected due to Currency13.

Once Currency13 is adopted for online banking transfers, the company will begin to market the product as a way to make payments to small businesses both online and through a consumer's cell phone. Additionally, because of the unique nature of Currency13, the product can be used for gift certificates, international payments, loan transfers, and payroll as the most secure form of currency.

Target Market and Currency13 Approach

In-depth research has shown that Currency13 is a desirable product for both consumers and financial institutions. The primary online consumers are middle to upper-class women, but the industry is fragmented. Therefore, Currency13 interviewed 9 women with household incomes of $62,000 or greater and 6 men with the same household income. The age of all consumers interviewed ranged between 25 and 60.

Through these 15 one-hour interviews, Currency13 ascertained that consumers are interested in a reliable way to make payments and transfers to their peers while also being provided a sense of security and no transaction fees. On average, consumers are making purchases online at least one time per month with the purchase amount being $200 or less. Typically, consumers pay using PayPal or a credit card.

Through these discussions, the company learned that consumers remain apprehensive about inputting personal information online, especially through websites that are not well known and established. This sentiment is also consistent with consumers who use ebay.com as they are not familiar with the consumer on the receiving end. PayPal does assist in alleviating the security concern; however, 3 consumers interviewed had their PayPal accounts breached and now are reluctant to use it. When asked if they would ever return to PayPal upon increased security, they were hesitant saying they were very nervous about dealing with the breach of security again.

Although security is a concern, it is not so prevalent that consumers are avoiding online shopping. Therefore, in order for Currency13 to be a reasonable alternative, adoption of the software must be streamlined and easy. Currency13 has solved that issue by looking at partnering with financial institutions and implementing the software on online banking interfaces. This entry strategy will allow banks to feel secure in that they will be rewarded their use of funds and members can easily "click" to opt into the system. Because consumers had concerns using unknown websites and entering personal information, the company is also looking at online banking interfaces as a way to get around the hurdle of building trust with Currency13. Consumers mentioned that they typically trust their online banking platforms as there are several security passwords that need to be utilized in order to reach their accounts. Therefore, the online platform is the perfect place to begin implementing Currency13.

There are more than 8,000 financial institutions in the United States, and while the largest banks are well known, the vast majority of these would be considered small to medium-sized, community, or local banks and credit unions. These institutions do not have the resources or time to develop their technology in-house and, therefore, leverage third party systems to provide core accounting, online banking, and other critical technical services to their customers. Within this context, Currency13 has spoken with multiple sources, including Online Banking and Bill Pay Product Managers at City National Bank, Metavante (now part of FIS), Corillian (now part of Fiserv), and Digital Insight (an Intuit company). All of this primary research has indicated that financial institutions are actively looking to offer peer-to-peer, mobile payments that integrate with their online banking platform, and the service providers listed are all in the process of rolling out a flavor of this service. What is clear is the demand, but what is not is the model that will enable the financial institutions and the service providers to offer a compelling and easy to use service to the end customer.

Competition and Currency13 Advantages

In the financial institution industry, peer-to-peer and mobile payments are "hot" spaces right now. There are many competitors for the Currency13 technology. These competitors range from established players, such as Visa, MasterCard, PayPal, and Google Checkout, to more recent entrants, such as Obopay, CashEdge, and WebMoney, to new startups that are coming online almost daily, such as PayQuicker. The competitive landscape is fierce, but none of these companies is focused on serving the small and medium-sized financial institutions, which is where Currency13 will play. Visa, MasterCard, Obopay, and CashEdge are currently targeting the largest financial institutions and/or mass consumers directly. Google Checkout and WebMoney are focused on online ecommerce sites. And PayQuicker, still in a beta phase, has yet to make its strategy known. So, although there are similar technologies, these companies are not positioned to serve the small and medium-sized bank at this time.

Currency13's unfair advantage is twofold: (1) The payment system is patent pending and (2) The model is bank friendly. In terms of the technology, one of the differentiators is that Currency13 leverages the concept of coupon payments, which decouples the sensitive information, such as name and sender's account number, from the transactional information, such as the dollar amount and reason for payment. Another Currency13 technology advantage is that the sender can place an expiration date on the payment, so there is a risk mitigation element to the system that other platforms do not offer.

The Currency13 business model is also unique in the market, in that the company does not rely on Use of Funds to remain profitable nor does it charge a per-transaction fee for financial institution users. To date, the primary reason that banks have not partnered with PayPal to offer peer-to-peer payments, an obvious choice in this arena, is that PayPal and the bank would fight for which account holds the funds. PayPal, in essence, is a competing bank and uses the excess funds to earn float revenue. To incentivize small and medium-sized financial institutions to adopt the Currency13 technology, there is no per transaction fee for FI users, which is not common across the industry. The strategy with this model is to drive user volume and allow the banks to determine the per-transaction pricing structure for the end customer.

Currency13 Business Model

Currency13 has a unique and simple monetization model. Unlike current peer-to-peer payment systems, consumers who utilize Currency13 will not be charged per transaction. Currency13 consumers will be able to utilize the benefits of the system for free if they are members of financial institutions that opt into the software. The banks will be charged one dollar per user per month. Upon installation of the system onto a bank's interface, consumers will be able to select Currency13 for transfers when they log into their banking account. The consumer information will be sent to Currency13 so that the company can accurately monitor consumer use. When a consumer is inactive for more than six months, Currency 13 will no longer charge the bank for that particular member. Consumers who are not members of Currency13 banks will still be able to utilize the software directly through the company website. Those consumers will be charged a 1.0 percent transaction fee when receiving funds.

Product Development Plan

Currency13 has an aggressive development plan. The online software has already been developed and can be utilized directly by consumers via the Internet. Because consumer findings derived from in-depth interviews showed concern about entering personal information onto unknown websites, Currency13 has decided to move forward on the white labeled version of the product for banks. At the same time, the company will work diligently to contract with financial institutions interested in the software. At that juncture, Currency13's white labeled product will be uploaded onto each bank's online interface. The company believes that installation can occur as soon as six months. After working with the first few institutions, Currency13 will hire an additional marketing employee in month ten to procure more accounts. From month twelve on, the company will continue to acquire skilled sales and customer representatives to assist with the rapid movement of the product. Currency13's unique closed system of one-time use codes is patent pending both nationally and internationally, and the success of the company is predicated upon building relationships with well known financial institutions. These relationships will help to create consumer awareness and security in the brand. Additionally, those relationships are also key for the product's rapid adoption.

Management Team

Ian James currently serves as Currency13's CEO and software programmer after co-founding the company in late 2007. He has over seven years of software and web programming experience in addition to a strong research capabilities. Christy Matson serves as the company's Chief Financial Officer and co-founder. She has over seven years of business experience, including serving as the accounting and financial expert during the startup phase of iOffer.com. Christy Matson and Ian James will be responsible for developing the company's white label software and managing the day to day operations of Currency13, including customer service. Whitney Kalscheur has over seven years of marketing, brand management and entrepreneurial experience that will help to propel Currency13 forward. In addition to beginning her own sunglasses company, her expertise will enable the company to develop the essence of the company's brand image and strategically determine how to best approach potential partners. Bryan Walley has 10 years of technology and banking experience with a track record of delivering technical and process improvement results for both external clients and internal stakeholders. The company has one foreseen gap within its management team that can be easily overcome: a valuable sales manager. This person will assist in developing a team of qualified sales representatives responsible for building relationships with local banks in order to build the Currency13 network.

Financial Projections and Forecast

The financial projections rely on the following assumptions:

Financial Institution Assumptions	
Monthly Fee / FI User	$ 1.00
Average Number of Users / FI	7,500
Integration Fees / FI	$40,000

The $1.00 per FI User is at or below the expected cost per user for an online banking or online bill pay user that many of the competitors listed above charge financial institutions. The 7,500 users per financial institution is an industry average number for online banking and bill pay usage for a bank with more than 12,000 total customers.

Consumer Transactions Assumptions	
Average Payment Amount	$20.00
Fee per Consumer Transaction	0
Net Consumer Transaction Growth Rate	14.0% (includes 1.0% churn)

And as a result, the following metrics are a result:

Cash Flow Positive	Month 15
Breakeven	Month 34
Total FI's on Month 36	46
Total FI Users on Month 36	$322,500

In order to achieve the forecasts above, Currency13 estimates the following capital raise will be required:

Startup Capital Needs (SUCN)	$ 532,172
Safety Factor (SF)	$ 120,000
Total Startup Capital (SU)	**$652,172**

Timeline and Major Milestones

In conjunction with the financial projections above, Currency13 has laid out the capital, human, and physical resources plan against the major milestones below.

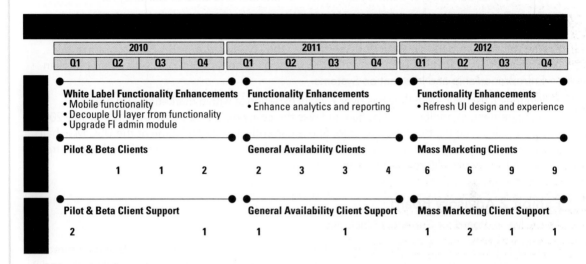

Harvest Strategy

To exit the peer-to-peer payment industry, acquisition would be the most viable option. This option becomes even more important once the company acquires consumers and financial institutions because they will rely on the product for transfers. This will enable the company's management team to maintain their reputations for future entrepreneurial business opportunities and allow the financial institution to continue to use the product for its peer-to-peer payments. An IPO is also possible; however, because Currency13 will rely heavily upon relationships with financial institutions, it would be challenging to receive approval from each institution within the network. If acquisition were not possible, the steps to shutting down the business would be to shift the funds from consumer's Currency13 accounts into their checking accounts prior to shutting down the system. For consumers who are not part of member banks, Currency13 would take measures to notify consumers in order to enable them time to empty their Currency13 accounts. The company would reduce its staff to the original two founders so that they could monitor consumer account elimination.

Exhibit 1 Key Management Team Bios

The Key Management for Currency13 includes:

- Ian James – Ian has 7 years of software and programming experience in addition to strong research capabilities. This experience includes working as a network consultant at Mark Chow Insurance and Investment planning and as a programmer at GizmoLabs. In addition, he has experience in directing and managing a software development team. He holds a B.S. in Physics from the University of California at Berkeley and is the co-founder and CEO of Currency13.

- Christy Matson – Christy has 7 years of management and financial experience, including several years as the lead accountant and financial expert at the startup iOffer.com. She has worked as an auditor at State Street Corporation in Boston, MA, holds a B.A. in Legal Studies from the University of California at Berkeley, and is the co-founder and CFO of Currency13.

- Bryan T. Walley – Bryan has 10 years of technology and banking experience with a track record of delivering technical and process improvement results for both external clients and internal stakeholders. He is currently enrolled in the USC Marshall MBA.PM program and has an undergraduate degree from the USC Marshall School of Business with an emphasis in Entrepreneurship and Information Systems.

- Whitney Kalscheur – Whitney has over 7 years experience within marketing and brand management. In addition, she began and was the co-owner of Oculus Eyewear until July 2008, upon which time the business was sold. She is currently enrolled full time at the USC Marshall School of Business with an emphasis in entrepreneurship and marketing and holds a B.A. from the University of California at Berkeley.

Exhibit 2 Advisory Board

The Advisory Board for Currency13 includes:

- Keith Matson – Keith has over 30 years of business experience. In addition to being a retired naval aviator, Keith has begun and sold several businesses within the realm of real estate and is an owner of the Padres. He received his bachelor's from the University of California at Berkeley in 1976. He became an angel investor in iOffer.com in 2001 and in OpenCuro.com in 2007. He also serves at the company's lead advisor.

Exhibit 3 Industry Analysis, Value Chain, and Business Process

Life cycle and industry demographics

NAICS 52232: Industry is established but growing as consumers become increasingly more reliant on ecommerce to meet their shopping needs. Ecommerce and online auctions are the means by which online payment software is typically utilized, and the industry is highly fragmented. The most well recognized payment system is PayPal. The focus within payment systems are convenience and safety. Consumer disposable income and changes in technology are the biggest areas of volatility. Household consumers and individuals make up 80 percent of the market and tend to be affluent, followed by online small businesses making up the second largest group at 8.9 percent. The online consumer is typically middle to upper class educated women. Market estimates that alternative payments could reach $1.6 trillion by 2016 with global mobile payments volume could reach $600 billion by 2011.
Source: IBIS World.

Trends, gaps, and disruption possibilities

Banks / Financial institutions need to capture low-cost deposits and most competitor systems do now allow use of funds. Financial institutions are still dealing with the aftermath of credit crunch and recognize technology as a means to reduce costs and/or increase revenue. They are grappling with how to serve younger demographics and are looking at mobile technology as a means to do so via the nearly 3 billion mobile phones worldwide. More robust mobile content and increasing functionality of phones will help drive mobile payments adoption. There is also a gap within internet banking that also has strong youth adoption as they are comfortable with ecommerce. There is an overall shift to electronic payments but also a merchant pricing revolt which will allow Currency13 to being adopted due to the company's reasonable pricing model. Prior to the 2008 recession, the money transferring industry grew by an average annual rate of 6.2 percent due to an increase in consumer spending and improvements in technology.

Barriers to entry

They are low but include:

- R&D costs – minimal
- Security concerns
- SAS 70 II audit
- Banks can be very slow to adopt
- Regulations
- Integration to online banking platforms
- Insurance
- Liability for consumer information
- Driving traffic to site
- Consulting fees
- No reputation in established industry

3 Industries and at least 6 customers where solution can be deployed

Industries:

- Banking / consumer-oriented financial institutions
- Telecommunications (mobile payments)
- Ecommerce

Customers:

- Online marketplaces (eBay/iOffer)
- Online gaming
- Blogs
- Credit unions
- Small online businesses
- Peer-to-peer payments / bank transfers

Five forces

Rivals: PayPal, Obopay, WebEx, WebMoney, Electronic Payment Systems, eBillme, Moneta, Secure Vault Payments, Noca, Mazooma, Revolution Money, Bill Me Later, Acculynk, Google Checkout, Amazon Payments, Decoupled Payments

Suppliers: Developers, hardware, infrastructure

Buyers: Financial institutions via established partnerships, financial institutions, new ecommerce sites, new small businesses, blogs, online gaming systems, consumers

Subs: Cash, credit cards, ACH, bill pay, debit

Comps: Online banking and mobile apps, ecommerce

Lead informants

- Alex Falk and Steven Wildemuth, City National Bank Product Managers
- Eric Jamison, FIS P2P Initiative Leader
- Rob Killoran, Fiserv Sales Manager
- Janice Cheung, Intuit Senior Product Manager
- Bank Technology News
- FierceFinanceIT and FierceMobile
- CNET
- Gartner, Tower, Javelin, etc.
- NACHA
- OpenCuro Founders – Christy and Ian
- Hoover's
- IBISWorld
- GonzoBanker

Primary and Secondary Research Summary

The Financial Institution Industry Research conducted included speaking with Alex F. and Steven W., the Online Banking and Bill Pay Product Managers at City National Bank, Eric J., the P2P Initiative Leader at Metavante (now part of FIS), Rob K., Sales Manager at Corillian (now part of Fiserv), and Janice C., Senior Product Manager at Digital Insight (an Intuit company). Some of the highlights from these conversations include:

- Alex F. noted repeatedly that he is already looking for a solution of this type, that there is strong demand for this type of product in the market, and that City National Bank would be a candidate for the Currency13 offering. Further, he helped with ensuring that the business model is bank friendly.

- Steven W. brought a commercial, not consumer, perspective to the interview. And from that vantage, he felt that there is a convergence of commercial functionality, like being able to pay anyone from anywhere, that is heading down market toward the consumer.

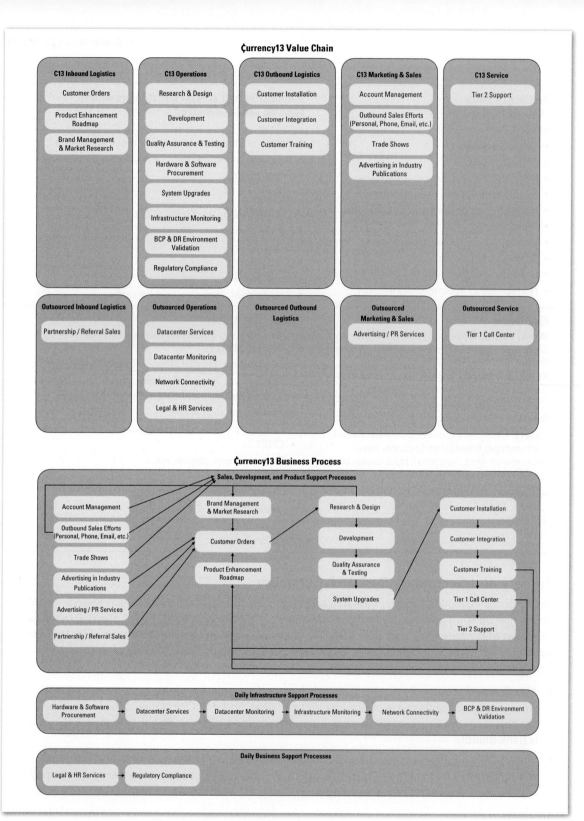

- Eric J. was interested in the coupon aspect of the Currency13 technology, as he stated that it is a unique offering in the market. He noted that the biggest hurdles this type of technology faces is brand recognition and number of users on the system (i.e., the positive network effect). He also commented that the typical rollout strategy for Metavante / FIS on this type of technology involved 3X the number of clients that Currency13 was forecasting, so that was a safe and sound projection.
- Janice C. offered many industry resources and reports, noting that peer-to-peer payments both for the consumer and the commercial space, was "hot" these days. She was also extremely helpful in validating the cost and support structure in our financial model.

Based on the information gathered in the company's industry analysis posted above, Currency13 performed 15, one-hour interviews with consumers who make electronic payments and/or electronic banking. The information represents an aggregate of the most important information derived from these findings.

Demographics of Interviews

- *Gender:* 9 Female, 6 Male
- *Age:* 25 to 60 for Female, 33 to 58 for Male
- *HH Income:* $62,000+

The results of these interviews include:

- *Online Shopping Habits*: Shop online at least 1 time every two months, spending on average $50 but typically no more than $200. They pay using PayPal or credit card.
- *Mobile Highlights*: None had made peer-to-peer payments through their mobile phone but were interested. Seems cumbersome to log into current peer-to-peer payment accounts. 11 interviewees had phones that could be classified at smart phones.
- *Banking Habits*: 8 out of 15 consumers consistently banked online. They had mentioned that they could transfer money within their own accounts. None had made transfers to other consumers using their online banking platform. They were intrigued by the concept of a way to transfer money between bank accounts but were skeptical of the security of the operations. Consumers felt comfortable logging into the bank's platform because there were typically several security measures a consumer had to go through prior to reaching his personal account information.
- *Fraud*: 3 consumers had their PayPal accounts breached. Only one had lost money because of the breach. The other two were able to update their profiles after being notified by PayPal of the breach. They are all reluctant to use it and prefer to use credit cards. When asked why they felt comfortable using credit cards, they mentioned they did not have many other options and felt comfortable that the credit card company would rectify any wrong doing. One consumer had her car broken into and her credit cards were stolen. They were charged several thousand dollars. She was able to get the funds returned; however, the process was a hassle.
- *Overall Sentiments About Pricing*: Consumers would prefer to not be charged a fee to make peer-to-peer payments and felt that 3 percent was exorbitant. Several were not aware that PayPal charged a Purchase Payment upon receiving money in a transaction. "PayPal is becoming a credit card company."

- *Overall sentiments about shopping on unfamiliar websites*: Consumers will not shop on unfamiliar websites that require personal information. They would especially be hard pressed to enter banking information onto an unfamiliar site.
- *Overall sentiments about shopping online*: Consumers love it. It is convenient and a big time savings. While they are concerned about security, it is not a large enough deterrent to stop consumers from entering personal information/credit card information to make purchases. They mentioned that they would definitely be willing try a new more secure product as long as using the product was seamless and streamlined.

Exhibit 4 Pro Forma Financial Statements

Below are the summary section and the assumptions section for the Currency13 financial model.

Total Startup Capital	**652,172**
Capital Expenditures (CE)	**450,000**
R&D Expenses	450,000
Soft Costs (SC)	**465,495**
Net 30 AR Balance	465,495
Startup Costs (SU)	**3,925,410**
Salaries	880,000
Commissions	522,460
FTE Workstations	25,000
Office Space w/ Utilities	186,250
Office Equipment	27,000
Advertising	40,500
Travel & Entertainment	81,000
Accounting	36,000
Legal	54,000
Insurance	36,000
FTE Load	308,000
Server Lease	794,700
Transportation	805,500
Installation Costs	41,000
Cell Phones	44,000
Internet	44,000
Working Capital (WC)	**4,308,733**
Working Capital Needs	4,308,733
Startup Capital Needs (SUCN)	**532,172**
Startup Capital Needs	532,172
Safety Factor (SF)	**120,000**
Safety Factor	120,000

Note: SC is Month 36 A/R, SF is 3 x Installation Fees.

Assumptions

Monthly Fee / FI / User	$1.00
Average OLB & BP Users / FI	7,500
Server Lease / FI	$1,500.00
FI Integration Fee	$40,000.00
Salary / Month / FTE	$5,000.00
FTE Load	35.0%
Sales Commission	10.0%
Office sq.ft. / FTE	500
Office Cost / sq.ft.	$2.50
Income Tax Rate	45.0%
Average Payment Amount	$20.00
Fee per Consumer Transaction	1.0%
Consumer Transaction Growth	15.0%
User Churn Rate	1.0%

Model Results

Cash Flow Positive Month	15
Breakeven Month	34
FI's Month 12	4
FI's Month 24	16
FI's Month 36	46
FI Users Month 12	22,500
FI Users Month 24	105,000
FI Users Month 36	322,500
Consumer Transactions Month 12	2,132
Consumer Transactions Month 24	10,270
Consumer Transactions Month 36	49,480

Assumptions

Monthly Fee per FI User	$1.00			Average Payment Amount	$20.00		
OLB & BP Users per FI	7,500			Fee per Consumer Transaction	1.0%		
Server Lease / FI	$1,500			Consumer Transaction Growth	15.0%		
FI Integration Fee	$40,000			User Churn Rate	1.0%		

Milestones	Mo. 1	2	3	4	5	6	7	8
New FI's on System	0	0	0	0	0	1	0	1
Cumulative FI's	0	0	0	0	0	1	1	2
Consumer Transactions	500	575	656	747	852	971	1,107	1,262
Salaried FTE	2	2	2	2	2	2	2	2
Lease Office Space	0	0	0	0	0	0	0	0

Cash Inflows	Mo. 1	2	3	4	5	6	7	8
FI Revenue								
FI Users (Net 30)	0	0	0	0	0	0	7,500	7,500
FI User Churn	0	0	0	0	0	0	0	0
Total FI Users (Net 30)	0	0	0	0	0	0	7,500	7,500
Integration Fees (Net 30)	0	0	0	0	0	40,000	0	40,000
Total FI Revenue	0	0	0	0	0	40,000	7,500	47,500
Consumer Revenue								
Transactions (Net 30)	0	100	115	131	149	170	194	221
Total Consumer Revenue	0	100	115	131	149	170	194	221
Total Cash Inflows	0	100	115	131	149	40,170	7,694	47,721

Cash Outflows	Mo. 1	2	3	4	5	6	7	8
Fixed Costs								
Salaries	10,000	10,000	10,000	10,000	10,000	10,000	10,000	10,000
Commissions	0	0	0	0	0	4,000	750	4,750
FTE Workstations	5,000	0	0	0	0	0	0	0
R&D Costs	250,000	0	0	0	0	0	0	0
Office Space w/ Utilities	0	0	0	0	0	0	0	0
Office Equipment	500	500	500	500	500	500	500	500
Advertising	750	750	750	750	750	750	750	750
Travel & Entertainment	1,000	1,000	1,000	1,000	1,000	1,000	2,000	2,000
Accounting	1,000	1,000	1,000	1,000	1,000	1,000	1,000	1,000
Legal	1,500	1,500	1,500	1,500	1,500	1,500	1,500	1,500
Insurance	1,000	1,000	1,000	1,000	1,000	1,000	1,000	1,000
FTE Load	3,500	3,500	3,500	3,500	3,500	3,500	3,500	3,500
Total Fixed Costs	274,250	19,250	19,250	19,250	19,250	23,250	21,000	25,000
Variable Costs								
Server Lease	1,200	1,200	1,200	1,200	1,200	2,700	2,700	4,200
Transportation	1,500	1,500	1,500	1,500	1,500	3,000	3,000	4,500
Installation Costs	500	500	500	500	500	1,000	500	1,000
Cell Phones	500	500	500	500	500	500	500	500
Internet	500	500	500	500	500	500	500	500
Total Variable Costs	4,200	4,200	4,200	4,200	4,200	7,700	7,200	10,700
Total Cash Outflows	278,450	23,450	23,450	23,450	23,450	30,950	28,200	35,700

Total Cash In/Outflows	Mo. 1	2	3	4	5	6	7	8
Net Cash In/Outflow	−278,450	−23,350	−23,335	−23,319	−23,301	9,220	−20,506	12,021
Tax Liability	0	0	0	0	0	4,149	0	5,410
Cumulative Cash Flow	−278,450	−301,800	−325,135	−348,454	−371,754	−366,683	−387,189	−380,577

Metrics	Mo. 1	2	3	4	5	6	7	8
Revenue / User	0.0	0.0	0.0	0.0	0.0	0.0	6.3	12.7
Cost / User	0.0	0.0	0.0	0.0	0.0	0.0	57.5	62.3
Margin / User	0.0%	0.0%	0.0%	0.0%	0.0%	0.0%	−89.0%	−79.7%

Assumptions

	Salary / FTE	$5,000		Office sq.ft. / FTE	500
	FTE Load	35.0%		Office Cost / sq.ft.	$2.50
	Sales Commission	10.0%		Income Tax Rate	45.0%

9	10	11	12	13	14	15	16	17	18	19
0	1	0	1	1	0	1	1	1	1	1
2	3	3	4	5	5	6	7	8	9	10
1,439	1,640	1,870	2,132	2,430	2,770	3,158	3,600	4,104	4,679	5,334
2	3	3	3	4	4	4	4	4	4	5
0	0	0	0	1	1	1	1	1	1	1

9	10	11	12	13	14	15	16	17	18	19
15,000	15,000	22,500	22,500	30,000	37,500	37,500	45,000	52,500	60,000	67,500
−75	−75	−150	−150	−225	−225	−300	−375	−375	−450	−525
14,925	14,925	22,350	22,350	29,775	37,275	37,200	44,625	52,125	59,550	66,975
0	40,000	0	40,000	40,000	0	40,000	40,000	40,000	40,000	40,000
14,925	54,925	22,350	62,350	69,775	37,275	77,200	84,625	92,125	99,550	106,975
252	288	328	374	426	486	554	632	720	821	936
252	288	328	374	426	486	554	632	720	821	936
15,177	55,213	22,678	62,724	70,201	37,761	77,754	85,257	92,845	100,371	107,911

9	10	11	12	13	14	15	16	17	18	19
10,000	15,000	15,000	15,000	20,000	20,000	20,000	20,000	20,000	20,000	25,000
1,493	5,493	2,235	6,235	6,978	3,728	7,720	8,463	9,213	9,955	10,698
0	2,500	0	0	2,500	0	0	0	0	0	2,500
0	0	0	0	100,000	0	0	0	0	0	0
0	0	0	0	5,000	5,000	5,000	5,000	5,000	5,000	6,250
500	500	500	500	750	750	750	750	750	750	750
750	750	750	750	1,000	1,000	1,000	1,000	1,000	1,000	1,250
2,000	2,000	2,000	2,000	2,000	2,000	2,000	2,000	2,000	2,000	2,500
1,000	1,000	1,000	1,000	1,000	1,000	1,000	1,000	1,000	1,000	1,000
1,500	1,500	1,500	1,500	1,500	1,500	1,500	1,500	1,500	1,500	1,500
1,000	1,000	1,000	1,000	1,000	1,000	1,000	1,000	1,000	1,000	1,000
3,500	5,250	5,250	5,250	7,000	7,000	7,000	7,000	7,000	7,000	8,750
21,743	34,993	29,235	33,235	148,728	42,978	46,970	47,713	48,463	49,205	61,198
4,200	5,700	5,700	7,200	8,700	8,700	10,200	11,700	13,200	14,700	16,200
4,500	6,000	6,000	7,500	9,000	9,000	10,500	12,000	13,500	15,000	16,500
500	1,000	500	1,000	1,000	500	1,000	1,000	1,000	1,000	1,000
500	750	750	750	1,000	1,000	1,000	1,000	1,000	1,000	1,250
500	750	750	750	1,000	1,000	1,000	1,000	1,000	1,000	1,250
10,200	14,200	13,700	17,200	20,700	20,200	23,700	26,700	29,700	32,700	36,200
31,943	49,193	42,935	50,435	169,428	63,178	70,670	74,413	78,163	81,905	97,398

9	10	11	12	13	14	15	16	17	18	19
−16,765	6,020	−20,257	12,289	−99,226	−25,416	7,084	10,844	14,683	18,466	10,513
0	2,709	0	5,530	0	0	3,188	4,880	6,607	8,310	4,731
−397,342	−394,031	−414,288	−407,529	−506,755	−532,172	−528,276	−522,311	−514,236	−504,080	−498,297

9	10	11	12	13	14	15	16	17	18	19
7.3	11.0	8.3	11.1	10.6	9.5	11.6	11.5	11.6	11.8	12.1
33.3	36.5	26.3	28.5	27.0	23.3	25.2	22.7	20.9	19.7	18.9
−78.0%	−69.9%	−68.3%	−61.1%	−60.6%	−59.2%	−54.1%	−49.1%	−44.4%	−39.8%	−36.0%

Milestones	20	21	22	23	24	25	26	27
New FI's on System	1	1	1	1	2	2	2	2
Cumulative FI's	11	12	13	14	16	18	20	22
Consumer Transactions	6,081	6,932	7,903	9,009	10,270	11,708	13,347	15,216
Salaried FTE	5	5	5	5	5	5	6	6
Lease Office Space	1	1	1	1	1	1	1	1

Cash Inflows	20	21	22	23	24	25	26	27
FI Revenue								
FI Users (Net 30)	75,000	82,500	90,000	97,500	105,000	120,000	135,000	150,000
FI User Churn	−600	−675	−750	−825	−900	−975	−1,050	−1,200
Total FI Users (Net 30)	74,400	81,825	89,250	96,675	104,100	119,025	133,950	148,800
Integration Fees (Net 30)	40,000	40,000	40,000	40,000	80,000	80,000	80,000	80,000
Total FI Revenue	114,400	121,825	129,250	136,675	184,100	199,025	213,950	228,800
Consumer Revenue								
Transactions (Net 30)	1,067	1,216	1,386	1,581	1,802	2,054	2,342	2,669
Total Consumer Revenue	1,067	1,216	1,386	1,581	1,802	2,054	2,342	2,669
Total Cash Inflows	115,467	123,041	130,636	138,256	185,902	201,079	216,292	231,469

Cash Outflows	20	21	22	23	24	25	26	27
Fixed Costs								
Salaries	25,000	25,000	25,000	25,000	25,000	25,000	30,000	30,000
Commissions	11,440	12,183	12,925	13,668	18,410	19,903	21,395	22,880
FTE Workstations	0	0	0	0	0	0	2,500	0
R&D Costs	0	0	0	0	0	100,000	0	0
Office Space w/ Utilities	6,250	6,250	6,250	6,250	6,250	6,250	7,500	7,500
Office Equipment	750	750	750	750	750	1,000	1,000	1,000
Advertising	1,250	1,250	1,250	1,250	1,250	1,500	1,500	1,500
Travel & Entertainment	2,500	2,500	2,500	2,500	2,500	3,000	3,000	3,000
Accounting	1,000	1,000	1,000	1,000	1,000	1,000	1,000	1,000
Legal	1,500	1,500	1,500	1,500	1,500	1,500	1,500	1,500
Insurance	1,000	1,000	1,000	1,000	1,000	1,000	1,000	1,000
FTE Load	8,750	8,750	8,750	8,750	8,750	8,750	10,500	10,500
Total Fixed Costs	59,440	60,183	60,925	61,668	66,410	168,903	80,895	79,880
Variable Costs								
Server Lease	17,700	19,200	20,700	22,200	25,200	28,200	31,200	34,200
Transportation	18,000	19,500	21,000	22,500	25,500	28,500	31,500	34,500
Installation Costs	1,000	1,000	1,000	1,000	1,500	1,500	1,500	1,500
Cell Phones	1,250	1,250	1,250	1,250	1,250	1,250	1,500	1,500
Internet	1,250	1,250	1,250	1,250	1,250	1,250	1,500	1,500
Total Variable Costs	39,200	42,200	45,200	48,200	54,700	60,700	67,200	73,200
Total Cash Outflows	98,640	102,383	106,125	109,868	121,110	229,603	148,095	153,080

Total Cash In/Outflows	20	21	22	23	24	25	26	27
Net Cash In/Outflow	16,827	20,659	24,511	28,388	64,792	−28,523	68,197	78,389
Tax Liability	7,572	9,296	11,030	12,775	29,156	0	30,688	35,275
Cumulative Cash Flow	−489,043	−477,680	−464,199	−448,586	−412,950	−441,474	−403,966	−360,851

Metrics	20	21	22	23	24	25	26	27
Revenue / User	12.4	12.8	13.1	13.5	14.3	14.2	14.2	14.3
Cost / User	18.3	17.9	17.6	17.4	17.3	17.0	16.2	15.6
Margin / User	−32.3%	−28.7%	−25.3%	−22.1%	−17.2%	−16.7%	−12.6%	−8.6%

28	29	30	31	32	33	34	35	36	TTD
2	2	2	3	3	3	3	3	3	
24	26	28	31	34	37	40	43	46	
17,346	19,774	22,543	25,699	29,296	33,398	38,074	43,404	49,480	
7	7	8	8	9	9	10	10	10	
1	1	1	1	1	1	1	1	1	

28	29	30	31	32	33	34	35	36	TTD
165,000	180,000	195,000	210,000	232,500	255,000	277,500	300,000	322,500	
−1,350	−1,500	−1,650	−1,800	−1,950	−2,100	−2,325	−2,550	−2,775	
163,650	178,500	193,350	208,200	230,550	252,900	275,175	297,450	319,725	
80,000	80,000	80,000	120,000	120,000	120,000	120,000	120,000	120,000	
243,650	258,500	273,350	328,200	350,550	372,900	395,175	417,450	439,725	5,224,600
3,043	3,469	3,955	4,509	5,140	5,859	6,680	7,615	8,681	
3,043	3,469	3,955	4,509	5,140	5,859	6,680	7,615	8,681	69,965
246,693	261,969	277,305	332,709	355,690	378,759	401,855	425,065	448,406	5,294,565

28	29	30	31	32	33	34	35	36	TTD
35,000	35,000	40,000	40,000	45,000	45,000	50,000	50,000	50,000	880,000
24,365	25,850	27,335	32,820	35,055	37,290	39,518	41,745	43,973	522,460
2,500	0	2,500	0	2,500	0	2,500	0	0	25,000
0	0	0	0	0	0	0	0	0	450,000
8,750	8,750	10,000	10,000	11,250	11,250	12,500	12,500	12,500	186,250
1,000	1,000	1,000	1,000	1,000	1,000	1,000	1,000	1,000	27,000
1,500	1,500	1,500	1,500	1,500	1,500	1,500	1,500	1,500	40,500
3,000	3,000	3,000	3,000	3,000	3,000	3,000	3,000	3,000	81,000
1,000	1,000	1,000	1,000	1,000	1,000	1,000	1,000	1,000	36,000
1,500	1,500	1,500	1,500	1,500	1,500	1,500	1,500	1,500	54,000
1,000	1,000	1,000	1,000	1,000	1,000	1,000	1,000	1,000	36,000
12,250	12,250	14,000	14,000	15,750	15,750	17,500	17,500	17,500	308,000
91,865	90,850	102,835	105,820	118,555	118,290	131,018	130,745	132,973	2,646,210
37,200	40,200	43,200	47,700	52,200	56,700	61,200	65,700	70,200	794,700
37,500	40,500	43,500	48,000	52,500	57,000	61,500	66,000	70,500	805,500
1,500	1,500	1,500	2,000	2,000	2,000	2,000	2,000	2,000	41,000
1,750	1,750	2,000	2,000	2,250	2,250	2,500	2,500	2,500	44,000
1,750	1,750	2,000	2,000	2,250	2,250	2,500	2,500	2,500	44,000
79,700	85,700	92,200	101,700	111,200	120,200	129,700	138,700	147,700	1,729,200
171,565	176,550	195,035	207,520	229,755	238,490	260,718	269,445	280,673	4,375,410

28	29	30	31	32	33	34	35	36	TTD
75,128	85,419	82,270	125,189	125,935	140,269	141,137	155,620	167,733	919,155
33,808	38,439	37,021	56,335	56,671	63,121	63,512	70,029	75,480	675,721
−319,531	−272,550	−227,302	−158,448	−89,184	−12,036	65,589	151,180	243,433	243,433

28	29	30	31	32	33	34	35	36	TTD
14.5	14.7	15.0	15.5	15.5	15.6	15.7	15.9	16.2	
15.3	15.0	14.8	14.7	14.3	14.0	13.8	13.6	13.6	
−5.1%	−1.7%	1.1%	4.9%	8.2%	11.4%	14.2%	16.9%	19.4%	

Exhibit 5 Narrative Assumptions for Financial Statements

The table below lists the line item, value, and reasoning behind the assumptions contained within the financial statements rendered above.

Revenue Figures

FI Adoption Rate	See Model	The forecast for the FI Adoption Rate is based on conversations with Eric J. as well as experiences of multiple product rollouts at City National Bank.
Monthly Fee / FI User	$1.00	Market rates for online banking and bill pay users in a similar model are above or near this value.
Average OLB & Bill Pay Users	$7,500.00	OLB and BP penetration rates across in the industry averages 60+%. Target FI's have more than 12,000 customers, which lead to an average user base of 7,500.
FI Integration Fee	$40,000	This is a professional services arrangement for 320 hours at $125 / hour. This time would be allocated across 2 – 3 individuals.
Server Lease / FI	$1,500	This is a dedicated hardware fee per financial institution.
Monthly Salary / FTE	$5,000	This rate yields a $60,000 salary to allow employees to live but also keep them very motivated.
FTE Load	35%	This is to account for taxes and other costs associated with full time employees.
Sales Commission	10%	This is to incent the sales representatives.
Office sq.ft. / FTE	$500	Nate C., a Commercial Real Estate professional, stated that this would be a conservative estimate.
Office Cost / sq.ft.	$2.50	Nate C., a Commercial Real Estate professional, stated that this would be a conservative estimate and include utilities.
Income Tax Rate	45%	This includes both CA State (9%) and Federal (35%) corporate tax rates.
Average Payment Amount	$20.00	This average payment amount was based on several different factors: Current usage patterns in the OpenCuro.com platform, a sampling of check payments from City National Bank, and the assumption that if users did not have cash on hand, this would be the smallest amount owed to a peer where the peer would demand payment.
Fee per Customer Transaction	1.00%	This is below or near industry average, as credit cards and online payment systems can charge up to 2.5% of the transaction amount in fees.
Consumer Transaction Growth	15%	This figure is taken from the trends being shown in the OpenCuro .com system to date.
User Churn Rate	1.00%	This is to allow a percentage of users to opt out of the system after a 90 day period.

Cost Figures Not Already Discussed Above

FTE Workstations	$ 2,500	This is a new computer expense during the month of hire.
R&D Costs	$450,000	This is a development fee to enhance the product. In Month 1, there is a $250,000 spend. And there are $100,000 spends in Year 2 and Year 3.
Office Equipment	$ 500	This is an allocation for paper, supplies, and miscellaneous work equipment.
Advertising	$ 750	This is a monthly allocation to build brand awareness, which increases in Year 2 and Year 3.
Travel & Entertainment	$ 1,000	This is a monthly allocation to allow Currency13 employees to travel and meet with prospects and customers. It increases in Year 2 and Year 3.
Accounting	$ 1,000	This is a monthly allocation based upon a price quote from Schubert & Company.
Legal	$ 1,500	This is a monthly allocation based upon a price quote from Good, Wildman, Hegness & Walley.
Insurance	$ 1,000	This is a monthly allocation based upon a price quote from Aon Insurance.
Transportation	$ 1,500	This a monthly allocation that increases in line with the total number of financial institutions on the system.
Installation Costs	$ 500	This is the expense that would be incurred to procure a new domain name and other technical requirements when a new financial institution comes onto the system.
Cell Phones	$ 500	This is an allocation of $250 per FTE for their work related mobile phone.
Internet	$ 500	This is an allocation of $250 per FTE for internet access at home.

Exhibit 6 Success and Risk Factors

Success Factors:

- Reputation – It is important to build a reputation within the banking community and with consumers. Currency13 is a company that consumers can trust and that values identity protection. In addition, the company stands behind all agreements.

- Marketing/Sales – Because Currency13 is a closed system and is monetized per consumer, rapid adoption is key. Therefore, having the right marketing and sales team is imperative to drive sales.

- Bank Partnerships – Without these relationships, the software will not get over the hurdle of consumer trust with the product. Additionally, it is imperative for adoption.

- Pricing – Consumers dislike current pricing models for peer-to-peer payment transactions. Currency13 has the simple model of charging banks one dollar per user. This pricing model will be a success factor in increasing adoption of the product.

Risk Factors:

- Security Breaches – While the company is currently confident in the Currency13 business model, security breaches are an area of concern. The company has consumer information stored offsite at a high security location and takes many steps to monitor information, therefore this risk factor is low.

- Competition – Currency13's niche is within the online banking realm; however, key competitors have the resources to build relationships quickly and may attack that niche fast. Because the product is superior to competitor products, competition may slow down adoption but not stop it completely.

- Technology – Changes in technology may be the largest threat to Currency13. In order to mitigate this risk, the company has patented its system. Once a network of banks is developed, the likelihood that a new technology will take over is low as the company plans to contract with institutions for an extended period of time.

- Cyclicality in Consumer Disposable Income – Currency13 has mitigated this risk because the banks will pay the company per consumer per month. The consumer lapses after six months and by that time, new consumers will likely utilize the product.

NOTES

Chapter 1

1. Schumpeter J.A. (1934). *The Theory of Economic Development*. Harvard University Press: Cambridge, MA.
2. Schendel D. (1990). "Introduction to the Special Issue on Corporate Entrepreneurship." *Strategic Management Journal*, Summer Special Issue 11: 1–3.
3. Gartner, W.B. (1985). "A Conceptual Framework for Describing the Phenomenon of New Venture Creation." *Academy of Management Review*, 702.
4. Churchill N.C., and D.F. Muzyka (1994). "Defining and Conceptualizing Entrepreneurship: A Process Approach." In Hills G.E. (ed.), *Marketing and Entrepreneurship*. Quorum Books: Westport, CT, 11–23; Shane S.A., and S. Venkataraman (2000). "The Promise of Entrepreneurship as a Field of Research." *Academy of Management Review* 25: 217–226; and Venkataraman S. (1997). "The Distinctive Domain of Entrepreneurship Research." In Katz J., and J. Brockhaus (eds.), *Advances in Entrepreneurship, Firm Emergence and Growth*. JAI Press: Greenwich, CT, 119–138.
5. Stevenson H.H., and J.C. Jarillo (1990). "A Paradigm of Entrepreneurship: Entrepreneurial Management." *Strategic Management Journal*, Summer Special Issue 11: 17–27.
6. Lumpkin, G.T., and G.G. Dess (January 1996). "Clarifying the Entrepreneurial Orientation Construct and Linking It to Performance." *Academy of Management Review*, 21(1): 135.
7. Morris, M.H., P. Lewis, and D.L. Sexton (Winter 1994). "Reconceptualizing Entrepreneurship: An Input–Output Perspective." *SAM Advanced Management Journal*, 59(2): 21–31.
8. Ronstadt, R.C. (1984). *Entrepreneurship*. Dover, MA: Lord Publishing Co., p. 39.
9. Gartner, W.B. (1985). "A Conceptual Framework for Describing the Phenomenon of New Venture Creation." *Academy of Management Review*, 702.
10. Schumpeter, J. (1934). *The Theory of Economic Development*. Cambridge: Harvard University Press; Solow, R.M. (1970). *Growth Theory: An Exposition*. Oxford: Oxford University Press; and Grossman, G.M., and E. Helpman (Winter 1994). "Endogenous Innovation in the Theory of Growth." *Journal of Economic Perspectives*, 8(1): 23–44.
11. Romer, P. (1986). "Increasing Returns and Long-Run Growth." *Journal of Political Economy*, 94: 1002–1037.
12. Allen, K.R. (2003). *Bringing New Technology to Market*. Upper Saddle River: Prentice Hall.
13. *Trading Economics* (June 23, 2010). "China GDP Growth Rate," www.tradingeconomics.com; *The Economist* (2002). "Self-Doomed to Failure." (July 6): 24–26; and Liao, D., and P. Sohmen (Spring 2001). "The Development of Modern Entrepreneurship in China." *Stanford Journal of East Asian Affairs*, 1: 31.
14. Wooldridge, A. (2009). "Global Heroes." *The Economist*, (March 14): 3.
15. Bosma, N., and J. Levie (2009). *Global Entrepreneurship Monitor: 2009 Executive Report*, 23.
16. Jovanovic, B., and G. MacDonald (1994). "The Life-Cycle of a Competitive Industry." *Journal of Political Economy*, 102(2): 322–347.
17. "All in the Mind," (March 14, 2009). *Special Report on Entrepreneurship. The Economist*, p. 5.
18. U.S. Dept. of Commerce, Bureau of the Census and International Trade Admin.; and Advocacy-funded research by Kathryn Kobe, 2007 (www.sba.gov/advo/research/rs299tot.pdf) and Advocacy Small Business Statistics and Research, http://web.sba.gov/faqs/faqIndexAll.cfm?areaid=24, accessed September 26, 2010.
19. "'The Job Generation Process' Revisited: An interview with author David L. Birch." *ICSB Bulletin* (*International Council on Small Business*, St. Louis, MO). Fall, 1993, p. 6.

20. Kane, T. (July 2010). "The Importance of Start-ups in Job Creation and Job Destruction." *Kauffman Foundation Research Series: Firm Formation and Economic Growth*, p. 2.

21. Small Business Administration Office of Advocacy (2010), www.sba.gov/advo.

22. Acs, Z.J. (2008). "Foundations of High Impact Entrepreneurship." *Foundations and Trends in Entrepreneurship*, 4(6), 535–620; and Autio, E. (2007). *Global Entrepreneurship Monitor 2007 Global Report on High Growth Entrepreneurship*. London, UK: London Business School and Babson Park, MA: Babson College.

23. Op.cit. Bosma and Levie, 2009, p. 9.

24. Schumpeter, J. (1934). *The Theory of Economic Development*. Cambridge: Harvard University Press.

25. Kirchhoff, B. (1994). *Entrepreneurship and Dynamic Capitalism*. Westport, CT: Praeger.

26. Reynolds, P.D. (July 1995). "Family Firms in the Startup Process: Preliminary Explorations." Paper presented at the 1995 annual meetings of the International Family Business Program Association, Nashville, TN.; Shane, S., and S. Venkataraman (2000). "The Promise of Entrepreneurship as a Field of Research." *The Academy of Management Review*, 25(1): 217–226; and Begley, T., and D. Boyd (1987). "Psychological Characteristics Associated with Performance in Entrepreneurial Firms and Smaller Businesses." *Journal of Business Venturing*, 2: 79–93.

27. Bhave, M.P. (1994). "A Process Model of Entrepreneurial Venture Creation." *Journal of Business Venturing*, 9: 223–242; and Reynolds, P.D., and B. Miller (1992). "New Firm Gestation: Conception, Birth, and Implications for Research." *Journal of Business Venturing*, 7: 405–417.

28. Block, Z., and I.C. MacMillan (1985). "Milestones for Successful Venture Planning." *Harvard Business Review*, 85(5): 184–188.

29. Carter, N., W.B. Gartner, and P.D. Reynolds (1996). "Exploring Startup Events Sequences." *Journal of Business Venturing*, 11: 151–166.

30. Reinertsen, D.G. (1999). "Taking the Fuzziness Out of the Fuzzy Front End." *Industrial Research Institute, Inc.* (November/December): 25–31.

31. Townsend, D.M., L.W. Busenitz, and J.D. Arthurs (2010 in press). "To Start or Not to Start: Outcome and Ability Expectations in the Decision to Start a New Venture." *Journal of Business Venturing*, JBV-05466.

32. Birley, S., and P. Westhead (1993). "A Comparison of New Businesses Established by Novice and Habitual Founders in Great Britain." *International Small Business Journal*, 12(1): 38–60.

33. Knaup, A.E. (May 2005). "Survival and Longevity in the Business Employment Dynamics Database." *Monthly Labor Review*, 128(5): 50–56; and Heald, B. (August 2003). "Redefining Business Success: Distinguishing Between Closure and Failure." *Small Business Economics*, 21(1): 51–61.

34. Headd, B. (January 2001). *Factors Leading to Surviving and Closing Successfully*. Center for Economic Studies, U.S. Bureau of the Census, Working Paper #CES-WP-01-01; and advocacy-funded research by Richard J. Boden (Research Summary #204).

35. Cohen, W., and R. Levin (1989). "Empirical Studies of Innovation and Market Structure." In R. Schmalensee and R. Willig (eds.), *Handbook of Industrial Organization*, 2nd ed. New York: Elsevier.

36. Case, J. (1992). *From the Ground Up*. New York: Belknap Press, p. 44.

37. Ibid., 46.

38. Ibid., 64.

39. Gupta, U. (1989). "Small Firms Aren't Waiting to Grow Up to Go Global." *The Wall Street Journal* (December 5): B2.

40. McDougall, P.O., S. Shane, and B.M. Oviatt (1994). "Explaining the Formation of International New Ventures: The Limits of Theories from International Business Research." *Journal of Business Venturing*, 9: 469–487.

41. Reuber, A.R., and E. Fischer (1997). "The Influence of the Management Team's International Experience on the Internationalization Behaviors of SMEs." *Journal of International Business Studies*, 28: 807–825.

42. Ibid.

43. Drucker, P. (November 3, 2001). "The Next Society: A Survey of the Near Future." *The Economist*.

44. Thornton, P.H., and K.H. Flynne (2003). "Entrepreneurship, Networks and Geographies." In Z.J. Aes and D.B. Andretsch (eds.), *Handbook of Entrepreneurship Research*. Boston: Dordrecht Kluwer Academic Publishers.

45. Op. cit., Audretsch and Thurik, 2005.

46. Occhino, F., and K. Fee (2010). "Three Headwinds on the Current Recovery." *Federal Reserve Bank of Cleveland*, June 4.

47. "Kauffman Index of Entrepreneurial Activity." Kauffman Foundation, www.kauffman.org/research-and-policy/kiea-interactive.aspx, June 25, 2010.

48. Minniti, M., I.E. Allen, and N. Langowitz (2005). "2005 Report on Women and Entrepreneurship." *Global Entrepreneurship Monitor*. Sponsored by Babson College and the London Business School.

49. "The Economic Impact of Women-Owned Businesses in the United States." *Center for Women's Business Research*, October 2009, p. 1.

50. Barletta, M. (2006). *Marketing to Women*. Berkeley, CA: Kaplan Business.

Chapter 2

1. Vogelstein, F. (2004). "14 Innovators." *Fortune* (November 15): 2004.

2. Hofman, M. (October 2002). "Until You Get It Right." *Inc. Magazine,* www.inc.com; and www.idlabelinc.com.

3. Eng, S. (July 10, 2001). "Impress Investors with Your Firm's Endgame." *The Wall Street Journal Startup Journal,* www.startupjournal.com.

4. Davidsson, P. (2005). "The Types and Contextual Fit of Entrepreneurial Processes." *International Journal of Entrepreneurship Education*, 2(4): 407–430.

5. Bird, B.J. (1989). *Entrepreneurial Behavior.* Glenview, IL: Scott, Foresman and Co.; and Volery, T., N. Doss, T. Mazzarol, and V. Thein (1997). "Triggers and Barriers Affecting Entrepreneurial Intentionality: The Case of Western Australian Nascent Entrepreneurs." 42nd ICSB World Conference. June 21–24, San Francisco.

6. Greco, S. (October 2002). "A Little Goes a Long Way." *Inc. Magazine,* www.inc.com/magazine/20021015/24779.html.

7. Aspelund, A., T. Berg-Utby, and R. Skejevdal (2005). "Initial Resources' Influence on New Venture Survival: A Longitudinal Study of New Technology-Based Firms." *Technovation*, 25(11): 1337.

8. Roberts, M.T., and L. Barley (December 2004). "How Venture Capitalists Evaluate Potential Venture Opportunities." *Harvard Business School Press.*

9. "All in the Mind," (March 14, 2009). *Special Report on Entrepreneurship. The Economist*, p. 5.

10. Abdul, A., I.E. Allen, C. Brush, W.D. Bygrave, J. DeCastro, J. Lange, H. Neck, J. Onochie, O. Phinisee, E. Rogoff, A. Suhu, Global Entrepreneurship Monitor. (2008). *2008 National Entrepreneurial Assessment for the United States of America, Executive Report.*

11. Drucker, P.E. (1985). *Innovation and Entrepreneurship.* New York: Harper & Row.

12. Gorman, G., D. Hanlon, and W. King (1997). "Some Research Perspectives on Entrepreneurship Education, Enterprise Education, and Education for Small Business Management: A Ten-Year literature Review." *International Small Business Journal*, 15: 56–77.

13. Nicolaou, N., S. Shane, L. Cherkas, J. Hunkin, and T.D. Spector (2008). "Is the Tendency to Engage in Entrepreneurship Genetic?" *Management Science*, 54:1: 167–179.

14. Op.cit. Abdul, et al. 2008.

15. Shane, S., and S. Venkataraman (2000). "The Promise of Entrepreneurship as a Field of Research." *Academy of Management Review*, 25(1): 217–226; and Begley, T., and D. Boyd (1987). "Psychological Characteristics Associated with Performance in Entrepreneurial Firms and Smaller Businesses." *Journal of Business Venturing*, 2: 79–93.

16. Tozzi, J. (January 25, 2010). "Home-Based Businesses Increasing." *The New Entrepreneur. Bloomberg Businessweek*, www.businessweek.com/smallbiz/running_small_business/archives/2010/01/home-based_businesses_increasing.html.

17. "Frequently Asked Questions." *Small Business Administration Office of Advocacy*, www.sba.gov/advo, accessed September 26, 2010.

18. Westhead, P., D. UcBasaran, and M. Wright (2005). "Decisions, Actions, and Performance: Do Novice, Serial, and Portfolio Entrepreneurs Differ?" *Journal of Small Business Management*, 43(4): 393.

19. Rosa, P. (1998). "Entrepreneurial Processes of Business Cluster Formation and Growth by 'Habitual' Entrepreneurs." *Entrepreneurship Theory and Practice*, 22: 43–61.

20. Schmedel, S. "Making a Difference as a Social Entrepreneur." *The Wall Street Journal Online*, www.wsj.com (accessed January 5, 2007).

21. Zahra S.A., D.F. Karutko, and D.F. Jennings (1999). "Guest Editorial: Entrepreneurship and the Acquisition of Dynamic Organizational Capabilities." *Entrepreneurship Theory and Practice* 23(3): 5–10.

22. Quinn, J.B. (1997). *Innovation Explosion*. New York: The Free Press.

23. Deutschman, A. (March 2005). "Building a Better Skunk Works." *Fast Company*, 92: 68.

24. Hawkins, J. (October 23, 2002). Stanford Thought Leader Lectures, Palo Alto, CA.

25. Barnett, William P., H.R. Greve, and D.Y. Park (1994). "An Evolutionary Model of Organizational Performance." *Strategic Management Journal*, 15 (Winter Special Issue): 11–28; and Baum, Joel A.C., O. Christine (1991). "Institutional Linkages and Organizational Mortality." *Administrative Science Quarterly*, 36: 187–218.

26. Ramesh, G. (July–September 2005). "Entrepreneurial Traps: Autobiography of an Unknown Entrepreneur." *South Asian Journal of Management*, 12(3): 79.

27. Aldrich, H., and C. Zimmer (1986). "Entrepreneurship Through Social Networks." In D.L. Sexton and R.W. Smilor (eds.), *The Art and Science of Entrepreneurship*. Cambridge, MA: Ballinger.

28. Granovetter, M. (1982). "The Strength of Weak Ties: A Network Theory Revisited." In P.V. Marsden and N. Lin (eds.), *Social Structure and Network Analysis*. Beverly Hills, CA: Sage.

29. Burt. R.S. (2004). "Structural Holes and Good Ideas." *The American Journal of Sociology*, 110(2): 349.

30. Fisher, D., and S. Vilas (2000). *Power Networking: 59 Secrets for Personal and Professional Success*. Marietta, GA: Bard Press.

31. Hatala, J.P. (2005). "Identifying Barriers to Self-Employment: The Development and Validation of the Barriers to Entrepreneurship Success Tool." *Performance Improvement Quarterly*, 18(4): 50.

32. Lounsbury, M., M. Glynn (2001). "Cultural Entrepreneurship: Stories, Legitimacy, and the Acquisition of Resources." *Strategic Management Journal*, 22: 545–564.

Chapter 3

1. Shane, S. (2003). *A General Theory of Entrepreneurship: The Individual-opportunity Nexus*. Northampton, MA: Edward Elgar.

2. Kirzner, I. (1973). *Competition and Entrepreneurship*. Chicago, IL: University of Chicago Press, p. 17; and Shane, S. (2003). *A General Theory of Entrepreneurship: The Individual-opportunity Nexus*. Northampton, MA: Edward Elgar.

3. Alvarez, S.A., and J.B. Barney (2007). "Discovery and Creation: Alternative Theories of Entrepreneurial Action." *Strategic Entrepreneurship Journal*, 1: 11–26.

4. Baker, T., and R. Nelson (2005). "Creating Something from Nothing: Resource Construction Through Entrepreneurial Bricolage." *Administrative Science Quarterly*. 50:329–366; and Sarasvathy, S.D. (2001). "Causation and Effectuation: Toward a Theoretical Shift from Economic Inevitability to Entrepreneurial Contingency." *Academy of Management Review*, 26(2): 243–263.

5. Op. cit. Alvarez and Barney (2007), p. 15.

6. Gryskiewicz, S.S. (1987). "Predictable Creativity." In S.G. Isaksen (ed.), *Frontiers of Creativity Research: Beyond the Basics*. Buffalo, NY: Bearly: 305–313.

7. Noller, R.B. (1979). *Scratching the Surface of Creative Problem Solving*. Buffalo, NY: DOK.

8. Isaksen, S.G., M.I. Stein, D.A. Hills and S.S. Grayskiewicz (1984). "A Proposed Model for the Formulation of Creativity Research." *Journal of Creative Behavior*, 18: 67–75.

9. Singh, B. (1986). "Role of Personality Versus Biographical Factors in Creativity." *Psychological Studies*, 31: 90–92; Barron, F., and D.M. Harrington (1981). "Creativity, Intelligence, and Personality." *Annual Review of Psychology*, 32: 439–476; and Gardner, H. (1993). *Frames of Mind*. New York: Basic Books.

10. Amabile, T.M. (1988). "A Model of Creativity and Innovation in Organizations." In B.M. Staw and L.L. Cummings (eds.), *Research in Organizational Behavior*, Vol. 10. Greenwich, CT: JAI Press, pp. 123–167; Oldham, G.R., and A. Cummings (1996). "Employee Creativity: Personal and Contextual Factors at Work." *Academy of Management Journal*, 39: 607–634; Mumford, M.D., and S.B. Gustafson (1988). "Creativity Syndrome: Integration, Application, and Innovation." *Psychological Bulletin*, 103: 27–43; and Payne, R. (1990). "The Effectiveness of Research Teams: A Review." In M.A. West and J.L. Farr (eds.), *Innovation and Creativity at Work*. Chichester, England: Wiley, pp. 101–122.

11. Wallas, G. (1926). *The Art of Thought*. New York: Franklin Watts.

12. Seeff, N. (2010). *The Triumph of the Dream*. Norman Seeff Productions.

13. Reuters. (February 23, 2006). "Work More, Do Less with Tech." *Wired News*, www.wired.com/techbiz/media/news/2006/02/70274.

14. Ophira, E., C. Nass, and A.D. Wagner (2009). "Cognitive Control in Media Multitaskers."

Proceedings of the National Academy of Sciences: 106(33), August 25.

15. Kanter, R.M. (Winter 2005). "How Leaders Gain (and Lose) Confidence." *Leader to Leader*, 35: 21.

16. Ibid.

17. Stewart, B. (2006). "A Butterfly Business Takes Flight." *Fortune Small Business* (November): 23.

18. Guilford, J.P. (1977). *Way Beyond the IQ.* Buffalo, NY: Bearly.

19. Newell, A., J.C. Shaw, and H.A. Simon (1962). "The Process of Creative Thinking." In H.E. Gruber, G. Terell, and M. Wertheimer (eds), *Contemporary Approaches to Creative Thinking: A Symposium Held at the University of Colorado.* New York: Atherton, p. 63.

20. Isaksen, S.G., K.B. Dorval, and D.J. Treffinger (2011). *Creative Approaches to Problem Solving* 3rd ed. Thousand Oaks, CA: Sage Publications, p. 31.

21. Jones, M.D. (1998). *The Thinker's Toolkit.* New York: Three Rivers Press.

22. Girotra, K., C. Terwiesch, and K.T. Ultrich (April 2010). "Idea Generation and the Quality of the Best Idea." *Management Science.* 56(4): 2.

23. Stroebe, W., and M. Diehl (1994). "Why Are Groups Less Effective Than Their Members: On Productivity Losses In Idea Generation Groups." *European Review Of Social Psychology,* 5, 271–303.

24. Op. cit. Girotra et al. (April 2010), p. 23.

25. Isaksen et al. (2011), p. 44.

26. Rogers, M. (May 1998). "The Definition and Measurement of Innovation." *Melbourne Institute of Applied Economic and Social Research, The University Melbourne*, Working Paper No. 10/98.

27. OECD (1997). The Oslo Manual: Proposed Guidelines for Collecting and Interpreting Technological Innovation Data (OECD: Paris), p. 28.

28. Chakravorty, B. (Summer 2007). "Innovations without Borders." *Innovations,* MIT Press Journals: 2(3): 113–124.

Chapter 4

1. Drucker, P.F. (2008). *The Five Most Important Questions You Will Ever Ask About Your Organization.* Jossey-Bass.

2. Shafer, S.M., H.J. Smith, and J.C. Linder (2005). "The Power of Business Models." *Business Horizons,* 48: 199–207.

3. Hamel, G. (2000). *Leading the Revolution.* New York: Plume.

4. Linder, J., and S. Cantrell (2001). "What Makes a Good Business Model, Anyway?" *Accenture Institute for Strategic Change*, www.accenture.com/SiteCollectionDocuments/PDF/business_model_pov.pdf.

5. Tucker, R.B. (2001). "Strategy Innovation Takes Imagination." *Journal of Business Strategy,* 22(3): 23–27.

6. Op. cit., Shafer et al. 2005, 204.

7. Friedman, T.L. (2005). *The World Is Flat.* New York: Farrar, Straus & Giroux.

8. Lounsbury, M., and M.A. Glynn (2001). "Cultural Entrepreneurship: Stories, Legitimacy, and the Acquisition of Resources." *Strategic Management Journal* 22: 545–564.

9. Glynn, M.A., and R. Abzug (1998). "Isomorphism and Competitive Differentiation in the Organizational Name Game." In Baume JAC (ed.), *Advances in Strategic Management,* 15. Greenwich, CT: JAI Press: 105–128.

10. Hamermesh, R.G., P.W. Marshall, and T. Pirmohamed. "Note on Business Model Analysis for the Entrepreneur." *Harvard Business School* (January 22, 2002): 2.

11. "Building a Business Model and Strategy: How They Work Together" (October 30, 2004). Excerpted from *Entrepreneur's Toolkit: Tools and Techniques to Launch and Grow Your Business.* Cambridge, MA: Harvard Business School Press, p. 5.

12. Linder, J., and S. Cantrell (2001). "What Makes a Good Business Model Anyway? Can Yours Stand the Test of Change?" *Outlook: Point of View,* www.accenture.com/SiteCollectionDocuments/PDF/business_model_pov.pdf.

13. Stuart, A. (December 2002). "This Year's Model." *Inc. Magazine*, www.inc.com.

14. Niraj, R., M. Gupta, and C. Narasimhan (July 2001). "Customer Profitability in a Supply Chain." *Journal of Marketing.*

15. Magretta, J. (May 2002). "Why Business Models Matter." *Harvard Business Review*, p. 6.

16. Allen, L.H., and C.K. Prahalad (May/June 2004). "Selling to the Poor." *Foreign Policy,* 142: 30–37.

17. Helmer, H.W. (2005). "A Lecture on Integrating the Treatment of Uncertainty in Strategy." *Journal of Strategic Management Education,* 1(1): 94.

18. Knight, F. (1967). *Risk, Uncertainty, and Profit.* New York: Sentry Press, p. 233.

19. French, N., and L. Gabrielli (2005). "Uncertainty and Feasibility Studies: An Italian Case Study." *Journal of Property Investment & Finance,* 24(1): 49.

20. Simon, M., and S.M. Houghton (2003). "The Relationship Between Overconfidence and the Introduction of Risky Products: Evidence From a Field Study." *Academy of Management Journal*, 46(2): 139–149.

21. Op. cit., Helmer, 2005, 193–114.

22. Delmar, F., and S. Shane (December 2003). "Does Business Planning Facilitate the Development of New Ventures?" *Strategic Management Journal*, 24(12): 1166.

23. Carter, N.M., W.B. Gartner, and P.D. Reynolds (1996). "Exploring Start-Up Event Sequences." *Journal of Business Venturing*, 11: 151–166.

24. Bhide, A. (2000). *The Origin and Evolution of New Businesses*. Cambridge: Oxford University Press, January.

25. Allinson, C.W., Chell, E., and Hayes, J. (2000). "Intuition and Entrepreneurial Behaviour." *European Journal of Work and Organizational Psychology*, 9(1): 31–43.

26. Bird, B. (1988). "Implementing Entrepreneurial Ideas: The Case For Intentions." *Academy of Management Review*, 13: 442–453.

27. Merkle, R.C. (April 2001). "That's Impossible." *Foresight Nanotech Institute*, www.foresight.org/impact/impossible.html.

28. Based on a feasibility study developed by David Dobkin, while a graduate student at the University of Southern California.

Chapter 5

1. Kirsner, S. (July 6, 2008). "Incubator Polishes Gem of an Idea." Boston.com, www.boston.com/business/articles/2008/07/06/incubator_polishes_gem_of_an_idea.

2. Porter, M.E. (2008). "Total Strategy: From Planning to Execution." *Presentation given to HSM Expomanagement, Buenos Aires*, http://docs.google.com/viewer?a=v&q=cache:rTAJVFXNu9MJ:ar.hsmglobal.com/adjuntos/15/documentos/000/052/0000052960.pdf+Profitability+of+Selected+US+Industries+1992-2006&hl=en&gl=us&pid=bl&srcid=ADGEESge0regu2_t0ZOqlYgYQbO1RRMnXwIhixf7dZiKFKuU_u1-smm_BH3MTYPajDi2BIacWZWn0Ghg2_T1Bea8NbjvdF-cO_8-_RS32ivprL99SdOXeL0LRGBEGz3z-ufOy7cQxpTm&sig=AHIEtbSUFdnE0K6H0MTKWcR_7JC7kmDcvA.

3. Bisson, P., E. Stephenson, and S.P. Viguerie (June 2010). "Global Forces: An Introduction." *McKinsey Quarterly*, www.mckinseyquarterly.com/Strategy/Globalization/Global_forces_An_introduction_2625.

4. Anthony, S.D., and C.G. Gilbert (Spring 2006). "Can the Newspaper Industry Stare Disruption in the Face?" *Nieman Reports*, 60(1): 43.

5. Schrage, M. (2006). "The Myth of Commoditization." *MIT Sloan Management Review*, 48(2): 12.

6. Jin, J.Y., J. Perote-Pena, and M. Troege (2004). "Learning by Doing, Spillovers and Shakeouts." *Journal of Evolutionary Economics*, 14: 85–98.

7. McGahan, A.N. (2004). *How Industries Evolve*. Boston, MA: Harvard Business School Press.

8. Ibid., 10.

9. Porter, M.E. (1980). *Competitive Strategy: Techniques for Analyzing Industries and Competitors*. New York: The Free Press, p. 3.

10. Rivkin, J.W., and A. Cullen (January 7, 2009). "Finding Information for Industry Analysis." HBS 9-708-481, p. 19.

11. Dees, J.G., J. Emerson, and P. Economy (2001). *Enterprising Nonprofits*. New York: Wiley; Ashbury Images, www.ashburyimages.org, July 2010; and "REDF Partners for Profit with San Francisco Ashbury Images." Press release, April 2, 2004.

12. Slater, S.F., and E.M. Olson (2002). "A Fresh Look at Industry and Market Analysis." *Business Horizons*, January–February, p. 20.

13. Gray, R. (2000). "The Relentless Rise of Online Research." *Marketing* (May 18).

14. Ulwick. A.W. (2002). "Turn Customer Input into Innovation." *Harvard Business Review*, product number 858X.

15. Chen, M.I. (1996). "Competitor Analysis and Intercompany Rivalry: Toward a Theoretical Integration." *Academy of Management Review*, 21(1): 100–134.

16. Bergen, M., and M.A. Peteraf (June–August 2002). "Competitor Identification and Competitor Analysis: A Broad-Based Managerial Approach." *Managerial Decision Economics* 23(4)5: 157–169.

17. Op. cit. Slater, S.F. and Olson, E.M. (2002), p. 18.

Chapter 6

1. Nauyalis, C.T., and M. Carlson (March 2010). "Portfolio Pain Points." *PDMA Visions Magazine*, p. 13.

2. Ulrich, K.T., and S. Pearson (1998). "Assessing the Importance of Design Through Product Archaeology." *Management Science*, 44(3): 352–369.

3. Ullman, D. G. (1992). *The Mechanical Design Process.* NY: McGraw-Hill.

4. Nauyalis, C.T., and M. Carlson (March 2010). "Portfolio Pain Points." *PDMA Visions Magazine,* p. 13.

5. Wolff, M.F. (2003). "Innovation Is Top Priority Again." *Research Technology Management,* 46(4): 7.

6. Cooper, R.G., and S.J. Edgett (2003). "Overcoming the Crunch in Resources for New Product Development." *Research Technology Management,* 46(3): 48.

7. Cooper, R.G. (2001). *Winning at New Products: Accelerating the Process from Idea to Launch,* 3rd ed. Boston: Perseus Publishing.

8. Crawford, C.M. (1992). "The Hidden Costs of Accelerated Product Development." *Journal of Product Innovation Management,* 9(3): 188–199.

9. Stevens, G.A., and J. Burley (2003). "Piloting the Rocket of Radical Innovation." *Research Technology Management,* 46(2): 16–26.

10. Teece, D.J. (1986). "Profiting from Technological Innovation." *Research Policy,* 15(6):285–305.

11. Pisano, G.P., and D.J. Teece (Fall 2007). "How to Capture Value from Innovation: Shaping Intellectual Property and Industry Architecture." *California Management Review,* 50(1): 277–296.

12. Ibid, p. 281.

13. Op. cit. Crawford, 1992.

14. Mankin, E. (2004). "Is Your Product-Development Process Helping—or Hindering—Innovation?" *Strategy & Innovation.* Harvard Business School Press, p. 4.

15. Quinn, J.B. (2000). "Outsourcing Innovation: The New Engine of Growth." *Sloan Management Review,* 41(4): 13–29.

16. Reitzig, M. (Spring 2004). "Strategic Management of Intellectual Property." *Sloan Management Review,* 45(3): 35.

17. Op. cit. Pisano, 2007, p. 282.

18. *Diamond v. Chakrabarty,* 447 U.S. 303 (1980).

19. Whitford, D. (2006). "Vision Quest." *Fortune Small Business* (April): 46.

20. "Qualifying for a Patent." NOLO Law for All, www.nolo.com/legal-encyclopedia/faqEditorial-29120.html.

21. Bonisteel, S. (2001). "Bounty Hunters Get Bonus for Effort on Amazon Patent." *Newsbytes* (March 14).

22. *Amazon.com, Inc. v. BarnesandNoble.com, Inc.,* 73 F. Supp. 2d 1228 (W.D. Wash. Dec. 1, 1999).

Amazon's patent is U.S. Patent No. 5,960,411 (issued September 28, 1999).

23. *State Street Bank & Trust v. Signature Financial Group Inc.,* 149 F.3d 1368, 47 USPQ2d 1596 (Fed. Cir. 1998).

24. Love, J.J., and W.W. Coggins (2001). "Successfully Preparing and Prosecuting a Business Method Patent." www.immagic.com/eLibrary/ARCHIVES/GENERAL/AIPLA_US/A010510L.pdf.

25. Oddi, A.S. (1996). "Un-Unified Economic Theories of Patents: The Not-Quite-Holy Grail." *Notre Dame Law Review,* 71: 267–327.

26. Trademark Act of 1946, 15U.S.C. § 1127.

27. Brown, J.D., and J.E. Prescott (2000). "Product of the Mind: Assessment and Protection of Intellectual Property." *Competitive Intelligence Review,* 11(3): 60.

28. 2001 Duke L. & Tech. Rev. 0018, May 31, 2001.

29. Levine, R. (2006). "Unlocking the iPod." *Fortune* (October 30): 73–74.

30. Ibid., paragraph 22.

Chapter 7

1. Davidsson, P., and B. Honig (2003). "The Role of Social and Human Capital Among Nascent Entrepreneurs." *Journal of Business Venturing,* 18: 201–331.

2. Ruef, M. (2002). "Strong Ties, Weak Ties, and Islands: Structural and Cultural Predictors of Organizational Innovation." *Industrial and Corporate Change,* 11: 427–429.

3. Bird, B.J. (1989). *Entrepreneurial Behavior.* Glenview, IL: Scott Foresman; and Kamm, J.B., J.C. Shuman, J.A. Seeger, and A.J. Nurick (1990). "Entrepreneurial Teams in New Venture Creation: A Research Agenda." *Entrepreneurship Theory and Practice,* 14(4): 7–17.

4. Ensley, M.D., J.W. Carland, and J.C. Carland (2000). "Investigating the Existence of the Lead Entrepreneur." *Journal of Small Business Management,* 38(4): 59–88.

5. Aldrich, H., and C. Zimmer (1986). "Entrepreneurship Through Social Networks." In D.L. Sexton and R. W. Smilor (eds), *The Art and Science of Entrepreneurship.* Cambridge, MA: Ballinger, 3–23.

6. Dubini, P., and H. Aldrich (1991). "Personal and Extended Networks Are Central to the Entrepreneurial Process." *Journal of Business Venturing,* 6(5): 305–313.

7. Owen-Smith, J., and W.W. Powell (2003). "The Expanding Role of University Patenting in the Life Sciences: Assessing the Importance of Experience and Connectivity." *Research Policy* 32(9):1695–711.

8. Lin, N. (2001). *Social Capital: A Theory of Social Structure and Action.* Cambridge: Cambridge University Press.

9. Ruef, M., H.E. Aldrich, and N. Carter (2003). "The Structure of Founding Teams: Homophily, Strong Ties, and Isolation Among U.S. Entrepreneurs." *Amercian Sociological Review* 68(2):195.

10. Roure, J.B., and M.A. Madique (1986). "Linking Prefunding Factors and High-Technology Venture Success: An Exploratory Study." *Journal of Business Venturing*, 1(3): 295–306.

11. Murray, A.I. (1989). "Top Management Group Heterogeneity and Firm Performance." *Strategic Management Journal*, 10: 125–141.

12. Kamm, J.B., J.C. Shuman, J.A. Seeger, and A.J. Nurick (1990). "Entrepreneurial Teams in New Venture Creation: A Research Agenda." *Entrepreneurship Theory and Practice*, 14(4), 7–17.

13. Seifert, R., and B. Leleux (Decebmer 2007). "Shape Up Your Technology Start-ups." *Perspectives for Managers*, 153:1.

14. Anonymous (2002). "Making Virtual Collaborations Work." *Research Technology Management*, 45(2): 6–7.

15. Gersick, C.J.G., and J.R. Hackman (1990). "Habitual Routines in Task-Performing Groups." *Organizational Behavior and Human Decision Processes*, 47: 65–97.

16. Kozlowski, S.W.J., S.M. Gully, P.P. McHugh, E. Salas, and J.A. Cannon-Bowers (1996). "A Dynamic Theory of Leadership and Team Effectiveness: Developmental and Task Contingent Leader Roles." In G.R. Ferris (ed.), *Research in Personnel and Human Resource Management.* Greenwich, CT: JAI Press, pp. 253–305.

17. Friedman, M. (2002). "Create the Virtual Company." *Canadian Business and Current Affairs*, accessed via LexisNexis on September 30, 2003; Trialto Wine Group Ltd., www.trialto.com; and Altovin International, Ltd. www.altovin.ca.

18. McDougall, P., S. Shane, and B. Oviatt (November 1994). "Explaining the Formation of International New Ventures: The Limits of Theories from International Business Research." *Journal of Business Venturing*, 9: 469–487.

19. Oviatt, B., and P. McDougall (1994). "Toward a Theory of International New Ventures." *Journal of International Business Studies*, 25(1): 45–64.

20. Miesenbock, K.J. (1988). "Small Business and Exporting: A Literature Review." *International Small Business Journal*, 6(2): 42–61.

21. Eisenhardt, K.M., and C.B. Schoonhoven (1996). "Resource-Based View of Strategic Alliance Formation: Strategic and Social Effects in Entrepreneurial Firms." *Organization Science*, 7(2): 136–150.

22. Fiegner, M., B. Brown, D. Dreux, and W. Dennis (2000). "CEO Stakes and Board Composition in Small Private Firms." *Entrepreneurship Theory and Practice*, 24: 5.

23. Kidwell, R.E., and N. Bennett (1993). "Employee Propensity to Withhold Effort: A Conceptual Model to Intersect Three Avenues of Research." *Academy of Management Review*, 18(3): 429–456.

24. Goodstein, J., K. Gautam, and W. Boeker (1994). "The Effects of Board Size and Diversity on Strategic Change." *Strategic Management Journal*, 15(3): 241–250.

25. Jonovic, D.J. "Professionalizing: The Key to Long-Term Shareholder Value, Part 1." Baylor University, www.fambiz.com/Orgs/Baylor/legacy/jonovic.cfm.

26. Clifford, S. (2006). "The Worst-Case Scenario." *Inc. Magazine* (November): 111.

27. "Financial Outsourcing Used by 75% of Multinationals; Benefits Mixed, Say 44%." *GlobalHR*, www.globalhrnews.com/story.asp?sid=617.

28. "Offshore Outsourcing on Rise for Small and Midsize Companies in 2009." *RUS®SOFT*, www.russoft.org/docs/?doc=1765, accessed September 30, 2010; and "IT Outsourcing Statistics 2008/2009." August 2008, *Computer Economics*, www.computereconomics.com/article.cfm?id=1378.

29. Barthelemy, J. (Spring 2001). "The Hidden Costs of Outsourcing." *Sloan Management Review*, 42(3): 60–69.

30. Sovereign, K.L. (1999). *Personnel Law,* 4th ed. Upper Saddle River, NJ: Prentice-Hall.

31. Butcher, D.R. (June 22, 2010). "Cooperative Purchasing: Buy More for Less?" *Industry Market Trends*, http://news.thomasnet.com/IMT/archives/2010/06/cooperative-purchasing-procurement-more-for-less.html.

Chapter 8

1. Blank, S. (July 22, 2010). "The Phantom Sales Forecast - Failing at Customer Validation," http://steveblank.com/2010/07/22/what-if-the-price-were-zero-failing-at-customer-validation.
2. McGrath, R.M. (1999). "Falling Forward: Real Options Reasoning and Entrepreneurial Failure." *Academy of Management Review*, 24: 1, 13–31.
3. Collis, D., and C. Montgomery (1995). "Competing on Resources: Strategy in the 1990s." *Harvard Business Review* (July–August): 118–128; and Wernerfelt, B. (1984). "A Resource-Based View of the Firm." *Strategic Management Journal*, 5: 171–180.
4. Covin, J., and D. Slevin (1990). "Content and Performance of Growth-Seeking Strategies: A Comparison of Small Firms in High and Low Technology Industries." *Journal of Business Venturing*, 5(6): 391–412.
5. Docters, R.G. (September/October 1997). "Price Strategy: Time to Choose Your Weapons." *The Journal of Business Strategy*, 18(5): 11–15.
6. Hogan, J.E., and J. Zale (February 15, 2005). "The Top 5 Myths of Strategic Pricing." MarketingProfs.com, www.marketingprofs.com/5/hoganzale1.asp.
7. Fishman, C. "Which Price Is Right?" *Fast Company* (February 2003): 68: 92.
8. "After the Techcrunch Bump." *Redeye VC*, accessed July 22, 2010, http://redeye.firstround.com/2008/01/after-the-techc.html.
9. Based on a feasibility study undertaken by Cassio Goldschmidt and Scott Webb, University of Southern California, 2006.
10. Johnson, W.K., and Walley, B.T. *Currency13, Enabling Bank Trusted Peer-to-Peer Payments,* a feasibility studying conducted at the University of Southern California as part of the requirements for a course in Technology Feasibility, Fall 2009.

Chapter 9

1. Gumpert, D.E. (2002). *Burn Your Business Plan! What Investors Really Want from Entrepreneurs.* Needham, MA: Lauson Publishing.
2. Logan, D., and H. Fischer-Wright (Fall 2009). "Micro Strategies: The Key to Successful Planning in Uncertain Times." *Leader to Leader*, p. 43–52.
3. Ibid, p. 46.
4. Kahneman, D., and G. Klein (March 2010). "Strategic Decision: When Can You Trust Your Gut?" *McKinsey Quarterly*.
5. Ibid.
6. Lovallo, D., and O. Sibony (March 2010). "The Case for Behavorial Strategy," *McKinsey Quarterly*.
7. Kelly, P., and M. Hay (2000). "The Private Investor—Entrepreneur Contractual Relationship: Understanding the Influence of Context." In E. Autio et al. (eds), *Frontiers of Entrepreneurship Research*. Wellesley, MA: Babson College.
8. Ibid., 65.
9. Caggiano, C. (October 2002). "A Strategic Misalliance," *Inc. Magazine*, www.inc.com/magazine/20021015/24786_Printer_Friendly.html.
10. Hankin, R.N. (July 17, 2000). "Creating and Realizing the Value of a Business." *Entrepreneur's Byline*, www.entrepreneurship.org/en/resource-center/creating-and-realizing-the-value-of-a-business.aspx.
11. Mason, C.M., and R.T. Harrison (2000). "Investing in Technology Ventures: What Do Business Angels Look for at the Initial Screening Stage?" In E. Autio et al. (eds), *Frontiers of Entrepreneurship Research*. Wellesley, MA: Babson College, p. 293.

Chapter 10

1. "Number of Tax Returns, Receipts, and Net Income by Type of Business: 1990 to 2006." *The 2010 Statistical Abstract*, U.S. Census Bureau, www.census.gov/compendia/statab/cats/business_enterprise/sole_proprietorships_partnerships_corporations.html.
2. Wagenseller, L. "Fighting Partnership Lawsuits – Five Threshold Issues." *Ezine Articles*, http://ezinearticles.com/?expert=Laine_Wagenseller.
3. Davidoff, H. (April 2006). "Understanding Buy-Sell Agreements," *The CPA Journal*, www.nysscpa.org/cpajournal/2006/406/essentials/p58.htm.
4. Toder, E., and J. Koch (August 6, 2007). "Fewer Businesses Are Organized as Taxable Corporations." *Tax Policy Center, Urban Institute and Brookings Institution*, p. 491.

Chapter 11

1. Cohen, R. (2007). *The Second Bounce of the Ball: Turning Risk into Opportunity*. Great Britain: Weidenfeld & Nicolson, 233–234.
2. Barrier, M. (March 1998). "Doing the Right Thing." *Nation's Business,* http://findarticles.com/p/articles/mi_m1154/is_n3_v86/ai_20401415, accessed April 2007.

3. Payne, D., and B.E. Joyner (2006). "Successful U.S. Entrepreneurs: Identifying Ethical Decision-Making and Social Responsibility Behaviors." *Journal of Business Ethics*, 65: 203–217.

4. Adler, P. (2010). "Ethical Action: The ABCs of IOUs." Workshop presented at the University of Southern California, June 7, 2010.

5. Ibid.

6. Anderson, D., and K. Perine (March 6, 2000). "Marketing the DoubleClick Way." *The Industry Standard Magazine*, www.infoworld.com/d/the-industry-standard.

7. Baker, S.L. (May 22, 2009). "Cancer Studies Published in Respected Journals Biased by Medical Industry Money." *Natural News*, www.naturalnews.com/026314_cancer_research_studies.html.

8. Brodsky, N. (October 2002). "Street Smarts: The Unkindest Cut of All." *Inc. Magazine*.

9. Evan, W., and R.E. Freeman (1996). "A Stakeholder Theory of the Modern Corporation: Kantian Capitalism." In T. Beauchamp and N. Bowie (eds), *Ethical Theory and Business*. Englewood Cliffs, NJ: Prentice Hall.

10. Robinson, D.A., P. Davidsson, H. van der Mescht, and P. Court (2007). "How Entrepreneurs Deal with Ethical Challenges—An Application of the Business Ethics Synergy Star Technique." *Journal of Business Ethics*, 71: 411–423.

11. McDonald, G.M., and R.A. Zepp (1989). "Business Ethics: Practical Proposals." *Journal of Business Ethics*, 81: 55–56.

12. Josephson Institute for Ethics, http://charactercounts.org.

13. Kant, I. (1964). *Groundwork of the Metaphysics of Morals*. New York: Harper & Row.

14. Cavanaugh, G.F., D.J. Moberg, and M. Valasquez (1981). "The Ethics of Organizational Politics." *Academy of Management Review*, 6(3): 363–374.

15. Dees, J.G., H.J. Emerson, and P. Economy (2001). *Enterprising Nonprofits: A Toolkit for Social Entrepreneurs*. New York: Wiley.

16. Ten Thousand Villages, BSD Global, www.iisd.org/business/viewcasestudy.aspx?id=89, accessed February 10, 2011.

17. The Nature Conservancy, www.nature.org, accessed August 16, 2010.

18. Ransom, D. (September 12, 2008). "Starting Up: Funding Your Social Venture." *The Wall Street Journal*, http://online.wsj.com/article/NA_WSJ_PUB:SB122124827514029295.html.

19. Roper, J., and G. Cheney (2005). "Leadership, Learning, and Human Resource Management: The Meanings of Social Entrepreneurship Today." *Corporate Governance*, 5(3): 95.

20. Thompson, J.L. (2002). "The World of the Social Entrepreneur." *International Journal of Public Sector Management*, 15(4/5): 412–431.

21. Working Assets, www.workingassets.com/About.aspx, accessed August 16, 2010.

22. Collins, J., and J. Porras (1997). *Built to Last: Successful Habits of Visionary Companies*. New York: Harper Business.

23. Ibid., 76.

24. Nash, L. (1988). "Mission Statements—Mirrors and Windows." *Harvard Business Review* (March–April): 155–156; and Schermerhorn Jr., J.R., and D.S. Chappell (2000). *Introducing Management*. New York: John Wiley.

25. "Drucker Foundation Self-Assessment Tool: Content—How to Develop a Mission Statement." Leader to Leader Institute, www.leadertoleader.org.

26. Boyd, D.P., and D.E. Gumpert (1983). "Coping with Entrepreneurial Stress." *Harvard Business Review* (March–April): 44–64.

Chapter 12

1. Ward, An., E. Runcie, and L. Morris (2009). "Embedding Innovation: Design Thinking for Small Enterprises," *Journal of Business Strategy*, 30(2/3): 78–84.

2. Fraser, H.M.A. (2007). "The Practice of Breakthrough Strategies By Design." *Journal of Business Strategy*, 28(4): 66–74.

3. Barth, H. (2003). "Fit Among Competitive Strategy, Administrative Mechanisms, and Performance: A Comparative Study of Small Firms in Mature and New Industries." *Journal of Small Business Management*, 4(2): 133–148.

4. Hanks, S.H., and G.N. Chandler (1994). "Patterns of Functional Specialization in Emerging High Tech Firms." *Journal of Small Business Management*, 32(2): 22–37; and Jennings, P., and G. Beaver (1997). "The Performance and Competitive Advantage of Small Firms: A Management Perspective." *International Small Business Journal*, 15(2): 63–75.

5. Stone, M.M., and C.G. Brush (1996). "Planning in Ambiguous Contexts: The Dilemma of Meeting Needs for Commitment and Demands

for Legitimacy." *Strategic Management Journal*, 17(8): 633–653.

6. Churchill, N., and V. Lewis (1983). "The Five States of Business Growth." *Harvard Business Review*, 61: 30–50.

7. Reed, M.I., and M. Hughes, eds (1996). *Rethinking Organizations: New Directions in Organization Theory and Analysis*. London: Sage; Hassard, J., and M. Parker (1993). *Postmodernism and Organizations*. London: Sage; and Boje, D.M. (1996). *Postmodern Management and Organization Theory*. Thousand Oaks, CA: Sage.

8. Gumm, D.C. (2006). "Distribution Dimensions in Software Development Projects: A Taxonomy." *IEEE Software* (September/October): 45.

9. Bryne, J.A. (1993). "The Virtual Corporation." *Business Week* (February 8): 98–102.

10. Schenker, J.L. (April 8, 2010). "Cloud Computing Boosts Virtual Companies." *Bloomberg Businessweek*, www.businessweek.com/globalbiz/blog/europeinsight/archives/2010/04/cloud_computing_boosts_virtual_companies.html.

11. Fitzpatrick, W.M., and D.R. Burke (2000). "Form, Functions, and Financial Performance Realities for the Virtual Organization." *S.A.M. Advanced Management Journal*, 65(3): 13–25.

12. Garaventa, E., and T. Tellefsen (2001). "Outsourcing: The Hidden Costs." *Review of Business*, 22(1/2): 28–32.

13. Watkins, M. (2004). "The First 90 Days." *Association Management*, 56(8): 44–54.

14. Smircich, L. (1983). "Concepts of Culture and Organizational Analysis." *Administrative Science Quarterly* 28, 339–358.

15. Davis, S. (1984). *Managing Corporate Culture*. Cambridge, MA: Ballinger.

16. Deal, T., and A. Kennedy. (1982), *Corporate Cultures: The Rites and Rituals of Corporate Life*, Reading, MA: Addison-Wesley.

17. Ulrich, D., and D. Kale. (1990). *Organizational Capability: Competing from the Inside/Out*. New York: John Wiley & Sons.

18. Tosti, D.T. (2007). "Aligning the Culture and Strategy for Success." *Performance Improvement*, 46(1):21.

19. Wortmann, C. (2008). "Can Stories Change a Culture?" *Industrial and Commercial Training*, 40(3):134–141.

20. Sloane, J. (2007). "Cure Your HR Ills." *Fortune Small Business* (March): 65.

21. Osborne, R.L. (1992). "Minority Ownership for Key Employees: Dividend or Disaster?" *Business Horizons*, 35(1): 76.

Chapter 13

1. Murray, A. (August 21, 2010). "The End of Management." *The Wall Street Journal*, www.wsj.com.

2. Hammer, M. (2004). "Deep Change." *Harvard Business Review* (April): 1.

3. "You Can't Manage What You Can't Measure: Maximizing Supply Chain Value." *Knowledge@Wharton* (September 6, 2006), http://knowledge.wharton.upenn.edu/article.cfm?articleid=1546.

4. Anderson, E., and B. Weitz (February 1992). "The Use of Pledges to Build and Sustain Commitment in Distribution Channels." *Journal of Marketing Research*, 29: 18–34; and Doney, P.M., and J.P. Cannon (April 1997). "An Examination of the Nature of Trust in Buyer–Seller Relationships." *Journal of Marketing*, 61: 35–51.

5. Lusch, R.F., and J.R. Brown (October 1996). "Interdependency, Contracting, and Relational Behavior in Marketing Channels." *Journal of Marketing*, 60: 19–38; and Noordewier, T.G., G. John, and J.R. Nevin (October 1990). "Performance Outcomes of Purchasing Arrangements in Industrial Buyer–Vendor Relationships." *Journal of Marketing*, 54: 80–93.

6. Horsfall, G.A. (November 1998). "How to Leverage a Bad Inventory Situation." *Hospital Materiel Management Quarterly*, 20(2): 40.

7. "Feigenbaum's 40 Steps to Quality Improvement." www.scribd.com/doc/23251743/Armand-V-Feigenbaumrename-1.

8. Ibid.

9. "Basic Concepts: Process View of Work." *American Society for Quality*, http://asq.org/learn-about-quality/process-view-of-work/overview/overview.html, accessed April 22, 2007.

10. Challener, C. (July 16, 2001). "Six Sigma: Can the GE Model Work in the Chemical Industry?" *Chemical Market Reporter*, www.findarticles.com.

11. Bartholomew, D. (September 2001). "Cost v. Quality." *Industry Week*, www.industryweek.com.

12. "Play Big." *Fortune Small Business* (November 2006): 30.

13. "The Future of Outsourcing." *BusinessWeek Online* (January 30, 2006), www.businessweek.com/magazine/content/06_05/b3969401.htm.

14. "As the BPO Business Grows, There's a Greater Focus on Metrics and Measurement." *Knowledge@ Wharton* (January 14, 2005), http://knowledge .wharton.upenn.edu/article.cfm?articleid=1102.

15. "Playbook: Best-Practice Ideas." *BusinessWeek Online*, www.businessweek.com/magazine/ toc/06_05/B39690605outsourcing.htm, accessed April 22, 2007.

16. "HSBC's Lessons in Outsourcing." *BusinessWeek Online* (January 30, 2006), www.businessweek .com/magazine/content/06_05/b3969426 .htm, accessed April 22, 2007.

Chapter 14

1. Christensen, C.M., S. Cook, and T. Hall (2005). "Marketing Malpractice: The Cause and the Cure." *Harvard Business Review*, December.

2. Anderson, C. (2006). *The Long Tail*. New York: Hyperion Books.

3. Golder, P.H., and G.J. Tellis (Spring 2004). "Growing, Growing, Gone: Cascades, Diffusion, and Turning Points in the Product Life Cycle." *Marketing Science*, 23(2):207–218.

4. "The Diffusion Process." Ames: Agriculture Extension Service, Iowa State College, Special Report No. 18, 1957; and Rogers, E. (1962). *Diffusion of Innovation*. New York: The Free Press.

5. Moore, G. (1999). *Crossing the Chasm: Marketing and Selling High-Tech Products to Mainstream Customers*. New York: HarperBusiness.

6. Woodruff, R. (1997). "Customer Value: The Next Source for Competitive Advantage." *Journal of the Academy of Marketing Science*, 25(2): 139–153.

7. Cooper, R.G. (2001). *Winning at New Products*, 3rd ed. New York: Perseus.

8. Woodall, T. (2003). "Conceptualization 'Value for the Customer': An Attribution, Structural and Dispositional Analysis." *Academy of Marketing Science Review*, 12.

9. Op. cit., Woodruff, 1997, 141.

10. Smith, J.B., and M. Colgate (2007). "Customer Value Creation: A Practical Framework." *Journal of Marketing Theory and Practice*, 15(1): 7.

11. Frey, D. (February 19, 2002). "Your Seven-Step, One-Day Marketing Plan." www.marketingprofs. com, accessed April 27, 2007.

12. MacInnis, D. (2006). "Just What Is a Brand, Anyway?" *Marketing Guides*, www.marketingprofs .com, accessed April 29, 2007.

13. MacInnis, D., and C.W. Park. (2006). "Branding and Brand Equity: Clarifications on a Confusing Topic." *Marketing Guides*, www.marketingprofs .com, accessed April 29, 2007.

14. Shipley, M. (March 13, 2007). "Keeping the Brand Health: The Annual Brand Checkup." www .marketingprofs.com, accessed April 29, 2007.

15. Zeisser, M. (June 2010). "Unlocking the Elusive Potential of Social Networks." *McKinsey Quarterly*, www.mckinseyquarterly.com/ Unlocking_the_elusive_potential_of_social_ networks_2623.

16. Ellis, D. (October 13, 2009). "Are Your Marketing Dollars buying Customers—or Just Renting Them?" MarketingProfs.com, www .marketingprofs.com/articles/2009/3083/are- your-marketing-dollars-buying-customersor-just- renting-them.

17. "Surviving Silly Bandz: Prolonging the Shelf Life of Fads." *Knowledge @ Wharton*, July 21, 2010, http://knowledge.wharton.upenn.edu/article .cfm?articleid=2551.

18. Levinson, J.C. (2005). *Guerrilla Marketing for the New Millennium: Lessons from the Father of Guerrilla Marketing*. Boston: Houghton Mifflin.

19. "Turning Social Capital into Economic Capital: Straight Talk about World-of-Mouth Marketing." *Knowledge @ Wharton*, July 21, 2010, http://knowledge.wharton.upenn.edu/article .cfm?articleid=2554.

20. McConnell, B., and J. Huba (November 26, 2002). "Top 6 Tips to Understanding Customer Evangelism." www.marketingprofs.com.

21. "US Online Advertising Industry: $300 Billion and Counting." *EconomyWatch*. Boston, June 26, 2009, www.economywatch.com/ economy-business-and-finance-news/US- online-advertising-industry-300-billion-and- counting-21-6.html.

22. Hausman, L. (June 22, 2010). "Seven Key Metrics for Rebalancing Your Social Strategy." MarketingProfs.com, www.marketingprofs.com/ articles/2010/3721/seven-key-metrics-for- rebalancing-your-social-strategy.

23. Ibid.

24. Sciortino, J. (2006). "Sharing a Lobster." *Fortune Small Business* (October): 45.

25. "How to Create High-Conversion Content for Lead Generation: 5 Key Questions Answered." *MarketingSherpa*, www.marketingsherpa.com, accessed September 26, 2010.

26. Corey, C.W. "Africa: Agoa Ministers Learn Importance of Adding Value to Commodities." allAfrica .com, August 10, 2010, http://allafrica.com/ stories/201008110794.html.

Chapter 15

1. Venkataraman, S. (1997). "The Distinctive Domain of Entrepreneurship Research." *Advances in Entrepreneurship Research: Firm Emergence and Growth*, 3: 119–138, JAI Press.
2. Barney, J. (1991). "Firm Resources and Sustained Competitive Advantage." *Journal of Management*, 17(2), 99–120.
3. Brush, C.G., P.G. Greene, M.M. Hart, and H.S. Haller (2001). "From Initial Idea to Unique Advantage: The Entrepreneurial Challenge of Constructing a Resource Base." *The Academy of Management Executive*, 15(1): 64–78.
4. Ibid.
5. Ibid.
6. "2008 National Entrepreneurial Assessment for the United States of America." *Global Entrepreneurship Monitor*. Executive Report, www .gemconsortium.org.
7. Gage, D. "VC Investment in Startups Keeps Falling." SFGATE.com, April 28, 2009, http://articles.sfgate.com/2009-04-18/business/ 17193792_1_venture-capitalists-national-venture-capital-association-clean-technology.
8. MoneyTree Report, *PricewaterhouseCoopers and the National Venture Capital Association*, www .pwcmoneytree.com/MTPublic/ns/index.jsp, accessed October 4, 2010.
9. Moore, G. (2002). *Crossing the Chasm*. New York: HarperBusiness.
10. "Business in a Bag." Vision Spring, www .visionspring.org/blog, accessed February 10, 2011.
11. "Impact Investing: Harnessing Capital Markets to Drive Development at Scale." *Beyond Profit Magazine*, http://beyondprofit.com/impact-investing-harnessing-capital-markets-to-drive-development-at-scale, March 5, 2010.
12. Ransom, D. (September 12, 2008). "Starting Up: Funding Your Social Venture." *The Wall Street Journal*, http://online.wsj.com.
13. Bhide, A. (1992). "Bootstrapping Finance: The Art of Startups." *Harvard Business Review*, 70(6): 109–117.
14. Siriwardane, V. (September 20, 2010). "How to Build a Bootstrapping Culture." *Inc. Magazine*, www.inc.com/guides/2010/09/how-to-build-a-bootstrapping-culture.html.
15. Welch, L. (October 1, 2010). "The Way I Work: Michael Arrington of TechCrunch." *Inc .com*, www.inc.com/magazine/20101001/the-way-i-work-michael-arrington-techcrunch.html.
16. Wellner, A.S. (December 2003). "Blood Money." *Inc. Magazine*, www.inc.com.
17. Mayer, M. (2003). "Taking the Fear Out of Factoring." *Inc. Magazine* (December): 90–97.
18. "Creative Business financing Options: Customer Financing." *Startup Nation*, www.startupnation .com/articles/1301/1/creative-business-financing-customer.asp, accessed October 20, 2010.
19 "Small Business Innovation Research (SBIR) and Small Business Technology Transfer (STTR) Programs." (August 16, 2010). U.S. Department of Health & Human Services, Office of Extramural Research, http://grants.nih.gov/grants/ funding/sbirsttr_programs.htm.

Chapter 16

1. PricewaterhouseCoopers/National Venture Capital Association MoneyTree™ Report, Data: Thomson Reuters, www.pwcmoneytree.com/ MTPublic/ns/nav.jsp?page=notice&iden=B, accessed October 15, 2010.
2. Franke, N., M. Gruber, D. Harhoff, and J. Henkel (September 2006). "Venture Capitalists' Evaluations of Start-up Teams: Trade-offs, Knock-out Criteria, and the Impact of VC Experience." *Entrepreneurship Theory and Practice*, 12: 8–20.
3. Shepherd, D. (1999). "Venture Capitalists' Introspection: A Comparison of 'In Use' and 'Espoused' Decision Policies." *Journal of Small Business Management*, 27: 76–87.
4. "VC Super Angels: Filling a Funding Gap or Killing the Next Google?" *Knowledge@Wharton*, September 1, 2010, http://knowledge.wharton .upenn.edu/article.cfm?articleid=2580.
5. Ibid, p. 2.
6. Baker, M., and J. Wurgler. "Market Timing and Capital Structure." *Journal of Finance* (February 2002) Vol. 57, No. 1, pp. 1–32.
7. Reardon, M. (June 4, 2006). "Investors Sue Vonage over IPO," www.zdnet.com/news/investors-sue-vonage-over-ipo/148306?tag=content; search-results-rivers.
8. Renaissance Capital, www.renaissancecapital.com, accessed February 10, 2011.

9. Hamm, A.F. (February 11, 2005). "Small Start-ups Look to Foreign IPO Markets." *Silicon Valley/San Jose Business Journal*, www.bizjournals.com/sanjose/stories/2005/02/14/story3.html.

10. Ahmad, Z., and Lim, S.M. (2005). Operating Performance of Initial Public Offerings in Malaysia. *Capital Market Review*, 13, pp. 21-32; Wang, C. (2005). Ownership and Operating Performance of Chinese IPOs. *Journal of Banking and Finance*, 29, pp. 1835–1856; and Mikkelson, W.H., M. Partch, and K. Shah (1997). "Ownership and Operating Performance of Companies That Go Public." *Journal of Financial Economics*, 44: 281–308.

11. Peristiani, S., and G. Hong (2004). "Current Issues in Economics and Finance." *Federal Reserve Bank of New York*, 10(2), www.newyorkfed.org/research/current_issues, accessed September 2004.

12. Ibid.

13. Welbourne, T.M. (2010). "Want to Make Money on the New Initial Public Offerings?" *Center for Effective Organizations, Marshall School of Business, University of Southern California, HRM, the Journal,* http://ceo.usc.edu/pdf/IPOs_HRM.pdf.

14. Brokaw, L. (1992). "The First Day of the Rest of Your Life." *Inc. Magazine*, 15(5): 144.

15. Feldman, A. (September 2005). "Five Ways That Smart Companies Comply." *Inc. Magazine*, www.inc.com.

16. "Sarbanes-Oxley Compliance Costs Decline." May 1, 2008, Business Law Prof Blog, http://law professors.typepad.com/business_law/2008/05/sarbanes-oxley.html.

17. "IPO Basics: Investment Bankers, Underwriters, and Other Key Players." *Inc. Magazine*, www.inc.com, accessed May 11, 2007.

18. Parsons, B. (August 8, 2006). "GoDaddy Pulls Its IPO Filing! Why I Decided to Pull It." www.bobparsons.com/WhyIPOPulled.html.

19. Hise, P. (2006). "Off-the-Grid IPOs: An Underused SEC Exemption That Deserves Another Look." *Inc. Magazine* (December): 40.

20. Spekman, R.E., L.A. Isabella, and T.C. MacAvoy (2000). *Alliance Competence: Maximizing the Value of Your Partnerships*. New York: John Wiley & Sons.

21. Anon. (2003). *Managing for Growth: Enabling Sustainable Success in Canadian SMEs,* http://business.queensu.ca, accessed May 11, 2007.

22. Ahuja, G. (2000). "The Duality of Collaboration: Inducements and Opportunities in the Formation of Interfirm Linkages." *Strategic Management Journal*, 21(3): 317–343.

23. Weaver, K.M., P.H. Dickson, and B. Gibson (1997). "SME-Based Alliance Use: A Three Country Comparison of Environmental Determinants and Individual Level Moderators." Paper presented at the International Council for Small Business Conference, San Francisco, California.

24. Birchard, B. (1999). "Intangible Assets Plus Hard Numbers Equals Soft Finance." *Fast Company* (28): 316, www.fastcompany.com, accessed September 2004.

25. "A Universe of Value." *Inc. Magazine* (January 2007): 100–101.

26. Lerner, J., and J. Willinge (April 8, 2002). "A Note on Valuation in Private Equity Settings." *Harvard Business School*, Reprint 9-297-050.

27. Ibid.

28. Ibid., 3.

29. Tuller, L.W. (1994). *Small Business Valuation Book*. Holbrook, MA: Bob Adams, p. 43.

30. Schilt, J.H. (1991). "Selection of Capitalization Rate—Revisited." *Business Valuation Review*, www.nacva.com/FTT_PDF/Chapter5+.pdf.

31. Boer, F.P. (2000). "Valuation of Technology Using 'Real Options,'" www.boer.org/files/RTMOptions2.doc, accessed September 2004.

Chapter 17

1. Kaplan, S., and R. Foster (2001). *Creative Destruction: Why Companies That Are Built to Last Underperform the Market—and How to Successfully Transform Them*. New York: Doubleday/Currency.

2. Mackey, J., and L. Valinkangas (2004). "The Myth of Unbounded Growth." *Sloan Management Review* (Winter): 89–92.

3. Stanley, M.H.R., L.A.N. Amaral, S.V. Buldyrev, S. Havlin, H. Leschhorn, P. Maass, M.A. Slainger, and H.E. Stanley (1996). "Scaling Behaviour in the Growth of Companies." *Nature*, 379: 804–806.

4. Golder, P.N., and G.J. Tellis (May 1993). "Pioneer Advantage: Marketing Logic or Marketing Legend?" *Journal of Marketing Research*, 30(2):158.

5. Roberts, M.J. (1999). "Managing Growth." *New Business Venture and the Entrepreneurs*. New York: Irwin/McGraw-Hill.

6. Hannan, M., and J. Freeman (1984). "Structural Inertia and Organizational Change." *American Sociological Review*, 49: 149–164; and McKelvey, B., and H. Aldrich (1983). "Populations, Natural Selection, and Applied Organizational Science." *Administrative Science Quarterly*, 28(1): 101–128.

7. Bishop, S. (1999). "The Strategic Power of Saying No." *Harvard Business Review* (November/ December).

8. Hamm, J. (December 2002). "Why Entrepreneurs Don't Scale." *Harvard Business Review*, pp. 2–7.

9. Gunther McGrath, R., and I.C. MacMillan (2005). "MarketBusting: Strategies for Exceptional Business Growth." *Harvard Business Review* (March): 4.

10. Ibid., 5.

11. Terpstra, D.E., and P.D. Olson (1993). "Entrepreneurial Startup and Growth: A Classification of Problems." *Entrepreneurship Theory & Practice* (Spring): 5–20.

12. Charitou, C.D., and C.C. Markides (2003). "Responses to Disruptive Strategic Innovation." *Sloan Management Review* (Winter): 55.

13. Porter, M.E. (2007). "Total Strategy: From Planning to Execution." Presentation to HSM Expomanagement, Buenos Aires, October 27, 2008.

14. Strauss, S. (February 28, 2005). "Five Reasons Why Franchises Flop." *USA Today*.

15. Buchanan, L. (2007). "Find it. Use It." *Inc. Magazine* (May): 93.

16. Mannion, M.J. (July 2003). "Advice on Acquisition Advisors." *Inc. Magazine*, www.inc.com.

17. Ibid.

18. Kline, S.R. "Growth and Diversification Through Vertical Integration." *PF Online*, www.pfonline.com/articles/growth-and-diversification-through-vertical-integration, accessed February 10, 2011.

19. Karra, N., and N. Phillips (2004). "Entrepreneurship Goes Global." *Ivey Business Journal* (November/ December): 1.

20. Oviatt, B.M., and P. McDougall (1995). "Global Start-ups: Entrepreneurs on a Worldwide Stage." *The Academy of Management Executive*, 9(2): 30–44.

21. Owens, J.B. (2007). "Who You Need to Know and How to Find Them: Building a Global Network." *Inc. Magazine* (April): 116.

22. *Doing Business: Measuring Business Regulations.* 2010, www.doingbusiness.org/Rankings.

Chapter 18

1. Knight, F.H. (1921). *Risk, Uncertainty, and Profit.* Boston, MA: Hart, Schaffner & Marx; Houghton Mifflin Co.

2. Borison, A., and G. Hamm (Fall 2010). "How to Manage Risk (After Risk Management Has Failed)." *MIT Sloan Management Review*, pp. 51–57.

3. Mackey, J., and L. Valinkangas (2004). "The Myth of Unbounded Growth." *Sloan Management Review* (Winter): 89–92.

4. Smeltzer, L.R., and S.P. Siferd (1998). "Proactive Supply Management: The Management of Risk." *International Journal of Purchasing and Materials Management*, 34(1): 38–45.

5. Krause, D.R. (1999). "The Antecedents of Buying Firms' Efforts to Improve Suppliers." *Journal of Operations Management*, 17(2): 205–224.

6. Lee, H.L., V. Padmanabhan, and S. Whang (1997). "The Bullwhip Effect in Supply Chains." *Sloan Management Review*, 43(4): 93–102.

7. Robertson, T.S., and H. Gatignon (1998). "Technology Development Mode: A Transaction Cost Conceptualization." *Strategic Management Journal*, 19(1): 515–531.

8. "Employer Costs for Employee Compensation." Bureau of Labor Statistics. United States Department of Labor, September, 8, 2010, www.bls.gov/news.release/ecec.nr0.htm.

9. "Navigating Legal Challenges." Fortune.com (January 2007): S3.

10. Shankar, B. (September 15, 2010). "Software Piracy Costs $142 Billion, 500,000 Jobs Globally." *International Business Times*, www.ibtimes.com/articles/62542/20100915/software-piracy-idc-business-software-alliance-economic-jobs-pc-stimulus-intellectual-property-ip.htm.

11. Richardson, R. (2008). *CSI Computer Crime and Security Survey*, http://gocsi.com.

12. Parker, P. (2006). "Racing Back." *Fortune Small Business* (March): 79; and Pro-Gate, www.progate.net, accessed October 27, 2010.

13. Zsidisn, G.A., and A. Panelli (2000). "Purchasing Organization Involvement in Risk Assessments, Contingency Plans, and Risk Management: An Exploratory Study." *Supply Chain Management*, 5(4): 187.

14. Buchanan, L. (2003). "How to Take Risks in a Time of Anxiety." *Inc. Magazine* (May), www.inc.com.

15. Bachrach, L. (January 22, 2007). "Global 500 CEO Departures at 15 Percent and Sweep All Regions." *Weber Shandwick Worldwide*, www.webershandwick.com/Default.aspx/AboutUs/PressReleases/2007/Global500CEODeparture-sat15PercentandSweepAllRegions.

16. Noe, R. A., J. R Hollenbeck, B. Gerhart, and P. M. Wright (2003). *Human Resource Management* (4th ed., pp. 406–407). New York, NY: McGraw-Hill Irwin.

17. Pasmore, W., and R. Torres (2007). "The Best Next CEO." *Leadership Excellence, 24* (8), 16–17.

18. The Family Firm Institute of Boston, www.ffi.org, accessed October 21, 2010.

19. Needleman, S. (July 16, 2010). "In Sports, Managing the Team Is Often a Family Affair." *The Wall Street Journal.*

20. Astrachan, J.H., S.B. Klein, and K.X. Smyrnios (2002). "The FPEC Scale of Family Influence: A Proposal for Solving the Family Business Definition Problem." *Family Business Review,* 15(1): 45–58.

21. Westhead, P., and C. Howorth (2006). "Ownership and Management Issues Associated with Family Firm Performance and Company Objectives." *Family Business Review,* 19(4): 301–316.

22. Dyck, B., M. Mauws, F.A. Starke, and G.A. Mischke (2002). "Passing the Baton: The Importance of Sequence, Timing, Technique and Communication in Executive Succession." *Journal of* Business Venturing, 17(2):143–162.

23. Malinen, P. (2004). "Problems in Transfer of Business Experienced by Finnish Entrepreneurs." *Journal of Small Business and Enterprise Development,* 11(1): 130–139.

24. Bjuggren, P.O., and L.G. Sund (2001). "Strategic Decision Making in Intergenerational Successions of Small- and Medium-sized Family-owned Businesses." *Family Business* Review, 14(1): 11–23.

25. Katz, J.A. (1995). "Which Track Are You On?" *Inc. Magazine* (October): 27.

26. National Employee Ownership Association, www.nceo.org.

27. Miller, SD. (March 2010). "The ESOP Exit Strategy." *Journal of Accountancy,* 209(3): 32.

INDEX

Note: *f* indicates *figure*, *p* indicates *profile*, and *t* indicates *table*.